The World According to Alex

A Russian Living in Los Angeles Writing Reviews for a Dallas-Based Publication Called www.IrishFilmCritic.com

Dedicated to Irish Film Critic… & All My Cinematic Idols

Other Works by Alex Saveliev:

Stranded with Stu – *A Novel*

Maid – *A Novella*

Taken Too Far – *Screenplay, Co-Writer*

Alex Saveliev's Book of Short Stories – *Short Story Collection*

Hello Dear Reader,

I know at this point there may not be many of you; my sincere hope is that this unfortunate fact will change. I welcome feedback, the more the merrier. And if we happen to disagree – well, just keep in mind that my opinion is better than yours. ☺ ☺ Regardless, here's my email: alex.saveliev83@gmail.com. Go crazy. Please.

I have written all the reviews featured in this book for the entertainment website called Irish Film Critic, run by the prodigious James McDonald. He and I do our best to edit the reviews. Forgive us our mistakes. We do this for free, during our free time. We do have day jobs. Until our site "blows up" and we all become millionaires, that is.

I love film more than anything else in life. It's been there for me throughout my many travels, when jetlag became unbearable, when fatigue and alienation took over. In strange, otherworldly landscapes, film always welcomed me with its grainy familiarity. While literature has always been an important means of escape, film gradually *become a part of me*; I *think* in cinematic terms, I regard life as a narrative, I sometimes tear up at music cues, and my heartbeat accelerates when a light dims just so.

So you can imagine my excitement when Irish Film Critic began to grow and appear on major studios' press lists, providing us with numerous opportunities to see films months before the rest of you suckers, as well as meet our cinematic idols.

I sincerely hope you enjoy the random rants, essays, reviews and thoughts published here – all written between the years 2015-2017 – and anticipate your responses, filled with admiration and awe!

PS I have no shame admitting that my own produced film, "Taken Too Far", is so devoid of any sort of cinematic merit, that it will take me a while before I'll even get to being able to review it. Does it render me hypocritical when I bash other filmmakers? Not really. Sometimes, films just don't come together. Look at Roger Ebert's "Beyond the Valley of the Dolls". If you do, however, happen to watch the atrocious mess of a film – also called "Deadly Dance Mom" – feel free to send me as much hate as you like. I'll attempt to explain myself.

Much Love,

Alex Saveliev
April 7, 2018

TABLE OF CONTENTS

5-Star Reviews

Annihilation - 8
Band of Outsiders - 11
Donnie Darko - 15
Heat - 18
Le Trou - 22
mother! - 24
The Handmaiden - 27

4.5-Star Reviews

45 Years - 30
BPM: Beats Per Minute - 32
Coco - 34
La Notte - 37
Meru - 40
Neruda - 43
Personal Shopper - 45
Summer 1993 - 48
The Girlfriend Experience (TV Series, Season 1) - 50
Time Out of Mind - 53

4-Star Reviews

A Hard Day - 56
A Monster with a Thousand Heads - 58
Aquarius - 61
Boy & The World - 63
Bridge of Spies - 65
Cartel Land - 68
Digging for Fire - 71
Embrace of the Serpent - 74
Ghost in the Shell (Original Anime Version) - 77
Guardians of the Galaxy Vol. 2 - 80
Halt & Catch Fire (TV Series, Seasons 1-2) - 83
Letters from Baghdad - 87
Miss Sharon Jones! - 90
Moana - 92
People - 95
Raw - 97
Sky Ladder: The Art of Cai Guo-Qiang - 100
The Beauty Inside - 102
The Good Dinosaur - 105
The Jungle Book - 108
The Music of Strangers - 111
The Salesman + Interview with Director Asghar Farhadi - 114
The Second Mother - 119
The Tiger - 122
Things to Come - 124

Thor: Ragnarok - 126
Tragedy Girls - 128
Victoria - 131
We Are the Flesh - 134
Since: The Bombing of Pan Am Flight 103 - 137

3.5-Star Reviews

A War - 140
Burden - 143
Cezanne et moi - 145
Dina - 148
Doctor Strange - 150
Eden - 153
Graduation - 155
Kahlil Gibran's "The Prophet" - 158
Louder Than Bombs - 161
Mojave - 164
Norman - 167
Phantasm (Series Review) - 170
Salt and Fire + Interview with Actress Veronica Ferres - 175
T-Rex - 180
Tab Hunter Confidential - 182
The BFG - 185
The Dinner - 188
The Endless - 191
The Innocents - 194
The Wolfpack - 197
Thelma - 200
Train to Busan - 203
Tumbledown - 206
Zootopia - 209

3-Star Reviews

#From Jennifer - 212
A Brilliant Young Mind - 215
Born in China - 218
Breaking a Monster - 220
Cardboard Boxer - 222
Dig Two Graves - 224
Everybody Loves Somebody - 226
Film Stars Don't Die in Liverpool - 228
Finding Dory - 230
From Hollywood to Rose - 233
Gimme Danger - 235
Ice Guardians - 237
In the Fade - 240
Jack of the Red Hearts - 242
Julian Schnabel: A Private Portrait - 245
Mifune: The Last Samurai - 248
My Golden Days - 251
Other People - 254

Pete's Dragon - 257
Queen of Katwe - 260
Rogue One: A Star Wars Story - 262
Sleeping with Other People - 264
Star Wars: The Last Jedi - 266
Stink! - 268
The Creeping Garden - 271
The Hollow - 273
The Insult - 275
The Phenom - 277
Till We Meet Again - 280
Truman - 283

2.5-Star Reviews

A Space Program - 285
Blind Sun - 288
Bluebeard - 290
Captain America: Civil War - 292
Churchill - 296
D.O.A. - 299
Flower - 301
Growing Up Smith - 303
Jim Henson's Turkey Hollow - 305
Love - 308
Max Rose - 311
Northmen: A Viking Saga + Interview with Actor Jonah Hegg - 314
Ordinary World - 319
Pirates of the Caribbean: Dead Men Tell No Tales - 321
Polina - 323
Railroad Tigers - 325
Red Trees - 327
That Sugar Film - 329
The Commune - 331
The Death of Stalin - 334
The Finest Hours - 337
The Landing - 340
The Man Who Knew Infinity - 342
The Ritual - 345
The Take - 347
The Timber - 350
The Void - 353
The Wilde Wedding - 356
Zoology - 359

2-Star Reviews

A Boy Called Po - 361
Aimy in a Cage - 363
Alleycats - 366
Beauty and the Beast - 368
Black Panther - 371

Blackbird - 373
Cars 3 - 376
Decanted - 378
Frank the Bastard - 380
Front Cover - 382
Gurukulam - 385
Ismael's Ghosts - 387
LBJ - 390
Les Cowboys - 393
Ozzy & Jack's World Tour - 396
Phantom of the Theatre - 398
Power Rangers: Dino Charge - 401
Radio America - 404
Suburban Cowboy - 407
The Backseat - 409
The Light Between Oceans - 411
The Young Karl Marx - 414

1.5-Star Reviews

A Family Man - 416
Abe And Phil's Last Poker Game - 418
Doobious Sources - 420
Freedom - 422
Sweethearts of the Gridiron - 424
The Automatic Hate - 427
The Bet - 429

1-Star Reviews

A Wrinkle in Time - 432
Dark Moon Rising. - 434
Honeyglue - 436
Ripped - 440
Tales of Poe - 443
The River Thief - 445
Voodoo Black Exorcist - 447

0-Star Movies

We Make Movies - 449

ALEX'S BEST & WORST FILMS OF 2016 - 451

ALEX'S BEST AND WORST FILMS OF 2017 - 453

ALEX'S TOP 38 HORROR FILMS OF ALL TIME - 455

About the Author – 471

5-STAR REVIEWS

Why Alex Garland's "Annihilation" – and Not "Black Panther" – May be the Most Important Film of 2018

Synopsis: *A biologist signs up for a dangerous, secret expedition where the laws of nature don't apply.*

With next-to-no fanfare, Alex Garland's gorgeous mind-bender "Annihilation" slipped into theaters this February. Based on the speculative eco-fiction / sci-fi head-trip by prolific author Jeff VanderMeer ("Annihilation" being the first part of his "Southern Reach" trilogy), "Annihilation" kept on slipping under the radar; while gathering impressive critical acclaim, confused audiences stamped it with a harsh "C" Cinemascore. It opened to a dismal $11 million.

This disparity between critical admiration and the general public's disdain, along with the lack of proper marketing and poor U.S. box-office, brings to mind Darren Aronofsky's "mother!", which just came out last year. Both are misunderstood, important, bold artistic films that are either destined to gain cult status over years, similarly to "Blade Runner" or "Donnie Darko", or will sadly disappear into the ether of forgotten masterpieces, overshadowed by massive, message-hammering monstrosities that reign over Hollywood these days.

Take "Black Panther", for example. Already, Jimmy Kimmel is waxing poetic at the Oscars about how this film will change everything in 2018. Currently, "Black Panther" is quickly becoming one of the top-grossing films of all time. It consists of primarily an African-American cast. Its message is that of inclusion and battling prejudice.

These are all admirable, undoubtedly history-making facts. Yet "Black Panther" still distills down to a story about a dude wearing a silly cat costume, hailing from an Atlantis-like, CGI kingdom that's fueled by a magical substance called Vibranium (I hear it's also a popular product on Pornhub). It contains a series of pixelated fights that lead up to the Ultimate Superhero Showdown. Yes, they attempted to make the villain less "villain-y", more ambiguous in his "villainess", but the attempt is so clearly forced, it's as if someone at Marvel *finally* took a look at their very long list of freakin' boring villains and said, "Hey, how about we add a modicum of depth to this one?"

Never for a second does one doubt the outcome of the "Black Panther" story. The whole thing is hard to take seriously, due to the campy nature of it all. Just because a silly comic book is infused with a degree of relevance does not all of a sudden make it The Greatest Thing Ever and a candidate for the next Oscar nominations (see what happened with the "just-okay", plot-hole-filled horror flick "Get Out", which all of a sudden is described as a masterpiece on par with P.T. Anderson's work and receiving Best Script golden dudes).

For a tiny fraction of "Black Panther"'s budget, "Annihilation" achieves something infinitely more subtle and thought-provoking. It contains memorable, relatable characterizations, as opposed to heroic and antiheroic archetypes. It's about humanity trying to come to grips with itself and the nature it's destroying, linking our capacity for self-destruction to the annihilation we inflict upon the very thing that birthed us. It utilizes its special effects more cunningly and sparingly, creating a hallucinatory world that grows on you like its emerald moss. It questions our perception of reality, and takes a peek beyond, posing the following inquiry: what if we were to see the world from nature's perspective?

It's also arguably more diverse - I'm talking both cultural and sexual diversity (it casually, without ever making a big deal about it or hammering the message into our heads, makes its four protagonists intelligent, independent females, all from different backgrounds), as well as biodiversity (the variety of life in Garland's cinematic ecosystem, a.k.a. "Area X", is mind-blowing, putting to shame "Black Panther"'s by-the-book (albeit splendidly colorful) Wakanda). Most importantly, like Garland's "Ex-Machina" before that, "Annihilation" reiterates the importance of hard sci-fi, as a mirror to humanity, as an artistic means to express our innermost dreams, fears and aspirations.

I know it may be unfair to compare the two films - one may argue they serve different purposes, are of different genres, etc. Yet it's not like I am comparing apples to oranges, "August Osage County" to "The Incredible Hulk". Both "Annihilation" and "Black Panther" can be described as fantasy epics; both contain special effects; both serve to frighten, enlighten and entertain the audience. Yet the former was made by an auteur who, after a tumultuous studio battle, got free reigns of the final cut and managed to share his singular, unapologetic vision with the world. The latter was constructed by a studio who dumped an auteur into the mix to imbue the enterprise with some class and gave the audiences exactly what they wanted, a zeitgeist theme in capital letters, so powerful it masks the hollowness beneath it.

Again, I am not arguing "Black Panther"'s cultural importance. I can't argue facts - audiences are loving it, it's crushin' it at the box-office, change is a-comin'. Yet,

I don't know about you, but it's "Annihilation"'s half-evolved bear - one of the most terrifying creations to ever grace celluloid - or its deer with antlers sprouting flowers, or Natalie Portman's sorrowful eyes as she gets submerged deeper and deeper into her own consciousness / into the mysterious Area X, or its hallucinatory ending, up there with "2001", "Under the Skin", "Arrival" or "Martyrs" in terms of utilizing hypnotic visuals for a both deeply unsettling and stunningly gorgeous effect - those are the things that will stay with me throughout 2018.

I will ponder the film's themes of nature vs. nurture, our effects on nature and each other. I'll mull over the meaning of some of its exchanges and flashbacks. Upon re-watching it many times, I will marvel at how it all gels together, and how Garland may have discovered a new cinematic language (like Villeneuve did with "Arrival" two years ago), filled with mystery and discovery, mind-bending questions and visceral thrills. As for "Black Panther", I *may* watch it one night with my wife on Netflix.

5 out of 5 stars

"Band of Outsiders" - A Classic Masterpiece Restored - Feels as Fresh as It Did in the 1960s

Synopsis: *Two crooks with a fondness for old Hollywood B-movies convince a languages student to help them commit a robbery.*

"We can't forget: classic equals modern. Everything that is new is automatically traditional."
- from "Band of Outsiders".

One could write an essay detailing cinema audiences' waning attention spans, based on the majority of films currently being produced, identical in structure (it's reassuring when you know what's coming) and pacing (it gets boring when a shot lasts longer than 10 seconds). While certain older films remain ageless, somehow having managed to transcend space and time and still captivate audiences just as powerfully as they did when they came out ("The Wages of Fear", "One Flew Over the Cuckoo's Nest", "The Exorcist", most of Hitchcock's oeuvre all come to mind), a friend of mine, for example, had trouble sitting through the first five minutes of Nicolas Roeg's classic "Don't Look Now".

I tried to explain to him that without Roeg's horror masterpiece, there would be no "American Horror Story", and how it inspired Danny Boyle's "28 Days Later", and the effect it had on cinematographer Anthony Don Mantle when he was shooting Lars von Trier's "Antichrist"… But by the time I was finished waxing poetic, he was deep in his iPhone, Instagramming my cats to a friend. It's really rather incredible how films have sped up the pace, and how folks either forget, or are clueless, that most of them are just regurgitating masterpieces, at twice the speed, to pander to our rapidly-growing collective ADD.

That is frustrating for many reasons. People may be hooked on Tarantino's "Pulp Fiction" - one of my favorite films, mind you - but few are aware that the dance sequence in that film is almost directly lifted from Jean-Luc Godard's 1964 masterpiece "Band of Outsiders", or that Tarantino named his company "A Band Apart" as an ode to this defining classic of the French New Wave movement. Fewer yet would force themselves to watch a black-and-white artistic gangster flick from the 1960s - which is too bad, as the film is more suspenseful, witty and clever than 99% of the crap floating into theaters today. Both in their early 30s, Godard and Tarantino each made a masterpiece that changed cinema forever - the exception being, Godard's stuff was 100% original and forgotten by all but the true cinefiles amongst us.

Described by the auteur himself as "'Alice in Wonderland' meets Franz Kafka" (legendary critic Pauline Kael referred to it as such as well), "Band of Outsiders" is one of the seven collaborations between the adventurous filmmaker and his star - and then wife - Anna Karina, whom he first spotted in a modeling ad. After turning down the lead in the director's classic debut "Breathless", due to the nudity involved, Karina was convinced by an obsessed Godard to star in his second feature, "Le Petit Soldat", which in turn led to the 5-year collaboration between them, up until their divorce.

There are no hints of the upcoming separation in "Band of Outsiders", Godard's infatuation with Karina (and filmmaking) very much evident in the way he shoots her, Raoul Coutard's camera tenderly caressing her soft features, large eyes and full, luscious lips. Yes, "Band of Outsiders" is highly erotic, in the subtlest of ways. (Side note: sometimes, watching the sexual innuendos in, say, Hitchcock's classics, just reiterates the point that "less is more", and a few words and glances can be much more arousing than a graphic portrayal of coitus - unless, of course, it's "Showgirls" we're talking about.)

From the first minute, during the rollicking, jazzy credit sequence, Godard thrusts a zippy montage in our faces, meshing the three main characters - Odile (Karina), Arthur (Claude Brasseur) and Franz (Sami Frey) - together, making it clear that they are One, a Team, a Band. We then follow Arthur and Franz, two stylish, albeit underprivileged, young French men and B-movie lovers, as they drive through Paris, on their way to the house they are planning to rob. They exchange sparse remarks, again bringing to mind the opening sequence in "Pulp Fiction", with Jules (Samuel L. Jackson) and Vega (John Travolta) waxing poetic about Big Macs, prior to shooting some gangsters. Only instead of fast food chains and foot massages, the main subject of Arthur and Franz's conversation is Odile, the men's playful rivalry taking precedence over their upcoming heist.

While we follow them, Arthur's narration sparsely, but helpfully, catches us up with the plot: "For latecomers arriving now, we offer a few words chosen at random: Three weeks earlier. A pile of money. An English class. A house by the river. A romantic girl." Having met the gorgeous Odile in class, Franz learned about the stash of money in her aunt's house, and the trio hatches a plan to steal it - only love comes in the way, as it tends to, Arthur's uncle gets involved, and things go horribly awry.

If that sounds like a flimsy plot, it does so for two reasons: I purposefully oversimplified it to let you discover the twists and turns of this 90-minute roller-coaster ride yourself, and the film is not so much about the plot as it is about the style, the performances, the tiny nuances and graceful moments peppered throughout the story: the trio exchanging looks and notes in class, as their teacher recites a tragic passage from "Romeo and Juliet" (premonition!); the consequent semi-improvisational dialogue between the uber-confident Arthur and naive Odile by the stairs, so sexually charged it almost climaxes; Arthur and Franz reading grim obituaries, while an excited Odile rushes over to meet them; Odile's hesitation, barely perceptible in the reflection of a restaurant mirror; or the remarkable sequence where the trio break "the record set by Jimmy Johnson of San Francisco", by running through the Louvre in 9 minutes and 43 seconds, as practice for the heist. And of course, there's the impromptu dance sequence, worth the price of admission alone, with its groovy soundtrack, highly stylized dancing and narrative interruptions. Pure brilliance.

Anna Karina exemplifies both innocence and boiling sexuality and playfulness; Claude Brasseur and Sami Frey, whom Godard called "Belmondo's suburban cousins", are the embodiment of "cool". Their acting complements the style, and vice versa: it's a symbiotic relationship wherein they feed off each other, an organic, fluid synthesis. A great example of this is a scene where Arthur and Odile share a joyous moment, walking down dimly-lit Parisian streets and squares, their love for each other palpable, as the narration wistfully comments: "It brought them back to the present, the past, and their intrepid future. Whereupon they went down into the center of the earth" - and the couple descends into a subway, where Odile half-sings, half-recites a poem, through the screeching of the train, directly into the camera.

"Band of Outsiders" is one of the purest examples of the French New Wave movement: defying conventional narrative structure with offbeat editing choices, non-sequiturs, a poetic narration ("Vegetation invaded the desolate prospect, its blackness recalling the Sea of the Dead"), the balancing act of objective and subjective realism, and a certain… coolness that was indispensable to those films. The characters are rascals, smoking and goofing off, but they also whiff of menace, and you kinda want to *be* them - another trait Tarantino frivolously adopted in pretty much all of his films.

Godard's film is about love: love of life, film, people; it's about ugly betrayal, the sweet (and swift) magic of youth, friendship and trust; it's a thriller, a comedy, a drama, a cautionary tale (that "happy ending" is one of the most acute and hilarious commentaries on the perils of living out a film fantasy ever committed to celluloid) and a heist flick, all seamlessly packed in one. There's a reason a master filmmaker like Bernardo Bertolucci paid an ode to "Band of Outsiders" in "The Dreamers", its 1960s-set story focusing on two young men and a young woman, also obsessed with film, life and each other. "Band of Outsiders" will linger in your mind, and you'll keep coming back to it to discover new things about it, just as a generation of filmmakers did (by utilizing its most profound elements).

"Band of Outsiders" is alive, each shot blistering with originality and passion; it's filmmaking at its most exuberant, and it still feels fresh, innovative, pulsating with more energy than a dozen "Transformers". It also happens to be Godard's most accessible, least experimental work, which should render it at least somewhat digestible for the current generation of filmgoers hooked on guarding the galaxy.

And yes, "Band of Outsiders" contains a minute-long scene of silence (the soundtrack cuts off, and the silence actually only lasts about 40 seconds) between the three main characters, filled with tension, the storm of emotions subtle yet palpable… to those of us who seek it. I assume audiences jaded on Marvel will find this sequence - and the entire film, in fact - borderline-unwatchable. To them, I'd like to echo Franz's sentiment, who interrupts the silence at the end of Godard's famous silent sequence with the simple words: "That's enough." Put away your iPads and revisit the classics, guys. You may learn a thing or two.

5 out of 5 stars

15 Years Later: Revisiting Richard Kelly's Paradigm-Shifting "Donnie Darko"

<u>"Why are you wearing that stupid man suit?"</u>

We've all been there.

At one point in our lives, be it at the dawn of adolescence or in the dank pit of midlife crisis, the shattering "Truth" breaks through the mold and overwhelms us, floors us. There may be many moments when we ask ourselves, "What's the point of it all?" - but we tend to do it fleetingly, our hearts accelerating a bit as we touch upon that void and swiftly withdraw, as if it were a hot coal. But there is that ONE instant, when our skin, our brains and organs, our very essence and its relation to our surroundings comes into question. Concepts of "time", "relativity", "success", "happiness" along with the plethora of human emotions, all become meaningless, due to the inevitability of it all. Some cannot help but dwell in that state, which society defines as "depression" or "severe alienation", others snap out of it and decide to make the best of it, capitalize on each minute, live each day as if it were their last.

<u>"Some people are just born with tragedy in their blood."</u>

Donnie Darko (Jake Gyllenhaal), the titular character of Richard Kelly's 2001 metaphysical masterpiece, perpetually lives in that moment. He sees through the thick bubble that society has created, his young mind struggling to understand and cope with the grim reality, and where it's all headed. Set in the paradigm-shifting 1980's, juxtaposed brilliantly against Donnie's own pubescent changes, where you feel like you are about to burst through your own skin, the film's aura is wondrous, alien, apocalyptic and harrowing, reflecting Donnie's continuous state of being. "Every living creature on Earth dies alone," Donnie says, so simply and accurately reflecting our collective greatest fear as humanity: "I don't want to be alone."

<u>"What if you could go back in time and take all those hours of pain and darkness and replace them with something better?"</u>

And so Donnie is given an opportunity, by a celestial force in form of an anthropomorphic bunny, to break through that societal membrane, led by one of the film's unforgettable creations, the Liquid Spears. Those "Abyss"-like gel formations, waltzing to Michael Andrews' minimal, otherworldly score, show Donnie what "redemption" may seem like, were he able to foresee the future: get together with the girl of his dreams (Jenna Malone, in what is still arguably her best role), corrupt a local charlatan (a fully committed Patrick Swayze), morally demolish his teacher (a formidably uptight Beth Grant)… And yet, being in "God's corridor" just makes

Donnie realize how futile it all is, and how his happiness comes at the expense of other people's misery - and so he makes the ultimate sacrifice.

"They just want to see what happens when they tear the world apart. They just want to change things."

"Donnie Darko" flopped at the box-office. Its commercial failure may be attributed to a variety of factors: being released right after the tragedy of 9/11, a lack of a real marketing push, the film's off-kilter amalgamation of styles and vague plot, blockbusters overshadowing the underdog… It did, however, find a massive audience on DVD. Richard Kelly's dark, uncompromising vision spoke to a generation of film lovers like myself, who emphasized with Donnie, trying to radically alter a crumbling world that resembled Kelly's so much. We all felt the need to connect with the cosmos, with eternity, come face-to-face with existential questions, break through the mold - or, we knew deep in our bones, it would all end in a catastrophe. Donnie's "teen existential angst" transcended those of your average high-schooler - it resonated with all ages and races, piercing though time and space, taking shape of a microscopic bubble, in which we all fester, akin to ants. Kelly's film was a call to action, to "think outside the box". By casting a retrospective look at our volatile past, "Donnie Darko" urged us to change the future, see the Liquid Spears in front of us.

"I want you to watch the movie screen. There is something I want to show you."

Richard Kelly's film is one of those miracles, like Michel Gondry's "Eternal Sunshine of the Spotless Mind", where it's as if the director's flow of consciousness were directly translated - unfiltered - onto celluloid, touching upon a number of nerves ever-so-gently but powerfully. It's a thing of wonder to behold, a dream-like, seamless blend of directing, writing, acting, cinematography and score. On a measly budget, Kelly managed to put together one of those seminal, generation-defining films, like Kubrick's "2001: A Space Odyssey" or Tarkovsky's "Solaris". If you think it's an overstatement, watch "Donnie Darko" again and see for yourself how it holds up even better 15 years after its initial release, a true sign of a lasting masterpiece.

I can't think of a single scene that doesn't work, or that doesn't serve a purpose in driving the narrative in "Donnie Darko". Who could forget Frank the Bunny Rabbit and the knife sequence, or Darko's sleepwalking, or the tracking / upside-down shot, or the Tears for Fears tunes… The list goes on and on. Donnie's family (played perfectly by real-life sister Maggie, the wise mother Mary McDonnell and sarcastic dad Holmes Osborne) may be one of the most realistically depicted American families in film. The entire Grandma Death sub-plot, which would be normally delegated as redundant in a similar feature, plays a crucial role and gains power upon multiple viewings. Even off-kilter dialogues, such as Donnie's unforgettable Smurfette "thesis", serve to delve deeper into Donnie's penetrating, sardonic mind.

As for Donnie himself, I admire Gyllenhaal's impressive body of work, but I don't think he has yet topped the gentle, angry, implosive/explosive performance he gives here, carrying the film on his fragile shoulders, each glance burning its way through the screen right into your heart. You *are* Donnie while you're watching this film, no matter your age or gender or race, because he is all of us - and that's quite the feat to pull off for a young actor. "I'm painting and stuff," he stammers. "Writing. I want to be a writer, or maybe a painter, I don't know, or maybe both. I'll write a book and draw pictures. Then maybe people will understand me. I don't know, change things."

Alas, Richard Kelly has not been able to top this effort either. Far from it in fact, with the lackluster (but ambitious) follow-ups "Southland Tales" and "The Box", the former of which featured Justin freakin' Timberlake and the latter of which even went so far as to replicate Donnie's Liquid Spears, making me wince bitterly. I met the director recently; he is an intelligent, passionate man, and I believe he just needs to reign in the ambition, and let his creativity speak for himself, get back in touch with that dreamlike "Donnie Darko" state, where consciousness and cinema are in perfect harmony.

5 out of 5 stars

An Ensemble Cast on Fire: Revisiting Michael Mann's "Heat"

Synopsis: *A group of professional bank robbers start to feel the heat from police when they unknowingly leave a clue at their latest heist.*

"Don't let yourself get attached to anything you are not willing to walk out on in 30 seconds flat if you feel the heat around the corner."

Say what you like about Michael Mann's recent string of misfires, but, in a swarm of lookalikes, the director remains a true auteur. His career did peak over 20 years ago, with the 1995 soulful crime drama "Heat". Throughout he 1980's, Mann's work in TV ("Miami Vice", "Crime Story") and film ("Thief", "The Keep", "Manhunter") served as creative workouts that led to the instant-classic. The director gained confidence, increased his scope while narrowing down on his recognizable style: cold, neo-noir-ish, gritty/violent character studies, basked in frigid blues and blurry browns, with slim sociopolitical currents slithering through them. He's never married style and content as successfully as he did in "Heat".

Based on his own 1989 TV pilot, which in turn was based on a true story, "Heat" is built on contrasts - between good and evil, monochrome light and shadowy darkness, aching tenderness and brutal violence, sweat dripping of the nose of a wounded criminal and the visible breath of a half-frozen cop. The film juxtaposes its two polar opposite protagonists: Al Pacino's aging Lieutenant Hanna, whose private life is in shambles, and notorious robber Neil McCauley, "alone but not lonely", on the brink of escaping to Fiji with his newfound love, Eady (Amy Brenneman). They both seek redemption, each other's dark mirror reflections. There is an inherent understanding between them, yet it's in their blood to do what they do best - a cat will never stop chasing a mouse. Both of the worlds those characters inhabit are appalling and seductive in equal measures, and Mann has Hitchcockian fun playing with conventions and having those worlds collide.

After a particularly elaborate bank heist gone awry, the heat closes down fast on McCauley and his gang of robbers. McCauley's right arm, Shiherlis (Val Kilmer), gets wounded, one thing leads to another - and to their eventual downfall. "Heat"'s simple tale is one as old as time, touching upon eternal themes of loyalty, regret and obsession. Like "Lawrence of Arabia" or "No Country for Old Men", a tale such as this doesn't need to be overly complex. At almost three hours, it moves swiftly, confidently, taking the time to flex its muscles, flesh out its characters, build the tension, revel in its own meticulously-structured sequences. And meticulous they are: Mann reportedly spent seven months riding along with the LAPD in preparation for the film.

Pacino delivers an astoundingly touching (and hilarious!) performance, one of fading resilience and strength; out of touch with humanity, lost in this constantly evolving world, Hanna clings to one thing he knows best, his gun. De Niro does his usual shtick, but let's face it - he does it best, the whole "steely-demeanor-with-hints-of-kindness" thing. The trio of Pacino / De Niro / Kilmer get stellar support from a remarkable roster of talent Mann managed to put together: Jon Voight, Ashley Judd, Amy Brenneman, Tom Sizemore, Mykelti Williamson, Dennis Haysbert, Natalie Portman (in her second screen role!), Tom Noonan, Hank Azaria, Ted Levine, Wes Studi, Danny Trejo… Even the small parts are memorable: who could forget the heartrending sequence, with Ashley Judd's loyal Charlene exchanging one last despondent look with husband Chris out of a bedroom window - a brief glance that speaks volumes.

Speaking of volumes, how about that epic, 10-minute shoot-out, orchestrated by maestro Mann with ear-deafening gusto, where geysers of bullets are sprayed, and which, at the time of writing this, has been YouTubed almost six million times. The sequence was so accurately portrayed, with the actors undergoing three months of rigorous firearm training, it caused real robbers to attempt to replicate it and allegedly inspired the 1997 North Hollywood shootout.

And of course, there is THAT coffee shop scene. "I do what I do best, I take scores," McCauley nonchalantly says, as he sips on his cuppa. "You do what you do best, try to stop guys like me." Today, one would barely wink at De Niro and Pacino sharing the screen, but in 1995, this was Don Corleone having a cup of coffee with Jake La Motta, for the first time - and the chemistry was so electric, sparks were actually known to injure audience members. Creating such an impact in less than 10 minutes, in a film spanning 170+ minutes, is no small feat.

With several exceptions (Natalie Portman, Dennis Haysbert), "Heat" marked the beginning of the end of the careers of mostly everyone involved. De Niro had a few decent-to-good 'uns left in him - "Wag the Dog", "Great Expectations", "Ronin", "Analyze This" - before slipping rapidly into cinematic hell, the gates of which were unlocked by Rocky & Bullwinkle and are still held wide open by Dirty Grandpa's Hands of Stone.

Similarly, after a final leftover streak of memorable titles like "Donnie Branco", "The Devil's Advocate" and "Insomnia", Pacino must have switched agents, or for some mysterious reason ceased to recognize good scripts, blemishing his incredible career with crap like "Gigli", "88 Minutes" and, worst of all, "Jack and Jill". Lately, both actors seem desperate to return to their glory days, the former chewing scenery in the second-rate "The King of Comedy", a.k.a. "The Comedian", the latter slumming it in the morose "Danny Collins". Echoes of that glory can be glimpsed in their eyes, mere remnants of that greatness - and yet this just proves the adage: one has to know when to quit.

As for Val Kilmer, he decided not to hold off and immediately plummetted straight into the abyss, with the triple-punch of "The Island of Dr. Moreau", "The Ghost and the Darkness" and "The Saint", followed by an avalanche of non-stop dreck: "At First Sight", "Red Planet", "Hard Cash", "Mindhunters", "Wyatt Earp's Revenge"… The list goes on - and yet, despite the slew of horrid titles, a capable director may just resuscitate his career (the man's still got chops, judging by his knockout live Mark Twain performance).

Ashley Judd, as much as I love her (the gorgeous actress exudes a sophistication and charm one cannot ignore), and yet, aside from carrying William Friedkin's mind-fuck "Bug" and appearing briefly, albeit vividly, in Julie Taymor's "Frida", I struggle to think of a single film that lived up to the actress' clear potential. As for Tom Sizemore… the epic demise of his career is worthy of a film - aptly named "Heat" - itself.

So it seems, Michael Mann managed to assemble the "avengers" for one last, gargantuan smackdown. He himself never managed to top the pure ambition, razor-sharp precision and inspiration smoldering in "Heat" - certainly not with the meandering "The Insider", which reunited him with Pacino, to a much lesser impact. I know the film got praised, but honestly, do you ever hear anyone go, "Let's do an 'Insider' night this Friday'?" No, because that finger-wagging nag of a film evaporated from public consciousness a year after all the praise died off, "Monster Ball"-style.

By then Mann was busy tidying up his Muhammad Ali biopic, creatively titled "Ali", which ended up awkwardly paced and, despite the awards and nominations, dissolved into that same murky ether left by the cigarette smoke of "The Insider". "Collateral", "Miami Vice" and "Public Enemies" were oddly stiff affairs, with two-dimensional characters mumbling monotone dialogue, style presiding over substance. His latest flick, the hacker thriller "Blackhat", proved so alienating, it made a measly $7 million domestically, losing over ten times that amount in the process.

"Heat" marks the zenith prior to the nadir of (mostly) everyone involved, and I use the term "(mostly) everyone" liberally - production designer Neil Spisak, for example, went on to pursue a wildly successful career slinging webs for Spider-Man. At the very least, those who creatively struggled after "Heat" can confidently state that "went out with a bang". Cloaked in neo-noir shadows, paced like a bullet, bristling with dynamite dialogue, both gripping and emotional, "Heat", akin to "Pulp Fiction" and "The Usual Suspects" is a seminal 1990's crime flick that deserves to be re-watched, its nuances coming vividly to life with multiple viewings. Christopher Nolan, for example, saw it many times, citing it as the defining influence on "The Dark Knight". Despite its director's trademark cold stylistic flourishes, "Heat" generates enough of it to melt Mr. Freeze and his entire headquarters in one of the next inevitable Batman iterations – which, for all I know, will mark Kilmer's return as the now-aging masked crusader, facing off De Niro's cryogenically-frozen icicle dude.

5 out of 5 stars

Jacques Becker's Prison Break Classic "Le Trou" Shows Wannabes How It's Done

Synopsis: *In prison, four long-sentence inmates planning an elaborate escape cautiously induct a new inmate to join in their scheme which leads to distrust and uncertainty.*

The French have always been ahead of the curve when it comes to filmmaking. Jacques Becker's 58-Year-Old "Le Trou" (translated as "The Hole"), now restored in crisp 4K restoration and presented by Rialto Pictures, serves as another example of a film that was well ahead of its time, and is as riveting today as it must have been almost six decades ago. Its laser focus on the minutiae of the prison break itself, its refusal to delve deep into character backgrounds, its long takes (one lasts almost four minutes; take that Mr. Iñárritu!) and lack of score form a minimalistic approach that heightens the suspense and propels the story along. Though quite different in style, the Coen Brothers' "No Country for Old Men" is similarly scaled-back, focusing on the ages-old battle of good vs. evil, the film's vast, painterly canvas rendering its relatively straightforward proceedings grand and epic. The bros must have studied "Le Trou", for a similar effect is achieved here - on a tight, claustrophobic canvas - a tale of morals and ethics, of loyalty and perseverance, told with clenched-teeth determination - a gargantuan world revealed through the tiniest of peepholes.

In jail for alleged attempted premeditated murder (that's a mouthful!) of his wife, Claude (Marc Michel), a good-looking fellow in his late-20's, joins four inmates in a tiny cell. They are: Manu (Philippe Leroy), the dashing leader, Vossellin (Raymond Meunier), the gentle, welcoming one in the bunch; Roland (Jean Keraudy), the expert who has "pulled off three breakouts", and the gruff, grumpy Geo (Michel Constantin), who instantly interrogates the newcomer about his sex life. Stuffed in the cell like sardines in a can, marinating in their own testosterone, the gang bickers, bonds and gets excited about inedible soup; they piss next to their dining friends and perform monotonous errands like folding thousands of boxes… Those errands in fact conceal their Grand Escape Plan. After a little consideration, Manu's crew decides to involve the new guy, and a highly detailed and nail-biting breakout follows, culminating in a heartrending final revelation.

Becker was a master at establishing characters, their dynamics and surroundings, and in "Le Trou" he excels at revealing a lot - about our protagonists, the prison, their plan - by actually saying very little. His camera, like a curious observer, shows just the right thing at the right time, never letting go of the audience's immersion. And yes, it's an adventure that requires patience, similarly to that of its scheming protagonists. This isn't a thrill-a-second ride, but rather a meticulously detailed study of what it would really be like, built on close calls and prolonged sequences of intensity. The characters' guilt or innocence - save for Claude's, perhaps

- is beyond the point. "Le Trou" is solely about the escape. I wouldn't be surprised if the makers of such classics as "The Great Escape", "Papillon", "Escape from Alcatraz", "The Shawshank Redemption", "The Green Mile" and even the ongoing Netflix series "Orange is the New Black", used "Le Trou" as a blueprint for how this stuff is done.

To list all the highlights in a film that happens to be one of the shining beacons in our vast cinematic world would be impossible, but here are a few standouts. A guard slices through salami and butter, inspecting it for contraband, in a weirdly queasy sequence. Our gang eats in silence for a good minute, a moment of bonding, where one can almost taste how delicious their simple food must be. Two of our "heroes" loudly cut through a bar and consequently hide from a couple of chatty guards - just to discover they have to dig another tunnel in the sewers. There is the ingenious invention of a sand-clock, an assault on thieving plumbers, and a rubble avalanche that traps one of our heroes.

Guards have become more brutal, plots increasingly complex, and prisons more advanced (and certainly less stylish) - yet filmmaking has never improved upon the standards established by Jacques Becker and his peers. Don't let the black-and-white photography, gorgeous in its stark contrasts, or the subtitled dialogue, sharper and more eloquent than anything coming out of Sam Jackson's mouth these days, stop you. "Le Trou" is Le Real Deal.

5 out of 5 stars

Darren Aronofsky's Masterpiece, "mother!" is Not for the Faint of Heart

Synopsis: A couple's relationship is tested when uninvited guests arrive at their home, disrupting their tranquil existence.

Talk about word of mouth. Darren Aronosky's "mother!" got the rarefied "F" Cinemascope among frustrated, confused audiences, who either expected a conventionally-structured Jennifer Lawrence vehicle or an elegant character study, in the vein of the director's "Black Swan" or "The Wrestler". Unable to digest the steadily deteriorating allegorical world of its protagonist, audiences fled, stamping the film with the score previously attributed to films like "Disaster Movie, "Alone in the Dark" and, infamously, Richard Kelly's "The Box". Consequently, "mother!" earned a measly $7.5MM on its opening weekend, and a total of $18MM so far, on a $33MM budget. A month later, Christopher Landon's "Happy Death Day" - a teen-slasher-horror-retread of "Groundhog Day" - made on $5MM, raked in $55MM domestically. Go figure.

Sometimes audiences get it wrong. In the pantheon of "exiled" F-Cinemascore films, at least six are, in fact, good-to-excellent: William Friedkin's "Bug", Robert Altman's "Doctor T and the Women", Jane Campion's "In the Cut", Stephen Soderbergh's "Solaris", Greg McLean's "Wolf Creek" - and now, "mother!". Whether it's the case of misguided marketing, audience expectations or the director being ahead of his time remains to be seen, but I have a strong feeling that, upon repeated viewings, those same haters will grow to appreciate Aronofsky's mastery of craft in a sublime, ballsy, once-in-a-decade example of filmmaking.

Yes, it may be flawed, just because it's ambition geysers out in shocking, brutal streams, as if the director were unable to contain himself. He wrote the first draft in less than a week, and it shows: the inspiration, the fevered intensity, the cerebral rumination of its creator is all there, on the grainy, 16mm screen. The film itself - following the descent into madness of its nameless, motherly protagonist, played by Jennifer Lawrence - is structured like a linear-albeit-mad dream, an evocation of an artist's subterranean existential wanderings. Organized chaos. Paranoia. A woman scorned. Heaven and hell. Environmental disaster. Apocalypse. It's all there, folks, in a seemingly simple tale of a young woman falling prey to her writer husband's (a nameless Javier Bardem) obsessions.

What starts off as a tranquil story of an interior decorator and a writer, living in an idyllic, undefined h(e)aven rapidly spirals into a "I can't believe this is happening" deconstruction of said h(e)aven. The arrival of Ed Harris's sickly Man and Michelle Pfeiffer's overly inquisitive Woman signals the beginning of the end. As the walls that she so carefully sculpted crumble around her, Mother finds herself helpless against humanity's remorseless assault. The climactic, stratospherically intense, stirring and violent sequence may have been the reason for the audience's dismay, but logically, in this illogical world, there was no way to end but The End. And yet, Aronofsky hints at another beginning. In the words of Samuel R. Delany, "Apocalypse has come and gone. We're just grubbing in the ashes."

The direction is impeccable, as fluid as the cinematography, Aronofsky and long-time collaborator Libatique forming a symbiotic duo, the camera gliding over increasingly corroded walls and surfaces, but mostly staying focused on Lawrence's features. And boy, does she hold the screen. A gamut of emotions - from contentment to bewilderment to stoic heroism to grief - plays out on her face, lit in soft, angel-like colors, for she is the Good amongst the unraveling Chaos. In the masterful hands of her director, Lawrence's painful journey is more than justified. Unlike her glitzy, Oscar-Winning roles, this one gets under your skin. Think Scarlett Johansson in - no pun intended - Jonathan Glazer's "Under the Skin" or Kate Winslet in Michel Gondry's "Eternal Sunshine of the Spotless Mind", but even more harrowing in its rawness.

While Lawrence runs the show, Bardem is right up there with her, counterbalancing Lawrence's gentleness and our sympathy with a heavy, dreadful presence, a symbol of our collective penchant for greed, fanaticism, disguised under a smarmy facade of charm. Harris and Pfeiffer are equally memorable in smaller but crucial parts, the former exuding both menace and vulnerability while the latter's invasive, eccentric nature is a welcome comical - albeit creepy - counterpoint to the heavy proceedings. Kristen Wiig shows up in a truly unforgettable, rabid cameo.

The beauty of "mother!" is that it can be scrutinized from multiple perspectives. It can be viewed as a minimalist retelling of the Bible, or as a feminist parable / desperate shriek into the abyss, or as an environmental allegory, or as a global political statement, or simply as a psychedelic horror thriller. Essays could be written about the film being one or all - or none - of the above. And that's the beauty of this film, that makes its poor box-office performance, its reportedly arduous shoot (Lawrence allegedly walked off set, fed up by the insanity of it all) and the mixed critical reception worth it. Brave, divisive art such as this tends to stand the test of time.

And in tumultuous times, we turn to art. These days, "mother!" is a breath of fresh air, despite its dark, dark themes. I applaud Aronofsky's audacity. I thank him for daring to release something unconventional, something jarring and horrifying and mesmerizing and unforgettable. "mother!" ripped my heart out. It is the best film of 2017.

5 out of 5 stars

"The Handmaiden" Marks Another Unadulterated Success in a Great Director's Career

Synopsis: A woman is hired as a handmaiden to a Japanese heiress, but secretly she is involved in a plot to defraud her.

Split into three chapters, each mirroring and revealing clues about each other, "The Handmaiden", in the words of its director Park Chan-wook, is "a thriller movie, a story about swindlers, a dramatic story with some unexpected twists, and more than anything else, a romance." He's being modest. I would add "feminist parable", "psychological study", "sneaky satire of the 'romance' genre", "heist flick", "Cronenbergian dissection of human anatomy/sexuality", and "one of 2016's best films" to the list. The director, known for handling hard-to-pinpoint genres (check out, if you dare, his "Vengeance" trilogy), navigates through these currents with the ease and grace of a seasoned pro, constantly snatching the rug from under his audiences' feet and making the film's 144 minutes whizz by. Now that's quite an accomplishment for what initially may seem like a basic, subtitled (gasp, the horror!) period-piece romance.

I hesitate to reveal much of the plot - it's one of those films where every detail may be a spoiler for the attentive - so I'll attempt to provide it in a nutshell. The conniving Count Fujiwara (Ha Jung-woo) hatches a plan to get the inheritance of Lady Hideko (Kim Min-hee) by stealing her away from the incestuous Uncle Kouzuki (Jo Jin-woong) and committing her to a mental institution. He uses Sookee (Kim Tae-ri), a self-proclaimed young pickpocket, to scheme his way into Kouzuki's gargantuan Gothic mansion. Under the pretense of being the Lady's handmaiden, Sookee begins to experience feelings for the seemingly fragile - and slightly unhinged - Hideko, while Count Fujiwara arrives to seduce the Lady. He teaches her art, completely confident in his hypnotic effect on women, and the mission's success. The three of them manage to elope to Japan… Only things don't quite work out they - or the audience, for that matter - anticipated.

By the time Part Two arrives, Chan-wook has inserted a twist to the aforementioned proceedings, leaving one intrigued and disoriented. Without saying too much, there is a flashback to Lady Hideko's harsh upbringing, revealing a depth to her relationship with the sadistic Uncle and caring-but-hollowed Aunt (Moon So-ri). The narration of Part One proves to be not-entirely-reliable, and everything is put in perspective: objects and their significance, characters' motivations and their feelings - everything mirrors each other, adding tiny brush strokes here and there, until a complex and beautiful painting appears on the canvas. The film is crammed with tiny-but-crucial details, such as a pin in Sookee's hair that also happens to be a key (literally) to salvation. Plot points unravel seamlessly, Park Chan-wook carefully peeling away the onion's layers until we get to the film's nerve-shredding core. If there ever were a film that demanded multiple viewings, this one's it, folks. Part Three plays more like an Epilogue, a natural sequence of consequences and tying of loose ends.

"The Handmaiden" is both a breath of fresh air and a powerful parable that will take your breath away. (Speaking of, breathing is a crucial aural aspect of the film, continuously reappearing on the sublime soundtrack, the breath of an orgasm juxtaposed against the Dying Breath.) Scenes wedge themselves into your brain: a woman hanging from a tree; Sookee fixing Lady Hideko's tooth in the bathroom… I've never seen anything quite like the reading of an erotic tale, Geisha-style, in front of an audience of horny men, prior to an auction - and a consequent mid-air suspension that is terrifying, artful and beautiful, embodying this unique film.

The sex scenes are some of the most genuinely erotic since the days of Roeg's "Don't Look Now". They are somehow both palpably real and sumptuously filmed with flair, radiating passion and awkwardness, heat and alienation. Another auteur, Gaspar Noé, recently attempted to approach this level of realism in "Love" (read my review **here**) but failed at it; perhaps the French director can take cues from his South Korean compadre. The passionate sequences are as "spellbindingly beautiful" as a certain part of the female anatomy, at which Sookee gapes in awe, before her and Hideko's bodies morph into one. Through the cunning use of lighting, editing - and a magic touch the secret to which only the filmmaker knows - the viewer is fully immersed, forgetting they are in a theater with dozens of other aroused spectators (insert bad Pee Wee joke here).

"Everyone's performing their roles so well," Sookee narrates, spying on the Count and the Lady, and the same can be said about the acting. Tae-ri Kim, a newcomer, portrays alluring innocence and carries the film on her deceptively fragile shoulders. Kim Min-hee is an ethereal presence, astoundingly beautiful and mysterious. Ha Jun-woo's transformation from suave chauvinist to a man coming face-to-face with his demons is effective and memorable. The women in this film are powerful and sensual, feeding off of each other's constrained energy. All criticism aimed at Chan-wook for chauvinistic male-gazing are completely unjustified - he admires those women, purposefully displaying them as objects of men's affection lovingly, luring us in, and then, "Audition"-style, reversing expectations. In the meantime, men are portrayed as shallow, scheming, sex-obsessed and self-absorbed, feeding on women like testosterone-filled predators. Only the joke's on them. This is a much more potent female empowerment tale than the shit Hollywood forces down our throats - it just expects its audiences to keep up with it.

This, of course, would not be a Park Chan-wook film without at least one scene of gasp-inducing violence. He also clearly has a thing for octopi, here a symbol of the penetrating tentacles of oozing, slithery men. The director has no tolerance for sap - something I had presumed/feared would occur in a Gothic love story. Akin to Sookee gagging at the Count's cheesy sentiments, Chan-wook would gag at the soap-opera-ish sentimentality of, say, a lot of Jane Austen adaptations. This is about as hard-edged a romance as you're going to witness. Yet a romance it is, the cinematography, by Chan-wook's "brother-in-arms" Chung Chung-hoon (who's worked with the director before on "Stoker" and "Old Boy") simply astounding, every shot charged with such eroticism and grace it would make Bernardo Bertolucci proud. "The Handmaiden", to use the old chestnut, oozes sexuality, and does so effectively, keeping the audience mesmerized (and, ahem, again, I assume, um, slightly aroused) throughout its lengthy running time.

Sadistic and beautiful, biting and romantic, it's a high-voltage, part-Shakespearean, part-psychedelic brew that only Park Chan-wook, one of the best current auteurs in cinema, could concoct. Imagine "The Talented Mr. Ripley" clashing with Marquis De Sade, then add a heavy dose of Gothic drama to the mix, and you won't even come close to picturing the experience of "The Handmaiden". It shocks, titillates and provokes in equal measures. Half-Japanese, Half-Korean, it even manages to smoothly incorporate the tumultuous political past of the two countries. Unabashedly old-fashioned in its epic sweep and grand romantic gestures, "The Handmaiden" succeeds in harkening back to the glory days of filmmaking, but also twists the genre inside out. Above all, it's hugely entertaining, always teetering on scandalous and melodramatic but never tipping over, thanks to the firm directorial grasp. Bravo.

5 out of 5 stars

4.5-STAR REVIEWS

"45 Years" Piercingly Examines the Effects of Time on a Marriage

Synopsis: *A married couple preparing to celebrate their wedding anniversary receive shattering news that promises to forever change the course of their lives.*

Sometimes a drama comes along that's so intense on a purely emotional level, it plays out like the most visceral of thrillers. Director Andrew Haigh's "45 Years" achieves that feat with the subtlest of plots, the most understated glances, a film of insinuation and longing and dread, and two formidable lead performances than propel the minimalist storyline forward with heart-wrenching momentum. Similarly to Ruben Östlund's recent "Force Majeure", in which a minor snowslide triggers a major emotional avalanche, "45 Years" also begins with a fragile, seemingly inconsequential occurrence, a flutter of a butterfly wing, that sparks a glowing remnant and eventually causes an existential inferno.

Aging couple Kate and Geoff Mercer (Charlotte Rampling and Tom Courtenay) live peacefully in the British countryside. Their 45th anniversary approaches (they had to skip the 40th, due to Geoff's bypass surgery). One day, during breakfast, they receive news of the discovery of a body, Geoff's long-lost love, Katja, frozen and presumably preserved under the ice of a Swiss mountain glacier. Geoff's immediate impulse is to go to Switzerland to identify the body, but Kate gently tells him he's too old to climb mountains.

Kate inspects the venue for their upcoming party, a museum-like building, frozen in time like Katja, where, the organizer informs her, the "Trafalgar ball" was once held. She clarifies that they specifically don't want to recreate their wedding… Is her memory of the momentous day already tarnished by the reappearance of a past love in her husband's life?

The news haunts them. Geoff reveals to Kate that he happened to be Katja's next of kin, because they had to pretend to be married for the "authorities", for some vague housing reasons. Kate is understandably suspicious, asks Geoff why he hasn't told her about this before. He is sure he has, but if he hasn't, "It's hardly the sort of thing you tell your beautiful new girlfriend, is it?"

Thus begins Kate's reevaluation of her marriage: she wonders about their absence of photos, reminisces about their days together, confronts her own insecurities, her resentments and jealousy. In the meantime, Geoff delves deep within himself, mourning the loss of his adventurous spirit, and the woman that shared it ("I think that's the worst part of getting decrepit... Losing that purposefulness.") He starts smoking again, doesn't shave, loses interest in the upcoming party. "Do you think the library will have anything on climate change?" Geoff asks, in vain hope that the ice of the past will melt away, and he may yet reconnect with a thawed-off Katja.

Katja becomes an apparition, haunting Kate's every step. She confronts Geoff, with a tremendously affecting exchange, that results in Kate saying, "I think I was enough for you. I'm just not sure you do." The final scene, the wedding anniversary, is so multi-faceted - Is Geoff's touching speech honest? Does Kate believe it? Is there a "happily-ever-after"? - it puts to shame even glorified, beautifully shot Hollywood pictures that claim to be the zenith of psychological nuance, such as Todd Haynes' beautiful, but cold and hollow, "Carol".

And talk about great acting. Charlotte Rampling, an international stalwart, known for baring it all in controversial films such as Liliana Cavani's "The Night Porter" and François Ozon's "Swimming Pool", is mesmerizing here, vulnerable and distraught and loving and tender. There is a scene where Geoff recollects the tragic past he shared with Katja, and Rampling's face conveys more during those couple of minutes than, say, Megan Fox managed in all of her films combined. Tom Courtenay gives an equally touching performance, filled with quiet regret and torment and, ultimately, what I would like to think is love.

There is a particularly beautifully-orchestrated sequence that comes about halfway through the film. It begins in dialogue, morphs into a dance and ends in passionate but ill-fated lovemaking. Their attempt to grasp onto their youth is brilliantly exemplified here, but the ultimate, for lack of a better word, climax of the sequence, involving an attic and an old photo, adds a whole other layer that makes it unforgettable.

The concepts of time, memories and aging permeate the film, whether it's in the day-by-day segment structure, as if counting down to doom; or Katja being frozen in eternal youth - something Geoff aches for (perhaps there's a reason Kate's name so closely resembles his lost love's?). It's a film of small gestures (I loved the "blink-and-you'll-miss it" look Kate gives a painting of a glacier mountain), which speak volumes of truth. With echoes of Michael Haneke's "Amour" - but not as dreadfully pragmatic about life's futility - and Paolo Sorrentino's "Youth" - but more grounded in reality - "45 Years" is about life itself and is one of the best films of the year.

4.5 out of 5 stars

"BPM: Beat Per Minute" Will Give Your Heart a Workout

Synopsis: *120 BPM. The average heart rate. The protagonists of 120 Battements Par Minute are passionate about fighting the indifference that exists towards AIDS.*

French filmmaker Robin Campillo has a penchant for lengthy running times. One could also describe his aesthetic as Dardenne-esque (sans the Belgian siblings' in-your-face grimness and keen sense of spiritual enlightenment). Campillo's features hold a dark (though not quite black) mirror to our society. The 134-minute "Time Out", which he wrote, focused on an unemployed man desperate to hide his status from loved ones, fearing inadequacy and shunning. Campillo's directorial debut, "They Came Back", twisted horror conventions, turning "the zombie film" into an exploration of time, change, familial relationships and humanity's continuously shifting values (as well as spawning a French TV spin-off, which led to the A&E remake, "The Returned"). Cannes darling "The Class" - scribbled by Robin and running at over two hours - revolved around a classroom of eager but underprivileged students, and a teacher desperate to organize chaos. "Eastern Boys", with its epic 130-minute length, examined homosexuality, gangs, prostitution and immigration. With a minimum of stylistic flourishes, Campillo's films take their time to develop and lure us into relatable worlds of familiar characters overcoming hardship and struggling to fit in.

True to form, Campillo now brings us another 140-minute study of fighting injustice, its title, "BPM", reflecting humanity's collective heartbeat. This time the setting is the late 1980's, and the subject is ACT UP, the confrontational movement of young people - mostly consisting of HIV-positive gay men - who committed a variety of shocking, inflammatory acts to bring attention to the AIDS epidemic. Purposefully avoiding incendiary drama or heart-pounding action, Campillo's focal point is the everyday lives of the protestors, their debates and passions and fears. The result is a powerful story about fighting injustice - arguably Campillo's best effort yet.

The film opens with ACT UP's scheduled Tuesday meeting, during which they argue over a particularly violent publicity stunt that got out of hand (involving a politician and a balloon filled with fake blood). Segregation and major disagreements flare up within the faction. When ACT UP invades the offices of a pharmaceutical company, the HIV-positive members group together in the elevator - the rest take the stairs. A potential new treatment method raises a heated debate about its efficiency, the unproven drug potentially eclipsing established (albeit ineffective) treatment methods. Campillo takes his time pulling us into their world, slyly narrowing the focus on the film's two protagonists: Sean Dalmazo (Nahuel Pérez Biscayart, resembling a young Vincent Cassel) and Nathan (Arnaud Valois).

The director observes, never judging, allowing us to question ACT UP's sometimes-horrific methods of conveying their message. Smearing unsuspecting employees in fake blood while blaring horns and tearing up their offices could be seen as a bit, well, extreme. Yet it's not all guerrilla warfare. ACT UP is led by well-spoken, clear-minded individuals that hold their own at meetings with corporate bigwigs about, say, the futility of lengthy, painful, lymph-node-puncturing trials. That said, most of the protestors are kids, raucous young men and women who want to live their short lives to the fullest, partying in clubs to the sounds of early rave music. (One such hallucinatory clubbing sequence morphs into a virtual depiction of a T-cell being destroyed by HIV.) Despite the stink of death lingering in their nostrils, they joke about how much their photographer bends when he takes photos, jab each other, fall in love… There is a highly tender, prolonged lovemaking sequence between Sean and Nathan, with them sharing their innermost secrets and insecurities with each other, that's as frank and realistic a depiction of sex as I've seen in a while in cinema - gay or straight.

There are also unexpected lyrical interludes, such as the bitter and vivacious Sean looking out a train window, marveling at the stunning mandarin sky hanging over the city, its eternal vastness a stark contrast to Sean's own ephemeral existence. Another young man collapses unexpectedly during a meeting, his condition deteriorating at an accelerated pace - a powerfully poignant moment in a heartrending but never manipulative character arc. The film really picks up in its final hour, with a tighter focus on Sean's own tragic trajectory, Nathan by his side, the actor's soulful eyes conveying every emotion, (titular) beat by beat. Biscayart better clear that shelf for some major awards coming his way.

Searingly affecting, with minimal music cues letting us know how to feel, "BPM" is a sobering look at the lives of the ignored, by turns tragic and joyous. More importantly, it (for the most part) avoids the languid pratfalls of the director's previous lengthy efforts. Unraveling gracefully, gradually, "BPM" will wedge itself into your consciousness, beat by beat.

4.5 out of 5 stars

"Coco" Reminds Us Why Pixar is the Best

Synopsis: *Aspiring musician Miguel, confronted with his family's ancestral ban on music, enters the Land of the Dead to work out the mystery.*

The best films work on multiple level, engaging different parts of the brain. Pixar knows this better than most. After several recent missteps - "Finding Dory", "Cars 3" and the widespread derision towards what I personally think is a perfectly charming little adventure, "The Good Dinosaur" - "Coco" marks the company's attempt to scale the heights of their best film so far, "Inside Out". While not quite reaching them, Pixar doesn't sear its wings against the sun either. Far from it. A story of a young Mexican boy reconnecting with his ancestors in the Land of the Dead during Día de Muertos celebrations, "Coco" provides a wondrous feast for the eyes and a great emotional workout; there wasn't a dry eye in the house. It may lack the searing poignancy of "Inside Out" and follow a somewhat-predictable structure, yet sometimes formula works if done right, and such is the case with "Coco".

Born into a family of shoemakers, Miguel (Anthony Gonzalez) is obsessed with Ernesto de la Cruz (Benjamin Bratt), a famous guitarist and soap actor, who was tragically crushed by a... well, I won't spoil one of the film's many comic highlights for you. Miguel's great-grandmother, Mamá Coco (Ana Ofelia Murguía), used to be married to a musician, whose face ended up torn out of their family photo; a dark past which led to the family turning their back on music. Despite their disapproval, Miguel signs up for a Day of the Dead contest - but after grandmother Abuelita (Renée Victor) smashes Miguel's handmade guitar, the boy has no choice but steal (or "borrow") his idol's, from de la Cruz's shrine at the local cemetery.

This leads Miguel to the spectacular Land of the Dead, a breathtaking vision that surpasses anything Pixar has done so far, by far. Filled with layers of railroads and highways, magnificent twisted buildings, a wild variety of skeletal inhabitants and neon spirit creatures, the metropolis has its own districts, from the slums to the most prestigious areas, each vibrant and dazzling, connected by ephemeral golden bridges.

Miguel, seeking his family's blessing so that he could get back to the Living before sunrise - or he will turn into a skeleton himself ("La Cenicienta", anyone?) - embarks on a search for de la Cruz, with the help of the misshapen Héctor (Gael Garcia Bernal). On the way he encounters many imaginative characters, among them none other than Frida Kahlo (Natalia Cordova-Buckley), unibrow and all. When Miguel finally meets his idol, de la Cruz isn't quite what the boy imagined...

Pixar has always nailed the what I call "tiny detours". They're not pop-culture puns or marvels of animated pixels (though there's an abundance of both - the jaw-dropping dragons of the underworld are a particular standout, both a splendid visualization of the mythological alebrijes and a sly/loving reference to the spirit animals of Philip Pullman's "His Dark Materials" trilogy and Hayao Miyazaki's "Princess Mononoke"). No, what I'm specifically talking about are the small gestures and expressions, the tiny, very human asides that give the characters their depth, their strength, their personality quirks. Lee Unkrich and his creative team clearly spend an inordinate amount of time studying human behavior and translating its nuances into animated magic.

They evidently spent just as much time studying Mexican culture, as it is depicted in all its glorious - if perhaps embellished - detail with much reverence and sensitivity. The team of animators went to Mexico and delved deep into its traditions. The Día de Muertos festival is about families honoring the journeys of their dearly departed, and one of "Coco's" many memorable sequences involves Miguel making his way through tombstones and graves, all candle-lit altars with the deceased's memorabilia. Every frame is peppered with some authentic detail. My friend from Mexico City, where the film premiered ahead of its U.S. release - raves about how "Coco" nails the tiniest of nuances. She would know. She's Mexican.

One of the film's many strengths is its refusal to shy away from adult themes. "Coco" does not underestimate its young audience's intelligence, dealing with death (and murder), the loss of a father, living up to parental expectations; there are even timely references to illegal immigration. Its overall message of acceptance couldn't be more relevant in our tumultuous times. Some of this will go over right over the young 'uns heads, some of it will resonate but they won't quite know why, and the stuff that sticks - well, it's quite profound, calibrated to inspire and challenge a child. Just don't blame them for belting out "Remember Me", "Coco"'s lead tune (of which there are thankfully few, especially for a self-proclaimed musical), on par with "Moana"'s "How Far I'll Go" (...before my parents shoot themselves) or "Frozen"'s "Let It Go" (...because I will never stop singing it).

Whether it's Disney's heavy-handed touch or a fear of *too* much "adultness", there are moments in "Coco" that could have used more subtlety. Most of the film's themes are spelled out by Ernesto de la Cruz, in snippets: "Never underestimate the power of music", or "When reaching for the dream, [make sure to] hang on tight, make it come true", or "One cannot deny what one is meant to be." Thankfully, a clever mid-point reversal makes you reconsider the earnestness of those statements, rendering the obviousness somewhat forgivable. What's harder to disregard is the film's predictability. While the final scenes are surely powerful, I could see the exact beat-by-beat conclusion about halfway through the film. The sentimentality may be well earned, but it would have been nice to see Pixar slip the rug from under us a little instead of sticking to what works.

Regardless, this is superior entertainment, whether you're nine of fifty-nine - and it's because Lee Unkrich's odyssey functions on so many levels: as a heart-tugging drama, rip-roaring adventure, subtle societal critique and splendid eye-candy. If "Cars 2" were Drakkar Noir, "Coco" is Pixar's Chanel No 5.

4.5 out of 5 stars

"La Notte": Italian Maestro Antonioni Dissects a Crumbling Marriage

Synopsis: *A day in the life of an unfaithful married couple and their steadily deteriorating relationship.*

As the French New Wave movement was gradually changing the shape of cinema forever, itself spawned by the splurge of Italian neorealist films of the 1950s, Italian directors such as Michelangelo Antonioni and Federico Fellini (himself one of the originators of neorealism) began to redefine the "art film". Antonioni particularly favored atmosphere and mood over conventional narrative structure, producing films that would be felt on a subconscious, visceral level rather than an overtly intellectual one. He made seemingly obtuse cinematic offerings mainstream. Fellini, in the meantime, fully embraced surreal/magical realism, both alienating a good portion of his devoted fans and gaining a new cult audience. Some of the world's greatest screen legends starred in their films, including Marcello Mastroianni, Monica Vitti, Alain Delon and Jeanne Moreau. One cannot underestimate those celluloid maestros' significance when it comes to tracing modern cinema's past.

The central film of Antonioni's "trilogy on modernity and its discontents" - which started with the Cannes Jury Prize Winner, the convention-shattering drama "L'Avventura", and climaxed with the Palme d'Or nominated, poetic "L'Eclisse" (a film that influenced the majority of Martin Scorsese's work) - "La Notte" won the Golden Bear at the Berlin International Film Festival in 1961, but encountered censorship upon release due to its tame-by-today's-standards nudity and sexual innuendoes. It also appeared on Stanley Kubrick's top 10 list, its shadows, silences and uncanny, symmetrical visuals evident in most of the late director's work (as they are in pretty much everything, from Cassavetes' ouvre to the Dardenne brothers' modern masterpieces). Looking back at "La Notte" now, it's shockingly ironic how fresh it feels, amongst the deluge of clone-like Hollywood by-products. It makes one long for the days of true cinematic innovation, pity those that avert their ADD-addled glances in favor of bombastic, shut-your-brain-off entertainment, and be grateful that those films exist, their imprint still palpable in the small portion of truly innovative films that come out today.

"La Notte" opens with an ambient, sterile, desolate soundtrack that accompanies blankly geometric visuals of Milan construction sites. The camera slides down the side of a modern skyscraper, instantly setting the mood of a downward spiral, an alienation felt in the New substituting the Old, as the lens' gaze shifts to a stunning shot of the historical part of Milan. Author of a just-published book called "The Season", Giovanni (Marcello Mastroianni) and his wife Lidia (Jeanne Moreau) visit their terminally-ill friend Tommaso (Bernhard Wicki), nary exchanging a word on their way to the hospital. Tommaso is filled with regret, but ends his sad soliloquy with a bright note: "A little self-criticism puts things in perspective and gives you courage." He then longingly looks out the hospital window, at a helicopter tracing its way through the concrete jungle. "Quite a place, eh?" he dryly states. "Everything I used to hate in terms of style. I never thought I'd end my days in such luxury. I feel like a fraud." His sardonic, pessimistic outlook reverberates throughout the rest of the film, as does the theme of change.

Lidia leaves to cry outside the hospital, while Giovanni gets sidetracked by a mentally-unstable-but-gorgeous patient, who - almost successfully - tries to seduce him in a highly unexpected, erotically-charged sequence. When Giovanni relates this incident to his wife, Lidia's response is that of apathy. Their relationship is deteriorating as fast as poor Tommaso, as rapidly as the Old City is being replaced by the New One. We follow the couple to Giovanni's book party - but Lidia promptly leaves, to go wandering through the streets of Milan, where she encounters an abandoned child, witnesses a street fight and joins some guys who are setting out fireworks. Giovanni soon reunites with Lidia and brings her home. Somehow both restless, sensual and forlorn (Moreau's acting prowess on full display here), Lidia, nude in a bathtub, asks Giovanni if they could leave the house; Giovanni suggests going to the filthy rich Gherardini's, but, just as they get dressed for the occasion, in a desperate attempt to sustain their relationship, Lidia asks to go elsewhere, just the two of them. They end up in a burlesque jazz club (featuring a highly memorable dance sequence), where Lidia, bored, changes her mind about going the Gherardini's.

They crash a celebration, where the cynical Valentina Gherardini (Monica Vitti, a force to be reckoned with) comes in, sweeping Giovanni off his feet (quite literally). In the meantime, the mysterious Roberto (Giorgio Negro) lurks in Lidia's shadows, an alluring and somewhat-alarming presence. The party a background of jazz and distant laughter, Lidia spots her husband making out with Valentina. A sudden downpour sends the entire party diving into the pool (and, in my favorite non-sequitur moment, a young woman making out with a statue). A pivotal moment occurs when Giovanni and Valentina emerge after an intimate session, to come face-to-face with Lidia and Roberto, soaked from the rain - and a consequent heartrending confrontation between the couple, out in the vast and quiet Italian fields.

If this all doesn't exactly sound like a thrill-a-second ride, well, it's because it's not. "La Notte" is about moods: those of doubt, jealousy, despair, alienation, reconciliation. It's an immersive aural and visual experience, an artistic statement on the disillusionment of marriage. The jazzy, sparse, seductive and melancholic soundtrack echoes the film's dualities of serenity and melancholia, graceful eroticism and empathy for its characters. The long stretches of silence serve as moments of reflection, as much for the film's characters as they are for the audience. Each shot is perfectly composed, the camera movement fluid, the gorgeous black-and-white accentuating its thematic contrasts. Antonioni pulls you in with his visuals, into his world of space between words, of change and nostalgia, of dissipating love. In a sparsely-verbal film, the phrases that *are* uttered matter. "But sometimes beauty can really be depressing," a character observes, and dammit if it weren't true. "I no longer have ideas, just memories," another character states. There is an incisive dissection of writing and why humans aspire to greatness and strive to leave behind a legacy. A beautiful-but-inaudible moment of conversation in a rain-soaked car wedges itself into your consciousness. My favorite line of dialogue comes towards the end, from Valentina: "You two have really worn me out tonight."

The film's acting is (almost) uniformly top-notch. Antonioni's protagonists say a lot more with gestures, glances and movements than words ever could, particularly Moreau, in a masterclass showcase, a highlight of an incredible career. If I have one gripe with the film, it's Mastroianni's wooden performance, especially compared to the wildly expressive women that surround him. Perhaps it was the director's intention, to paint Giovanni as abstract and unreadable as the future he faces, a faceless object, but towards the end his lack of readability becomes a nuisance (almost saved in the film's final, unforgettable shot).

The film's profound minimalism, its unconventional editing - sometimes a cut anticipates an action within the shot, at other times it accentuates a certain object or expression - coupled with its infinite artistic merits and historical significance in the annals of cinema, marks it as one of those "can't miss" experiences. If you're a true cinefile - or an appreciator of culture in general - you owe it to yourself to see "La Notte" - or Antonioni's entire trilogy, for that matter, or most films from that magical, transformative era of filmmaking. I promise, the journey will leave you "Breathless" (couldn't help myself). Indeed, how marvelously ironic - to delve into the past, in order to get a breath of fresh air.

4.5 out of 5 stars

"Meru" Reaches the Summit of Bold Documentary Filmmaking

Synopsis: *Three elite climbers struggle to find their way through obsession and loss as they attempt to climb Mount Meru, one of the most coveted prizes in the high stakes game of Himalayan big wall climbing.*

In October, 2008, renowned alpinist Conrad Anker, along with fellow daredevils Jimmy Chin and Renan Ozturk, arrived in India to tackle Meru, a 21,000-foot summit in Northern India. The notoriously difficult climb is riddled with absurd obstacles, such as the 4,000 excruciating feet leading up to a "smooth, clean, nearly-featureless" Shark's Fin, a vertical cliff, on top of which rests the much sought-after summit.

Jimmy Chin' and Elizabeth Chai Vasarhelyi's visceral account of the trio's adventure doesn't beat around the bush. The very first shot sees them sleeping in a tent strapped to a steep precipice, virtually frozen under layers of clothes and sleeping bags. The next scene finds our heroes climbing - at night! - up a treacherous cliff, as an ethereal dawn descends upon them. It's a quiet and breathtaking opening to a deeply exhilarating film.

The characters' rich backgrounds unravel as the story progresses. Conrad, the leader, calls mountain-climbing the most dangerous extreme sport, and excitedly states: "Meru is a combination of all I've done and all I've wanted to do." His wife, Jenny, seems to get her husband's passion but then, as his family history deepens, the stakes rise. Renan is described as borderline homeless, an insane climber and artist, who takes part in any expedition offered to him. And then there's Jimmy, a climber and filmmaker, who's photographed both K2 and Mount Everest. His parents escaped from China during the Communist revolution, coming to the US to build a new life, and had high expectations from him, his father particularly tough, shaping him into a hardened, impassioned man. Jimmy's mother made him promise not to die before her…

Famous climber and author Jon Krakauer ("Into Thin Air") adds extra validity to the film, providing an articulately reverential narration of their journey; he describes the peak as "the point where heaven and earth and hell all come together". He points out that Jimmy and Conrad have climbed Mt. Everest four or five times; Jimmy even skied off the top. But Meru is different - there's no sherpas to hire to help carry stuff and secure the ropes. You're on your own.

Our climbers' planned seven-day trip turned into a 20-day odyssey, bringing them to within 100 meters of the elusive summit. Each carried a 200-pound load, most of which was meant for the last high-altitude stretch, where the body needs significantly more energy to keep functioning. Yet an unexpected storm came, delaying their climb by days and depleting more than half of their food supply before they even got to the halfway point. Conrad's persistence in attempting to reach the summit against all odds (they split their last frozen cubes of cheese, roasting them over fire) turned into severe disappointment when he realized that there was no way they could succeed. So close and yet so far… In Conrad's own words: "The center of the universe is… unattainable." They came back with frostbite, blackened and bloodied feet (a condition called trench foot); Jimmy was confined to a wheelchair for a while… Yet Conrad was possessed, already planning their next Meru climb.

After another famous alpinist failed to reach the summit of Meru, Conrad took it as a sign: time to try again. But a series of horrid events occurred: Renan received a severe head injury during a skiing/shooting project, which almost killed him. Jimmy got mauled by an avalanche, and miraculously survived. The two events shook the crew up - especially Jimmy, who, for a while, was in a "bad way, psychologically". Conrad himself had lost a friend in an avalanche during an earlier climb, an event that haunts him to this day (he is now married to the friend's wife, who is clearly attracted to alpinists).

So the decision to go back wasn't easy. In 2011, the three of them ventured into hell again, under even harsher circumstances: equipment shattered; Renan broke down emotionally (but overcame his demons and became the team's leader); icy blizzards scarred their bodies; and an overdose of couscous almost happened. The final moments of the film, albeit brief, are sublimely powerful.

With no reenactments, no fancy visual embellishments (save for one helpful tracing of their route), "Meru" is about as raw, nerve-shredding and, for lack of a better word, authentic as documentaries get. The fact that the trio filmed their own adventures under the harshest circumstances a human being can possibly endure - and that those shots are so overwhelmingly gorgeous - is astonishing. This is a straightforward account of three men's perseverance in the face of insurmountable obstacles, both emotional and physical.

I did wonder why the filmmakers decided not to show the alpinists' descents, which, as far as I know, having read Krakauer's book, may be even more treacherous. But that's a minor flaw in a transcendent parable on human endurance, friendship, obsession and a ceaseless passion for exploration. Hopefully, films like "Meru" or its thematic brothers, "Touching the Void" and "Man on Wire", will inspire folks to get out of their grey cubicles and challenge themselves, for the world is a wondrous, magnificent and fragile place, and our lives are fleeting. Films likes this makes one wonder why so many of us wage wars, pollute, run massive corrupt corporations - or, for that matter, surrender ourselves to what we established as "societal norms", the day-to-day nuclear existences. Whatever drives Conrad, Jimmy and Renan to keep risking they lives, those guys are badasses, the few remaining true explorers among us, and their feats should be applauded. If the Academy Award voters have any sense left in them, "Meru", along with "Cartel Land" and "The Look of Silence", will be an Oscar contender this year.

4.5 out of 5 stars

Bernal Hunts Down Gnecco in Larraín's Poetic "Neruda"

Synopsis: *An inspector hunts down Nobel Prize-winning Chilean poet, Pablo Neruda, who becomes a fugitive in his home country in the late 1940s for joining the Communist Party.*

"Tonight I can write the saddest lines.
Write, for example, 'The night is starry and the stars are blue and shiver in the distance.'
The night wind revolves in the sky and sings.
Tonight I can write the saddest lines.
I loved her, and sometimes she loved me too."

– an excerpt from Tonight I Can Write (The Saddest Lines) by Pablo Neruda (Translated by W.S. Merwin).

Pablo Neruda – "the greatest poet of the 20th Century in any language," according to Gabriel García Márquez – led a tumultuous, extravagant, wildly romantic life. A senator for the Chilean Communist Party, Neruda had to flee his homeland after the regime was outlawed in the late 1940s, escaping through perilous mountains – on a horse! – to Argentina. His poetry deemed offensive, Neruda himself labeled a traitor, he could only return home years later. In 1971, Pablo Neruda won a Nobel Prize for Literature; two years later he died in his native Chile. A complex, sardonic, deeply affectionate man, he led a passionate life; director Pablo Larraín's "Neruda" is as poetic, surreal and eloquent as its prolific titular character.

Though he's worked on countless projects, Larraín is arguably most notable for the Gael García Bernal starrer, political satire "No," where Bernal played an ad exec going after Chilean president Augusto Pinochet. This time the chameleon-like actor appears as Óscar Peluchonneau, a Prefect who doesn't read much poetry and whose name reflects his bloated personality, sent on a mission to "catch and humiliate Pablo Neruda." Desperate – and unable to – understand the artist, his poetry and motivations, Peluchonneau is deeply envious of his nemesis, as he has no clearly-defined identity of his own – except striving to live up to his esteemed father's reputation. Driven by this jealousy, awe and bitterness, but also by a canine-like perseverance, Óscar will stop at nothing to capture the poet.

But Bernal, while melancholic, funny, despicable and sympathetic in equal measures, wisely takes a step back to let the star of the show, Mr. Luis Gnecco as Pablo Neruda, shine. And shine he does, lighting every scene in more nuanced colors than the brilliant cinematographer Sergio Armstrong (who has worked with the director on "No"). Both Gnecco and Larraín portray the artist as a fantasist, to whom the entire dangerous escape from Chilean authorities is wildly exciting, another elaborate verse in the artist's glamorized existence, one in which the Prefect and his girlfriend and the authorities are all romanticized characters. A man whose pen "has the ability to change a thousand minds," Pablo never loses sight of his sense of humor. When told that 300 policemen are after him, an intoxicated Neruda remarks, "That's quite a lot, isn't it?" At another point he states, "You think exiling us will help? No. You have to kill us."

His personality too large to be confined in cramped apartments, ("Neruda is a man of bare land and eagles, not of mattresses…"), Pablo seeks solace in brothels, parties where he dresses as Lawrence of Arabia, and provoking scandal by badmouthing the new president – until he finally decides to go for the border. His partner – and later, for a brief time, wife – Delia Del Carril (a perfectly-calibrated performance from Mercedes Morán), stays by the genius, through all the infidelities and borderline-abusive behavior ("Kill yourself, Delia," Pabloa spits in her face at one point. "That way I'll write about you for another 20 years."), basking in his adventurous spirit.

Apart from being an incisive character study, Larraín's stunner of a film plays like a thriller, such as in the tense sequence, where 30 poems are distributed anonymously, one of them sent to – and later publicly read by – Pablo Picasso himself; or in the final, lyrical mountainous escape scene. It plays like an acute indictment of the suppression of the freedom of speech and creative expression, with numerous portrayals of the horrid conditions of the Chilean Communist camps. It plays like a comedy: Peluchonneau thinks he's seduced Neruda's bitter wife, only to be proved very wrong when she publicly professes her admiration of the artist instead of condemning him ("He's not a traitor, he's very kind. He owes me a lot of money, but he's a great man.") It plays like a metaphysical exploration of art itself, the impact it can have culturally, socially, politically, personally, breaking the fourth wall subtly, such as when Óscar whines, "I'm not a supporting character!" We all are either leaders or supporting characters; we either lay in the shadows or bask in the sun – and sometimes it's impossible to escape the shadows.

"Neruda" celebrates life, love, music, the art of storytelling – poetry's impact specifically, but it also challenges the norms of narrative through it's "mostly-linear-sometimes-fragmented" structure, mirroring Pablo's writing – and it's filled with stunning prose, courtesy of screenwriter Guillermo Calderón. That's how you write a script, folks. Surely to be a contender for the Academy Awards this year, "Neruda" is a cinematic poem worth reciting over and over.

4.5 out of 5 stars

"Personal Shopper" Marks Another Hit for Assayas & Stewart

Synopsis: *A ghost story that takes place in the fashion underworld of Paris.*

"Personal Shopper"'s IMDB synopsis is so deceptively simple, those not familiar with the psychologically-complex films of French director Olivier Assayas may assume that this is just another cheap-o horror flick churned out by the House of Blum, in the vein of "Insidious", "Oculus" or "Jessabelle". Considering that the lead star is known for a certain little vampire franchise, I wouldn't blame those suckers either. Assayas seems to have found his muse in Kristen Stewart, who became the first American actress to win the prestigious Cesar award for her supporting role in the director's 2015 drama "Clouds of Sills Maria".

So folks are either in for a major disappointment or a pleasant surprise. While "Personal Shopper" is indeed a ghost story, it does not contain your usual murderous talking dolls, demonic clowns or vampire fangs. One could argue that all the makings of a stereotypical horror flick are here - a dilapidated house with loudly creaking doors; a young woman hell-bent on making contact with the spiritual world, a jump scare or two, a ghost even - yet they are seen through a sophisticated, minimalist prism, one cloaked in a foreboding atmosphere of building tension, which compensates for outright shocks.

Assayas' film is first and foremost a hypnotic rumination on life and death, social status and art, mourning and moving on, faith and identity, and our connection to our loved ones, which transcends the spiritual realm. It's a tough task to pull off, and in less capable hands it could have easily slipped into a laughable disaster, but with Olivier's assured directorial grip, honed by three decades of filmmaking, and Kristen's take-no-prisoners central performance, "Personal Shopper" leaves you breathless. The experienced helmer subverts horror film staples, insinuating rather than showing, posing questions rather than answering them. He understands that the human imagination has the ability of conjuring monsters infinitely more disturbing than any of the translucent deities in, say, James Wan's 2013 hit.

Stewart plays Maureen, a self-proclaimed medium, whom we first see dropped off at a spooky Paris mansion by Lara (Sigrid Bouaziz). She hears noises at night and sees a glimpse of an apparition. "Lewis?" she calls into the darkness. Unlike idiotic Hollywood characters that venture into the clearly-dangerous unknown, Maureen has a purpose, and the spirit seems somewhat benevolent. "You must make contact," Lara insists next morning.

Maureen also works as a personal shopping assistant for the uptight fashionista Kyra (Nora von Waldstätten), picking out the uptight control freak's expensive jewelry and clothing. Maureen resembles a ghost herself, all pale, trying on Kyra's shoes, picking up things left behind by the boss, standing in for her photo shoots… The girl becomes so immersed in her research of the spiritual realm, the world around her dims, including her boyfriend, who tempts her to come visit him by the seaside. But Maureen is waiting, always waiting, for a sign, for closure, for Lewis to respond to her, her own identity dissipating.

Who Lewis is, I'll let you discover. Twenty-five minutes in, it's not a major plot twist. Most reviews will probably spoil it, but in this particular case, I think it's best to leave most things unspoken, mirroring Assayas' style. I will, however, say that the plot gets increasingly and deliciously complex. Maureen meets Ingo (Lars Eidinger), Kyra's boy toy; she comes in contact with an angry female spirit and starts receiving creepy texts. The world begins to close in on the young woman, with the manipulative mysterious texter increasingly threatening - until the discovery of a grisly murder scene, and Maureen's closure (of sorts) at the heartrending finale.

"You need to avoid physical efforts and intense emotions," Maureen's doctor advises her. The film's dialogue, written by Assayas, is sparse and, it seems, partially improvised. "When you're a medium, you're just attuned to a vibe," Maureen says. "It's an intuition… a feeling… you see this door, and it's only slightly ajar." Determined to summon Lewis' spirit when it shows itself in form of a running faucet, Maureen exclaims, "I'm gonna need more from you."

"Personal Shopper" raises fascinating questions about the inspiration behind forward-thinking works of art. It's filled with moments of unbearable tension, birthed by great characterization and intricate plotting, as opposed to cheap shock tactics. There's that unforgettable, nerve-racking text exchange on a train to and from London, with the beautiful cities fading to a blur (the power of texting!). Maureen's state of mind is so vividly portrayed - and depicted by Yorick Le Saux' stunning camerawork - the films sinks its fangs into you deeper than "Twilight"'s Edward could ever muster. And this film is weirder than any beast in the epic Meyer trilogy. It has an enigmatic, unpredictable pace of its own, with unexpected fade-outs, plot detours, purposefully unresolved plot points and a meticulous attention to detail. I loved every second of it.

On occasion, it does verge on the ridiculous, especially when the apparition shows up - a cross between the library ghost in "Ghostbusters" and "Donnie Darko"'s liquid spears. Lines like, "She vomited ectoplasm and then she left," don't help either. Somewhat reminiscent of Brit Marling's fare, it's filled with dialogues about the soul, other realms, etc. There's even an extended Victor Hugo flashback/interlude, beautifully written but, like, huh?! I reiterate: I loved every second of it. Here's a director that goes for it, takes chances, and ends up with mesmerizing entertainment. He deconstructs a typical ghost story into its most basic elements, but also emphasizes all the mournful aspects inherent to a ghost story, skillfully avoiding stereotypes in the process. Hats off.

Final note. Stewart really gets a chance to show off her acting chops here, folks. No more pouty Bella. Fully shedding her "Twilight" persona, Stewart inhabits her chain-smoking character, in constant waiting, drawn to forbidden things, reserved, focused, very upfront, but also vulnerable and questioning her own sanity. Stewart and Assayas may just be the new Scorsese and DiCaprio, or Hitchcock and Kelly, leaving the days of Edward and Bella far in the past.

4.5 out of 5 stars

Drenched in Filtered Sunlight, "Summer 1993" Evokes Pure Nostalgic Bliss

Synopsis: *After her mother's death, six-year-old Frida is sent to her uncle's family to live with them in the countryside. But Frida finds it hard to forget her mother and adapt to her new life.*

Coming-of-age films aren't exactly rare. From "Stand by Me" to "Boyhood", from "The 400 Blows" to "I'm Not Scared", from "Kids" to last year's fantastic "The Florida Project" - numerous visionary directors have painted that fragile, heartrending moment of transitioning from innocence to adulthood. Now it's Carla Simón's turn to join the ranks of Rob Reiner, Richard Linklater, François Truffaut, Gabriele Salvatores, Larry Clark and Sean Baker.

Her feature-length debut, "Summer 1993", also brings to mind the works by the Belgian Dardenne brothers (see: "The Son"), in its pseudo-documentary approach, languid pace and a borderline-spiritual ending, both deeply revelatory and as delicate as porcelain. The film didn't quite make it to the Oscars, although it was in the run to be nominated in the Best Foreign Language Film category. Too bad. With its hushed, wondrous, colorful, tragic and joyous look at childhood - one afflicted with trauma - Simón used the subtlest of brushtrokes to create one of the prettiest painting on the cinematic canvas of 2017. She has a bright future ahead of her.

Kudos go out to her cast. It all comes down to four principal roles: the six-year-old Frida (Laia Artigas), whose parents just passed away and who is thrust from the urban landscape of Barcelona into the jungle-like environment of the Catalina countryside by her somewhat-insistent grandparents; Anna (the adorable Paula Robles), her younger cousin (but really a new sister), precocious and infinitely trusting; and Anna's parents, Esteve (David Verdauger) and Marga (Bruna Cusí), the latter of whom commands a sequence of such tenderness it's almost painful to write about. It involves her lying down next to a distraught Frida and caressing her gently, like only a mother could.

I mentioned that Simón "portrays" an actor - this may be a mistake, for the actors seem to live a life of their own, the camera glimpsing them vérité-style, in prolonged scenes that folks jaded on Marvel may find coma-inducing, but I found striking in how authentic they are. The camera assumes Frida's perspective, sometimes literally following her from behind, the back of her curly head in focus, the world behind her a kaleidoscope of colors both familiar and muted, exciting and distressing. The film is clearly autobiographical, the director drawing from her own experiences, all nostalgic images that seem to come unfiltered from her mind straight to the screen.

Chickens plucking at their own spilled eggs. Children dancing on a dimly-lit porch. Two stalwart farmers bleeding a sheep to death. Endlessly wondering through the countryside, touching trees and stone walls and dirt. An argument between parents, both distant and incomprehensible and deeply affecting. Running after a car as your family abandons you. Abandoning a child out of spite, because you didn't know better. Stringing together those images into a lyrical narrative, Simón creates a tangible, vivid representation of what it's like to be a lost child, on the brink of bursting through your own skin.

But what really ties the film together is its final sequence, so keenly observed, poignant and heartbreakingly real, it lends even more depth to the preceding proceedings. It's Laia Artigas' shining moment, her Frida finally tearing through the hazy veneer of childhood and getting a raw glimpse of reality. It's an astounding feat of acting, a rare moment that caught me off-guard, left me wondering how this tiny, inexperienced actress managed not to only hold the screen for over 90 minutes, but also so subtly portray such a complex spectrum of emotions. But it's not just her. All four leads play a crucial role in how this magical scene unfolds - and ends - and deserve equal credit. Both intimate in scope and epic in its depth of feeling, "Summer 1993" hits all the right notes, ending with the perfect one. Seems like Carla Simón has come of age, artistically speaking. And just like Frida, she had nothing to worry about. Things will be okay.

4.5 out of 5 stars

"The Girlfriend Experience": Lawmaker by Day, Lawbreaker by Night

Synopsis: *TV series based on Steven Soderbergh's "The Girlfriend Experience", which centered on the life of a New York call girl.*

Steven Soderbergh's "The Girlfriend Experience", similarly to most of his films, was technically-sound, not without its artistic merit - but also detached, cold and, like its protagonist, hard to read and ultimately vacant. So it's fitting that the co-creator of the STARZ spin-off, Lodge Kerrigan, decided to expand upon the film's themes and infuse the show, and its central character, with some much-need dimension and context (if not necessarily warmth). Kerrigan directed the heartrending "Keane", after all (if you haven't seen that film yet, order it now), and he utilizes his knack for subtle characterization and empathy here to great advantage. His "partner-in-crime", Amy Seimetz (who shows up in a few episodes as sensible sister Annabel), starred in the mind-bending, experimental "Upstream Color", directed by Shane Carruth, who composes the ethereal score to "The Girlfriend Experience", echoing its otherworldly vibes.

My feeling is that the show's blend of incisiveness/poignancy and coolness/artfulness is the result of the meeting of those disparate yet symbiotic minds. It doesn't always work - there are moments when the series' self-awareness becomes a little grating - but "TGE" is certainly more intriguing / captivating / absorbing than Soderbergh's big-screen effort, a relatively rare case where a celluloid TV interpretation one-ups its cinematic source material. It's a genuinely one-of-a-kind, cerebral experience, which renders it one of the best shows of 2016 so far.

Christine, played by Riley Keogh (Elvis's granddaughter!) gets seduced by her friend Avery (Kate Lyn Shell) into the dark shadows of the Chicago underworld, following her on a "date", the titular experience. A focused and cynical law intern by day, Christine, instantly seduced, becomes the sultry Chelsea by night, at first just "listening and asking" over dinner with a client. Curiosity killed the cat, yet this feline doesn't seem aware of the phrase, as she consequently delves into repeated coitus with a number of men (and women). When Christine/Chelsea threatens to branch out, her pimp Jacqueline (Alexandra Costillo) threatens right back by placing an envelope with Christine/Chelsea's nude photos on her work desk. Let the power-(p)lay/blackmail games begin!

The allure of sexual pleasure and the feeling of empowerment it provides leads Christine/Chelsea to sleep with Avery and then her own married boss, lawyer David Tellis (Paul Sparks), which in turns stirs up sociopathic behavior on her behalf that steadily spreads, akin to an STD. Spurred by her newfound rebellious lifestyle, a psychotic stalker, and the recent threats from Jacqueline, Christine/Chelsea gathers the balls (ha!) to blackmail David. Eventually she's fired in a mesmerizing sequence of events, and escapes to see more - progressively shadier - clients in Toronto. In the meantime, her identity goes public, an explicit, NSFW video appearing on the cover of all Chicago newspapers and blogs. Eventually, Christine/Chelsea may have to decide which one she really is.

For all the seemingly scandalous drama (in a sub-plot that initially seems random but eventually gets intertwined with Christine/Chelsea's plight - and the show's prevalent themes - David and his partner, Erin (Mary Lynn Rajskub), fight over a case), the filmmakers adopted a muted, chilly approach to the proceedings. Things unfold without any eccentricity of flare for the overly dramatic. This isn't "The O.C."... Or look at it as "The O.C." re-imagined by Lars von Trier.

Christine/Chelsea becomes a therapist for these men, most of them needy and desperate, lonely and ashamed, others arrogant and vulgar and sadistic. One touching moment comes when a desolate client professes his love to her but has to take out loans in order to keep seeing her - an uncomfortable but powerful sequence. In another memorable bit (of which there are many), a disheveled wife pays off/threatens Christine/Chelsea never to see her husband again. The stalker scenes are extraordinary for avoiding the pratfalls of your standard slasher thriller antics - the suspense comes unexpectedly and escalates swiftly, to plateau and dissipate just as effectively.

In another exemplary prologue to a chapter, a client seems to have died and then (literally) resurfaces - a sustained, highly intense moment that culminates with respite… just to have that same man die a few moments later in the episode. I have seen my share of TV and films, but this was truly something new - the rug was pulled out from under my feet, making me contemplate not only life's fragility, but the staple narrative structures we all adhere to, both in cinema and life.

Among other moments that stuck with me were Christine's (faked?) panic attack and the call she has with her concerned parents, as she's escaping a rapidly escalating, brutal reality. But "TGF" is more than the sum of its lovely parts. It's an acute commentary on the de-romanticized, sanitized state of current relationships and the corresponding paradigm shift in our collective consciousness. It examines sex as the ultimate power play. It's a thriller, a crime procedural, an artistic experiment, an incisive psychological study, a meditation on alienation and identity. Its seemingly unresolved storylines, ambiguousness in terms of morality and characterization (what drives Christine/Chelsea? Does she ever watch TV or snack on ice-cream?), and the general blurriness, for lack of a better word, all aids the show's transcendental feel.

Riley Keogh is perfect in the role. "You have the smartest eyes," a client tells her, and she really does - a juxtaposition with her steely demeanor and the mystery behind her actions.

For a series that mostly takes place inside bedrooms, buildings and offices, "TGF" represents Chicago's winterly chill surprisingly well, portraying those moments when you're confined to your apartment or office, and the blizzard outside makes your imagination - and fantasies - run wild. With unusual angles and a rhythm of its own, Kerrigan and Seimetz's creation defies every expectation in the book. Leaping forward through time, it doesn't follow conventional trajectory, which to some may be off-putting, but I found the approach wholly original, one of the reasons behind "TGF"'s greatness. It's as titillating and appalling as its heroine's lifestyle, similarly pulling us in, almost unwillingly, into its unethical but sexy world. Despite moments of pretentiousness and some off-putting scenes here and there, this is an experience well-worth immersing yourself into, whether you have a girlfriend or not.

4.5 out of 5 stars

"Time Out of Mind" Showcases Richard in High Gere

Synopsis: George seeks refuge at Bellevue Hospital, a Manhattan intake center for homeless men, where his friendship with a fellow client helps him try to repair his relationship with his estranged daughter.

Films about homeless people are inherently compelling - it could happen to any one of us. What would it be like, to live off the cold, uninviting streets, to be both free of societal norms and a slave to deprivation? What does "home" mean, when you don't have one? How would it feel, to be unnoticed, to know, with certainty, that nobody cares whether you live or die?

Classics, such as Terry Gilliam's mythical "The Fisher King" and Satoshi Kon's animated masterpiece "Tokyo Godfathers", touched upon those subjects in ways that were both insightful and artistic. Oren Moverman's deliberately paced "Time Out of Mind" comes closest so far to depicting that state of constant perplexity, brought on by desolation and a steady disassembling of one's humanity, from its opening shot of a crummy apartment, to the extraordinarily sublime conclusion.

At its center is a career-defining performance from Richard Gere, an actor who's displayed quite the range throughout his impressive filmography, but here reveals a side previously unseen in the notorious charmer. The stalwart's long overdue for an Academy Award nomination, and he surely deserves one for "Time Out of Mind" - he's absolutely mesmerizing.

The film begins in the aforementioned rundown New York apartment. The building manager (Steve Buscemi) discovers George (Richard Gere) in the bathtub. George mumbles about someone named "Sheila" coming back ("She's not gonna lie to me, I'm here with her, this is my home!"), but is assured that no one is coming back, and hurriedly ushered out, with nothing but a trash bag and a feeble suitcase to carry his few belongings. He later attempts to return to the building, with the same result - an action one could define as a symptom of insanity.

More traces and shades of George's condition become apparent, as we follow him through the rainy, late-winter streets of the Big Apple. He has a large scar on the side of his head. He sleeps on benches. He sells his clothes off for booze. He swigs vodka out of the bottle and rests on cold asphalt. He watches a young barmaid from a distance (Jena Malone).

He sleeps in the waiting room of an unusually (for New York) empty ER, where a friendly nurse recommends a shelter for him. "Sheila is going to be worried sick, I better get back home," he says absent-mindedly. The nurse's kindness turns into discomfort the more they talk, and then another gentleman - not-so-politely - asks him to leave. He has to go through a bunch of bureaucratic paperwork to get a bed at a shelter. He strains the entire time, struggling to piece his life together, and the paperwork is just too much for him.

Everywhere George goes is alienating, numbingly inhumane - until, that is, an older homeless man, Dixon (Ben Vereen), brings a little substance and meaning to his life. Dixon claims to be a jazz musician, but can't play (and by "can't", he means that he doesn't allow himself to touch upon a remnant of a life he once led, a life that has since shattered into fragments he cannot reassemble). Dixon follows George around, both angry at the world and a kindred spirit.

One day George seems to recognize "Sheila", who turns out to be another homeless woman, Karen, (Kyra Sedgwick). Karen has adapted to the streets, her strategy involving a copious amount of collected soda and beer cans. They make love. George ends up literally stripped - off his clothes, and down to man's basic desires: warmth, shelter, food, water... contact.

"Time Out of Mind" is a portrayal of a man who's hit rock bottom... and keeps falling. "I'm really no good right now", he declares grievously at one point. He is torn, impatient, emotionally imbalanced (who wouldn't be?), lost, regretful. A faint glimmer of damp hope propels him through his delusions, and a stubborn denial, a refusal to admit he needs medical help and that he is, in fact, homeless ("It's temporary", George resolutely states), out of pride and sophistication he must have once possessed.

It must be reiterated how magnificent Gere is. Appearing in pretty much every shot, he channels his established charisma into a delicate, devastatingly real performance. If the film has one flaw, it's the choice not to reveal a little more backstory, which renders it a bit distant - but Gere's warmth thaws the frigid portrayal of the city and brings much depth to the impenetrability of his character. Ben Veeren provides outstanding support (best line: "Okay, I'm a cartoon, at least I'm animated!"), turning a potentially clichéd character into a tragic and complex figure.

Bobby Bukowski, Moverman's cinematographer on both "The Messenger" and "Rampart", supplements every shot with gloom and urban beauty, such as one of George standing by a shop-window, with a blurry-but-vivid yellow haze obscuring the right side of the screen, in stark contrast to the wet, monochrome despair of the left side. The duo's decision to shoot mostly from inside or outside buildings, at a distance from George, pays off, directly isolating the viewer with shields of raindrop-covered glass, making the basic comforts of life seem that much more unattainable.

A lot of the dialogue is barely-audible, in resistance to most films' crisp-clear soundtrack. This is real city noise, where distant murmurs intertwine with random ramblings and discussions. The technique further adds to New York being urgently, realistically represented.

If the film sounds like a total downer… well, it is. But one can't expect all art to be optimistic and, you know, "happily-ever-after". Gere and Moverman infuse the film with so much nuance, it's more of a beautiful, existential painting - but also a meditation on the roots of homelessness, loneliness, friendship, forgiveness, and the humanity in us. It never for a moment resorts to sermonizing. "Time Out of Mind" is a poetic call to action, an ode to a city and its inhabitants, and a stellar showcase for the protagonist. Next time you look at a homeless person, you may just stop and wonder…

4.5 out of 5 stars

4-STAR MOVIES

"A Hard Day" Takes Viewers Through an Adrenaline-Fueled, Darkly Comedic Journey

Synopsis: *Homicide detective Geon-soo Go is having a hard day: in less than 24 hours, he receives a divorce notice from his wife, his mother passes away, and along with his coworkers, he becomes the focus of a police investigation over alleged embezzlement. And that's just the beginning...*

South Korean filmmakers have been steadily emerging into the worldwide spotlight within the past decade or so. Directors such as Bong Joon-ho ("The Host", "Snowpiercer"), Park Chan-wook ("Oldboy") and Kim Ki-duk ("Spring, Summer, Fall, Winter... and Spring"), just to name a few, have had international festival recognition and box-office success, due to their distinct perspectives that defy conventional narrative structures and blend accessibility with artistic (and, at times, wonderfully bizarre) flourishes.

That novel approach to filmmaking - call it the SoKo movement - feels like a breath of fresh air in an age of cinematic regurgitation, filled with remakes, sequels, prequels and re-imaginings (in fact, "Oldboy" has already been "reimagined" by Spike Lee, for some odd reason that no one understood). Whether "A Hard Day" will propel its writer/director Kim Seong-hoon to join that auteur movement remains to be seen, but this sophomore effort certainly marks the filmmaker as "one to watch".

In a way, of all the aforementioned titles, "A Hard Day" comes closest to mimicking Hollywood's traditional approach to a high-concept thriller, yet it skillfully avoids the usual trappings - excessive sentimentality, excessive heroism, and, well, excess. An exercise in prolonged tension, the film wisely adopts a minimalist approach: a relatable character, a short time frame, and a domino-like sequence of events that progressively pulls the protagonist - Detective Go - into a nightmarish, almost "Fargo"-esque, cobweb of intrigue.

The film starts off at "pedal-to-the-metal" speed: Go, driving tipsy from a funeral gathering, smashes into a man on the highway. Panic-stricken, he stuffs the body into the trunk of his car, barely avoiding the cops at the last moment, and drives right into a DUI checkpoint. As the plot unravels further, Go's former extortions surface, turning his partners against him; and a mysterious caller comes into play, claiming he witnessed Go's murder.

Some of the intricate ways Go gets out of ostensibly impossible situations are ingenious, particularly one involving a remote-controlled G.I. Joe action figure and a few yellow balloons; or a scene where Go deliberately drives his car into a police vehicle, in order to seem innocent. Other memorable moments include a giant block of cement unexpectedly smashing a car into a pancake, and a particularly well-timed explosion towards the end... To reveal anything else would be a major disservice to the film's many breathless twists and turns. Let's just say, "A Hard Day" proves Edward Murphy's ol' adage, that if anything can go wrong, it will - though it does end on a much-needed note of redemption (or is it *truly* redemption?).

The seemingly convoluted plot is easy to follow, laid out in brisk, suspenseful sequences that, granted, sometimes verge on the ridiculous, such as the extended - and very loud - office bathroom brawl that, of course, *no one* heard, or a pointless "dream recap" of events, or numerous little plot holes riddling the script... But none of it matters in the moment, nor does it prevent the film from achieving its primary goal - to shock, startle and intermittently induce outbursts of laughter for over 100 minutes. "A Hard Day", bound to soon be remade by some Hollywood hack, falls neatly into the category of unusual and entertaining South Korean cinema, and will hopefully pave the way for more features from that highly creative part of the world.

4 out of 5 stars

"A Monster with a Thousand Heads" is a Powerful Indictment of the Healthcare System Under the Guise of a Taut Thriller

Synopsis: *When her insurance company refuses to approve the care her husband needs to survive, Sonia takes things into her own hands. Up against an unyielding bureaucracy and disinterested workers, she is pushed to her breaking point: with her son in tow, she attempts to fight the system.*

Though it sounds like a horror film, "A Monster with a Thousand Heads" doesn't deal with Kaiju creatures slamming into each other with multiple craniums. Instead, its thrills come from the searing, heartbreaking sight of a woman driven to the edge of sanity by the System - in this case, the bureaucracy of the Mexican healthcare system. Rodrigo Plá's small-but-explosive dramatic thriller, running at a succinct 70 minutes (sans end credits), plays almost like a chamber piece, a struggle of One against an Army that is both claustrophobic in its intensity and epic in its thematic scope. Yes, the plot may not be all that novel (look at it as a better "John Q") - or plausible for that matter - but the fierce central performance and the director's confident control of pacing make you overlook the film's inherently clichéd/somewhat-preposterous set-up. The claws this "Monster" bares happen to be much sharper than any of the ones in Guillermo del Toro's Kaiju throwback "Pacific Rim".

The film opens with an unbroken, two-and-a-half-minute shot that initially brings to mind the "Paranormal Activities'" gimmicky, static sequences… and proceeds to wipe the floor with them. While the horror anthology's shots were designed for the sole purpose of creating an extended build-up to a shock that rarely came, "Monster'"s opening is filled with so much quiet drama unfolding on screen, the camera becomes a passive observer, immersing us into a tragedy that could hit us all at any moment. Sonia (Jana Raluy) wakes up to find her husband Guillermo collapsing on the floor. Her family comes down, sleepy, reality slowly settling in. She calls the ambulance, asking them to hurry. Simple and devastatingly real.

From that moment on, cinematographer Odei Zabaleta spends a good portion of the film focused on Sonia's facial expressions, as she grows from victim-in-denial to savage avenger. The ambulance nurse informs her that the situation is only going to get worse. She refuses to accept it, "It will get better when he resumes treatment. We're just waiting for the approval." The approval never comes - in fact, Sonia doesn't even get to see her doctor, met with blatant indifference at the clinic after waiting for hours. When Dr. Villalba (played by Hugo Albores) literally attempts to sneak by, Sonia snaps.

Bringing her son Dario (Sebastián Aguirre Boëda) along for the ride, Sonia follows the doctor to his home. She greatly inconveniences him by interrupting his upcoming squash session and next thing they know, Sonia has a gun pulled on him and his wife. "Not all applications are approved. That's how insurance companies work," Dr. Villalba says in panic. As it turns out, only "the board" can reevaluate Sonia's application… And so it keeps going, the determined Sonia climbing up the echelons of the healthcare "net" and doing whatever it takes to get to the "main guy", who may or may not solve her issue - or it may even be beside the point. You'll see what I mean when you watch it.

The sequence leading up to the title credit - which has the balls to arrive at the 10-minute mark in this short film, mind you - is worthy of the price of admission alone. We know what Sonia is holding in her hands, we know why she's torn and what's coming; an intense electronic wail builds up, mirroring/foreshadowing "Monster"'s upcoming accumulation of momentum - and then it cuts off harshly. Another scene involving Maria speaking into a security camera inaudibly - but conveying every word with her desperate face - is a standout. A fired shot, followed by a resounding, prolonged silence, perfectly arrives at a crucial, edge-of-your-seat moment. There are even tidbits of hilarity, such as a naked man barging in on a female water-exercise routine. Alas, those moments of wit are purposefully brief. The world in this film consists of harsh, dimly-lit-halogen, geometrical environments with no soft corners, warm colors or kind people.

The filmmakers employ an ingenious technique of juxtaposing the witnesses' current testimonies in court, via voice-over, against what actually unfolded. It's best exemplified in an early sequence of Dr. Villalba disregarding Sonia, as the witness narration blankly states, "I told [the doctor] she had been waiting for him for hours." Another great example occurs during a rather shocking moment of Sonia inadvertently shooting someone in the leg, with the witness's narration pointing out the suspect in court.

Jana Raluy dominates the screen. From the initial voice message she leaves when trying to reach her doctor, to her trying to maintain some traces of dignity while escorting naked men out of a steam room, the actress displays enormous range and a sense of urgency vital to this film's pace. She bares it all on screen, similarly to what Charlize Theron did in "Monster" (another character forced to resort to violence by the society that birthed her), but without all the make-up. When her son smacks the bejesus out of a character with a baseball bat, Raluy's torn expression is a sight to behold.

Sure, some events seem a little forced and hard-to-buy, some characters are overtly demonized and, like I mentioned, a certain amount of disbelief has to be suspended to buy into the notion of a single person laying down the law in a cold, emotionless world. However, if you overlook those flaws, you will discover a superlative, step-by-step examination of what it would be like to be in that situation, taken to the extreme to emphasize its grueling point, without over-sentimentalizing it. "Monster" can also be interpreted as a subtle feminist allegory: a resilient, resourceful woman fighting the society that keeps shunning her. ("Did you order the erotic massage?" one of the male board members asks another, when Maria barges in on them, naked in a sauna. "She knows you only last a minute.") The title itself lends itself to questions: Who's the monster in this film? The bureaucratic culture, or the borderline-demented human that it spawned?

The filmmaking team keep surprising us with unexpected camera angles, sudden cuts and heart-wrenching moments of unbearable suspense. Best of all, Rodrigo Plá's "A Monster with a Thousand Heads" represents an important shift in Mexican filmmaking, reminding us of its elegance, subtlety and power, and hopefully signaling more to come. Guillermo del Toro, a fellow Mexican, should take note when he's making his next monster bash.

4 out of 5 stars

Sonia Braga Prepares for the Age of "Aquarius"

Synopsis: Clara is the last resident of the Aquarius, an original two-story building, built in the 1940s. All the neighboring apartments have already been acquired by a company which has other plans for that plot. Clara has pledged to only leave her place upon her death, and will engage in a cold war with the company.

When I was a kid, I had a favorite painting of a burning forest. I remember looking at it, sunburnt after a day of troublemaking, and getting utterly lost in the scarlet, aquarelle embers, feeling like I was going to burst out of my own charred skin. Throughout years, that painting gained value to me; when I look at it, I see my late grandfather's kind face as he raises a toast; I see my bloodhound Dumbo crunching on watermelon, parched on a thirsty day; I see my entire life in those brushstrokes and hues. It's more than just a painting - it's an extension of my identity, and no one can take it away from me, like a lung or an artery. Director Kleber Mendonça Filho's "Aquarius", which was rightfully nominated for the Palm d'Or at the 2016 Cannes Film Festival, is about a woman, Clara (Sonia Braga) whose apartment is as much a part of her as her organs. While a mastectomy may have left her with one breast, Clara is not about to part with that organ, which serves as her soul, heart and brain. With a mesmerizing lead performance and as many brush strokes as that burning painting, "Aquarius" will quietly tear you up inside.

Told in three parts and set in the beautiful city of Recife, Brazil, "Aquarius" begins with the chapter entitled "Clara's Hair", set in 1980, a year after young Clara's intense battle with cancer. Her hair still short (and very stylish), Clara rushes back from a carefree evening at the beach to her Aunt Lucia's 70th birthday party, where her husband gives a touching speech - the cancer cast a dark shadow, but also brought the family closer together. The music swirls - and then we seamlessly transition to today, as Clara, now a widow and prominent writer, her dark hair long and luscious, hears the same upbeat tune out of her window. She leads a quiet, unassuming life, attending yoga-like "energy" classes, swimming in tumultuous ocean waters under the watchful eye of a lifeguard (who literally becomes her life's guard as the film progresses) - until, that is, a construction company approaches Clara about selling her apartment, offering her way more than the market value. They are calling the project "The New Aquarius", in memory of a building that, as Clara points out, hasn't even been demolished yet.

Part two, "Clara's Love", sees the matriarch take a stand, refusing to abandon her place, despite the rest of the residents absconding, while the evil corporation, along with her own family, continuously urges her to leave. Clara has essentially become Aunt Lucia, clinging to the remnants of her past, reliving memories, her nephew being the closest person in her life. In an incredibly touching sequence, Clara goes out with her giggly friends and meets a handsome widower, who, upon finding out about her breast surgery, wants nothing to do with her. Like life itself, what starts as a night of debauchery ends in grimly nostalgic retrospection, loneliness… and a bit of dancing. Aroused by the orgy of new residents next door, Clara promptly gets a gigolo. Unlike the young love that blossoms around her, this brief "affair" resembles a wilting flower. Part three, entitled "Clara's Cancer", brings everything full circle, a malignant lump of termites spreading and consuming everything in its path.

"Aquarius" is about many things. It's about the power of memories, how certain places and objects can carry tremendous nostalgic value, never better personified than in the scene where Aunt Lucia gazes longingly at a cupboard, as her kids read birthday speeches. Lucia is immersed in memories of her first sexual encounter on top of that furniture piece with Augusto, a married man and her consequent partner of 30 years. "Aquarius" is about the passing of time, time's relevance and role in our lives. It's about transition; in an era where everything is digital, Clara still listens to vinyl records - "this is like a message in a bottle", she explains. It's about generational differences, exemplified in a scene where Clara is confronted with changing her whole life by an arrogant kid, the grandson of the main architect, who gleefully announces the project to her. Finally, Filho's film is about inevitability. As the construction company closes in, akin to death, putting stickers on apartment doors, Clara is "pissed but not stressed"; it affects her, but like the looming presence of death, she deals with it calmly and resolutely.

Sonia Braga is astounding in the lead. Gorgeous, classy, determined, fragile and lonely, her Clara is a sight to behold, a powerful depiction of a middle-aged woman trying to assert herself, distinguish her place in the modern, constantly-changing world. Despite the film's intimidating length - at well over two hours, it could have used a bit of trimming - you will never be able to take your eyes off Braga. It's a powerhouse of a performance. The rest of the cast keeps up, but she is the sun around which the small planets revolve.

4 out of 5 stars

"Boy & the World" Dazzles with Its Simplicity and Scope

Synopsis: *A little boy goes on an adventurous quest in search of his father.*

Inexplicably - though deservedly - nominated for the Best Animated Feature Academy Award three years after its original 2013 release, Alê Abreu's visual feast aims high - for the grandiose, epic scope of Hermann Hesse's "Siddhartha", no less. While it never quite reaches those heights (and who could?), its protagonist, Merino, does become wise, and even finds his own personal Eden towards the end. Until that sublime moment occurs, we are treated to a true spectacle, a lyrical coming-of-age story, told wordlessly, its sensational imagery speaking volumes about growing up and coming to terms with humanity and all its sins.

In the beginning, little Merino's world is pure and white, ripe for filler. As the boy discovers it, traces and brushes of color punctuate the screen, until it's filled with them, and joyful music erupts, emphasizing his excitement with every note and hue. He runs up horses and trees and clouds, looking down upon the real world from his fantasy land. A dark breeze eventually blows him back to earth, and reality settles in: his father leaves him alone with his mother, playing a few sorrowful notes on his flute (one of which the boy manages to capture) before a train takes him away into the whiteness.

When a strange man replaces him, Merino embarks on a quest to find his dad. On the way, he gets a ride in an old cotton picker's carriage and encounters his tyrannical cowboy boss; he floats in a balloon through a fleeting parade; he barely survives the tidal waves of a dark-emerald storm; he witnesses the drone-like existence of a textile factory; and, finally, he ends up in the Big City.

Chaotic, oppressive and hostile, the City's staircases, vehicles, buildings, cables and roads are jumbled together, all jagged edges and spikes. The mechanical factories and gloomy ship harbors overwhelm the boy, but with the help of a bicyclist/street performer, he sees the bright side of humanity. His adventure starts with the search for his father and ends with a grown-up Merino finding himself.

Society in this world exists in a Gestapo-like regime, taken over by corporations, machine-like factory workers doing the same perpetual tasks for the Man. As the boy leaves his innocence behind, he realizes that yes, life is vibrant and mysterious, but also unforgiving, cruel, a juxtaposition of geometrically-structured factories and blazing celebrations, of low and high classes, of compassion and callousness. We all grow up; the film is a reminder to embrace our childlike wonder and see the world through a kaleidoscope sometimes.

Simplicity is key here, and "Boy"'s lively animation - sometimes detailed, sometimes crayon-like, abstract - reminded me a bit of Don Herztfeldt's approach. With just a few strokes, moments shine, like a music note, caught in a red jar; or a reflection of a bucket, dropping into a well; or a guileless swim through a heap of cotton. As the film progresses, those moments gain texture: a brown splotch of people stuffed into a bus, carrying them down into a labyrinthine city; a devastating destruction of a vibrant bird by tanks and an evil black crow…

If I had to pinpoint a niggle, it's that the messages of industrialization are laid on a bit too thick at times, such as when the film jarringly switches to real-life footage of construction factories, melting icebergs, and Amazonian rainforests being chopped down - a bold move, mind you, but an unnecessary one. By that point, we already got the point.

"Boy & the World" may be a bit too experimental and dark and cerebral for young kids, but adults and animation purists will marvel at its ambition and scope, created with the most basic of techniques. A Brazilian "Triplets of Belleville", Alê Abreu's feature is by turns touching, darkly moody, dazzling to the eye and, most importantly, thoroughly - and wordlessly - engaging throughout. I urge you to discover this boy's world.

4 out of 5 stars

"Bridge of Spies" Almost Bridges the Gap Between the Youthful and Mature Sides of Steven Spielberg

Synopsis: An American lawyer is recruited by the CIA during the Cold War to help rescue a pilot detained in the Soviet Union.

One will be hard-pressed to find a more ardent defender of Steven Spielberg than yours truly. "Jaws" blew my mind the first time I watched it at the tender age of five. Its score, performances and stubborn refusal to showcase the shark until the end were so groundbreaking, even then my tiny brain acknowledged I was experiencing something special, something that transcended the boundaries of films I had seen before. "E.T." infused my childhood with an existential wonder, which consequently led to my obsession with film.

I could go on about how I will totally overlook the sentimentality and unnecessarily drawn-out triple-ending of the otherwise incredible, deeply unsettling "Artificial Intelligence", or the astonishing power and sincerity of "Schindler's List". With the sole exception of "Hook", which I thoroughly despise, I'll even come to the defense of Spielberg's lesser-known, not-as-well-received efforts, such as "Always" (a dead Richard Dreyfuss extinguishing forest fires!) and "Empire of the Sun" (a young Christian Bale as a prisoner of war!). The director knows film magic, and each of his films contains at least several sequences of pure awe. Remember, he's the guy who made us believe in aliens, dinosaurs, and that a man can rip another man's heart out with his bare fingers.

Spielberg's films can be grouped into two categories: those that embrace his youthful, "go-for-broke" spirit and boundless imagination, and those that display a somber, "mature" side of the great director. Lately, he's been dabbling with the latter: the monochrome "Munich" dealt with terrorism; "War Horse" told a classical tale of a boy and his horse; "Lincoln" was a painting-in-motion, depicting a crucial moment in the President's life… So I approached "Bridge of Spies" with a dose of caution, worried that its solemnity may induce a yearning for the audacious, "let's-do-insane-freakin'-sequences" of, say, "Minority Report".

My fears proved mostly groundless, as I sat gripped from start to (almost) finish of this courtroom-cum-spy drama. Yes, the director again adopts a classical style of filmmaking Frank Capra would appreciate, but it's so beautifully shot by his regular cinematographer extraordinaire Janusz Kaminski ("Saving Private Ryan", "Catch Me If You Can"), and so eloquently written by Ethan and Joel Coen (no surprise there), that the subliminally tense story propels itself along, making the almost two-and-a-half-hour run-time zip by. Spielberg's gleefully audacious side is intermittently evident too, especially in the moments of literary and visual humor, peppered throughout the film's narrative. Spielberg's magic is on full display, making one - for the most part - overlook the minor flaws of "Bridge of Spies".

The plot, in a nutshell: After an alleged Russian spy, Rudolph Abel (Mark Rylance), gets caught in an intense, precisely-choreographed opening sequence, set in the nuclear-1950s, a seasoned insurance lawyer, James Donovan (Tom Hanks), is assigned to defend him. A parallel story-line introduces a team of "drivers" being trained for a stealth-like mission to take photos of potentially hostile territories; another follows a young reporter, as he's arrested in the tumultuous, Cold War-stricken Berlin. The film switches from courtroom drama to espionage thriller, as Donovan's journey takes him to Germany, where he has to negotiate a complex, triple-prisoner exchange.

That Spielberg hooks you from the first second is a given, considering the director's captivating repertoire. There are many things going for "Bridge of Spies". Mark Rylance is serene and intriguing as Abel. Tom Hanks, who can do no wrong, gives a commanding central performance that anchors the film; his eyes keep filling with wisdom as he grows older. Spielberg's filmmaking fluency is remarkable, per usual. The cinematography smoothly morphs from strikingly beautiful imagery of a plane soaring through a blue sky, to a pirouetting, nerve-shredding crash of said plane, to dismally gorgeous shots of the Berlin Wall being built in a grey, highly hostile environment.

Most importantly, the Coen brothers' script evokes philosophical musings on the meaning of patriotism; the "difference between 'enemy' and 'criminal'", cowardice and humanity. The film resolutely doesn't take sides. The East-German, Russian and U.S. agendas get muddled, each pursuing their own intentions, and one can't help but see the parallels between the film's themes and the current situation in Syria. It strikes a profoundly resonant note, perhaps without even meaning to do it.

As Spielberg's biggest defender, I have to admit his films are almost never without flaws, and "Bridge of Spies" is no exception. The "arrested journalist" subplot is under-developed, while the "U.S. drivers" subplot is over-cooked; neither reveal much about the characters. The film loses momentum in its second half and becomes tonally inconsistent. Sebastian Koch ("The Lives of Others") hams it up as Wolfgang Vogel, and there is a confusing car-swerving-through-icy-Berlin scene that could've been left on the chopping room floor. The music, by Thomas Newman, is just *too* much sometimes - another Spielberg trope. The triple-ending syndrome strikes the director once again; the guy's prone to sentimentality, and he ain't backing away from it!

Gripes aside, the director masterfully guides us through an intricate and powerfully poignant story. I thought it would be overtly patriotic, but its subjectivity, sensitive performances and humor keep it this side of nationalistic. My sole real objection would be: now it's time for Spielberg to remember his roots, embrace his inner child again. I hope his next film will involve anthropomorphic manifestations of dreams, or parallel dimensions, or transgender space odysseys (yes, it's quite obvious that I hoped that Spielberg would direct "Interstellar"… dammit) - or reach new frontiers that only this cinematic wizard can dare to explore.

4 out of 5 stars

"Cartel Land" Casts an Unflinching Gaze into the Heart of Darkness

Synopsis: A physician in Michoacán, Mexico, leads a citizen uprising against the drug cartel that has wrecked havoc on the region for years. Across the U.S. border, a veteran heads a paramilitary group working to prevent Mexico's drug wars from entering U.S. territory.

Humanity has always been on a quest for power. It's difficult to argue with the fact that most wars were essentially caused by our animalistic desire to lead, to reign over others. That feeling of superiority and control - be it over dozens or thousands or millions - drives us to rob and pillage and slaughter. And no matter how idealistic their cause, leaders tend to become corrupt, overwhelmed and aroused by their own authority - the line between right and wrong, between philanthropy and self-interest, becomes increasingly blurry.

Matthew Heineman's edge-of-your seat documentary portrays the trajectory of such doomed idealism, through the prism of a Mexican cartel's comparatively short lifespan. From the very first shot until the last unforgettable frame, it holds our attention like a first-rate thriller (the director's intention), breathlessly taking us right into the midst of the action, making us participants, as opposed to mere passive observers. "Cartel Land" traces the rise and fall of a small empire, one of thousands, in a land riddled with warfare and unthinkable acts of violence - but it's also a statement on our penchant for violence, a reflection on the state of current affairs... and a humanity that's perhaps beyond exoneration.

The "empire" Heineman depicts began as the Autodefensas: a small-town citizen uprising in Michoacán, led by the charismatic Dr. Jose Mireles, also a physician, known as "El Doctor." After his neighbors were beheaded by the Knights Templar cartel - and an innocent farmer family massacred by the same criminals (a heart-wrenching scene shows a family member describing the massacre in vivid detail), Dr. Mireles took matters in his own hands. He, along with fellow townsmen, "identified the houses where the Templars lived" and struck back (an edge-of-your-seat sequence follows them on their "hunt", a prime example of the striking verisimilitude Heineman achieves in his documentary). They were met by "corrupt government forces", who confiscated Autodefensas' weapons - but the town rebelled and cornered the military, until their weapons were returned. Was it truly a "victory"? And was Mireles driven by a strong need for justice, or did he have a hero complex and merely craved recognition and servitude (after all, he's shown as unfaithful, with numerous mistresses, of whom his saddened wife is bitterly aware)?

The beauty of Heineman's documentary is that it's never manipulative, and the emotions it evokes are always conflicting: small victories result in horrific consequences. In Cartel Land, one man's justice is another man's tragedy; the heroes become villains, but the concept of "right" and "wrong" is questioned; a quest for peace gradually reveals itself as an exorcism of personal demons…

This latter observation may be applied to "Cartel Land"'s other "cartel" leader, leathery-faced Tim "Nailer" Foley, a veteran living in Arizona's Altar Valley (known as "Cocaine Alley"), right on the Mexican border. Abused by his father, and consequently resorting to drug abuse, Tim managed to quit, but grew appalled by the number of "illegals" after the economy crisis, working "under the table" and not paying taxes. This led to Tim forming the Arizona Border Recon, a paramilitary group, whose tracking of illegal immigrants morphed into a quest to hunt down drug cartels. Similarly to the Autodefensas, Tim was labeled a vigilante by the media. His unclear intentions lead to questions of motivation - is Tim just projecting the anger of his abusive childhood, searching for recognition (when asked why he does it, he says, "If not me, who else?")? His troops' reasoning differs wildly too: one man spews out nonsensical rhetoric about needing a wall to separate two groups of people who will never get along.

The film switches between Foley's and Mireles' stories: as Mireles' troops became more violent, spinning out of his control and forming their own cartel, led by "Papa Smurf" (a frightening, insipid, chubby little man, lacking Mireles' charisma but possessing an affinity for violence, who quickly lost the Autodefensas leadership to the Michoacán government, who, in turn, formed their own cartel, called the "Rural Defense Force"), Foley's band of troops observed the news, approving of the cartels without any real understanding of their logistics and attempted their own vigilante justice. If the film does have a flaw, it's that Tim Foley's story is under-developed, especially when compared to the "City of God"-like, deeply thorough portrait of the Autodefensas clan.

There are countless scenes of such power, they'll wedge themselves into viewers' minds forever. A girl recounts how she witnessed her entire family massacred by the Templars; she was later thrown in the graves with their dismembered bodies, raped and left alive to "live with it". This leads to the viscerally intense apprehension of her captors. Another scene shows the Mexican President, assuring the civilians a "state of law" will be enforced - a statement that rings even more absurd from the perspective of the Autodefensas, to whom law, by this point, is an abstract term. Heineman is wise and true to his cinematic ambitions when it comes to portraying violence: at one point, Dr. Jose tells Chago, a member of the Autodefensas, to kill a member of the Templars, and Heineman wisely doesn't show the consequences, letting the viewer's imagination run wild.

Heineman's goal to make his documentary as cinematic as possible was a success: "Cartel Land" is jam-packed with tremendously affecting, tragically beautiful visuals, such as the milk-white vapor building around a man cooking meth in pitch-blackness; or the outline of a guard, holding his rifle against the tangerine sunset, the warfare of violence and beauty never more apparent; or a shot of white balloons, soaring into the air, an image of freedom in a world that knows none.

"Cartel Land" was criticized by some for lacking scope and answers - but that's its point. There *are* no answers. Of all the competing drug lords and politicians, the reigning king in Cartel Land is chaos - and Heidelman's brutally efficient documentary, an early contender for the Academy Awards, simply shows us the atrocities that happen, how they came to be, and how nothing is being done about them, making us question our own humanity.

4 out of 5 stars

"Digging for Fire", Joe Swanberg's Rumination on Marriage and Mid-Life Crisis, Digs Deep

Synopsis: *The discovery of a bone and a gun send a husband and wife on separate adventures over the course of a weekend.*

Joe Swanberg is a busy man. According to his filmography, since 2003 he has been involved in over 76 films, 25 of which he directed. Often shot in the "mumblecore" style - introduced to the world by the Duplass Brothers with their 2005 cult indie "The Puffy Chair", it involves focusing on the story over production quality - Swanberg's films often have a loose format, paying less attention to narrative structure, and letting their actors' mostly-improvised performances carry the film.

The director/writer/editor/actor/producer/cinematographer has come a long way since his modest 2006 effort "LOL" (which featured Greta Gerwig in one of her first starring roles). The budgets of his films went up - but not by much. The star power went up too - but instead of hiring A-listers for their mass appeal, Swanberg tends to find actors that fit their roles. He stays true to his indie roots, letting the story unfold naturally and in a uniquely entertaining fashion. He grips our attention - gasp! - not with dinosaurs and bombastic thrills, but with dialogue and little nuances.

Swanberg's most recent directorial venture, the "dramedy" "Happy Christmas", starred Anna Kendrick and Lena Dunham, and displayed a maturity and poignancy reminiscent of Cassavetes' early works. "Digging for Fire", which he co-wrote with his "Drinking Buddies" star (and one of the leads on the popular sitcom "New Girl"), Jake Johnson, marks yet another step in the right direction for the young director (he's only 33 years old), this time bringing to mind the works of Belgian Cannes festival darlings, the Dardenne brothers. "Digging for Fire" is comparable to their masterpieces in its verisimilitude, affection for the low-middle class, credible performances, and a lyrical, deeply touching ending that sneaks up on you.

"Digging for Fire'" is less of a story and more of a peek at a couple's life, over the course of a weekend. Having just moved into a new home with a young child, Tim (Jake Johnson) and Lee (Rosemarie DeWitt) resort to yoga sessions to relieve their post-pregnancy/mid-life crisis anxiety. Tim is more of a blue-collar guy, who works at a public school, and Lee comes from a wealthy family, and is lost after the birth, attempting to define herself as more than just a "mom" (she reads books on marriage early on in the film, signaling trouble-to-come). One day, Tim discovers an old bone and a gun in the woods; Lee dismisses it as nothing, but her husband instantly becomes fixated on unraveling the mystery.

Tension rises - they disagree on their choice for a pre-school for their child, each prejudiced by their own upbringing. She resents him for having low aspirations, and he resents her for being the provider. Lee goes to visit her parents, leaving Tim at home to do taxes; instead, he gets stoned and barbecues with his friends. The story-lines separate: we follow Tim and his buddies (including the sensible Phil, played by comedian Mike Birbiglia, and the "ticking-time-bomb" Ray, played by one of the best and most versatile actors currently working, Sam Rockwell), as they party and help Tim with the digging; while Lee confronts her parents, her friends - and herself - about her feelings.

The more Tim and his friends dig, finding old license plates and bones that may or may not be human, the more obsessed Tim gets. The timid Phil leaves, but Max (Brie Larson), Alicia (Anna Kendrick) and Tango (Chris Messina) show up, distracting everyone with cocaine, skinny-dipping and general rowdiness.

In the meantime, Lee struggles with her wealth and its connotations, and getting used to... well, reality. Unable to connect with her parents - played by Sam Elliot (without the iconic mustache - what did you do, Sam?!) and Judith Light - Lee visits her rich friends Bob (Ron Livingston) and Squiggy (Melanie Lynskey. Lee ends up at a bar with handsome Ben (Orlando Bloom), who protects her from a drunkard, which eventually leads to stitches and a moonlight walk by the ocean.

As Tim and Max bond, first somewhat-passionately, then steadily more awkwardly, Lee bonds with Ben... well, I've already described too much. What Tim finally finds in the grave I'll also let you discover. As with most Swanberg films, it's about the journey. Let's just say, sometimes it's best to leave certain things buried.

"Digging for Fire" is brimming with insightful dialogue. There's a beautiful and succinct "cremation vs. burial" discussion, which functions as a metaphor for our past, for hidden secrets that sometimes need unraveling, and at other times demand complete eradication. Here's another memorable tidbit, voiced eloquently by Sam Elliot (how else can he voice stuff?): "Being in love... What is that? Getting what you want? Or is it giving somebody what they want... Sacrificing, if you want to call it that?"

The film touches upon acute observations on marriage, death, friendship, love, wealth, growing up, obsession - and even the unexpected wisdom of Uber drivers... The smallest parts get to shine - Swanberg's specialty - such as Rockwell, stealing scenes shamelessly, per usual; or the talented Brie Larson, whose career I've been following since she was in the popular show "The United States of Tara", and who has since become a mainstay in great indie films like "Short Term 12" and "The Spectacular Now". Jake Johnson and Rosemarie DeWitt both give their most subtly complex performances to date.

The film's minor flaws include its slightness (c'mon, Swanberg, make an even bigger (thematically-speaking), more complex/intricate study of marital foes!), and the Orlando Bloom storyline, which could have used a bit more flesh. But those are minor quibbles. More films like this should be made in America, and it's a shame that, in this day and age of superhero-driven multiplex fare, they're restricted to limited screenings and VOD channels. Bravo to Swanberg, and here's to his next project.

4 out of 5 stars

"Embrace of the Serpent" Slithers Its Way into Your Subconsciousness

Synopsis: The story of the relationship between Karamakate, an Amazonian shaman and last survivor of his people, and two scientists who work together over the course of 40 years to search the Amazon for a sacred healing plant.

Theodor Koch-Grunberg and Richard Evans Schultes were scientists and explorers, who ventured out into the Amazon to learn about its esoteric powers. Both recorded the horrors, magic and eccentricity of the jungle and its inhabitants in their diaries. Based on those diaries, Ciro Guerra's "Embrace of the Serpent", Academy Award nominee for Best Foreign Language Film (marking Colombia's first Oscar nomination), is a psychedelic journey into the heart of darkness, a deeply disturbing look at human nature/evolution and thirst for power, seen through a hallucinatory Amazonian prism. It condemns humanity, and yet ends on a transcendentally buoyant note - there may be hope for us yet.

Karamakate (Nilbio Torres), a.k.a. "world traveler", lives deep in the jungle, having utterly secluded himself from civilization. One day, he reluctantly agrees to help a dying Theodore (Jan Bijvoet) and his friend/servant Manduca find the mystical Yakruna plant, which may heal Theo, and lead Karamakate to his Cohiuano tribe... or whatever remains of it. They embark on a long and arduous journey, Theodore kept alive by Karamakate blowing a cocaine-like powder up the scientist's nostrils. On the way, they encounter many tribes, ravaged in one way or the other by the Rubber War and the "white man"'s wrath.

The shaman dreams of a jaguar who declares him the Protector of Theodore. Ironically - and symbolically - it's the "white man" that holds the key to Amazon's survival. When they do discover Yakruna, it's been harvested for all the wrong reasons, and Kalamakate would rather burn it all down to ashes than let its holiness be desecrated. "You bring hell and death to Earth," he proclaims bitterly, as flames engulf him.

The second storyline takes place many years later: Evan (Brionne Davis) follows Theodore's footsteps by reading his diaries, looking for the same magical plant. He enlists an older Karamakate (Antonio Bolivar) to assist him, initially offering him $3 for his services.

The older Karamakate is sadder, more reflective, surrendered to his fate. He weeps bitterly for his people, for his own identity, deep in the murky depths of the Amazonian night. "My memories are gone," he states. "Now I'm empty… What have

I become?" He's the embodiment of all the indigenous peoples, lost to modern civilization's depravity.

Eventually, the shaman convinces Evan to get rid of his possessions and embrace Caapi - the Jungle spirit that prevails throughout both plots - at the Workshop of the Gods, a mountain overlooking the endless Amazon. It's the last Yakruna in the world, and it's Caapi's "gift to the white man" - again, salvation rests upon the devil's shoulders.

"Embrace of the Serpent"'s authenticity is palpable, and its languid rhythm is key to that verisimilitude. Despite the deliberate pace, the film is never less than entertaining, precisely because it allows the viewer to marvel at the beauty and horror of the jungle and its stories. The effect is psychedelic; the filmmakers wisely let the jungle speak for itself, with next-to-no music, its resonating voices that much more entrancing. The performances are so lived-in, they defy the term "acting" - it feels like we're there, with them by that fire, taking a sip of some ethereal substance.

My initial reservations about the filmmakers' choice to film in black and white in such a gorgeous location proved unwarranted, as the stark contrast emphasizes every detail on screen: every wrinkle of old Karamakate's wise face, every hieroglyphic on an ancient wall, every ripple in the serpentine Amazon, coiling its way through the jungle - which itself almost gains a fabric-like, suffocating texture when reduced to two opposing colors. It's all depicted vividly by David Gallego's stunning camerawork. Several shots of men surrounded by butterflies are standouts in this "you are there" cinematic experience.

"Embrace of the Serpent" defies convention: events mirror each other, things occur unexpectedly, there are prolonged moments of reflection, followed by abrupt violence, and it ends on an unexpected - yet wholly credible - note. The "Rubber War" is a never-ending cycle, which in itself represents our thirst for resources and power, at the expense of knowledge and wisdom that took thousands of years to evolve.

Guerra carefully avoids sentimentality, and is never as manipulatively brutal as, say, Cary Joji Fukunaga's "Beasts of No Nation". "Serpent" has moments of levity that come as welcome relief to the violent imagery, such as when Karamakate laughs heartily at Theo's sappy love letters to his Dear Love in Germany. "I enjoy expressing affection," Theo says defensively. "Before or after you cry?" Karamakate asks, before collapsing into a heap of giggles.

That said, the powerful moments are the ones that will stick in your memory for days after watching "Serpent". A sequence, which starts with Theodore singing joyfully and ends with a tense compass exchange negotiation, perfectly illustrates cultural differences and how conflict may arise from our attachment to possessions.

Other, similarly powerful and heart-wrenching set pieces, include a one-armed slave, tortured and begging for death; and a priest, who hates "Pagan languages" and enslaves children, whipping them into servitude, whipping everything that shapes them as a culture - as humans - out of them. Also worth mentioning is the cult-like "Eden", led by a Jesus-like (crown of thorns and everything) self-proclaimed messiah, who declares, "The only thing sacred in this jungle is me!" His grisly demise I'll let you discover - but it's very apt - *the* ultimate ego trip.

There are a few small missteps, here and there. Theodore's story is more developed than Evan's, and yet Evan's ends more coherently. An off-kilter, unnecessary sequence of a jaguar facing off against a snake is pretentious and jarringly shot, as if it were done so in two separate locations and then clumsily stitched together. The film's pace does slow to a crawl intermittently - at least ten minutes could have easily been chopped.

The flaws are minor and easy to overlook in this film. Guerra's jungle trip is as accessible as Fernando Meirelles' "City of God", as balls-out nuts and authentic as Werner Herzog's "Fitzcarraldo", and as inventive and hallucinatory as Ben Wheatley's "A Field in England". What an amalgamation! And yet, in the capable hands of the talented filmmaking team, "Embrace of the Serpent" joins the league films that both condemn and embrace humanity - and do so with a healthy dose of Yakruna.

4 out of 5 stars

Looking Back at the Future: Revisiting Mamoru Oshii's "Ghost in the Shell"

Synopsis: *A cyborg policewoman and her partner hunt a mysterious and powerful hacker called the Puppet Master.*

I remember watching "Ghost in the Shell" for the first time when I was a 12-year-old kid and though the convoluted plot lost me about 10 minutes in, its cyberpunk, neo-noir, psychedelic visuals have haunted me since. Now, 22 years after the original's release, Scarlett Johansson is about to don the cybernetic suit in Rupert Sanders' live-action Hollywood remake. An acquaintance of mine in the animation world worked on the 2002 TV spin-off, "Ghost in the Shell: Stand Alone Complex"; she recently expressed much excitement about the new film from the director of "Snow White and the Huntsman". While I totally get her involvement in the project, I can't say I share her enthusiasm. Hence my joy at the opportunity to re-watch the original feature, in its full remastered glory, packaged in a beautiful Mondo Steelbook® case.

A line out of something I saw the other week stuck with me: "How does one define sanity in an unstable society?" Released at the peak of the mid-1990's cyberpunk craze, "Ghost in the Shell", based on the popular manga series by Shirow Masamune, poses similar questions, with a "Matrix"-like twist: "What defines a human in a society that has the ability to replicate us? Is it our soul? At what point, exactly, does a machine become sentient?" Those themes crystallized in front of me two decades later, unnoticed back then by my distracted, adolescent mind (which was more focused on the exposed flesh in the film). The plot is still murky, yet the visuals hold up, and most importantly, the themes that starkly shine through the murk - those of human nature, artificial intelligence, existentialism, immigration/deportation, hacking, invasion of personal freedom and disregard for basic human rights - are still relevant - particularly so! - in 2017. Watch Mr. Sanders gloss over them with a thick coat of bombastic thrills (okay, perhaps I am pre-judging a bit harshly here - let's give ScarJo a chance.)

The film starts with the iconic shot of the gorgeous cyborg, Motoko a.k.a. The Major, undressing herself and leaping backwards off a skyscraper, all stealth-like in her "optical camouflage", to assassinate a crooked diplomat. A visceral-but-brief bloodbath ensues - followed by a Matrix-like credit sequence (there is a reason why I keep bringing up the Wachowskis' flick, it's so freakin' heavily indebted to "Ghost"). We see the cyborg dismantled and reassembled, the eerie visuals complemented by Kenji Kawai's genuinely unnerving score that combines tribal, choir, trip-hop and even gothic elements to great effect.

Daisuke Aramaki, the Chief of Public Security, assigns his cyborg agents to "ghost-hack government officials". Our hero Motoko's new task is to hunt down a crooked politician. While the suspicion falls on Mares, a prominent public figure, Motoko - or her "ghost" (her consciousness) - believes the chain of corruption ultimately leads to a mysterious entity, referred to as the Puppet Master. "Wanted internationally for stock price manipulation, information gathering, political maneuvering, terrorism, cyberbrain ethics violation, and several other crimes," the Puppet Master seems to be pulling the government's strings - until it becomes Motoko's mission to cut them. With me so far?

An investigation begins, led by the "command center", communicating with Motoko through an apparatus, which in itself resembles a pair of strings, plugged into the back of her neck. This allows her to do nifty things, like access "a wide range of information and a network", track down a moving target - basically making her the ultimate GPS. She and her infatuated partner Batou encounter suicidal cyborgs and question their own past and mortality - until the Puppet Master slips right through their fingers. Twist upon twist lead to a final showdown, Motoko subjected to the ultimate temptation, a fusion of cyborgs that would spawn a God-like entity. In other words, Motoko's own strings prove binding, and Geppetto may have to go down.

Like I said, the plot may be needlessly complicated (the cyber-talk especially gets monotonous, and fast), but it's the strong characterizations, themes and imagery that power the story along. There's a melancholy to the proceedings, an apocalyptic current running through the narrative, as if it's all futile anyway (including trying to figure out the minute plot details). The stunning animation goes a long way in conveying that sense of decay: synthetic skin flaking off; a vacuum-cleaner-like machine, pumping tech/coding directly into a young female cyborg's brain; Motoko diving into the tangerine depths of a lake; a melancholic interlude that portrays the segregated, broken city; Motoko facing off against a giant, crab-tank… Those large, expressive eyes, so prominent in Japanese animation, accentuate each flicker of emotion, infusing the cyborgs with life. The backgrounds, fluid character motions and intense action sequences have all aged remarkably well, proving again that hand-drawn animation is timeless.

Though I watched the subtitled version and can't speak to the accuracy of the translation, I can certainly attest to its sporadic lyricism, wit and insight. "Your brain has a lot of noise," Motoko is told. "I'm on my period," she replies nonchalantly, before unplugging the cords from the back of her neck. "Life is like a node, born out of the flow of information," the Puppet Master Himself explains at one point. "Would you ghost-hack your wife to find out how she feels?" a character asks another. "For now, we see through a glass, darkly, but then face to face," Motoko's "ghost" whispers to Batou on a boat. Lines such as, "I'm not interested in other people's photos", are particularly resonant in a world where invasion of privacy is so commonplace.

A futuristic take on "Frankenstein" of sorts, "Ghost in the Shell" doesn't match Katsuhiro Otomo's equally-convoluted "Akira"'s scale and epic nature. It's not as poignant as Isao Takahata's brilliant meditation on war, "Grave of the Fireflies". It lacks the magic and searing emotion of Studio Ghibli's output, or the otherworldliness - and plain trippiness! - of Satoshi Kon's oeuvre. So yes, one could make a good argument that there are better entry points into the anime world than Mamoru Oshii's "Ghost in the Shell".

Yet none of those films is getting a live-action Hollywood remake. This "Ghost" has clearly implanted itself into our collective consciousness, not unlike the hacked minds it depicts.

4 out of 5 stars

"Guardians of the Galaxy Vol.2" Finds Gunn Firing on All Cylinders

Synopsis: Set to the backdrop of Awesome Mixtape #2, 'Guardians of the Galaxy Vol. 2' continues the team's adventures as they unravel the mystery of Peter Quill's true parentage.

As my friend and I sat at the press screening of #GotGVol2, staring at the giant projected image of James Gunn's ragtag team of anti-Avengers searing through space, Blue Swede's "Hooked on a Feeling" latched on to my brain. Catchy and lightly rebellious, the song perfectly illustrates the first volume's wit and anarchic vibe (it certainly got $800 million-worth of global audiences hooked on its feelings). Studio honcho Kevin Feige took a gamble on a relatively inexperienced, indie horror director, who got his start with cheap-o Troma films ("Tromeo & Juliet") and moved on to a career in screenwriting ("Dawn of the Dead"), with the occasional directorial venture ("Slither").

Feige's gamble paid off, big time. Gunn's talents - his trademark wit and visual energy - were magnified by the first volume's giant budget, instead of getting lost amidst the FX (see: Colin Trevorrow's disastrous "Jurassic World"). Gunn maintained the perfect equilibrium of weird but not too weird, bombastic but not too overwhelming, funny but not too cocky, its humor steeped in characters rather than pop-culture references or, for that matter, references to other Marvel films.

So, as I hummed the tune, my apprehension grew. I began reading too much into the cheesy poster in front of me: was it going to be yet another soulless Marvel SFX extravaganza, a retread of the first film, its originality recycled and blown-out to the *n*th degree? To my relief, my rising fears were swiftly eradicated with the opening sequence, which again showcases the director's incredible skill at knowing exactly what the audience wants and how to deliver it: the GotG crew, all together, exchanging quips and light banter in face of imminent peril. And then *that* Groot credit sequence starts, putting any doubts I may have had to rest. Taking over scripting duties, Gunn has taken over entirely; we are in his world now. Vol. 2 doesn't achieve the near-impossible feat of topping the original, but it comes damn close, and it left me breathlessly anticipating Vol. 3, already in pre-production by the director and his team.

The cast being in on the joke is part of the reason why it all works so well. There's barely any slapstick or forced improvisation, but the delivery is constantly on-point. Chris Pratt's Star-Lord remains the actor's best character since his gut-bustlingly clueless Andy Dwyer graced the small screens in "Parks and Recreation". The palpable camaraderie on set - I imagine Gunn kept it low-key despite the stratospheric budget - allows Pratt to be natural, which grounds the film's insane happenings in a much-needed relatability. Unusual for a Marvel flick, he has real (and really self-aware) chemistry with Zoe Saldana's emerald-hued Gamora, who, unlike most women in this testosterone universe, is a fully fleshed-out, kick-ass character, with a violent sister rivalry (a returning Karen Gillan as the Frankenstein-like Nebula). Dave Bautista's Drax surprised me to no end the first time around, an intimidating beast with a warm heart and absolutely no speech filter, and here continues to shine in some of the film's highlights - most involving his scenes with the "ugly on the outside, beautiful on the inside" alien Mantis (the otherworldly Pom Klementieff).

Gunn's frequent collaborator Michael Rooker returns as Star-Lord's adoptive father Yondu, in an expanded role - and you can never give *too* much screen time to Michael Rooker. As for the film's central digital characters - Bradley Cooper's Rocket Raccoon and Vin Diesel's Baby Groot - the former's storyline delves deeper into the furry character's insecurities, while the latter actor continues to cash in the millions, Vin's voice now contorted by computers to sound child-like and barely recognizable.

That said, there's no denying that Baby Groot is friggin' adorable. Other memorable characters include Kurt Russell's Ego - his plot-line with Star Lord is an apocalyptic reunion that literally echoes through space; Elizabeth Debicki's High Priestess Ayesha, a golden, statuesque, prideful goddess; Chris Sullivan as the hilarious TaserFace… and a cameo that I will let you discover. Sometimes I like a good cliffhanger.

Giddy on the ridiculousness of its own scope and concept, the film jets along from well-structured scene to scene: Drax hanging on to the back of a spaceship as it hurtles through a forest; Gamora slicing a beast in half with her sword; Baby Groot trying to help his friends escape from prison… The list goes on and on: I never thought a David Hasselhoff reference would make me bend over in laughter again, but there you go; a scene involving an immediate need of scotch tape is one of the year's highlights so far; Yondu descending through the air, grasping his "magical whistle stick" and shouting, "Yo, I'm Mary Poppins!" may just be another.

The soundtrack, from Fleetwood Mac's "The Chain" to Cheap Trick's "Surrender", matches the first film's retro catchiness, and Gunn does a fine job contrasting the futuristic space visuals against old-school tunes, but there's a tad of "too muchness" to it. Scale it back a bit next time, Jimmy. Despite a subtly satirical undertone running through it, "GotGVol2" also can't help but give in to the well-established Marvel tropes from time to time - FX overload, stretched-out ending (do these films really need to be over two hours?), some expositional dialogue - yet for the most part it avoids most of the studio's output's tedious, predictable pratfalls.

Gunn steps into the same river twice and comes out a champion swimmer.

PS Stay after the credits for FIVE post-credit scenes!

4 out of 5 stars

"Halt and Catch Fire" Halted in Its First Season, Catches Fire in the Second

Synopsis: *Set in the early 1980s, this series dramatizes the personal computing boom through the eyes of a visionary, an engineer and a prodigy whose innovations directly confront the corporate behemoths of the time. Their personal and professional partnership will be challenged by greed and ego while charting the changing culture in Texas' Silicon Prairie.*

In its first season, the Dallas-set "Halt and Catch Fire" went for the "'Mad Men' set in the 1980s pre-digital era" vibe, and while succeeding intermittently, the struggle was evident. Joe MacMillan (Lee Pace), a conceited ex-IBM employee with an ambiguous sexuality and a penchant for lashing out in the most extraordinary ways (e.g. smashing his own apartment windows, fighting off storms with flashlights and burning down trucks), was basically Don Draper on speed, smart and unstable. He single-handedly fooled and collapsed a small computer empire, Cardiff Electric, in Dallas and then rebuilt it from scratch, with the help of his chosen partners: the weaselly Gordon (Scoot McNairy, extraordinarily good at playing "weaselly") and the rebellious Cameron (Mackenzie Davis), a punk-ish computer geek.

Yet, "HACF" was no "Mad Men", missing the latter's assured pacing, impeccable class (in every aspect) and top-notching ensemble cast (the "ad execs bickering" show received - get this - 355 different award nominations throughout its seven-season run). Nor did it come close to matching another AMC series it sort of resembles in its rags-to-riches "power" trajectory: "Breaking Bad", whose style and shock value it just couldn't match. "Halt and Catch Fire"'s creators' - newcomers Christopher Cantwell and Christopher C. Rogers - lack of experience surfaced often and glaringly. Imagine a serious "Silicon Valley" and you'll have an idea of what the series was like: full of tech speak, tech drama and tech relationships.

What they lacked in experience however, the creators made up in ambition. The show held promise, mostly due to its protagonists who, while flawed, each had their own secret and, most importantly, chemistry. Despite the borderline-irredeemable shit their unethical characters did, the lead acting trio are pros, and kept our attention hooked - as did the show's themes, touching upon consumerism, leadership, power-play, feminism/sexism and, of course, the Dawn of The New Era in Technology.

Sure, the series had its share of silly exchanges, peaking when Joe ripped his shirt right off, revealing a body covered in scars, to consequently (tearfully) share a sad/inspirational childhood tale. But even in that overblown moment of eccentricity, his manipulative nature kept us guessing whether any of it was actually true (it wasn't; the moment he revealed the real reason behind his scars was actually quite poignant).

The show also contained sharp snippets of dialogue and nuanced scenes, counterbalancing the silly bits. The season ended with the success of Cardiff Electric and the portable computer (ironically titled "The Giant") at a Las Vegas expo, a great review of "The Giant" in the press, and Cameron forming her own renegade company, aptly named Mutiny, with internet's birth looming heavily in the horizon. (Fun fact: While its initial ideas were indeed conceived in the early 1980s, with the adoption of TCP/IP by ARPANET (which "HACF" mirrors), the actual World Wide Web was invented by computer scientist Tim Berners-Lee in 1990. I know, I'm smart enough to be a part of Mutiny. Or I'm good at Googling).

Season Two of "Halt and Catch Fire" matures significantly. It wisely spends more time on Gordon's wife Donna (a tricky role, impeccably played by Kerry Bishé), an intelligent, strong woman who broke through bureaucratic barriers in the first season with enviable resilience and patience, earning a place in Mutiny. The trio has become the Fearless Foursome and then reassembled, Avengers-style, only Tony Stark (a.k.a. Joe) is now exiled to Siberia (it's a metaphor; you'll see what I mean).

Mutiny is portrayed as the "original Google", its home offices resembling the colorful/anarchy/hipster/geek open work environments of the corporation that owns us all (Cameron even discovers someone's glasses molten into stale pizza). We meet the characters 20 months after the events of the first season. Donna (the sensible one) and Cameron (still the outlaw who doesn't give a damn about rules), are now running their online (on-phone?) gaming office out of the house, blowing the power surge in the entire neighborhood - a definite premonition of things to come.

In the meantime, Gordon (torn and addicted to cocaine - about time someone touched upon *that* staple of the 1980s) and Joe (back from "Shangri-La") reconnect at Cardiff Electric to collect their checks. Only Joe's check gets shredded by Cardiff's bitter owner and, unhireable due to his past shenanigans, he's left with no choice but to take the job filing docs in the basement for his fiancée Sara's (Aleksa Palladino) father, oil tycoon Jacob (played by a stoic James Cromwell).

Of course, things don't stay stagnant for any of these characters. Joe hatches a brilliant scheme in the pits of Jacob's firm. Cameron's entire enterprise almost crashes due to Gordon's unintentional error. Cameron and Machiavellian Joe's relationship, fueled by their flare for drama, takes a new spin when they finally reconnect halfway through the season. When Mutiny tries to dupe Joe during a gaming demonstration, what potentially could have led to disaster ended up a revelation: Mutiny are IP geniuses (read: early internet inventors).

A company called WestNet steals all their tech innovations, and whether it was Joe's intention (directly or indirectly) is one of the titillating aspects of this season. There are small moments peppered thorough the story that stick out: Gordon's reunion with an old flame and his debilitating sickness; the casual invention of online dating (and "catfishing") based on a homosexual chat; a molly trip in a neon-lit nightclub, where Joe waxes prophetic; and my favorite: Donna singing to her daughter over the phone to soothe her after a series of highly traumatic events. Best of all, "HACF" substitutes the claustrophobic, grey setting of season one with golden hues and a generally more expansive palette.

The actors feel more comfortable in their roles: McNairy cuts back on the sleaze in a nuanced turn (his trajectory from "coked-out-of-his-mind Gordon trying to impress Joe" to "gradual deterioration in his basement" is a sight to behold); Lee Pace is more humble and toned-down - yet still keeps us guessing what the character's real intentions are; Mackenzie Davis is more fleshed out and less irritating, her anarchic vibe a much-needed jolt to the show (take "the creation of a shooter" sequence), and special kudos to the aforementioned Kerry Bishé for not merely playing a conflicted character but subtly embodying oppressed women, and John Bosworth (aka "Boz", poignantly played by veteran actor Toby Huss), a tragic figure, a requiem of a man lost in a new world who gradually finds his way back.

Hefty themes of pride, redemption, finding oneself, alienation, "free-wheelin' it" vs corporatization, "focusing on numbers" vs "bringing people together" (and how the two aren't mutually exclusive), the rise of the internet and start-up companies are all incisively explored… Cantwell and Rogers toned down on the melodrama, replacing it with subtler moments, such as Joe's very real confession to Gordon over dinner and Cameron's panic attack after a blow-out leaves them with zero users…

In season two, past clashes with the future more evidently: Joy Division "Clash"es (see what I did there?) with Bonobo on the soundtrack; characters' demons resurface and clash with their ambitions; complicated algorithms clash with abacuses…

The creators learned from past mistakes and don't let all the nerdy tech jargon get in the way of deep characterization, intricate plot strands and, let's face it, a bit off scandalous drama thrown in. The dialogue has become even sharper, the characterizations deeper, the fluidity of the filmmaking gives off more of a purpose, and the stakes are infinitely higher. Most importantly, it's addictive, my wife as hooked as I was marathoning through both seasons.

It's not revolutionary or groundbreaking; while it still can't hold an LED light to "Mad Men", the punk-rock, nerdy, thought-provoking and engrossing "Halt and Catch Fire"'s quality is steadily rising, the buzz around it spreading, like a virus.

4 out of 5 stars

The Highly Relevant "Letters from Baghdad" Pays Tribute to a Great Woman

Synopsis: Gertrude Bell, the most powerful woman in the British Empire in her day, shaped the destiny of Iraq after WWI in ways that still reverberate today.

While Gertrude Bell is certainly very well-known and respected as a highly influential historical figure, her fascinating life story has been utterly neglected by the entertainment industry. To my knowledge, apart from Werner Herzog's recent under-the-radar Nicole Kidman vehicle "Queen of the Desert" (which currently boasts a 16% rating on Rotten Tomatoes) and a little-seen early 1990's made-for-TV flick, there's no film or series depicting Bell's tumultuous journey. And her journey certainly warrants an epic motion picture, if not several seasons of an HBO binge-watching experience.

One of the most respected women of her - or all - time, Gertrude spoke half of the world's languages (Arabic, Persian, French, German, Italian and Turkish!), explored and mapped several Middle Eastern territories, witnessed WWI and the Armenian Genocide, played a crucial part in the creation of the modern state of Iraq, investigated archaeological sites, changed the course of female history - and that's not even skimming the surface. What have YOU done lately?

Filmmakers Sabine Krayenbühl and Zeva Oelbaum decided to rectify this abhorrent omission in cinema with "Letters from Baghdad", a wonderful documentary that sheds more light on the figure than her actions. Tilda Swinton's eloquent narration as Bell herself infuses the film with a resonant intimacy - to quote the beginning, "This is her story, told in her own words and those of her contemporaries, taken entirely from private letters, secret communiques and other primary sources". T.E. Lawrence (THE Lawrence of Arabia), Sgt. Frank Stafford, Sir Percy Fox and other real-life figures are played by actors, interviewed on camera, the footage made to seem old. This highly stylized approach works in the film's favor - it flies by.

"The only woman allowed to come up to Baghdad", the Yorkshire-born Bell's "swim against the current" started early, when she was one of the first women allowed to attend college in Oxford, based solely on her blistering intelligence. After a brief and tragic love affair in Tehran, Gertrude became fixated on "doing all the most impossible peaks in Switzerland." Though she made some "remarkable ascents", her "destiny was fixed by that first visit to Persia." She returned to the East, drawn to its people, culture and languages.

Bell proceeded to travel hundreds of miles to the Ottoman Empire by foot and camel, where she was deemed a spy. Her own government turning its back on her, she continued her journey, encountering tribes and taking photos of important historical sites on the way. "Letters" accentuates the highlights of her colorful/tumultuous life: Bell's solitary confinement, her involvement in the British Red Cross, her travels to Egypt ("She knows more about the Arabs and Arabia than almost any other living Englishman or woman") and Baghdad, in the role of Assistant Political Officer, which caused major controversy. But her "knowledge of inter-tribal relationships" became very useful and she "gathered and sourced information" for the British government.

Adored be the Sheikhs, convinced that "no people likes permanently to be governed by another", she then fought for transition from British to native rule in Mesopotamia, fighting for an Arab Head of State. The Americans came in, and the great battle for oil commenced. "Oil is the trouble, of course," Bell bitterly commented. "Detesting stuff. [...] We had promised an Arab government with British advisors, and instead we have a British government with Arab advisors." Bell's report caused ripples in England, leading to her role as the "oriental secretary" and eventually drawing up Iraq's borders in pursuit of establishing a steady Arab government. We all know how that turned out...

The letters (along with Swinton's & Co's narrations) portray Bell as passionate, determined, sophisticated, endlessly curious, fiercely intelligent, but also, at least according to one source, "abrupt and intolerant, snoozy... [and] downright rude", which made her unpopular outside the elite group with whom she traveled. Magnificent with words, Bell's letters unsurprisingly provide the film's best quotes:

"In the desert, every newcomer is an enemy till you know him to be a friend."
"Don't tell them that the 'me' they knew won't come back in the 'me' that returns."
"Perhaps there's just not enough sun to keep us all warm."

In the words of another "acquaintance", "Do read her letters. They are splendid"

Major kudos to the filmmakers for enlivening the doc with countless absorbing bits. For example, we find out that she "she never mastered the art of spelling". Bell's deep affection for her father is vividly and touchingly brought to life. Smaller scenes stick out, like Bell's visit to the ruins of Babylon, or setting up screenings for Arabian women, or Winston Churchill expressing admiration for the woman. The actors all do commendable jobs, giving the film a theatrical flair, but also broadening its scope and entertainment factor. Archival photos come to life, real footage gets seamlessly interweaved with reenactments - all devices that complement Bell's story and spice up the documentary format's predictable structure.

If there is a minor flaw, it's that the doc's reliance on letters leads to skimming past some important bits of Bell's life and focusing too much on others (e.g. her love affairs). Some events are displayed in a somewhat choppy manner, hopping from one highlight to another without much context. Quite a great deal of historical knowledge is expected from the viewer in order to fully get all the references... But that's okay. This is more of a study of a heroic woman who spoke her mind and broke through barriers than a detailed historical account. If you're curious - go pick up a book. It would be impossible to distill Bell's life into 90 minutes anyway, as each "episode" could make a captivating feature-length film.

In a society ruled by men comparing a woman writing an article to a "dog standing on its hind legs", Bell managed the impossible: "she told the man what she wanted to be done." Sabine Krayenbühl and Zeva Oelbaum's "Letters from Baghdad" avoids most of the dry documentary trappings, even making its series of testimonials more than palatable. The stylistic techniques they utilize keep things entertaining and original. Now let's hope David Fincher is deep into Bell's letters, working on a grand outline as I write this.

4 out of 5 stars

"Miss Sharon Jones!" Pays Tribute to a Living Legend

Synopsis: *Miss Sharon Jones follows the talented and gregarious soul singer of the Grammy nominated R&B band "Sharon Jones and the Dap Kings." As she struggles to find her health and voice again, the film intimately uncovers the mind and spirit of a powerful woman determined to regain the explosive singing career that eluded her for 50 years.*

Barbara Kopple knows a thing or two about brave, intrepid musicians. She helmed the award-winning doc "Shut Up & Sing" about Natalie Maines, member of the country band The Dixie Chicks, who took a stand against George Bush in 2013. Now Miss Kopple gives us another look at a magnificent performer, Sharon Jones, who took a stand against her own Stage 2 pancreatic cancer in the years 2013-2014. And though I generally have an issue with fictional cancer dramas (see my review of the atrocious "Honeyglue" here), a powerful documentary that examines a real-life struggle of a performer, who has inspired generations of fans, is an entire different ball game. "Miss Sharon Jones!", a delightfully entertaining and poignant treat, earns the exclamation point of its title: Kopple's doc is by turns heartbreaking, insightful and ultimately inspirational, without a shred of sentimentality. Its joy is infectious.

Combining elements of funk, R'n'B, soul - and wrapping it all in a fuzzy throwback blanket of 1950s doo-wop, Sharon Jones and the Dap Kings barely ever graced the pop charts, nor was tabloid popularity their goal. A "female James Brown", Sharon has won over thousands of devotees all over the world with her relentless energy, extraordinary vocal range and the uniqueness of her band's genre-blending.

Struck with the horrific news of the disease, Sharon held her head high. Her friend, Megan Holken, a Holistic Nutritionist, invited Sharon to stay with her during the seven-month recovery. As Sharon faces a struggle against near-impossible odds, watching countless talk shows and eager to get back to work, the documentary smoothly introduces us to her past, her band members, how they formed and consequently perfected their sound. But Kopple wisely keeps the focus on Jones and the music, never straying too far into the murky depths of an archive-overloaded, visual Wikipedia.

The film contains plenty of moments that will make you smile and cry - or both, at once. Sharon's deep friendship with her manager Alex is palpable. A touching scene sees Sharon fishing while recollecting moments from her past. The singer belting out "Somewhere Over the Rainbow" at Megan's wedding in an all-too-brief VHS glimpse showcases why she's a natural-born genius. A memorable moment involves Sharon watching the video to her song "Retreat", a parable for beating cancer. Miss Jones singing at a church while reconnecting with God, bringing herself to a near-ecstatic frenzy, is a sight to behold. The band practicing with a post-chemotherapy Sharon, who is on top of her game - and the band's conversation after she leaves - resonates deeply, as does Sharon's excitement at the news of being on Ellen (and the dancing with the talk show host after). We also get to see a wilder side of Sharon, briefly flipping out over Thanksgiving dinner plans. And, of course, there is the incredible comeback, Sharon hesitant to return, but not succumbing to weakness.

Kopple's glimpse inside the life of a living legend is stuffed to the brim with fascinating facts. Being told that she was "too dark, too short" to be a star in the 1980's, Sharon Jones played in a wedding band. She had a stint as a corrections officer (badass!), never took any vocal lessons, and her trumpet player left the band to perform with The Roots on the Jimmy Fallon show. And of course, there's the spine-tingling, get-up-off-your-seat music, joyful and inspiring, influencing everyone from Beck to Amy Winehouse to LCD Soundsystem. if you don't enjoy this sort of thing, there's no talking to you.

Sharon herself is a goddess: brimming with humor, goodwill, honesty, striking intelligence and resilience, channeling her sorrow into creative things like painting (she's a pro, by the way) and exorcizing her demons through music. Just watch her try on wigs early on in the film: "I should go for the Oprah look," she comments dryly. "I gotta sing," she tells her doctor later. "I can't be sitting here… Hell, I'll go bald! Put some make up on, I'll look cute!" At another point, she exclaims, "I don't want to be like Whoopi Goldberg with no eyebrows."

The film never focuses solely on cancer, nor does it wallow in sentiment; its focus instead is on the joys of life, its every precious moment, as personified in its titular heroine. Kopple's film may not side-step some of the pratfalls of a doc biopic - there are some dry patches, its structure is a tad too predictable - but there's no denying its verisimilitude and power. I'm a vinyl collector who happens to spend way too much money on those beautiful shiny discs. Hell, there goes another $20 for "Give the People What They Want", an appropriately-named Sharon Jones and the Dap Kings classic. I suggest you do the same. It's money well-spent.

4 out of 5 stars

Note: Since I wrote this review, Miss Sharon Jones has tragically passed away. I dedicate this review to her.

An Amalgamation of Disney's Past and Present, "Moana" Soars High

Synopsis: *A young woman uses her navigational talents to set sail for a fabled island. Joining her on the adventure is her hero, the legendary demi-god Maui.*

An ode to classic Disney animation, "Moana" also happens to adhere - almost too insistently - to the current cultural "standards" set by Hollywood: a strong-willed central female protagonist fits in nicely into the current zeitgeist of female empowerment; the themes of man vs. Nature remind us of the looming environmental crisis (though Moana does destroy an entire coral eco-system in one scene with her foot - talk about human's effect on Nature…) - and so on and so forth. There is nothing wrong with those commendable thematic elements - but nowadays, they do feel a bit forced, instead of just being, you know, like, the norm. I guess humanity needs to be spoon-fed and hammered more than ever.

Luckily, "Moana" never becomes finger-wagging or overly sentimental, its evident love for the staples of the Disney animation of yore - a dangerous quest, joyful musical numbers, stunning visuals, a goofy animal side-kick and a variety of weird and wonderful creatures - counter-balancing the "relevant" contemporary themes and propelling the story along. Though I refer to them as "staples', those elements indeed feel fresh in this polluted ocean of product-placement, ice-cold computer animation; "Moana"'s like a lung-full of crystal-clear air.

"In the beginning," Moana's Gramma Tala (velvety voice of Rachel House) announces at the start, "there was only ocean - until a Mother Island emerged." When vain and powerful Demi-God Maui (not-so-velvety voice of Dwayne "No-Longer-The-Rock" Johnson) steals the literal emerald heart of this mythical island during one of his quests to impress humankind, a Demon of Earth and Fire is unleashed upon the world, gradually destroying everything in its path. Even Maui's magical fish hook, which transforms him into any animal he desires, cannot defeat the fire demon - and so he flees. Someone needs to "find Maui and restore the island's heart", Tala concludes, to an audience of mesmerized children, Moana particularly entranced. Not long after Gramma Tala's tale, little Moana is parting the ocean like a tiny Moses; a strikingly beautiful sequence that sets the vibrant visual tone of the film. Will she be the one to accomplish this challenging task?

Moana is drawn to water and she sings about it, arms spread wide, ready to embrace her uncertain (well, to her, not to us) fate. "You are the future of our people, Moana," her traumatized-by-past father, Chief Tui (voice of Temuera Morrison) insists, "and they're not out there, they're right here." He briefly convinces her to "take the throne" - until the darkness reaches the island, killing the fish and turning the coconuts into ash. Prompted by her dying Grammy, Moana sets out to find Maui, get his hook back and return the heart of the island to its rightful place. Will they bond and accomplish their task?

Like in most classic fairytales, the conclusion is evident and it's about the journey. This is quite a journey. Dazzling in its colors, exhilarating in its assured sense of pace and a knowing balance of danger and comic relief, "Moana" easily falls amongst the best the studio has offered (excluding its affiliation with Pixar). Tiny coconut pirates that seem to have emerged out of a Miyazaki fable; a glittering hoarder crab, deep in an underwater world, surrounded by a wild variety of creepy and dazzling critters; the aforementioned Earth and Fire Demon, made out of lava that solidifies when struck against water - these are just some of the more memorable elements in this timeless story.

"Hamilton" creator Lin-Manuel Miranda wrote several songs for the film, and while I am by no means a fan of musicals, I found myself tapping along to the exhilarating visuals and tunes that actually didn't grate me as badly as they normally do. (There is one funny line in the film that reflected my attitude towards musicals, uttered by Maui: "If you start singing, I'm gonna throw up.")

The dialogue, warm and fuzzy, also defied my expectations, pleasantly wrapping me in its wholesomeness. Auli'i Cravalho's debut voice-acting is a superb feat, Moana a fully-formed, fleshed out middle-finger to all the weak-spirited Disney princesses dependent on men to save the day. The Rock - sorry - *Mr. Johnson* does surprisingly well, even when belting it out about how awesome he is. Apart from one groan-inducing stinker that produced more chuckles in the theater than it should have - "Use a bird to write with, it's called tweeting" - it's evident that the film's myriad screenwriters paid attention to avoid the usual trappings of pop-culture references and lame slapstick.

Some questions did arise, the cranky ol' critic that I am. Why didn't Maui just carry Moana on his back, in his giant eagle form, to the destination, once he got his magical hook back? The ocean's involvement in Moana's adventures also seems randomly intermittent - she could have surely used more of its tremendous power, although it would have diminished the themes of human perseverance against all odds. I also felt like Jemaine Clement's Tamatoa turtle was a little underused, considering he's gut-bustlingly hilarious and a total scene-stealer.

Forget my bitc… - sorry, *kids' review* - moaning. "Moana" is a winner. Adults will be in awe of its visuals, appreciate its IMPORTANT themes and get all nostalgic about animated films like "Beauty and the Beast" and "Aladdin" - oh, and enthused about the inclusion of a powerful female hero to set the standard for future generations of "voyagers".

4 out of 5 stars

"People" Will Make You Ponder Humanity

Synopsis: *Six vignettes featuring an ensemble of characters who grapple with each other in order to gain control of their own perspectives.*

It's rare to see an indie film that is littered with people just… talking to each other, pondering existential issues, be it over dinner, or at a party, or in a car. It's even more rare to see such a film succeed (the suspenseful "Locke" with Tom Hardy comes to mind). Shane McGoey, having gained some experience as a PA on major Hollywood productions, had the balls to come up with such a concept - folks challenging each other's perspectives of existential issues in contained spaces - and follow through with it, as a result producing one of the better micro-budget films this year. His "People" comes with a discloser - "This film is meant to be taken in small doses" - and while I don't necessarily agree with it, I see McGoey's point: each segment is stuffed with so many themes and ideas, it's a lot to take in. That said, he never lets the film get bogged down in its own pomposity - the acting is so natural, the dialogue so well-written that the only frustration "People" may cause is the desire to pause and rewatch a sequence, to see how it so naturally went from point A to point B.

Split into six seemingly random segments, "People" starts its unconventional journey with "Being for Others", a study of sex, identity, generational differences and power. A young woman, Rainey (Christine Lekas) etches an ouroboros into a table (the film's central theme of wholeness is hinted at here) at her psychiatrist's (Greg Homer) office, as she reveals a history of family abuse and her consequent inability to feel pleasure, resorting to sexual asphyxiation. "I don't think I know how to love," she says. "It's necessary for my happiness." The session swiftly becomes a power play, with the protégé becoming the mentor, so to speak, resulting in a somewhat-awkward and hilarious finale.

"The Lacked", "People"'s second chapter, finds two young men, Jeffrey (Rane Jameson) and Richard (Jake Wynne-Wilson) in a Chinese restaurant, after sleeping together. They have entirely different perspectives on sexual identity, sex, monogamy and commitment. "I make myself every day," Richard tells Jeffrey when confronted with being a "fag". "I'm not a light switch, like you," Jeffrey snaps back. The non-sequitur ending to this episode actually made me pause the film and re-think the entire segment from a new angle.

"Control" - the most assured, entertaining and resonant chapter, finds four men - a conflicted war veteran, an acerbic and eloquent "gangster", a mysterious silent observer and a nurse - debate the futility of war, as they do drugs and bet on a fight unfolding on TV. They conversation gets progressively more heated, and it becomes impossible to take your eyes off those charismatic actors. Poignant, unpredictable, with razor-sharp dialogue that deals with the implications of war, the reasoning behind joining the military, and yes, control, this is the best segment by far, breathlessly twisting stereotypes inside out. It's the best Tarantino scene Tarantino never wrote.

In stark contrast, "Values" happens to be the weakest point of the film, and the shortest (if you discount the madcap ending). Conspiracy theorist Baldwin (Baldwin Justice) and his exasperated girlfriend Taylor (Margot Bienvenu) drive to a hospital after Baldwin had a mishap at a fountain that resulted in a foot injury. They bicker the entire way about religion, privilege and ultimately their relationship - until the harshest, most abrupt ending in "People".

In "Bad Faith", screenwriter Franz (Mustafa Harris) has a bad conference call during the strangest party you'll ever crash. "Where's the meat and potatoes?" the disembodied producer voices on the other end of the line demand. "What's at risk here? Where are the character arcs?" They go on like that for a while. A self-referential statement on narrative structure, selling out, creativity vs marketability, having faith in the artist and their audience, "Bad Faith" is also a showcase for Mustafa Harris, who goes through a wide spectrum of emotions while being on the phone throughout the entire segment. His rant about the hollowness of Hollywood is a sight to behold.

The final chapter, "Nothingness", connects all the characters in an amusing and surreal fashion, tying the film together in a satisfying way. To say anything else would ruin a borderline-berserk finale that somehow makes sense in the context of the aforementioned proceedings. Think of "People" as an indie "Crash" on acid, or a contemporary take on Neil LaBute's "Your Friends & Neighbors".

Despite some issues with editing (some shots don't match), Shane McGoey's film is a well-written and audacious effort, filled with wonderfully odd moments - such as a boom mic purposefully appearing in the shot at one point - that tend to accentuate/complement the film's unusual structure and surreal undertones (which, in turn, point out the absurdity of life). The acting is uniformly excellent, especially for a fresh, "untested" cast. Let's hope this one doesn't entirely slip under the radar. Kudos to the filmmaking team for making a compelling film, imminently watchable from start to finish, comprised of nothing more than people… being people.

4 out of 5 stars

"Raw" is Bloody Well Done

Synopsis: *When a young vegetarian undergoes a carnivorous hazing ritual at vet school, an unbidden taste for meat begins to grow in her.*

Julia Ducournau's French arthouse horror flick "Raw" begins with a serene moment: a long, empty road at dusk, heavy clouds hanging low and threatening to burst, a lone figure walking towards us quietly in the distance. A car appears, heading towards her. This moment of tranquility is jarringly interrupted when the stranger leaps in front of the car and smashes against it violently, making it swerve into a tree. As the vehicle emits dying fumes, the figure slowly gets up, seemingly unscathed, approaches the car, looks inside… Does the victim become the perpetrator?

This defiance of expectations, already quite palpable within the first two minutes, is just one of the many goals first-time feature director Julia Ducournau achieves with aplomb in "Raw", her darkly funny, beautifully-shot, deeply disturbing and unbearably sad cinematic treatise on adolescence. Propelled by a powerful central performance from the enigmatic Garance Marillier, who exudes both tenderness and savagery, "Raw" lives up to its title, built on stark contrasts and uncompromising truths about humanity. With echoes of David Cronenberg's early "body horror" oeuvre and Michael Haneke's clinical dissections of humanity, "Raw" reveals what we all secretly already know: all vegetarians are actually cannibals. It'll also make you think twice before digging into that medium-rare steak.

After the effective prologue, we meet Justine (Marillier), having a difficult time being vegetarian, meatballs finding their way into her mashed potatoes at a quiet, grimy-looking cafe. Her supportive parents (Joana Preiss and Laurent Lucas in small-but-crucial roles) drop her off at a desolate vet boarding school, where - to quote the synopsis - a "carnivorous hazing ritual", led by masked seniors, finds its way into her quiet, grimy-looking dorm room at night. Animal-like, on all fours, Justine is forced to crawl through air ducts towards what the initiators refer to as "freedom". When Adrien (Rabah Nait Oufella), a fellow student, notices her fear, he reassures her, "Hey, it's just a game. What do you think could happen?" Famous last words.

Justine's sister, Alex (Elia Rumpf), who has been at this school for a year now, shows up at the initiation party. After a brief moment of reconciliation, she takes Justine to a pitch-black animal morgue, effectively filmed with Alex's flashlight, embalmed creatures in giant jars materializing every time its beam flicks on. In a striking contrast to those grisly images, framed pictures of former valedictorians hang on the walls, among them Mom and Dad - it runs in the family.

Tension builds slowly but effectively: a scene that pays homage to THAT "Carrie" moment, here acts as a catalyst for the proceeding events, as opposed to the Grand Guignol finale in the Brian De Palma classic. The fraternity-like initiators, who prefer to be called elders ("veterans" in French; play on words here - veterinarian/veteran) force Justine to eat raw rabbit kidneys as part of the hazing. This awakens an appetite in Justine, previously suppressed by her family's insistence on being vegetarian, a craving that she has to satisfy, be it a shawarma at a local gas station, raw salmon as a midnight snack… or her sister's sliced-off finger. Upon witnessing the gruesome act, Alex looks shocked… but for the wrong reason, which I will let you discover.

"Raw" is a deft examination of sociological tendencies, such as herd mentality, the effect of peer pressure on a naive young soul, female oppression and empowerment. "I bet a raped monkey suffers like a woman," Justine argues at lunch, defiantly standing behind her argument that a raped monkey and a raped woman are no different. Her humanity then gets stripped away, (skin) layer by layer, until she is forced to resort to her own most animalistic tendencies. "An animal that's tasted human flesh isn't safe," Justine's father says. "If he likes it, he'll bite again."

Which leads to another important theme in Julia Ducournau's deceptively minimalist film: genetics, and whether we can escape what's inherently embedded in our DNA. As Justine comes of age and to term with her awakening sexuality, she begins to hunger the flesh in more ways than one. On one hand, the effect of her ecosystem certainly plays a part in this violent change, but towards the end doubt settles in, until the film leaves you with a sense of inevitability that resonates for days after.

Ducournau sure loves Cronenberg - and that's meant as a compliment. She never directly mirrors the great helmer's literal dissections of humans, but rather pays subtle homage: in both of the directors' work, it's the vomit, excrement, pubic hair, urine and, yes, flesh (all exposed in great abundance in "Raw", so stay clear, sensitive ones!) that makes us human, our primal instincts taking precedence over rationality. Built on juxtapositions of warmth and beauty vs. clinical coldness, human vs. animal, light whimsy vs. visceral psycho-horror, Ducornau proves to be a worthier Cronenberg successor than his own son Brandon did with the lurid, emotionally-vacuous "Antiviral".

The young director fills her debut with striking images that burrow their way into your head - and under your skin. A horse gallops on a treadmill in magnificent slow-motion. Justine vomits a seemingly endless strand of hair, or mane. A car horn won't stop blaring for a very nasty reason. Justine gets trapped under bedsheets, suffocating in her own skin. Her first, multi-colored, bloody sexual experience, swiftly followed by another one of brutal intensity (along with some eyeball-licking, I kid you not), may count as one of the highlights of the film. The score is great too; I'd like to point out one song in particular, Orties' "Plus Putes Que Toutes Les Putes", the rapping French girls wiping the floor with Eminem with their, ahem, daring lyrics.

There are moments of levity amidst the darkness, such as when Justine gets caught for stealing a burger, or her first Brazilian wax experience, or when she tells her sister, "You taste like curry" - or especially when she and a guy get splashed, head-to-toe, in blue and yellow paint respectively, then thrust into a room, "seven-minutes-in-heaven-style", and told not to come out until they're both green. Marillier, who appears in nearly every scene, leads us through the tonal changes with her utterly believable performance.

A cautionary tale above about the perils of adolescence and sending your kids to college, the film should only be regarded metaphorically, and not subjected to too much scrutiny. It never really delves into the minute details of what it means to become a vet. It doesn't really deal with the moral repercussions that the girls must experience after their hideous acts (one murder of an innocent couple in the middle of the film in particular gets dismissed, rendering it that much more horrific). Ducournau is not interested in explaining why, of all places, this vet hospital is so frat-like, harboring depraved human beings. Nor does she explain how exactly Justine managed to never notice the scars on an important character's chest.

Never mind all that. Just go with "Raw"'s demented flow, and it will eat you… raw.

4 out of 5 stars

"Sky Ladder: The Art of Cai Guo-Qiang" is Documentary Dynamite

Synopsis: Trace the rise of contemporary artist Cai Guo-Qiang from childhood in Mao's China to global art world superstar, and join his quest to realize his lifelong obsession: Sky Ladder.

Cai Guo-Qiang has had a dream of going to space ever since he saw the Americans land on the moon. Who could have predicted that a young boy from a small town in the Fujian Province of Mao's China would go on to realize his dream, perhaps indirectly, but no less astonishingly. "Art could be my space-time travel, connecting me to the universe," the man himself says wistfully in director Kevin Macdonald's ("The Last King of Scotland") immersive and beautiful documentary, "Sky Ladder: The Art of Cai Guo-Qiang". Cai's pieces defy easy categorization - some of them literally explosive, others implosive - but all representing the inner torment and, ultimately, optimism of Cai, who is haunted by the tumultuous past but, like all great artists, exorcizes his demons through his astonishing work.

"Sky Ladder" starts with a montage of things exploding, an assault on the senses that pulls us into the mindset of its outwardly serene protagonist. Inspired by gunpowder - its historical significance in Chinese culture, as well as its representation of something simultaneously lethal and ephemeral - Cai went on to turn a conduit for violence into a source of eye-melting beauty. In 1993, hell-bent on making contact with extraterrestrials, the artist decided to prolong the Great Wall of China by stretching a gunpowder fuse all the way to the Gobi desert. His grandiose opening/closing of the 2008 Beijing Summer Olympics ceremony was a sight to behold. His fireworks leave effervescent, aquarelle mists that dissipate, resembling souls, once joyful, now deteriorating.

His love for his 100-year-old ill grandmother is one of the driving factors behind Cai's relentless strive for greatness. The entire "Sky Ladder" project, on which the artist has been focusing for over 20 years - and the running thread of Macdonald's doc - is dedicated to the woman that clearly means the world to Cai. After three failed attempts, he finally manages to assemble the right team at the right time for the 1,650-foot ladder (anchored by helium balloons!) to work.

Before that happens, the film delves into his past, mostly told by Cai himself, with his family and friends contributing thoughtful tidbits about what drove the artist, tracing his meteoric rise to international fame. He readily talks about his move from China to Japan and then to New York, where he hit the zenith of popularity. We also get to see some of Cai's less physically explosive, but equally awe-inspiring work, a few influenced by his love for the environment (a pack of wolves, stretched in an arc that leads into a glass cubicle), others projecting socio-political statements (oil dripping into viscous smudge, a ghastly/gorgeous image) - all in one way or another influenced by his country's Communist regime, a personal way of defying it. He denies being overtly political, but this film's philosophical stance - and his work - raises the question: "Is Cai in denial?"

Whether that's the case or not, there's no question that Cai is wondrously talented, eloquent and perseverant-as-all-hell. When Steven Spielberg himself is in awe of your creations, you know you've made it. Built on contrasts between the artist's explosive art pieces and the humble, soft-spoken artist himself, his country's mythical serenity and violent regime, and of course, the brutality and fragility of the work itself, "Sky Ladder" is, above all, a poetic statement on the importance of art.

Evoking James Marsh's masterpiece "Man on Wire", Macdonald's film is about the pursuit of dreams against all odds; both films culminate in searing sequences of impeccable power, visions of dreams come true. While "Sky Ladder" lacks Marsh's scope, suspense and nuance, it's nevertheless a gorgeous little reminder that we should all make lo…, sorry, art, not war and, like Cai, always reach for the heavens.

4 out of 5 stars

"The Beauty Inside" Gives Heartstrings a Good Workout

Synopsis: Woo-jin wakes up in a different body everyday, regardless of age, gender and nationality. Each time he transforms, Woo-jin must figure out how to return to his own body and reunite with his girlfriend, Yi-soo.

Folks have been discussing the dearth of romantic comedies - and romances in general - lately; some even describe them as a "dying genres". Films such as this summer's hit "Trainwreck" attempt - and to a certain degree succeed - to revitalize romcoms by resorting to raunchiness, so prominent and hip nowadays. Others, like the deluge of Nicholas Sparks and John Green YA adaptations, wholeheartedly embrace the inherent sentimentality of the "romantic" genre, manipulating audiences into weeping by resorting to cheap cliches (e.g. Ryan Gosling proclaiming his love in the rain to Rachel McAdams in the much-beloved atrocity "The Notebook").

America's history of romcoms seems too steeped in sappy sentiments and overtly forceful moralizing; so it doesn't come as a surprise that it took South Korea's film industry, known for its inventiveness and defiance of conventions, to come closest so far this decade to bringing us a well-made, funny, insightful and honest romance.

"The Beauty Inside" introduces a spectacularly assured talent to the world of cinema: director Baek Jong-Yeol, previously known for his work on commercials. Here, he elicits subtle performances, complementing them with elegant images and a smooth flow, barely resorting to maudlin, manipulative tactics to make his audiences feel deeply for the fate of his protagonists.

The film starts with a nifty montage, quickly depicting our hero's - the 30-year-old Woo-jin's - predicament: for the past 12 years, he has been waking up in a different person's body every morning, be it a child, woman and/or foreigner. The colorfully mournful prologue briskly establishes the overall, Charlie Kaufman-esque (yes, I am officially coining that term) tonal juxtaposition of lightheartedness and melancholy.

Woo-jin makes furniture in a spacious but desolate studio, where no one, save for his best friend and work partner, Sang-bek (Lee Dong-Hwi), has to interact with him. Sang-bek takes Woo-jin out to clubs and parties; when Woo-jin is in an attractive young girl's body, Sang-bek proposes they make love, just once, for he would never be able to sleep with a girl like that (Woo-jin declines the offer). Whenever Woo-jin finds himself in a handsome man's body, he takes advantage and sleeps with women. Some hilarity ensues: what if you fell asleep with a charismatic stud and woke up with the same man, but in an old, wrinkly body? "I can never fall in love", Woo-jin proclaims.

Only he does - with Yi-soo (Han Hyo-ju), a stunning young woman who works at a different furniture shop. It's love at first site, and Woo-sin patiently waits until he is in a body of a good-looking guy to ask her out. They "click", and he stays up all night to see her again. "People say true beauty lies inside," Woo-jin says dreamily, "but first impressions are equally important." After a few nights, his exhausted body caves in… His struggle to stay up for the girl he loves, while maintaining his sanity, functions beautifully as a metaphor for our strive to be as charming on a second - and third, and fourth - date, to live up to established, fragile expectations, as the initial mystery begins to subside. How he explains his dilemma to Yi-soo, and the consequent blossoming - and possibly disintegrating - romance, I'll let you discover.

A variety of international actors play Woo-jin, which may sound confusing, but it all gels surprisingly well; the sparse, lyrical narration, for one, holds it together seamlessly - you never, for a minute, doubt it's him, and it's all in the little gestures and mannerisms and vocal intonations of the impressive cast. The lead actress, Han Hyo-ju, gives an incredibly memorable performance, by turns subtle and funny and touching. The chemistry between the leads truly sparks.

"The Beauty Inside" consists of almost-unbearably heartrending moments, such as when Woo-jin comes to his mother after his first transformation, and she recognizes her son almost instantly; or when Woo-jin states longingly about Yi-soo, "She's the only person that understands me", a well-worn phrase that takes a whole new meaning; or the lovely sequence where he taunts her to find him in a crowded square; or even something as simple as a description of a chair - "Once a tree, then a ship, and now a chair" - which reiterates the film's theme of the passage of time… I loved how the custom-made furniture, carefully carved to fit individual postures, mirrored so brilliantly our tendency to "customize" ourselves to fit expectations.

That's not to say it's all philosophical musings - this romcom surely lives up to its "com" element; the film is sprinkled with great, bizarre moments of humor, such as when Woo-jin turns into a… young boy. Yi-soo takes him on a somewhat-uncomfortable date - but he gets drunk quickly ("The body doesn't lie"), and then, completely inebriated and hanging off her neck, insists on picking up the check, confusing the waitress.

Upon closer scrutiny, certain questions do arise. Whose bodies does he take, exactly? Are they real people? If so, do they keep leading their lives, while he's in their bodies? What if he met his counterpart? Would it be a "Back to the Future",

Armageddon-type scenario? What about allergies? A bit of a passport issue there? The film is also a little too long, and never really delves into the psychological toll frequent transformations like that would have on a body and mind… but then again, that would be too heavy for an allegorical romantic comedy.

If you buy into this admittedly far-fetched premise, you'll find a moving parable about alienation, loneliness, friendship, identity, sexuality, societal expectations and, well, the meaning of beauty. What the film truly nails is the wrenching heartache of being in love. Forget your Sparkses and Greens and go see "The Beauty Inside". I'll be honest, I was never a fan of "romance" as a film genre. But this one got to me.

4 out of 5 stars

"The Good Dinosaur" Finds Pixar Stomping Its Way to the Top Echelon of Contemporary Animation... Again

Synopsis: *An epic journey into the world of dinosaurs where an Apatosaurus named Arlo makes an unlikely human friend.*

Pixar rightfully takes pride in its consistently stellar output of computer-generated wizardry. While I'll always be a proponent of good ol' hand-drawn animation (no pixel can ever convey the warmth of a paintbrush), I have to admit that the studio's attention to detail, undeniably gorgeous visuals and inventive plots make it tower above the current competition. Even Pixar's lesser efforts, like "Cars 2" and "Monsters University" (both of which caught a case of "sequelitis"), wipe the floor with the likes of DreamWorks' lackluster "Home" or Sony Pictures Animation's assault on the senses, "Hotel Transylvania" (partial blame for the latter falls on "auteur extraordinaire", Adam Sandler).

This year's "Inside Out" blew me away - arguably the deepest, most complex and heartfelt of Pixar's offerings. "The Good Dinosaur" marks the studio's second release in one year - a first! - and while it doesn't quite scale "Inside Out"'s dizzying heights, it's a sublime, suspenseful and unusual take on the Mesozoic era, filled with existential messages, told in sensational, photorealistic detail. In other words, it's a typical Pixar film.

"The Good Dinosaur" starts with a bang - not the Big One, mind you, just a few million years later - by putting a different spin on evolution: dinosaurs look up at the asteroid - the one that was supposed to hit Earth and destroy most life - as it misses by an inch and soars by harmlessly. Cut to a few million years later (modesty of scale has never been Pixar's forte): dinosaurs now talk and study agriculture. Poppa (Jeffrey Wright) and Momma (Frances McDormand) give birth to three children. As the siblings grow, it becomes clear that flimsy Arlo (Raymond Ochoa) is way too sensitive and cowardly to survive in this harsh Cretaceous world.

Poppa grows especially concerned when Arlo fails to kill a human "critter", later nicknamed Spot (Jack Bright), who keeps stealing their food. So Poppa takes his son on an epic journey, to get Arlo ready for life's Big Obstacles. And boy, does Arlo learn his lesson the hard way, as things take a drastic turn for the worse, in a scene that evokes "Bambi"'s brutal lack of sugarcoating in its portrayal of death. When Arlo later attempts to avenge his father's demise, he literally gets swept up, hopelessly lost, and consequently has to find his way back home, encountering a variety of extraordinary creatures on the way, and forming a bond with Spot. In essence, "The

Good Dinosaur" becomes a survival tale, with nods to "127 Hours" aplenty (I'm only half-kidding).

As "Wall-E" demonstrated in its first half, Pixar is best at creating silent sequences, where actions speak significantly louder than any carefully-scribbled word: behold the numerous, wondrous scenes of Arlo fighting nature - and himself - or the laugh-out-loud comedic set pieces. "The Good Dinosaur"'s parallel universe - where the Apatosauruses speak and grow crops, while human children resemble wolf cubs - works marvelously. Magical moments, that left the theater in awed silence, include a night walk with prehistoric fireflies; a different spin on "Wack-A-Mole" (Blow-A-Mole? no, that sounds wrong); a hallucinatory trip-out sequence; and - by far the film's highlight - the dry and bonkers Styracosaurus, Forrest Woodbush (the voice of Peter Sohn, also the film's director) and his entourage of critters, whose appearance I won't spoil any further, in fear of ruining... well, the entire, brilliant - albeit way too short - sequence. Forrest deserves his own spin-off. "The Loopy Dinosaur", anyone?

Other quirky characters include a gang of playful T-Rexes, led by the gruff-voiced Butch (Sam Elliott); the vicious pterodactyls, whose leader, Thunderclap (Steve Zahn), has "seen the eye of the storm", which rendered him "wild and fearless"; a herd of buffaloes, and a group of hillbilly dinos.

"The Good Dinosaur" does flirt with the sentimentality "Inside Out" so successfully avoided. While the emotion-driven drama managed to convey a wide spectrum of said emotions without resorting to preaching, Pixar's latest can't help but venture into "Obvious Land" here and there. "Someday you'll all make your mark," Poppa promises, as he forms a footprint against the wall of a shack, "and I can't wait to see it." He also repeatedly assures Arlo, "You're me, and more." The film's final message, while laudable, is piled on a bit too thick, as are its themes of achieving goals, overcoming adversities, and abundant lessons about facing your fear ("Sometimes you gotta get through your fear to see the beauty on the other side," Poppa says).

It's a familiar story, but a familiar story told well, and the juxtaposition of such genre tropes and state-of-the-art animation weirdly works in the film's favor. The fact that it doesn't resort to cheap pop-cultural references, product placement gags and hit songs gives it a timeless quality. Most importantly, we believe the central friendship, care for the unlikely heroes, and understand the importance of letting go at the end.

Overall, while not quite a gargantuan achievement, "The Good Dinosaur" has the feel of classic fairy tales and delivers where it's most important. The comic timing is spot-on throughout, the colors are gorgeous, and the film's swirls of rain, dust, clouds, tornadoes and floods represent the turmoil of adolescence perfectly. Pixar nails it again - let's hope we don't have to live through several more "Ice Ages" before the studio's next release.

4 out of 5 stars

"The Jungle Book" Covers All the "Bear Necessities"

Synopsis: The man-cub Mowgli flees the jungle after a threat from the tiger Shere Khan. Guided by Bagheera the panther and the bear Baloo, Mowgli embarks on a journey of self-discovery, though he also meets creatures who don't have his best interests at heart.

Jon Favreau has come a long way since his role as the brute Mike in Doug Liman's seminal indie film "Swingers" (which the actor also wrote). Since those glory days of 1990's micro-budget experimentations, both Liman and Favreau have established themselves as Hollywood A-list directors, the former catapulting Tom Cruise out of an airplane in "Edge of Tomorrow", and the latter catapulting Robert Downey Jr. out of... well, a variety of structures in "Iron Man". After the bomb that was "Cowboys & Aliens", Favreau returned to his indie roots with the charming "Chef" - which, as it turns out, was just prep work for his next big outing.

Now Favreau brings us the much-anticipated remake (rework? new take? retelling?) of the Disney's classic "The Jungle Book", in live-action - though about 80% of the film seems to have been animated, albeit with pixels instead of brushes. While usually it's those damn pixels that suck all the magic out of big-budget extravaganzas, Favreau's film happens to be one of the rare exceptions, like Ang Lee's "Life of Pi" (which also had a ferocious CGI tiger), where the almost-never-distracting effects actually enhance the narrative, instead of assaulting our eyeballs, "Transformers"-style. The magic is palpable, kids. Welcome to the jungle.

In true spirit of Rudyard Kipling's classic, Favreau's film is about the disparity of human and animal. Where do those distinct separations lie, if a human were to be raised by a pack of wolves? Could humans and animals ever live together in peace - or, at the very least, mutual respect? The phrase "fight like a man" takes a whole new meaning in this film. At the very beginning, as Mowgli (Neel Sethi) is being chased by his mentor, panther Bagheera (voiced by Ben Kingsley), through a deep jungle of vines and exotic shrubbery, the latter inquires, "I realize you weren't born wolf, but could you at least act like one?"

The dry season devastates the jungle. The exotic shrubbery dissipates, unraveling the Peace Rock in the sole water reservoir, where animals - both predator and prey - gather to drink peacefully, under the solemn oath of the Water Truce. The presence of Mowgli and his human inventions, causes a furor, especially maddening the mighty tiger Shere Khan (Idris Elba), who growls, "Man-cub becomes Man, and Man is forbidden!" He warns Akela (Giancarlo Esposito), the wolf pack leader, that as soon as "the water rises, this rock disappears and the truce will end... Ask yourselves, how many lives is a man-cub worth?"

Intimidated by the tiger's threats, the wolf pack debates its next steps, until Mowgli volunteers to leave, and Bagheera takes him on a journey back to the "man village". On their adventure they encounter a herd of God-like elephants who "created this jungle", separate in a suspenseful moment, just to soon reunite; in the meantime, Mowgli's backstory is revealed, and (spoiler alert!) Akela is murdered by Shere Khan, to lure Mowgli back for the Ultimate Showdown.

"The Jungle Book" is fast-paced, beautifully photographed by Bill Pope ("The Matrix") and most importantly, filled with obvious love of the material. Favreau always approaches his projects, even the failures, with strenuous attention to detail, and here his passion for the book - and the Disney original - shows. A lot of care went into bringing Kipling's classic novel to life, to attract a new generation of film-goers.

And what life! An edge-of-your seat sequence of Shere Khan battling Bagheera leads to a wild chase through a buffalo stampede. A wildly original overture sees Mowgli help Baloo out by getting him honey from a tall hill edge (Baloo, to an irritating critter, as he watches Mowgli perilously approach the bees-infested honey combs: "You have never been a more endangered species than you are now"). Mowgli's kidnapping by King Louie's monkey army is a sight to behold - and that's followed by an insane musical number and a thunderous, fire-thirsty Louie (the animals refer to fire as the "red flower") crashing through a Mayan temple...

The voice-acting is uniformly stellar. Idris Elba is savage, roaring and snarling as the villainous tiger. Ben Kingsley's Bagheera is wise and dependable. Lupita Nyong'o is compassionate as Akela's sweetheart Raksha. Christopher Walken does a hilarious King Louie (and he sings!). Though Scarlett Johansson appears for a mere three minutes as the sexy, coiling, hypnotizing snake Kaa ("I know what you are... I know where you come from... Let go of your fear now..."), she leaves an impression with her recognizable husky voice that the actress infuses with a slithery seductiveness. And, of course, there's Bill Murray who, after a couple of recent missteps ("Aloha", "Rock the Kasbah"), comes back with a... well, I wish I could say vengeance, but it's really more like a cave-full of delectable honey, as the lovable, legendary Baloo, who doesn't exactly "hibernate" so much as "take long naps". Each scene involving the somewhat-dry (in that trademark Murray fashion), clumsy and loyal bear ups the already-entertaining film's ante considerably.

Though newcomer Neel Sethi does a commendable job in the action sequences, his lack of experience behind the camera does show in the scenes where the CGI critters around him out-act the little guy. Not that Sethi doesn't give it a valiant try - I'm sure that under Favreau's assured guidance, the kid had a blast - it shows. The role of Mowgli is quite a hefty one, so at the very least, props to the filmmakers for hiring an unknown to shoulder it. Another department where the film falters a little is the dialogue - there are quite a few jokes that fall flat, some of the otherwise-laudable "man against nature" themes are overstated, and "sentimentality fatigue" settles in roughly 75% into the film. I blame it on writer Justin Marks, whose only "notable" work before this was the 2009 "classic", "Street Fighter: The Legend of Chun-Li".

Though it doesn't quite live up to the original - and what film ever could? - Favreau's "The Jungle Book" is about as efficient a re-"whatever-you-wanna-call-it" as one could wish for. Absent of product placement, cheesy contemporary dance routines or pop-culture puns, it's filled with wonder, a palpable love of nature (as well as the source material), edge-of-your-seat action, a commendable ecological message and gorgeously-animated, perfectly-voiced animal characters. The rendition of "Bare Necessities" - Mowgli lovingly splashing water onto Baloo's mug as he rides the scruffy bear down the river - is worth the price of admission alone. You'll envy their pure, unadulterated mirth. Favreau's next project is "Magic Kingdom", written by Michael Chabon (Pulitzer Prize winner and writer of "Spider-Man 2") and Ronald D. Moore (mastermind behind the brilliant TV series "Battlestar Galactica"). Judging by "The Jungle Book", there will be plenty of magic to go around in that Kingdom.

4 out of 5 stars

"The Music of Strangers: Yo-Yo Ma and The Silk Road Ensemble" Proves that Music, Like Math, is a Universal Language

Synopsis: *Cellist Yo-Yo Ma and other international artists of The Silk Road Project discuss their philosophies on music and culture.*

I am quite proud of the fact that I learned to read when I was merely 3 years old, and never fail to bring it up when it comes to "tooting your own horn" at social gatherings. Reading quickly led to writing, and consequently developed into a (so far) moderately successful career in film criticism and screenwriting. I don't envision myself doing anything else, and naively hope that one day my passion and "talents" will be recognized on a global scale… and perhaps even change the world a little bit. That said (false modesty aside) I would never refer to myself as a "prodigy", and envy those born with the inherent ability to create works of art effortlessly, provoke change and retrospection, evoke awe and reverence with a few brush strokes - or, in the case of world-renowned cellist Yo-Yo Ma, several plucks of a $2.5 million 18th-Century Montagnana cello. At the age of 7, I was reading "Goosebumps" and emulating R.L. Stine's gripping-but-simplistic writing with my own series entitled "Bedtime Stories". At the age of 7, Yo-Yo Ma performed in front of packed audiences for presidents Eisenhower and Kennedy. Bastard.

Yo-Yo went on to make over 90 albums (you're almost there, Rihanna!), and win 18 Grammys (you're almost there, Kanye!). "It's all statistics, you know," the genius humbly states at one point in director Morgan Neville's "The Music of Strangers", whose previous film, the "back-up singers doc" "20 Feet from Stardom", won an Academy Award in 2013. The director now focuses his lens on Yo-Yo Ma's "Silk Road Project", a collection of "musicians from across the globe" that the talented cellist brought together in 2000. "Since that time," the opening titles reveal, "the Silk Road Ensemble has recorded 6 albums and performed for nearly 2 million people on 33 countries."

"Being good at something can carry you really far for a long period of time and not require a lot of introspection," says Nicholas Ma, Yo-Yo's son, "because you're good at it - and everyone tells you that." From early on, Yo-Yo never had a choice, "never committed to being a musician, fell into it". He went on to accept and explore his talents and attempt to use them to "find himself at home again." This project embodies Yo-Yo's struggles and goals: to achieve a certain cohesiveness, connect with other cultures through music on a borderline-spiritual level - and as a result, find his own identity.

Neville's film focuses on each member of the diverse troupe individually: their backgrounds, how they miss home, the definition of home, what their ambitions are… The Syrian musician expresses his sadness through music, unable to write songs during tumultuous times ("Can a piece of music stop a bullet? Can it feed someone who's hungry?"); the Chinese performer leaves her conservatory in search of individuality; the Iranian musician muses about his fascination with the West, and tells a gripping story of how he ran from his own country's revolution with nothing but a backpack and a musical instrument; the Spanish musician from Galicia, a "culturally rich but economically poor" part of Spain, recollects how she was the rock star of bagpipes… "Finding [their] voice" in the most culturally diverse group imaginable, each of those musicians brings a fascinating tale and tells it through his or her instrument.

There are quite a few standout moments in "The Music of Strangers": Yo-Yo Ma going through a trance ritual; how 9/11 pushed the musicians to keep going, gave them a reason; Keyhan and Yo-Yo performing a piercing tune on stage by themselves to a montage of a violent revolution; a hip-hop/ballet medley; or - my favorite - when Yo-Yo refers to a certain sound as a "giant horse fart." Neville's doc travels from Lincoln, Nebraska to San Diego, to the National Conservatory in Beijing, to Iran, to Spain, to New York, to Tehran, to Boston, to Istanbul, to Lebanon, to Jordan, and to the Tanglewood Workshops in the Berkishers, MA, where the musicians first met and practiced. The film's structure and geographical reach reflects its themes, and at its center is a true melting pot of musicians, exorcizing their demons through music. "We are not our political identities," one musician states - but the thrilling music speaks louder than any words could.

The music itself is electrifying, a sweltering amalgamation of diverse sounds that combine to form an ethereal and joyful stream, something you would send to space for aliens to discover and learn about us. It's music as a representation of "the power of the human spirit", demonstrating how it unites us in tumultuous times. The doc truly hits its high notes (pun intended) when we are watching the musicians fuse their diverse styles into one otherworldly orchestra.

Neville keeps the pace going with fast editing, fascinating archival footage and great cinematography that complements the energetic music. Contributions from the likes of legendary composer John Williams spice things up even further. The running thread is the charming Yo-Yo himself, speaking candidly to a crowd about his life and career - and the theme of music transcending background, nationality, gender, cultural and religious differences. "The Music of Strangers" may not say anything new, it may run 10-15 minutes too long, and it may a bit repetitive, but it reiterates important points and reminds us what truly good music is, and why it matters. I'll be grateful to achieve even a fraction of what Yo-Yo Ma's terrific ensemble - or Morgan Neville for that matter - managed to do with their careers, especially considering the turmoils the former had to endure. Kudos to them all (with a dash of resentment).

4 out of 5 stars

"The Salesman": A Crumbling Building, a Crumbling Marriage and a Director on the Rise

Synopsis: Forushande (The Salesman) is the story of a couple whose relationship begins to turn sour during their performance of Arthur Miller's Death of a Salesman.

Prior to winning countless major accolades for his brilliant "A Separation", director Asghar Farhadi used to be a playwright. It comes as no surprise, then, that his latest feature, the remarkably subtle and affecting "The Salesman", centers around Arthur Miller's famous play. While the titular "salesman" doesn't die in Farhadi's film (at least not in real life), Miller's spirit is fervently alive throughout the narrative, its protagonist, similarly to Willy Loman, gradually coming to grips with reality. A deft meditation on political and personal oppression (and how the two intertwine), the crumbling of a marriage, revenge, status and the pursuit of happiness, all wrapped in a "contemplative-to-the-point-of-leisurely" thriller-like package, Farhadi's commendable new entry into a decaying cinematic world is bound to bring him even more awards and recognition. Man's already snagged A Palm d'Or nomination and two awards in Cannes: one for Best Screenplay and another for Best Actor.

The film starts with a rumble, and then a roar, as a building begins to cave in for no discernible reason, its inhabitants fleeing through shards of broken glass and down collapsing steps - among them, our "hero", schoolteacher/theater actor Emad Etesami (Shahab Hosseini). A camera pan reveals a giant tractor, ripping through the building with its mechanical claws, disregarding the fact that there are still people inside.

Emad's friend, Babak (Babak Karimi), offers temporary shelter to Emad and his "partner and wife" - and theater acting mate, Rana (Taraneh Alidoosti). An abandoned apartment, its previous female resident leaving next-to-no trace behind - except for a locked little room stuffed with her belongings - it doesn't seem like the worst choice… at first. As things get revealed about that stranger - and a traumatic event occurs, rendering the Etesamis unsafe in their new abode - their relationship begins to disassemble, akin to their old building. Unable to seek help from the police - this would embarrass them for eternity in the eyes of the entire neighborhood, and lead to nothing anyway - Emad resorts to personal investigative methods, and a side of him, previously unknown to Rana, starts to surface.

The intense, heart-wrenching finale takes place in the same apartment the Etesamis fled at the start of the film, exemplifying the ouroboros-like nature of Farhadi's narratives, but also displaying how cracks in a political regime that spawn such atrocities may ultimately lead to cracks in a personal relationship (the giant cracks on the walls of Etesamis' apartment speak for themselves) - a catalyst, so to speak, that brings out the best and worst in people by putting them on the very edge of sanity. For instance, the Etesamis perform their play, over and over again, almost joylessly, because it's an outlet for their creativity, but also, maybe subconsciously, to give the oppressive government - the same government that confiscated Emad's "questionable" textbook choices and cut entire scenes out of Miller's play - a big middle finger. "What a disaster, this town," Emad says bitterly at one point. "If we could raze it all and start again…"

Those are the things that struck me in the film, but the beauty of "The Salesman" is that it's open to interpretation (see interview with the director below, conducted after this review), raising controversial questions that will lead to hours of deliberation. Be warned: Farad's film is a slow-burn drama-cum-thriller, with strong emphasis on "slow-burn". While thoughtful, assured and incisive, it doesn't exactly get your heart racing until its final, gut-wrenching sequence, nor does it reach the epic heights of the director's transcendent "A Separation". But nor does it try. The acting from the two leads, filled with compassion, remorse, guilt, pride and love, is expectedly stellar (I wouldn't have it any other way from the remarkable helmer). Compassion is key here, as all characters display moments of empathy that resonate in the grim setting: helping a disabled man out of a collapsing apartment complex; friends and neighbors sticking together during tumultuous times in this tainted, new setting; the offer of shelter in itself - though later rebuked - means a lot to our two hapless protagonists.

I had the privilege of sitting down with Asghar Farhadi after the film. The man is eloquent, soft-spoken, passionate and very intelligent. All of those qualities are palpable in his work. Here's hoping no salesman in the world could get the humble award-magnet to follow in the footsteps of his fellow indie directors, like Taika Waititi or J.A. Bayona, and make "Thor: Lost in Jurassic Park" next.

4 out of 5 stars

ROUNDTABLE: ASGHAR FARHADI'S TAKE ON HIS OWN LATEST FEATURE, "THE SALESMAN" (SPOILERS!)

How did the idea for the film come about?

For many years I had the idea of a couple who would go rent a place, whose previous tenant was a prostitute. But the story was never complete enough for me to decide to make it - until one day, I came to the realization of what it was they did in life. I thought, if [Emad and Rana] are theater actors, it would help me a great deal to find a part that's missing in my story. For them to be actors, what that means, is that they are individuals who know how to put themselves in the shoes of another. And now I was thinking these characters, in reality, how well do they succeed [at that]? This was what completed the story for me. I made the decision that they would be rehearsing a play, and the story came together for me.

The film is about dealing with guilt, which ultimately leads to revenge. What are your thoughts on vengeance, a major theme in "The Salesman"?

We need to look at what "revenge" means. When someone does us harm, and we pronounce judgment, and sentence, and execute that sentence against that person - this is what we call "revenge". It's a very risky process, because it is liable to go wrong at many turns. This is why revenge is something we consider a negative value.

Rana does warn Emad that he has [embraced] revenge. It is very specific.

Two things I can say. Women, on the whole, tend to be more forgiving than men. In my previous film, "The Past", I also make a point to this. Because women are capable of childbearing, their gaze is pointed toward the future more. And men - perhaps because they worked the land for so many eons - are more rooted to where they are, so they are looking behind more. But here, the woman is also speaking to another point. She's saying, "I am the one who has undergone harm." She wants to have a part in the judgment against the old man. The other point that's significant is that a man has intruded on their private space and attacked their honor. She's upset by the fact that her husband now wishes to act in the same way. She doesn't want to force her husband to forgive the old man. She says, "The way you're [doing it], the method you're applying points to revenge, and this is action that is not moral."

At which point does Rana achieve closure in the film, or will she ever achieve it?

This is something that will remain with her like a wound for her entire life. But she, at the same time, seems to have the capacity to understand the situation of that old man.

What was the first job that you ever had? If it wasn't film-related, what was the moment you knew you wanted to get into filmmaking?

[Laughs] I had no time to have another job! I was 13 when I made my first film, and then made a short film each year. Then I quickly moved on to a university where I studied theater. Now I regret it. I entered cinema too early. I started to ponder the serious questions too soon. I feel like my childhood was diminished. I wish I could go back and start these things a little later. I am now coming to discover that cinema is not the most important thing in the world. Childhood and living are much more important things.

From "A Separation" to this film, the theme of communication is very [prevalent]. Can you speak about that?

It's very important to me. In today's world, where the networks of communication have expanded so much, it seems to me we have so many more tools and devices for communicating. But then why are we so alone? And those who are not alone, pretend to be. We have become very alone. The more progress we make, the more we expand the abilities of language, the less we're communicating. Relative to the past, humans have become more complicated. Like an object that has hundreds of facets. For [Emad and Rana] to meet, where they can join - there's a very limited surface, whereas in the past, there were not hundreds of facets to the object, there were just a few. So the possibilities for common sighting and for communicating were greater. I'm not trying to say that the modern world is a "bad" world. It's a much more comfortable world. But misunderstandings are far more frequent in it than in the old world. People believe they know one another. For instance, a man and wife, who have been in love and lived together for some time - and then [comes] the moment of crisis, where they don't know each other at all, they're just strangers. This is why people get separated all the time. Because they receive a new image of the other.

Is there a special significance to using "Death of a Salesman" as the play they are [performing]? Is it common for American plays to be done in Iran?

"Death of a Salesman" is no longer an American play. It belongs to the whole world. It's a very well-loved and famous play in my country. It's staged frequently, maybe once every couple of years. I like that play a great deal for a number of reasons. In the play, Arthur Miller emphasizes with all of his main characters. It's not easy to say whether it's Willy Loman or his son that is responsible for the crisis. At the same time, he's describing a social situation, in America, at that moment, an American Dream, on the way to which people are sacrificing themselves. A significant theme in that play is humiliation. Willy Loman commits suicide because his son, coworkers, neighbors humiliate him. The tragedy of that play is that that individual feels completely useless in his family, he's a nobody. Do you know why Willy Loman's job [entails] going to different cities? When he goes away, no one feels he's gone in that house. He thinks, "even if I'm gone, I'm dead, this family is okay, it's going to carry on the same." Truly, when I think it, I want to cry. It's the most difficult situation for a father to be in. We have an Iranian version of Willy Loman and Linda in our film - the old man and woman who come in at the end. That father, the old man, is like Willy Loman. Maybe it's what he's lacking that prompted him to go establish that relationship with the prostitute, this sense of loneliness, not wanting to accept that he's old.

In "The Salesman", the series of events is spawned by the demolishing of a building, with people still in it, which sends its protagonists on a downwards spiral. Was that a way for you to comment on how a political climate can seep into, intimately infiltrate, and ultimately demolish private lives?

It's hardly related to anything political. In the first instance, it's related to the movement of the story. The progress of the story moves the characters out of that building, but it's also a prologue, a sort of foreshadowing of the way in which the relationships between people are undermined at their foundation. As the film advances, the greater the fissures and cracks become in the relationship [of its protagonists] that have not been apparent before. Just like the cracks in the building.

"The Second Mother" Provides a Welcome Antidote to Bloated Hollywood Blockbusters

Synopsis: *When the estranged daughter of a hard-working live-in housekeeper suddenly appears, the unspoken class barriers that exist within the home are thrown into disarray.*

In a summer swarmed with silver-screen dinosaurs, hot pursuits and earthquakes, director Anna Muylaert's "The Second Mother" is a pleasant reminder that films don't need huge budgets to be huge crowd-pleasers. One could even argue that the film's inflated production costs may serve as detriments to their overall entertainment factor: characters get overwhelmed by special effects, a coherent plot takes second place to a constant assault on the senses, and dumbed-down dialogue seems pasted-in to transition one vapid sequence to the next. The majority of it set within the confines of a privileged São Paulo family household, "The Second Mother" mesmerizes with piercing gestures, simmering resentments and astute characterizations, and does so much more powerfully - and with a longer-lasting effect - than any given chase from, say, "The Transporter Refueled".

The film introduces us to Val (Brazilian soap opera and film star Regina Casé), a hardened maid, going about her chores. Her ambiguous role is established within minutes: she is a laborer, ready to serve at the matriarch's, Bárbara's (Karine Teles), every whim, a "second mother" to her privileged son Fabinho (Michel Joelsas), and a nurse to Bárbara's ailing - or perhaps just severely depressed - husband Carlos (Lourenço Mutarelli)… On top of that, Val has a daughter of her own, Jéssica (Camila Márdila), whom she hasn't seen for over ten years.

Bárbara, an imperious fashion mogul, is too busy to pay proper attention to her family, which has led to her husband's dreary isolation. Carlos is a sad, broken man, whose inheritance is - somewhat-surreptitiously - the reason behind the family's wealth ("Everybody dances, but I'm the DJ," he proclaims sadly at one point), and who, long ago, had dreams of being an artist. His paintings are now confined to the garage; some hang on the walls, as lifeless and forgotten as the man who once painted them. Fabinho, the son, is equally lost, his alienation bringing him almost disturbingly close to Val, who cuddles him to sleep, stroking his hair while singing sweet lullabies.

Val is a slave on one hand, but an essential part of the family on the other. Life in this film unfolds from her perspective, represented by a reoccurring shot from inside the kitchen, with only a fraction of the living room visible. The family eats their dinners in silence, each immersed in his or her cellphone (ah, upper-class bliss!).

One evening, Jéssica calls and asks Val if she can come stay with her, while she studies to apply to a university. Val is utterly delighted; upon asking Bárbara, Val's excitement is met with a tight-lipped "of course!", and even an oh-so-gracious offer to pay for a mattress, to stuff inside Val's five-foot closet of a room, already dwarfed by the enormity of the house.

When she finds out she has to stay at her mom's "boss"'s abode, Jéssica is appalled, "You're taking me to someone else's home." But the family is impressed by how much of an erudite Jéssica is, and by her ambitions as an architect. They show her around the house, Val trailing behind, turning on the pool lights. Jéssica discovers the beautiful guest room and brashly invites herself to stay there. In a perfectly-pitched sequence, the creepily enamored Carlos quickly caves in, leaving Bárbara no choice but to reluctantly oblige.

Jéssica's arrival leads to a rapid succession of unraveling developments: Val is torn between being a good mother to her daughter and the loyalty to her second family; Carlos temporarily rediscovers his former self, albeit in an awkward, humiliating manner; Bárbara resents Jéssica and has to eventually reevaluate her life; and Fabinho has to grow up and overcome his Oedipal tendencies. As for Jéssica… Jéssica is a symbol of hope, of an eager, educated generation that just may eventually bring an end to those societal discrepancies and injustices, still so prevalent today.

If all the intrigue sounds scandalous and soap-opera-ish, it sometimes verges dangerously to being so, but Muylaert's assertive, deft directorial touch ensures the film largely stays within the realms of sincerity. The dramatic, at times lightly-comedic, tone, is well-sustained in keenly observed scenes, such as Val's thoughtful birthday gift to Bárbara, promptly dismissed, but touchingly, though predictably (at least in my "desensitized-by-films" mind) reappearing later.

Another standout scene shows Val accidentally oversleeping, and Jéssica taking it into her own hands to make breakfast and sit at the "master"'s table. When Val dashes out, apologetic and panicking, Bárbara harshly scolds her and storms off. Val yells at her daughter for overstepping boundaries; Jéssica nonchalantly finishes her breakfast. Soon after, Fabinho comes in, and sits at the table, and Val kisses him, and strokes his hair lovingly, and makes him breakfast.

Muylaert chose a naturalistic approach, letting the camera linger to catch the little nuances in the performances. There are images that stick: Carlos, left alone in the shadows, in front of his unwanted painting; Val, and then Bárbara - the two mothers - comforting Fabinho, one by one in the bedroom; drenched Val, running after her fed-up daughter in the rain…

With traces of Sebastián Silva's "The Maid", "The Second Mother" does flirt with excessive sentimentality at points (especially towards the end), and remains a bit too slight to be labeled a masterpiece, but it's an acute study of class and family bonds, with a marvelous central performance. While it's a pleasure that films like that are still produced, distributed internationally and recognized at festivals, it's a pity that contemporary audiences will surely be turned off by "The Second Mother"'s modest scale and subtitles, for they'll be missing a true little gem. Make time for "The Second Mother". It's not an impossible mission, after all.

4 out of 5 stars

"The Tiger" is as Majestic and Rare as Its Titular Animal

Synopsis: *While the Kingdom of Korea is under occupation by the Japanese, an old and experience hunter is challenged by the hunt of the last tiger.*

South Korean director Park Hoon-jung wrote the excellent "I Saw the Devil" and wrote/directed the innovative-but-flawed crime drama "New World". "The Tiger", which he both scripted and helmed, sees him find his footing as a filmmaker with an epic vision, a distinct voice and an artful sensibility, preserved among all the big-budget mayhem. While overlong - and sometimes overblown - "The Tiger" is a thoughtful blockbuster, a truly pleasant oddity these days.

The prologue takes place in 1915: Father Chun Man-duk (Choi Min-sik, who worked with the director on "New World") teaches his son how to hunt, passing on his highly enviable skills. He goes hunting, promising his wife he'll bring something back this time. "Bear with me," he says (pun intended? lost in translation? regardless, made me smile). He follows a bloody trail that leads him to a tiger, and an intense confrontation.

A decade or so later, the occupying Japanese authorities send out their own group of hunters, to eliminate all the tigers from Korea - particularly one legendary beast that has been massacring their troops, the "King of all Korean tigers", weighing "over 850 pounds". They enlist a drunk, decrepit Chun for the next-to-impossible task. "Why would you dare provoke the mountain lords?" Chun reasonably asks. When his own, angsty son joins a gang of hunters - led by the villanous Gu-kuyng (Jeong Man-sik) - and tragedy (involving, yes, a tiger - but also a pack wolves) strikes, Chun "comes back from retirement" to face the beast, with whom he shares a deep, personal history.

Bing-sik as the wise, aging hunter seamlessly blends with the scenery, bringing to mind DiCaprio's performance in the somewhat-similar "The Revenant". One with nature, his Chun is multi-faceted and intriguing, a borderline-mythical character who stepped off the pages of some ancient legend. Cinematographer Lee Mo-gae catches every wrinkle in the actor's face - but also every snowflake in the air, every exhaled breath; he quite literally paints on screen, his strokes of blizzard, landscape and aquarelle contrasts absolutely mesmerizing.

Hoon-jung sustains a contemplative, unhurried mood, complemented by sounds of wind whistling and feet crunching in the snow. It's assured filmmaking: engrossing and gorgeous to behold. The hunting scenes are masterfully done - starting from Chun's first, pre-credit encounter with a tiger and ending with the final, lyrical, extended confrontation. The tiger-killing scenes are both exhilarating and hard-to-watch, those heavenly beasts mercilessly slayed by soldiers. The film's biggest success is its portrayal of the relationship between man and nature (in this case, exemplified by the Tiger) that transcends Earthly realms, and how it's juxtaposed against the tyranny, cynicism and banal evil of humankind.

When it comes to politics, the film falters a little. The Japanese-Korean conflict isn't really explored; the Japanese villains come off as thinly drawn and one-dimensional. Some dialogue exchanges are a bit silly (especially in a scene involving a father impressed by his son's penis size). "Use any means necessary to catch that tiger," a Japanese commander bellows, as if the hunter has a choice in the matter (were the restrictions regarding the tiger's killing methods prior to that statement?) The film can't help but delve into sentimentality here and there, especially in its flashback sequences. At well over two hours, the film is too long for such a minimalist plot. At 100 minutes, this would have been a lean, mean killing machine, without losing its contemplative tone.

Hoon-jung's epic film reiterates the magnificence of wild animals, their grandeur and savage beauty, and the importance of animal preservation. An action/horror hybrid, a survival tale, a historical account and an art film - "The Tiger" is an almost-perfect symbiosis. Its main statement is: "Look at how puny and stupid we are, compared to the natural world we're steadily annihilating." Seek this tiger out. Just please, for Christ's sakes, don't kill it.

4 out of 5 stars

"Things to Come" Displays a Newfound Maturity from a Talented Filmmaker

Synopsis: A philosophy teacher soldiers through the death of her mother, getting fired from her job, and dealing with a husband who is cheating on her.

Mia Hansen-Løve pulls the rug from underneath you with her latest foray into the human psyche, the quiet-but-ferocious drama "Things to Come". The young filmmaker - and wife of French auteur Olivier Assayas - seemed to have established a unique vision with her previous films, the stylish and deeply personal examination of young "amour", "Goodbye First Love", and the neon-lit, energetic "Eden" (read my review here). She abandons the stylistic flourishes of those features in favor of a more subdued/grounded cinematic study, anchored by a tremendous performance from French acting goddess Isabelle Huppert. The film's borderline-lethargic pace does not lessen its powerful impact.

"Things to Come" is a delicate portrayal of a middle-aged woman dealing with a bad case of Murphy's Law, faced with a fresh start, both apprehensive of and elated by the sudden freedom. While there's no pulsating Daft Punk beats to complement her travails, nor is there a slew of twisted perspectives or blurry interludes to enhance the narrative, the film leaves you with a lasting impression, joining the top ranks of incisive French cinematic offerings. Yep, the French know how it's done.

Huppert plays Nathalie, a philosophy teacher and married mother of two, living in Paris. After a lyrical prologue that takes place by the sea (which, incidentally, happens to say more in under two minutes than the entire "By the Sea" did in over two hours), when things seemed certain and time eternal, the film skips forward a decade. Surrounded by faceless tomes of textbooks, with a discontent academic husband (André Marcon) and a depressed mother (Edith Scob) who calls the fire department at every whim, Nathalie overcomes all obstacles in a Zen-like manner. No wonder her book sales are plummeting - the layout/design of Nathalie's philosophical texts is about as drab as her existence… And yet she seems comfortable, referring to her team as "marketing fiends" and refusing to amp up the colors and covers of her transcribed ruminations.

When things start going terribly awry - her husband announces nonchalantly that he is moving out; her mother dies in a retirement community - Nathalie finds herself stranded without a compass. "I thought you'd love me forever," she tells her husband quietly upon hearing the news - a somewhat naive and touching sentiment from a philosopher, to whom the term "forever" either means nothing or the world. Luckily, a former adoring student, Fabien (Roman Kolinka, who worked with Hansen-Løve on "Eden"), happens to resurface in her life, infusing it with a tempting, rebellious, anarchist vibe. It's against that backdrop of a tumultuous, politically active youth-in-revolt that Nathalie has to try to reassert herself. "My husband left me, my mother died," she tells Fabien wistfully. "I've never experienced such freedom. It's extraordinary." She doesn't add that it's extraordinarily confusing too - but she doesn't need to, Huppert's eyes doing all the talking her lips won't.

"Things to Come" is filled with quiet revelations. At one point, Nathalie reads a passage from her own book that is so heartrendingly true and beautiful, it's almost difficult to watch - we as audiences are not used to such celluloid honesty. "We are happy only before becoming so" may be the most resonant line of any film out this year. An obese black cat that Nathalie adopts, freeing it from "10 years by her mother's feet", embodies Nathalie's plight: the animal's instincts kick in and it brings home a mouse. Like the cat, Nathalie's instincts take a moment to sharpen - she wholeheartedly embraces Fabien's remote farm, a place where time and age are almost irrelevant… but does she fit in?

Watching Huppert do her thing is always a revelation. Each stance, each flutter of an eyelid communicates a plethora of emotions. Nathalie stands her ground and overcomes life's obstacles with grace; she is a determined, fiercely intelligent character in search of meaning. When was the last time you saw Hollywood focus on a middle-aged woman's daily predicaments? Hansen-Løve and Huppert certainly set the example. There are no major conflicts, no pulse-pounding scenes of suspense - it's the dry wit, the insight and the magnificent central performance that serve as the film's momentum. Filled with fascinating philosophical discussions about the nature of truth, time and art, at its core "Things to Come" is about a woman who has to quickly reassemble her goals, in order to prepare herself for the foggy future. Perhaps it's time for Hollywood to take note and do the same.

4 out of 5 stars

"Thor: Ragnarok" Marks the Rebirth of Marvel

Synopsis: Imprisoned, the mighty Thor finds himself in a lethal gladiatorial contest against the Hulk, his former ally. Thor must fight for survival and race against time to prevent the all-powerful Hela from destroying his home and the Asgardian civilization.

Marvel / DC films have become painfully repetitive. I used to crave more darkness and depth in superhero fare. Be careful what you wish for. Post-Nolan's "Dark Knight" trilogy, the deluge of increasingly ponderous, $200 *mil.*+ films, revolving around God-like men and women in frankly ridiculous-looking outfits experiencing existential angst, has ironically rendered them more and more laughable.

Taika Waititi, a New Zealand director known for the cult HBO series "Flight of the Conchords", as well as oddball, charming indie comedies ("Eagle vs Shark", "What We Do in the Shadows" and last year's "Hunt for the Wilderpeople"), infuses the "Comic Book Movie" with a much-needed shot of irreverence. With "Thor: Ragnarok", Waititi nails the humor/action balance, while also managing to adhere to the conventional Marvel structure: there is a villainess that a ragtag team of pseudo-Avengers must confront, and it all ends with an epic showdown.

The filmmaker peppers "Ragnarok" with all his auter-ish trademarks. There are the self-referential puns: he voices one particularly memorable character and stages a meta play-within-a-film, with cameos that I am dying to reveal here. There are the non-sequiturs and lightness of tone, particularly welcome in this day and age of "the darker the better". "Thor"'s third stand-alone adventure plays more like a tongue-in-cheek fantasy, without (quite) venturing into "Flash Gordon" / "Batman & Robin" camp (although Waititi did make the actors watch the former cult classic prior to shooting).

Plot in nutshell: Thor has to defeat his evil sister Hela (Cate Blanchett, having a blast out-hamming every villain in comic-book history), who wants to take over Asgard. Thor's team is quite something to behold. Thor and Hulk (the always-perfect Mark Ruffalo) are joined by the beautiful/powerful Asgard refugee, Valkyrie (Tessa Thompson), as well as Korg - a character made out of rocks (quietly voiced by the director), and good ol' Machiavellian Loki (the, let's face it, much-overpraised Tom Hiddleston). Jeff Goldblum makes a memorable, flamboyant appearance as the Grandmaster, who engages Hulk and the titular hero in a gladiatorial smackdown.

Waititi mentioned in interviews that there was quite a lot of improvisation on set, and it's obvious: there's a joyous, "anything-can-happen" vibe that's evident not just in the action (watch Hulk battle a monstrous wolf) but the dialogue as well (see:

the gradually developing friendship between Hulk and Thor). "Thor" pokes fun at all the things that make superhero movies ridiculous: the heroes' righteousness, the solemnity of tone, the inherent concept of all-powerful, death-defying deities battling it out. It does so wisely, Waititi proving that he can sustain that intricate balance of comedy / self-awareness / zaniness and actual, you know, intrigue, with maybe a dash of drama that he displayed in his indie fare. What may be even more impressive is his adept handling of gargantuan smackdowns, as "Marvel"-conventional as they may be - something he's never done before.

The word "Ragnarok" comes from Norse mythology, meaning both Armageddon and celestial rebirth. This Ragnarok, along with "Deadpool" and "Guardians of the Galaxy", marks the dawn of the gleeful, self-aware Marvel superhero - one who gives himself the finger, while traveling through an inter-dimensional portal called "The Devil's Anus".

4 out of 5 stars

"Tragedy Girls" is #BloodyAwesome

Synopsis: *A twist on the slasher genre, the film follows two death-obsessed teenage girls who use their online show about real-life tragedies to send their small mid-western town into a frenzy and cement their legacy as modern horror legends.*

Back in 1996, "Scream" cleverly subverted "teen-horror" genre clichés, while also managing to stay true to them. Both an ode and a satire, Wes Craven's seminal slasher thrilled as a tongue-in-cheek send-up of 1980s "masked killer" classics like "Friday the 13th" and stood on its own as a gore-filled "whodunit".

In addition to being an effective comedy/chiller, the original "Scream" perfectly captured the zeitgeist of the tremulous late 1990's. Haunted by major events like Osama bin Laden's declaration of war - a war that, similarly to the Ghostface murderer in "Scream", no one really understood - and OJ's acquittal, it represented a confused, scared nation, as seen through the prism of its rebellious, nerdy, film and popularity-obsessed teenagers. Media was becoming more bias (see: Gale Weathers' reporter, hilariously played by Courtney Cox), teens more angsty (see: Never Campbell's pseudo-goth Sidney Prescott) and violent (see: Skeet Ulrich's deranged Billy Loomis) and the cops more useless in the face of overwhelming forces they did not comprehend (see: David Arquette's goofy Deputy Dewey).

It was a neat trick to pull off - and a difficult one, as "Scream"'s three increasingly inferior sequels proved. Then came a slew of imitators that failed to capture Craven's subtly political, razor-blade satire, instead fully resorting to "dumb teens dying in grisly ways" cliché: "I Know What You Did Last Summer" (and its sequel, where the killer STILL knew), "Urban Legend" (and its sequel, where the Legend was STILL Urban), the "Final Destination" series - and so on. The trend still continues, with the terribly-titled "Happy Death Day" raking in money at the box-office as I write this. Those horror flicks seem to be missing the essence of what made "Scream" so great.

Thankfully, recently a sub-genre of intelligent "teen-slasher" flicks began to emerge, puncturing the "teen slasher" vacuousness with directorial flourishes, clever genre subversions and a healthy dose of irony. That small-but-growing "movement" - which includes "It Follows", "The Cabin in the Woods", "The Descent", "Martyrs" and "Creep", to name a few - is now joined by director Tyler MacIntyre's horror/comedy hybrid "Tragedy Girls" (which even references "Martyrs"). Focusing on a friendship between two sociopathic high-school BFFs, it's a spicy cocktail of relevant commentary, dark comedy and outright horror.

It doesn't take long for the film to kick into high gear and defy expectations. The young, fiery Sadie (Brianna Hildebrand, Negasonic Teenage Warhead in "Deadpool") makes her escape from a masked killer. His machete still covered in her boy toy's blood, the psycho proceeds to trip over a strategically-installed wire and is then tasered by Sadie and her best friend McKayla (Alexandra Shipp, who, somewhat coincidentally, played Storm in "X-Men: Apocalypse"). The title credit blares in neon. Welcome to the world of "Tragedy Girls".

Sadie and McKayla - sporting hip hairdos and nonchalant attitudes - strap Lowell the Killer (Kevin Durand), a "Texas Chainsaw reject", to a chair in their "lair" and, after a small "pep talk" ("Do you know how many hand jobs this girl had to give to get you you?"), reveal their plan to him: the girls want him to be their guru, to teach them in the ways of mass murder.

Both girls have cozy homes with loving parents. At school, they cheerlead, lead the prom board committee and get jealous over boys. Sadie's obsession, the suspicious Jordan (Jack Quaid, of "Hunger Games" fame), edits their popular "Tragedy Girls" video blog, in which they "investigate" their own murders and provoke controversy, while McKayla's crush, the dreamy Toby (Josh Hutchinson, of, um, "Hunger Games" fame) has a competing popular blog.

Of course, anyone who stands in the way of "Tragedy Girls" has gotta go, in various ways: a motorcycle killing followed by a brutal stabbing, a (botched) masked art-room attack, a memorable gym tussle that ends with one of the more inventive decapitations in recent cinematic history... As their blog jeopardizes the actual police investigation and provokes a furor of the entire town, Jordan narrows down his own list of suspects to - you guessed it - our heroines. In a wild turn of events, Sadie becomes the local town hero, which leads to a fallout between the girls, and gives her a taste of humanity... which she doesn't seem to like very much. It all culminates in a very "Carrie"-esque prom night.

The acting is top-notch throughout, with the two leads effortlessly dishing out both cutesy charm and despicable evil. The film hinges on their performances and they pull it off with aplomb. Josh Hutchinson - in vein of the film's overarching goal, it seems - hilariously subverts his own "cool guy" image, enunciating each word with a James Dean-like indifference. A special shout-out goes to the always-reliable Craig Robinson (also a producer on the film), who plays local firefighter and community leader Big Al.

I bet the cast relished reciting such deliciously nasty dialogue: "To make an omelet, you have to kill some ex-boyfriends", or "That is some serious 'Final

Destination' shit". The film is briskly paced, maintaining that uncanny, disturbing "jolly/vicious" balance, with its twinkling (kick-ass!) soundtrack and 1980's teen-flick staples blending smoothly, as opposed to clashing, with the blood-soaked elements.

In what could be a slyly Hitchcockian move, MacIntyre actually makes us root for the girls at certain points throughout the film, making us sick participants, a-la Michael Haneke via "Hunger Games". But that's just one of the perverted pleasures "Tragedy Girls" offers. By turns deeply twisted, side-splitting, bitter and resonant, the film, like "Scream", works on many levels: as a straightforward horror flick, a feminist parable and a clever satire of our social media-dependent culture, where tragedy is milked for "likes", abbreviated, memefied and capitalized upon, and the line between true feeling and pixelated emotion becomes increasingly blurry. ("If I'm gonna be murdered," utters one victim, in a mockingly poignant moment, "I'm so happy it's you.") If there's a flaw, it's the didactic lack of any background - or any sensible trace of actual emotion - in the girls.

But perhaps that's the generation we live in, defined by its vapid chasm of explanation for, or reasoning behind, its malignant actions. Like "Scream", one could argue, "Tragedy Girls" also functions as a parable of our tumultuous times, with senseless, glorified crimes committed - and consequently showcased - at an alarmingly increasing rate. With the stench of looming attacks, hurricanes and war stinging our collective nostrils, we turn to social media for solace. So, remember, "You can follow us. It's @TragedyGirls… Two, plural."

4 out of 5 stars

"Victoria" Casts an Unblinking (Camera) Eye on the Seductive Nature of Crime

Synopsis: *A young Spanish woman who has recently moved to Berlin finds her flirtation with a local guy turn potentially deadly, as their night out with his friends reveals a dangerous secret.*

Long, single-shot camera takes have been a popular cinematic technique since Hitchcock played with it in his classic "Rope", where the mystery unravels like the titular coiled thread, in one continuous, seemingly unedited narrative. Hitch skillfully cut his shots by panning close over characters' backs, or zooming in tight on objects, and while it's quite obvious where the cuts occur to the desensitized eye of the current moviegoer, back in 1948 it was revolutionary, and paved the way to such contemporary classics as "Children of Men", "Birdman", "Gravity"… and the not-so-classic "The Silent House". Sebastian Schipper's "Victoria" doesn't have the technical precision or production values of those Hollywood giants, but the lack of gloss plays in its favor. It's not a mere gimmick; the "one-take" approach is crucial to the story.

Right off the bat, the film establishes its propulsive rhythm by plunging us into Berlin's kaleidoscopic club scene, the electronic soundtrack's four-by-four beat resembling the human pulse. Victoria (Laia Costa), recently relocated from Madrid, dances by herself, then flirts with the waiter, somewhat-desperately. She seeks a connection in a new city, which has left her alone and dejected - that is, until she meets the persistent and charming Sonne (Frederick Lau) on the way out of the club.

Sonne hangs out with his gang of self-proclaimed (on multiple occasions) "true Berliners": hotheaded Boxer (Franz Rogowski), goofy Blinker (Burak Yigit), and increasingly wasted Fuss (Max Mauff). After casually trying to steal a car and escaping from its owner, they promise to show Victoria the "real Berlin". Exhilarated by their acceptance, Victoria eagerly joins them, to soon discover that the "real Berlin" involves stealing booze from a liquor shop, whose elderly clerk is deep asleep. When Victoria questions the theft, Sonne assures her, "I'll pay him back tomorrow. I've known him a very long time." She's not quite buying it, but goes along with it, even grabbing a bag of peanuts on the way out.

Sonne's entourage of misfits is brash, intimidating, careless - but also goofy and intriguing. Sonne focuses on flirting with Victoria, while his gang bounces and causes havoc around him, shifting from playfulness to animosity within seconds - particularly the violence-prone Boxer. Police cars drive by, faceless cops eyeing them suspiciously, a foreboding presence.

Minor misdemeanors lead to bigger stakes, with Sonne eventually asking Victoria to take part in an impromptu heist. She sinks deeper and deeper into the quicksand, as the audience watches helplessly. The film does a great job evoking tension through language barrier: we understand what's unraveling sooner than Victoria, who doesn't speak German - another nifty ode to Hitchcock. We know the bomb is ticking under that table, always seconds ahead of the film's hapless lead.

There are many standout sequences in "Victoria", a few particularly worth pointing out, such as when the characters' dialogue fades, and a minimalist piano score (courtesy of composer Nils Frahm) follows them for a while, making Victoria seem trapped, naive and helpless in the company of daunting hoodlums. There is also a beautiful little detour, when Victoria plays piano for Sonne - a tender moment, the calm before the storm. Other gripping scenes include a sudden panic attack; a car engine dying at a crucial moment; a breathless, white-knuckle escape, and the consequent prolonged chase sequence which, while lacking credibility at times, never loses momentum.

The cinematography by Sturla Brandth Grøvlen is spectacular. The single-take approach works seamlessly, making one forget they're watching what is essentially an extended cinematic stunt - quite the feat. Without the experience or budgetary resources of, say, "Gravity"'s Emmanuel Lubezki, Grøvlen pulls it off with aplomb, demonstrating a proficiency that's truly awe-inspiring. Whether or not digital editing trickery was used, the fact that my trained eye wasn't able to tell makes "Victoria" a stunning technical achievement.

The unflinching, almost intrusive camerawork also serves the story, emphasizing its heroine's claustrophobic spiral into the depths of immorality, and the film's central theme of circular fate: we revisit locations, which all seem within driving distances of each other, but take on different connotations as the story progresses; the film ends virtually the same way it begins, with one major difference I won't spoil here. "Victoria"'s "rope" forms an ouroboros, both visually and thematically.

Laia Costa in the titular role brings to mind Carey Mulligan with her doe eyes, an endearing fragility and reserves of hidden/unexpected strength. If there's one nag, it's Victoria's naiveté, which at times approaches pure stupidity. There are several moments in the film where she should have just said "no". Sonne even offers to take her back to safety at a crucial point, to which she firmly - and inexplicably - responds, "I want to go back with you." Perhaps it's an intentional choice, showing the lengths to which one would go to avoid solitude, but Victoria's past is not clearly enough defined to make her actions justifiable. While there are definitely traces of attraction, she is not expressly in love with Sonne either; "love at first sight" would have at least provided a semblance of rationale.

That said, it was the filmmakers' choice, and Costa manages to overcome her character's lack of concrete motivation with a commanding, soulful performance. Frederick Lau almost steals scenes as the by turns mischievous, affectionate and precarious Sonne, the leader of the pack.

Schipper, a German director who has worked with Tom Tykwer on several occasions, clearly learned from the auteur, and brings an energy and flow to "Victoria" that brings to mind Tykwer's "Run Lola Run". The suspense builds fast, beat by beat, the director layering it on like a master pastry chef.

Despite my niggles with the protagonist's (lack of) reasoning, "Victoria" does effectively demonstrate how easily susceptible we all find ourselves to perilous influences, especially when displaced, lost and alone. It's also a visceral portrait of current-day Berlin's seedier side, focusing on the lower-middle-class youth, its aimlessness and pathos. Above all, "Victoria" succeeds at being a thrill ride, and sustaining our breathless attention, in one take, for over two hours. It shows that, when used well, long takes can have a powerful and lasting effect. Bring on "The Revenant."

4 out of 5 stars

"We Are the Flesh" Cuts Right to the Bone

Synopsis: *After wandering a ruined city for years in search of food and shelter, two siblings find their way into one of the last remaining buildings. Inside, they find a man who will make them a dangerous offer to survive the outside world.*

Some filmmakers gradually crawl their way to fame. Others announce their arrival with a hot film that breaks the mold. Emiliano Rocha Miner blares his entrance into the cinematic arena with the wickedly funny, absolutely deranged psychological drama / art-house / horror hybrid "We Are the Flesh". It may not be for everyone, but those willing to stomach its dementia will be rewarded with a surprisingly thoughtful - albeit gruesome - existential study, anchored by an unforgettable central performance.

The opening shot - 45 seconds of a black screen and heavy breathing - sets the claustrophobic, desperate tone of pure agony and helplessness. Sweaty, filthy Mariano (Noé Hernández) mixes fuel in a rundown, post-apocalyptic Mexican apartment. He uses the most basic elements - bread, water, bucket, hose, fire - his lips curling in joy, as he immerses his hands into the mucus-like, viscous moonshine sludge, which later finds its way into his gullet.

He rips apart a table with brutal force and rage, to use the splinters for firewood. He beats a drum to death, breaks windows, smashes through furniture… He destroys things because they hold no more value, reflecting his own moral vacuum and sense of self-worth, but also because he's reached the peak of depravity, where his own skin no longer feels safe.

When a young woman, Fauna (Maria Evoli) and her brother, Lucio (Diego Gamaliel) break in, having "wandered the city for days", Mariano feeds them eggs and agrees to provide them with shelter. His psychedelic world and odd charisma begins to affect the new inhabitants. They rapidly fall under his crazed spell, leading to: a rather intense corruption of a vegetarian, death by ejaculation, an oral ingestion of menstrual fluids, an incestuous sex scene, cannibalism, brutal murder, and yes, necrophilia. Mariano becomes their God - or Satan, depending on how you look at it - in their own little h(e)aven - or more like a womb that they plaster and tape together, "the last monument of a rotten society".

There are no soulful remnants in this grimy world, all of their humanity stripped down to "rotting meat". Akin to the dilapidated environment - cave-like rooms, membrane-like windows and skeleton-like furniture - the characters devolve into mere shells of human beings, acting upon their most basic, animalistic desires and impulses. They fully embrace their darkest perversions, succumb to their demons, get lost in their subterranean nightmares. The final scene / twist powerfully reinforces those themes of humans essentially amounting to nothing more but heaps of sentient flesh, seeking solace from a corrupted world in the darkest recesses of their minds.

Sparse but focused, lyrical but lurid, profound but daringly in-your-face, the film is based on contradictions. Noé Hernández gives a similarly ambiguous performance of contrasts - the maniacal monster, cooped up for 47 years, beating away on his drum as he welcomes the morning sun vs. the sorrowful man, lost in his own city, in his own skin, spouting poetic monologues vs. the sick, manipulative pervert. "When you embrace solitude," Mariano stammers, "your head spins around like crazy. And with every turn, you take more space in the void." By turns menacing, deplorable, sad and weirdly sympathetic, Hernández is a force to be reckoned with. Evoli and Gamaliel are totally game too, by the way - particularly in the highly candid, infrared sex scene, which puts any 3-D ejaculation in Gaspar Noe's "Love" to shame.

Running barely over an hour - which is a good thing, for I'm not sure how much of its artsy tendencies (a full minute of a character dancing naked in the mud, anyone?) and intensity audiences would be able to take - the film is both sparse and crammed with detail, contemplative and relentlessly brutal, confined to one location but somehow epic in scope, its themes and images resonating deeply. The scene of a National Anthem being sung right before a grisly demise of a helpless victim is not easily shaken.

Made on the cheap, Minter's film utilizes some ingenious techniques to keep its vicious narrative propelling forward: the body horror is very Cronenberg; the frenzied, spinning camera shots bring to mind Noe's "Enter the Void" and "Irreversible"; sustained periods of black-outs and an overall Dogme-like approach recall some of the ballsiest Lars von Trier choices; the perfect framing and silences, interspersed with assaultive musical cues, evoke Stanley Kubrick; the madness of isolation and a world constructed of your own consciousness scream Friedkin's "Bug"; the last "party" sequence, scored to a bit of classical music, could be a nod to Ben Wheatley's psychedelic oeuvre… The list of references goes on. If Minter cannibalizes those filmmakers' techniques, he does so effectively - in a film that's partially about cannibalism anyway.

Among its many influences, "We Are the Flesh" brings to mind Jim Mickle's "We Are What We Are" and Pascal Laugier's "Martyrs". These films, like Minter's horrific journey, transcended the torture-porn genre and elevated sadistic fare to borderline-spiritual meditations on what actually makes us human: our flesh, our agony, our sacrifices, our masochistic tendencies, the last dying embers of feeling, love. An end-of-year surprise that's most certainly not for the faint of heart, "We Are the Flesh" just may rip yours out and eat it.

4 out of 5 stars

"Since: The Bombing of Pan Am Flight 103" is a Powerful Ode to the Victims of Terrorism

Synopsis: The 1988 bombing of Pan Am Flight 103 over Lockerbie, Scotland, killed 270 innocent people and began the new age of terrorism. Bound together in tragedy, the victim's relatives fought for justice, only to watch it unravel for Libyan oil.

When I asked my friend whether he knew anything about the bombing of Pan Am flight 103 over Lockerbie, he shook his head. Several other (relatively) erudite friends of mine had similar reactions. This awful tragedy, which happened in 1988, failed to embed itself into the annals of U.S. history and our collective consciousness, due to political reasons Phil Furey's debut documentary "Since: The Bombing of Pan Am Flight 103" masterfully exposes. Told mostly through the eyes of the victim's relatives, without resorting to fancy visual embellishments or over-sentimentalizing, the film tensely and touchingly reveals the plight of those people, as they embark on a long and arduous crusade for justice.

"Since" begins with grainy images from the crash. The regularly scheduled Pan Am transatlantic flight from Frankfurt to Detroit just had its stopover in London and was on its way to New York, when the bomb exploded over Lockerbie, Scotland, killing 270 people. The town's residents rushed to help, but their efforts were futile. "Everyone's life hangs by a strain," the narration laments at one point, "and in one minute, it can all be over for you."

While the investigation led to conclusive evidence that a detonated explosive caused the crash, the reaction from the U.S. government was… muted. Neither Pan Am reps nor anyone from the State Department was present at the funerals. As one mother states, "The coffins left Lockerby with the dignity they deserved, then came to the United States and were received like garbage." The bombing was even shockingly left out of George Bush's inaugural speech.

Two months after the crash, the victims' families formed an organization and had their first formal meeting at a restaurant. Their goal was simple: to determine what happened, and why was there next to no response from the government. 103 days after the tragedy, they marched on Washington. Five relatives demanded a meeting with the president; in fear of negative media portrayal, Bush agreed. This paved way to further investigation, whereby Pan Am was found willfully negligent when it came to baggage control. The relatives of the deceased pressed on, with a direct address to the U.S. government, accusing them of cold-shouldering the case. The trail led to Libya - specifically intelligence agents Abdel Basset Ali Al Megrahi and

Lamen Khalifa Fhima, allegedly ordered by Muammar Gaddafi to plant the explosives.

In an "unprecedented legal arrangement", the two fugitives were finally flown into the Netherlands to be tried under Scottish law, looking "unperturbed" as they boarded the plane (in fact, smiling and waving). Lamen Khalifa Fhima was eventually set free (still smiling and waving), while his "buddy" was sent to jail, with a sentence equaling a "month for each victim". He eventually got prostate cancer, and after serving 8 years of life sentence, was released on compassionate grounds and allowed to return to Libya to die. Gaddafi admitted responsibility and offered almost $3 billion in compensation to the families.

The fascinating reasons for such an inexplicable act are revealed at the end; let's just say BP, and the U.S., British and Libyan governments were involved. "Justice and law were thrown out of the window for the sake of Libyan oil," a journalist comments, "and that disgusts me." The Pan Am 103 investigation is still open today.

"Since" focuses on fascinating tidbits, such as the families' disagreements over where the blame needed to be placed: some thought it was the Libyans, some the Syrians, some wanted the trial on American soil, others on Scottish... The emotional turmoil, anger and confusion, spurred by a lack of guidance or support, is cringingly evident. There are multiple searing recollections, like a mournful and bitter monologue by a long-suffering mother: "I entered a parallel universe. You are the enemy of the airline. You are the enemy of the government. You are the enemy, more than the people who created this horrible thing."

Many other of the film's most memorable parts come from the personal stories of the victims. A photographer, an actress, a surfer - they all had dreams and aspirations, some of which their parents decided to continue pursuing for them. Poetic testimonies from the kind residents of Lockerbie are compassionate and mournful, as opposed to the blatant disregard witnessed by the "people in charge" on the news. An incisive commentary from Special Agent Richard A. Marquise, retired lead FBI investigator on the case, brings gravitas and validity to the film.

One sequence in particular struck me. Suse, mother of one of the young victims, Alexander, is a sculptor. She comes to visit his grave in Lockerbie, her attitude shockingly nonchalant, making one wonder whether she came to serene terms with her son's death, or is in denial - or perhaps Suse shaped her mourning into her sculptures: a memorial which consists of all the victims in various states of distress, both beautiful and eerie. In stark contrast, another couple refuses to go to Lockerbie and face the sight of their daughter's death.

The doc gets its main point across: as one gentleman puts it, the "Scotts cared, and… it hurts me to say that my government… didn't care. It's a terrible thing for me to say." "The women of Lockerbie actually laundered every piece of clothing," another family member muses. I paraphrase here a passage from the film: "There used to be honor and dignity, and now it's all money… So long as the oil flows… and Pan Am is all but forgotten." We're nothing but ants, fighting a giant eagle.

While not especially mind-blowing and a tad manipulative at points (such as in the quick montage of the victim's photos towards the end), composer Phil Furey's first foray into filmmaking impresses. The decision to split "Since" into successive fragments, each detailing the unfurling investigation, was a clever one, as it shows the passage of time, and how memories may fade, but resolve and love burn on like embers until we die; it also makes the investigation easy to follow.

"Since: The Bombing of Pan Am Flight 103" is an important documentary, an indictment of the U.S. government, both right and left wing, and the larger political machinations that out-shadow the victims that get in the way. It focuses on the repercussions, roots and ultimate pointlessness of terrorism and the importance of sticking together in its face. Furey's documentary especially resonates in the current times of political unrest. It's not just about Pan Am. It's about 9/11, and Iraq, and Katrina, and the BP oil spill, and Syria, and countless other incidents where innocents die, while those responsible reign on rapaciously. It's important to know about Pan Am 103. I'm going to tell my friends about it.

4 out of 5 stars

3.5-STAR REVIEWS

"A War" Brims with Intelligence and Passion but Lacks Novelty

Synopsis: *During a routine mission in an Afghan province, company commander Claus and his soldiers are caught in heavy crossfire. In order to save his men, Claus makes a decision that has grave consequences for him - and his family back home.*

While I was watching Tobias Lindholm's Oscar-nominated drama "A War", a scene from Ricky Gervais' bitingly satirical British show "Extras" came into my mind. Gervais plays one of the titular extras. In one episode, he encounters Kate Winslet on the set of a ridiculously over-the-top Holocaust drama. When he inquiries why she's doing it, Kate's response is something in the vein of, "It's a guaranteed Oscar." Lo and behold, in a bit of meta-reality clash, just a few years later Winslet received the golden statue for Holocaust drama "The Reader" - a frankly mediocre film that got a lot of Academy attention, most certainly due to its controversial subject matter.

Now, Lindholm's latest directorial feature is definitely less emotionally manipulative and glossed-over than Stephen Daldry's by-product of adhering to Academy expectations. It's a Serious Drama whose focal point is not the war in Afghanistan, but a man at war with himself, challenged to recollect an event that defies rationale. Yet I never felt true originality or incisiveness; beat-by-beat, the story feels rehashed, already covered, to various degrees of success, in many films, from William Friedkin's "Rules of Engagement" to Susanne Bier's "Brothers". It's all very familiar, but well-told by a capable cast and director, with a subject matter - War Itself - ripe for Academy picking.

Michael Shannon-lookalike Pilou Asbæk plays Claus, leader of a small troop of Danish soldiers stationed in the vast, open mountains of Afghanistan, whose sheer enormity and grandeur are gracefully portrayed by cinematographer Magnus Nordenhof Jønck. The DP switches between those admiring shots of nature, and shaky, "you-are-there" moments of intense combat, as well as Claus' wife Maria's (Tuva Novotny) grey-hued, solitary existence back at home in Denmark. She lives with their three children, in constant anticipation of her husband's call, which weighs heavily upon the family.

One day, Claus and his soldiers encounter an Afghan family, in need of medical assistance. This leads to a prolonged, and steadily mounting, conflict. "We'll come tomorrow, we'll secure the area, and we'll drive the Taliban out," Claus promises the family. This results in a disastrous confrontation and innocent victims. Claus is brought home and put on trial for the dubiousness of his actions, while Maria observes, firmly believing in the virtue of his orders, and even of the orders that may or may not have been given to him at a crucial point. Early in the film, Claus justifies their actions to his traumatized soldiers by claiming they are liberating civilians - by the end, he is put through the ultimate grinder, a reminder that no such action can truly be justified.

Tobias Lindholm wrote the brilliant "The Hunt" for fellow Danish director Thomas Vinterberg, so it doesn't come as a surprise that the film is sharp: it covers a lot of issues, the prevailing one being a lack of communication when it comes to war - communication between loved ones, communication between commanders, communication between man and himself. The verisimilitude is there, Lindholm getting the minute details right, down to the terminology: "Commander? He must mean CO", one of the soldiers muses. Men are known merely as "7-5"'s and "0-2"'s. "A War" displays how an event of such enormity - the deaths of civilian lives - can be reduced to a simple term, such as "PID", which basically means "visual on the target". Among all this simplification, the unattainable answer lies in a manner of interpretation: what, exactly, did Claus mean when he said, "Tell them I know who's in there"?

There are several highlights worth noting. A scared soldier wants to go home, but all Claus can do is reassure him with a cigarette. A child accidentally ingests a bottle of pills and goes through a painful-to-watch medical procedure. A sequence involving a group of children, a sniper and a biker is the most striking one - the sniper hums before taking a shot, and our hearts skip as he pulls the trigger.

Yet, like Vinterberg with the recent well-made but middling "Far from the Madding Crowd", Lindholm seems to have gone a bit soft, "A War" lacking bite, of all things. While, say, Lars von Trier still shocks and provokes and screws with your mind with films like "Nymphomaniac" and "Melancholia", this war flick just stirs it a little.

What aggravated me the most was how poorly the two stories - Claus' and Maria's - gelled, her subplot underdeveloped in comparison to the visceral war scenes. When the plots merge in the second half, the film loses drive, becoming a courtroom procedural (another staple Hollywood loves). Pilou Asbæk conveys a storm of emotion with subtlety while on trial, but it's repetitive and talky, like a vice-versa "Full Metal Jacket", in which the first half's talky scenes were masterful, while the second half's war scenes dragged.

Yes, war is terrible and dehumanizing and unnecessary, filled with casualties, and has physical and emotional repercussions, but we all know that, right? Perhaps "A War"'s intelligence and passionate execution IS its novelty, but I'd like to think that we still live in a world where those aspects are a given, not Oscar-worthy commendable traits. There are foreign films out there that stirred a war of emotions within me in 2015 with a single shot - Abderrahmane Sissako's "Timbuktu" comes to mind - but "A War" left me somewhat cold. With all due respect.

3.5 out of 5

"Burden" is a Breeze to Sit - or Lie Under a Sheet of Glass -Through

Synopsis: *A probing portrait of Chris Burden, an artist who took creative expression to the limits and risked his life in the name of art.*

How you feel about performance art will most likely not affect your feelings towards directors Richard Dewey and Timothy Marrinan's impressive first feature documentary, "Burden", which focuses on THE performance artists of them all, the (in)famous Chris Burden. He arguably started the whole "performance art" trend, leading to the likes of Marina Abramović covering James Franco in honey and golden leaves (no, really, look it up!), Johnny Knoxville shooting himself in the balls with a BB gun and Vito Acconci masturbating underneath a gallery (though it's possible that Acconci was the "PA initiator", who knows, whatever). I myself am skeptical towards the whole thing and its artistic merits, but I cannot deny its entertainment/shock value. Dewey and Marrinan's doc is plenty entertaining, detailing Burden's life in vivid detail, but it's never really shocking, avoiding, for the most part, the difficult task of examining the machinations behind the troubled artist.

And troubled young Burden was, his last name oddly standing in as a metaphor for his existence. A borderline-sadistic man back in the late-1960s and early-1970s, Chris performed a variety of wild feats, such as locking himself in a locker for 5 days, nailing himself to a VW, putting a knife to the neck of a woman, dropping large beams from an impressive height and shooting a gun at a departing passenger airplane. The most famous stunt involved Burden, fueled by gun violence and the Vietnam War, having a friend shoot him in the shoulder with a real rifle. "Jackass"? Or "genius provocateur"? it's up to you to decide.

Towards the end of the 1970s and early 1980s, Burden went through drug-related issues and a concurrent curious transition from performance artist to sculptor, which he describes as quite similar in nature: "What is the essence of sculpture? Sculpture is action." His later pieces, quite impressive by anyone's standards, involve the world-famous "Metropolis" - a giant model reconstruction of Los Angeles with hundreds of moving parts ("It took nine months to reinstall") - and, of course, his "Urban Light" piece, the much-photographed lanterns that illuminate LACMA every evening. In a lovely passage, Burden reminisces about strolling through the lanterns at night and seeing the tourists take pictures. Not a lot of folks know his name, but the piece transcends the artist, and Burden is perfectly content.

The man himself, captured in the final stages of cancer (he died shortly after filming wrapped, right before the unveiling of one of his works), is eloquent, soft-spoken, living out his days in a large studio, located in the vast emptiness of Topanga Canyon. "Some of the publicity I got helped me change direction," he says, looking at his coyote-hunting dogs. The documentary switches between the quiet present, with the meticulous Chris and his proud workers relentlessly pursuing that next piece that achieves the "equilibrium" he's looking for, and the punk-rock past, with a young Burden - "Art-Martyr", as newspapers labeled him - rolling down a flight of stairs in public.

Consisting of archival footage, a plethora of photos, interviews with colleagues, lovers and friends, "Burden" is a pretty straightforward documentary that wisely keeps its lens on the fascinating subject, which keeps it rollickin' along. While never less than entertaining, it doesn't reveal enough of Burden's personal life, touching upon but never fully exploring his somewhat-abrasive relationship with women (did he fear/resent them?), or the drug addiction, or the aforementioned sadistic streak to his early work. It's almost like his later pieces are atoning for the brutality of the earlier work… with a hint of nostalgia to them, which, again, I wish the doc more fully explored.

Whether you consider Chris Burden's art goofy or radical, whether you're a cynic, skeptic or admirer, chances are, you will enjoy Dewey and Marrinan's brisk and witty doc. The directors could have scaled back a bit on their almost-reverential approach to the subject, but they certainly show promise. "Burden", like the performance artist's work it depicts, may not be art, but it's certainly fun as hell.

3.5 out of 5 stars

"Cézanne et Moi" Examines a Tumultuous Relationship Between Two Legendary Artists

Synopsis: A historical drama that traces the lifelong friendship between two renowned 19th century French artists - painter Paul Cézanne and writer Emile Zola - from their first meeting as schoolmates to their creative rivalry, as fame and success continue to elude Cézanne.

"The artist is nothing without the gift, but the gift is nothing without work." - Émile Zola

Most artistic rivalries are spawned from admiration, either one-sided, as was the case with Antonio Salieri, who envied Mozart's effortless skills, or mutual, like that of Post-Impressionist painter Paul Cézanne and writer Émile Zola. Director Danièle Thompson delves into the nuances of their relationship in the well-written and shot but plodding period drama "Cézanne et moi". Theatrically staged, with long repetitive stretches of characters frolicking in 19th Century garb, and the two protagonists loving or hating each other eloquently (there is a strong homoerotic subtext that the film never fully explores), the film has its share of memorable moments, yet certainly poses a challenge to sit through for anyone but the most rabid enthusiasts of the two highly influential artists.

One of its issues is the conventional narrative structure. We begin in the "present" - or 1888 - as Zola (Guillaume Canet) reunites with Cézanne (Guillaume Gallienne), for another one of their countless confrontations about the merits of art. This time, it's personal, a broken-down Cézanne passionately accusing Zola of plagiarizing the painter's turbulent life, at times transcribing their most private moments in his books. With frequent flashbacks, the film reveals the duo's lengthy friendship, starting in or around 1860, when Zola was piss-poor, feeding his mother plucked city birds (yeah, you heard me), while the rebellious Cézanne flees his privileged family and elopes to Paris to hang out with (and secretly lust after) the talented writer.

A rascal and a provocateur, Cézanne throws tantrums, breaks into fights at highbrow parties, his ostentatious, judgmental nature forming a striking contrast to the timid, reclusive Zola. Having an art dealer would "paralyze" Cézanne. Of course, bashing the world of which you are a part eventually leads to exile, and the artist ends up banished to the glory of France's nature, spending his miserable days painting stunning vistas and his wife's, Hortense's (Déborah François), naked flesh, refusing to adhere to the "standards" imposed on him by the art world. In the meantime, inversely-proportionally, Zola's stratospheric rise to fame leads to him marrying one of Cézanne's ex-sweethearts, Alexandrine (Alice Pol) and setting down in a mansion outside Paris.

The two meet, over and over, mingling with other notorious figures, their rivals, such as Édouard Manet (Nicolas Gob) and Guy de Maupassant (Félicien Juttner). They debate over art's merits and its reflection of the truth. Cézanne despises the bourgeoisie and becomes more and more of a hermit, while Zola doesn't exactly embrace it either, but kind of goes along with it, leading to a poignant final confrontation that displays both men at their most vulnerable and poses the question: which one of them has been truer to himself?

The women luckily also get their moments to shine, apart from being mere subjects for the Artistes' inspirations. Déborah François delivers an astonishing monologue halfway though the film that serves as one of its highlights. Sick of her husband's infatuation with the projected images on a canvas, she dares him to fuck his painting, an applause-worthy zinger. Another such moment comes several scenes later, with Alice Pol verbally massacring Cézanne, as a train approaches in the background, intensifying her speech. The dinner sequence - "Cézanne et moi"'s centerpiece, later referenced in Zola's works - is another standout.

Unfortunately, those inspired moments are rare. One can't fault the dialogue, which is uniformly elegant, but the film comes dangerously close to the tedium of watching (Cézanne's) paint dry. Perhaps it's because we don't get to see enough of the great painter's pieces. Or maybe Thompson could've infused her film with a few more artistic flourishes - it's not like there aren't enough skinny-dipping shots she could've easily replaced with a grandiose, inspired sequence. But no - the film adheres to a classical style, all tiny umbrellas and corsets and friendly kisses (just do it already, dudes!). As for Jean-Marie Drejou's beautiful cinematography - it certainly reflects Cézanne's work but lacks his warmth and grandeur.

"Your writing is so modern," Cézanne tells Zola at one point, until his gaze falls on the writer's furniture. "Don't all those old things weigh down on you?" This is just an example of Thompson's dialogue, which I now have to point out, for it so powerfully buoys the otherwise-somewhat-boring flick. One can quote pretty much any part of this film, it's so erudite and expressive. Zola, the writer that he was, in particular gets moments to shine: "Discouragement can also make the pen fall from my hand… We know each other too well to ever fall apart… Two friends who understand each other at a glance." He utters my favorite line to his friend/nemesis: "With you, I never know whether I'm dealing with a dog, a cobra or a butterfly." Both of the actors fare well, playing multiple ages and chewing on scenery, especially Guillaume Gallienne, in the showier role. Shy and intimidated by women, Guillaume

Canet surprisingly fares better as Zola, in the subtler role. Two Guillaumes playing mirror opposites - coincidence... or design?

When it comes to great Artiste's biopics, I'd recommend starting with Andrei Tarkovsky's dark and somber "Andrei Rublev", or Milos Forman's genial "Amadeus" - or for those of you who think the world did not exist before the 2000's, Ed Harris' complex "Pollock", Julie Taymor's dreamlike "Frida", Mike Leigh's epic "Mr. Turner" or Pablo Larraín's recent masterpiece, "Neruda" (read review here). But one could also do much worse than hanging out with Thompson and Cézanne, which reveals some truths about rivalry, leaving behind a legacy, love and friendship... Though, let's face it, "Cézanne en Moi" would've been WAY more interesting.

3.5 out of 5 stars

"Dina" Takes a Look at the Lives of Ordinary People Through a Magnifying Glass

Synopsis: *An eccentric suburban woman and a Walmart door greeter navigate their evolving relationship in this unconventional love story.*

If one were to judge humanity solely by the dreck that Hollywood dishes out, they would most likely assume that our population consists of gorgeous, privileged people, whose issues can be resolved with just a wee bit of perseverance. From Will Smith's perfect teeth and homeless chic in "The Pursuit of Happyness" to Eddie Redmayne's recent Oscar-winning portrayal of mental illness (as Stephen Hawking himself, no less!) in "The Theory of Everything", the Dream Factory's perspective of "common folk" is skewed, to say the least.

In direct opposition to such glamorized representation of the lower-middle classes and people with mental disabilities, filmmakers Antonio Santini and Dan Sickles structured their documentary "Dina" like a conventional romcom, albeit one populated with real characters as opposed to their flashy big-screen stereotypes. The simple-but-profound "Dina" reminded me of films like "The Station Agent" - rare heartfelt gems that lack so much as a hint of glamorizing.

Dina (Dina Buno) is a middle-aged woman with a heavy past: she's been stabbed several times and tragically lost her husband. Nine years later, she's developed a neurological disorder and bad habits that lead to the dentist's office ("I like sweets", she says). She wears oversized sweatshirts, Pink jumpsuits and big bows in her hair. She is obsessed with kangaroos, speaks in a frank monotone and adores the Kardashians.

She and her autistic groom Scott (Scott Levin) go to the movies and ride the bus together. Scott works at a nearby Walmart, lives with his parents in a crammed little house and says "uh-huh" a lot in response to Dina's ramblings. Early on, he moves in with Dina, his first time away from the hoarders - which leads to a gentle but incisive study of sexual frustrations and insecurities, one of the running threads of the doc.

To ignite their sex life, Dina and Scott watch "Sex and the City" together, read sex books and discuss fetishes and masturbation. She takes Scott to the ocean for his first time. The filmmakers follow the couple through their nuptials, Adam Uhl's still, observant camera catching all the complex nuances of a seemingly simple sequence of non-events. Dina confides in her friends at a mini-golf course. Scott plays Richard Marx's 1980's classic "Right Here Waiting". Those little moments resonate. "Dina" is peppered with levity: the couples' honeymoon suite is truly something to behold, as is Dina defending Caitlyn Jenner's transition to her mom at a nail salon.

How much of Santini and Sickles' documentary was staged by the directors remains debatable. Some shots seem a bit premeditated - the gorgeous sunset-field-set scene on a bench and the following poignant ending particularly striking me as more of reenactments than captured moments. For the most part, though, Dina's life feels so real, you can almost feel the texture of her rumpled bedsheets. It's difficult not to see yourself in Dina and Scott, though, paradoxically, you most likely don't notice those people as they pass you by on the street or open a Walmart door for you.

"Things will be positive and filled with sunshine and hope," Dina says early on in the film. Funny, unconventional, if slight, "Dina" may not be a thrill-a-second experience or particularly revelatory - but nor does it contain Margot Robbie as an uglified housewife. At its heart, it's a love story, a romcom about a real guy proposing to a real woman. In other words, a cinematic rarity these days. "Dina" strives for authentic and achieves it - mostly - with aplomb.

3.5 out of 5 stars

"Doctor Strange" Awes with Visuals, Disappoints with Story

Synopsis: *A former neurosurgeon embarks on a journey of healing only to be drawn into the world of the mystic arts.*

Marvel films have issues avoiding the tropes of a new superhero introduction: a more-or-less regular human is confronted with a magical power, learns how to harness it, encounters a formidable foe and ultimately defeats it, just to pave the path for an even more gargantuan, world-destructing force in the sequel (see: "Spider-Man", "Captain America", "Ant-Man", "Iron Man", etc). Who can blame them - the formula clearly works; the box-office numbers speak for themselves. We are now in Marvel's Phase II, where barely any of the dots between films connect, but they try oh-so-hard, and the public laps it up. Who cares that there are now three Spider-Men, three Hulks and eight members of the Fantastic Four? No one pays too much attention that the Avengers "are busy" during the apocalyptic events of "Captain America", or that the X-Men are conspicuously absent from the majority of non-X-Men Marvel outings.

Even off-kilter films like James Gunn's berserk "Guardians of the Galaxy" (still the best Marvel offering, along with "Deadpool"), which attempted to redefine the formula - and came THIS close - still adhered to the aforementioned structure and tried to tie it all together into a coherent universe. Actually, make that universes, as Scott Derrickson's "Doctor Strange" boldly takes Marvel into parallel dimensions, with spectacular, psychedelic visuals and a strong central performance by Mr. Sherlock Holmes himself, Benedict Cumberbatch - or B.Cumbs, as I like to call him. Unfortunately, despite the phantasmagoria on display, all the occult mumbo-jumbo becomes a little too much, derailing the plot into "uber-silly" territory in the film's second half. However, the main issue I had with this Doctor is that he didn't take a scalpel and trim all the fat - specifically, the unnecessary city-destructing plot with a weak, spacey villain, and the random references to other Marvel entries (including the groan-inducing post-credit sequence).

The film starts off with a bang: as a city folds upon itself, "Inception"-style, Mads Mikkelsen's baddy, Kaecilius (I'm still waiting for a villain with the name Orneosciliorocious), along with his posse of samurai-like warriors, escape a power-wielding monk. In the meantime, the arrogant-but-brilliant Dr. Stephen Strange (B.Cumbs), along with the help of his beautiful assistant - and potential love interest - Christine (Rachel McAdams - a "Night Nurse" spin-off is probably in the brewing as we speak), extracts a bullet from a patient's brain, ever-so-gently. Soon after, a car crash leaves our fame-hungry hero with paralyzed hands. "No one could've done it better," Christine reassures him in the hospital. "I could've done it better," the doctor vehemently replies. "You ruined me." This kind of attitude rapidly alienates him from his colleagues and friends; in search of a cure for his limp shaking hands, Stephen travels to Kathmandu, to seek a magical place that cured another patient, Jonathan (Benjamin Bratt, in what amounts to little more than a cameo).

Mr. - sorry - Dr. Strange encounters Mordo (Chiwetel Ejiofor) who, with a cryptic "forget everything you know", leads him to The Ancient One (an androgynous Tilda Swinton), an "unpredictable, merciless yet kind" Buddha-like being - and therein, the trip begins. And by "trip" I literally mean a hallucinatory assault on the senses, as The Ancient One "pulls [Stephen's] astral form out of his physical form" and introduces the pragmatic doctor to numerous parallel worlds, scrambling his scientific brain. Apparently, there are multiple sanctums all over the world that protect humanity from mystical threats, while the Avengers focus on physical dangers (though it can be argued that Thor's storyline does a fine balancing act there). Spatial paradoxes abound, along with time leaps, inter-dimensional portals and space-time continuums. The evil villain, striving for nothing less than eternal life, resurfaces, with an even bigger villain behind his back. Ultimately, it's up to Stephen, now sporting a cape and a frankly ridiculous-looking outfit, to save the day.

"Doctor Strange" is crammed with pseudo-spiritual musings, the best of which brought to mind the entire moral of the brilliant horror film "Babadook": "We never learn to leave our demons. We only learn to live above them." Aside from a few more resonant lines, it's best not to take any of the doctor's travails too seriously or think too deeply about the events unfurling on screen, like the jaw-dropping but nonsensical time-reversal battle at the end. Steeped in the occult but never seeming to know how to properly utilize its teachings (a-la Alan Moore), "Doctor Strange" is more "Bulletproof Monk" than "Watchmen". Perhaps that's a bit harsh, considering the truly awe-inspiring visuals (seemingly intended for HEAVY drug consumption) and the dedicated lead performance, but after a promising start, the film's potential depth dissipates into a series of fortune-teller Chakra-speak.

B.Cumbs excels as usual, the theatrical, Baritone-voiced pro that he is - although I couldn't quite figure out what he was doing with the accent (Britamerican?). Rachel McAdams, a charming actress, is a bit underused but does shine in the small reaction-shot moments. The producers figured, in this day and age of feminist progression, it makes sense to delegate a couple of moderately funny one-liners and goofy facial expressions to one of our more promising young actresses. Go figure. Benedict Wong - as Wong (original!) - has some funny one-liners, but again, plays a one-dimensional character in a multi-dimensional universe. The standout would have to be the stunning Swinton, who can act anything, anytime, anywhere.

Doctor Strange succeeds at defying the laws of physics yet struggles when it comes to defying the established Marvel narrative structure. Props for trying, but, akin to Stephen Strange himself, voluntarily trapped in a time loop in the film's finale, Marvel seems to be stuck in a swamp of self-plagiarism. Maybe it's time to transport the entire enterprise to a parallel dimension, with storytelling that matches the $170 million visuals.

3.5 out of 5 stars

Eden: Neon Lights, Drug-Fueled Nights and Daft Punk

Synopsis: *Paul, a teenager in the underground scene of early-nineties Paris, forms a DJ collective with his friends and together they plunge into the nightlife of sex, drugs, and endless music.*

Daft Punk has remained one of the most popular electronic music acts since Guy-Manuel de Homem-Christo and Thomas Bangalter formed the duo back in the mid-1990s. The key to their success has always been accessibility - from house to funk to electro to techno, they evolved with the music, constantly introducing new elements and euphoric sounds to their repertoire. "Eden" is not about Daft Punk, though they are prominently featured throughout the film. The film, amongst many other things, is about the deejays that emerged around the same time but failed - or consciously refused - to keep up with the trends, forever remaining in the increasingly less-welcoming "cubby hole" of 1990s rave culture, their personal "Edens".

Based on the experiences of Sven Hansen-Løve - brother of *Eden's* director, the uber-talented Mia Hansen-Løve ("Goodbye First Love") - the film explores the allure of the 1990s underground dance scene, when house music was at its glorious peak, and traces its evolution (or, as some would argue, its *de*volution) through the 2000s.

Some things have changed significantly along with the music (the novelty / sense of discovery has worn off; the clothes lost their acidic tones and eight-inch platform shoes), some have not (ecstasy and cocaine still mostly go hand-in-hand with the EDM clubbing experience). "Eden" touches on a wide variety of subjects - the fleetingness of young love, the rebellious nature of artists, the deceptiveness of creative impulses, the bitterness of rivalry - but at its heart it's about the necessity to change and adapt. Paul, the film's protagonist (and Sven's alter ego), resolutely refuses to change, clinging to the brief glory of the old days, as the club scene gradually wedges him out. And Daft Punk is always in the background, leading the electronic dance movement, as if taunting Paul, showing him how it's done - but he refuses to listen.

The protagonist's murky existence is reflected by the film's kaleidoscopic, "stop-and-go" momentum - delving into the neon-spotted darkness of the clubs, and then back out into the sobering light of day; going from girlfriend to girlfriend (the always-stellar Greta Gerwig makes an appearance early on, and disappears for most of the film, just to reemerge at the end, in one of the most affecting sequences in the film); shifting from year to year - and sometimes skipping *through* years - like flipping through a radiant, acid-tinged sketchbook. This approach is both effective in demonstrating the larger, epic scope, and intermittently problematic, as it rarely gives one the opportunity to truly understand Paul (Félix de Givry's muted central performance doesn't help much), or allow scenes to dramatically evolve - or, for that matter, truly grip the audience.

There are many highlights, such as one character's ardent - and weirdly sensible - championing of Paul Verhoeven's 1990s "disaster-piece" "Showgirls"; or the brutal and unexpected death of another central character, which emphasizes the film's main theme of unrealized potential and failed ambitions. But, for all its four-by-four beats and grandiose ambition, "Eden" often lacks forward momentum of similarly-themed films like Mathieu Kassovitz' classic exploration of aimlessness "La Haine", or even Doug Liman's glimpse of 1990s rave culture "Go", or Harmony Korine's recent, basked-in-neon-lights "Spring Breakers". Those films may not possess "Eden"'s ambition and scope, but "Eden" could certainly use some of their drive and amaranthine energy.

Paul, in all his aimlessness and poetic waxing, resembles the central protagonist of the Coen Brothers' "Inside Llewyn Davis", which "Eden" also brings to mind, substituting folk music with house beats - the irony is that "Inside…" is more compulsively watchable, because it truly gets inside Llewyn's head, tracing his morose existence through a series of darkly-funny and compelling sequences, but Paul remains somewhat of an enigma throughout "Eden". Even the long musical interludes, while beautiful and nostalgic, begin to get repetitive.

But perhaps that's the point. For Paul, this club life *is* Eden, and the repetitiveness serves as a reminder that, sooner or later, everyone gets exiled.

3.5 out of 5 stars

"Graduation" (Hopefully) Concludes Cristian Mungiu's "It's Hard Out Here for a Romanian" Trilogy

Synopsis: *A film about compromises and the implications of the parent's role.*

It's not easy to be Romanian - at least, according to Christian Mingu's cinematic oeuvre of depressing sociopolitical commentaries. "Occident" told a complex story of youth fleeing the country. "4 Months, 3 Weeks and 2 Days" followed a woman, step-by-step, through a grueling abortion in the 1980's. I haven't had the "pleasure" of watching Mingu's "Beyond the Hills", but "Graduation", again, subjected me to a 130 claustrophobic, despairing minutes of corruption and heartlessness, before I got to the glimmer of hope at the very end.

Reminiscent in style to the Dardenne brothers' films (who act as co-producers on "Graduation"), the film's focus is on everyday men and women, struggling to survive in a bleak, heartless world. Traces of Hollywood "gloss" - rapid-fire editing, spelled-out themes, predictable narrative beats, swooping camerawork, Jennifer Lawrence - are nowhere to be found in this exercise of ultra-realism. There's no score, no embellishments - just a straight-up account of a man, somewhat-ironically called Romeo (a brilliantly restrained performance by a desperate, bordering-on-reprehensible Adrian Titieni) battling uphill against a corrupt society, and himself.

While a bit dry, and lacking the Dardennes' spiritually-cleansing conclusions, "Graduation" is a worthy addition to the talented director's filmography, whose next film should perhaps shift its lens on a different topic. Though he manages to convey a multitude of ideas and themes through that prism of contemporary Romania, I would love to see the director try his hand at another genre. Unless, of course, he has found his niche - the multiple Palm d'Or awards on his shelf speak for themselves, after all.

Romeo is a morally-torn man. His wife, Magda (Lia Bugnar), is depressed, homebound, and aware of Romeo's affair with Sandra (Malina Manovici), a teacher at their daughter's school. His daughter, Eliza (Maria Dragus), gets attacked and potentially raped. Romeo's primary goal, however, is to make sure Eliza graduates with honors and gets a scholarship in the "more civilized" UK - her (and, vicariously, his) golden ticket out of the hellhole that is Romania. Unable to escape himself, finding temporary solace in infidelity, he fervently pursues this goal, at the expense of disregarding everyone's actual needs. "My daughter wasn't raped, just assaulted," he hesitantly corrects his reassuring neighbor. In denial much?

Romeo projects his insecurities and desires onto his loved ones, believing he will ultimately find redemption when his daughter flees to greener pastures. He keeps reiterating to poor Eliza that a top score on the exam is top priority, even when she cries at night, traumatized from the incident. "You know if your heart hurts, this isn't right," Magda says. "That's not the path I want her to take... Why this burden on her shoulders?" Romeo instills Eliza with fear and a need to please him, as opposed to finding herself - something most parents unknowingly do, in one way or another.

Perhaps not so surprisingly, it's Romeo's mother (Alexandra Davidescu), a symbol of Romania's past, who provides the most acute insight regarding her granddaughter: "She should stay and change things. If they all leave..." She trails off. Romeo, who represents the country's tumultuous, ever-changing present, can't accept that fact. It may ultimately be up to Eliza - Romania's future - to decide her own path. Mingu plays heavily with this generational juxtaposition, to great effect.

The city itself seems to be against Romeo. It all starts with a rock thrown through his window, and later through the windshield of his car. He runs over a dog. A complication leads to a school board confrontation, which in turn leads to bribes and a general defiance of principles. His mother collapses. Eliza finds out about Sandra, the other woman. A dying patient under investigation may prove to be the pivotal point. And the entire time, in the background, a phone rings incessantly, a nagging, invasive sound. "Why did we abolish the death sentence?" Romeo inquires solemnly. I have a felling he would murder quite a few people, if he legally could, just so that Eliza could ace that baccalaureate.

Disregarding the soulless individuals and crumbled-down city, the country's natural scenery actually looks stunning, courtesy of cinematographer Tudor Vladimir Panduru and, of course, the beautiful country itself. That said, the film is basked in 50 shades of grey, reflecting the moral areas its characters inhabit. Two scenes stood out to me: one involving a policeman, who found a way to deal with depression through... marbles, each representing a day in his life; and another, in which our stoic doctor breaks down sobbing uncontrollably in the woods.

A tad repetitive, and not nearly as razor-sharp, succinct, emotional and focused as "4 Months, 3 Weeks and 2 Days", "Graduation" is nevertheless a beautifully-written, assuredly-directed (as acknowledged by Cannes), incisive critique of a corrupt society. It's a study of parenthood, of a man driven to obsession, of a crumbling marriage and crumbling values. It's filled with searing exchanges, subtlety that's uncommon in contemporary film and powerful performances. Things may be tough today, but the future holds sparks of hope.

Perhaps Mingu's palette will broaden too. I'm glad that, after such a dismal education, this graduation may lead to a promising scholarship.

3.5 out of 5 stars

Kahlil Gibran's "The Prophet" Aims High but Sears Its Dazzling Wings

Synopsis: Exiled artist and poet Mustafa embarks on a journey home with his housekeeper and her daughter; together the trio must evade the authorities who fear that the truth in Mustafa's words will incite rebellion.

Kahlil Gibran's 1923 collection of philosophical, poetic essays "The Prophet" has since become a massive international hit. Translated into 40 languages, with millions of copies sold, the book's sweeping themes of love, freedom, sorrow, religion, death - among many other deep, esoteric subjects - resonated with folks worldwide. Roger Allers' animated adaptation took a risky approach and split the narrative into segments, each illustrated by a top contemporary artist, such as Bill Plympton ("Idiots and Angels"), Nina Paley ("Sita Sings the Blues") and Tomm Moore ("The Secret of Kells"), all strung together - or "directed" - by the helmer of "Open Season" and "The Lion King". For the most part, the effort pays off, though the film does lack coherence.

Salma Hayek's passion project - she is the lead producer, who got Liam Neeson for voicing the protagonist, came up with the idea of having separate vignettes, and voices what I assume is a Lebanese character in a blatantly Spanish accent - begins with Almitra, a young, fatherless, troublemaker girl who hasn't spoken a word since her father's death. She upsets and alienates her village with pranks and general trouble-making, and her mom, Kamila (yep, Salma Hayek), has to defend her daughter against the frankly justified anger of the villagers. They live in the home of an imprisoned poet Mustafa (a highly elegiac Liam Neeson), where Kamila serves as his maid.

Mustafa tells Almitra he's not really a prisoner, and that he's "flown away many times" (followed by a short but beautiful sequence about imagination's limitlessness, and how "we are spirits, free as the wind.") Yet now he's being exiled, and on their journey to a doomed ship, escorted by guards, the trio encounters a legion of thankful villagers. Mustafa is a Christ-like figure, whose poetic readings are visualized in the animated sequences, ranging from Monet-like painterly impressionist overtures to briefly outlined sketches, dazzling in their simplicity. Almitra discovers that the guards have a plan brewing, which involves having Mustafa renounce all of his creations, and she attempts to stop them. The film ends on a profound note - by far "The Prophet"'s high point.

It's genuinely refreshing to see hand-drawn animation; the warmth and artistry is palpable - but while it's a joy to behold for the most part, the sketches do vary in quality, one particularly psychedelic piece resembling a trippy screen-saver. The sketch-to-sketch narrative is both exciting, as one never knows what will appear on the screen next, and off-putting, giving the film an episodic structure that doesn't flow as well as it should. The main plot, connecting Mustafa's cabalistic stories together, is jarringly straightforward and sophomoric.

Which brings me to the film's big flaw: its elegant, poetic, mythical, and at times passionately political narrative gets regularly interrupted by moments of juvenile humor, apparently to appease the young 'uns, but the flow stumbles, hard. For example, there's silly "guard-chasing-bird" slapstick, or a character proclaiming, for no reason: "I'll stick with the baklava." (Worst punchline of 2015?) Maybe some things got lost in translation, as it's an international effort; the United States, France, Lebanon, Quatar and Canada were all involved in the film's production.

But does that excuse the film's dearth of tonal consistency? Passages, such as "For you can no longer be free, when you think of freedom as a goal", or "Give your hearts, but not into each other's keeping, for only the hand of life can contain your hearts" are lovely sentiments… that will totally go over the little heads of children amused by poop jokes. I'm all about not underestimating the kids' intelligence, and parents pausing the film and explaining the meaning behind each sequence, but then why bore those parents with frequent immature shenanigans and bad dialogue?

In addition, while in the Gibran's book the authority's intentions - to suppress artistic expression with despotism - were clearly defined, many kids may be left confounded as to why Mustafa's harmless teachings are deemed so evil by those mean guards. Say what you want about Pixar, but they do the fine balancing act of "accessible to both kids and their parents on multiple levels" better than anyone else, as proven by the recent, brilliant "Inside Out".

The film could have done without the musical interludes, which sound like diluted, Disney-like numbers, barely saved by the animation driving them. The "Children Are Not Your Children" song is particularly laughable. Again, it's like the filmmakers didn't trust their instincts to stick to the darkness of the source material; imagine "Persepolis" with Looney Tunes interludes, and a Phil Collins soundtrack.

I realize I may have been a bit harsh on the film. A lot of care and attention went into this ambitious project, and while it's not quite the masterpiece it wanted to be, and has trouble defining its audience, it's a gorgeous story, with inspired passages, and certainly better than most of the computer-generated animation coming out of the Dream Factory these days.

Similar in structure to the sketch-like narratives of "Fantasia" or "Fear(s) of the Dark", it's best enjoyed as a visual poem, a feast for the eyes that gets the imagination buzzin'… and driftin' a little bit.

3.5 out of 5

"Louder Than Bombs" Proves that Words Can Resonate Louder than Any Explosion

Synopsis: *The fractious family of a father and his two sons confront their different feelings and memories of their deceased wife and mother, a famed war photographer.*

After his award festival darling "Oslo, August 31st", director Joachim Trier follows up with the English-language debut, "Louder Than Bombs", displaying real filmmaking proficiency and firmly placing himself on the list of "Ones to Watch". Darkly humorous and insightful, if overly convoluted, it's a study of a family dealing with loss and coming to terms with each other, and themselves. If the plot sounds a bit familiar and "blah", the acting from the four main leads, and Trier's nimble directorial touch, save it from becoming just another low-key drama that disappears into the cinematic ether of granola indies.

Gene (Gabriel Byrne) is putting together a memorial for his celebrity war photographer wife Isabelle (Isabelle Huppert), who died in a tragic - and mysterious - car crash. It involves an article/expose, written by Richard (David Stathairn), a journalist and Isabelle's ex-lover (scandalous!). In the meantime, Gene's older son Jonah (Jesse Eisenberg) comes home, in denial after having a baby, to revisit his past, try to make sense of it.

Jonah's younger brother Conrad (Devin Druid) is reclusive, constantly immersed into music (he wears noise-canceling headphones everywhere he goes), video games, and unadulterated resentment. While Jonah's relationship with Gene is strained but at least amicable, Conrad refuses to even speak with his father, dreaming about the popular girl he loves and waking up to the ghost of his mother. Gene's attempts to bond with Conrad reach an apotheosis, when the poor dad spends days creating a video game character, to attempt to reach out to his son in a virtual reality - just to swiftly end up decapitated.

Gene also happens to sleep with Jonah's teacher, Hannah (Amy Ryan). "It's uncomfortable," she tells him, "looking at Conrad in class and thinking he's just like the other kids." The article gets published, revealing facts about Isabelle previously unknown to Jonah, leading to a series of incidents, where the characters' lives get intertwined, and each protagonist goes through a process of self-cleansing.

Trier expertly handles sequences and fluctuations in tone, the film dexterously shifting between searing drama and dark comedy. I loved how Gene, concerned for Conrad's well-being, spies on his son; he calls him, watching Conrad lie about being with friends, while alone on the playground swings, and then follows him to the cemetery, where the boy collapses onto one of the graves.

Other memorable scenes involve Conrad pulling a plastic bag over his head in a crazed attempt to isolate himself from his dad; Jonah and Conrad bonding over their father's old soap opera footage and video games; Conrad's diary montage - a haiku-like, lyrical insight into a troubled psyche ("Dad is everywhere… I swallowed a bullet. Maybe it's still inside of me."); a fantastic monologue Jonah delivers to Conrad during a cheer-leading practice that encapsulates everything one needs to know about teenage angst; Conrad confronting his teacher in front of his entire class, after finding out about her affair with his father…

You may have noticed that most of the sequences I described involve Conrad. That's because in a film that sometimes feels a bit overstuffed and aimless, the young actor Devin Druid, known for his memorable appearances in TV's "Louie", manages to anchor the narrative with a realistic, tender portrait of teen angst, melancholy and grief.

The rest of the stalwart cast all get moments to shine. Every scene is haunted by the ghost of the mother, and Isabelle Huppert was the perfect casting choice - her naturally enigmatic, alluring presence dominates every shot. While Druid is the anchor, Huppert, appearing only in a few flashback and voice-over sequences, is the beating heart of the film. There is a moment where she spots her own photograph in a newspaper, casually being flipped by a stranger, and a single glance of hers speaks volumes about humanity's ignorance. That's Acting. Gabriel Byrne is always reliable, and here brings another understated, touching performance. Jesse Eisenberg shows range, toning down his "nerdy wise-ass" shtick. Amy Ryan and David Strathhairn both get their moments to shine in small-but-pivotal roles.

Therein lies the film's flaw. Each of the characters is so compelling, a film could be made revolving around them - and yet "Louder Than Bombs" feels both overstuffed and sparse. Its moments of sublimity are powerful, but rarely get the chance to truly stand out - there's just such a rapid succession of them! Let's take a look at the multitude of story arcs: Isabelle's intense journey as a war photographer, which leads to depression and a possible suicide; her family's consequent dealing with her death; Conrad's coming-of-age; Gene's love affair with Conrad's teacher; Jonah facing his demons, with the arrival of a new baby and ex-girlfriend (the one sort-of unresolved storyline that could've frankly been left on the cutting room floor); the brothers bonding after years of alienation; the infidelities that surface… Don't get me wrong, Trier deftly handles each of the sequences with subtlety and gravitas - it's just that the abundance of them makes the film lack a strong central focus. A lot of really good stuff is being thrown at you, but little of it truly sticks, unfortunately.

There are a few stylistic choices that leave you baffled. The voice-over narration by several characters feels tacked-on and unnecessary. The dreamy, artsy dream interludes jar with a pretentiousness absent in the rest of the film. Some scenes drag a little too long, while others - especially ones between Byrne and Huppert - made me long for extended versions.

That said, Joachim Trier's film has plenty of moments of real gravitas, moments that resonate and ring very true. It's about how our perception of people can alter based on circumstances. It's about grief and reconciliation. It skillfully avoids sentimentality, which so many similar dramas get trapped into. Its melancholic narrative effortlessly cuts back and forward in time, and between parallel story lines, and if there are too many of them, it's simply too much of a good thing. With his next feature, I hope the director scales back and focuses more on exploring one or two subjects, as opposed to twenty. I'll be the first one in line.

3.5 out of 5 stars

"Mojave" Over-Intellectualizes and Mesmerizes in Equal Measures

Synopsis: *A suicidal artist goes into the desert, where he finds his doppelgänger, a homicidal drifter.*

Screenwriter William Monahan has displayed a stratospheric rise to fame and prestige within the past decade. His very first major gig was the 12th-Century crusades epic "Kingdom of Heaven", directed by Ridley Scott in 2005 (who collaborated with Monahan again three years later on the vastly inferior political actioner "Body of Lies"). Monahan worked with Martin Scorsese ("The Departed", for which he won an Oscar) and Martin Campbell ("Edge of Darkness"), and wrote the recent Mark Wahlberg starrer, "The Gambler". He has promptly become the go-to guy in Hollywood for gritty dramas, fueled by morally-questionable characters seeking retribution and, ultimately, salvation.

While Monahan is clearly a gifted (though somewhat patchy) writer, the lackluster Colin Farrell/Keira Knightley gangster flop "London Boulevard", which he wrote and directed in 2010, gave signs that maybe the man should stick to his day job. Sure, it was atmospheric and had moments of cleverness, but its dullness, lack of memorable characters and heavy-handed approach weighed the film down, deep into the murky depths of forgettable cinema. Monahan's proverbial hand is no lighter in "Mojave", his second stab at directing his own script, but he scales back on the characters and plot, and, with the help of a talented lead, adds enough enthralling moments to compensate for the occasional moments of artificiality and tonal inconsistency.

Thomas (Garrett Hedlund) is a rich celebrity filmmaker, who decides to isolate himself from a life of wealth, sleazy agents and coked-up producers. He goes off to the desert, seeking solace. He taunts howling coyotes, as if daring them to eat him ("Come on what are you waiting for?" he bellows into the darkness). He drinks and drives erratically, crashing his car ("Good," he says, looking at the mess). With not much more than a gallon of water and a pack of smokes, he goes into nowhere, seeking certain death… Until he spots a figure in the distance.

The figure turns out to be Jack (Oscar Isaac), a pseudo-intellectual hillbilly, who joins Thomas by the fire and talks about Jesus, quotes Shakespeare, spouts government hate and pretends to be the Devil Himself. Tension builds, erupting in a duel of sorts, wherein Thomas leaves an unconscious Jack by the fire.

Things unfurl rapidly. Thomas, all riled up from the encounter, his own demons gnawing at him, accidentally shoots a cop with Jack's rifle, as Jack observes from the distance. Newspapers reveal that Jack's been at it for a while, murdering naturalists in the desert. Upon discovering the news, Thomas, rather abruptly, decides to return home, putting his suicide mission on hold. Jack, of course, follows him, murdering and assuming a rich man's identity on the way.

When Thomas' agent, Jim (Walton Goggins) asks him what happened in the desert, Thomas glumly says, "Nothing". Though married with a kid, Thomas sleeps with Milly, an actress (Louise Bourgoin), pissing of his producing partner Norman (Mark Wahlberg, a coked-up embodiment of every Hollywood producer cliche in the book), who whines, "He can't sleep with the talent!". Everyone's emotionless, rigid and sleazy in this real world, sheltered as it may be from the sparse and lethal Mojave.

It comes as no surprise that Jack soon finds Thomas, which leads to a "Heat"-like confrontation in a bar - the film's highlight. Jack promises to kill Thomas, "and you need it", he says, "just as a brother needs to be served." Thomas threatens to go to the cops, and yet Jack retorts with an ingenious monologue, which I paraphrase here: "You shot a brother in the desert… but you gotta be Elvis Beetle. That's bad press of the show. You'd have to say you're psychologically unequal… You'd have to admit to deficiencies - deficiencies you don't really have. So you cover it up, at an expense of a man life… So which one of us is the sociopath, brother?" Ultimately though, Jack doesn't "want to be defined by that sequence of accidents" any more than Thomas does, and is ready to "move on", challenging Thomas to a talky stand-off at the end.

"Mojave" is essentially a story of men (literally) confronting their demons - and what better setting to do this than the infinite, rocky plains of the titular Mojave? To quote one of the characters, "You go to the desert to find out what you want, what you are." Don Davis' beautiful cinematography does the film's contemplative mood justice, with its wide shots of moonlit landscapes and close-ups of equally enigmatic, almost-mythical characters.

Oscar Isaac ("Inside Llewyn Davis") is quickly becoming one of the great contemporary actors, elevating "Mojave"'s rougher patches with an utterly commanding presence; all of the scenes involving his Socrates-quoting, existentially mournful and malevolent character mesmerize. "The devil came to me and I said yes," he says, with much conviction. In fact, Isaac shamelessly steals scenes away from Hedlund, who tries his best to carry a minimalist-but-epic story with next-to-no words… or expressions, for that matter. Wahlberg plays as if he just stepped off an "Entourage" set, though he does get some of the film's funniest lines ("I don't need any of you, pieces of shit!" he bellows out the balcony), which provide some relief from Monahan's at-times oppressively heavy narrative.

Yes, we are deep in Monahan world here, inhabited by mean-spirited, lost people, ready to pull the trigger at every whim. Which leads me to some of the film's bigger issues. The highly-stylized, literate-but-overly-poetic dialogue is beautiful if, perhaps, read on a page, but just doesn't ring true when spoken by these characters, especially since it fluctuates between highbrow and ordinary at every twist and turn. "Mojave" therefore comes off as a peculiar blend of a cerebral art film, Hollywood satire, and film noir. Folks seeking to get their fix in any one of those genres are probably going to be left... well, confused. It's as if George Bernard Shaw met Samuel Beckett and decided to write a 1950s-style pulp fiction novel, with a Western twist. Characters remain obscure - albeit fascinating - sketches rather than fully-fleshed out individuals with clear motivations.

"Mojave" does deal with a number of hefty issue, ripe for discussion, such as: appearances vs. intellect, and the effect appearances may have; the meaning of identity, fiction vs. reality, villain vs. hero, and the "duality of man" (Jack: "Do you know yet which one of us is the bad guy?"). It may be off-putting to some, with its brainy approach to a very basic story and jumbling of tones, yet true film connoisseurs will appreciate what it has to offer and overlook most flaws. Looks like Monahan won't be directing for a while - he's listed as the screenwriter on his next 10 slated projects - but "Mojave" certainly shows signs of an oasis for him as a great director.

3.5 out of 5

"Norman" Stumbles but Never Falls on Its Way to Redemption

Synopsis: Norman Oppenheimer is a small time operator who befriends a young politician at a low point in his life. Three years later, when the politician becomes an influential world leader, Norman's life dramatically changes for better and worse.

It's safe to assume there is a powerful creative bond between filmmaker Oren Moverman and actor Richard Gere. Oren co-wrote Todd Haynes' "I'm Not There", where Gere played (one of the versions of) Bob Dylan; he later directed him in the sublime study of homelessness "Time Out of Mind" (read review here) and, more recently, in the social-satire-cum-drama "The Dinner" (read review here). Israeli filmmaker Joseph Cedar's political drama "Norman" (shortened from "Norman: The Moderate Rise and Tragic Fall of a New York Fixer") marks another collaboration between the two, this time Overman assuming a comfortable spot in the producing chair. His trademark visual flair, deft handling of characters, sociopolitical critique and unexpected, beautiful "left turns" are occasionally glimpsed, Gere yet again displays major acting chops and Cedar deserves credit for keeping this at-times unwieldy story flow together as smoothly as it does.

Split into several acts, each one depicting a stage in the titular character's existential trajectory and steeped in Jewish culture - a running thread throughout his career - Cedar's film is, like his previous efforts, both a love letter to his people and a condemnation of his country's turbulent regime and its political leaders. "Norman" marks a fresh, somewhat-lighter approach - just as cynical and scathing, perhaps, but more focused, examining the effect of prioritizing politics and the pursuit of "the greater good" over actual, you know, human beings. The writer/director's at-times overt preaching is now masked under an astute character-study sheen, buoyed by its powerful lead performance.

Norman Oppenheimer (Gere), a self-proclaimed fixer, is perpetually making moves, lingering among the financial and political elite, building connections that go nowhere - until they do. His go-to "inside guys" like Philip (Michael Sheen) and Bill (Dan Stevens) try to avoid being associated with him, but he presses and presses, provoking pity / irritation, until they're backed into a corner. He hunts them down while they're jogging, "bumps" into them at parties, and, in the case of the Israeli Deputy Ministry of Trade and Labor, Eshel (Lior Ashkenazi), goes so far as to follow them through the streets of New York. "You're like a drowning man, trying to wave in an ocean liner," Philip tells Norman. "But I'm a good swimmer," Norman replies.

A gesture of either kindness or self-interest - or both; let's call it "alleged goodwill" - leads to major political ramifications. Norman ends up befriending Eshel, though the basis for their brotherly love remains purposefully dubious throughout. "Three Years and Many Small Favors Later", as the title card announces, Norman is hesitant to meet Eshel, now a political bigwig, at a convention. They reconnect - but then Norman's synagogue falls under the threat of closure - unless he raises millions of dollars. A montage both heartrending and hilarious displays the man desperately going through his network of dismissive bigwigs, including Eshel, trying to make sense of his life by achieving closure. Who is using whom? As Esher's career takes a dive, crucial information is revealed about Norman's background - and then their seemingly disparate storylines get intertwined in the most meticulous of ways. "History is full of anonymous heroes," Eshel tells Norman over the phone towards the end. Perhaps, this gives Norman the closure he so desperately seeks.

Cedar showcases a deft handling of sequences. There is a formidable muted exchange between Norman and Eshel, seen through inside of a store, their body language telling us everything we need to know about the dynamics of their interaction. Norman desperately shoving herring and crackers into his mouth is a sight to behold. The director isn't afraid to spice up his narrative with surreal touches, mirroring his protagonist's journey and the absurd nature of his country's political regime: everyone freezes at a convention, segueing into a visual sequence of Norman going through each potentially-lucrative encounter he'd had in his head on a rainy ride home.

Richard Gere, after a slight stumble with "The Dinner", where he played second fiddle to Steve Coogan's maniacal central character, here gives another "can't-take-your-eyes-off-him" performance. His Norman, always "very happy to introduce" you to someone, is constantly scheming in his beige overcoat, growing more weary and conflicted, his skin flaking from exhaustion. One wishes he shared more scenes with the charismatic Lior Ashkenazi, whose Eshel is self-pitying, "radiating optimism" but internally conflicted. "The shoes I buy today will last longer than the government they're serving," he proclaims dismissively. He wants to go down in history as the leader who ended the conflict - and worse comes to worst, God will be blamed.

As for the rest of the film's impressive cast, Charlotte Gainsbourg stands out in a minor but key role. A scene where she calls Norman at a train station and observes his reaction as they converse, demonstrates what a powerful actress she is: her Alex sees through Norman, and that mixture of compassion, empathy and just a trace of pity is quite a feat to pull off in less than a 20-second shot. "I need the satisfaction of knowing I'm doing good in the world," Alex proposes, the one thing Norman cannot provide.

As for the rest of the cast - Sheen, Stevens, Steve Buscemi as a Rabbi, Hank Azaria - they are unfortunately not given enough room to breathe, delegated to plot requirements. As good as they are, they each also serve a purpose, limited by the director's vision. That same vision gets in the way of a fully-fleshed out story, which is so busy racing towards tying it all together, it meanders between its two leads, never truly gaining raw, jaw-dropping moments of power a film like this requires. It's all entertaining and occasionally quite touching - but also rather inconsequential, the film disappearing from your mind as quickly as Norman's business cards do from most folks' coats. Were it not for the superb ending and its central performance, this would merely be another exercise of a director showing off considerable skills in an otherwise-flat affair (think "The King's Speech").

That said, Norman's gradual and painfully funny climb to success is portrayed with brutal, and brutally hilarious, accuracy. Taking cues from Overman's surreal touches, Cedar's intricately-structured, well-paced script covers hefty subjects like the meaning of friendship / loyalty and personal vs political priorities, clever in the way it's both a character study, a sociopolitical critique of our increasingly disconnected culture and a somewhat-suspenseful Man vs Goliath tale. Cedar continues his streak of explorations of the different facets of Jewish culture and politics through the prism of his (anti) heroes - incisive, sometimes absurd, cynical and unpredictable… sort of like life itself. While Norman's life may resemble a rollercoaster ride of ups and downs, "Norman" is more of a pleasant stroll through New York streets, where a surprise just may lurk around the corner.

3.5 out of 5 stars

Evil Dwarves, Head-Drilling Spheres & Parallel Dimensions: Revisiting Don Coscarelli's Cult Horror Saga "Phantasm I-V"

In the history of horror film sequels, there has never been a phenomenon quite like Don Coscarelli's "Phantasm" series. Three years before Sam Raimi put Bruce Campbell through the C-movie grinder in game-changing "The Evil Dead", the 25-year-old Coscarelli concocted a similarly wild hybrid of exploitation, artistic flourishes (that established both directors as auteurs) and pure dementia: severed wriggling fingers spurting yellow aquarelle, dwarves, parallel dimensions, an enigmatic central antagonist simply known as The Tall Man (played by the recently departed Angus Scrimm with delectable gusto in all five of the films) - oh, and let's not forget those flying Spheres that drill into people's foreheads. Even more so than Raimi's creature feature, it played for both horror and laughs and was utterly surreal in its dream-like narrative, forgoing plot and logic in favor of an atmosphere of dread and otherworldliness. Yet it also had something more going for it: before Spielberg explored sci-fi through the prism of childlike wonder in "E.T.", Coscarelli valiantly strived for a similar perspective: all the events in "Phantasm" unfurl through the eyes of a young teenage boy, Mike (A. Michael Baldwin, a series mainstay), making this horrific, hallucinatory phantasmagoria of gore and acidic flashbacks relatable to young, impressionable boys (such as myself). So, yes, it can be argued that Coscarelli was way ahead of both Raimi (with whom he's allegedly good friends) and Spielberg. The fact that he proceeded to write and produce four increasingly out-there sequels, three of which he directed, makes "Phantasm" a true oddity in the cinematic universe - and one that deserves revisiting.

Made on next-to-no money over a several-year period, the original **"Phantasm" (1979)** feels like the work of a highly ambitious artist finding his footing (and budget), which accounts for the fragmented structure and, one could argue, plays in its favor. Mike's super-groovy, womanizing brother Jody (Bill Thornbury - another reappearing character in the ongoing "Phantasm" cannon) comes to take care of the motorbike-riding kid after their parents' death. Mike spots The Tall Man outside the mortuary, single-handedly picking up a coffin and stuffing it into the back of a hearse. This just adds to Mike's continuous worries that Jody will leave him all alone. The Tall Man starts to haunt poor Mike, both in dreams and reality. A midpoint confrontation with a vicious Sphere, a ballistic Dwarf behind the wheel of a car and the Man himself leaves the brothers no choice but to face off against Evil. This leads them, along with ice-cream-vendor-turned-road-warrior Reggie (Reggie Bannister, yet another member of the "Phantasm" family), into the depths of the mortuary, where they discover a futuristic portal… Well, I'll let you chew on the rest.

"It was little, brown and low to the ground," Mike explains exasperatedly to his brother after his first glimpse of a Dwarf. "It was probably just a gopher in heat," Jody responds with a straight face. Whether intentional or not, "Phantasm" tickles the funny bone as much as the nerves. For every goofy, amateurish or even offensive moment ("I just don't get off on funerals, they give me the creeps" or "You sure it wasn't that retarded kid Timmy up the street?" are just two of the film's dialogue samples) there is a scene that tugs on a nerve. Dealing with themes of adolescent fears, loneliness and curiosity, "Phantasm"'s most memorable for its sustained sense of surreality, of things gone terribly awry deep in the recesses of the sub-conscious, where demons lurk and darkness prevails. The fact that Coscarelli directed, wrote, shot and edited the entire picture renders it that much more impressive. Fred Myron' and Malcolm Seagrave's soundtrack twinkles menacingly like an amalgamation of "The Wicker Man" and "Halloween", with a dash of a phantasmagoric organ-led beat here and there. The marble interior of the mortuary is a memorable piece of set design. And yes, there are 1970's staples: shaggy haircuts, multiple close-ups of female breasts… and a sequence of Jody and Reggie jamming out with their funky guitars. But if you don't find all of this freakin' endearing, as Roger Ebert used to say, "there's no talking to you".

Despite "Phantasm" making a healthy return at the box-office, it wasn't until almost a decade later that Coscarelli mustered up the courage to venture back into the universe he created, backed by Universal. Armed with a much higher budget and a cast revamp, **"Phantasm II" (1988)** sees James Le Gros step into the shoes of the older Mike, with Jody nowhere to be seen, while Reggie and Angus reprised their roles as, well, Reggie and The Tall Man, respectively. Incidentally, Ebert despised "Phantasm"'s sequel. "No character development, logic or subtlety is necessary," the critic wrote in his scathing review, "just a sensation every now and then to provide the impression that something is happening on the screen." That pretty much summarizes the criticism aimed at the film upon its release. Watching it again three decades later, it doesn't quite hold up as much as the first one, despite its higher budget and younger age, but doesn't deserve such scathing backlash either. Funny, because I actually remember liking part two more as a kid.

"Phantasm II" picks up where the original left off: Reggie (looking bafflingly ageless throughout most of the series) battling an army of Dwarves - whose horrific faces we now get to see - in a kitchen. "Burn, you bitches," he says, before storming out of the exploding house, little Mike in tow. They watch The Tall Man drive off in his hearse. Cut to: years later, a grown-up Mike is understandably in therapy. When he and Reggie find out that an entire graveyard is filled with empty coffins, they embark on a quest to find and defeat The Tall Man and - well, whatever his Evil Quest is. Like in the first film, that's all beside the point. Reggie himself says early on, referring to earlier events: "Mike, that wasn't real." The line between reality and fantasy continues to blur here: the two "road warriors" loot a convenience store filled with guns, encounter small towns devastated by The Tall Man and pick up a spunky hitchhiker called Alchemy (Samantha Phillips). Mike's girlfriend Liz (Paula Irvine) gets kidnapped towards the end, so our heroes go inside the mortuary to save her (Reggie: "Let's go and kick some ass"). The Tall Man ends up - spoiler alert! - meeting his gruesome, neon-yellow blood-soaked death…. or does he?

Gone is the childlike perspective - both the protagonists and the director have aged, after all - replaced by a more assured sense of pacing and a more knowing humor, at the expense of joyful bewilderment and an underpinning intoxication with unadulterated insanity. Basked in autumnal colors and different shades of darkness, it does convey the atmosphere more assuredly, and the acting is certainly better. While the highlight of the film is Sphere 2.0 - which has three drills and lasers! - the film isn't short for memorable bits. We get a more thorough glimpse into the "other dimension". There's a nasty suction machine straight out of "Hostel". I love that moment when Liz recognizes her grandma in one of the Dwarves. The funniest sex scene this side of "Bride of Chucky" is followed by a witty Sam Raimi gag - and there's the batshit crazy sequence that puts the recent "spine burst" of "Alien: Covenant" to shame. Unfortunately, despite making its budget back, part two failed to ignite a fire as widespread as its predecessor's, sending the consequent chapters into the murkier depths of straight-to-video fare.

Six years later came **Phantasm III: "Lord of the Dead" (1994)**. Sporting ludicrous key art that doesn't do the film justice, part three reunites series regulars A. Michael Baldwin and Bill Thornbury, albeit - and thankfully - briefly. A back-from-the-dead Jody shows up nonchalantly, the brothers get kidnapped by The Tall Man and don't reappear again until the grisly finale. In the meantime, Reggie takes off with Tim (Kevin Connors), the most violent kid this side of Damien (whom we meet in an uproarious "Home Alone" send-up) to save them. The fastest-moving and most inventive of the bunch, Coscarelli inspired by the previous entry's box-office failure, "PIIILOTD" delves head-first into maniacally preposterous territory. Spheres 3.0 are now sentient, with brains and eyeballs and a nasty tendency to emerge out of demons' skulls. At one point, a zombie's head spins so wildly it literally pops off, which I think was the effect the filmmaker wanted his film to have on audiences. The zinger-filled third part may lack the first one's enigmatic, rugged appeal or the sequel's assured pacing and high aspirations, but "Lord of the Dead" makes up for it in plain outrageousness and obvious glee of its creators. Reggie summarizes the entire "Phantasm" universe perfectly when, after Rocky (Gloria Lynne Henry), a black female ex-Army ninja warrior with nun chucks (!) demands, "What the fuck was that?", his nonchalant response is, "That… kinda hard to explain."

This brings me to **Phantasm IV: Oblivion (1998)**, which sees Coscarelli return to his ultra-low-budget roots, stretching out the running time with clumsily-interwoven flashbacks to previous entries and unused footage from the original film. This time, Reggie embarks on a Mission to rescue Mike, who himself is on a Mission to destroy The Tall Man (you may have noticed that Quests and Missions form the backbone of "Phantasm"). Attempting to tap into fans' love for the series, Coscarelli puts the frankly lackluster A. Michael Baldwin front and center, his Mike spending the entire first third of the film tripping out while driving a hearse to Death Valley, and the rest of it hopping through time and space in said valley. There are random Civil War flashbacks. Spheres 4.0 now come in hordes - though much more rarely - and emerge out of female breasts. The womanizing, ponytail-sporting, wisecracking Reggie proves yet again that he's the most compelling actor of the bunch, but he's given little to do. I counted exactly two standout moments: one involves a face-off between Reggie and a zombie cop, and the other sees Mike randomly go back in time to encounter The Tall Man… before he became The Tall Man. Otherwise, the "Phantasm" Sphere is running on empty… which didn't stop David Hartman to take over the directing reigns from Coscarelli on **"Phantasm: Ravager" (2016)** (though Don remained on board as a co-writer and producer).

Known for his work on the animated "Transformers" and "Tigger & Pooh" series (his filmography is rather eclectic), Hartman boldly took cues from his mentor and shot/produced/wrote/directed/edited "Ravager" - all on his abacus, by the looks of it. Reggie escapes from a bunch of Spheres in his car, before embarking on another vague quest through at least two timelines. As old Reggie wrestles with dementia and confides in Mike at a mental institution, a younger Reggie (the actor has aged remarkably well in four decades) encounters a very old Tall Man, before teaming up with a sardonic little person called Chunk (Stephen Jutras) to kick some ass. The film attempts to take the whole myth to an epic, apocalyptic level. The effects are pitiful: Spheres 5.0 somehow manage to look worse than all the ones preceding them, this time attacking horses and blowing up to gargantuan, city-demolishing sizes. Dialogue that was once knowingly stupid is now just plain redundant: Mike: "Everything is different. Nothing is the same." Hartman's "odyssey" amounts to little more than non-stop, confusing exposition. Were it not for the touching ending, it would be a next to worthless addition to the "Phantasm" saga.

Part of "Phantasm"'s appeal is its rugged charm and naivety, as if it were unaware of its own flaws. Another is its "fever dream"-like ambience; through the hazy fog of almost Dali-esque absurdity, themes of childhood paranoia, family (it's as much about the importance of family as "The Fast & The Furious" saga wants to be) and rumination on quantum physics emerge. But let's face it, at the end of the day, it's just a fun ride, a glimpse inside the schizoid mind of a borderline-brilliant auteur. Coscarelli's opus may not have the mass cult status of horror series like "Halloween" or "Friday the 13th", but the man, along with his devoted cast and crew, carved out a niche of his own, with a small but rabid fan base. Despite the diminishing returns there's a continuous, contagious sense of joy and love for its characters. Coscarelli has done other work: the trippy 1982 oddity "The Beastmaster", the "Elvis-meets-Mummy" horror comedy "Bubba Ho-Tep" and the spaced-out nightmare "John Dies at the End" - but his legacy will forever remain as the Tall Man behind the "Phantasm" series.

Phantasm - 3.5 stars
Phantasm II - 3.5 stars
Phantasm III: Lord of the Dead - 3.5 stars
Phantasm IV: Oblivion - 2.5 stars
Phantasm: Ravager - 2 stars

Overall Collection Score: 3.5 out of 5 stars

Werner Herzog's Quintessential Dementia Gets Slightly Watered-Down in "Salt and Fire"

Synopsis: *A scientist blames the head of a large company for an ecological disaster in South America. But when a volcano begins to show signs of erupting, they must unite to avoid a disaster.*

A few weeks ago, I had the privilege of speaking with one of the greatest directors of all time, Mr. Werner Herzog, at a special screening of his stunning doc, "Cave of Forgotten Dreams". We talked about "beautiful melancholy", the future of humanity, and how his films may, like the titular cave, eventually become chronicles of our own forgotten dreams. He confessed that he will keep making films until he's taken away in a straight jacket; I told him, as long as he documents his own demise... Made him laugh - and made my month.

There's no denying the director's legendary status. From 1972's almost-wordless "Aguirre, the Wrath of God", which follows a Spanish conquistador - played by Klaus Kinski, with whom the director had a tumultuous relationship, later depicted in the 1999 doc "My Best Fiend" - through the Amazonian jungle, to the remote icebergs of the stunning 2007 documentary "Encounters at the End of the World," Herzog has consistently churned out audacious studies of humans pushed to the very edge of sanity. Himself a provocateur and renowned prankster, as well as a philosopher and prophet, Herzog casts a unique outlook that's both wondrous and pessimistic, lyrical and pragmatic - and at times, very, very funny. Though lately his focus has been primarily on documentaries, an occasional detour - a feature film or a bizarre acting choice (e.g. the villain in "Jack Reacher") - tends to pop up in the fascinating man's vast filmography.

The latest one marks Herzog's second collaboration with Michael Shannon, after 2009's bonkers drama "My Son, My Son, What Have Ye Done". At least on paper, it's the definition of a match made in heaven: an eloquent-but-unhinged director and one of the most intense actors working today (I mean, Shannon made his scenes in freakin' "Man of Steel" resonate with a subliminal dread). "Salt and Fire", however, is not quite on that "Herzog/Kinski" level of pure cinematic lunacy, of controlled chaos. Rather tame by the helmer's standards, this environmental drama/thriller seems to be at conflict with itself, as exemplified by its two wildly disparate - both narratively and tonally - halves.

A brief intro sees Laura (Veronica Ferres), a United Nations professor, captured by a group of accommodating masked terrorists, who take off her handcuffs and offer her tea. The film flashbacks to Laura traveling to South America with her colleagues: creepy Fabio (Gael Garcia Bernal) and stoic Dr. Meyer (Volker Michalowski). They're a delegation, on a mission to study an "ecological disaster" - the enigmatic Diablo Blanco, which "will soon be a household name".

Before she can say "chlorobenzene", Laura and her team are abducted by a mysterious, terrorist-like group of masked men, led by Matt Riley (Michael Shannon), the "CEO of a Consortium" and a "prisoner of his own plans". Matt's goals are hazy; he tells Laura that "there's no reality, only views and perceptions". They proceed to engage in prolonged conversations that touch upon subjects of art, the search for identity, family ("having children invites tragedy") - until she is whisked away to the second half of the film, where the tone abruptly changes.

Matt reveals that the Matt - sorry - man made effects on the environment may soon be overshadowed by the apocalyptic threat of Nature Itself - a nearby gigantic volcano that could erupt at any moment ("Here lies a monster on the verge of waking."). He then drops Laura off in the middle of nowhere with two little blind boys, as an endurance test of sorts - and an astonishing sequence of spiritual transformation follows, reveling in silences: just Laura, the kids, and eternity itself. Though the film's anticlimactic conclusion is so earnest it verges on preposterous, the final shot, bringing to mind Voyager 1, exploring space millions of miles away, lingers long after the credits roll.

Filled with non-sequiturs (e.g. a character exclaims, "I forgot my toothbrush!" at an odd moment), the film itself resembles a non-sequitur in Herzog's career. It seems to have several aims: to steadily build tension, to be an existential parable, to tackle hefty issues of environmental pollution and natural disasters… As a whole, it never quite gels - there's never a real threat, the evil guys switching between physically hurting their prisoners and allowing them to take pictures on their iPads - nor does the thoughtful, haiku-like second half ever truly coalesce with the action-y first.

This is the kind of film where a flight attendant (Anita Briem) politely inquires, "And what, if I may ask, is your joyful party all about?" Fabio describes the line at the airport as "listless, torpid, moribund…" At another point, he exclaims, "There is a horde of protozoea running around my intestinal tract!" The wheelchair-bound Krauss (Lawrence Krauss), one of Matt's henchmen, gets all the best lines, which must be heard to be believed (okay, here's one: "I only use the wheelchair when I'm tired of life."). Alexander the Great, Nostradamus and Eclesiastés are all quoted in abundance. As literate as it is, the dialogue comes off as over-written, a bit clunky, partially due to the some of the actors' delivery.

That's not to say the film isn't filled with wondrous little moments. An abandoned "alien train" sequence is almost trance-inducing, as is the stunning cinematography by Herzog's regular DP, Peter Zeitlinger. His shots of vast salt fields, consuming our Earth at a rapid pace, scored to Ernst Reijseger's uncanny, tormented music, will sear themselves into your heads. Under Herzog's ambitious direction, this would-be eco-thriller morphs into a somewhat-muddled, unintentionally funny, but endlessly watchable rumination on humanity, and how we are overshadowed by the sheer power of nature, retaliating against us.

Shannon is unhinged, delivering lines like "'We' is basically 'me'", or "I bow to you" with much fervor and conviction. Ferres has a forceful presence, tall and determined and beautiful. Her moment to truly shine comes in the film's second, melancholic half. Bernal is barely there at all, playing a weasel - the actor probably leaped at the opportunity to list Herzog amongst the greats he's worked with, no matter how small the part.

Whatever the film's flaws may be, they are spawned from ambition and a need to express intimate statements by one of our living legends - and that by itself is worth acknowledging. "Salt and Fire" marks another volcanic fusion of two major contemporary cinema icons, with mixed but never-less-than-entertaining results. "It's okay to be afraid of the dark," a character says. "But the real tragedy in life is when men are afraid of the light." Herzog is one of the brave cinematic souls to wholeheartedly embrace the light.

P.S. For those of you interested in exploring Mr. Herzog's riveting body of work, here's my personal "Top 5 List", which may not fully reflect the artist's scope, but will surely provide a proper introduction to his magnificently oddball fare:

1. "Stroszek" (1977) - an underrated, hilarious critique of the American Dream, and a great entry point.
2. "Fitzcarraldo" (1982) - Herzog makes Kinski drag a giant ship into a jungle; need I say more?
3. "Grizzly Man" (2005) - perhaps the director's best, most minimalist, poignant and multidimensional doc.
4. "Rescue Dawn" (2006) - teaming up with Christian Bale to tell a real-life story of a captured U.S. fighter pilot in Vietnam, it sees Herzog at the peak of his "man vs. himself" mode.

5. "Encounters at the End of the World" (2009) - while "Grizzly Man" may be the "best", this one's my favorite - a nature doc, seen through Herzog's existential prism ("Is there such a thing as insanity in a penguin?").

3.5 out of 5 stars

INTERVIEW WITH VERONICA FERRES

What drew you to the role of Laura?
I've been wanting to work with Werner since I was studying in the university. I saw "Fitzcarraldo", and it had such a strong impact on my life. The relationship of its characters to nature and the power of your own greed [affected me]. Werner Herzog made me become an actor and after I saw "Fitzcarraldo" I wanted to become [a Herzog] character. Being an actor is nothing more than being a storyteller. Since then I've done 90 movies and 20 English-language films. Two-and-a-half years ago I was traveling, it was a domestic flight, and I saw Werner Herzog and his wife sitting in the first row. The day before this flight, I started reading one of his novels called "Walking on Ice." I thought it would be great if he could give me an autograph. I was shy, I thought, "I can't do that, I'm not a groupie!" Finally, I came up to him, I said, "Mr. Herzog, my name is Veronica Ferres..." And he said, "I know who you are." And he gave me this autograph. Two months later he called me and he said, "I wrote a feature film for you. It's a lead part. Do you want to be in it? Do you want to read it? What's your email?" I said, "Sure I want to read it!" - so I was reading it the same night. We started shooting a couple of months later, in Bolivia, 16,000 feet of altitude. No civilization, no internet, no TV, no Wi-Fi - nothing. Just the altitude and the incredible beauty of nature. It was quite a physical and emotional challenge.

Tell me a little bit about what it's like, working with the great Werner Herzog.
He treats actors like kings and queens. He loves actors. [He has] a very strong vision about his film and about every scene. You work under pressure - only one or two takes. He loves that pressure on actors, you really have to be focused and deliver the best you can. It was an incredible time in my life, a beautiful time. We had no distractions. At night, we were so close to the stars, and felt so close to God, to Creation. It was really breathtaking - and exhausting! [laughs] When you wake up in the morning, Werner wants you in front of the camera. He didn't want any make-up, nothing.

"Salt and Fire" is split into two quite different parts - the action-filled, talky first, followed by a sort of quiet spiritual awakening, with you and the children alone in the desert. Can you talk about that disparity?
For me, as an actor, it was just an incredible way of working. The first half of the movie I worked with one of the most talented actors in the world, Michael Shannon. Working on a very high, professional level. I also worked with two non-actors, two blind boys. They really were blind, they only

had a visibility of 5%. I couldn't speak their language, they couldn't speak my language. We had no way to communicate except our voices and body language. Using my hands - touching them, guiding them, holding them.

What Werner created there was that they were two little boys who lost their mother and kind of become attracted to this woman, whom they don't really know and cannot see. At night they are hugging and cuddling, as if they [have known] each other for decades. She feels responsible and wants to protect them from the danger of the desert. They don't know if they are going to die or survive in those next couple of days.

The day before yesterday, Trump changed the laws about protecting the environment. A movie like that will show, very emotionally and with a lot of poetry, what disrespectful behavior does to our environment. One of the reasons [Michael Shannon's character] is taking us hostage is because [his viewpoint is], "You should feel how it feels for local people, like us, what an ecological disaster does to you. I lost my wife, the mother of those kids, now they are blind, and I have to live with that every day." She could be a scientist and only do her measurements, but he wants her to be a voice for the rest of the world, because he made her really feel the loneliness and the sadness of the result of the ecological disaster. I think it's very modern.

Finally, what do you think will resonate with contemporary audiences?

I think it's a very unusual movie. Nothing is predictable. It's a thriller, it's about nature, it's about love. Michael Shannon is at his best. It's a typical Werner Herzog movie - unpredictable! The beauty of nature is breathtaking. I've never seen that before in my life. It touches upon our emotions and talks about disrespectful behavior to nature.

"T-Rex" Stomps Its Way to a Cinematic Bronze Medal

Synopsis: 17-year-old Claressa 'T-Rex' Shields dreams of being the first woman in history to win a gold medal in Olympic boxing. But in order for her to succeed, she'll need to stand her ground both inside and outside the ring.

Rather incredulously, 2012 marked the first time women's boxing was included in the Olympics. Even more incredulously, a teeny-tiny number of films cover the subject of female boxing (the sappy, overrated "Million Dollar Baby" comes to mind, as well as the "just okay" "Girlfight", and a film I distributed while working for Vision Films, Jill Morley's ambitious little doc, "Fight Like A Girl"). Directors' Zackary Canepari and Drea Cooper's latest real-life account of a young girl's struggle to get an Olympic gold medal is a commendable addition to the small sub-genre of female boxing films, but does little to renovate the genre itself, coasting along on the strengths of its protagonist and undeniably winsome underdog storyline.

Early on, we see Claressa, discouraged and inconsolable after a tournament. The 17-year-old narrates about dreaming of being in the Olympics: "In my dream, I'd be looking around and thinking to myself, 'how did I get here?'" Undefeated, with a record of 24-0, she knocks her opponents out on the ring, her approach relentless, aggressive. The titles announce: "She must win her next tournament in China to qualify for the Olympics."

We follow her through the six-month arduous training, also delving into Claressa's underprivileged background in Flint, Michigan (fun fact: also the birthplace of celebrity documentarian Michael Moore). Raised by an alcoholic, abusive - but loving - mother and an incarcerated father (as well as what seems like a series of, AHEM, "stand-up" individuals), Claressa didn't let those challenges affect her, and Canepari/Cooper's documentary examines her origins-to-success trajectory, with occasional slips into banality.

The film goes from Michigan to China to England, following Claressa's journey, with several great insider shots of what it's like to actually be a part of the Olympics. There are many standout moments. Due to lack of funding, Claressa cannot take her beloved coach Jason with her to China and has to work with a team of USA boxing coaches, which leads to a poignant series of phone conversations over the phone. When she loses a match, her palpable disappointment is heart-shredding. The finale is suitably enthralling, an ambiguous note. In fact, the film's most resonant line comes from the coach at the end: "Only in America. Won a gold medal and still gotta work. If she were a man, we'd be rich right now."

My favorite moment, however, comes from a scene outside the ring, involving Claressa's sister. During an interview at her house, the 14-year-old gets interrupted by her mother's boyfriend, who, after listening to her honest admittance that she wants to "get away from all these lowlifes", accuses her of doing nothing but smoking weed all day. Her response? "And you a crackhead, bitch!" The mother quickly steps in, "Now don't you start…" A pause hangs in the air. "Fuckin' pervert," the girl mumbles, then snaps back to it. "Anyways, like I was sayin'…" That's reality, right there, folks. It's a darkly funny, sad and humbling moment - a subtle and endearing call to action.

Weighing 165 pounds, all pure muscle and stringent focus, Claressa is a sight to behold. Determined, passionate, candid and strong-as-hell, the young athlete will stop at nothing to get to that medal. "Every Friday, when everyone was going to a party, I was down [at the gym]," she says. "It made me feel important." She delivers another memorable line later on: "My goal, before boxing, was to have 10 kids before I was 26." After a win in London, when her coach tells her they'll meet her on the train, she declares, "That's low class. I'm a celebrity now." At the end, she summarizes the film: "Respect me as being a woman, respect me as being black, respect me as being an athlete who represented the United States!"

The story's predictable structure is a given (just like most real-life underdog sports dramas), but the stylistic choices the directors implement are merely functional as opposed to groundbreaking. This simplicity works for the most part, as the story is interesting, but I did wish for a more thrilling pace, more unexpected shots and generally more novelty. This is no Werner Herzog. "T-Rex" is not deeply psychological. It's a bit repetitive (she wants to win and she'll stop at nothing, we get it, what else?). The bigger picture - Claressa's socioeconomic background and proposed methods to fight it - is barely touched upon, and the whole issue of female boxing JUST becoming relevant is left largely unexplored.

Perhaps that was the filmmakers' point - to just focus on Claressa during this journey, and nothing else -but it leaves one craving more. That said, the training / fighting scenes are invigorating, well-staged and edited throughout. The documentary definitely makes a strong point for the power of perseverance, achieving your dreams, and contains moments of genuine suspense. A young, black woman literally boxes her way to the heights of success, fighting - perhaps unknowingly - against the society that ostracized her. Add to that the fact that you can count the number of films about female boxers on one hand, and you got a worthy little cinematic achievement here. Kudos to the filmmakers - and especially Claressa - for setting an example, for all of us.

3.5 out of 5 stars

"Tab Hunter Confidential" Flings Open the Doors of a Closet, Revealing a Hollywood Icon Behind Them

Synopsis: *The story of matinee idol Tab Hunter from teenage stable boy to closeted Hollywood star of the 1950s.*

The Coen Brothers recently touched upon the persecution of homosexuals after the Cold War in their black comedy "Hail, Caesar!". Closeted gay actors, such as Tab Hunter and Rock Hudson, found refuge in Hollywood, the duality of being an actor arguably helping them deal with their double identities. (Hobie Doyle, as hilariously played by Alden Ehrenreich in the Coens' film, even somewhat resembles a young, naive and inexperienced Tab.)

Director Jeffrey Schwarz's documentary, "Tab Hunter Confidential", delves deep into the story of the titular 1950s icon, who, despite his sexual orientation, overcame a slew of obstacles and paved himself a lasting career in Hollywood. A heartthrob, Tab appeared in dozens of commercials and films, such as "The Burning Hills" with Natalie Wood, "That Kind of Woman" with Sophia Loren and "Damn Yankees!" with Broadway star Gwen Verdon. It's an inspiring - albeit somewhat run-of-the-mill and unfocused - story of resilience and the pursuit of dreams against all odds.

The doc starts off intriguingly, resembling a film noir: "Los Angeles, CA, October 14, 1950", the credits announce. Tab remembers being arrested at a gay party. "What would my mother think?" was the first terrifying thought that came to Tab's mind. "Will it affect this career I'm trying to get started in motion pictures?"

Born Arthur Andrew Kelm, raised by a single mother, whose abusive husband left the family when Tab was a young boy, Tab grew up feeling "lost in many ways - introverted… and extremely shy." His sole escape was the cool darkness of a movie theater, where he sat mesmerized by the moving pictures on the silver screen. The term "gay" didn't yet exist, people referring to homosexuals derogatorily as "fairies and queers". Tab readily admits that he may have called someone those names himself back then, "not wanting to be different."

The girls adored him at school, but all the attention made him seek solace in the Coast Guard and, when that didn't work out, horses (as in, horseback riding, etc., for those of you thrown off). His reputation as a "chick-magnet" followed him into Hollywood, where he signed a deal with the legendary agent Henry Wilson, who tended to "take the pretty boys". Good-looking, talented, popular, Tab, in the words of one of the interviewees, "had the star quality and he had the X-factor."

Then came the promotional tours with Natalie Wood, with "thousands and thousands" of adoring baby boomers, along with Tab's recording career (his hit single "Young Love" hit #1 on the pop charts). The "Tab-Hunter-ytus" disease spread through the nation, the young actor at the apex of his professional career.

The irony, of course, was that, unbeknownst to the public (at least, at first), it was all a show for Tab, a fake identity he created for himself. His first real relationship with a figure-skater apparently only spread amongst vehement, bigoted ice-skaters, somehow never reaching the mass media (I guess those were the 1950s…). "I had the ability to live behind this wall," Tab says, and it summarizes the juxtaposition of him relishing the fame, while painfully hiding his true self from his adoring fan base. "You were rewarded for pretending to be someone you're not," he says.

Until, that is, an article surfaced, which led to a rapid studio cover-up and forced romances with the likes of "Lafayette Escadrille" co-star, the gorgeous Etchika Choureau. "I think it was a soul-searching period of time about his sexuality," the actress reminisces. "It must have been very painful for him. You know, actors always have two faces." A tumultuous romance with Tony Perkins followed, along with acting for directors such as Sidney Lumet and John Frankenheimer - and, of course, "Gunman's Walk", which he proudly calls his "best work as an actor".

Soon after, he left Warner Brothers - a self-proclaimed "career suicide" - and a young lookalike Troy Donahue began to replace him. A swiftly sinking career led to a comedy show Tab refers to as "bottom of the barrel" - "The Tab Hunter Show". He then returned to his beloved horses, reconnected with his roots, got into a long-term relationship, and revitalized his career via John Waters' scandalous cult classic "Polyester".

"Tab Hunter Confidential" feels bit disjointed, careening from the whole "ice-skater bigotry" issue, to the intensely dark story of Tab committing his mother to a mental institution, to becoming a commentary on Hollywood's recycling of actors, to Tab's relationship with God… Despite all those stories and themes, the film never truly delves deep into Tab himself. His inner turmoil is touched upon but never really scrutinized. I'm sure there were some dark, dark demons with which he had to deal. The entire film is about torn identity, but this notion is not thoroughly explored.

The same applies to Tad's relationship with his mother, or him aspiring to be like his brother - and consequently dealing with Walt's death in Vietnam ("I really looked up to him so much," is about as deep as this film ventures.) I wish the film focused on one or two of those potentially jaw-dropping and heart-shredding aspects of Tad's life, instead of piling them all at once. That said, it does make for a fascinating "best of" kind of story, akin to flipping through Tad's album, with some little footnotes and flourishes here and there.

The documentary is chockfull of anecdotes, from how Tab got his fake name and his early struggles as an actor (his mother's reaction to Tab's first big film: "You were lousy!"), to his ascension to the upper echelons of the Hollywood elite. (After a publicity event, Natalie Wood would go out the back door and see Dennis Hopper, while Tab would go see Tony Perkins). Yet the film never truly transcends the pitfalls of a biography. It sometimes feels and looks like a PBS special, with its talking heads, archival footage and an overarching theme - that of acceptance and "being who you are" - that's highly commendable, but lacking the substance of groundbreaking films that dealt with similar subjects (see: "The Celluloid Closet", "Paris Is Burning", "How to Survive a Plague", "The Times of Harvey Milk", "Stonewall Uprising", "Vito" and the harrowing "Paragraph 175"). That said, those previously unaware of Hunter's life and career should enjoy - though perhaps not LOVE - the film as much as the cinefiles among us. A bit dry in places, it does tell a good story… with 10-15 minutes that could have been left on the chopping room floor.

Hollywood icons, such as John Waters, Robert Wagner and George Takei, all contribute curious-to-fascinating tidbits (Takei, laughing: "In every picture, [Tab] managed to take his shirt off! […] He was the embodiment of youthful American masculinity."). But the highlight and the centerpiece is, of course, Hunter himself - a droll, nostalgic, intelligent and passionate man, whose indelible career has been tarnished by the secret he's been harboring most of his life. "It's been difficult for me my whole life to talk about that side of me," he says. "I was always told: If there's something bad, push it from your mind. So I never confronted those things, even though [they] were there, and [they] were very powerful."

Amongst other memorable snippets, my favorite is: "Girls were very attracted to me and it made me extremely uncomfortable." It's good to see Tab let loose. His by turns wistful, witty and laid-back nature gives us hope - false as it may be - that times of such bigotry will soon be left entirely in the past.

3.5 out of 5 stars

"The BFG" is 100% Spielberg, for Better or Worse

Synopsis: *A girl named Sophie encounters the Big Friendly Giant who, despite his intimidating appearance, turns out to be a kindhearted soul who is considered an outcast by the other giants because, unlike them, he refuses to eat children.*

"It was the witching hour." That's the opening line of narration in Steven Spielberg's adaptation of Roald Dahl's beloved classic novel "The BFG". It's a fitting one, for the cinematic fable is both as dark and wondrous as its source. Many directors have brought the children's author's wonderfully odd books to the silver screen, with mixed results. The latest one from the man behind the awe-inspiring "Jaws", "E.T.", "Jurassic Park", "Schindler's List" and "A.I." falls in the "above average Dahl visualizations" category.

I touched upon the director's ability to create pure magic in my review of "The Bridge of Spies" (read it here). A mix of old-fashioned entertainment and futuristic special effects, "The BFG" harks back to the glory days of Spielberg's groundbreaking features, but rarely truly breaks new ground itself - except, perhaps, in the motion-capture technology it utilizes.

The opening narration comes from Sophie (Ruby Barnhill), a determined, book-smart troublemaker living in a London orphanage. "Don't 'little missy' me," she snaps back at a bunch of hooligans, sending them scurrying into the foggy, cobblestone darkness of the city. As with all the children protagonists in Spielberg films, underneath the veneer of confidence Sophie is lost and vulnerable. "Never get out of bed, never go to the window and never look behind the curtain," she chants, terrified and alone. Of course, she does, spotting the titular giant (an impressively digital Mark Rylance), wandering the shadowy streets.

This leads to a jaw-dropping sequence, shot from Sophie's POV, of the BFG kidnapping her, maneuvering and masquerading himself through London, and then hopping across vast plains and rocky terrains, to a mythical land called Giant Country. Those three or so minutes are magnificent; pure "can't-take-your-eyes-off-the-screen" Spielberg.

Sophie promptly realizes that the BFG is harmless and simply doesn't want the word to spread among the humans about the giants' existence. Yes, there are many giants that populate Giant Country - though only six or seven are featured - all of whom are evil, dumb and much larger than our softie hero. They roam the land, interacting in a very Dahl-esque language that includes phrases like "trouble humper", "bugs winkles" and "wiz poppers" (I'll let you discover what that last one stands for - to quote the BFG, they are signs "of true happiness").

The giants seem to spend the majority of their time sleeping under blanket-like layers of grass and violently harassing the BFG, literally using him as a football for their amusement. He therefore hides inside his workshop - for he is a dreamcatcher, you see, storing dreams inside colorful jars, which bring to mind the vibrant, sublime emotions of "Inside Out". When Sophie, the lil' hellion that she is, tries to escape, assuring the BFG that she is "an untrustworthy child", he plants a nightmare into her head from one of his jars to scare her into staying. The way the BFG sees it, Sophie will live there with him, "for the rest of our lives". "You mean my life," she corrects him brashly. " I *will* run away." Of course, she doesn't, they bond, embark on numerous adventures, separate, and (spoiler alert) end up at the Queen's Palace.

The film is filled with visual splendor, courtesy of Spielberg's prodigy cinematographer, Janusz Kaminski. One standout sequence involves Sophie and the BFG visiting the Dream Country, where a Tree of Life (Dreams?) grows both up and down under the Aurora Borealis sky, with firefly dreams surrounding it, all birthed by its ethereal leaves. Another stunning display of the Maestro's skills can be observed in a beautifully-rendered sequence of a little boy's visualized dream - the director himself, as a child, dreaming up motion pictures in his head.

And - I have to mention it - there's a flatulence joke (the title may as well stand for Big Farting Giant) that at first grates, but then ends up being the set-up for a later scene that takes "breaking wind" to such an extreme, it becomes funny... sort of. After the non-stop farting of "Swiss Army Man", and now this, I think I've had my fill of cinematic, um, gastric gases for the week.

There are gripes: the story is highly predictable, especially the giant's "tragic" backstory. Dull stretches slow an already-thin plot; this film could have made for a five-star 95-minute roller-coaster ride, but Spielberg bloats it with unnecessary sentiment and sweltering music to almost two hours. Ruby Barnhill is fine but unremarkable in the lead (Haley Joel Osmond absolutely OWNED "A.I."); perhaps she's yet to gain the charisma/experience to carry a film. The rest of the giants, whose names include Fleshlumpeater (Jemaine Clement) and Bloodbottler (Bill Hader), sort of blend together, and their world is never truly fleshed out. Worry not though, Mark Rylance is there to make up for most of those flaws.

Rylance, in his second collaboration with Spielberg after the aforementioned "Bridge of Spies" (which deservedly bagged him an Academy Award for Best Supporting Actor last year), shines beneath all the pixels, making you (mostly) forget about the whole "uncanny valley" thing (though it's still there, gobblesmoockle it, and it's creepy). By-turns rambling, uneducated, gentle and eager, the BFG is one of the only truly developed CGI characters (yes, yes, I know, Gollum), and all kudos go to Rylance for imbuing him with so much warmth and range.

Spielberg's film stays true to the spirit of the book: it's cozy, with laudable themes of friendship, a childlike naivety, and just enough visual wonder, muscular direction and prescient acting to keep the parents invested. "The BFG" is a few notches above Tim Burton's schlocky Dahl adaptation "Charlie and the Chocolate Factory", yet a few below Nicolas Roeg's terrifying - and arguably truest vision of Dahl's twisted world - "The Witches". Stuffed with visual gags, slapstick, both subtlety and "in-your-face" sentiment, it's exactly what you would expect from the director these days. Oh, and as for the nonsensical bits, to quote the great author himself: "A little nonsense now and then, is cherished by the wisest men."

3.5 out of 5 stars

Warning: Oren Moverman's Heartrending Drama "The Dinner" May Cause Appetite Loss

Synopsis: A look at how far parents will go to protect their children. Feature film based on a novel by Herman Koch.

"How much do you know?" - Laura Linney, "The Dinner"

That's the central question of director Oren Moverman's latest exploration of class separation and human ethics. How much do you know your brother, your wife, your children? How much do you know about the poor, the privileged and wealthy? "The Dinner"'s selfish characters' priorities, their morals and ethics, are distorted, reflecting the worst tendencies in all of us. Reuniting with Richard Gere after directing him in the sublime "Time Out of Mind" (read the review here), Moverman structures the less-successful but ambitious film like a chamber-piece-cum-mystery-thriller, under the guise of a talky drama. "The Dinner" takes its time unfolding, peeling off layer after layer of tinted glass until a picture crystallizes… only you may want to avert your eyes.

After a startling opening, which cuts from ambient images to a hip-hop-scored sequence of youth partying, we meet history professor and writer Paul Lohman (Steve Coogan), by listening in on his borderline-demented thoughts. Acerbic and hateful, Paul doesn't want to go to THE dinner and "meet these apes", yet his wife Claire (Laura Linney) insists - it's a very exclusive restaurant, after all. "These apes" turn out to be his brother, congressman Stan Lohman (Gere), who's running for governor, and his loyal wife Katelyn (Rebecca Hall). The restaurant is indeed quite exquisite, gold-plated columns and all - though their first table ends up too noisy and they switch to a quieter room. Character backgrounds unravel, as they all dance around the tense, "real reason" why they are here - their sons, and something awful they did.

Split into six roughly 20-minute sections - Aperitif, Appetizer, Main Course, Dessert and Digestif - the film's structure mirrors the Lohmans' meal, described in great detail by their waiter, Dylan (Michael Chernus). Frequent flashbacks interrupt the dinner to show us the lead-up: sons Michael (Charlie Plummer) and Rick (Seamus Davey-Fitzpatrick) committing the horrific act, as well as Michael's troubled upbringing and the Lohmans' consequent handling of the issue. Moverman's trademark themes of elitism vs idealism, societal clashes, parenthood, familial resentment, deep trauma / mental illness and homelessness - are on full display: Paul, obsessed with Gettysburg and all things war, believes in shedding blood for the greater good, while Stan may be willing to sacrifice his own future to do what's morally right.

Coogan has long since shifted gear from his comedic Alan Partridge persona, and here displays a range only hinted at before. By turns bitter, sarcastic, morose, self-loathing, literate, his character has no filter. When they toast to their wives and children at the start of the catastrophic dinner, he drily adds, "To getting through this dinner in one piece." He is resentful of his brother but proud of his work; he loves his kids but happens to be a terrible father… Does his wife's sickness haunt him, the guilt preventing him from drawing boundaries for his son?

Laura Linney is incapable of delivering a bad performance and here again is the epitome of calm and class, counterbalancing her husband, at one point literally preventing him from slapping himself. Yet an unraveling corrosiveness is lurking underneath that tranquil exterior, a blissful ignorance bordering on pure evil. Gere and Hall get smaller, less meaty role, but still shine, the former's Stan insecure underneath all that composure, and the latter's Katelyn a bubble about to burst. Since I'm discussing acting, I have to give a special shout-out to the great Michael Chernus in the small-but-crucial (and very funny) role as Dylan Heinz, the waiter.

Moverman knows his way around a scene. "The Dinner" may not be greater than the sum of its parts, but what parts they are! Katelyn prematurely joins Paul and Claire at the dinner table and makes awkward conversation, as her popular husband shakes hands with everyone inside ("Sometimes it's very hard to avoid people.") Coogan reads about the Gettysburg weapons, his focused, dark thoughts barely audible, blending in with a hilariously light dialogue (interestingly, Moverman does venture into that Altman-esque voice overlap thing quite frequently here). An exchange outside the restaurant between Paul and his son ends with Michael telling his dad to "shut the fuck up" and calling him a "fucking child". Another memorable sequence has Paul screaming, "May I please have your fucking attention?" at his class, before proceeding to talk about their miserable lives and the importance of wars.

"The Dinner" is so filled with so many biting exchanges, it at times makes you feel like you're having dinner with your own relatives, albeit a highly intense one. "I love you too, I really do," Paul says blankly to his wife. "It's pretty much unbearable." He goes on later, describing his scrumptious meal: "You taste the war and plagues and fire-bombings, lightly dressed with a drizzle of famine, polished off with some volcanic eruptions." There is a car scene that stuck out to me. Stan and Paul sit there, sharing a rare relatively-peaceful moment with each other. "There's no shame in getting help, Paul," Stan says, to which Paul retorts, "there's help in getting shame." "Am I causing you shame?" Stan wonders. "You're shaming my cause." It then dawns on Stan. "Are you just gonna flip every sentence I say?" Paul grins. "I'm just gonna say every sentence you flip."

The film does occasionally stumble, so eager to get its point across, so overwhelmed by its own ambition, it forgets coherence. The flashbacks are a bit jarring, the Civil War references are a bit too much - particularly evident in an acid-tinged, off-kilter, ear-splitting sequence that hammers the point home and becomes too artsy and psychedelic, like something out of a Ben Wheatley film. Moverman's script becomes too talky/expository at points, in stark contrast to his laconic "Time Out of Mind". Though "The Dinner" starts off with a bang, it becomes increasingly, both tonally and stylistically, jarring. It would have almost worked better if it completely confined itself to the restaurant, like Polanski's underrated "Carnage" did - just four characters and an apartment. Go full-theatrical, man. As it stands, "The Dinner" gradually slips into overindulgence, drunk on its own aperitif, running around in circles, especially in its latter part.

But that's okay. It's still well-worth seeing. It remains a grim reflection of the ethics behind contemporary politics, an incisive character study and a fantastic showcase for its tremendous cast. Bobby Bukowski's cinematography recalls "Time Out of Mind"'s jarring-but-gorgeous use of color and framing. Though he should scale back next time, I'm glad Owerman is still making those kind of psychologically probing films, bound to be discussed with relatives and friends, ad nauseam, over dinner. How much DO you know about them, after all?

3.5 out of 5 stars

Benson & Moorhead Reach for Infinity but End Up with "The Endless"

Synopsis: *Two brothers return to the cult they fled from years ago to discover that the group's beliefs may be more sane than they once thought.*

Some independent films baffle you with mere ambition - and if, like Icarus, their wings are singed in the process, so be it. On a limited budget, they attempt to convey grandiose, existential ideas. Brit Marling is one of those filmmakers, whose "Another Earth", "I Origins" and the recent Netflix series "The OA" all deal with parallel dimensions, mankind's origins, the capabilities of the human mind and, well, other trippy stuff. But it's Marling's "The Sound of My Voice" that perhaps most closely echoes Justin Benson and Aaron Moorhead's "The Endless"… with dashes of Alex Garland's recent "Annihilation" and a heavy dose of Lovecraftian eccentricity thrown in for good measure. If that sounds intriguing, it mostly is, the brothers managing to sustain the tone of building dread - yet it begins to unravel in its second half, Icarus' wings igniting in the film's apocalyptic finale.

The directors play the leads, Justin (Benson) and Aaron (Moorhead), brothers who escaped from a cult when they were young. Antisocial and depressed, they go to deprogramming sessions and secretly long for the warm embrace of the cult, particularly Aaron, who thinks they should have stayed in the first place. There is a nice juxtaposition happening here, the dim and dreary normalcy of everyday existence set against the lunacy of living in a welcoming cult (it brought to mind prison films where inmates commit suicide upon experiencing freedom).

So the brothers go back to what now is ostensibly a camp. They reconnect with old "friends", who welcome them with open arms, albeit not without a trace of creepiness. There's Hal (Tate Ellington), the leader, though he claims he isn't one. There's the bearded Tim (Lew Temple), a bit of an outcast in the group, along with Dave (David Lawson Jr.), who always smiles. There's clothing designer Anna (Callie Hernandez). There's Lizzy (Kira Powell), who upon wandering out of a nearby mental health facility decided she's better off here. There's Jennifer (Emily Montague), so sick of the gang partying all the time, she leaves notes everywhere for people to shut up - but also has an agenda of her own. According to Justin, they are all castrated and in their 40's… "they just look young." He thinks it's all bullshit and wants to go home, but Aaron is enthralled and asks him to stay one more day.

Things get weird. A chalkboard equation Hal is working on solves… what exactly? "Wouldn't believe me if I told you," Hal intones mysteriously. A physically impossible trick involving a baseball may not be a trick at all. There's a rope-pulling contest, the other end of it attached to something invisible - and impossibly strong -

in the sky. Bullets ricochet against an invisible barrier, one that is most apparent at night, when it reflects this world's three moons. A shack stands in the middle of a hay field, with a clock on it on repeat, and something uncanny happens inside, over and over again. According to Hal, the "answer" is at the bottom of a nearby lake, a Rorschach-like stain in the midst of which Justin discovers a rusty container with a tape. "It's how It communicates with us," Hal explains at a viewing ceremony. "With images."

"The Endless" may or may not reveal what "It" is, along with answers to all the other questions it steadily poses. Perspectives shift. What if Justin is wrong, this isn't a cult, and there is, in fact, a god-like entity ruling over this domain? What if, as the outcast, half-crazy Carl (James Jordan) stutters, the brothers are, indeed, trapped in a series of time-loops - a time-loop zone if you will - and all the humans are nothing but mere pawns entertaining this terrifying, all-consuming entity until it kills them, therein resetting the loop?

This is nutty territory and one has to tread carefully to avoid stumbling headfirst into silliness. Thankfully, for the most part, Benson and Moorhead succeed, pulling the viewer into a world where one has to both suspend disbelief and have their feet firmly planted on the ground, a world of illusion and hyperreality, of freedom and surrender, where time is both crucial and irrelevant. They incorporate themes of finding connection in a crumbling society and, like I mentioned, are best at contrasting the alienation of the "normal" world against the warmth and acceptance of the alien one. One could perceive "The Endless" as a treatise on the nature of time and/or an allegory of defying God - or neither.

The problems occur in the film's second half, when it strays away from the cult into the aforementioned "Annihilation" territory. Things get weird - and by weird, I mean Weird - and if you don't know what I mean, check out Jeff VanderMeer's work. The worlds he creates consist of things both familiar and alien, existential and minute, tangible and surreal. And it all somehow resonates, achieves the goal of striking senses in us that perceive the imperceptible. If the filmmakers harbored those kind of aspirations with "The Endless", they took a few major missteps. The brothers' constant wandering in-between time-loop zones verges on unintentionally hysterical in how earnest and serious those sequences are. Upon the brothers' discovery of the time loops, their nonchalant attitude is somewhat confusing (I'd be freaking the hell out). They banter about sleeping with Anna and jab each other - WHILE STUCK IN A FREAKIN' TWILIGHT ZONE.

One a positive note, frequent moments of humor come from the brothers' rapport, which is never forced - their chemistry is a crucial grounding factor in an otherwise-demented narrative. The way the directors utilize slow motion shots and music helps build and sustain suspense. Their imagery is striking, some of the dialogue exchanges thought-provoking. I just wish they reigned it in a little. Benson and Moorhead reached for the stars and ended up imploding.

But it's the reaching that matters.

3.5 out of 5 stars

"The Innocents" Revisits a Dark Moment in Our History Through a Painterly Prism

Synopsis: *In 1945 Poland, a young French Red Cross doctor who is sent to assist the survivors of the German camps discovers several nuns in advanced states of pregnancy during a visit to a nearby convent.*

Director Anne Fontaine, known for the glossy-but-entertaining biopic "Coco Before Chanel", strives to dial down on gloss and up the ante on grim realism in her latest directorial feature, "The Innocents", which tells a terrifying true tale of pregnant Polish nuns in hiding during World War II. The helmer can't help but resort to artful - or what some would mockingly call "artsy" or "showy" - displays of craftsmanship, but in this case, the perfectly-framed shots, sentimentality and flawless set designs mostly aid the story, instead of overshadowing it. A little well-earned tear-squeezing and eye candy doesn't hurt - just look at Spielberg's undeniably powerful - and undeniably glossy - "Schindler's List".

Thing is, Spielberg knew he was making big-budget, accessible entertainment, which he also happened to make personal and artistic. Fontaine seems to go the other way, reaching for the great artistic heights of, say, Pawel Pawlikowski's "Ida", which dealt with similar (and similarly bleak) themes, but resonated more due to the strict adherence to its style. "Ida" reflected the inner-workings of a conflicted nun in a more believable fashion; "The Innocents" doesn't so much delve inside the minds of its protagonists, as cooly observe their horrific circumstances from a distance. (A bit of trivia: Agata Kulesza and Dorota Kuduk, who play Sisters Mère and Wanda in "The Innocents" respectively, happen to appear in both films). While this approach does have its merits, one can't help but wonder what Michael Haneke would have done with this material - just watch his "White Ribbon" and you'll see what I mean.

Poland, December, 1945. The film starts with the Polish nuns lined up across from each other, singing a choir, then bowing to each other - all but one sister, who stands straight, her face obscured by doubt. She then escapes the confines of the convent and has a group of stray children in a nearby desolate town lead her to a French doctor, Mathilde (Lou de Laâge), daughter of "die-hard Communist parents". Mathilde promptly sends the nun to the Polish Red Cross - not out of prejudice, but due to a lack of alternative. A few hours later, she spots the woman praying outside the hospital in the snow and ends up driving her back to the convent, where, she discovers, many pregnant nuns are hiding out. "We were persecuted by the Germans," a Sister says, "and then the Russians arrived... an indescribable nightmare. Only God's help will allow us to overcome it." "How many more are in that condition?" Mathilde wonders. "Seven," Maria replies. "God's help will not be enough," Mathilde concludes.

If evicted, the Sisters become "objects of shame". Mathilde soon gains their trust and starts helping the nuns, bonding with them and guiding them through their pregnancies. Some are devout, some lost they faith after the Russians' assault and seek refuge in the convent - all are conflicted, bitter, resilient, strong women (whom we, unfortunately, know a little too little about). Mathilda brings back penicillin and assists in their pregnancies, in secret… Until, that is, she has no choice but to involve her lover, the Head Doctor back at the Polish Red Cross, Samuel (Vincent Macaigne). Samuel is Jewish and loathes the Polish: "I can't stand them," he says after a night of coitus with Mathilde. "They got what they deserved with the Russians and the Germans." He eventually puts his "ethics" aside and helps out, the kind-hearted bastard.

Fontaine achieves moments of grandeur and awe on numerous occasions. "Faith is 24 hours of doubt and one minute of hope," a character says - a poetic and resonant line. There is a graphic depiction of a caesarian section early on in the film, performed under the worst conditions imaginable, which is as hard to watch for the viewer as it is for the nuns (you'll feel every flutter of their eyes). Another striking moment arrives during an examination sequence, Mathilda taking in the pregnant Sisters, one by one, urging them to "set God aside", until they bolt, in "fear [of] damnation". A terrifying encounter with the Russians is highly suspenseful (goddamn those heartless Russkis!). The choirs, as performed by the nuns, are beautiful and ethereal (take note, a-ca-"Pitch Perfect"). There is also the murder of a newborn child in a patchy-white field with a cross; a suicide; and an ambiguously "happy ending" which, depending upon your investment in the film, will either make perfect sense within its context or infuriate you.

Cinematographer Caroline Champetier, who shot the wonderfully kaleidoscopic, neon-extravaganza "Holy Motors", tones down the approach here. The world created in "The Innocents" is basked in monochrome grays, starkly contrastive snowy whites and hues of pure visual sorrow. Lou de Laâge is fantastic in the central role, Mathilde's expressions conveying every shade of emotion with utmost subtlety. Her character has little choice but to obey, yet we can see how torn she is. She essentially plays a Christ-like figure in a hellish world, and pulls it off with aplomb. In addition, Fontaine's film deals with important subjects and themes, such as women ostracized by society; faith shattered by war; resilience and the power of friendship; holding on to traces of humanity in an inhumane world; and the resolute belief in God.

All that said, the pacing is uneven - "The Innocents" lags, especially when it gets deeply bogged down in political discussions, or the "racist doctor" sub-plot. There's probably two or three birth sequences too many in the film. The villains - in this case, the perpetually-evil Russians - are a little one-dimensional, especially if they are supposed to represent the male-dominated society that exiles females. The film takes patience to sit through - all the murk and gloom becomes overwhelming. Oddly, for such a slow film, we learn next to nothing about everyday nun life, or what drives them. As with Haneke's (sharper) visions, there's no doubting "The Innocents'" artistic merit, but you won't want to immerse yourself into Fontaine's beautiful gloom more than once.

3.5 out of 5 stars

"The Wolfpack" is a Study of Isolation and the Power of Film

    Synopsis: *Locked away from society in an apartment on the Lower East Side of Manhattan, the Angulo brothers learn about the outside world through the films that they watch. Nicknamed the Wolfpack, the brothers spend their childhood re-enacting their favorite films using elaborate homemade props and costumes. With no friends and living on welfare, they feed their curiosity, creativity, and imagination with film, which allows them to escape from their feelings of isolation and loneliness. Everything changes when one of the brothers escapes, and the power dynamics in the house are transformed. The Wolfpack must learn how to integrate into society without disbanding the brotherhood.*

    The Angulos live in a weirdly anachronistic apartment, both spare and over-stuffed, plastic chairs next to wooden ones, leaning against walls with tacked-on old calendars and photos. It's stuffy and claustrophobic. Told mostly through the eyes of one of the boys (the other siblings largely remain unidentified, until the end credits), "The Wolfpack", a documentary by Crystal Moselle, unravels itself quietly, with no narration or text, the camera observing passively, which only amplifies the oppressive - and highly resonant - vibe. But the film's ambition is also its downfall, as the subject matter is so utterly compelling, the gaping holes in the narrative become that much more frustrating.

    The father, who is absent for most of the film, a self-described "recluse", refers to his family as "the tribe", and to himself as the "landowner" - and at a different point, "god". The children fear him. A man of contradictions, he sees the world as a prison, and though he vehemently avoids corporate slavery by secluding himself, and his family, from society, he does have musical aspirations and wants a record deal with a production label. When he finally appears towards the end of the film, the father doesn't say much, except that his "power is to influence everybody", and how he wants his children to be unaffected by the world outside, and truly discover themselves - but contradictorily allows them to watch "thousands" of violent films like "Blue Velvet" and "Pulp Fiction", without real context or discussion.

    The father's enforced imprisonment led to the children's addiction to film, and consequent reenactments with elaborate - but shockingly detailed - outfits. The Angulo boys have no choice but to fully delve "into the minds of their characters"; a searing sequence depicts one of the siblings in a Batman outfit, longingly gazing at the city of New York through a glazed window, both inspired and saddened by his discovery of "The Dark Knight". This scene brilliantly depicts the overwhelming effect of cinema, how it makes one wish to be a hero as much as long for a better world.

A brief reference to her husband's abusive past suggests why the mother never followed her ambition, to raise the kids in the "farm land", where she grew up. She met him while on a trip through South America; impressed by his complete lack of consumerist inclinations, so prevalent in modern society, she fell in love, or, to quote the film, they found "common ground". She's remained a helpless victim since their wedding, living out her life in deep regret, while also functioning as a saint to their children, a source of calm and stability in a four-walled world of cinema.

Moselle's debut directorial feature is filled with undeniably powerful moments, such as the unsettling archive footage, showing the family dancing in costumes during a Halloween, a scene that verges on satanic; or another shot depicting everyone squished on mattresses and cushions in a tiny, suffocated room, a vision of helplessness and despair. The story of the protagonist's first escape from the apartment in a Michael Myers mask - and subsequent incarceration in a psychiatric ward - is revelatory, as it so succinctly shows how difficult it is for the kids to adapt to the real world.

This escape led to others, which in itself led to a gradual change, during which Moselle's crew seems to have entered their lives: the film takes place in the present, as the boys discover the world in "Reservoir Dogs" outfits. Trains, bridges, cars - everything seems new and glorious to them. The pure exhilaration the siblings experience after watching "The Fighter" is palpable and contagious.

The film falls apart a little in its second half, when the editing becomes sporadic - brief, quickly-cut shots depict the family members pursuing their lives, but glaring holes remain. Where did the blonde girlfriend come from? What prompted them to go strolling through the orchard, after years and years of relentless inaction?

The film could have also delved a little deeper into the characters' psyches: the mother, and the reasoning behind her passivity; the father, and how exactly did he plan to make money in New York and move to Scandinavia, of all places; and especially the kids who, while shown as sheltered but bright, ambitious and talented, are never fully explored.

Some parts of the film seem staged. While the mother's call to her mom after fifteen years of silence is touching, it feels prompted and a little forced. The siblings' moments of child-like wonder are intermittently touching but also induce skepticism (for example, one brother's discovery of new words - including an unexpected racial slur - should have long been a part of his lexicon, from the thousands of films he watched).

A real-life, twisted amalgamation of "Dogtooth" (whose bite it lacks) and "Be Kind Rewind" (whose humor it lacks), "Capturing the Friedmans" ("Capturing the Angelos"?) and "Catfish" (whose suspense it lacks), "The Wolpack" is nevertheless by turns deeply disturbing, mordantly funny, confusing, frustrating and ultimately a perspicacious statement on isolation, the power of escapism, and how films, while reflecting real life, cannot prepare one for the challenges of the real world. It will stay with you, but you'll also wish there was more to it.

3.5 out of 5 stars

"Thelma" is a Queer, Horror, Quasi-Religious Parable About Coming of Age... And It Somehow Works

Synopsis: *A woman begins to fall in love, only to discover that she has fantastic powers.*

After his U.S. debut, the subtle indie drama "Louder Than Bombs", Norwegian director Joachim Trier returned to his motherland to make the unnerving art-house horror "Thelma". The same issues that plagued Trier's 2016 film now seem to invade this one. At the end of my "Louder Than Bombs" review I wrote, "With his next feature, I hope the director scales back and focuses more on exploring one or two subjects, as opposed to twenty." He tackles quite a lot of subjects in "Thelma", yet another take on a demonic teenager - not all of them fleshed out, but endlessly fascinating nevertheless.

The opening scene is masterfully staged. A father takes his young daughter hunting. They walk over a large frozen lake, deep in the wilderness, with fish gazing up at them from underneath the ice. Deep in the woods, they encounter a young deer. Dad aims his rifle at the animal, then slowly shifts it to his daughter, who is too entranced by the deer to notice. Spoiler alert: after a sustained moment of suspense, the father can't go through with it. What would make a father attempt to murder his own daughter? That thought will linger with you throughout the rest of the film.

A decade or so later, Thelma (Eili Harboe) is a somewhat-reclusive college student, studying chemistry in a remote Norwegian town. Shaped by her rigid Christian upbringing, she lives by herself, finding solace in swimming. Thelma is sad, because she feels superior to most. "When I see girls with friends and boyfriends," she confides, "they seem uglier than me."

Odd things begin to happen. Thelma has a violent seizure in a classroom, as birds smash against its large windows. Unable to determine the cause, the doctors advise Thelma to contact home, yet she doesn't want her uber-religious parents (Henrik Rafaelsen and Ellen Dorrit Petersen, both excellent) to know about the incident. She has lucid fantasies, dreams of snakes crawling over wrinkled throats, and throws up a lot. Tests rules out brain tumors or epilepsy yet reveal an early addiction to a powerful anti-seizure drug.

In the meantime, Thelma meets Anja (Kaya Wilkins) at the indoor swimming pool she frequents. There is an instant spark. They meet at a bar, where they share secrets, then a club, where they share Thelma's first-ever alcoholic drinks, then a rooftop, where they share Thelma's first-ever cigarette, and eventually the theater -

with Anja's mother in tow - where the girls' hands and lips interlock during an ethereal ballet. Thelma begs God for forgiveness, for she has sinned.

Yet sin she does, with more alcohol consumed, and her first (pseudo)marijuana experience turning into a hallucinatory, snake-infested make-out session with Anja. A series of intense flashbacks, involving a baby, reveals Thelma's Terrible Secret. The film morphs into a genre piece, a "Carrie"-esque tale (fiery finale and all) of adolescent rebellion, involving telepathy, hereditary superpowers and/or a possible possession - all wrapped under the guise of a coming of age tale about a young girl overcoming her religious background and discovering herself.

As such, the film works wonders, steadily building tension, its lead protagonist carrying us even through its uneven patches. Eli Harboe is a bona fide star. We see the guilt she feels when doing something she's been raised to think of as "wrong"; we feel every twinge of pain during her seizures; she even makes us relate to the somewhat-horrendous act she performs towards the end, using her, um, powers.

Kudos must go out to Joachim Trier, who paints a dark allegory with vibrant, confident strokes, helped greatly by his cinematographer Jakob Ihre. His lingering lens captures frigid landscapes, apocalyptic flocks of birds circling grey skies and psychedelic snakes straight out of the Bible, but its true achievement is capturing every nuance of Harboe's performance, from the moment she's singled out in a square of busy people, to the final shot of her, in the same square, though not quite alone this time.

Trier fills "Thelma" with such mirroring imagery, its reflections slightly off or just plain twisted. An insightful conversation between Thelma and her parents during one of their visits, touching upon religion and acceptance - with Thelma quickly being shut down for expressing her beliefs - is mirrored later, when Thelma defends her family's faith to her friends over drinks (her being non-alcoholic). A nightmarish "trapped in a swimming pool" sequence mirrors that "fish gazing up through the ice" opening shot. In this way, the films reflects Thelma's own duality of identity, her revelatory present mirroring her dark past, Thelma's twisted notion of herself mirroring her actual self. Trier also twists our expectations: what starts off as a tender love affair, rather quickly culminates in a passionate kiss and a strand of hair, caught in a window. Thelma's initial, earnest prayer, is later closely observed by her father, sitting inches behind her as she expresses her anger at him, head against the wall.

There is a lot to juggle here, and Trier does lose grasp. Hefty themes of nature vs. nurture, leaving behind a religious upbringing, unleashing restrained desire (at times manifested in violence), and a parental quandary that's up there with the one in the final scenes of this year's "The Killing of a Sacred Deer" in terms of its ambition, grisliness and ludicrousness, wedge themselves in-between a deeply sympathetic love story and horror tropes, such as reptiles entering human orifices. It all gels, but barely. Had he stripped the film down a bit, it would've made for a much more effective and chilling character study. As it stands, the film walks a razor-thin line between artistic and silly.

In its desire to combine the mundane with the fantastical, art-house with accessible mainstream fare, "Thelma" is also very much in the vein of Tomas Alfredson's snowy, cold masterpiece "Let the Right One In" or this year's powerful, succinct, "cannibal coming of age" drama "Raw". Definitely worth seeing for its ambition and central performance, its cinematography and unexpected detours, as well as Ola Fløttum's deeply unsettling soundtrack, "Theresa" is as conflicted and torn as its titular character.

3.5 out of 5 stars

"Train to Busan" - Call It "Snowpiercer 2: Attack of The Zombies" - Derails into Cinemas

Synopsis: *While a zombie-virus breaks out in South Korea, a couple of passengers struggle to survive on the train from Seoul to Busan.*

Ever since George A. Romero's "Night of the Living Dead", the zombie genre has seen every reincarnation imaginable. We've had domesticated zombies ("Fido"), Nazi zombies ("Dead Snow"), hell-bent-on-apocalypse zombies ("28 Days Later", "World War Z"), beaver zombies ("Zombeavers") and even, yes, cockney zombies (in the aptly titled "Cockneys vs. Zombies"). While stylish and consistently inventive, "Train to Busan" borrows freely from these films (well, maybe not the cockney beavers), struggling to spice up the undead genre with a limited setting and a ferocious, "assault on the senses" approach. It winds up highly entertaining but treading familiar ground nonetheless. Kudos to director Yeon Sang-ho ("The Fake") for all the legitimate thrills and spills - he's limited by the genre itself. What's next, half-alligator, half-alien Slovakian zombies? (I would actually watch the shit out of that.)

The film's intro is intensely effective. A man drives down to a biohazard outpost and has his car sprayed down. "There was a tiny leak at the biotech district," he's informed. Uh-huh. We all know what this means. Next thing he knows, the guy runs over a deer. In a superbly creepy scene, as he drives off, the deer shakily gets back up, pupils missing. (Zombie deer! Yes!) In the meantime, Seok-wu (Gong Yoo), a "fund manager", is having a bad day. Not only is his financial institution on the brink of bankruptcy, he's also getting divorced - AND it's his daughter Su-an's (Kim Su-an) birthday. Clearly not a "Father of the Year" contender, Seok-wu gets her a Wii, forgetting she already has one, the dimwit. No wonder Su-an begs him to take her to see her mother in Busan, a town apparently only reachable by train and impossible to get to in Seok-wu's brand-new, slick ride. "While you're down there," his mother urges, "have a heart-to-heart with your wife."

Signs of the looming apocalypse are everywhere - armed guards, squealing fire trucks - but, in a (purposeful?) nod to "Shaun of the Dead", they are only apparent to the viewer and not to the film's preoccupied protagonists. Just as the train is about to depart, an injured girl stumbles in, with what looks like bite marks on her legs… And so the mayhem begins. And by mayhem, I literally mean utter chaos is unleashed. Those zombies don't fuck around. They turn instantly, post-bite, and attack the closest bystander with unstoppable fury. The caveat? They can't slide doors open, ramming up against them like a bunch of morons instead - which provides the survivors a means of escape, and the film with several white-knuckle scenes. Oh, and those zombies are useless in the dark. Comes in handy during those nifty tunnel sequences.

Sang-ho builds the tension well, immersing the viewer in a suitably claustrophobic setting, with superb make-up and special effects. Fans of the genre will find plenty of reasons to gorge on this cinematic treat: standouts involve the devouring of a baseball team; the inventive use of a bottle of water with some newspaper; a weirdly funny conversation with a zombie-turning mother over the phone… I loved the bit where the train goes past a station, with folks throwing their bloody selves against its windows. The station attack halfway through "Train to Busan" is by far one of the film's two major highlights, the second involving three central characters, steadily, and gruesomely, making their way through the zombie-infested locomotive.

A train in flames derails (I was a spoken-word artist before this gig). A horde of zombies form a centipede, attached to the moving train. Sang-ho's loving tribute doesn't skimp on memorable bits (or trains, for that matter). I also loved how bleak the film is. Not a lot of folks survive on this ride. To counter-balance the moroseness, there are dashes of humor. In a misleading scene, a husband is patiently waiting for his presumably zombie wife by the bathroom. "Are you okay, honey?" he asks, receiving a harsh knock on the door in response, which sends him stumbling back. "It's okay, take your time," he mumbles. Talking to a terrified zombie witness, the train conductor warns Su-an: "If you don't study, you'll end up like him." "Why is your ring tone so tacky?" Seok-wu asks the "alpha-male" at one point, making the dude question his masculinity.

The film's messages about compassion and not just "looking out for yourself" in a time of crisis are especially - and surprisingly - potent. However, as a cautionary tale, the film lacks credibility. The political subtext is where the film particularly falters occasionally. So potent in the similar (but better) "Snowpiercer", here it gets muddled - and when it's not, it's painfully obvious. The film's also too long; clocking in at two hours, the zombie attacks and limited location become repetitive. Not to beat a dead horse, but at least in "Snowpiercer" the train represented social hierarchy, each cabin a different, invigoratingly imaginative setting. Some moments of sentimentality are also unnecessary. Without revealing crucial plot points, let's just say that ONE cheerleader with common sense among dozens of sensible human beings barricading themselves - well, that's a hard pill to swallow… As is the "twist" towards the end (involving Seok-wu's job), for that matter.

The director clearly knows how to choreograph action, pace and structure a film. Though we've seen it all before, one can't blame the filmmakers for failing to bring the dead genre back to life. However, one CAN blame them for not utilizing their prowess and making a more original film. Let's hope Sang-ho takes cues from fellow South Korean filmmaker Bong Joo-ho, who made the unpredictable and wonderful "The Host" and takes us on a truly original ride next time, be it plane, train or automobile.

3.5 out of 5 stars

"Tumbledown" Triumphantly Pairs a Toned-Down Jason Sudeikis with an Uptight Rebecca Hall

Synopsis: A young woman struggles to move on with her life after the death of her husband, an acclaimed folk singer, when a brash New York writer forces her to confront her loss and the ambiguous circumstances of his death.

Jason Sudeikis, mostly known for his prolonged stint on Saturday Night Live and leading roles in lowbrow, high-concept Hollywood comedies ("Horrible Bosses", "We're the Millers"), has recently taken a more restrained approach to acting, leaning away from straightforward slapstick and snappy one-liners to subtler, endearingly witty and warm characterizations. The recent, raunchy, charming-but-flawed "Sleeping with Other People" marked the beginning of this trend. Sean Mewshaw's first directorial feature, the romantic dramedy "Tumbledown", sees Sudeikis continue down that path, once again imbuing his potentially one-dimensional character with much-needed warmth, while maintaining his playful persona that we all know and love so much. Ironically, it's the lightly comedic bits that "Tumbledown" nails, while the film's granola, folk-music-infused dramatic core sags a little.

Hannah (Rebecca Hall), a small-town journalist/biographer, mourns the death of her folk singer husband Hunter, who tumbled to his demise in the titular Tumbledown ravine while hiking. She's secluded herself deep in the Maine wilderness, attempting to piece Hunter's life back together by writing his biography.

One day, while visiting his grave, Hannah briefly spots Andrew (Jason Sudeikis), riding in to the cemetery on a motorbike, a striking presence in her otherwise-mundane, sorrowful existence. He leaves her numerous voice-mails, introducing himself as a "scholar" and "writer of pop culture in America", interested in writing a biography about her deceased husband, but she initially ignores his insistent requests. Andrew keeps stalking her, resulting in Hannah's mother (Gwyneth Paltrow Sr., a.k.a. Blythe Danner) interrupting a frigid lovemaking session between Hannah and her boy-toy, Curtis (Joe Manganiello), to let her know that Andrew won't back down until he meets her.

"You parasites are done running Hunter through the rumor mill," Hannah informs Andrew upon their first meet-ugly (is that the opposite of a "meet-cute"?). She initially shuts him down, even ripping up his notebook, but then Andrew gradually wins her over with his guileless passion for Hunter's music. Lonely, deeply entrenched in reliving her husband's life, Hannah gives in and allows him to join her in the writing process. As they bond together over a past life, their own lives begin to make sense.

"Tumbledown" deals with universal issues - such as loss, grief, atonement, the meaning of true artistic prowess, and the rekindling of love - with gentle humor, intermittently observant nuances and patience, albeit it does so with rare traces of novelty. It never digs deeper than the 2-inch snow of Maine. The music also becomes grating, as do the banal melancholy bits, some montage sequences particularly as moth-eaten as Hannah's sweaters.

Hunter, who only wrote 12 songs, is no Kurt Cobain or David Foster Wallace, both of which are referenced in the film, which takes away from the gravity - his music just never resonates. Andrew says it best himself, "There's nothing cutting-edge about him." He does proceed to describe Hunter as "timeless". Timeless? Hell, he's not even as good as Llewyn Davis - and that guy had it rough.

It comes as no surprise that the best lines in the film come from Sudeikis and are hence its funniest. "That crazy 'widow routine' of yours, does that work on people?" he asks Hannah, half-seriously, as only Sudeikis can. "Seems a little over the top." When confronted by her at one point, he retorts, "Nothing stinks like a pile of unpublished writing… a quote from Sylvia Plath before pre-heating herself to 350." There is also a "deer condom" line that made me burst out laughing. The actor effortlessly conveys his established natural charisma, but it's the deeper shades of poignancy that make Andrew one of Sudeikis' most intricate characters so far.

Rebecca Hall ("The Gift") is always dependable, and her character could have easily slipped into "despisable", but the actress's natural charm and astute command of her performance prevents that from ever happening. Hannah is conflicted, bitter, possessive, egotistical, by turns rude and vulnerable, refusing to let her husband go. Andrew, who could never replace Hunter, comes in as her savior, not just from the trauma of her husband's death, but from her own personal demons.

Some of the film's finest moments come from Hannah and Andrew's interactions, such as when they discuss the rationale behind writing Hunter's biography. "You are condemning a genius to obscurity," Andrew shouts, as she slams the door in his face. "Work on this with me!" Their chemistry is especially palpable in the film's highlight, a sequence that comes late in the film, where they discuss one of Hunter's songs. It starts off with Andrew thinking he's nailed down the essence of a song, and ends with Hannah ostensibly twisting his notions, and the actors handle the fragile interaction deftly.

The rest of the supporting cast is somewhat underused: Joe Manganiello hams it up as Hannah's deer-hunting fuck-buddy, Griffin Dunne barely makes an impression as Hannah's boss and Dianna Agron seems like a last-minute addition to the script as Andrew's girlfriend Finley. Blythe Danner and Richard Masur, stalwarts that they are, make the most out of the short-but-very-funny Easter (Andrew: "Passover? Both?") dinner scene, as Hannah's parents.

Mewshaw's film is the definition of a charming, predictably paced and plotted little indie. It doesn't break any new grounds, nor does it attempt to plumb the depths of human emotion, but its predictability is almost reassuring, like a mother's hug. Akin to a pleasant perfume that leaves a pleasant-but-brief scent, "Tumbledown" doesn't soar, but due to Sudeikis' and Hall's charismatic lead turns, its moments of genuine humor, and a generally amicable vibe, it never tumbles down into the murky depths of pretentious indie dramas.

3.5 out of 5 stars

"Zootopia", Like a Caged Animal, is Beautiful to Behold but Needs to Be Set Free

Synopsis: *In a city of anthropomorphic animals, a fugitive con artist fox and a rookie bunny cop must work together to uncover a conspiracy.*

"Don't call me cute," Judy, the bunny protagonist (voiced by Ginnifer Goodwin) proclaims at one point in Disney's latest animated spectacle, "Zootopia". "A bunny can call another bunny cute, but when another animal does it…" She trails off, letting the kids in the audience giggle and gush, while their parents reflect on racial intolerance and appreciate the sly way the gag/political message was interpreted into the scene. This approach pretty much summarizes directors' Byron Howard and Rich Moore's energetic tale, which is crammed to the brim with sharp humor, laugh out-loud visual gags and relevant themes, but still manages to adhere to Hollywood's laws of narrative structure, with some of the bootlicking and predictability that comes with it. In other words, a little more "The Talented Mr. Fox" - or even "Rango" - and a little less "Madagascar" wouldn't have hurt.

"Zootopia" takes place in an alternate universe, where humans (presumably) never evolved, and neither - presumably - did anyone but mammals, who did evolve past their differences and grew to get along… to an extent. Judy, a young bunny living in a remote farm town called Bunnyborrow (the population of which keeps steadily rising), dreams of working for the Zootopia Police Department (ZDP), yet her friends and family don't support her ambitions. "You know how your mom and I remained so happy?" her father Stu (Don Lake) relates dryly about his relationship with Bonnie (Bonnie Hunt). "We gave up on our dreams and we settled."

Fifteen years later, fueled by everyone's scorn, Judy aces the Zootopia Police Academy Training, fighting and climbing and clawing her way to the 1st Rabbit Officer position. Before departing to the Big City, Judy is warned by her folks about predators… especially foxes. Stu and Bonnie stuff her with all sorts of fox repellent (profound "racial fear" analogy here), and off she goes to the wondrous land of Zootopia.

And wondrous it is, an amalgamation of everything from the recent retro-futuristic look of "Tomorrowland" and the mind-island trippiness of "Inside Out", to the works of Chuck Jones and a real, New York-ish vibe, angry neighbors and all, each animal an all-too-real archetype. Judy delves right into her work, but instead of getting a cool assignment, she gets delegated to parking duty by her mean Chief Bogo (Idris Elba). Undeterred by the dull task, she goes for a record amount of tickets -

until she stumbles upon Nick (Jason Bateman), a hustler fox who runs a shady popsicle selling business (profound "drug war" analogy here). She attempts to stop him, but the mean Nick puts the bunny in her place, momentarily crushing her dreams (profound "big city crushing naive aspirations" analogy here).

One day, Judy stumbles upon an intriguing case and gets 48 hours to solve it, her file consisting of a single vague picture. It eventually brings her back together with Nick, and together they embark on a perilous investigation, which leads them to a clawed limo filled with polar bear fur, the tiniest and most evil crime boss in animated history, and, of course, a massive, "Chinatown"-like conspiracy. This is where the more adult themes kick in, as Judy unravels something that makes her a hero, but also ignites prejudice and social unrest throughout the city. "I came here to make the world a better place," she says despondently. "But I think I broke it."

Despite the lofty motifs and needlessly convoluted plot, "Zoolandia"'s chief saving grace is its assault of visual puns and clever lines of dialogue. "Our killer instincts are still in our denim," an overalls-wearing critter threatens, while his friend corrects, "I think you mean DNA." In the classroom, the teacher starts off by saying, "We have to acknowledge the elephant in the room…", and then wishes Francine, an elephant student, a happy birthday. A chase sequence through a tiny rodent city is exhilarating in its breakneck pace and imaginative twists on films like "Godzilla", every buddy-cop chase ever made, and even the Buster Keaton oeuvre of nonstop, borderline-demented slapstick hilarity. Some other standout bits include a "Carrot for One" microwaveable dinner; "The Mystic Spring Oasis" nudist/hippie retreat; the sloth DMV sequence (renowned from the trailer); Mr. Big, a Scorsese-meets-Corleone pastiche; and a character who calls himself The Duke of Bootlegs.

While delivering commendable messages about tolerance and fitting in, and by all accounts succeeding on the comedy front, "Zootopia" never quite transcends its generic roots in a way, say, "The Lego Movie" did (by being so "meta" it redefined the term). Some of its pop culture references already give off a stale whiff, and the pedestrian Shakira opening - and closing - number surely doesn't help the film achieve a timelessness of, for example, Pixar's recent "The Good Dinosaur". The solution to the Big Mystery is a bit cobbled-together and formulaic (may be the result of the story being originated by no less than eight writers).

The film frequently made me wish it were a collection of anecdotes from the city of Zootopia, the ambitious but somewhat-contrived story getting in the way of the real fun: watching those characters interact and mirror our behavior in eccentric fashion. "We may be evolved, but deep down we are still animals," one of the characters poignantly says, reflecting on our tendency to resort to our primal, often violent and impulsive, instincts. With any luck, the inevitable "Zootopia 2"'s script will evolve past the antiquated narrative structure that Hollywood loves so much and deliver a full-blown extravaganza of carrot-crunchin', inspired zaniness.

3.5 out of 5 stars

3-STAR REVIEWS

"#FromJennifer" is Social Critique Under the Guise of a Demented Video Blog

Synopsis: *An actress becomes obsessed with internet fame after her manager drops her for not having enough of a social media presence.*

It's not often you get two horror villain icons in one film, especially one made on a shoestring budget. Yet writer/producer/director Frank Merle's audacious low-fi follow-up to 2013's "The Employer" (a clever little thriller, starring Malcolm McDowell and Billy Zane) does exactly that. Behold: the legendary Tony Todd (known for his memorable performance as the titular "Candyman" in Bernard Rose's 1992 horror classic), sharing the screen (fine, not exactly, but they're in the same movie) with Derek Mears, who donned Jason Voorhees' hockey mask in Marcus Nispel's 2009 reboot of "Friday the 13th".

Don't expect a "Freddy vs. Jason"-style smackdown (though Merle should really consider a "Candyman vs Voorhees" spin-off, involving lots of bees and swampy lakes). A continuation of sorts to 2016's under-the-radar "2 Jennifer", which Merle produced, the film uses its two cult stars sparsely, with Mears getting the juicier part, while Todd amps up the "creepy ham" factor in what must have been a few hours of shooting. Most of its flaws seem to stem from budget limitations; an astute satire is buried underneath the GoPro pixels and horror flick conventions. This one's well worth checking out for all the things it gets right - because when it does, it nails 'em.

Stephanie (a hilariously OTT Meghan Deanna Smith) is a social media star sensation. Her claim to fame? "Revealing" clips of Stephanie making out with herself and sharing lists of things she can't live without ("cotton swabs, your mom, pickles, margaritas, pooping, coconut water" - just to name a few). The recently-fired actress Jennifer (Danielle Taddei, in an effectively humble performance) also happened to break up with her boyfriend and envies Stephanie's popularity. Inspired by her wildly eccentric manager Chad (Todd), she starts her own blog - though her life, at least at first, proves significantly less enticing than that of her idol / friend.

One leaked sex tape and misunderstood audition later, Jennifer's left with no manager and a hilariously nonchalant, psychotic revenge ploy. It consists of three Phases and involves an eager-but-cautious bodyguard, Butch (Mears), who assists her in the increasingly screwed-up travails. "We just broke the law," Butch says nervously, after committing robbery early on, "and everything just seems really risky to me." "Once we get to phase three, we are going to be famous," a calm Jennifer reassures him.

Butch does not remain so apprehensive. As Jennifer phrases it, he seems to "have impulse control problems." We find out that Phase 3 involves wolf masks. A botched attempt to drug an unsuspecting chauvinist douche - who gets his dues moments later, mind you - and multiple kidnappings follow. As for the blood-soaked Phase 3… well, it involves a lumberjack, a popular fairy tale reenactment and Jennifer's ultimate social media statement ("it's going to need a lot of editing").

Everything is viewed from the main characters' perspectives, Merle slyly juxtaposing Stephanie's vapid rants against Jennifer's disturbing video diary. Breaking the fourth wall - when the characters address the camera - can be jarring (see: all the "Paranormal Activity"-inspired shlock), but "#FromJennifer" utilizes it as a technique to emphasize its sly critique of social media and the narcissism it spawns, while also pulling the viewer deeper into the experience. Merle and his team had very little money to work with and used it to their advantage. Akin to the splendid British sitcom "Peep Show", it may take a second to get used to, but the approach ultimately serves the film.

Apart from touching upon themes of social media worship (see also: Matt Spicer's recent "Ingrid Goes West"), "#FromJennifer" emerges as an incisive and relevant critique of the male ego. At about the halfway point, Jennifer goes off on an extended monologue about gender misrepresentation in media that eloquently summarizes the current sociopolitical climate. "Our society is fucked," she concludes. Amen.

Her steadily-escalating rampage is more subversive than the one in, say, Austin Chick's "Girls Against Boys", bringing to mind classic female-centric revenge horror films like "Audition", "Under the Skin", "Lady Vengeance" and "I Spit on Your Grave" - but on a minuscule scale. Without Merle's sure-handed approach, or Daniel Taddei's eerie calm and naivety ruling the show (just don't call her Jenny!), this may all have fallen apart. Special props go out to Mears' trusting and naive - but demented - Butch, who leaves a long-lasting impression.

Sure, it's a tiny film with minor aspirations, and flaws come with the territory, such as uneven acting from the supporting cast, some repetitive scenes and at times distractingly low production values. Yet it's entertaining on its own humble terms, has a sustained atmosphere of building dread, is frequently very (darkly) funny and, most importantly, it showcases a talented filmmaker having some fun. Given a larger budget, Merle may just be the next Blumhouse mainstay. "Michael Myers vs. Hannibal Lecter", anyone?

3 out of 5 stars

"A Brilliant Young Mind" Achieves the Unique Feat of Being Both Subtle and Obvious

Synopsis: A socially awkward teenage math prodigy finds new confidence and new friendships when he lands a spot on the British squad at the International Mathematics Olympiad.

The British film industry loves a good underdog story. From the dancing feats of outcast Billy Elliot, to that "One Chance" Billy Corden gets in the recent tearjerker, the desolate weather of the otherwise-beautiful Kingdom of Great Britain clearly needs to be counterbalanced by the occasional serving of inspirational fluff. (That trend doesn't so much translate to British television programming, which is as dry as the streets are wet, and utterly fatalistic, often to hilarious effect). Some of those feel-good films work (the recent "Pride", about gay activists, was touching and relevant), some not so much (see (or, rather, don't): "Blow Dry", "Pirate Radio"); Morgan Matthews' "A Brilliant Young Mind" falls right in the middle. It goes through all the usual motions of such fare, but its dependable cast and unexpectedly subtle ending keep things from becoming too maudlin.

The tone and characters are swiftly established from the outset. The prologue, scored by an almost-unbearably twangy soundtrack, wastes no time introducing us to the dismal world of the Ellis family: the young child, Nathan, is declared "unique" by his doctor, who goes on to - somewhat harshly - state that the boy will remain socially awkward for the rest of his life. Nathan's parents, Julie (Sally Hawkins) and Michael (Matin McCann), are naturally horrified. "I have lots of things to say," Nathan's voice-over whispers, "I'm just afraid to say them... I've always been like that". (Asa Butterfield plays the older version of Nathan, while Edward Baker-Close shows up as the young Nathan in frequent flashbacks that halt the story-line.)

Michael is your definition of the perfect father, sticking french fries up his nostrils to amuse his kid, but never forgetting to sprinkle a little wisdom here and there. One day, as they're driving, just as Michael utters another "gem" - "You shouldn't be afraid", to be exact - a car smashes into them, instantly killing the father, and forever scarring Nathan and his mom.

Cut to the present. A pot-smoking, foul-mouthed, self-loathing math professor who suffers from a debilitating illness and depression (yep, that's some heavy stuff right there), Martin (Rafe Spall), recognizes Nathan's incredible arithmetical talent and agrees to tutor the boy. From that point on, we see the events unfold mostly from the boy's perspective, as he is accepted into the International Mathematics Olympiad; travels to Taiwan with another tutor, Richard (Eddie Marsan), meets a girl, learns how to play piano and speak Chinese (!!), bunks with another socially-awkward teenager, and has his triumphant moment, overcoming his fear and figuring out a math sequence, making everyone smile/nod in recognition, and then proceed to clap uproariously. In the meantime, Julie and Martin engage in a little romance of their own - a minor but affecting subplot that buoys the film in much-needed sincerity, maturity and novelty.

Matthews is a TV veteran, and while his direction is confident, his filmmaking roots are apparent: "Brilliant"'s visual approach and structure are quite pedestrian. Its pretty shots of despondent city districts, courtesy of cinematographer Danny Cohen ("The King's Speech"), keep the film just this side of having that "Lifetime special" feel.

The cast, saddled with sometimes-overbearing characters, handle their roles with aplomb. And therein lies the strange juxtaposition: the film's thoroughly predictable story beats are counterbalanced by the actors, whose little mannerisms (one scene, involving an awkward kiss between Julie and Martin, is particularly memorable), gentle humor and barely-perceptible nuances keep all the triteness imminently watchable.

The same disparity can be applied to the film's dialogue: for every obvious mathematical analogy ("It's about adaptability... Sometimes we have to change our shapes to fit in"; "Music is math") there are shining moments, perhaps improvised by the actors, such as when Richard calls Martin a "wasted opportunity", and then proceeds to describe his flock of genius outcasts as the "sixteen cleverest young brains in the country".

Matthews made the sensible decision to focus the film on the characters, not the competition. Butterfield is quickly becoming one of the more promising contemporary young actors, though, to be hypercritical, his performance here does lack a little depth (the blame is on the director, who seems to have failed to elicit more from the actor than a mystifying blankness). The kid does show range and growth, after his roles in "Hugo" and "Ender's Game". Sally Hawkins reunites with her "Happy-Go-Lucky" co-star Eddie Marsan; though they barely share the screen, both have moments of real warmth. But the heart and soul of the film is Rafe Spall, making his character a lonely, passionate, caring bear of a man.

There is a commendable anti-bullying message - especially powerful in a scene where an angry, socially-awkward boy cuts himself ("If you're not gifted, you're just weird"). Other themes have been explored before - and better - such as those of loneliness, physical ailment, depression, the meaning of success and how there's no mathematical formula for love (ugh). What Matthews nails is the ending. In fear of spoiling it, I'll just say that, instead of the usual victory you get in such films, there is another one, infinitely more powerful, involving two hands connecting over a car's stick-shift.

In Britain you get "Full Monty" and "The Theory of Everything". In the United States, Land of the Underdog, filmmakers clone the uplifting plot over and over: "A Beautiful Mind", "Dead Poets Society", "The Emperor's Club" and "Good Will Hunting", just to name a few. At one point in Mathews' film, a fellow young mathematician tells Nathan, "we're painstakingly average". "A Brilliant Young Mind" comes close to that definition, but - by a hair - progresses to the finals.

3 out of 5 stars

Disney Nature's "Born in China" is More "Panda Express" than "Planet Earth"

Synopsis: Venturing into the wilds of China, "Born in China" captures intimate moments with a panda bear and her growing cub, a young golden monkey who feels displaced by his baby sister, and a mother snow leopard struggling to raise her two cubs.

Disney manages to put its stamp on everything it releases, sometimes to great nostalgic effect (that opening Disney logo tune that always send a lump careening up my gullet), at others evoking groans (extreme sentimentality, from its song-and-dance numbers to the reduction of a spectrum of emotions and themes to two, maybe three obvious ones). Chan Lu's gorgeously-shot documentary is pure Disney, through and through, from its positive, age-old messages of conversation (most evidently enforced in the PSA leading up to the film), to the obviously-edited storylines of its animal protagonists. Goofily narrated by John Krasinski, who goes all out by even voicing animals sliding on ice, one almost expects Carmen Twillie to croon about life's circles towards the film's end, when the doc gets as tangled up in metaphors about life and rebirth as its adorable snub-nosed monkeys do in tree branches.

Those little golden simians are just some of the animals the documentary anthropomorphizes by awarding them names and tracking their very human-like lives throughout the four seasons in various parts of China's wilderness. Misleadingly putting pandas - one of humans' most beloved creatures - on the poster (evidently to draw a bigger crowd), this film is only partially about Ya-Ya and her cute cub. Dao, the snow leopard, attempts to save her two babies from starvation; there are inconsequential shots of grazing antelopes, the chiru; while the crane, "a symbol of longevity and good fortune", gets the feces end of the stick by appearing as a mere symbol within the film, in the prologue and at the very end.

"Born in China" was designed to provoke two strong responses: "Aww, how adorable!" and "Aww, how sad!" The only grays in the doc are the effervescent fogs descending over endless alleys - everything else is as black and white as the pandas. There are plenty of embellishments, which I guess are forgivable, considering its target audience: young children, who would most likely get bored / frightened by anything too static / violent. So it's right there, in the middle, never showing us the full glory of the hunt, but not settling down for a moment of contemplation either.

It's actually rather impressive, how well-orchestrated (read: edited) some of the sequences are: the filmmaking team actually managed to pull of an entire storyline of an underdog monkey, Tao-Tao, who joins a gang of outcasts led by a violent Rooster (allusions to "The Warriors"?) and then returns to his loving sister and tough-love father. "He's certainly a hero in his sister's eyes," Krasinski comments gently, and one can't help but BELIEVE.

In my cynical mind, none of this ever happened. One shot in particular, involving the baby panda encountering a red panda, has me convinced it was filmed at different locations, at different points in time. I may be wrong - but the fact that the film made me constantly consider this renders those fabrications a distraction, at least for those of us over the age of eight.

Nature needs to be preserved and loved and cared for, and so I applaud the existence of "Born in China", fake as its "plot" may be. It's hard to hate on a film about freakin' pandas after all, they're just so adorable. Kids at the press screening dug it - the fact that their ADD-addled minds stayed focused is a commendable feat for an 80-minute nature doc. Chuan Lu essentially made an extended early-morning PBS nature episode with a higher budget. It's an (animated) step or two away from becoming Disney / Pixar's "Pandas 3-D", with a moderately-violent Bambi moment thrown in here and there for good measure. Enjoy it with the wee ones, and then let Sir David Attenborough take you on a real journey through nature's majesty.

3 out of 5 stars

"Breaking a Monster" Rocks Without Breaking Boundaries

Synopsis: *Follow 13-year-old members Alec Atkins, Malcolm Brickhouse and Jarad Dawkins as they first encounter stardom and the music industry, transcending childhood to become the rock stars they always dreamed of being.*

Luke Meyer's entertaining but by-the-numbers "rockumentary" "Breaking a Monster" follows the trajectory of three talented 13-year-old black boys from Brooklyn, who defy their hip-hop-rooted culture by embracing metal music and rocking their way to relative stardom. Instead of examining the ramifications of such a young, resolute trio of performers breaking monstrous racial and ageist stereotypes, Meyer adopts a different approach, simply following Alec, Malcolm and Jarad through their first year of ascension to nationwide popularity. It proves engrossing, and the subjects are charming, but, like the music they perform, "Breaking a Monster" evaporates from your mind as soon as you press "stop".

The kids are talented well beyond their years; it's startling to see them play songs influenced by decades of punk rock and metal - a reservoir that their young minds managed to absorb, filter and shape into a sound of their own. It may not be the most original or memorable sound - Malcolm himself admits that his lyrics and vocals need work - but there's no denying the skill. As the band goes through its ups and downs - from practicing in a basement to appearing on "The Colbert Report" after signing a five-album, $1.8 million deal - the trio stays grounded and focused, no small feat for any band. The fact that those kids managed to do it against all odds - playing punk rock and painting their nails black didn't exactly sit well among their peers, in a neighborhood "known more for hip-hop than heavy metal" - makes their success that much more admirable.

The kids are thoughtful and charming, but they also avoid the aged-too-fast "Dakota Fanning" syndrome, remaining, you know, *kids* at heart: goofy, lounging on their Spider-Man sheets, playing GTA and watching Naruto cartoons. The most endearing parts of the doc focus on Malcolm, Alec and Jarad and their everyday lives: practicing in the studio, skateboarding, exchanging wisecracks and sharing their thoughts on camera. In one standout scene at the record label offices, the boys are about to sign a major deal, but their attention is on an iPhone video game - that naivety is disarming, a stark juxtaposition to the adults around them, the titular monsters, hungry to exploit their fresh talent.

The boys do stand their ground when it comes to maintaining their artistic integrity: they argue over their logo design, refusing to seem juvenile ("Not the cartoon… We want to be taken seriously"); Malcolm continuously perfects his "childlike" vocals in fear of alienating their core audience; during a branding meeting, Malcolm gets frustrated at the shallowness of it all, while Jarad and Alec become "easily distracted." "I'm too young for responsibility," Malcolm says at one point, which makes him that much more mature in an industry of arrested development. The boys' nonchalant response to negative criticism, unaffected by years of dependence on media reaction, is particularly poignant. In the words of their meditating manager Alan Sacks: "They're relating to everything in L.A. because of 'Grand Theft Auto'."

There is a moment in the doc, where Alan reads an aggressive comment on a message board, basically stating that the kids' popularity is an "act of liberalism", their quick rise to fame based solely on the uniqueness of their being black metalheads. "I'm not stupid, Alan," Malcolm replies. "That's exactly what happened. And I don't care." At a later point, he says: "They don't know me. They know the kid with the afro. They don't know Malcolm Brickhouse." The doc doesn't reveal much about the enigmatic little guy either, and neither does it delve any deeper into the nuance and depth that aforementioned scene hinted at. In general, Meyer's film doesn't transcend the biography format - talking heads, shaky cam, skimming the surface - but its protagonists pull it through. We may not get a lot of socio-political context, or dig too deep into what drives the protagonists, but it's never less than entertaining to observe them breaking the monster that is pop music these days.

3 out of 5 stars

"Cardboard Boxer" Throws a Lot of Punches but Fails to Land a Vital Blow

Synopsis: *A homeless man is recruited by a bunch of rich kids to fight other impoverished people.*

Few things are more tragic than human beings reduced to shadows of themselves, left without an identity or home by circumstance. They wander the streets, largely ignored by some, repulsing others; some search for meaning, sustained by memories of their former selves, others just exist on a minute basis, hopping from one tiny accomplishment (a leftover meal, a couple of quarters) to the other. The number of films that examine the lives of those people unfortunately happens to be quite low. Knate Lee's "Cardboard Boxer" falls somewhere in the middle of the pantheon of those movies, which range from admirable failures ("The Caveman's Valentine") to ambitious-but-flawed efforts ("The Soloist") to, well, so far one masterpiece I've seen that dealt with the issue, Oren Moverman's "Time Out of Mind" (read my review here). While it certainly has noble intentions, moments that stick and a few memorable performances, "The Cardboard Boxer" fails to truly pack a punch.

Willie (Thomas Haden Church) is a broken man without a past, desperate for friendship, his creased features, deadened eyes and slouchy posture revealing a long, desolate life out in the streets. Three events occur that arguably change the course of Willie's future: he finds a little girl's burnt diary; a local cabdriver (Terrence Howard), nicknamed Pope for taking care of the homeless, gives him a blanket; and a couple of rich kids force him to engage in a street fight, whereby a hidden talent is discovered and he is nicknamed - you guessed it - The Cardboard Boxer. As the fights become more intense, Willie creates an imaginary friend out of the diary, clinging to it, a last ember in his charcoal life, even learning to read and write cursive through spelling cards. "I don't want to be alone when I die," he says. But then he befriends the wheelchair-bound Pinky (Boyd Holbrook), a young man who lost his legs in the war, and a spark of hope appears… Until about an hour in, that is, when the film takes an unexpected, grisly turn that almost derails the entire plot.

Willie's skewed interpretation of "friendship" - a burnt diary, a bitter young veteran, a couple of maniacal kids that use him for kicks - is an effective prism through which writer/director Lee condemns society. "Look what you've done to this man," he accuses us. His film is about people who live minute to minute, cent to cent, spending their hard-earned cash on overpriced motel rooms, just to feel momentarily alive. These men and women shed their dignity a long time ago, glimmers of it peeking through intermittently. Macy Gray shows up in what amounts to barely more than a resonant cameo as a prostitute who gives blowjobs for $5 - the ultimate embodiment of stripped-away humanity - but all Willie wants for the money is a minute of love, a hug, to feel.

Other accomplished scenes include Willie's simple-yet-lyrical recital of his day-to-day living, Pinky's tragic fate, a wise and heartbreaking ex-piano player reminiscing about his glory days ("You gotta filer through the memories, pick the best one and hold that shit tight. Let the rest of them fade away")... When Willie tries to enlist in the army and doesn't meet the age requirements, he desperately insists, "I want you to use me as a human shield. I want you to throw me away." The film sustains a dismal, melancholic tone well.

Unfortunately, when it comes to the fighting - the central concept - the film starts to resemble a cardboard "Fight Club", and not in a good way. Bordering on mean-spirited, the film revels a bit too much in scenes of helpless, homeless folks beating the last semblance of life out of each other for the rich kids' amusement - whose exchanges, by the way, come off as both overwritten and shallow ("From now on, you are Romans, and these bums are gladiators!", their leader, JJ (an eccentrically evil Rhys Wakefield), proclaims). I know they are supposed to be terrible and stupid, but the film goes way overboard, a stark contrast to the more effective, quieter scenes. Perhaps it has something to do with the director's background - he has been involved in one way or another in all of the "Jackass" movies - but scenes like Willie beating the pulp out of an arguably mentally-challenged man evoke the horrid "Bumfights". The film is also a little one-sided and repetitive. We don't know anything about Willie's past, which makes it hard to relate to him, as he's borderline-psychotic. Last but not least, Terrence Howard appears in a few more-or-less powerful scenes, but one can't shake the feeling that the man's just cashing in his paycheck.

While "Cardboard Boxer"'s intentions are admirable and clear, and Thomas Haden Church truly commits to his character, it inadvertently leaves a bit of a sour taste in your mouth. Lee should have stuck to his guns, like Moverman did in "Time Out of Mind", and made his film a study of a man, driven to this point by a corrupt system that sends many lives spiraling down into the gutter. Instead what we have is an uneasy combination of true insight and a somewhat-forced, sentimental/derivative tale that borders on exploitation. Not quite a knockout then, but definitely worth a look.

3 out of 5 stars

The More You "Dig Two Graves", the More Surprises It Reveals

Synopsis: A girl's obsession with her brother's disappearance leads her on a nightmarish journey through a small town's Gothic landscape where she is faced with a deadly proposition. How far will she go to save the people she loves?

A pale, quiet young girl. A desolate lake. A grieving sheriff. Slithery snakes. While all the ingredients of your typical horror flick are here, filmmaker Hunter Adams subverts them into an effective little drama about redemption - one with slashed throats and blood guzzling. In that way, it's similar to "Personal Shopper", another horror-cum-redemption-drama I just reviewed, yet "Dig Two Graves" lacks the French film's assuredness, wackiness and depth.

That said, it would be unfair to expect Hunter Adams to be on Olivier Assayas' level, and in his feature debut the young director gets a lot of things right. Its outcome may be obvious from a mile away, and there are a few niggles on the way, but "Dig Two Graves" still manages to tickle heartstrings, as opposed to shredding nerves. This is the kind of film that marks its writer/director team as "one to watch".

Dedicated to Candy and Pam, "DTG" starts in 1947, with Deputy Waterhouse (Ted Levine) threatening to shoot Sheriff Proctor (Danny Goldring), after they dispose of two wrapped-up bodies in The Lake. Waterhouse clutches an occult-looking pendant in his hands, his eyes filled with remorse. 30 years later, siblings Sean (Ben Schneider) and Jake (Samantha Isler) are living out their halcyon days, riding bikes and exploring the wilderness surround their suburban little town - until Sean dies, that is, in The Lake.

Time passes. We find out that Waterhouse - now the town's sheriff with hemorrhoid issues and a predilection for Confucius - is Jake's grandfather. Upon hearing the news that a baby sibling is on the way, Jake escapes to his house and has feverish dreams about drowning in The Lake.

Mysterious, dirty, hillbilly-looking men appear in Jake's life, led by the creepy Wyeth (Troy Ruptash), who wears a top hat and seems to know a bit too much about the night Sean died. Upon making Jake perform the grisliest magic trick of her life, Wyeth "assures" her that Sean "is not dead, he's just hard to find." They bring her back to their devilish headquarters and offer an exchange: her brother, back from the dead, in exchange for Willie (Gabriel Cain), her bullied friend at school.

What follows is a gradually unfolding mystery, with weird side-tracks into the occult that bring down an otherwise-solid, and at times touching, story of two men (and a girl) dealing with grief, guilt and revenge - until the ultimate face-off (and plunge). Stomped and chomped snakes mesh uneasily with a resonant shot of blood mixing with egg yolk; half-naked characters mumbling occult gibberish and dancing around the fire precede a tense stand-off in the forest; there are laughable lines, like "put the goddamned egg salad down and listen to me" or "don't speak fucking gypsy to me" - but then most of what come out of Waterhouse's mouth is borderline-profound.

Which brings me to Ted Levine's performance, going a long way in buoying the film. Though at times he chews scenery as slavishly as his character chomps on his cigars, the actor brings gravitas and depth to an otherwise quite straightforward film. When he says, "you about done sucking' my dick?" to his kiss-up deputy, one can't help but wonder what this film would have been like if it focused solely on his character.

Samantha Isler needs a stronger directorial grip, but there's a steel shade in her eyes and a poise in her demeanor. She certainly has her standout moments, such as when she defends William from bullies by smacking one of them in the face with a bar of soap, or brings to mind Jennifer Lawrence's Ree, in the way she nonchalantly guts a deer.

The ending got to me, even though I saw it coming. Perhaps the film caught me at a vulnerable time. There's no denying its ominous atmosphere, the effectiveness of Eric Maddison's icy-cool camerawork or the gravity of its lead actor's performance. Hunter Adams went for something more than your average spook-house here, and for that her must be applauded. Candy and Pam, I'm sure, are very proud.

3 out of 5 stars

(Mostly) Everyone Will Love "Everybody Loves Somebody"

Synopsis: A successful and single career woman asks her co-worker to pose as her boyfriend at a family wedding back home in Mexico. Her situation gets complicated when her ex shows up at the ceremony.

Though Hollywood has recently made valiant strides to include more diversity in its roster of films, focusing primarily on African Americans in response to the 2016 #OscarsSoWhite backlash (an immediate slew of Afrocentric films was released: "Moonlight", "Sleight", "Hidden Figures", "Fences", "All Eyez on Me"), other demographics are still being severely underserved. Asian Americans - almost 6% of the U.S. population - were "presented" with the lousy "The Great Wall" as the sole 2016 studio film featuring a predominantly Asian cast (led by a predominantly white Matt Damon).

As for the Hispanic/Latino market (17% of U.S. population), after the unexpected (but completely rational) success of Eugenio Derbez's 2013 comedy "Instructions Not Included", the Dream Factory has been trying to cash that cow, producing similar, mid-grade fare, to progressively diminishing returns. That said, the intermittent popularity of films like the recent "How to Be a Latin Lover" proves that folks are willing to overlook shoddy filmmaking just to see their people and culture represented on silver screens.

Whether it's due to a lack of good marketing or the film's somewhat generic premise, writer/director Catalina Aguilar Mastretta's "Everybody Loves Somebody" failed to generate much buzz, at least Stateside. Too bad - it's inspiring to see films like this being produced, even if they do wholeheartedly embrace some of the oldest rom-com staples in the book. No one would label "ELS" "revelatory", yet it's a delightful little concoction, a representation of the Mexican culture that's both realistic and mega-glorified.

The self-absorbed Clara (Karla Souza), a doctor in Los Angeles, has a somewhat pessimistic outlook on love: "It's the privilege of a chosen few. And if you're lucky enough to find it, you lose it." Consequently, she avoids attachment - until she has to find a "cute Mexican" to make her parents happy, who are getting married after 40 years (!) of being together. Her Australian co-worker, Asher (Ben O'Toole), happens to fit the bill... despite being, you know, Australian - don't ask, just go with it - but just when sparks start to ignite, Clara's hunky ex, "adventure Daniel" (José María Yazpik), shows up at the ceremony, charming everyone with his wonderful Doctors Without Borders stories. Clara ends up in a love triangle, with secrets surfacing (e.g. one of the characters is a widow) and emotions boiling.

If the story doesn't exactly sound original, it's not. What propels the film along is the effortless charm of its leads, the panoramic scenery (there's no shortage of stunning Mexican vistas in this colorful postcard of a motion picture; Mastretta's Mexico may as well be Monaco) and just a little extra much-needed depth the filmmaker injects into the proceedings that grounds it all in reality, making both the dramatic and comic bits resonate.

There are nifty snippets of dialogue along the way. "Dad, when will you learn Spanish like him?" a kid asks. "As soon as your mom starts fasting on Yom Kippur," his father deadpans. "He's nice and cute," Clara says. "He's koala," Daniel responds, "you're seeing a koala." I also like the line: "It was a laughter that made you fly." There are other standouts, like when Clara talks about "reinforcements" and "neutralizers", or when she goes off, in a fit of rage, at a couple of expecting parents. A dinner sequence, and the next-morning poker game, are particularly well-directed, with tensions rising between our sparring trio.

Of course, a film such as this does not come without its trappings. There's the predictability, the cheesy melodrama (Clara and Daniel riding bikes through sun-swept hills; Clara's mother even proclaims at one point: "Who would've ever thought you'd be my cheesy daughter?"), the perfunctory secondary characters, the annoyingly twinkling soundtrack, the obligatory drunken karaoke sequence, and, oh God, the regrettable speechifying (Asher waxing poetic to Clara towards the end: "It'd be adorable if it wasn't so pathetic.")

Whatever. All is forgiven - because "Everybody Loves Somebody" doesn't talk down to its audience, it has three leads who share real chemistry, it's not stupefyingly rudimentary and, most importantly, it is infinitely better than a lot of similar, all-white, Katherine Heigl stuff that Hollywood churns out. The industry seems ready and willing to embrace more cultures, expand the horizons. It should give more films like "ELS" a chance.

3 out of 5 stars

Annette Bening and Jamie Bell Shine in the Otherwise Forgettable "Films Stars Don't Die in Liverpool"

Synopsis: *A romance sparks between a young actor and a Hollywood leading lady.*

Director Paul McGuigan made exactly one memorable film, and that was 18 years ago: the sadistic "Gangster No.1", mostly resonant due to Malcolm McDowell's deranged lead performance and the in-your-face grotesque violence. That was McGuigan's second directorial feature, after his "'Trainspotting' wannabe" debut, the hollow but colorful "Acid House". A chain of tepid releases followed, negligible-to-average thrillers that had their rare moments but failed to connect with audiences: "The Reckoning", "Wicker Park", "Lucky Number Slevin", "Push" - and the most recent box office bomb, "Victor Frankenstein", as poorly hobbled together as its monster.

Now, in an admirable move, McGuigan shifts gears and visualizes screenwriter Matt Greenblah's (who wrote the superb "Control") adaptation of Peter Turner's memoir, the nostalgic May-December romance "Film Stars Don't Die in Liverpool". While its leads try their best to anchor the film in depth, it treads shallow waters. One can't help but imagine what a more visionary/adventurous/capable director like, say, Michael Winterbottom or Danny Boyle, would have made of such a poignant real-life story. McGuigan does his best to follow all the rights beats - but sometimes stepping wrong is what makes a film such as this special.

Liverpool, 1981. Gloria Grahame (Annette Bening), a washed-up Hollywood star who hit her peak in the 1950's when she won an Oscar, shows up with "stomach gas" at her young bisexual lover Peter's (Jamie Bell) Liverpool home. It's immediately apparent that her "gas" is actually terminal sickness, and Gloria's in denial, hiding from the world in Peter's bedroom, convinced she'll get better. Flashbacks to 1979 reveal their "meet-cute". They dance together in an extended sequence. He takes her to see "Alien", where they giggle and make-out. She in turn takes him to her play - where she states, "Everybody here wants to fuck me", with a grace that only Bening can manage.

Smitten and fascinated by the star, Peter follows her to a green-screen Los Angeles, then to a greener-screen New York. Back in 1981, once Peter finds out what's really wrong with Gloria, he tries to convince her to be with family, but, delusional, she is resolutely staying in Liverpool. Who wouldn't? Of course, she doesn't get any better. The second half of "FSDDIL" devolves into a weepy-of-the-week, albeit with Hollywood polish: nifty cinematography courtesy of Urszula Pontikos and Eve Stewart's gold-hued, suitably retro production design.

There are sequences peppered throughout the film that provide glimpses of how much more fun and unexpected it all could have been. Peter's terrified at the movies, while she laughs at him - a rare honest moment, untouched by Hollywood gloss and/or schmaltz. In another touching scene, Gloria gets offended when Peter deems her too old to play Juliet in Shakespeare's play. Peter's mom's reluctance to go to Manila (a running thread through the film) is lukewarm but at least provides SOME insight into his family.

And of course, the leads are magnificent. While Bening carries the film - no surprise there - embodying a sophisticated has-been who's prone to eccentricities and bad moods, Bell becomes the emotional epicenter of "FSDDIL". Whether they fight or make love, the two actors' chemistry is palpable - and the film's saving grace.

Problem is, "FSDDIL" doesn't fully function as an examination of what it means to have fallen off the peak of stardom. Nor does it probe deep enough when it comes to its two protagonists' relationship. Stale and generic, energized only by the sparks of its leads, McGuigan's bio-pic chugs along, predictable every step of the way, never too boring, but never exhilarating either.

From time to time, the director utilizes stylistic techniques - meta sequences of Bening-as-Grahame watching herself on the silver screen; pseudo-1950's flashbacks - but they do little to elevate the affair above its cancer drama tropes. For a film that deals so much with faith, it never takes a leap of it. While I wouldn't call McGuigan's eighth feature "memorable", it's certainly diverting due to its lead performances, and marks the second minor highlight in the director's somewhat-unremarkable career.

3 out of 5 stars

"Finding Dory" Searches for Deep Meaning but Ends Up in Shallow Waters

Synopsis: *The friendly-but-forgetful blue tang fish reunites with her loved ones, and everyone learns a few things about the real meaning of family along the way.*

The fact that Pixar is making a "Cars 3" is disheartening, to say the least. Not only is it the least successful offering by the typically "can do no wrong" studio (nothing about the "Cars" universe makes sense to me), it also continues their "sequelitis" trend. Why make a third part to a critically-panned sequel? With the exception of the "Toy Story" trilogy (about to become a quadrilogy, by the way), which built upon its subtle themes, developed its characters and made it all feel like a fluid story, Pixar's other prequel, "Monsters University", proved to be a mere rehashing of the original, with nary an original bone in its flimsy plot. Oh, and "The Incredibles 2" is on the way. Yay.

Now Andrew Stanton, the man who helmed two instant classics, "Wall-E" and "Finding Nemo", returns with a similarly half-baked retelling/sequel of the original tale. There's nothing particularly wrong with it, the voice cast delivers, and some scenes verge on pure brilliance (Pixar wouldn't have it any other way), but I found myself asking the question: Is the gargantuan production house, now owned by Disney, running out of original ideas, or just cashing in on proven successes?

"Finding Dory" starts off briskly enough, and the way it incorporates the original film's storyline into part two is rather ingenuous. Ellen DeGeneres reprises her role as Dory, a secondary character, now taking central stage. Dory's folks Charlie (Eugene Levy) and Jenny (Diane Keaton) attempt to deal with her disability - memory loss - by making sure little Dory remembers the line "Hi, my name is Dory and I have short-term memory loss" and finds her "way home" by following a carefully paved-out sequence of shells. Those scenes mirror Nemo's struggle with his little fin and adjusting to the adult world in Stanton's first film. (Being Different and Proud are two of the many, many themes spelled out in this undersea adventure, and there's nothing wrong with that - it's just that they are all both too blunt and diluted, a myriad of motifs, such as reinforcing the horrors of animal captivity, living in the moment, etc, etc).

Dory, of course, gets lost, and meets Marlin (Albert Brooks) and Nemo (Hayden Rolence) two years later. After their rollickin' adventure, Dory spends her days pestering father and son, even joining Nemo on his school field trips, to the dismay of teacher Mr. Ray (Bob Peterson). Mr. Ray speaks of the Undertow, which leads to Dory gradually remembering her parents. Marlin reluctantly agrees to join her on another adventure; "I know a guy," he says. The "guy" turns out to be Crush

(Andrew Stanton), the buzzed-out sea turtle, a favorite from the first film, that takes Marlin, Nemo and Dory to California. On their way, the trio escapes a vicious sea creature and get separated at the Marine Life Institute, where Dory's parents may or may not be held captive. As a result, Marlin and Nemo try to find Dory, as Dory tries to find her folks… and herself.

Dominic West and Idris Elba provide one of the highlights as sea lions Rudder and Fluke - replacements for the "mine, mine, mine" hilarity of "Finding Nemo"'s seagulls. Their deadpan delivery, and verbal abuse of a Groucho-Marx like character, provide a glimpse of what the film could have been, had it contained more non-sequiturs and humor like this. Becky, a one-eyes bird-like…thing, is another marvelous (and bonkers) creation. Other new characters include the snarky octopus Hank (Ed O'Neill); the visually-impaired whale shark Destiny (Kaitlin Olson); Bailey (Ty Burrell), a beluga whale, whose way of communication is not dissimilar to that of Batman's digital vision at the end of "The Dark Knight"; and a pearl oyster, whose heart was broken by a clam.

I know it's all animation and you're not supposed to wonder about the probabilities of it all. That said, the best animation makes you buy things within the magical universes it creates. In "Cars", it creeped the engine fuel out of me that the Roman Colosseum still exists in a world solely inhabited by cars… did vehicles take over Earth, Skynet-style? In "Finding Dory", how the urchin do the fish know what their species are, without ever interacting with humans? How do they travel so effortlessly between Australia (in "Finding Nemo") and friggin' California, without the climate changes making their little bodies float up lifelessly to the shimmering ocean surface? Little Nemo gets slapped around so much and goes through so many polluted containers - both (I assume) salt-water and not - he must be made of Adamantium.

The animation is very pretty - one can only imagine the amount of work that went into making Ed O'Neill's Hank, an octopus (well, technically "septopus") desperate to get to Cleveland ("30 Rock" made Clevelan funny a million years ago), blend in and out of things, his texture changing with every move. The underwater scenes are pure eye candy - but, shockingly, not that big of an improvement over the 2003 original. After the jaw-dropping effects of the recent "The Good Dinosaur", this feels like a minor step back. There is an intricate, POV shot at one point that takes you in and out of water - but again, it's a replica of the "escape the aquarium" sequence in "Finding Nemo".

The film certainly does not side-step sentimentality. "Not everything in life is easy to do" is one of the Buddhist-like teachings in this film. "Someone with three hearts shouldn't be so mean", Dory tells another character. There is also a dearth of witty one-liners (the Sigourney Weaver "thing" is funny at first, and then gets increasingly less so each time the joke's used). The best one comes from one of the human scientists, who tells off her goofing colleague: "We're scientists. We've talked about this." Another title for the film could also be Ex Machina (shout out to Jeremy Scott of Youtube's brilliant Cinemasins), as so many darn coincidences happen in this film, it's a wonder Dory got lost in the first place.

At times, it feels like the film is desperately fishing (sorry) for moments of enchantment that came so effortlessly in the earlier Pixar offerings. The synopsis speaks for itself: "everyone learns a few things about the real meaning of family along the way". The vague generalization of that consensus represents the unfocused nature and watered-down (pun intended) values of "Finding Dory", age-old truisms that are wearing thin in family entertainment - especially when compared to Pixar's boundary-breaking, sharp-as-a-blade "Inside Out." Not nearly as incisive and mind-blowing as that film, nor as photo-realistically beautiful as the studio's recent, similarly by-the-numbers (but with an "at least" original story) "The Good Dinosaur", "Finding Dory" is nevertheless a pleasant, slight little distraction. Judging by the "oohs" and "aahs" at the jam-packed, toddler-infested press screening, Pixar's latest, strategically-placed bait will make the wee ones bite in hordes (or should it be schools? I'm all punned-out, guys), while the adults will find it as exciting as… well, bait-fishing. Here's hoping Pixar's upcoming "Coco" brings back some of that much-needed ingenuity, for which the epic studio is known.

3 out of 5 stars

"From Hollywood to Rose" Resonates in Unexpected Ways

Synopsis: *When embarking on a mythic quest, its best to take the bus.*

After the recent catastrophe that was the micro-budget "We Make Movies" (read review here), here's an example of what a talented filmmaking team can achieve on a minuscule budget. Liz Graham and Matt Jacobs' "From Hollywood to Rose", a poignant little ode to L.A. and its outcasts, is far from perfect, but, unlike the aforementioned sorry excuse for a film, it's honest, has a style of its own and an original story to tell, while its robust lead performance carries us through the rougher patches. I thoroughly enjoyed it, flaws and all.

An aging woman in a cheap wedding gown (Eve Annenberg) - never named - waits for the bus at night in Hollywood. Her "mythic quest": get to Venice. On her journey, she encounters transgender ladies, a compassionate businessman who believes he's a reptile, a bus driver having a mental breakdown - and two arguing film geeks (Maxx Maulion and Brad Herman), who proceed to befriend her. Together, they eat burritos, ride a skateboard and divulge intimate secrets. Her background is revealed, as is theirs… And then the film boldly separates them in its last third, putting her back on another bus to complete the journey.

The woman rarely talks at first, but gradually starts to open up. Mascara runs down her face. She wears thick-rimmed party glasses and a giant white bow. She tends to get "panicky" and her "brain freezes up". She waxes poetic about "Blade Runner" ("I used to feel sorry for the replicant") and fried food ("I know it's bad but I eat it anyway.") She's afraid to swim in the ocean because she's scared of sharks. She also loves her fish-lamp and knows surprisingly a lot about Bruce Lee's signature moves.

Basked in shadows, lovable oddballs and half-broken neon signs, the film is quintessentially "L.A.": a melting pot of crazy, wonderful, dangerous and quirky people, where no one will bat an eye at a disheveled-looking lady in a gown strolling down a beach. The film functions as a somewhat-demented tour guide through the city's nightlife, where a surprise lurks around every corner, and a myriad of deep issues oozes through the glossy exterior.

That said, the heightened reality of the film does get overbearing. Liz and Matt lack the grasp of, say, Jim Jarmusch, who gets away with outlandish characters and non-sequitur lines. "FHTR"'s dialogue could have been a bit sharper - especially the supposedly "witty" exchanges that just hang there, such as, "you look like a retarded 12-year-old" or "remain dauntless in your pursuit." The film geeks' continuous debates over Christopher Nolan, "Willow" and "X-Men" turn tedious. Some of the acting is (understandably) amateurish.

The film is at its best when it's at its weirdest, like when the woman encounters a butch, tattooed haute couture connoisseur, who talks about Betsy Johnson and Alexander McQueen, in-between… choking her. That sequence is borderline-perfect in its hilarity, darkness, weirdness. If only the film sustained that perfect pitch throughout its duration, it would have been something really special.

Major points for trying. There's a lot of potential on display here. I can't wait to see what Liz and Matt do next; with a slightly bigger budget and a tighter focus, it could end up magnifique.

3 out of 5 stars

"Gimme Danger" Could Use a Shot of Adrenalin

Synopsis: *An in-depth look at the legendary punk band, The Stooges.*

Iggy Pop (aka Jim Osterberg), Ron Asheton, Scott Asheton and Dave Alexander. They were the original The Stooges, a grungy punk band that changed the future of rock music in the late 1960s - early 1970s with its raw, uncompromising approach and nihilistic attitude. In 1973, they were dirt - now they are legends. In the words of a young Iggy himself, "It isn't too easy being The Stooges sometimes."

Jim Jarmusch's doc, narrated by Iggy, traces it all, from Iggy's childhood and the band's formation, through the rise-and-fall of their career, to their 2003 Coachella reunion and 2010 induction into the Rock and Roll Hall of Fame. Music highlights and some primitively animated interludes are peppered in-between. Pretty standard stuff. Gimme more danger, Jarmusch.

Interviewed in front of a laundromat, perhaps as a nod to the good old days of stuffing fresh marijuana into a tumble drier, the 69-year-old Iggy is witty, animated, a little spacey, very leathery and surprisingly clear-minded. There's obvious rapport between him and Jarmusch, which is crucial to the one aspect the doc really has going for it: candidness, leading to some truly fascinating tidbits.

Did you know, for example, that the spontaneity of 1950s comedian Soupy Sales' act was a major influence on Iggy's career? Or that the band's name came from a tripping-on-LSD Ron: ""Let's just call it The Stooges, 'cos we don't do anything wrong, but everyone is picking on us." I bet you had no idea that Iggy happened to be neighbors with Andy Warhol, who suggested Iggy "sings the newspapers", or that he declined the offer to be Peter Pan (!) on Broadway, suggesting he play Charles Manson instead.

Iggy refers to Bob Dylan as "blah blah blah blah" and remembers how he "smoked a big joint one day by the [Chicago] river and realized [he] was not black". He reminisces about the radical 1960's Ann Arbor days, smoking weed and dropping acid. Yes, most memories include drugs, lots and lots of drugs, from LSD to cocaine to the big H. "We started looking dirtier and skinnier and more and more used," Iggy recollects. "Upsetting people because of me wherever we went."

Live archive footage of Iggy working the crowd provide some of "Gimme Danger"'s most exhilarating moments. The band barely moves, just jamming out, while Iggy crowd-surfs, curses and gives his mic fillatio - and then gets back up on stage and resumes singing, and the band's right there with him. Their unique brand of giddy energy, "don't give a fuck" attitude and pure rawness paved the road to The Ramones, Sex Pistols, The Damned, Sonic Youth, Nirvana, The White Stripes and even Bowie himself, whom we see do a "Black Dog" cover in a fascinating - and too short - bit of archival footage.

While I appreciate the intimate, laid-back approach - which I believe Jarmusch chose purposefully, to defy people's expectations of the rebellious, backward-bending, naked Iggy - it renders the doc a little tame, considering it's, you know, about the freakin' Stooges, made by THE ultimate cinematic rebel. Jarmusch's idle "Paterson", still out in theaters, has more tension than this doc. Though insightful and bound to satisfy hardcore Iggy fans, "Gimme Danger" titular's request may as well be aimed at itself.

3 out of 5 stars

"Ice Guardians", or "Hockey: Making Dentists Rich Since 1875"

Synopsis: *On-ice enforcers struggle to rise through the professional ranks of the world's most prestigious hockey league, only to be confronted with a new found fight for the existence of the role itself.*

"Hockey's not just played on ice, hockey's played on hormones." - Howard Bloom, Author & Mass Behavior Expert, *Ice Guardians*

Brett Harvey's documentary "Ice Guardians" opens with a split in opinion: some folks think hockey brawls interrupt the games' flow, others come purely for the bashed-in helmets and shattered noses. What's hockey aboot? Is fighting just as much a part of hockey as the game itself? Do the players feel bad aboot it? Those are the central questions permeating the very Canadian study of hockey enforcers - the bulky guys hired to protect the stars of the team - and their struggles, both on ice, with the media, and ultimately with themselves. A bit too neatly/predictably structured - skimming through the players' personal lives, split into many chapters, siding with its giant heroes every step of the way - the film is nevertheless eye-opening, because it examines the players' "purpose" from many angles, but mostly due to the testimonies coming from the players themselves, massive fellows who prove to be quite fragile.

The aforementioned chapters speak for themselves. "Why Hockey?" inquires why hockey, of all sports, is defined by the number of teeth left on the ice. As it turns out, it's the higher speed, players attacking each other "with a massive stick in your hand that could be used as a weapon". As another player states, "the danger, the adrenalin level is far higher" than in other sports. The players seem to be drafted based on their physical self-preservation skills, lured in with the golden ticket into the NHL. "I waited by the phone all day," remembers Todd Fedoruk, an NHL/AHL player (the difference between NHL/AHL is explained in the film), "and I got the call from the Philadelphia Flyers, and my father said, 'Well, you're their type of player, that's for sure!'" "Type" being bulky, eager and ready to punch.

"Welcome to the Jungle" delves into the enforcer's responsibility: to protect his inmates, and, (in)advertently, instigate the one thing that keeps hockey truly compelling - the fighting. There's no arguing the greats' success: Wayne Gretzky would be nothing without his enforces, particularly the beast-like Dave Semenko. It's the aggression, the concussions, the broken teeth and limbs that come along and get the crowds cheering that raise ethical and moral questions. Some of the players do resemble brutes, trained dogs snarling at each other toothlessly on the ring - or, regarded from a different perspective, Vikings, six-foot-five gladiators, showcasing their skills in front of an adoring crowd. "It is the league's responsibility to prevent cheap shots," a neurosurgeon states, "as long as they follow the rules." But where does one draw the line when the rules are blurry?

And so the documentary goes: "Power of Intimidation" reveals the power play dynamics within the game and how it's built on dominance and fear; "The Beginning" goes back in time to the first-ever hockey game that ended in a fight; "Welcome to Broad Street" traces hockey's past through the days of Philadelphia Flyers infusing it with overt testosterone; "Building a Warrior" scrutinizes the tactical aspects of a hockey fight… In "Injuries", the players proudly showcase deep-purple knuckles, talk about popped shoulders, knocked-out teeth and forehead gashes. The guys claim it doesn't even hurt in the moment, when all you see is red and adrenalin pumps through your veins. The emotional toll proves to be tougher to handle: anxious sweats, seeing your family after a bloody match, being embarrassed, getting knocked down, not wanting to let teammates down, the media's scrutiny - and, of course, the term "goons", to which the players seem averse.

"The enforcer is the most moral and ethical member of the tribe, because he is willing to go through such sacrifice," argues Howard Bloom, the Mass Behavior Expert, but then he adds that it's all about perspective: from within the group that's what an enforcer is, but from the outside, they look like enemies or goons. "Ice Guardians" then delves into more interesting territory, comparing hockey and the roles of teammates in sports to the way we structure societies. It's "the externalization of an old, emotional, deep human template," says Bloom, referring to the roles of enforcers. It's in our human nature to separate ourselves into certain roles within a group. It also happens to be in our nature to be mesmerized by violence, a "fundamental tribalism", an exorcism of our demons, an "innate desire to see justice being done" without killing each other.

One can't blame "Ice Guardians" for not being meticulous enough. Chapters like "Etiquette" show how such a thing can emerge "out of the chaos of hockey", and how there are rules, such as no sucker punching, no eye gouging, no breaking someone's head through the ice. The doc also discusses substance abuse, and how the media tends to perceive their drug use and concussions as causes of the deaths in the NHL - but the filmmaker is too adoring to truly dwell on the dark side of things. Among my chief few niggles with the doc is its clear awe of the protagonists, as if it doesn't dare to step into their shadows, in fear of being knocked out.

Candid tidbits from the players themselves form the heart of the "Ice Guardians". NHL/AHL player Dave Schultz shares, "I didn't start playing hockey to fight! That's the last thing I would've thought of. But once you start… I was never able to stop." "It's really not the safest thing to be doing," another player states, chuckling, "but that's why there are only a few of us maniacs that do it." "I used to wrap my hands in those chains and then go and whack trees," yet another player states nonchalantly. Hockey fan and actor Jay Baruchel (who directed the hockey-themed "Goon") pops up briefly to talk about momentum and its role in the game; he also dares you to "check your fucking pulse" if you don't feel the hair on the back of your arms stand up when witnessing a hockey fight.

The "rags-to-riches" process is laid out in detail, the doc portraying what it takes to make it up the NHL ladder, when your sole role is to fight, and the repercussions of such a life. Kudos to Brett Harvey for both directing and shooting the doc, though it's an odd jumble of styles: an in-your-face, biased, ESPN-like profile, clashing violently with a poignant, intimate study of what drives those "on-ice enforcers" and casts a dark mirror to society. At 105 minutes, it's also at least 20 minutes too long. If you're not a hockey fan, this may prove to be as dry as the ice on the ring, but if you're into the sport, you'll want to get on that ring with the "Ice Guardians".

3 out of 5 stars

Diane Kruger's Electric Performance Saves Conventional Drama "In the Fade"

Synopsis: *Katja's life collapses after the death of her husband and son in a bomb attack. After a time of mourning and injustice, Katja seeks revenge.*

From "Munich" to "Marathon Day", senseless acts of terrorism (is there any other kind?) and their repercussions have been widely depicted on film. Similarly, extensive is the history of thrillers about women hell-bent on revenge: from "Foxy Brown" to "Girl with the Dragon Tattoo". Fatih Akin's "In the Fade" attempts to tackle both subjects. Think of the JLo starrer "Enough", replace its lead with an infinitely subtler actress, add a political element and a heavy dose of artistic flourishes, and you'll have an idea of what "In the Fade" is like, its title quite aptly describing the length of time it stayed in my memory. A weird amalgamation of TV-drama-of-the-week and searing character study, the film is compulsively watchable but hollow. Were it not for Diane Kruger's revelatory, Cannes-winning performance anchoring the by-turns tedious, sappy and predictable elements, this would have been just another cautionary tale on Lifetime - albeit a particularly pretty one.

Split into three parts - the sorrowful first third, the courtroom-set middle and the thriller-like finale - the film always seems on the edge of taking off but never really does, each part settling into a comfortably conventional rhythm. After her husband Nuri (Numan Acar) and son get killed in an explosion, Katja and her lawyer set off to bring justice to the perpetrators: a blonde couple (Ulrich Brandhoff and Hanna Hilsdorf) who happen to be Nazis. With authorities digging into Nuri's shady past - he served time for smuggling drugs - and scrutinizing Katja's substance abuse, she is left to her own devices and realizes that it may be "A Time to Kill", going all MacGyver on the assailants' asses.

As a courtroom drama, it's nothing new - we've all lived through John Grisham's heyday; "The Rainmaker" this ain't. Haberbeck (Johannes Krisch), the Nazis' lawyer, is so purely evil, a nasty growth protruding out of his bald head, it's as if he stepped off a Leni Riefenstahl set, enunciating and spitting each syllable with utmost vehemence. "In the Fade" doesn't really function as a mystery either, for there is no real investigation. As a treatise on terrorism and its impact, the film's lukewarm, its message not extending beyond "terrorism is as senseless as the revenge it spawns" and "why can't we all just get along". As an examination of racism, it's simply inefficient: what's the conflict here? What are the Nazi couple's motivations, aside from Nuri being a foreigner, as a title card solemnly proclaims prior to the credits rolling? Yes, I get it, there are folks who bomb folks simply because of their race, but I'd still like to see them fleshed out beyond mere cardboard villains. I guess it works best as a character drama, thanks to Diane Kruger's powerful portrayal of grief.

And oh man, she brings it. Known primarily for her roles as Helen in "Troy" and Bridget von Hammersmark in "Inglorious Basterds", Kruger gets a chance to truly flex her acting chops here; she's up to the task. From the unforgiving close-ups of her face in the immediate aftermath of this immense tragedy, to pure exhaustion, to unadulterated fury, to clenched-teeth determination, it's all right there, in each flutter of her eyelids. In one of the film's truly original moments, Katja is in a field of hay, her straw-blonde hair blending with the swaying stalks, and the actress wonderfully morphs with her surroundings, a literal force of nature. She handles some of the film's other potentially-campy scenes - an interrupted suicide attempt, listening to painful autopsy report details about her child's death - turning them into highlights.

Despite her acting, there's not much we get to know about Katja, or her husband, or their circle of friends. The film is so minimal and so resolutely focused on one aspect of what I imagine would be a kaleidoscopic emotional spectrum in the wake of such tragedy, it has little room to breathe and doesn't attain the lingering effect for which it so clearly strives. Writer/director Akin's filmography dates back over 20 years, and while I'm ashamed to admit I'm not familiar with his films, judging by "In the Fade" it's clear that the man knows how to position a camera, sustain suspense, create a rewarding sequence… It also seems like he thinks that has more on his mind than he really does. A bit more depth next time, please, thank you.

3 out of 5 stars

"Jack of the Red Hearts" Doesn't Entirely Steal Yours

Synopsis: *A teenage con artist tricks a desperate mother into hiring her as a live-in companion for her autistic daughter.*

According to director Janet Grillo's vast - and gloriously mercurial - filmography, spanning from executive-producing both the second and third feature in the infamous "House Party" trilogy to working on sets with David O. Russell, she steadily gained experience, until hitting her stride circa 2008, winning an Emmy for her work on HBO's "Autism: The Musical", and being nominated in the Best Narrative Feature category for her autism drama "Fly Away" at the SXSW festival. Grillo continues her exploration of the subject of autism in "Jack of the Red Hearts", a well-meaning tale that rings true in ambition but false in execution.

Early in the film, Kay (Famke Janssen) and Mark (Scott Cohen), argue over whose life is more difficult; Kay is exhausted from staying at home 24/7 with their autistic daughter Glory (Taylor Richardson), while Mark claims he's too busy. Kay wants a career, too - but who's to take care of Glory?

Cut To: EXT.: Orphan sisters Jack (AnnaSophia Robb) and Coke (Sophia Anne Caruso) (Jack and Coke… because they blend so well together…) loiter outside a food mart, fooling folks into giving them spare change under the guise of being Red Cross workers. Jack - bratty and selfish but also street-wise - is under probation, her sister under the threat of being placed with a foster family. Unable to sustain themselves, Jack sheds her goth look and cons her way (a tad too smoothly, if you ask me) into serving as a live-in companion for Glory, for $20 an hour, under the pseudonym Donna.

Jack/Donna meets Robert (Israel Broussard), Glory's brother, who is a sarcastic prick at first ("Are you here to save the day?" he asks, munching on cereal), but then rushes over to his friend's car and rants about how "unequivocally hot" the new "babysitter" is. Kay takes Jack on a tour: the multitude of vitamins that needs to be consumed, Glory's "bible" that requires studying, Glory's classes that cannot be missed.

They say grace around the dinner table, while Glory walks around, grabbing mashed potatoes off everyone's plates. When Jack refuses to share hers, Glory reacts violently. "We are accustomed to Glory taking things off our plates while we eat," Mark explains, as the rest of the family eyes Jack disapprovingly.

Jack starts off by treating Glory like a spoiled child, is forceful and impatient. She sees her eating dirt and comments, "That's gross. What's wrong with you?", before taking a nap. This is followed by an extended yam-feeding sequence (which made me feel uneasy, but I guess it was supposed to).

More family dynamics unravel, such as father-son issues, but all gradually gets resolved: Jack bonds with Glory and her parents, she grows a conscience, a tween romance blooms, it all comes crashing down before... Well, you can probably guess the rest. And if not, by all means, watch the film and let it shock you with its twists and turns.

Sarcasm aside, there are some pretty good reasons to watch the film. Glory's POV, a murky yet shiny, muted world, out of which she keeps getting violently yanked, is vividly portrayed. Jack's relationship with her sister Coke is so real, I almost wished this whole story was about their travails. There are some standout sequences, most involving Glory getting herself into dangerous situations (a roof, a tall branch). A scene in the middle of the film involves Jack actually discussing a Jack of Red Hearts card with Glory, which not-so-subtly refers to the Red Cross shenanigans in the earlier sequences, and how much Jack has changed since then... Subtle? No, but effective nonetheless.

AnnaSophia Robb, after her turns in "Bridge to Terabithia" and the more recent "The Way Way Back", displays real maturity and grasp of character in the lead, although she is more believable when "fake-charming" than "real-goth". Cohen and Janssen are decent, but the formulaic script doesn't give them much leeway with nuance. Tonye Patano as Jack's probation officer, and Drena De Niro (yes! the young De Niro!) as Jack's counsellor, provide memorable albeit too-brief support.

The film is stuffed with the aforementioned formula. Sappy moments abound, most involving the central romance, which feels "Twilight"-ish and out of place; e.g. Jack rescues Robert from pretentious bullies by kissing him in front of them, and consequently putting them all in the right place. Another particularly abrasive, "sisters being forcefully separated" scene at the end, carried all the pathos of "Sophie's Choice" and none of its tragedy. And God, I'm getting so sick of all the twangy music in low-key American indie films! Scott Cohen literally picks up a guitar and twangs away - let's just say the actor should stick to his day job.

It's not that the film is poorly made or even unentertaining - it just offers virtually no surprises, delivering a predictable, made-for-TV storyline - "arrogant girl learns about selflessness" - in a somewhat-clunky fashion. What's admirable is how believable the details of "life with autism" are laid out, lacking the gloss of similar

Hollywood fare. ("Rain Man" is even referenced in a gently funny remark.) "Jack of the Red Hearts" clearly stems from personal experience and/or investment. "You look retarded," Jack says at one point, and Robert voices all of us by answering, "You're not supposed to say that." Janet Grillo's film is a reminder of how tough autism truly is, without embellishments. I just wish the film - its characterizations and plot turns - was less Lifetime and more lifelike.

3 out of 5 stars

"Julian Schnabel: A Private Portrait" Paints a Great Artist in Broad Strokes

Synopsis: *A look at the personal life and public career of New York artist Julian Schnabel.*

Neo-expressionist painter and award-winning director Julian Schnabel has, without a doubt, firmly established himself in the contemporary art world. From sculpting gargantuan "plate paintings" to helming intimate-but-epic biographies (five, to be exact: "Basquiat", "Before Night Falls", "The Diving Bell and the Butterfly", "Berlin" and "Miral"), Schnabel's work tends to revolve around the theme of testing one's psychological limits.

It's evident in Schnabel's own paintings, composed of curtains, sails, ceramic, wax, velvet, plaster and photographs - cluttered, torn expressions of an unsettled, beautiful mind. It's evident in the art of the public figures he depicts, be it the struggles of openly gay poet Reinaldo Arenas, or Lou Reed's tumultuous career, seen through the prism of German's chief gloomy city, or the heroic acts of a young Palestinian girl.

It's not, however, evident in Pappi Corsicato's breezy documentary "Julian Schnabel: An Intimate Portrait". Featuring contributions from Schnabel admirers Al Pacino, Bono and Willem Dafoe, this extended made-for-TV biography paints a well-rounded and entertaining portrait of the artist but fails to elicit a visceral emotional response that one would expect from such a controversial subject matter.

The theme of water is prevalent throughout the film, a significant part of his work - "I use water a lot in a subject matter and also as a material". The film starts with Schnabel diving from a towering cliffside into an azure ocean, akin to the Bell in his film (one of the doc's sole artistic flourishes). Corsicato then proceeds to cut between Schnabel working in his New York studio in 2014, different edits from a variety of sources, archival material and a variety of interviews with Schnabel's sister, his sons and daughters, his wives (all of whom speak fondly of him), gallery owner Mary Boone, friends, other artists, film producers, a former assistant and a curator/writer.

"He sees beauty where he looks," is a reoccurring motif, all of Schnabel's friends and critics agreeing that his work is of towering importance and beauty, yet rarely discussing what lies behind it. Executive-produced by Schnabel himself, this "Private Portrait" conveniently skips past his latest directorial feature, the critically-slammed "Miral", making one wonder how "private" (read: biased) this "portrait" really is. Charismatic, torn, full of himself and abrasive, Schnabel is a fascinating figure, but here, despite being featured in almost every shot, he's held at an arm's length, like a painting we cannot approach to study closer, but everyone tells us is so beautiful and complex. "He's playing with conventions in unconventional ways," says Willem Dafoe reverentially.

Constricted by the claustrophobic, blank "quarters" of his childhood, young Julian found solace in large-scale paintings and exuberant colors. "He was pretty wild, taking acid even day, skipping school and going surfing," his daughter shares. His early studios were "full of paintings, piled on top of each other", gargantuan ones, which immediately impressed gallery owners. In the late 1970s, his art exploded, and Schnabel began mingling with the likes of Warhol, traveling the world with his wife - living the life, in other words.

Ironically, for someone who freed himself from familial and societal restrictions by escaping into the vast freedom of the art world, once Schnabel birthed children, he became quite the restrictive parent. Everything had to be a certain way. "I grew to appreciate it," his despondent son says, "we weren't going to go on walks in the park or play basketball." Schnabel himself admits that that period is difficult for him to talk about. And so he doesn't, the documentary politely moving on.

In its second half, "A Private Portrait" delves into the cinematic part of Schnabel's career. Heavily influenced by "The Godfather" and "Spartacus", he always wanted to make films, the lines between painting and directing blurring. "He throws his actors at the camera like he does with paint!" exclaims actress Anne Consigny. Going film-by-film - except, that is, Schnabel's 2011 misfire, which never happened, according to Corsicato - the film gains momentum but loses poignancy, resembling a behind-the-scenes featurette. It all sort of concludes in the fisherman's village of Montauk, Julian's hiding place, where he spends time with his family - and, of course, paints.

Jarring in their wild combination of splattered colors and vivid, three-dimensional structures, Schnabel's "bigger than life" paintings really do provoke an immediate gut reaction - I just wish the doc had the same impact, or at least slowed down and spoke more about the pieces. "When you get attached to somebody," Schnabel says, discussing loneliness, "you find your mother in their arms." This is about insightful as his own commentary gets. There are tidbits here and there about what lies behind his art - say, how he depicted occurrences that stuck with him: a death, a moment of any given day, etc. - but I wish it were explored in more detail.

Corsicato's film does move along snappily, touching upon themes of "believing in yourself as an artist", "exploring your limits as an artist" and... "following your dreams... as an artist". It contains fascinating archival footage of Schnabel throwing cloth against a canvas, then wiping his hands against said cloth, in stark black-and-white. There is an episode involving Schnabel crying on a film set, touched by an image he himself composed - a weird amalgamation of poignancy and a self-congratulatory streak that could be applied to this documentary. Schnabel putting together the "Berlin" set for Lou Reed's live performance clearly meant a lot to him, and the affection is palpable.

Schnabel infuses all of his cinematic biographies about artists with a dash of his own artistic flourishes, recognizable auteur-ish trademarks, as well as reflecting said artists' styles. Corsicato fails to achieve the same with his documentary, which similar docs like "Exit Through the Gift Shop", "Cutie and the Boxer" or "Gerhard Richter Painting" did so gracefully. It's intermittently lyrical and incisive and certainly reverential of its protagonist, but it doesn't hold a brush to Schnabel's own cinematic eye. This "private" portrait could have used some privacy invasion.

3 out of 5 stars

"Mifune: The Last Samurai" Offers a Basic Overview of a Screen Legend

Synopsis: A feature-length documentary about the life and films of legendary actor Toshiro Mifune, weaving together film clips, archival stills, and interviews with such luminaries as Steven Spielberg and Martin Scorsese. Narrated by Keanu Reeves.

Keanu Reeves happens to be an avid fan of martial arts, specifically the samurai culture, as is evident in his recent cinematic oeuvre: the mega-flop "47 Ronin", where he starred as Kai, one the samurais on a quest to avenge their master, and the even-bigger-flop, the underdog fight flick "Man of Tai Chi", which he also directed. Both projects, while flawed, deserved more attention: Reeves embraced a passion that is palpable on screen in those ambitious efforts, which failed to live up to their grand potentials.

From "The Matrix" to "John Wick", there's a running streak through the star's career that harks back to the old-school martial arts movies and their insanely-choreographed fight sequences. I'm shocked Tarantino hasn't directed him yet. It comes as no surprise that Reeves narrates the latest documentary, "Mifune: The Last Samurai", which focuses on screen legend Toshirô Mifune, mostly known for playing the titular warriors in Akira Kurosawa's classics. Reeves reverential approach to one of the most inspiring figures on his career is palpable - and with fascinating tidbits from contemporary masters - and massive fans - like Spielberg and Scorsese, director Steven Okazaki's career retrospective of a screen legend is never less than entertaining and passionate, if unoriginal in its approach. It doesn't delve deep.

Okazaki traces Japanese filmmaking back to the Lumiere brothers; initially, its themes of feudal regimes reflected the tumultuous times and appealed to young people. Later, during the war, Japanese films - similarly to those produced in Russia, Germany and the U.S. - were used as propaganda tools. The Toho Studios went through its Golden Age during the 1950's and 60's with Toshirô Mifune and Akira Kurosawa producing some of the most influential films ever made. Without them, "Darth Vader wouldn't be a samurai."

Japan's "biggest movie star, along with Godzilla", Mifune's career took off rapidly. His first collaboration with Kurosawa was on a script the latter co-wrote. Kurosawa saw major potential in Mifune and proceeded to cast him in "increasingly complex" roles, frequently collaborating with lifelong friend Takashi Shimura. A sequence of classics followed, defying conventional narrative structure and the way audiences perceived film - "Rashomon", "Seven Samurai". "Throne of Blood", "Yojimbo" and "Red Beard" being the standouts among the 16 features the two made together - whose themes Okazaki and Reeves examine, their insights diverting but never deeply enlightening.

We learn how Kurosawa put the crew together, get several glimpses at his tough directorial approach and "volatile" sets, learn about each film's status and impact, delve into Mifune's exceptionally thorough preparation - to the point where Kurosawa didn't have to give him any instructions on set - and so on and so forth. The highlight comes when real arrows were shot at an uninsured Mifune by college students in a particularly dangerous scene - he did the sequence because he was indebted to Kurosawa. The film skips past most of Mifune's non-Kurosawa collaborations, only occasionally pausing to flip through a visual photo album of his career highlights. Sometimes the line becomes blurry: is the focus on Mifune or Kurosawa here?

Okazaki does skim through Mifune's work with another prominent Japanese filmmaker, Hiroshi Inagaki ("The Samurai Trilogy", which gave Mifune "the rare chance to play a romantic role"). Under contractual obligation to Toho, Mifune made over 20 films in four years, which took its toll on his career and dedication to the art of film. "We were in the studio 350 days out of 365," says his co-star, Yosuke Natsuki, who also shares that Mifune was an avid card player and loved to order Ramen during lunch breaks.

Eventually Mifune and Kurosawa fell off, Mifune "busy working on films overseas", while "Kurosawa's career floundered". Convinced by Toho studios, Mifune started his own production company but, unable to balance being a businessman and actor, this venture started to slide. Tabloids haunted him: a mistress, a divorce - it all began to tarnish the career of an intensely private man. One of his last roles was in Spielberg's "1941". "Toshiba understood what the movie was," Spielberg remembers. "He was always the first one to laugh." (And the only one, as the film's critical reaction and box-office indicate.) To keep his company afloat, Mifune turned to television, including the 1980 series "Shogun". He died of "Alzheimer-related causes" in 1997.

You surely can't fault the doc for its lack of talking heads. Kano Uni, swordfighting choreographer, was "killed by Mifune more than a hundred times"; Shiro Mifune, the actor's eldest son, was born the year "Rashomon" was filmed (1950); Teryo Nogami worked with Kurosawa on over 20 films as script supervisor; Kyoko Kagawa , "one of the great actors of Japanese cinema", recollects her time with the Man - they all reminisce and share anecdotes, though none particularly enthralling. Unsurprisingly, the best ones come from Mifune's most avid admirers and brilliant successors. Scorsese muses: "Mifune studied the movement of lions in the wild while preparing for "Rashomon", like a caged animal." Spielberg compares Mifune to Baryshnikov and speaks of Mifune's raw on-screen energy: "It felt like he had just been created by a form of seismic activity underground."

Perhaps more fitted for a cable channel, "Mifune, The Last Samurai" contains fascinating archival footage from the bygone silent era of Japanese samurai films, surprisingly forward-thinking and exemplarily shot. It's tightly-packed with facts and focused on its subject, informative but never truly galvanizing in its approach. The doc doesn't ever attempt to really get behind the mind of its protagonist. What drove him? What was Mifune's relationship with his beautiful actress wife? At one point, one of the talking heads comments, "Toho wasn't big on roles for women". Why not explore this subject, still relevant today, a little more? How did Mifune feel about women in cinema? Beyond the actor's dedication, uncanny ability to reassure actors, his relationship with Kurosawa, the influence of his films and the stalwart's affinity for alcohol, we really don't get much insight into the legend's actual brain.

Okazaki's documentary is a reminder of the incredible films that helped shape some of the best of contemporary filmmaking, even if it did include ambitious duds like Reeves' loving odes to the all-time greats. A visual Wikipedia of Mifune's career, "The Last Samurai" may have great passion and ambition but remains unremarkable, barely doing justice to one of the greatest actors to ever grace international screens.

3 out of 5 stars

"My Golden Days"' Stab at Pure Nostalgic Gold Ends Up Gold-Plated

Synopsis: *Paul is preparing to leave Tajikistan, while thinking back on his adolescent years. His childhood, his mother's madness, the parties, the trip to the USSR where he lost his virginity, the friend who betrayed him and the love of his life.*

From "Stand by Me" to "Boyhood", coming-of-age stories tend to strike a resonant note with viewers, due to the genre's fundamental relatability. We all throw the occasional retrospective glance back at our pasts, the hazy memories of childhood, the defining moments of our lives that shape us: our parents, getting into trouble for the first time, falling in love… But it also comes down to simple images that stir up profound emotions - something as insignificant as a vase, a gust of wind, a whiff of an aroma, a fleeting glance.

Just like the process of cells in our bodies constantly dying and being replaced (one could argue we are in a perpetual state of reincarnation), French director Arnaud Desplechin's examination of growing up, "My Golden Days", keeps reinventing itself - visually and tonally. While it has its share of moments bordering on profound, it's oddly uninvolving and disjointed. The experience of watching "My Golden Days" is like leafing through a stranger's random photo album, where several pictures may make you pause, but ultimately you're left feeling cold, rather than basking in the warm glow of bygone days.

Paul Dédalus (Mathieu Amalric) bids goodbye to his girlfriend and leaves Tajikistan to go back to Paris. Suspicious custom authorities stop him at the border and proceed to question him about his passport. This leads to Paul reminiscing about his childhood, starting from the early days, where a young Paul (Antoine Bui) fends off his insane mother with a bat, to early adolescence, where a grown-up Paul (Quentin Dolmaire) helps a Jewish couple escape the terrible woes of Russia back into the heavenly gates of Israel by - you guessed it - giving his passport to his look-alike (who looks nothing like him - therein lies the irony?). The narrative then switches, with an older Paul falling in love with the enigmatic (and frankly, quite slutty) Esther, who literally sleeps with all of his friends.

I expected the first, brutal "sadistic, crazy mother" bit to instinctively lead to some explanation of the passport being lost (after all, he is telling the story to a customs officer), but no - it's just there, briefly, and while his mother's ghosts haunt him throughout the film, that visceral scene is never really referred to again. When it does come to the passport scene, it's fun, and has a lot of potential (like, say, delving into the meaning of "identity", and two lives being branched off by that single event), but no - it sort of just fizzles away.

The way the film segues from his account to the customs officer to a third-person recollection is jarringly off-putting. The first 15% of the film is anecdotal and engaging, while the latter 85% is dedicated to a love story that fluctuates between moments of true poignancy and pretentious artistic flourishes. "My Golden Days" goes from a horror-like family drama (which happens to be the best part of the film, and also the briefest), to a political thriller, to an almost-heist movie, to a love story. All this is supplemented by Ingrid Bergman-esque filmmaking, mixed with highly-stylized split-screens, images show in silhouettes, characters waxing poetic directly into the camera, dead Grandmas (yeah, it's there) - and let's not forget the "Fight Club"-like sequence of self-mutilation, which made me cringe uncomfortably, primarily because I still don't get why that specific character would go through all the trouble. Those swings from naturalism to eccentricity, from heartfelt dialogue to pseudo-poetic nonsense, are, I assume, meant to portray the ups-and-downs of life, but come off as gratingly uneven when condensed into two hours.

Paul-the-teenager is a broke, chain-smoking, "idiot savant" hipster (a-la Llewyn Davis), well-versed in art, history and religion, especially those of Russia, Tajikistan, Turkmenistan, Uzbekistan, Iran and Israel. He is overly sensitive - at one point, he even faints at some (admittedly tragic) news. And yet, we never know his motivations, what truly drives him. Why is he so hell-bent on helping his friend? Why is he so invested in Eastern-European and Middle-Eastern politics? Why is he so nonchalant about his girlfriend's - the love of his life, mind you - promiscuity? The blame doesn't fall on Dolmaire, who actually makes a rather compelling feature acting debut - it's like Desplechin expects us to already know Paul, and therefore relate to his experiences.

There are moments of memorable dialogue, especially in the earlier scenes of Paul and Esther getting to know each other, which feel natural and sexy ("Men come", Esther states after a particularly passionate act of coitus, "but women go off.") Love lasts, as does bitterness, vocalized succinctly by Paul: "A love intact. My fury intact." Sadly, the script later becomes increasingly pompous, repetitive and inexplicable. "Take me," Esther says at one melodramatic "sexy" point. Another eye-rolling moment, and I paraphrase, comes when Paul utters: "Have you ever been loved more than life? This is how I'll love you."

That's not to say I don't recommend watching the film. Sometimes an ambitious failure is worth a million run-of-the-mill Marvel films. There is a lot here to like. Though Amalric, a great actor, has little to do in a thankless role, the rest of the primarily young cast carry the film admirably. There are passages of true visual poetry and humor (a clothing mishap being a standout). I like the notion of someone being "undone" by love, the concept of losing the alluring, mysterious veneer - both inaccessibility and vulnerability can be equally sexy and sad. Desplechin's commitment to the material is evident - he clearly feels for his characters, and probably went through a lot of it himself.

The problem is - he rarely gets us to feel the same. There's too little at stake, and the disjointed narrative doesn't help the lack of a drive, a forward momentum. Perhaps if it were more pensive and elegiac - or straight-up purely "artsy", a succession of heartrending images and sounds - then there wouldn't even be a need for that momentum. But the fact that it's neither here nor there is maddening, and the great moments just emphasize the poor creative choices. Perhaps next time the director throws that retrospective glance back at his golden days, he can select ones that shine brighter.

3 out of 5 stars

"Other People" Puts Things in Perspective

Synopsis: *A struggling comedy writer, fresh off a breakup and in the midst of the worst year of his life, returns to Sacramento to care for his dying mother.*

Nominated for the Grand Jury Prize at the Sundance Film Festival, Chris Kelly's "Other People" sees a wide array of top-notch character actors anchor a drama that is by turns comic and tragic, if overly dependent on manipulative tactics. Kelly's background as a writer for shows like the luridly hilarious "Broad City" and "Saturday Night Live" is evident - there are moments of genuine humor and insight amongst all the bathos. In his feature-length debut, the writer/director shows promise; he just needs to tone down on the melodrama.

The opening scene is fantastic, plunging us straight into the immediate aftermath of a mother's death. Stricken by grief, her family is sprawled in a darkly-lit bedroom, sobbing uncontrollably. The phone rings, goes to voice-message. Their deceased mother's oblivious friend just found out about the terminal sickness and decided to express her condolences, while in a Taco Bell drive-thru lane. Her dialogue with the Taco Bell employee, juxtaposed against the tremendous mourning of the family, sets up the tone perfectly: morbidly funny, incisive and relentlessly dark.

We then go back in time: a struggling comedy writer David (Jesse Plemons), a "New York City boy", comes home to Sacramento and awkwardly mingles at a New Year party. His spunky grandmother Ronnie (June Squibb), sisters Alex (Judd Apatow's offspring, Maude, all "growns up") and Rebeccah (Madisen Beaty), "asshole" homophobic father Norman (Bradley Whitford), and a slew of other mildly quirky individuals all torment him with twangy folk songs and questions about his career. He escapes to chat with his ailing mother Joanne (Molly Shannon).

David is pessimistic and self-absorbed, but he means well. "Now I'll have no mom, basically no dad, no boyfriend, no job," he rants to his friend at a club. "I just want my mom to die thinking I'm doing okay, that's all," he tells the same friend later. That pretty much summarizes the film's plot (or lack of thereof): David's struggle to self-actualize, as his mother dies slowly, and her family deals with their demons.

"Other People" amounts to a series of sketches, riddled with slight philosophical rumination and resonant little moments. Joanne stops her son from biting his nails after a brief-but-searing exchange. A grocery store employee takes her time scanning products, which leads to an unfortunate meeting. Joanne can't stand watching her dog lick its genitals while throwing up from chemotherapy. Norman refuses to come up to meet his son's boyfriend. David throws up during a date and then proceeds to manically search for laxatives in a supermarket... My favorite comes when a character tells David, "No, you're 'other people' to 'other people'", as a man in a wheelchair rolls by. It's all about perspective, you see. Those poignant moments display Kelly's mastery of tone, the "heartbreaking-drama-followed-by-unexpected-wit" thing he does so well

Jesse Plemons may currently be one of our most underrated actors. After terrific turns in TV's "Breaking Bad" and "Fargo", and a solid run of memorable supporting characters in films like "Black Mass" and "Bridge of Spies", he finally gets to lead a feature film. His David is conflicted, kind, arrogant and imminently watchable. Molly Shannon gives what may be her subtlest performance, in a career of manic, eccentric characters that haunted poor Molly ever since her prolonged stint on SNL. I can't imagine what she had to go through to get inside the mind of Joanne. Bradley Whitford, an always-dependable thespian, provides gravitas and elegance as David's father. Zach Woods, still mostly known for his characters Gabe in "The Office" and Donald in "Silicon Valley", portrays a less showy side in a scene where his character Paul discusses masturbation with David, his boyfriend. Oh, and an extra shout-out goes to the young J.J. Totah; an entire film could revolve around his character Justin, who appears up all-too-briefly in "Other People".

That said, the film is not without its glaring faults. Visually, it's pretty run-of-the-mill, with generic shots portraying suburban Americana - you've seen those frames a million times in similar indie dramas. The director fails to pack a punch when it comes to novelty in execution. Those who have been following my reviews know how I feel about cancer-centric dramas, and while this one thankfully has great actors to sell it, it still is manipulative by its very nature. You'd have to be heartless not to emphasize and care for a person - especially one as likable as Molly Shannon - who's slowly deteriorating into nothing.

That point is particularly emphasized in a heartrending - and scathingly manipulative - sequence of the family trio - dad, mom, son - discussing post mortem details over milkshakes. You'd have to be a robot not to cry, but I struggle to see its point. All it's doing is reinforcing the grimness of this all-too-real situation (I have dealt with it myself) and provides no answers on how to cope with it (how could it?). The monthly countdown to the day of death doesn't help matters.

Luckily, there are enough real, tender, funny and touching moments to counterbalance the viscous sap. "Other People" also gets props for what some would call a brave, minimalist approach to storytelling, especially in an age of high-concepts and talking dragons. It deals with self-absorption, reaching for the stars, basic human kindness and serves as a gentle reminder that we only get one life on this Earth, and every day counts. Here's hoping the overall impact of Kelly's next feature will be more visually (and aurally) stimulating - and less maudlin.

3 out of 5 stars

"Pete's Dragon", or "A High-Profile Indie Director Reads a Children's Book"

Synopsis: *The adventures of an orphaned boy named Pete and his best friend Elliot, who just so happens to be a dragon.*

Director David Lowery's 2013's ode to Terrence Mallick, the "shot-in-the-early-stages-of-twilight" drama "Ain't Them Body Saints", was an ambitious "art film", aimed at a steadily-declining group of cinema appreciators ("ATBS" earned a measly $400K in the U.S.): folks who would get all the subtle cinematic references, catch every nuance of Rooney Mara and Casey Affleck's performances, "ooh" and "aah" at Bradford Young's cinematography and dissect the film for hours, if not days, after watching it. So who would have thought that the director's leap to big-budget, studio filmmaking would be so drastic? Did the execs at Disney watched "ATBS" and say, "This guy would be perfect for a remake of 'Pete's Dragon'?"

One could argue the same thing happened to Colin Trevorrow, who zoomed from tiny drama "Safety Not Guaranteed" to the Everest heights of helming "Jurassic World", as well the upcoming "Star Wars: Episode IX". The situation is slightly different though: I can see how someone like Spielberg could see traces of 1980's fantasy magic in "Safety Not Guaranteed" and - far from a safe bet - assume the novice is ready for the big league, perhaps even with the potential to spice it up with some of that indie sensibility in the process. (Side-note: Spielberg was wrong, "Jurassic World" sucked, Trevorrow dazed and confused amidst all the dinosaurs). But... "Ain't Them Body Saints"? Really? So, I pose the question again: what was it that some (and I'm being presumptuous here) sleep-deprived, bloated-on-wealth studio exec saw in Lowery's film that made him hand the director the reigns to a $100+ million feature about a kid and his dragon friend?

Having just screened "Pete's Dragon", I can attest that one of those factors may be the poignancy that dominates every scene in "ATBS". The Disney SFX-laden extravaganza certainly capitalizes on the director's knack for creating touching moments, particularly between the central duo. However, his ability to flesh out characters, dial back on sentiment and infuse the plot with originality is not on full display here. As a result, we get a thankfully-brief (it runs just over 90 minutes), charming but clichéd fantasy melodrama - and by clichéd I mean this film is literally a retread of the "sad-child-befriends-creature" staple, seen in superior films like "The Neverending Story", "E.T.", "Dragonheart", "The Iron Giant" and even this summer's earlier "The Jungle Book" and "The BFG".

Pete (newcomer Oakes Fegley, compelling as the lead) befriends the chameleon-like dragon (voiced by John Kassir) after a terrible car accident leaves him an orphan. He calls the dragon Elliot, after a book his parents gifted him. (We later find out, from a character called Meacham, played by a wise, "twinkle-in-the-eye" Robert Redford, that dragons "come from the North… but sometimes a dragon gets lost.") Having spent six years in the woods, Pete now resembles a less-agile, Mid-West version of Mowgli, fighting off bears and sprinting through the flora - until forest ranger Grace (Bryce Dallas Howard being Bryce Dallas Howard) and her daughter Natalie (an animated Oona Laurence) discover the two. As you can imagine, this leads to quite unpleasant consequences. Grace's husband Jack (a cardboard Wes Bentley) cuts down trees for a living (makes sense, ying-yang kinda thing, I guess), while his "evil-but-not-really" brother Gavin (a hammed-up Karl Urban) helps him out. Gavin has an affinity for hunting, and when he finds out about the dragon, the action kicks into (relatively) high gear.

I would delve into the rest of the plot, but any more-or-less savvy moviegoers can see where it's going: danger-culmination-redemption. It's definitely been-there-seen-that stuff, enlivened by the charismatic lead, who had to converse with a bunch of pixels and make it looks convincing. The dragon's kinda cool, though his facial features are a little too eerily human. There's a scene or two that elevates the film to "recommended" status, one particular standout being Pete's escape from a hospital. The tiny guy in the little white gown hops over cars, growls at dogs and clings to a school bus - an exhilarating sequence, ALMOST ruined by the twangy soundtrack accompanying it (a factor prominent throughout the film - one of the times the director's indie (read: granola) musical tastes clashed with, instead if aided, the plot).

"If you go through life seeing only what's in front of you," a character spells out the film's main theme at one point, "you're gonna miss a whole lot." Profound observation - it's moments like this where the filmmaking team clearly took cues from the subtleties of "Ain't Them Body Saints." There are also themes of deforestation and nature preservation; adulthood and friendship. The FX are decent if unspectacular… But enough of that, I have questions. What does the dragon eat? His sharp fangs, strength, ability to disappear, breathe fire and fly clearly indicate he's not a vegan - but we never even see him consume a chipmunk or a rabbit. Why doesn't he turn invisible more often? How has he managed to survive with the boy for six gosh-darn years?

While it's not quite the artful, thought-provoking, fresh blockbuster it could have been (think Spielberg's "A.I."), "Pete's Dragon" does charmingly hark back to the days of old-fashioned filmmaking, albeit with modern technology in its every shot. As for the director, (the horror!) Lowery is now scripting/directing the 145th iteration of "Peter Pan", after 144 of them flopped miserably. Damn you, Hollywood - stop turning ambitious directors with great potential into millionaire robots who churn out sequels and remakes, forgetting one of the most important aspects of what makes cinema great: a distinct voice.

3 out of 5 stars

"Queen of Katwe" is an Underdog Story Seen Through a Colorful Disney Prism

Synopsis: At the age of 10, Phiona Mutesi sees her world rapidly change when the young girl from the streets of rural Uganda is introduced to the game of chess.

Spanning five years, specifically 2007-2012, Mira Nair's based-on-a-true-story "Queen of Katwe" follows a young chess prodigy who hails from the slums of Kampala, Uganda. Only don't expect another "Slumdog Millionaire" - itself a sanitized depiction of a highly violent, dog-eat-dog world. This "Queen" is gorgeous to behold, airbrushing tumultuous lives with a PG stylus to make it all a family-friendly, harmless affair. Visceral scenes of slumdog existence are absent - instead we get a kaleidoscopic, gorgeous depiction of the nation, with even the protagonists' struggles (eviction, a torrential downpour, poverty) coming off as whimsical and charming.

While some may find that approach offensive, I was pleasantly surprised by the assured direction, central trio of performances and a pace that manages to entertain but not awe. Don't let the sappy trailer fool you - while this film is certainly prone to glamorizing and could have used a bit of trimming, it nevertheless remains an interesting story that is accessible to kids and may even teach them a lesson or two - both about chess and overcoming struggles.

Phiona (newcomer Madina Nalwanga) is a feisty young girl who lives in the "ghetto" with her resolute mother Nakku (Lupita Nyong'o) and siblings. One day she spies the local football coach Robert (David Oyelowo) gathering a team of young "pioneers" in a warehouse to practice playing chess. It doesn't take long for Phiona's plucky attitude to show itself; impressed, Robert invites her to join ("This is a place for fighters," he says.) Amazed by the natural talent of the illiterate young girl - "So you just reasoned out this end portion on your own?" - Robert quickly recruits her.

Together they overcome her mother's reluctance to part with her child and fear that Phiona will forget her roots, as well as a little bit of prejudice and injustice ("I cannot bring a disease into this school," the Chairman says about Phiona when Robert asks him if she can join the championship) to eventually participate in major chess competitions - from Kings College ("the finest school in the country") to the U.N.-sponsored International Chess Tournament in Sudan to the Chess Olympiad in Russia.

And it's all oh-so-lighthearted and fun. Basked in sun-drenched hues and a wide color spectrum (courtesy of cinematographer Sean Bobbitt, who worked on the polar-opposite, grisly "12 Years a Slave"), the film resolutely avoids delving too deep into the issues that plague this beautiful African nation. All conflicts are resolved quite promptly, without too much effort or sacrifice. Most goals are accomplished with a bit of determination and spunk. A great example of this is the scene at Kings College, where Robert's "pioneers" are having panic attacks before the tournament, and he swiftly calms them down with an eccentric anecdote, followed by an inspirational speech. Anyone who's seen a movie will be able to tell where this is all headed from the first minute, but in this case it's more about the journey than the destination.

Thankfully, Nair got a trio of great actors to carry the film. While Nyong'o (gorgeous and passionate) and Robert (determined and kind) unsurprisingly give multi-dimensional performances, it's Nalwanga, in her very first role, who forms the backbone of the film. She is by turns spirited, goofy, charming and convincingly erudite. I have a feeling we're going to see a lot more of her in the near future. She even manages to hold our attention during the chess sequences, which, like the game itself, are somewhat boring, especially for those who don't know the intricacies of the game. The wee ones may be zoning out during those scenes, but the adults may stay mesmerized due to the young actress's natural talent. Nair's knack for an off-beat vibe and bright tone with little glimpses of darkness also helps to counter-balance all the polish, predictability and sentiment.

"Queen of Katwe" is packed to the brim with obvious chess metaphors: "In chess, the little one can become the big one. That's why I like it." "Do not be quick to tip your king." "What matters is when we reset the pieces and play again." At over two hours, this obviousness does become repetitive, and the film proportionally gets a bit muddled - 30 minutes could have easily been trimmed off. That said, the director knows a thing or two about society ostracizing folks ("The Namesake" dealt with immigration issues; "Amelia" examined the role of women in the early 20th Century), as well as keeping a lively pace. While not exactly a check mate, "Queen of Katwe" is a game well played.

3 out of 5 stars

"Rogue One" Goes Base Delta Zero

Synopsis: *The Rebellion makes a risky move to steal the plans for the Death Star, setting up the epic saga to follow.*

Mother of Kwath! I was sworn under the oath of the Rebel Alliance not to reveal any plot points about Gareth Edward's latest installment in the "Star Wars" saga. Chances are high that at least one limb of mine will be charred off by a lightsaber belonging to someone at Disney, if a spoiler were to pop up. No pressure.

Shrouded in secrecy, the screening - which took place in the Main Theater on the Disney lot - was crammed with diehard aficionados, ready to be whisked off to a galaxy far, far away. The level of hushed excitement for a new adventure in the Lucasverse was palpable. In this political climate, I don't blame them for being so desperate for escapism - I'd also rather stand off against with the evil Orson Krennic (a smarmy Ben Mendelsohn) than have a few rounds of Celebrity Apprentice with our current fearless leader, General Don Trumpo.

To start, I have to admit that I was never a huge "Star Wars" fan. It has (mostly) nothing to do with the quality of the films - I grew up in tiny Switzerland, shielded from the "Star Wars" furor and oddly exposed to the somewhat more disturbing / reality-based fantasy fare of the 1980s: "Ghostbusters", "The Neverending Story", Tim Burton's oeuvre… Whether my folks had some particular issues with George Lucas's films, or they just somehow slid by me unnoticed - point remains, I was a late bloomer, encountering the Wookies well into my teens. Therefore, my opinion is in no way as informed as that of, say, the excited gentleman sitting next to me; let's call him Lorrig.

As soon as the familiar booming soundtrack (Michael Giacchino taking over the reigns from John Williams) announced the most-beloved title credit of all time, Lorrig got up and wooed, barely able to contain his excitement. The film's protagonist Jyn (a one-note (read: determined) Felicity Jones) embarks - or, rather, is forced to embark - on her *mysterious* and convoluted quest, with the help of a conflicted Cassian Andor (a confused Diego Luna), a smartass robot sidekick (Alan Tudyk) and Chirrup (Donnie Yen), a blind (literally) believer in the Force who may or may not be a Jedi. Lorrig delved deep into their travails, absolutely transfixed by all the familiar references, tributes and sly nods. I found the meticulous adherence to fans' expectations in "Rogue One" both commendable and abhorring - it tries so hard to please and be original but ultimately adds up to one big ode to all things "Star Wars".

Back to Lorrig. He cheered and wowed during an admittedly impressive battle between Chirrup and a small army. He didn't seem to at all mind the fact that large chunks of the film's running time were mired in boring politics and seemingly endless aerial battles, mouthing *piu-piu* along with the lasers on-screen. He giggled and gushed at every loving/forced reference, his damp palms making echoing noises as he clapped. Most of all, he seemed to enjoy Forest Whitaker, reprising his haunting role as Ker in the classic scientology propaganda "Battlefield Earth" (here he goes by the name of Saw). Loaded with relevant political themes, its tone strangely dark and angry (both thematically and visually), "Rogue One" has the most basic of "sci-fi opera" storylines. Lorrig lapped it all up.

There were a few moments where both Lorrig and I couldn't help but quietly sit back and marvel at Greig Fraser's swooping cinematography, his palette smoothly transitioning from drenched in rain and desolate to sunny and victorious. We gave each other a knowing nod now and then, such as when the film took a gamble that paid off by finally finding a funny sidekick in K-2SO, almost completely erasing Jar-Jar from our memories, or its numerous digital vistas, transporting us to wondrous worlds. The first half of the film especially kept both of us in a state of suspense (Jyn's quest and determination are initially engrossing). The film's epic sweep is undeniable.

Yet Lorrig seemed way more invested during the lengthy battle scenes, planet eradications and relocations - oh yes, and lasers. So many lasers. Every wisecrack, no matter how lame, made Lorrig burst out in uncontrollable laughter. His fist pumped in the air so many times, it created airwaves not dissimilar to those of the sabers on-screen.

But what do I know? Chances are, if you're like Lorrig, you will enjoy the kriffing out of Edwards' loud, dark and long chapter (subchapter? spin-off? prequel?) in the "Saga That Will Never Go Away". However, if you're reviewing the film based solely on its cinematic merits, such as memorable performances and jaw-dropping moments, originality and depth, you may come out of the theater muttering, "What the Sith…"

3 out of 5 stars

"Sleeping with Other People" is Run-of-the-Mill with a Dash of Raunchiness

Synopsis: *A good-natured womanizer and a serial cheater form a platonic relationship that helps reform them in ways, while a mutual attraction sets in.*

In my recent review of the South Korean love story "The Beauty Inside" (read it here), I briefly wrote about how the rom-com genre is gradually fading in this cynical decade, with excess and straightforwardness replacing romance and subtlety in Hollywood fare. While Baek Jong-Yeol's film resolutely - and successfully - managed to embrace the genre's tropes, Leslye Headland's "Sleeping with Other People" takes a different route, and attempts to subvert the clichés, "Trainwreck"-style, with naughty humor and general explicitness amidst all the heartfelt sentiment. As with most films tagged with the "Produced by Will Ferrell and Adam McKay" credit, "Sleeping" lives up to the lewdness that we have come to expect from the two goofball moguls. Yet, while the two leads possess effortless charm and chemistry, the film falls short on delivering a profoundly affecting and incisive romance.

Headland showed promise with her debut directorial feature, the flawed, "Bridesmaids-lite" "Bachelorette", and even more so with her surprisingly subtle script for the remake of the 1980's classic "About Last Night". "Sleeping with Other People", her second stab at helming a feature, marks another step in the right direction, albeit a small one. If you're willing to go with its utterly predictable storyline and outcome, you'll discover a pleasant diversion, anchored by a stellar cast.

The plot is basic. It's all in the synopsis. You've seen this film many times before. In fact, I can summarize the entire story in two succinct sentences. Lainey (Alison Brie) and Jake (Jason Sudeikis), both late bloomers, "de-virginize" each other in college, just to accidentally meet again, years later, at a sex addict anonymous meeting. Despite their predilection to infidelity, they become friends and (spoiler alert!) grow to love each other.

The opening scenes are by far the sharpest, filled with memorable one-liners and a giddy, "anything goes" vibe. Once the plot jumps to the present, it, along with the characters, becomes more "adult", losing momentum by valiantly trying to be insightful and clever, while maintaining its profaneness. Headland never quite maintains the balance between a mature sensibility and juvenile, abrasive whimsy.

There are some keen little observations along the way. The film explores people's tendency to pretend to be assholes, in fear of their actual personalities not being "good enough". It deftly portrays the desire to constantly crave more in a partnership, and touches upon the age-old question of whether men and women can maintain non-sexual friendships. For the most part though, "Sleeping" is a breezy, light affair - like "Sleepless in Seattle", if it were directed by Judd Apatow and contained naughty words and dildos.

Memorable appearances by a top-notch supporting cast add depth to the narrative. Adam Brody has a funny cameo, throwing a tantrum in a classy restaurant. Billy Eichner pops up briefly as a member of a sex addict group. Amanda Peet plays Jake's boss with a touching sincerity. The always-hilarious Jason Mantzoukas steals scenes as Jake's "second-best friend" Xander (his shining moment comes during the end credits). Adam Scott (wearing a thin mustache) hams it up as Lainey's sleazy ex. Natasha Lyonne is… well, Natasha Lyonne (and there's nothing wrong with that), Lainey's best friend. It's a slew of cameos, and credit's due: everyone gets a moment to shine - with the sole exception of Katherine Waterston, who was so good in "Inherent Vice", and is massively underused here as a sex-bomb with no personality.

"Sleeping with Other People" is chock-full of great lines. Jake refers to Lainey's first fling as "the Pontiac Aztec of people". Other standouts include: "Sex is like shooting heroin in a controlled yet moist environment", and "I'm raising friendless children because of you." Both Sudeikis and Brie are expert comedians, their talents exemplified perfectly in the film's standout kid's birthday party sequence (featured on the poster). While Headland resorts to the somewhat-tired "our protagonists are on drugs, and hilarity ensues" cliché, the sight of Sudeikis drinking water from a swimming pool to come down from a molly trip is worth the price of admission alone. Some jokes fall flat - particularly the "Notting Hill"-style ludicrous fight towards the end.

Headland's film sticks to the well-worn rom-com structure. No stone is left unturned: from the "meet cute" staple, to the sappy piano music, to the issues our heroes face, to the exchange of text messages that pop up in adorable bubbles, to the split-screen, to the happy ending… Hopefully next time the writer/director will focus more on subtlety and plunge deeper into exploring what makes her characters tick. That said, you could do worse than spend an evening with Lainey and Jake. They may not be especially deep, but their raunchy shenanigans are never less than entertaining.

3 out of 5

Skywalker and Rey Unite in the Overlong "Star Wars: The Last Jedi"

Synopsis: *Having taken her first steps into the Jedi world, Rey joins Luke Skywalker on an adventure with Leia, Finn and Poe that unlocks mysteries of the Force and secrets of the past.*

Kudos to director Rian Johnson, the cult indie darling known for "Brick" and "Looper", for both writing and directing another chapter of arguably THE most popular saga in cinematic history. The man is so nonchalant about it in interviews, as if he were completely content with the end result. Good for him. While lacking J.J. Abrams' assured pacing, brevity and robust character development, "Star Wars: The Last Jedi" succeeds on other fronts: creative little detours, memorable imagery and plenty of easter egg moments targeted at the saga's most ardent fans. The press screening I attended was filled with a raving crowd, clutching their stuffed Porgs, applauding at all the knowing nods to previous entries and acts of intergalactic heroism. Yet the film, at over two and a half hours, gets too bogged down in its own pomposity, without really going anywhere.

Under the threat of being exiled to Jakku, I'll be brief and careful not to reveal major plot spoilers (I think I just glimpsed a pair of Mickey ears outside my window). Here's "The Last Jedi" in a nutshell: while Luke (Mark Hamill) teaches Rey (Daisy Ridley) the Ways of the Jedi on his remote island planet, filled with the aforementioned owl-chipmunk hybrids called Porgs, Finn (John Boyega), with the help of admirer and potential love interest Rose (Kelly Marie Tran), embarks on a heist mission - to disable a device that would allow the Rebel Alliance to successfully escape The First Order.

Okay, I'll stop there. As much as I'd like to reveal that Supreme Leader Snoke, played by green-screen master Andy Serkis, is finally seen in his full CGI glory, or that Laura Dern takes control of the Rebel ship - mostly thanks to her commanding lilac hairdo - I simply cannot spoil any more surprises. I will, however, praise Mark Hamill, who gives a touching, splendid central performance as the legendary Luke Skywalker, by far overshadowing Harrison Ford's self-referential, phoned-in turn as Han Solo in "The Force Awakens". An escape on a casino planet, involving Falkor-like horse aliens, bristles with imagination and intensity. There is a spectacular three-way lightsaber fight. The ending, with its stark contrast of red against white, almost straddles that fine line of art-meets-blockbuster.

Unfortunately, those are all bright glimpses in a patchy middle chapter. Daisy Ridley's Rey, previously the protagonist of the story, gets sidelined, her youthful determination and character arc sorely missing this time. Her performance isn't bad, she just doesn't have much to do except share longing looks - if not the screen - with

Kylo Ren (Adam Driver, in "whiny teenager" mode). Her comatose island training sequences made me long for "Kill Bill"'s Pai Mei tutorials. The rest of the cast uniformly ham it up. Even Oscar Isaac, so perfect as Poe in J.J. Abram's last entry, gets more screen time and loses the quirk here.

Johnson's entry feels like a filler, a bridge between two more substantial chapters. Worst of all is "The Last Jedi"'s preposterous running time - at 152 minutes, it's the longest film in the series, consequently coming off as self-indulgent and bloated. There's so much exposition, so many flashbacks, countless prolonged sequences that go nowhere and endless, monotonous space battles, that one can't help but consider how much better the film would have been, had 20 minutes or so been left for the Blu-Ray special features.

To a "Star Wars" fan, "The Last Jedi" may be a dream come true, for it has everything they could possible want: the return of the saga's most beloved character, lightsaber battles, lots of laser "piu-piu"'s, pseudo-Shakespearean soapy drama, grand special effects and introductions of new characters - both cute and evil - all bound to become this universe's mainstays. For folks who don't know or care much about the series, the film may provide a few colorful moments, but will most likely suck the... well, force out of them.

3 out of 5 stars

"Stink!" Reveals the Toxic Truth about Your Yankee Candle

Synopsis: A foul smell from his kid's pajamas prompts director Jon Whelan to embark on a madcap journey from the retailer to the laboratory, through corporate boardrooms, down back alleys, and into the halls of Congress, all trying to protect the darkest secrets of the chemical industry. You won't like what you smell.

"Who doesn't sniff a product before buying it?" Jon Whelan states at the start of his investigative report / socially-conscious documentary. A legitimate point. I know I twist off the occasional shampoo cap at Walgreens, to take a little whiff prior to selecting the optimal scent. Whelan's account proceeds to demonstrate how those pleasing odors of Wacky Melons and Caribbean Ocean Waves may actually lead to cancer, birth defects, and other long-lasting physical ailments. Deodorants, shower gels, detergents, dishwashing liquids, your girlfriend's new Chanel perfume - all those products contain the mysterious ingredient - "fragrance" - the chemicals of which are undisclosed by the corporations that manufacture them. I'll think twice now before indulging in Watermelon Frenzy.

Whelan proceeds to state that his doc is an amalgamation of "a love story, a mystery, a crime drama, a wakeup call, and a farce". I'll try to compartmentalize my review into corresponding segments. The Love Story involves his wife, Heather, who died from cancer in 2009, and is by far the most affecting aspect of the film, involving truly lyrical passages. "My wife, Heather, was perfectly healthy… And then she wasn't," Whelan narrates. "She left things better than she found them." Haunting archive imagery of Heather reappears throughout the film, infusing it with a much-needed emotional heft. After a journey of self-discovery through the United States, Whelan buys his two daughters pajamas for Christmas from the popular store Justice, and notices a weird smell…

Here's where the Mystery begins: fueled by his wife's death, Whelan goes on a crusade, to discover what "kind of chemicals would give off this sort of smell". When he can't get a straight answer over the phone - it's enigmatically referred to by the manufacturers as "proprietary information" - he proceeds to send the PJs to a lab for a chemical analysis - and discovers that they contain flame retardant chemicals, banned for decades and known to cause cancer.

"Stink!" then morphs into the Crime Drama, with the corporate "crime lords", such as Justice, or Unilever (the giant behind Axe), unwilling - or unable - to disclose the secret formula behind those chemicals. We, consumers, are enamored by the "mystique" behind the fragrance, but the lavender that we think is grown in gale-swept, vast fields of France is in fact manufactured in charcoal-black New Jersey factories. The "crime lords" get away with making them, because those chemicals are not regulated by the federal government.

One can't blame Whelan for not going the distance. He attempts to contact the CEO of Justice, and even buys a share of the company to get some answers. He finally attends a shareholder meeting and addresses the CEO directly, in one of the doc's highlights. Another highlight involves the absurdity of a Breast Cancer Foundation selling perfume, which contains cancer-causing chemicals, to raise money for breast cancer (this is where the doc ventures into Farce).

"Stink!" is chockfull of testimonies and facts, provided by experts in a variety of scientific fields. Christophe Laudamiel, "Master Perfumer" behind the Abercrombie & Fitch scent (that overwhelms your senses every time you step into that goddamn store), shares diverting tidbits, like: ingredients that start off smelling like sewage can end up "smelling like hazelnuts". There are also personal accounts, such as Brandon's - a young man, whose life almost ended from a reaction to some chemical scent in an Axe deodorant. Whelan assaults us with data: "women and teen girls typically use up to 20 products a day; men and boys - about half that"; the ingredients used in Chanel No5 are the same used in toilet bowl cleaner; phthalates, found in most of our everyday supplies, interfere with the function of our hormones (no wonder the smell of gasoline turns me on!) and can mutate our DNA… "We are quietly becoming genetically modified by toxic chemicals", Whelan gravely states.

While "Stink!" runs around in circles sometimes, hammering the same point over and over again, Whelan's aspirations are commendable. With a mix of archival footage, interviews and graphics, he traces the recorded birth of unregulated chemicals, sometime back in the 1950s, through the uprising protests of the 1980s, to the current day, and the introduction of the "Prop 65" California act, which warns people about cancer-causing chemicals. Whelan urges us to use caution, and reminds us, that there are politicians fighting the good cause, such as Hon. Steve Israel, who states that "the fundamental problem is that no one knows what those chemicals are… Inform them, and then let them make whatever decisions they want." It's politicians like him, Whelan argues, that can lead to fixing the toxic substances control act, and companies disclosing all the ingredients on their products.

The doc's budget limitations are apparent, Whelan never getting access to any major political leaders or CEOs of the companies he condemns - his most "exciting" interviews occur when he startles his subjects in hallways and proceeds to interrogate them about chemical regulations - an approach that left a sour taste in my mouth. He also extends the running time with news reports, extracts from political debates and redundant visuals.

Like this year's earlier "That Sugar Film" (read my review here), "Stink!" is an informative, if unspectacular, documentary that gets its point across. Unlike Damon Gameau's saccharine study though, the subject matter here is a bit more focused, and cuts deeper. We can control the amount of sugar that goes into our bodies - but how can we control something we don't know? "Stink!" does lack some of "Sugar"'s playfulness, and its didactic approach, overwhelming us with dreadful facts and expository graphics, can be wearying at times. For a film with an exclamation point in its title, it certainly could use an injection of adrenaline and humor.

While it may not entirely live up to its claims of being "a love story, a mystery and a crime drama", as a Wake-Up Call, "Stink!" gets the job done. I'm convinced. I'm going to get in so much trouble for throwing away my wife's new perfume…

3 out of 5

Aliens Among Us: "The Creeping Garden" Delves into the World of Sentient Slime

Synopsis: A feature length documentary exploring the work of fringe scientists, mycologists and artists, and their relationship with the extraordinary plasmodial slime mold.

Note: I will use the term "slime mold" quite a bit in this article, so I'll count the number of times I say it, and you can then multiply it by roughly 10, to get an idea of how often it's pronounced in the documentary.

The synopsis makes it seem like a rollercoaster ride, doesn't it? Who wouldn't want to spend 80 minutes watching plasmodial slime mold (1), when the visceral experience of drying paint / growing grass is a paintbrush / seed away? But don't scrub this slime mold (2) with bleach quite yet. In their odd little documentary, "The Creeping Garden", directors Tim Grabham and Jasper Sharp manage to morph what could have been a contender for "Most Boring Film Ever" into a sometimes-fascinating, probing study of the fungus/animal that plays more like science fiction than your average, run-of-the-mill plasmodial smile mold (3) doc.

"I'm mainly looking for mushrooms, with a sideline of slime molds (4)," says Mark Pragnell, an amateur mycologist. Feeding on decay, found on rotten logs, yellow/white/grey/purple, furry and bean-like and viscous and crusty, constantly morphing and oozing, the slime mold (5) is a sight to behold. As one of the scientists states, "the slime mold (4) is not animal, not vegetables, not fungi". It can survive vacuum and radiation. Quite the organism - any science fiction buff will surely geek out on the sheer peculiarity of the subject matter.

There are awe-inspiring, stop-motion shots of slime mold (6) making its way through a rat-like maze to find a pile of nuts, along with a plethora of gorgeous, magnified images of colorful slime mold (7), supplemented by Jim O'Rourke and Woob's drone-like, minimalistic score. Those shots are reminiscent of films like "Under the Skin" or "Invasion of the Body Snatchers": highly artistic, bringing to mind human veins and butterflies and death.

There are quite a few interesting tidbits along the way. The primary focus of the doc is examining whether the slime mold (8), does, in fact, exhibit behavioral patterns or is functioning based purely on mechanistic responses. A "human experiment", with folks tied together and acting like slime mold (9), examines parallels between human problem-solving skills and those of slime mold (10). Slime mold's (11) way of "branching out" gets compared to motorways, a scientist stating that "it imitated Roman roads in Italy - a perfect match". A piano is even plugged into a slime mold (12) petri dish, to gauge its responses to music. Whether or not it is, in fact, sentient, the slime mold (13) does like pasta, while "oats are its favorite"; a scientist uses a variety of food products to "coax" the slime mold (14) in a specific direction.

Amongst the few slime mold (15) scientists in this world, the ones on display exhibit passion, intelligence and, of course, quirks that come with the job. "I haven't spent a lot of time observing dog penises," one scientist comments drily in regards to a slime mold (16) whose name derives from that canine organ. Another scientist takes her slime mold (17) on holiday with her to keep it "fed and happy". The aforementioned amateur mycologist even admits to getting strange looks from people - a lone man, studying decaying logs in the deep woods, can seem quite odd to those unaware of slime mold (18).

As a film fanatic, the most fascinating part of the doc to me was how slime mold's (19) "pulsing, rhythmic movement" led way to the earliest forms of cinema, viewed through a kaleidoscopic prism of slides and microscopic time-lapse (back then called "time magnification"). I am currently seeking out 1931's "Magic Myxies", shot by lead naturalist/filmmaker Percy Smith, as it is clearly the trippiest thing from the last Century this side of Luis Bunuel's "Un Chien Andalou".

Of course, a film dealing solely with slime mold (20) can't go without its tedious passages, such as one of the scientists literally reading a book on screen, or the recurring shots of poorly-rendered molecules floating through vacuum. "The Creeping Garden" does stretch out its length; it could've been a stellar short. Quite pedagogical, it's not exactly edge-of-your-seat entertainment either, or a "must watch" - no one (unless they have a particular interest in mycology) is going to drag you out to see "that latest flick about slime".

Since I mention pedagogy, what DOES "The Creeping Garden" teach us, exactly? That slime mold (21) emulates road structures and/or human patterns? That we could learn from it? The doc's message is a little ambiguous. Yet it does transcend its nerdy roots and, at times, becomes an artistic look at the odd things that surround us, the mystery of nature, and how little of it we still understand.

PS: For an entertaining - and heady - look at human's literal fusion with nature - and slime mold (22!) - check out Alan Moore's brilliant graphic novel "Swamp Thing", an epic rumination on how the natural world is all connected through a consciousness we don't have the capacity to grasp.

3 out of 5 stars

"The Hollow", Soaked in Sweat and Scandal, is B-Movie Heaven

Synopsis: *When a U.S. congressman's daughter passing through a small town in Mississippi dies in a mysterious triple homicide, a team of F.B.I. agents descends to investigate.*

Miles Doleac has balls. The man wrote an intricately-structured (well, comparatively) script, assembled a cast of B-movie stalwarts, then proceeded to produce and direct "The Hollow" himself... and actually managed to get away with it. The result, while not a classic by any means, may catch you off-guard with its sly socio-political commentary, breakbeat pace, muscular acting and an unabashed commitment to its sleazy, murky, highly unethical roots. A vicious alligator in a swamp of terrible straight-to-VOD releases, this Southern action/thriller introduces a new, brave talent to the filmmaking world. Whether he lives up to the potential displayed here remains to be seen.

"The Hollow" starts with the ultimate "Bad Lieutenant" scene: Officer Ray Everett (Doleac) is getting a blowjob from a "lot lizard" while dealing drugs, parked in a shady alley in Small Town, Mississippi. It doesn't take long (a few seconds, really) for the film to establish him as a chauvinist, racist, filthy redneck, a corrupted man with a mean Southern drawl covered in beads of sweat and cum. When a horny couple asks him for directions to a nearby motel, Ray sends them to the titular Hollow instead ("Don't nobody bother you there."). I'm not spoiling much by revealing that the naive couple gets murdered - but not before hearing a shot ring out in the darkness of the Hollow.

Turns out it was a triple homicide, and one of the victims was a U.S. congressman's daughter. Divorced FBI agent Vaughn (James Callis) and his partner (both professionally and sexually) Sarah (Christiane Seidel) fly in from D.C. to investigate. In the meantime, the local Sheriff Beau McKinney (William Sadler) chews Ray out, suspecting he had something to do with the murder. Vaughn and Sarah encounter a "strict disciplinarian" football coach who beats his players with a paddle; Big John Dawson (William Forsythe), a country lawyer who "runs this town", and whose grandson is a quarterback in the local team (and who may or may not be involved in the case); and a slew of other toothless, tattoo-covered characters...

But the film is really about the world closing in on Ray, who's given a chance for "penance"; in the words of John Dawson, "This is scandalous, boy!" Not even Ray's father, Darryl (Jeff Fahey, in what amounts to little more than a cameo), can provide decent advice: "I can't blame you for using what little talent you got to provide for your family." It all leads to a rainy stand-off, heavily indebted to Morricone and Tarantino but effective nevertheless (and hilarious! the puking!). The conclusion of the film - and I'm referring to where Vaughn ends up at the very end - is hilariously misguided.

Miles Doleac gives a commanding presence as Ray, a force to be reckoned with, channeling all the bad cops - Denzel in "Training Day", Keitel in (and Cage in the Southern remake of) "Bad Lieutenant", Woody Harrelson in "Rampage". A somewhat-loving father at home, a cowering imbecile in front of his boss, and an unleashed beast everywhere else, he gives himself all the best lines, spitting them out with pure vehemence. The rest of the actors all seem in on the joke. James Callis, whom I loved so much in TV's splendid "Battlestar Galactica", revels in the clichéd role of a sulking divorcee; his shining moment comes about halfway through the film, where he delivers a speech to a hillbilly redneck worthy of applause.

Sure, this film ain't perfect. It's filled with expository dialogue; it could've been shorter (I'd cut out the twangy lovemaking sequence, for one; the women get severely underserved (Candice Michele Barley as Ray's wife Trish particularly could use more room to breathe, in a small-but-delicate performance)... But the film's combination of knowingly hilarious wisecracks and silly exchanges saves it. "What did I do to piss you off? It ain't like I asked to take you 'round back and fuck you sideways," a character exclaims. "There's an attorney general out back... U.S. attorney general," another character clarifies. "You know I don't like it when you do that, right?" a female character asks Ray. "What?" he snarls. "Sexually harass me," she replies nonchalantly. "A make-out session gone south," Vaughn says, leaning over the dead bodies. "No pun intended."

What primarily makes "The Hollow" worthy of at least a rental is that it's consistently entertaining, a near-perfect example of a B-movie. It's also a surprisingly hilarious satire of a certain area of the South and its ignorant, Bible-spouting, alcohol-loathing residents. Yes, it's not cerebral entertainment, nor will it change your life or linger in your memory for longer than the aftertaste of moonshine, but as midnight fare goes, this will do the trick. Robert Rodriguez - another auteur who "cuts", shoots, directs and even scores his B-flicks, should watch his back. Miles Doleac is coming for him.

3 out of 5 stars

A Glimpse at The Lebanese-Palestinian Conflict, "The Insult" Should Have Been More Scathing

Synopsis: *In today's Beirut, an insult blown out of proportions finds Toni, a Lebanese Christian, and Yasser, a Palestinian refugee, in court. From secret wounds to traumatic revelations, the media circus surrounding the case puts Lebanon through a social explosion, forcing Toni and Yasser to reconsider their lives and prejudices.*

Sometimes, a well-intentioned film can become so overtly political and blatant, it loses its bite. While "The Insult" never quite bores, thanks to its humanity, sharp performances and some effective sequences, it also could have been so much more. For such a controversial subject matter - the ongoing tumultuous Lebanese-Palestinian relationship - "The Insult" lacks a strong core, be it satire or heart-twisting drama or pulse-pounding thriller. As it stands, writer/director Ziad Doueiri's film is an earnest little tale that touches upon a variety of compelling subjects, but ultimately fails to add up.

Toni (Adel Karam) lives with his pregnant wife Shirine (Rita Hayek) in Beirut. She wants to move to a bigger house in another city, but Toni, a car mechanic and patriot, resolutely states, "I work here". Fiercely protective of his country, his city and especially his apartment, Toni refuses to let an illegal Palestinian City Hall construction worker, Yasser (Kamel El Basha), into his home, even after his illegal draining pipe splatters Yasser's face with water. A building violation, the pipe needs to be replaced, so Yasser does so from the outside - just to have Toni smash it with a hammer. A war between the two gentlemen ensues. Toni ends up with broken rib in lieu of an apology.

The first trial - one of the film's highlights, both wryly humorous and intense - is brief, however. The judge finds the evidence inconclusive and lets Yasser off the hook. Toni, who refused to hire a lawyer, is enraged, screams out insults at the judge and Yasser, including the scathing, "I wish Ariel Sharon wiped you all out." When Toni's wife goes into early labor and his child ends up on life-support, he decides to sue again. This time, he's backed by a team of lawyers, who advise him not to use such slurs, if he wants a shot at winning (for defending Palestinians is "trendy"). It's not money Toni's after though. His pride guides him on.

In a twist of sorts, it turns out Toni's lawyer is Yasser's lawyer's father. Politics and law intertwine, leading to chaotic testimonials and a revolting crowd outside the courtroom. Soon, the entire city of Lebanon is involved, the media avalanching down upon the two men. The city's streets burn with overturned cars and scorched flags. Secrets from Toni's past surface, potentially changing an inevitable outcome.

Adel Karam is a force of nature, a coiled spring, a seething, spouting, deeply bitter character, insulting everyone in his way, so morally and ethically misguided he cannot defy the prejudice embedded in his DNA, or overcome his traumatic past. Kamel El Basha is his direct opposite, a deeply empathetic man, saddled with years of abuse, the actor doing a wondrous job conveying his sorrows and anger. He makes the brief moments of elation count.

Ziad Doueiri ticks off many admirable themes, methodically. His film is about the stubbornness and misguided pride of individuals that leads to a collective denial, an inability to see past prejudices and recognize the human being. It's about the power of words and the age-old question of right vs. wrong. It's about the domino effect of a tiny mishap leading to an all-engulfing storm. It's about one's past, haunting him. Ultimately - oddly - the main query "The Insult" poses is a rather simple one: "Why can't we call just get along?"

Doueiri can't help but spell out some of the themes with a big bold permanent marker. "We're the n*****s of the Arab world," Yasser tells his wife at one point. Like, whoa. A little subtlety goes a long way. Here's an example of another passion filled statement: "As the Jews say," Toni proclaims bitterly in Yasser's face, "'Palestinians never miss an opportunity to miss an opportunity.'" As he's being escorted out of a courtroom, Toni screams: "It pays to be a Palestinian!"

While the first half of the film moves at such pace it may make one disregard the obviousness of some of its statements, the dry, courtroom-drama second half turns into a pedagogical treatise on Middle-Eastern politics. Add in the somewhat unnecessary sub-plot of the father/daughter courtroom face-off, as well as a healthy dash of sentimentality, and even Tommaso Fiorilli's beautiful cinematography, conveying both Beirut's corroded state and its majesty, cannot save the film from coming off somewhat "eh" - while it should have thrilled, infuriated and inspired. Undoubtedly filled with powerful moments, the "The Insult" is nonetheless never more than the sum of its parts.

3 out of 5 stars

"The Phenom" Reaches the Base but Plays It Safe

Synopsis: *A Major League rookie pitcher loses control over his pitching and is sent down to the minor leagues, where he begins sessions with an unorthodox sports psychologist. In the process, hidden conflicts with his overbearing father are brought to light.*

Writer/director Noah Buschel has had an interesting career trajectory. He's worked multiple times with Academy-Award Nominee Amy Ryans, as well as notable, top-notch actors such as Michael Shannon, Billy Crudup, Corey Stoll, Paul Sparks and Tate Donovan. He's dealt with serious, commendable subjects such as agoraphobia ("Sparrows Dance"), the repercussions of 9/11 ("The Missing Person") and the psychological effects of Kerouac's "On the Road" on its main inspiration ("Neal Cassady"). Yet none of his ambitious-but-flawed films seemed to have had much success when it comes to revenues - or made much of a cultural dent.

"The Phenom" continues that unfortunate trend, his second consecutive sport-centric flick in a row after the boxing drama "Glass Chin". This time the subject is baseball, the stars are multiple Academy Award Nominees Ethan Hawke and Paul Giamatti… and the box-office results are as low as ever. Whether the fault lies in the over-saturation of blockbusters, bad marketing, audiences' disinterest in the aforementioned topics, or Buschel's own lack of a directorial trademark and diluted visual approach, is difficult to determine. "The Phenom", as laudable as it is for being not so much about the game itself as it is about the implications behind it (kind of "Moneyball"-style, with Buschel's grounded dialogue instead of Aaron Sorkin's linguistic orgy), hints that the answer may be "all of the above". Buschel's film has its share of standout moments and a genuinely interesting approach to the subject but lacks directorial charisma to truly stand out in the field.

Hopper Gibson (Johnny Simmons) is a highly promising baseball player, who one day has a meltdown on the mound after some guy shouts out the word "coke" in the crowd. Hopper reveals that his memory is somewhat foggy to his psychologist, Dr. Mobley (Paul Giamatti), who comments, "Memory is a funny business. And sometimes we fog over the past, because of damage. Like in the old movies, when they put Vaseline on the camera lens to make faces prettier and softer." Savvy moviegoers will note that this pre-credit line spells out the film's main theme, as well as it's plot, and will certainly know the answers to the following questions: Could Hopper have a traumatic past that surfaced and is now affecting his game? Is Dr. Mobley his conduit to salvation? Will the film continue to mix the poetic with the mundane?

As the therapy sessions go on, we flash back to scenes of Hopper going through his self-discovery journey. He confronts his coach Eddie (Yul Vazquez), girlfriend Dorothy (Sophie Kennedy Clark) and his abusive, recently-imprisoned father, Hopper Sr. (Ethan Hawke), who puts him through the grinder, expecting greatness from his son that he himself never achieved (and bringing to mind J.K. Simmons' psychotic music instructor Fletcher from "Whiplash"). Hopper Sr. teaches his son to "always be on the mound", and view everyone in life as an opponent, which, as Dr. Mobley acutely notes, must make it pretty difficult for Hopper to confide in him.

All the actors shine, elevating the film a notch above your run-of-the-mill character drama. The ever-reliable Paul Giamatti is by far the highlight, turning in a relaxed, subdued performance filled with depth, remorse and empathy. Johnny Simmons in the lead manages to keep up with the stalwart in their intimate scenes together; the exchanges between Hopper and Dr. Mobley are the most memorable, two actors at the top of their game, managing to transcend the clichéd "at the psychiatrist" scene. The highlight comes during their final confrontation, the camera staying focused on their faces as they call each other out. Ethan Hawke is all smarmy aggression bordering on violence, filled with seething bitterness and resentment, disappearing behind his crew cut and tattoos. ("You must think you're pretty astonishing," he tells his son, shirt unbuttoned, beer in hand. "Everything that you accomplished, you owe to me.") When he asks Hopper to "check out steroids", you can't tell if he's kidding or not, just as when he states, "all drugs should be legal." It's a hammy but effective turn from the versatile actor.

I like that the film deals with the implications behind the making of a U.S. athlete star, and how institutions turn their backs on grades, as long as their star player "keeps pitchin'". "You have to work," Hopper's teacher June (the underused Elizabeth Marvel) says. "If you only do what comes easy to you, what you are good at, you are just an untrained thoroughbred, which isn't a race horse, at all." A similar indictment of the sports industry and its "false idols" comes from Dorothy in the beginning of the film. It's refreshing to see a sports drama examine the rudimentary nature and effect on society of the sport its depicting. The dialogue, several needless flourishes aside, is incisive and biting.

Tonally, the film seems a bit lost. A siren-blaring, crimson-red sequence of Hopper freaking out on the field as he watches his father getting arrested feels jarring and out of place in an otherwise subdued film, with grey tones and no sudden swerves into pretentiousness. Another scene involving Hopper talking to reporters in a locker room is laughably bad - obvious and unnecessary. It also goes from talky psychological drama to allegorical sports tale to underdog story to, yes, even a thriller at one point - all in odd little waves. The budget limitations become apparent when it comes to the surprisingly empty baseball fields. There are also dull stretches in an already-short film (just over 80 minutes) and, despite the convincing acting, a strange vacuousness when it comes to their backgrounds, goals and everyday lives.

I'm all about indie, artful films having exposure and firmly believe audiences crave more intellectually stimulating films that take a new look at well-worn subjects. However, in a world filled with baseball dramas ("Bill Durham", "Rookie of the Year", "A League of Their Own", "42", "Trouble with the Curve", the aforementioned "Moneyball", to name a few) "The Phenom" gets lost. If it attempts to use baseball as a backdrop and/or metaphor for the drama unfolding on screen, it doesn't entirely succeed due to lack of truly existential/philosophical insight. On the other hand, its misleading poster and synopsis makes one assume there's actual baseball in the film, of which there's next-to-none. Perhaps next time, in order to make his name, Buschel needs to focus more on his target audience, and the message he's trying to relay. If he wants to stand out from the rest, ambition is not enough - Buschel's gotta hit it out of the ballpark.

3 out of 5 stars

"Till We Meet Again" Resembles a Mumblecore "The Beach", sans DiCaprio or Cults

Synopsis: This film follows a couple through their completely different journeys in Thailand and simultaneously reveals their past in New York through flashbacks.

I've traveled to Thailand three times. At first overwhelmed by the boisterous, chaotic and extremely polluted City of Bangkok, I allowed the culture shock to wear off, until glimpses of the city's magnificence began to peek through: its extraordinary culture, history, people and food (OMG, the food!). By the time I left the capital to travel down to the islands of Koh Samui and Phuket, I was head-over-heels in love with the country. Its spiritual tranquility, its luminous golden steeples, its natural beauty, its gentle people speaking the soothing language of the gods formed a stark contrast to its poverty-stricken areas, political unrest and the ever-growing flood of tourism. Lounging on a beach after a day of scuba diving with the sharks, while eating fresh red snappers, I stared at the giant crimson setting sun and wholeheartedly considered leaving Western civilization behind and succumbing to the magic of Southeast Asia.

Alas, I didn't have the balls to do it. I still dream of Thailand and the uncanny-but-highly-pleasant feeling of being immersed in another dimension, all wondrous smells, exotic jungles and the spicy-tangy taste of Tom Yum Goong. The protagonist of director Bank Tangjaitrong's micro-budget "Till We Meet Again" at first comes off as a bit of a spineless twerp, but ultimately proves to have bigger balls than I do. (Is that too much testicle talk for a film review? It is? Well, then... BALLS!) While a bit unrefined - as in, unpolished, rough around the edges, you get the point - the film has a genuine, charming streak that runs through it, which I personally found rather contagious. It may not have the lasting impact of, say, "Lost in Translation" or "Eurotrip" (kidding!), but it certainly leaves a bittersweet aftertaste and is not the worst time to spend a few hours - similarly to lounging in a hammock by a beach.

I may have missed the exact profession of Joanna (Linnea Larsdotter), but I assume it's some sort of "artistic collage" type of work, as the film starts with her being criticized by a professor-type. "Your cultural references are a little too literal right now," the alleged "academic" tells a disheartened Joanna, in reference to the travel pictures she put together that we never see. "I just feel like this is a bit naive." Urged by her friend ("If you need to go," the somewhat-forceful dude says, ""you need to go now. Forget about the money. Just go."), Joanna embarks on a journey to Thailand. Her boyfriend of five years, Erik (John Matton, who also co-wrote and produced the film), generously buys her the ticket - well, two tickets, as he sort of invites himself too. We never really get to see what her "research" is, as the rest of the film focuses solely on their relationship.

In Thailand, tension between the couple amounts; Joanna tells Erik to finish his paid-for scuba diving lessons and leaves the poor dude to go see some friends "seven hours away." Waiting for her is sexy hunk David (Emrhys Cooper), whose girlfriend - wouldn't you know it - had to unexpectedly go back to New York. "Why didn't you tell me?" Joanna reasonably asks. "You were on your way and I didn't have time!" comes the highly unreasonable response. It seems to satisfy Joanna though, who smiles at David seductively and absconds back to her bungalow. Erik is understandably distressed at the news that his girlfriend, whom he bought a freakin' expensive ticket to Thailand, bailed to go sleep with a single, handsome, presumably Australian (!) dude.

But then Erik meets the uninhibited Miranda (Astrea Campbell-Cobb) - and, instead of reuniting with Joanna, goes off exploring the market with the beautiful blonde stranger. Sneaky, presumably Australian David spots the two of them flirting, gives them a disapproving look and proceeds to not tell Joanna about it, instead convincing her that she doesn't need "an anchor holding [her] down". We follow Erik and Joanna on their two paths until... well, "till [they] meet again".

Tangjaitrong and Matton's film conveys the feeling of paradise tainted by personal issues, how doubly alienating it can be to be left alone in an unfamiliar, albeit gorgeous, environment, its exotic nature just accentuating the isolation. The allure of the swaying palm trees, azure ocean waters and elephant rides through the jungle gets tainted by loneliness. I liked the juxtaposition of two separate breakfasts, served to Joanna by Erik and David, displaying the warmth of the former and the adventurous-but-somewhat-cold vibe of the latter. The acting is uniformly decent, if unremarkable, with Joanna (perhaps purposefully) coming off as self-obsessed and cruel and Erik as a pantsy - but that may be purposeful, as he does gradually transform into a ballsy dude (BALLS!).

Two particular moments stand out. The first one comes during a skinny-dipping sequence in a lagoon, when Miranda spontaneously kisses Erik. "Now you don't have to be mad at Joanna," she says, and swims off. It's a small but profound detail, where a tiny little kiss may resolve a convoluted mess of emotions and set one on the right path. The second moment comes during the ending, which as we all know is the hardest part of the film to pull off, and in this case verges on the profound, putting the aforementioned events in a new perspective. Stick with Tangjaitrong's feature till the end and you may just like it that much more.

Sure, "Till We Meet Again" lacks true novelty and depth, contains some clunky dialogue - and it's freakin' slow here and there. But while it provides next-to-no fresh insight into how relationships work, it doesn't resort to clichés either. Most crucially, it shows how a change in a physical environment can spur a change in one's personal life, act as a catalyst, its structure - the inception of romance vs. the "now" - bringing to mind films like "Eternal Sunshine of the Spotless Mind". Kudos for pulling it off, on what I assume was a minuscule budget. I'm booking my flight as I write this.

3 out of 5 stars

"Truman" is by Turns "Biutiful" and Banal

Synopsis: Julián receives an unexpected visit from his friend Tomás, who lives in Canada. The two men, accompanied by Julián's faithful dog, Truman, will share emotional and surprising moments prompted by Julián's complicated situation.

The first time I had the opportunity to witness a performance by the great Ricardo Darín was 17 years ago, in the twisty crime-caper, "Nine Queens" (later remade into an inferior sequel with John C. Reilly). He played a sleazy schemer, both smarmy and charming; you wanted to trust him, but he kept fuckin' with you. A screen actor since the early 1980's, Darín have always seemed to locate the core of each character he played, his very soul, his driving element, and then toy with our preconceptions of such a character. (For a great example, check out his haunted performance as Benjamín in Juan José Campanella's "The Secret in Their Eyes".)

Cess Gay's cancer drama "Truman" (which originally got released in 2015) presents another showcase for Darín. This time, he wisely takes a step back to let his acting comrade, Javier Cámara (Louie C.K.'s Spanish doppelgänger), take equal spotlight in a heart-piercingly restrained performance. The trio create a touching ode to friendship, a gentle meditation on life and death that, like life itself, is fleeting, with a few particularly memorable moments - all involving its two venerable leads.

As my longtime fans know (I'm speaking to all four of you), I am not a huge fan of cancer dramas, finding most of them manipulative and pointless. Yet Gay, who worked with both actors before on "A Gun in Each Hand", tries hard to avoid the trappings of, say, Julia Roberts' tearjerker-from-hell, "Stepmom". "Truman" is more nuanced, the cancer and impending doom a metaphor for the brevity of our lives, and how they can seem so long and yet end up so unfulfilled, rich but full of regrets. Also, the film happens to be unexpectedly funny - a rarity in films that deal with the slow deterioration of a human being.

The titular Truman happens to be Julián's (Darín) dog, with whom the stage actor resides in Madrid. Unexpectedly, his best friend Tomás (Cámara) comes to visit the cancer-stricken man from Canada - but only for four days. He's here to talk Julián out of something-I-will-not-reveal-but-is-quite-obvious. When Julian finds out he freaks out, "Go back to Canada and your penguins!"

The film follows the duo, as Julián makes amends, the running thread being their attempt to find a new owner for Truman. They visit an adoption shelter, an oncology doctor, a bookstore, a restaurant, pick a coffin, meet up with Paula (Dolores Fonzi) - a mutual acquaintance, surprise Julián's misinformed son, Nico (Oriol Pia) in

Amsterdam - and so on and so forth. Those moments - tear-jerking dialogues, long goodbyes, getting affairs in order before the imminent demise - do get a bit repetitive in their brash commitment to communicate the inevitability of death, how everything around you falls apart in those final days.

Were it not for Tomás' sardonic commentary, as if echoing our awareness of those staples, the film would have spiraled into the dreadful "cancer drama abyss". "Warn me before a next scene like this," he urges Julián, after they walk out of a heartbreaking visit to the vet. He is resistant to his friend's attempts to get him to open up, terrified of the darkness that may surface within himself. After Julián shares a very intimate and kind thought with Tomás and asks him to do the same, Tomás' response is both laugh-out-loud-funny and touching - a mixture of emotions that can be applied to the overall effect of "Truman". The conclusion is predictable but suitably poignant.

There are moments of magic sprinkled throughout the inescapable melancholy. When presented with a simple crayon drawing from Tomás' kids, Julián, overwhelmed, responds, "See, these are the moments we will have to avoid." "How do dogs experience grief?" Julián wonders at one point. In a bookstore, he compares a book about dealing with death to having a guide on a trip to Thailand. When a fellow actor ignores him at a restaurant, Julián proceeds to confront him; "People don't know what to say to me", he says. An encounter in a restaurant leads to an unexpected, heartfelt gesture from a longtime friend.

Upfront, witty, self-loathing and arrogant, Julián is a vibrant character, bringing to mind Javier Bardem's performance in "Biutiful". Truman is his last link to life, to everything vivacious within him, and watching him part with the dog, his best friend, is as heartbreaking for the viewer as it is for Tomás. Julián's polar opposite, Tomás is insecure, stoic and reserved. They have an easy, lived-in chemistry. "You're very nervous," Julián tells Tomás on an airplane. "Why don't you go jerk off? You remember how to jerk off, don't you?"

Straddling the line between grim manipulation and true-to-life observations (perfectly illustrated in the scene where Julián urinates on himself in a cafe, then says , "I used to be a romantic hero!") , "Truman" is insightful, funny and dire. Whether you'll want to watch it over and over again is highly debatable. Whether it is even necessary is an inquiry worthy of another essay. Ricardo Darín and Javier Cámara shine though, and those seeking to fill their time watching a well-directed, well-acted cancer drama (I know you're out there!) could do worse.

3 out of 5 stars

2.5-STAR REVIEWS

"A Space Program" Resembles a Bricoleur "The Martian"

Synopsis: *The artist Tom Sachs and his team of bricoleurs build a handmade space program and send two female astronauts to Mars.*

Imagine a college art project, the purpose of which was to recreate a manned Mars mission. Now imagine this project being assigned to a highly gifted and wealthy student, and you get contemporary New York artist Tom Sach's "A Space Program" - a filmed "art exhibit-cum-science lesson", which runs a little over an hour - exactly twice the length it should have been. While not without its merits, Sach's experiment leaves you feeling drained and claustrophobic, akin to being trapped in a space capsule.

It all beings promisingly, with evocative narration, supplemented by Shaman-like electronic soundscapes, quoting the visionary inventor Buckminster Fuller: "Science and religion are on a parallel course, to answer one question… [long pause] …are we alone?" We are then introduced to the team of pseudo-scientists (slash artists?) that Sachs assembled, Avengers-style, for his grandiose experiment, all set in a couple of massive stages. Impressively, Sachs managed to rally hundreds of folks, specializing in science, literature, film… and "imagination."

Among them are: Lt. Samantha Ratanarat, "a model-maker, astronaut, ironworker" (in that order), who focuses on steel - the most prominently used material for space travel; Commander Mary Eannarino, "an astronaut and carpenter", whose specialty is plywood, "the queen of all building materials"; Sgt. Pat McCarthy, "the shop foreman", who uses… a broom ("No one is above manual labor… Sometimes even a boss might shovel shit in Louisiana."); Lt. Nick Doyle, "a fifth-degree master bricoleur"… At the helm of the project is, of course, Col. Tom Sachs himself, known for such controversial work as a full-scale model of the atomic bomb that was dropped on Nagasaki.

And therein lies the entire point of this, well, I hesitate to call it a "film" - let's say, "piece". "Our space program is handmade, guided by the philosophy of bricolage," the narration informs solemnly. Everything is replicated using the most basic of materials and tools. The "trip" is led by two female astronomers (in memory of Ann Lee, inventor of the circular saw), which allows them to plunge-cut the

Martian surface (and, in one grisly shot, a human heart and brain), and is broadcast to the theater audience on multiple "telescreens", while it is led from stage to stage, as the events unfurl. The two women go to Mars "not to exploit the resources of a new planet, but to better understand our resources, here on Earth" - which, I guess, summarizes the whole goal of "A Space Program"… although, at a different point, Sach states that his mission is to find life on Mars and recoup their investment. So this part is a bit hazy.

The art exhibit itself is impressive in its scope and imagination. Sachs infuses all the technical jargon and self-seriousness with dashes of humor, such as a "turn off your cellphones, turn on your minds" sign at the start of the exhibit, an "Applause/Quiet" electronic board, an old-school globe on a string serving as a replica of Earth, and a detailed depiction of what it would be like to defecate in a space ship. The artist lands the ship on Mars using a prehistoric Atari landing emulator. The insemination of the Martian surface consists of poppy seeds and cream cheese from a bagel. Oh, and there's a "funky boom box", the first to grace the Martian surface.

There are some interesting factoids, such as the makings of a Martian suit, the length of time it takes to get to Mars without technology, and, of course, the aforementioned step-by-step reenactment of the entire mission - from boarding the space ship to the flight, from landing on Mars to exploring it. It demonstrates how close, claustrophobic proximity and isolation can get out of hand, shown through a quirky "Bitch Meter", old IBM footage, and crayon graphics depicting the heart-brain "feedback system". Whether or not they astronauts find life on Mars, I'll let you discover - but let's just say, funky music is involved.

Overall, "A Space Program" feels like an extended, artsy episode of "How It's Made" or "Mythbusters", if it were heavily dosed on opium. Some of the "do-it-yourself" science is dubious, leaving the viewer wondering what is plausible and what isn't. The "piece"'s amateur feel starts to become a detriment - it's just hard to take crayon drawings of space ships seriously. There is no sense of peril or suspense. After an engaging start the narrative lurches into long stretches of "floating through fake space" boredom. None of the characters engage - we are passive observers, somewhat fascinated at the possibility of "what if", but ultimately left cold. Perhaps the celluloid format distances the viewers from the experience of actual emotional involvement.

While Sach's ambition and imagination are admirable and impressive, and a lot of passion and effort clearly went into this project, it ultimately leaves you confused regarding its purpose. It's not really educational, doesn't work as a documentary or a narrative piece… Kudos for keeping the quest for space exploration alive, I guess?

Watching it, I wished I were there, wandering around the artist's bricolage inventions, instead of blankly staring at it on the screen, hoping for Matt Damon to show up and plant some damn potatoes already.

2.5 out of 5 stars

"Blind Sun" Will Require SPF 50 to Sit Through Its Oppressive Scorching

Synopsis: *Sometime in the near future, in Greece, a seaside resort gets struck by a heavy heat wave. Water is rare and violence is mounting. Ashraf, a solitary immigrant, is looking after a villa while its owners are away. On a dusty road crushed by the sun, he is stopped by a police officer for an identity check.*

I like minimalist art, for the most part. To me, the most satisfying art comes in form of books, music, films and paintings that evoke profound feelings and stir up turbulent emotions by revealing very little. A simple dot on a canvas can make you cry, if juxtaposed against the enormity of said canvas in just the right way (see Don Hertzfeld's work). A flinch of an eyelid or a tender hug at the finale of a film may have the capacity to tear a soul into shreds (see the Dardenne brothers' "L'Enfant"). A repeated note, struck at just the right tempo, can reverberate in your mind, like a liquid ripple effect (see Nils Frahm's discography).

Minimalist art may easily have the opposite effect, coming off as pretentious. To some, Malevich's work is profound, to others, it's just a black freakin' square. Arguing minimalist art's validity therefore becomes an ouroboros-like endurance test. I will, however, argue that Joyce A. Nashawati, in her debut feature-length film "Blind Sun", relies a bit too heavily on prolonged beautiful shots of scorched vistas to evoke feeling. At the same time, it piles on its themes, however valid and relevant they may be, too heavily, resulting in an ambitious and well-shot, but muddled and frankly tedious affair.

Ashraf (Ziad Bakri) is entrusted to look after a gorgeous villa by an arrogant French couple. On a solitary, parched road he encounters a cop, who proceeds to threaten Ashraf and confiscate the poor guy's documents. Ashraf's attempts to get them back from the police station prove futile.

Back at the house, the heat and thirst begin to affect the young man, whose vision blurs, along with the film's narrative. He stumbles upon an archaeological site - and later has sex with the beautiful young archaeologist. A woman visits him and reads his future in the bottom of a coffee mug. The house gets raided by invisible forces and shadowy figures. The visions and weird occurrences escalade, until it all goes down in flames / reaches its boiling point / [insert metaphor here]. Ashraf's not the best house-sitter, if you ask me.

All of this is set against the backdrop of a smoldering heat wave, protests and the looming presence of an Umbrella Corporation-like corporation: a water company called Bluegold, that promises redemption in form of crystal-clear hydration. "There's going to be a war," Ashraf declares despondently at one point, "and we're all going to burn."

"Blind Sun"'s themes of prejudice against immigrants, while resonant in light of the recent European crises, are laid on thickly, the protagonist treated like utter shit at every turn. "I know your type, free as a bird. All you think about is fucking," Gilles (Louis-Do de Lencquesaing - what a name!), the French owner of the house, proclaims before leaving Ashraf to take care of it. "This will teach you to respect the country you live off," the racist cop snarls, before roaring away on his motorbike - with Ashraf's freakin' passport!

Basked in scorched-orange hues, blinding sunlight and the ear-splitting chatter of cicadas, Nashawati's film takes wild swings: it has Lynchian moments of subliminal terror; real-life political currents run thread-like through the narrative; an angry outcry against the inevitability of global warming echoes in every fiery frame; a psycho-horror film and a tender touch of a love story appear then dissipate... Oh, and warning: the film is most definitely NOT for cat lovers.

If that all sounds intriguing, somehow, despite Bakri's best efforts (the lanky actor is in every shot), the film comes off as monotonous and exhausting, with its deliberate pace and roasting soundtrack and depravity and religious imagery and blinding sun and shot after shot of dried-out land weighing you down in the first ten minutes and making the remaining seventy feel like torture. Which, if that were the filmmakers' intention - bravo, mission accomplished. The only thing that's refreshing about this dry feature is the fact that the characters speak in three languages - Greek, French and English - giving it an authentic international flavor.

"Blind Sun" takes too long to get going and eventually doesn't really go anywhere, like looking at beautiful, smoldering embers for an hour and twenty minutes - or arguing about the merits of art. It tries so hard to both be a parable about oppression (human/weather) and an ambitious little arthouse horror flick, it never really achieves the right balance. Akin to Icarus, it scalds its wings against the sun it's blinded by - but points for attempting to soar that high.

2.5 out of 5 stars

"Bluebeard" Starts Off with a Bang and Ends with a Whimper

Synopsis: *Dr. Seung-hoon sedates his landlord before medical check-up, when the old man begins telling him a convincing murder confession.*

South Korea has consistently been a source of inspiring, off-kilter, original and engrossing cinema - Park Chan-wook's "Vengeance" trilogy, Bong Joon-ho's "The Host", Kim Jee-woon's "I Saw the Devil", Yeon Sang-ho's "Train to Busan" and Baek Jong-Yeol's "The Beauty Inside", to name a few. "Bluebeard" initially delivers, as it steadily builds momentum with a strong stylistic grasp - but its belligerent final third reveals that director Lee Soo-youn still has some ways to go to reach the level of his revered peers. A weird amalgamation of Agatha Christie, Brian De Palma and Eli Roth, by turns entertaining and infuriating, this strange beast is perhaps worth a look - if only to cause a heated debate with your film-geek friends over the twist-upon-twist insanity, which it delivers in such heaps, suffocation may be a factor for the uninitiated.

The film starts off on an ominous note: as a Seoul weather report announces longer but warmer winters, a body bubbles up through chunks of melting ice in the Han river - whose waters "used to unfreeze completely by April". The camera keeps elegantly panning up to the highway traffic, and into a bus, where Dr. Seung-hoon (Jo Jin-woong) wears an expression as desolate as the vast, empty construction sites through which he's driven.

Dr. Seung-hoon does not seem like a happy man. He works at a somewhat-decrepit, overfilled colonoscopy clinic in the Gangnam district that's on the verge of bankruptcy. He examines people's insides with his assistant Mi-yeon (Lee Chung-ah), whose offers to "air out" and get lunch he continuously declines. He looks for "answers" in mystery novels, falls asleep on the bus and comes to work early. He pays alimony, argues with his unstable ex-wife and barely gets any time with his smart-ass son. His boss is, well, a "douchebag".

He gets his meat at the local butcher's, run by an old man (Shin Goo) with a bad habit of consuming raw flesh, and his creepily cheerful son Sung-geun (Kim Dae-myung). Crucially, they also happen to be Seung-hoon's landlords. The monotony of Seung-hoon's life is shattered when, during the butcher's routine colonoscopy, his drugged rant about dismantling joints turns into a confession about dismantling human victims. What unfolds from here on is an enveloping sense of Hitchcockian paranoia, with news reports of body parts being discovered, cops snooping around, and our good doctor putting pieces of the puzzle together, desperately trying to "out" the butchers...

And then the film switches gears about half-way through, with a twist involving his ex-wife and a retired cop. This is soon followed by yet another twist, both predictable and far-fetched, plus way over-explained with damn flashbacks. Frequent nightmarish dream visions are… nightmarish, but been-there-done-that, the character waking up in sweat/screaming/choking/[insert verb here]. Put it this way: the film ends at the 84-minute mark, and then goes on for another half an hour to delve deep into the pits of convoluted absurdity.

Too bad. If only Soo-youn managed to sustain that borderline-Lynchian mood and perhaps take the film into a purposefully surreal, Takashi Miike territory, it could've worked. "Bluebeard" certainly has some splendid things going for it. Seoul is effectively depicted as a city running wild with rampant serial killers. Jo Jin-woong, appearing in nearly every scene, showcases his versatility, especially after his sleazy performance in last year's "The Handmaiden". Often morbidly funny, touching upon hefty themes of parenthood, apathy, alienation - and how it spawns paranoia and change - while balancing a fine line between hilarity and horror, particularly in the early scenes involving the doctor and the butcher's son, Soo-youn was really onto something here.

Even the darkest South Korean cinema tends to have moments of unexpected levity, and this one's no different. "Wrong hole!" a sedated female patient exclaims during a colonoscopy, startling our doctor and his assistant. "It's my first time doing anal." "It's like diaphragm in human," the butcher's jolly son tells a terrified Seung-hoon, while offering him thin skirt steak. During the culmination, a crazed Seung-hoon screams in panic: "Local police and the butchers are in league with each other!" And then the scene cuts away…

Speaking of, quite a few scenes fade out, or cut, or "stay behind the closed door" at crucial moments purposefully, letting your imagination work out the rest. Unfortunately, while intermittently effective, those abrupt shifts in tone and plot lead to a disjointed narrative, with major pacing issues and lapses in logic, escalating into pure madness towards the end. Director Lee Soo-youn seems to be flexing his cinematic muscles, this being his second feature after 2003's "Uninvited". Here's hoping he doesn't fly off the treadmill next time.

2.5 out of 5 stars

"Captain America: Civil War" Pits Iron Against (Superhuman) Flesh

Synopsis: *Political interference in the Avengers' activities causes a rift between former allies Captain America and Iron Man.*

The success of Christopher Nolan's "Dark Knight" trilogy signaled a drastic change in the approach to comic book movies. Lots of darkness - both internal (hero trauma; existential rumination) and external (dimly-lit, grisly scenes that pushed PG-13 to its limits) - became requisites. The most prominent theme that seemed to have spawned from the Caped Crusader's tortured journey, and consequently formed a thread through all the consecutive graphic novel adaptations, seems to be the duality of good vs. evil, the meaning of heroism, the internal struggle of an ultra-powerful being (see: "Avengers: Age of Ultron", "Batman v Superman: Dawn of Justice"). This motif is perhaps best exemplified in the current, second season of Netflix's "Daredevil", which has an entire episode centered around the titular character and The Punisher, debating whether vigilante justice causes even more violence instead of resolving it.

Anthony and Joe Russo's follow up to their first Captain America directing gig, the popular-but-overrated "Captain America: The Winter Soldier", continues the trend, the film's central conceit being the dubious actions of the Avengers, and whether the number of casualties in their epic stand-offs require regulation. As Secretary of State, Thaddeus Ross (played by a somnambulant William Hurt), dryly comments (and I'm paraphrasing, as the theater was very dark, and I had trouble scribbling dialogue verbatim in my 3-D glasses): "While a great deal of people see you as heroes, some prefer the term vigilantes." "Captain America: Civil War" splits the beloved Avengers team into two opposing gangs, with sometimes entertaining, but mostly wearying results.

To start, the narrative hops between locations like it's just done several rails of cocaine. BOOM: we're in Lagos, where Captain America and his team create chaos trying to stop a biological weapon heist from taking place. BOOM: Iron Man's at MIT, giving a solemn speech about the "correlation between generosity and guilt" and oh-so-generously gives a grant to every student's project (let's hope none of them is a Robert Oppenheimer in the making), just to be tearfully confronted by Miriam (Alfre Woodard), whose son died in Sokovia. "He's dead, and I blame you," she says vehemently, "victory at the expense of the innocent is no victory at all." (Central theme of film spelled out right there.) The events of New York, Washington D.C., Sokovia, and now Lagos have led to 117 countries calling a meeting at the U.N. to assign a panel that would tightly regulate the Avengers' actions.

BOOM! We're in Cleveland, where Evil Zemo (Daniel Brühl) obtains the Winter Soldier's (Sebastian Stan) activation codes, as well as other classified docs that will later lead him to… well, a Discovery, deep in Russia. In the meantime, Steve Rogers' and Tony Stark's confrontation begins, at first verbally: Cpt. America: "If we sign [the U.N. agreement], we surrender our right to choose." Stark: "We need to be put in check." Both act uncharacteristically, but my guess is that's intentional. The Avengers quickly start splitting into factions: Team Stark and Team Rogers. BOOM: the film takes us to Vienna, where the U.N. summit, just as a peaceful resolution is about to be reached - yes, BOOM! - explodes, and the blame immediately falls on Bucky (a.k.a. The Winter Soldier, for those of you a bit lost). BOOM: welcome to Bucharest, where Cpt. America catches up with Bucky, instantly believes his spiel about how he "wasn't in Vienna" and he doesn't "do it anymore", and together they attempt to escape a slew of Avengers, joined by a new masked vigilante called Black Panther (Chadwick Boseman).

From this point on, the film keeps dashing wildly between Berlin, where Bucky gets captured, escapes with Caps, and Iron Man gets 36 hours to find them; Queens, where Stark enlists Spider Man (Tom Holland) to help him track Caps; Leipzig, where the Showdown occurs: Caps, Falcon (Anthony Mackie), Ant Man (Paul Rudd), Scarlet Witch (Elizabeth Olsen), Bucky and Hawkeye (Jeremy Renner) vs. Stark, Black Panther, Spidey, War Machine (Don Cheadle), Black Widow (Scarlett Johansson) and Vision (Paul Bettany) (I hope I got this right). After quite a few minutes of this violent-but-pointless showdown, the film propels us to the blistering Siberian wilderness for the final, even more "intense" showdown, where two lifelong friends beat the living crap out of each other, for reasons not that well defined (c'mon, sit down, spark one, get laid, violence can't be the only way, dudes).

One of the issues is: the stakes are quite low. Yes, it's kinda awesome to see the Avengers go at each other, but they are never truly provided a compelling enough reason to bash the living hell out of themselves - it's almost as if they all sniffed some powder and went berserk - or an extension of that Thor vs. Stark sequence from the original "Avengers". I get that Tony, after messing up (to say the least) in "Age of Ultron", is all for regulation (though it does go against his character), and Cpt. America, the virtuous spirit that he is, seeks justice - but is that reason enough for them to engage in an extended, SFX-laden sequence, where nothing is at stake, which diminishes the intensity to an almost-zero-degree (spoiler alert: NO ONE dies during that episode)?

Another issue is the central character. Chris Evans has always been a non-presence for me, a step above James Franco and two below Ryan Reynolds, whose one "shining" moment, at least for me, will always remain the sequence in

"Snowpiercer" where he talks about eating babies. He resembles Chris Pine, who can't carry a non-"Star Trek" film. To me, Chris Evans, with his formidable-but-expressionless features, fails to infuse an inherently-blank, overly-righteous character with any zing or, for lack of a better word, pepper (speaking of, Potts is sorely missing from "Civil War"). He's the embodiment of the American Patriot Hero, and hey - audiences lap it up.

In contrast, Robert Downey Jr. continues his sardonic shtick as Tony Stark / Iron Man, and at least he's got energy and wit - but even his drollery is wearing thin. By far the best line in the film he utters is about 75% through the film, to Bucky, who keeps a sniper rifle aimed at him: "Hey, Manchurian Candidate… there's a truce going on over here, all right?" Tom Holland as the new Spidey (#14?) comes off as kinda wimpy, but does boast some exhilarating moments… Not to be a complete hater, but I am pointing out again: it's not so much the actor, as the wizards behind the computer screens, and millions and millions of dollars, with perhaps a dash of creative input from the directing duo.

The rest of the characters fare better than others (deep breath for the upcoming run-on sentence): Scarlett Johansson finally has more than one line and a single fight sequence; Anthony Mackie gets a few quips in as Falcon (although his costume really does resemble a flamboyant, bird-like drag queen from the future); Paul Bettany strains to emote through layers and layers of make-up as Vision (like, wtf is this character's deal, by the way?); Don Cheadle is way underused as the injured War Machine (check him out in "Miles Ahead", currently out in theaters, instead); Sebastian Stan frowns and smolders as Bucky; Chadwick Boseman gets the silliest, hate-filled lines as the Black Panther; Elizabeth Olsen, normally a reliable presence, fails to connect here, especially with her Russian accent (general point here: come on, Hollywood, hire some native Russian speakers for your $200+ mil productions!); Daniel Brühl, so memorable in "Rush" and "Inglorious Basterds", makes for a surprisingly bland villain; and, finally, Paul Rudd makes a welcome, albeit short, appearance as a (spoiler alert!) gargantuan Ant-Man. (Okay, this one's for the ultra-nerds: there's a new, sorta-kinda character called Red Wing, Falcon's "sidekick", whom Black Widow refuses to acknowledge, as did I.)

"Deadpool", flawed as it may be, at least thought outside the box, broke the fourth wall, added violence and an acute commentary on the ridiculousness of tent-pole comic book movies. Made for a fifth of "Civil War"'s budget, Tim Miller's film proved that less is more, and it's not the effects that are impressive, but the way they are sparingly used. When it's an assault on the senses, as we witnessed in "Age of Ultron", "Man of Steel", and its recent bombastic sequel, no amount of pseudo-intellectual rumination on the effectiveness of superheroes can compensate for what is essentially a polished turd. All this critic talk of Marvel infusing the film with "moral and emotional conflict" (Russ Fischer, The Playlist) makes it seem like we should be joyously grateful for a tiny bit of thought inserted into the mix, while it should simply be a given. Nolan's "Batman Begins" pulled it off with aplomb.

Also, can we just agree that, after several Hulks, Fantastic Fours, Spideys, War Machines, the (for now?) parallel X-Men universe(s), and all the other inconsistencies, the Marvel universe makes no sense? There's really no point in piecing the puzzle bits together, as hard as the studio tries to make it all fit. It's really a "shut-your-brains-off-and-gape-at-the-spectacle" sort of entertainment, overstuffed with eccentric characters, one-liners and top-of-the-line SFX, with a spontaneous dash of pretentious, oh-so-serious polemic now and then. If that's your thing - and no judgement there, we all need to shut down our brains from time to time - "Civil War" is right up your alley. Thing is, once you've seen one Marvel bash-'em-all-to-hell PG-13 sequence, no matter how inventive it is, you've pretty much seen them all. "Civil War" definitely feels like a minor step back into all-too-familiar territory, which is unfortunate, after films like the aforementioned "Deadpool", or even ""Guardians of the Galaxy" that had quirky tidbits, like a rocking' soundtrack, a mad raccoon and a talking tree.

I just watched "The Lobster", Yorgos Lanthimos' Cannes entry, which will be released on U.S. screens on May 13th. It stars a chubby Collin Farell in a dystopian, absurdist society, where relationships are determined based solely on compatibility, people hunt each other with tranquilizer guns - oh, and you get to pick an animal to turn into, if you fail to find a partner. Made for a fraction of "Civil War"'s budget, the film - also flawed, mind you - is exponentially more epic, affecting, morbidly funny, nerve shredding and yes, entertaining (at least for "cinefiles" like me) than the whole Marvel cannon put together so far. If it weren't for the likes of "Ant Man" and "Deadpool", I'd be tempted to say I'm at a point where Marvel is losing me, and it's sad, considering I am a graphic novel lover. Let's hope the upcoming "Sandman" adaptation (if it ever happens, dammit!) saves the day.

2.5 out of 5 stars

"Churchill" Goes Nowhere - Just Like Winston's Struggles

Synopsis: *A ticking-clock thriller following Winston Churchill in the 96 hours before D-Day.*

Brian Cox is one of our great character actors, whom everyone recognizes - "ah, it's that guy from 'Troy'!" - but not many can actually name. About half a decade before Anthony Hopkins tasted delectable human flesh in "Silence of the Lambs", Cox gave an equally harrowing, albeit significantly less heralded performance as the original Hannibal Lecter in Michael Mann's 1986 cult classic "Manhunter". The film underperformed and, instead of catapulting Cox to fame, led to a steady career of strong, memorable supporting parts, ranging from blockbusters ("Braveheart", "The Bourne Identity", "Rise of the Planet of the Apes") to indie gems ("Rushmore", "Adaptation", and my personal favorite Cox performance, Big John Harrigan in Michael Cuesta's little-seen, hard-to-watch 2001 drama "L.I.E."). Jonathan Teplitzky (director of the tepid 2013 Nicole Kidman vehicle, "The Railway Man"), must be a big fan of Cox's work, casting him as the lead in his low-budget biographical snippet "Churchill". Preachy, reverential and by-the-numbers, this heartfelt but misguided project serves as an excellent showcase of a great actor elevating sub-par material.

The film opens on the "1,736th day of WWII" (I wonder what the starting point of this "countdown" was, and whether Alex von Tunzelmann, the screenwriter, actually used a calendar and a calculator). As Winston Churchill, who's seen his share of battles, stands on the ocean shore, he watches its waves turn crimson with the blood of his memories and solemnly swears: "I mustn't let it happen again." Yet doubt shadows his eyes - doubt, as it turns out, regarding Operation Overlord, devised by Dwight Eisenhower (John Slattery) and approved by His Majesty Himself, King George VI (James Purefoy). "This plan may be admirable in its bravery," Winston warns them, "but in its risks, it is foolhardy." His efforts to stop it, however, are futile - he's a dinosaur stuck in a well-oiled machine, afforded, out of respect for his past heroic deeds, the courtesy of witnessing but not participating in any aspects of warfare. Only, according to Churchill, "It's not warfare, it's butchering, and I can't let them do it to our men."

Teplitzky follows the trials and tribulations Winston faces in his quest for having his voice heard: coming face-to-face with Eisenhower, the King, an army general - just to keep getting repeatedly rejected. His relationship with Clementine (poor Miranda Richardson, reduced to the "sensible wife role"), falters. "Why don't you just have me stuffed?!" he hollers at her, before receiving a hearty slap. It all leads to, well, nothing: Operation Overlord goes into effect on the north coast of France as planned. A glorious final speech, delivered by Churchill, feigning enthusiasm while realizing his own insignificance, almost saves the clichéd narrative - until it proceeds to end on another gag-inducing note.

This film is less a "ticking-clock thriller", as its IMDB description claims, than a languid study of a once-great man who's left with no choice but to surrender to the "perils" of evolution and take second fiddle to a new generation. An admirable theme, then, seen through the prism of an important figure at a crucial point in our history. The issue's that the film gets its point across within the first 20 minutes - and then proceeds to relentlessly pound us over the head with it for almost two hours. There's no discernible progress in plot or character development. It's all one-note: Winston's desperation and helplessness against the inevitable - the war, the future, death. Speeches about "slaughter" and "hope" are solemnly delivered, over and over again. A ponderous drama, "Churchill" relies on tropes and provides very little in the way of spontaneity or originality. The lack of subtlety is not helped by Lorne Balfe's insistent sentimental score, swooping in every several minutes to remind us how we should feel. Someone should check the battery in that "ticking-clock", because it seems to have stalled.

Prone to preaching, with cheesy lines like "Britain will thank you, Winston… forever", "Churchill" never gains momentum due to its lack of true insight. A character stating, "When you reach calm waters, it is easy to forget the captain who steered you through the storm", is as close to wisdom as this film gets. The rest of the dialogue is 95% filler sap like, "Men will die tomorrow. Do not let a single one of them die in vain", or "The men do their duties and we do ours", and so on, so forth. Winston's prayer to God about the weather, an orchestral choir "cheering" him on, takes the cake as "Most Blatantly Manipulative and Obvious Scene of 2017 So Far". "Who will I be, when it's all over?" he spells out the film's Big Theme towards the end. "You'll always be the man who led us through this," Clementine answers. Ugh.

Luckily, it's not all dire. Brian Cox is a live-wire, prone to violent outbursts, growling at his own reflection in the mirror, chomping on his cigar as forcefully as he does on scenery, reprimanding his assistant on her transcribing skills, but also deeply insecure, neglected, hanging on to his past and filled with remorse for the fallen souls of war. Hunched over, at times barely recognizable under layers of make-up, the actor's wise eyes shine through, guiding us through the morose proceedings. No amount of make-up could hide John Slattery though. I like the actor, but I have trouble seeing him as anything but Roger Sterling from the TV series "Mad Men" - it's the poise, the mannerisms, the intonations. He can't seem to escape from the shadow of this giant, like, say, his co-star Elizabeth Moss did (you don't see "Peggy" when you watch her Offred in Hulu's "The Handmaid's Tale"). When Slattery's Eisenhower proclaims, "The war you're talking about, that was 30 years ago. I don't think you appreciate how much things have moved on", he may as well be talking to Don Draper.

What could have been a nerve-shredding thriller a-la Roger Donaldson's underrated "Thirteen Days" or a blistering character study, like Spielberg's "Lincoln", ends up a lukewarm, repetitive slog, much like the Teplitzky's previous effort. It's not without its merits - dashes of poignancy, some nice cinematography, impressive costume / set design, and it's almost worthy for seeing the lead performance by Cox alone, who adds several much-needed notes to this otherwise one-note study. Perhaps the man will get a lead role in a film deserving of his talents yet. Someone should put him back in touch with Michael Mann.

2.5 out of 5 stars

Sex Pistols Causing Havoc: Revisiting Lech Kowalski's Cult Rockumentary "D.O.A.: A Rite of Passage"

Synopsis: *Documentary chronicling the rise and fall of the punk movement with rare interview footage of Sid Vicious and Nancy Spungen. Also featuring concert and news footage.*

Back in 1978, Lech Kowalski - the ultimate groupie who happened to be armed with a 16mm camera - embarked on a journey. He followed The Sex Pistols on their only seven-city U.S. tour. It was ultimately their last one, after which the band broke up, and Sid and Nancy tragically died. Non-invasive, filled with music but not much insight, "D.O.A." serves as a curiosity, a rare glimpse at some legendary footage, without much context or depth.

An actual rite of passage opens the documentary, juxtaposed against female fingers, putting on an LP - the last such flourish in an otherwise-basic doc. Kowalksi then delves deep into a Los Angeles punk rock club, a Sex Pistols gig, taking the viewer along for the tour and the U.S. audience's reaction to it. The energy is palpable before Johnny Rotten even begins to wail, "I wanna be anarchy", fist up in the air, the man an embodiment of said anarchy. Hearing the terrified U.S. audience's feedback is exhilarating (those clothes!), folks both shocked and aroused by the punk provocateurs. My favorite line comes about halfway through the film, when Sid Vicious is asked, "What's your impression of America, at this point?" by an eager journalist, and simply replies, "A load of shit."

Issues of authority are discussed. Interviews with folks opposing the movement, while amusing in their all-too-British uptightness, halt the doc's momentum, like the one with the elderly Mary Whitehouse, an "anti-smut crusader", who says, "I'm not shocked by punk. I'm shamed by it."

On the other hand, the doc could have used more interviews like the one with an intoxicated Sid - who wears a swastika T-shirt - and Nancy, months before their death. Toppled on top of each other, barely comprehensible, they smoke cigarettes and try not to pass out. Nancy asks the camera guy, "Should we kiss for you?" She makes Sid a cup of coffee. Later, she undresses and makes out with him, after snapping at him for spilling coffee and cigarettes on her. True artist geniuses, ladies and gents.

Kowalski's doc is chock-full of legendary live performances by The Sex Pistols, and lesser-known bands, such as Sham 69, the female-led X-Ray Spex, The Dead

Boys, Generation X (later famous for giving rise to the one and only Billy Idol) and, well, the less said about Terry and the Idiots, the better.

Shot mostly on grainy 16mm film in bars and clubs, "D.O.A." portrays a moment in time, with all of its fashion and anarchist movements. It shows how authority viewed it as a threat, and was, in return, regarded as such itself ("neo-punk" bands like The Prodigy still sing anti-establishment ballads). But at the end of the day, that's all it is, a musical snapshot, without much cultural resonance, significance or any deeper glimpses at the band itself. Yes, it's raw and grimy. Yes, it's seeped with a healthy dose of authenticity; unlike watching aging rock stars reminiscing about the good old days, with intermittent archival footage, this is the real deal. One just can't help but wish that the real deal was a little bit more... real.

2.5 out of 5 stars

Zoey Deutch Blooms into a Serious Actress in the Otherwise Tangled "Flower"

Synopsis: *A sexually curious teen forms an unorthodox kinship with her mentally unstable stepbrother.*

Max Winkler's "Flower" has all the hallmarks of a good movie: memorable performances (particularly from Zoey Deutch, the lead), a hip soundtrack, biting dialogue and even some glimpses of a new twist on the whole "coming-of-age" staple. Yet sometimes, films just don't gel. Whether it happened during the editing process, or the screenwriters weren't sure on which trajectory to focus, it's difficult to tell, but "Flower" does not cohere, its good bits serving as teasers of the superior films we never get to see.

Is "Flower" a commentary on misguided feminism? Its protagonist, Erica (Deutsch), sure sees of herself as a feminist, as she bribes cops for money after giving them blowjobs and taping it with their friends. She's very self-aware: yes, she has daddy issues (her father is in jail), yes, she beats up on her classmates, and yes, she loves to give head ("I'm extremely gifted," she says. "A dick is just like a thumb without a fingernail.") She's seemingly confident with a turmoil of issues hiding underneath the chirpy exterior.

Is "Flower" a dark tale of adolescence and first love? When her overweight, anxiety-ridden stepbrother Luke (Joey Morgan) gets released from rehab, Erica bonds with him, endeared by his panic attacks and anger management issues. They consequently embark on a quest to frame a potential child molester, Will (Adam Scott), who happens to frequent the same bowling alley as Erica and her rebellious girlfriends. The plan, of course, goes terribly awry, leading to Erica and Luke escaping, "Bonnie and Clyde"-style. From this moment on - let's say, the last 20 minutes or so - "Flower" gets increasingly more ridiculous, culminating in the line: "I think I love you."

Is "Flower" a dark satire of suburbia? There are numerous allusions to cult classic satires like Todd Solondz's "Happiness" and Michael Lehmann's "Heathers" and Larry Clark's "Bully". Some of the characters are caricatures, like Erica's shrill, desperate mother Laurie (Kathryn Hahn, in her 300th project), recently remarried to another stereotype, Bob (Tim Heidecker), a "loser who collects pinball machines" but also "a good, good person " - at least compared to her incarcerated ex.

Is "Flower" a slapstick/situational comedy? Erica certainly finds herself in amusing situations, rendered somewhat awkward by their deliberate controversial nature (themes of underage sex, molestation, incest, suicide and murder are all touched upon lightly). There are a lot of fat jokes that may have landed if they were punchier and in, say, a Coen brothers flick, but then I'm talking about a much different film.

Winkler seems to grasp for different straws to connect them into a sound narrative. He at least aims to explore teenage-hood from a different angle, taking a look at a middle-class family whose values are just a tad askew. It's clear he has a reservoir of things to say about sexual liberation and gender equality… it's just not clear what those things are. While certain sequences, most involving exchanges between Erica and either Luke or Will, provide hints of a natural director of actors, the uneasy combination of humor and grimness of the overall film betrays Winkler's relative inexperience behind the camera. Here's hoping his career blossoms as opposed to wilting.

2.5 out of 5 stars

"Growing Up Smith" Barely Reaches Adolescence

Synopsis: *In 1979, an Indian family moves to America with hopes of living the American Dream. While their 10-year-old boy Smith falls head-over-heels for the girl next door, his desire to become a "good old boy" propels him further away from his family's ideals than ever before.*

Although films about immigrants coming to the Unites States in search of the American Dream aren't necessarily new - Jim Sheridan's "In America" dealt with it beautifully, as did Tom McCarthy's "The Visitor" and Mira Nair's "The Namesake" - Hollywood could certainly use more features that study the obstacles families face upon arrival to the Land of the Free, the World's Melting Pot, now ruled by a man intent on building walls to "protect" the country from the very same people that helped shape it. Unfortunately, Frank Lotito's "Growing Up Smith", though oh-so-cute and endearing, doesn't really add up to much, or contribute to the aforementioned modest sub-genre of immigration films. Set aside its Indian protagonists' impediments, and it becomes the most basic of coming-of-age tales; do the opposite, and you get a by-the-numbers, surface look at what it means to be a foreigner, lacking subtlety or any major revelations.

The film is narrated by a grown-up Smith (Samrat Chakrabarti), looking back at his bittersweet childhood. Toni Akurati stars as the titular young version, living in the late-1970s American suburbs. Having recently moved from their homeland, Smith's folks strictly abide by tradition, his father (Annul Nigam) proudly showing Smith a picture of his bride-to-be. Tough luck - Smith happens to fall for the girl-next-door, Amy (Brighton Sharbino).

He relentlessly pursues the Dream, wearing a bike helmet with the nation's stars-and-stripes on its side, wanting nothing more than to be a "good ol' American boy" - until, that is, he chokes on a KFC chicken, because, duh, he's a vegetarian (but also, who wouldn't choke on that nasty crap?). "Nice bag, Pocahontas," the racist white kids - "cowboys", as Smith refers to them - taunt poor Smith. "The only good Indian is a dead Indian." They chase him down alleyways, until "the one cowboy that made up for all the others", the enigmatic Butch Brunner (a scruffy Jason Lee) - Amy's father, as it so happens - pulls up in his big ol' truck and tells those kids to take a hike.

Any more-or-less savvy moviegoer will see the pattern forming here. We follow Smith through his inconsequential (mis)adventures, as he deals with the threat of banishment from his oppressive-but-kind father, wrestles with neurology, befriends Butch, struggles to keep his sister's boyfriend a secret, woos Amy, and (sorta) stands up against the "cowboys". Everything is glossed over in an optimistic sheen, with frequent use of music cues and cheap pandering to stimulate emotion.

The cracks in the Dream do eventually appear and spread, at first not apparent to Smith, enveloped in the idyllic dawn of adolescence. But the seemingly happy Butch has to sell his chopper in order to survive, Smith faces humiliation in class, his mom Nalini (Poorna Jagannathan) wastes her English linguistics degree sowing away at home, and their Bible-spouting neighbors try to convert them to Christianity. For a moment, the family does achieve a semblance of the much sought-after Dream, after an unexpected hunting incident propels Smith to fame. That whole sequence is displayed in a quick montage, just to swiftly catapult back to more obstacles and trauma. The poignant ending almost saves the film's formulaic structure - although I would have rolled the credits precisely 7 minutes before they did.

It's unpleasant to criticize children, but the bulk of the narrative's weight falls on the fragile shoulders of Toni Akurati, and while unquestionably adorable, the kid's not exactly a magnetic screen presence in the league of, say, a young Haley Joel Osment or Jacob Tremblay. The rest of the cast fares well enough, the highlight being Jason Lee's Butch, who infuses the film with a much-needed shot of adrenaline and wit. Mysterious and exotic to the Bhatnagars, he shows up for Halloween wearing dirty bedsheets and a John Deere hat and comes over for dinner with his wife Nancy (Hilarie Burton) and a box of mangled Morton Apple Pie ("you just have to bake it, it's like two hours at 350…"). Lee knows how to carry a scene. Cruise, give your fellow Scientologist a decent role already!

As for the rest of the film, it lags - and the dialogue doesn't help. "So is Naan a chicken or a beef or something?" Butch wonders at one point, the Epitome of American Ignorance. "Oh, I didn't know you could grill vegetables!" his hillbilly wife adds. Lotito certainly doesn't side-step sap: "I don't want to lose my best friend", "What good Indian boy will marry you now? You've been enjoyed!", "What is wrong with our children? Whores, all of them!" (Okay, that last one's kinda funny.) The drama is forced and the comedy struggles, which makes for an uneasy jarring of tones: happy-go-lucky vs. forcefully dramatic. There is no real sense of suspense or involvement. Growing up Smith ends up growing up John Doe.

2.5 out of 5 stars

"Jim Henson's Turkey Hollow" Marks a Welcome - Albeit Awfully Slight - Return of the Legendary Creature Shop

Synopsis: *A recently divorced father and his kids head to the quaint town of Turkey Hollow to spend Thanksgiving at the farm of his eccentric aunt. The holiday threatens to take a bleak turn when a scheming neighbor frames the aunt for turkey theft, but the fractured family teams up, along with some surprising new friends, to save the day.*

Films about Thanksgiving have had a hit-and-miss run, ranging from classics ("Hannah and Her Sisters", "The Ice Storm", "Pieces of April"), in which Turkey Day serves as a catalyst to spark relationship turmoil, to utter - ahem - turkeys ("Dutch", "Son in Law", and the recent, computer-animated debacle "Free Birds"), which use the holiday as an excuse to assault audiences with slapstick gimmicks and clichés. Just as any American film revolving around a festivity, even the better examples tend to follow a familiar trajectory: families unite, argue and eventually come to realize the true meaning of love and reconciliation.

There aren't many Thanksgiving films aimed at the young 'uns, and as such, "Jim Henson's Turkey Hollow", a Lifetime film, falls squarely in the middle of the cinematic Turkey lore. It does not by any means redefine the genre, and adults will groan their way through the formulaic dialogue and gag-inducing sentimentality, but kids will enjoy its simplicity and adventurous spirit. As for the creatures, courtesy of the titular production house - they are a joy to behold for anyone, no matter the age.

"Turkey Hollow" starts with a narration by none other than a hilariously playful Chris "Ludacris" Bridges (an offbeat casting choice for a film aimed at toddlers), introducing us to the town of Turkey Hollow and the Emmerson Family: divorced father Ron (Jay Harrington), snarky teenager Annie (Genevieve Buechner) and the young, gullible Tim (Graham Verchere). They're on their way to spend Thanksgiving with Aunt Cly (Mary Steenburgen, who seems to pop up in every TV production these days).

A local at a souvenir shop reveals the town's "tall tale", the Hideous Howling Hoodoo monster, whose wooden statue graces the central square. "Should you hear that horrible, high pitched moan," the local warns, "run as fast as you can." Young Tim is terrified and excited, while his older sister has more of a pragmatic outlook. Ron asks them not to bring up the Hoodoo in front of Aunt Cly, as her husband was allegedly kidnapped by the monster and "nearly eaten alive".

Aunt Cly, a tree-hugging vegan who rescues turkeys and runs a sustainable farm deep in the woods, without internet or TV (the horror!), isn't nearly as excited about their arrival as Ron expected, instantly accusing him of feeding his kids too much processed meat. Her home resembles a hallucinogenic greenhouse, crammed with plants and lava lamps. Plot complications arise: turns out, Ron's ex-wife cleaned him out during the divorce (or, as he stubbornly refers to it, "mutual uncoupling"), leaving him no choice but to dump his kids on Aunt Cly to get some work done.

Little Tim soon discovers his uncle's secret diary, filled with mysterious names like Burble and Squonk. It eventually leads the kids to an enchanted forest, with a group of "monsters" who eat rocks; one of "Turkey Hollows'" unexpected highlights involve a slow-motion sequence of rock consumption, scored to Johann Strauss' "The Blue Danube Waltz". There's also the evil Eldridge Sump (Linden Banks), owner of a nearby turkey farm, whose turkeys "have more hormones than a high-school drama club." Tim accidentally lets a flock of his birds loose, which leads to the Emmersons having to pay off Eldridge ten grand within a certain time period - or else.

Jim Henson's creatures are a highlight, as was expected. A lot of work and care went into those monsters, and the practical effects are refreshing. Maybe it's my old-school upbringing, but I'll take an intricately-designed puppet, with fur characters can actually touch, over a million digitized hairs on Sully, any day. The magic is just more... tangible. In addition to the small group of aforementioned monsters, "Turkey Hollow" boasts pumpkins with faces and dancing trees... and, well, that's about it. The sparsity with which Henson's creations are displayed make the budget limitations that much more glaring. The Creature Shop, whose art was so rich and detailed in films like "Labyrinth", or "The StoryTeller" series, deserved a better comeback than a low-fi Lifetime movie.

The thin, plot-hole-ridden plot barely holds things together. Characters behave robotically and, at times, nonsensically (e.g. the truck chase sequence towards the end, which could have ended much faster - and to better effect - had our protagonists jumped to the side, instead of running down a straight path). Dad keeps calling his daughter Anne "Banana" - which proves as annoying to us as it is to her. (Harrington does get to deliver a surprisingly funny line that involves Liam Neeson.) Steenburgen embraces her zany side, fully committing to her portrait of Aunt Cly. "This room is nothing but bad vibes," she proclaims casually at one point. "There's a fine line between providing... and hiding" - another particularly memorable line the Academy Award-winning actress manages to utter with much conviction. The kids are just okay.

Ludacris' appearances are insane. The rapper-cum-actor hams it up, at one point appearing in ludicrous (yep, had to be done) camouflage, at another sitting behind a set of drums and actually saying "rimshots" with a straight face, and at yet another poised in front of a blatant green screen, reading the film's script, in a little dash of meta. It's goofy and weird… and strangely likable. I never thought I'd say this, but this film could have used more Ludacris.

Kirk R. Thatcher's direction is somewhat perfunctory - one expects more from the helmer of puppet-driven tales like "Muppet Treasure Island". Again, lest we forget, it's Lifetime, and the network's staple balance of cheesy line readings, sappy moments and easily-digestible themes (in this case, overcoming parents' divorce and, you know, Believing) are all on display. The filmmakers even managed to incorporate an environmental, anti-GMO message within the film, which is both laudable and a little jarring, in what should have been a wholly magical journey into "Henson Land". And the green screen is just too much, especially in the finale - c'mon, guys, America is a beautiful country, send your crew to Montana for a day, for Squonk's sakes!

"Jim Henson's Turkey Hollow" barely passes as family entertainment, mostly due to its nostalgic value, Steenburgen's stalwart presence, and appeal to youngsters. Perhaps one day there will be another children's Thanksgiving film to rival "It's the Great Pumpkin, Charlie Brown", but for now, the little ones will have to gobble-gobble this up.

2.5 out of 5 stars

"Love" Makes Gaspar Noé's World Go Round

Synopsis: Murphy is an American living in Paris who enters a highly sexually and emotionally charged relationship with the unstable Electra. Unaware of the effect it will have on their relationship, they invite their pretty neighbor into their bed.

Gaspar Noé is not exactly known for directing conventional, audience-friendly films. Anyone even remotely aware of the provocateur's oeuvre will know better than to expect pleasant, life-affirming experiences. There are no happy endings in Noé's raw, shockingly controversial stories. In fact, "Irreversible" twisted the entire concept of a "happy ending" by beginning with a brutal conclusion to a couple's journey, and then going backwards in time to a cheerful opening scene. He likes to make Statements.

Whether I personally respond to that in-your-face, brutal approach to filmmaking, I still can't say. I do know that "Irreversible"'s utter hopelessness and its horrid images will remain in my head forever (which is quite a feat, considering how desensitized I've become to graphic film violence over the years). Yet I also remember being infuriated at having my emotions manipulated so blatantly. Noé couldn't care less about subtlety (want to see someone's head bashed in with a fire hydrant? you got it!) - and yet I admire his fearlessness, and he certainly gets his points across.

Point being, don't expect "Love" to be reminiscent of Claude Lelouch's understated study of infatuation, the Oscar-winning "A Man and a Woman". One of the film's (admittedly attention-grabbing) posters displays a close-up of a penis, with a female hand cupped over it. It's in 3-D, to further immerse you into an over-two-hour long experience. I'm surprised the theater seats didn't vibrate.

Mr. Noé's latest ego-trip starts with a two-and-a-half-minute static shot of a couple stroking each other to what I assume is a simultaneous orgasm. The story then unfolds through the eyes of Murphy (Karl Glusman), a young American filmmaker living in Paris who wants to shoot a film "depicting sentimental sexuality". He lives, out of obligation, with his child and Omi (Klara Kristin), whom he loathes ("living with this woman is like living with the CIA"). We hear Murphy's thoughts, as he delves into depression upon discovering that his ex-lover, Electra (Aomi Muyock), is missing.

Noé, in typical fashion, throws chronology out the window. The film cuts between Murphy's present despondent state and the backstory of his and Electra's love affair. We are transported back in time to Murphy and Electra inviting Omi over for a threesome. ("I fucking love Europe," Murphy comments, in one of the director's many attempts at "stabs" at the United States' general ignorance.) It's to fulfill their "ultimate fantasy, sex-wise", you see.

And fulfill they do. You want to see some graphic porn? The film is punctuated by frequent sequences of explicit sex, including an orgy, a somewhat-offensive part involving a transgender character, and The Money Shot: a penis ejaculating, straight into the audience, in glorious 3-D.

Some of it is titillating; most makes one wonder why a visual artist like Noé shot it so… banally. That's not to say his cinematographer, Benoît Debie, did a bad job - au contraire, his stunning shot compositions are one of the film's saving graces. It's that Noé, for the most part, makes sex seem mundane, instead of passionate, sweaty, both awkward and magical - not something I expected from the guy who ventured into a vagina in "Enter the Void".

Murphy and Carmen's relationship is then explored from its origins, the story predominantly confined to their apartments and a few clubs, where they screw, do drugs, have long pseudo-existential conversations, and experiment with infidelity. There is one all-too-brief ayahuasca sequence (during which I prepped up, ready for the director to go nuts) - but alas, the visual flairs are over within minutes, and then it's back to close-ups of genitals and expressionless faces.

Which leads me to the acting. It would be generous to call the trio's performances "adequate". They are natural during the graphic sex scenes, which is commendable - and also about the only positive thing one could say about their work in "Love". I hesitate to put all the blame on them, since all they're essentially asked to do is, pardon my French, fuck, in-between delivering lines such as: "Open the door, you selfish cunt!"; "I'm just a dick. A dick has no brain."; "Hey, what's the meaning of life?"; "Life is what you make of it. Like a dream". The script and the acting really bring Gaspar's already-problematic film down, hard.

The stylistic flourishes barely save the film: frequent black flashes, massive screen credits, a haunting soundtrack, Debie's mastery with the camera… That said, "Love"'s pretentiousness becomes that much more apparent against the inept line readings. At one point, Murphy and Electra even contemplate calling their baby Gaspar, and Electra's ex-boyfriend's name is Noé - if that's not the epitome of self-admiration - or, more fittingly, mental masturbation - I don't know what is.

Unless, of course, Gaspar is messing with us. It's difficult to figure out if he's making one of his Statements, or whether the film's title is satirical, or if Noé's just playing an elaborate prank on his audience, a-la Michael Haneke with "Funny

Games". The film really doesn't amount to much more than a semi-soulful, beautifully-shot-and-scored wet dream.

For a great psycho-sexual study, check out Bernardo Bertolucci's "The Dreamers". This film also has an American coming to France, to consequently engage in a tumultuous sexual exploration - but Bertolucci's film is savvily juxtaposed against the revolution of the 1960s; it's a nostalgic look at a rebellious, adventurous (both sexually and politically) youth; it has more of a purpose, anchored by a trio of great performances. Gaspar Noé's film is an act of feckless provocation, a feeble attempt to trace the stages of love through the singular prism of sex. File it in the "Amateur" category.

2.5 out of 5 stars

"Max Rose" Marks Jerry Lewis's Return to the Big Screen - A Shining Beacon in a Dreary Film

Synopsis: A jazz pianist makes a discovery days before the death of his wife that causes him to believe his sixty-five year marriage was a lie. He embarks on an exploration of his own past that brings him face to face with a menagerie of characters from a bygone era.

There is no doubting Jerry Lewis's status as an American entertainment legend. An actor, filmmaker and comedian, he's arguably most famous for slapstick fare like "The Bellboy" and the original "The Nutty Professor" (both of which he also wrote and directed), as well as his team-up with Dean Martin on over a dozen films in the 1950s. Lewis gave his last truly memorable on-screen performance in Martin Scorsese's 1983 classic "The King of Comedy". Now, in Daniel Noah's "Max Rose", the 90-year-old Jerry Lewis makes a comeback of sorts, headlining his first film in over 20 years (I'm referring to Peter Chelsom's 1995 critical bomb / box-office disaster "Funny Bones"). Unfortunately, despite good intentions, the film gets bogged down by a somnambulant pace, manipulative moments and a distinct lack of originality.

Max (Lewis) is an aging actor from Hollywood's Golden Age, whose wife Eva (Claire Bloom) just passed away. His granddaughter Annie (Kerry Bishé, in a delicate performance) takes care of the old man; she tries to make him laugh at lame jokes, in an attempt to rekindle the spark in his eye. Max prefers to spend time alone, reading a Roosevelt biography, listening to records and going over his life's memorabilia. His son Chris (a scaled-back Kevin Pollack) comes to visit with comedy DVDs, but Max kicks him out. "I'm 87 years old and I lost my Eva," Max says at her funeral, "but the truth is, I lost her a long time ago." He concludes by stating that it wasn't Eva's fault, for she thought she married a better man, and he's "a failure."

Max is visited frequently by Eva's apparitions. "I feel better calling your name," he says into the void in a touching scene, before Annie brings him back to bed. Haunted by his wife's 65-year infidelity, Max "has to know 'why'". He ends up in an elderly home, run by Ms. Flowers (a welcome-albeit-underused turn from the always-reliable Illeana Douglas). "I'm here to try to help you find a little bit of happiness," she says. He reluctantly socializes with the other inhabitants and participates in the home's activities. Family issues intertwine with Max digging up the past, until it all culminates with a confrontation between Max and Eva's lover, Ben Tracey (a sardonic Dean Stockwell), the latter stating bitterly, "You don't know how disappointed I am. I was hoping you would go first."

If all that doesn't sound like a roller coaster ride of storytelling efficiency, it's because it's not. Let's start with the good news. Jerry Lewis is magnificent, the decades of experience evident in his sad eyes; in the most desolate performance of his career, he's an embodiment of past glories, of regret and memories and nostalgia, of wisdom accumulated through a lifetime of remarkable achievements. Though he technically plays a character called Max Rose, we are really watching Jerry Lewis, in a retrospective showcase, the line between his on-screen persona and real-life - sarcastic, gentle and silly - man increasingly blurry.

The issues lie in the fact that the film doesn't use that blurriness to its advantage. At times it feels like it tries, in the parallels between Max's past and his real-life counterpart's. But "Max Rose" could have been a fascinating study structured around that man, a film that on the surface was about aging and reconciliation, but if one were to dig deeper, would reveal itself to be an in-depth study of its protagonist, a reflection of a real-life legend. Though at times tender, eloquent and clearly well-meaning, the movie falters, pandering to its audiences with manipulative tactics - such as an oppressive soundtrack, or scenes like the one where Annie makes her grandpa laugh with a clown nose and 5th-grade jokes - instead of scaling back and letting the actor's eyes do the speaking.

The film has trouble establishing a mood - unless you count its suffocatingly dismal tone as one. The film drags; there's little momentum or novelty to the proceedings. The actors all do well, but their characters aren't fleshed out enough for us to truly emphasize. There's a scene in the middle where Chris sells Max's home and then tries to get his father to say that he loves him that feels particularly grating and incoherently structured. On top of that, there are some clumsy editing and shot composition choices - the film's production values leave much to be desired. Its morose ending is morally questionable.

The film does catch some nuances of what it must be like to go through twilight years - a demographic rarely addressed - especially in scenes where Max is having trouble with an electric can opener, or his inability to connect with his own family after opening up to an audience full of strangers. The highlight comes when Max hangs out with his friends, just shooting the shit, discussing death and reminiscing about the past. The film could've used more of that scene's jazzy vibe, levity, improvisational feel and honesty.

Michael Haneke's "Amour" or Paolo Sorrentino's "Youth" are two recent meditations on aging that happen to be more assured, subtle and generally mesmerizing than "Max Rose", which is about a man trying to come to terms with his past before he passes away. It could have been so much more. As a showcase of a legendary American stalwart, I guess you could also do worse. And yet "Max Rose" is too claustrophobic and been-there-done-that to truly recommend. "Did you hear about the restaurant on the moon?" Max asks Annie at one point, in another wistful nod to his real-life counterpart. "They serve good food, but no atmosphere." The joke can be applied to this film: there's some good food, but no atmosphere.

2.5 out of 5 stars

"Northmen: A Viking Saga" Falls Short of Reaching Valhalla

Synopsis: *A storm finds a band of Vikings stranded behind enemy lines on the coast of Alba. Their journey becomes a race for their lives, when the King of Alba sends his most feared mercenaries after them.*

Vikings have had a vast and uneven representation in cinema, from Roy William Neill's 1928 Technicolor phenomenon "The Viking" to John McTiernan's flawed-but-underrated 1999 box-office disaster "The 13th Warrior". The closest the medium has come to accurately capturing the Viking Age is perhaps History Channel's "The Vikings", now in its third season. The show's length gives characters ample opportunity to develop, and its sets and accents have been meticulously researched.

Sadly, "Northmen: A Viking Saga" never approaches that level of veracity or complexity. It surely gets points for ambition. A Swiss/German/South African co-production, filmed in the beautiful mountainous and ocean-side terrains of South Africa, it's clear the filmmakers aimed for an epic scope and a mythical, resonant story. The result is a derivative - but beautifully-shot - underdog adventure about a small group of Vikings, with its unfortunate dearth of originality outweighing its pretty pictures. Perhaps the fault lies with the Swiss director, a relative dilettante (Claudio Fäh's resume is dubious at best, including the 2006 "masterpiece" "Hollow Man II", and the more recent, edge-of-your-seat, cerebral Billy Zane thriller "Sniper: Reloaded").

"Northmen" starts off on a high note, depicting a breathtaking, three-minute sequence of a shipwreck on the Scottish Isles, our Viking protagonists getting submerged underwater, their symbolic necklaces and swords hitting the tremulous ocean's sandy floor. Apparently, that's when the majority of the film's budget ran out, for the characters spend the rest of the film's running length, *ahem*, running away from evil Scottish mercenaries, led by the determined and violent Hjorn (Ed Skrein).

Our heroes do get help from the Scottish King's daughter, Inghean (Charlie Murphy), who happens to possess mystical abilities, and "sees what the land reveals" when she touches the ground. They capture her as ransom for the King, but, afraid to seem cowardly in front of his potential enemies, he orders to kill her instead (yes, all perplexing plot points - how insensitive is this freakin' king? - but just go with it). While there are some sequences that engage mildly, all this running and following and setting traps and then running again becomes repetitive. Imagine a medieval "The Fugitive", written by a 13-year-old, and you'll get a sense of what "Northmen" is like.

A few of the film's improbabilities have to be pointed out: 1) How in the world do the mercenaries keep catching up with the clearly faster and more savvy Vikings? Do they have medieval tracking devices? 2) When a man falls off a vertical cliff, there is no way another man, who is also clinging to that cliff with the tips of his fingers, can catch his friend mid-air and hold on to him long enough to exchange meaningful glances, and subsequently *save him*. Even if this man possessed *ten times* the power of Hercules, this would not be feasible. 3) At one point, a monk leads our protagonists out of a seemingly impossible situation through a tunnel, at the last minute. Why he waited this long will forever remain a mystery. 4) Late in the film, the characters stumble upon a giant waterfall. Watch carefully how long it takes the characters to climb it, in relation to each other - it makes zero sense. 5) The worst thing to do when hiding out and setting traps is to scream into the forest, alerting the mercenaries to your presence. The Vikings in this film aren't aware of this basic fact. 6) In the climactic showdown - spoiler alert! - the villain jumps out of a muddy quicksand sinkhole, something that had been established as clearly impossible, and therefore executed purely for shock effect. 7) Okay, last one: all the Vikings survive a 200-foot fall into the ocean, unscathed. Just sayin'.

The dialogue is so poorly written, one wonders if Bastian Zach and Matthias Bauer used Google Translate for some of the passages. When prompted to climb a cliff, one Viking states resolutely: "I am a warrior. Not a climber." In another instance, a character proclaims ferociously: "There will be no bounty in hell."

The acting is on-and-off, at best. Ed Skrein, star of the upcoming 398th Marvel film "Deadpool", as well as the "reboot-that-no-one-asked-for" "The Transporter Reloaded", scowls away as Hjorn, attributing his character with next-to-no-depth, except unsubstantiated savagery. Ryan Kwanten (of "True Blood" fame) plays the sullen monk, who, for no apparent reason, decides to endanger his life and help the gang of Vikings, and, oh, happens to boast some *serious* Neo-level skills with his stick. Tom Hopper gives an adequately heroic - and stoic - performance as the gang's leader, Asbjorn, although those golden locks and blue eyes and bulging muscles and uber-serious one-liners make him resemble Thor's younger, wimpier brother. Leo Gregory plays Jorund, the staple nasty rapist member of the gang, who unleashes his little phallic swords at every urge to fornicate and/or murder but is ultimately presented as a character with whom we should sympathize. Everyone roars viciously during the modestly-scaled battles scenes, which are choppily edited and hard to follow.

This film could have been so much better. The dialogue scenes could have spawned deliberations over spirituality (something the film touches upon, briefly, and with utmost vulgarity); their journey could have functioned as a metaphor for the futility of running from imminent death, and/or evoked existential rumination (like Nicolas Winding Refn did so powerfully in "Valhalla Rising"). As it stands, the humorless "Northmen: A Viking Saga" doesn't bring anything new to the "Viking cinematic canon", but should at least appease (and/or infuriate, depending on their predilection for accuracy) Norsemen aficionados and those looking for a couple of hours to waste. It's certainly better than "Vikingdom".

2.5 out of 5 stars

Death Metal in Asgard: Amon Amarth's Frontman Johan Hegg Talks Vikings, Film Acting and Staying Fit

Swedish Death-Metal band Amon Amarth, whose songs primarily deal with the Viking era, has enjoyed a rapidly-growing international recognition since its inception in the early 1990s. Its lead singer, Johan Hegg, recently tried his hand at film acting, in Claudio Fäh's epic international production, "Northmen: A Viking Saga". At home in his native Sweden, Johan Hegg discusses the intricacies of the filmmaking process with Irish Film Critic's Alex Saveliev.

AS: You are the frontman of the uber-popular Swedish death-metal band, Amon Amarth, whose lyrics deal mostly with Norse mythology and the Viking Age. Why the fascination with Vikings, and is that why you were approached for the role of Valli?

JH: Yes, that's why I was approached for the role of Valli, it's as simple as that. One of the writers is a fan, so when they were casting the film, he mentioned my name. My interest in Norse mythology started when I was about 9 or 10 years old, and it just grew gradually. It's really a fascinating history, their sagas are simply amazing. I have a deep love of the subject.

AS: Did you contribute extensive Viking knowledge? Did the filmmakers ask you for tips/advice?

JH: Actually, the actors and the crew were very well-read on the characters from that time. They put in a lot of work to portray the characters the right way. So I didn't really have to do that much; from time to time they would ask me, "Is that something a Viking would say?", and I would go, "Yeah, sure!" (laughs). I wasn't there the whole time, so they were pretty much on their own.

AS: The film was shot primarily in South Africa over 8 weeks. How long were you on the set?

JH: I think it was about 16 days. I came in for a 12-day principal shoot, and then returned for another 4 days.

AS: Can you describe your impressions of the location; did it inspire you to get into your character more? Would you say it evoked a mythical atmosphere that was easier to delve into?

JH: I think the South African locations were absolutely fantastic. I definitely felt that it was easier for me to get into character, it was beautiful.

AS: Did you feel comfortable in front of the camera?

JH: (Laughs) It felt good. I had a lot of help preparing from the other actors, especially from Darrell D'Silva and Charlie Murphy [who play the characters of Gunnar and Inghean in the film, respectively]. They were tremendously supportive. Otherwise, it wasn't the first time I was in front of the camera. I've done several music videos, so I kind of knew the drill, but moviemaking is obviously on a much-bigger scale. On a video shoot, I don't really have to do any dialogue (laughs).

AS: Can you please talk a little about your experience working with the director, Claudio Fäh? Did you get along on set? Did he have a distinct vision and give clear, intuitive direction?

JH: I love Claudio, he's such a great guy. He knows what he wants, and he knows how to get it. He's a friendly guy, but also very straightforward. He's great to work with, I admire him a lot. From my perspective, he's a director any actor would like to work with. I don't have that much experience, but I would definitely work with him again.

AS: What was the biggest challenge you faced during the shoot?

JH: For me, it was the stunts. When I went down there, I was not prepared at how much physical work it would be… and I was *not* in great shape! I was also struggling with my asthma; this kind of stuff made it difficult.

AS: Are you now considering an acting career, or are you going to stay focused on your band - or juggle both?

JH: Well, the band is my priority, obviously. But if I get the chance to do more movies, I will gladly take it. It was a lot of fun and a great experience.

AS: When is Amon Amarth touring next?

JH: At the moment, we are writing a new album. We will record it this fall, hopefully the album will be out early next year. And after that we'll be touring in late-spring, early-summer, I guess.

AS: Any plans on coming to the States?

JH: Yes, we will, definitely! We are planning on doing an extensive North American tour, hopefully very soon after the album's release, but it all depends on how it all falls together, when the album comes out, that kind of stuff.

AS: Any words of advice for other musicians-turned-actors out there?

JH: You should definitely come prepared, read a few scripts, get an idea of what to expect. And, if you're going to be in an action movie, make sure you're in pretty good shape!

"Ordinary World": Green Day Frontman Billie Joe Armstrong Has a Blue Day

Synopsis: *An aging punk rocker copes with life after rock.*

Lee Kirk presumably met his wife, actress Jenna Fischer, on the set of NBC's acclaimed remake of the British sitcom "The Office". Kirk briefly appeared as a character called Clark (and even directed an episode of the show). He followed up with a feature-length directorial debut, the painfully contrived but earnest melodrama "The Giant Mechanical Man", which Fischer starred in and produced. The actress is nowhere to be found in Kirk's follow-up, the teeny-weeny more assured dramedy "Ordinary World". Seems like the director left his sitcom roots behind and dove deep into granola indie filmmaking, Brian Baumgartner's brief appearance serving as the only reminder of his television past.

In a case of "art imitating life", Bille Joe Armstrong plays an ex-rocker called Perry, his band resembling a somehow even more lo-fi Green Day. The film starts with black-and-white footage of the band performing in 1995, at the peak of their career. Cut to 20 years later: Perry is now a family man, working at Barry's Hardware with his brother Jake (Chris Messina), forgetting to take out garbage cans, begging for a quickie from his wife Karen (Selma Blair), who (allegedly) forgot his 40th birthday… His daughter interrupts his jam-out trips down memory lane and scrutinizes him about his lack of a job; his acquaintances call him a "pussy". "My night was awesome," Perry tells a friend. "I watched 'House Hunters' and went to bed." "House Hunters" comes up again later, as the ultimate embodiment of rock bottom. So yeah, life sucks for poor Perry.

Until, that is, Jake lends him a grand, and Perry wisely decides to spend it on renting the Presidential Suite at The Drake Hotel. In a desperate attempt to reconnect with his rebellious youth, he tries to put together a party, but alas, only his borderline-psychotic friend Gary (Fred Armisen) shows up with a friend and a stripper. Before things get rowdy, Perry's domestic life comes barging in: locked-out in-laws, woodwork, getting bought out of the family business… In the meantime, Gary tears the hotel suite up, inviting a dozen people, ordering hundreds of dollars worth of room service and kicking Perry out of his own band. I'll let you figure out how the rest turns out.

The novelty of seeing freakin' punk-rocker Billie Joe Armstrong play an everyman wears off, then becomes a humbling experience - watching the performer put himself out like that - and eventually turns aggravating, as the guy is clearly not up to the task. That's not to say he doesn't have his moments - I'll even go so far as to say that, with a little honing, he could become a charismatic screen presence - but as it stands, the musician just can't hold the weight of an entire film on his (surprisingly frail!) shoulders. The rest of the cast do decent albeit unmemorable jobs, sort of blending in with the environment, the one standout being the always-reliable Fred Armisen. When his insane Gary steps into that hotel room, the film comes alive.

"Ordinary World" touches upon some interesting ideas about reaching the zenith of one's life and then having the ability to accept normality and enjoy each moment. There are a few poignant exchanges. However, every time Kirk seems to find nuance, he side-steps it, teasing us with real depth but merely skimming the surface, as if afraid to drown. The film never seems to find its rhythm, vacillating between comedy and drama and only half-succeeding at both. It's also filled with age-old tropes, such as a lover resurfacing from the past (Judy Greer, in a thankless role), the father barely making it to his daughter's talent show, a heartwarming song towards the end that makes it all okay, a sappy reconciliation - and so on and so forth.

Die-hard Green Day fans are not likely to embrace the schmaltz, nor will cinefiles find much to appreciate. There are some moderately funny bits about coasters, and Armisen seems to improvise the best lines - but, as scripted, "you look like a goblin" just doesn't do the trick. Perhaps embracing your TV roots is not such a bad thing. Kirk's writing lacks zingers, memorable one-liners that made "The Office" such a hit; you'd think he'd learn a thing or two. He and Jenna should binge-watch season three.

2.5 out of 5 stars

"Pirates of the Caribbean: Dead Men Tell No Tales" is Dead in the Water

Synopsis: *Captain Jack Sparrow searches for the trident of Poseidon.*

It all started so splendidly. Gore Verbinski's original "Pirates of the Caribbean: The Curse of the Black Pearl" was an unexpected delight back in 2003, both to worldwide audiences and studio execs. It made over $650 million on a $140 million budget, putting behind bitter memories of pirate flops like Renny Harlin's "Cutthroat Island". "Curse" delivered all the requisite swashbuckling adventures, but its real appeal lay in Johnny Depp's madcap, Keith-Richards-like pirate Jack Sparrow. Our heavily-mascara-d anti-hero with an ambiguous sexuality, a penchant for booze and the uncanny ability to continuously get away from certain death, thanks to his skills but mostly luck (read: ex-machina), said or did something surprising at every turn. Depp's performance elevated a standard-albeit-entertaining yarn to "almost-classic" status. It certainly overshadowed the tepid romance between Orlando Bloom's dull Will Turner and Keira Knightley's one-note Elizabeth Swan.

But then came the sequels. "Dead Man's Chest"'s plot was "Godzilla-in-a-wet-suit" bloated, while "At World's End"'s almost-three-hour length induced seasickness. That didn't seem to bother audiences, as budgets grew proportionally to box-office - even when Verbinski stepped off, focusing on cartoons ("Rango") and cowboys ("The Lone Ranger"), and Rob Marshall, of "Chicago" fame, came on board. His slightly stripped-back "On Stranger Tides" was lukewarm, but big $$$ kept comin' in.

Now, 14 years after Jack Sparrow first hiccuped drunkenly on silver screens, part five sails in, titled "Dead Men Tell No Tales" - and the intention's clear: to bring back the spontaneity/magic of the original and keep the execs happy. With all the quality big-budget entertainment in theaters right now ("Guardians of the Galaxy, Vol. 2", "Alien: Covenant"), I'll be surprised (if not necessarily shocked) if the film delivers on the latter (dammit, folks seem to dig them ghostly bootleggers!). As for the former, Norwegian directorial duo **Joachim Rønning and Espen Sandberg, known for their Oscar-nominated sea fare adventure "Kon-Tiki"**, comes close but ultimately fails at rekindling the spark of Verbinski's seminal flick.

They do have Javier Bardem's evil Captain Salazar on their side. His heavily-CGI-d turn as the embittered pirate-hater, hell-bent on exacting revenge on Jack Sparrow after the young lad sunk his ship and turned him into a ghost ages ago, almost saves the film. Like its opening sequences - one involving a boy improbably surviving a deep-water dive, the other following Sparrow's misguided robbery - the film is sorta entertaining but preposterous and unoriginal, trying oh-so-hard to replicate instead of innovating. Moments of true originality come rarely and hence stand out.

The plot in a nutshell: Abandoned after the aforementioned robbery by his crew, Sparrow gets joined by Will Turner's son Henry (an instantly-forgettable Brenton Thwaites) and the determined Carina (Kaya Scodelario) on a quest to find Poseidon's Trident. With Captain Barbossa (a returning, tired-looking Geoffrey Rush) helping Salazar hunt down Sparrow, as well as MacGuffins, such as a magical compass and a book with a glowing ruby on it, Sparrow runs into all the expected obstacles, resulting in (spoiler alert!) a massive ship battle and a tidy resolution, doors left wide open for another billion-dollar sequel.

I may make it seem dire, but I'm just tired of Hollywood milking cash cows. It's not all bad. Scodelario, replacing Knightley, brings a dash of "feminine power" to her role, but it gets eclipsed by all the cleavage-gazing and sexual innuendo. There are some genuinely chuckle-inducing scenes, like when Sparrow, strapped to a sliding guillotine, spins in place over and over. Salazar's gawping, snarling ship is an inspired creation. There are zombie sharks, if that's your thing. Depp's nonchalant way of reacting to certain death, as if he knows he will surely avoid it, is charming - though, almost 15 hours of Sparrow's shtick does get a tad tiring. The intention to revisit the ad-libbing feel of the original is palpable. Oh, and we do get to see a "digi-young" Depp, which is always fun.

That said, let's face it, the plot is rubbish. There is a surprisingly high count of quite gruesome, undeserved deaths-by-sword. Secondary characters are reduced to either stereotypes or forgettable plot devices. The script could have used another polish or two: "The memory of my father will not be befouled by the tongue of a pirate!" - come on, Jeff Nathanson, you wrote "Catch Me If You Can" (okay, you also wrote "Speed 2: Cruise Control"). The fifth, painfully unnecessary, installment of Disney's "based-on-a-theme-park-ride" yarn proves that you can't step in the same ocean twice... or in this case, five times.

2.5 out of 5 stars

Ambitious Ballet Drama "Polina" Fails to Keep You on Your Toes

Synopsis: *A young girl studies classical ballet. As a young woman she turns to modern dance and choreography.*

What haunts Polina, the titular character in Valérie Müller's behind-the-scenes look at ballet / character study? The film never really answers that question. It's on the knife's edge of wisdom, but never quite reaches true depth.

Sure, there's Polina's shady father, making deals with some hoodlums and embarking on an unexplained trip to Afghanistan. And yes, our hero comes from an impoverished background, living in Moscow's "factory ghetto". But really, her life isn't so bad.

Her family sits around the table, singing songs. Despite not being able to afford ballet classes, she inexplicably still enrolls, for years. Somewhat dispassionately determined, taunted by her strict teacher (the wonderful Aleksey Guskov), Polina boldly turns down a great opportunity at Moscow's world-famous Bolshoi Theater. French boyfriend in tow, she embarks on a trip to Southern France, leaving her grief-stricken mother behind.

After encountering enigmatic ballet instructor Liria Elsaj (the wonderful Juliette Binoche), Polina runs off from another incredible opportunity to a small town in Belgium. Homeless at first (she sleeps at a laundromat), she then becomes a bartender and soon finds her true self - I guess - in modern dance.

The fragmented, episodic structure lets the film down, hopping between crucial scenes of Polina's development. What drove her to so abruptly leave Bolshoi theater behind, or Liria? I get that she's on a quest to "find herself", but that's me tacking on that theme forcefully - her character's vague motivations become irritating. The protagonist is kept at a stretched leg's length; the film runs itself into a corner in its tedious second half.

Anastasia Shevtsova's "scaled-back to vacuum" performance doesn't really help matters: while certainly a pro when it comes to dancing, the real-life ballerina happens to be a blank slate when it comes to acting. A good actor makes a hard-to-read character compelling (for two random examples, see Forest Whitaker in "Ghost Dog: The Way of the Samurai" and Garance Marillier in the recent "Raw"). Deeply affected by her teacher's insistence on feeling emotions, her character remains emotionless throughout the film.

"Polina" is your typical underdog story of a girl fighting against impossible odds to find herself, disguised as a somber, naturalistic Indie Drama. The Dardenne brothers this ain't, though Valérie Müller adopts a similar approach: a relentless focus on its main, lower-middle-class protagonist, a slow build-up to a soul-cleansing conclusion… and next-to-no humor. The Belgian brothers make it work. Müller valiantly tries, but doesn't quite get there, her film too dour to please "Step Up" fans and too shallow to satisfy connoisseurs of, say, Robert Altman ("The Company") or Darren Aronofsky ("Black Swan").

"Polina" briefly kicks into high gear when stalwart Binoche steps into the picture, her character's fusions of techno and contemporary dance propelling the narrative for a while. "It's too pretty," Liria yells at Polina, "I'm looking for something real." She may as well be talking about Müller's movie.

I'm being extra harsh on "Polina", because when it gets things rights, it's aces. It contains gorgeous music and astounding ballet sequences (props to Angelin Preijocaj, who co-directed the film with Valérie Müller). It especially comes alive when Polina dances in grimy surroundings to drone-like dance beats. Case in point: one of the film's opening scenes, where a young Polina (Veronica Zhovnytska) performs joyous pirouettes against the gloomy backdrop of filthy snow and steaming factories.

Which makes it all the more disappointing that I walked out of the theater feeling "meh". What haunts Polina? The lack of script rewrites, apparently.

2.5 out of 5 stars

"Railroad Tigers" Introduces Us to Jackie Chan's Not-So-Magnificent Seven

Synopsis: *A railroad worker in China in 1941 leads a team of freedom fighters against the Japanese in order to get food for the poor.*

My wife and I recently binge-watched the entire "Rush Hour" trilogy (because we have nothing better to do with our lives, apparently), and it's struck me how well the first one holds up, and how badly its two sequels aged, their blatant racism/misogyny/homophobia - mostly coming from the Ugly American embodiment, Mr. Chris Tucker - leaving a nasty taste in your mouth that overwhelms the pleasure of watching Jackie Chan do his thing. That said, his bits were by far the highlights of the films.

Now, 10 years after the third part of Brett Ratner's monumental contribution to the echelons of action cinema, Jackie Chan is still doing his thing - at 63, mind you! - in the latest $50 million extravaganza from China (which the star also produced). He hops on top of moving trains, glides down ropes, runs up brick walls and drop-kicks enemies - though not quite as, um, boisterously as he used to, with frequent questionable cuts that suggest the use of stunt doubles. The aging actor's golden years have passed, he's going through his Steven Seagal stage, and that's totally understandable - not so forgivable are the film's jarring pacing and a lack of cohesiveness. Like the its eminent lead actor, "Railroad Tigers" means well and is frequently entertaining, but its joints are creaky and it frequently falls flat on its ass.

The film opens in the modern day. When a child wanders off during a poorly-supervised British school excursion at a railroad museum, he comes upon a crude chalk drawing of a "flying tiger" on one of the trains. This segues to an eyeball-scorching title credit sequence - and then we are transported back to mid-20th-Century China. Has the kid opened a time portal in the back of that train? The introduction seems to serve no purpose - but we shall see.

One of the many animated, freeze-frame, graphic-novel-style title credits introduce us to Da Hai (Zitao Huang), an amateur tailor. He encounters Chinese freedom fighter Ma Yuan (Jackie Chan) - the "Head Porter", whose "catchphrase" is "Shut Up" (some characters have catchphrases like "What Now?"… don't ask, I have no idea) - on top of a speeding locomotive. Ma Yuan's gang knock out and rob the train's Japanese crew. Da Hai consequently joins the Robin Hoods of 1940s China.

To list off the rest of the plot would take many paragraphs, as it zig-zags along with relentless abandon, with a million characters and twice as many jump-cuts. In a nutshell: Ma Yuan sets out to avenge his mother's death and face off against the captain of the Japanese military police, by blowing up a crucial railroad bridge and cutting off enemy supplies. Obstacles arise - imprisonment, a failed attempt to steal explosives - all leading to a final, extended stand-off on top of the aforementioned bridge.

Ding Sheng's sixth directorial feature contains some nifty sequences. There are two standouts. The first comes during the gang's robbery of a warehouse and consequent escape on a train from a small army of Japanese soldiers, fighting them off with bags of flour. The second highlight arrives during the way over-extended finale - a tank battle on top of a train that has to be seen to be believed. The rest of the action is competently staged if unremarkable. I liked the scene where a member of the gang hides underneath a fire-pit, coals lighting him aflame. A particularly clever descent into a moving train from a bridge also stood out. Ma Yuan gang's camaraderie is apparent and there is an infectious spirit to the proceedings, like everyone involved had a blast doing this.

That said, the humor is wildly uneven, as is the editing and pacing (the filmmakers didn't seem to know how to go from one scene to the next, resorting to frequent fade-outs and chapter titles). The film reduces the turmoils of the Chinese-Japanese conflict to a slapstick comedy, most of it derived from the Looney Tunes fight scenes and silly verbal exchanges. Sheng's feature is overstuffed with so many characters, including an unfunny magician with a tragic fate, that the plot seems more needlessly convoluted that it actually is. Despite its overstuffed nature, most of the story beats here will be predictable even to the non-jaded action fans. Ma Yuan's characters aren't really fleshed out beyond comic stereotypes - but the Japanese fare way worse, reduced to cardboard villains who suffer grisly deaths for comedic effect. Stretched out over two hours, the train-hopping action becomes repetitive. Some of the special effects are questionable, and that's putting it kindly.

As for the weird introduction with the kid, it really was just that - a way to start and end the film, as if the writers just tacked it on for no apparent reason. It really isn't a storytelling technique - the child's not reading the unfolding events in a book, nor is he being told this story by the wise old spirit of Ma Yuan - it's just… there. Despite its frequent allusions to classic Westerns of yore, "High Noon", this ain't. It's not even "Rush Hour", where your jaw would intermittently drop at Chan's hijinks. If you're looking for prime Jackie Chan, watch the "Police Story" trilogy. As for "Railroad Tigers", the locomotive doesn't quite derail - but it does belong in a museum.

2.5 out of 5 stars

"Red Trees" is Better on Page than on Celluloid

Synopsis: Award-winning filmmaker Marina Willer ("Cartas da Mãe") creates an impressionistic visual essay as she traces her father's family journey, from war-torn Eastern Europe to the color and light of South America, as one of only twelve Jewish families to survive the Nazi occupation of Prague during World War II.

Here's an eloquent documentary about the Holocaust that has little reason for existence, beyond its maker's - Marina Willer's - personal desire to investigate her father Alfred's horrific plight during the worn-torn Czechoslovakia. Admittedly, his memoirs could have made for a thrilling, emotional story, but "Red Trees" rarely says anything new about that tragic period of our history and, after over 300 films made on the subject matter, its small scope, frequent reliance on "screensaver" footage and narration from the recently-deceased actor Tim Pigott-Smith may make it difficult for the doc to find a wide audience.

But perhaps that's beyond the point. Perhaps Ms. Willer, "humbled by what [her family] had to go through to stay alive, just to keep going, day after day", made the documentary for no one else but herself, as a sort of exorcism. It fails to function as an "impressionistic" piece, nor does it have enough momentum to truly shock or entertain, but it's certainly earnest and holds attention (barely) due to the narrated prose, courtesy of Alfred himself. "I've seen people murdered on the streets, on both sides," he says. "You learn not to look, but you never forget." Passages like this make one wonder if they'd be better off reading Alfred's fascinating biography rather than watching Marina's "best of" compilation.

Like her father, Marina does have a way with words. She describes the pre-war Prague as "a beautiful young model of democracy for the whole of Europe, borne out of the First World War and about to be strangled by the Second." The doc then follows the Willer family's plight, from living in a small apartment in Prague - where their passports were confiscated, eliminating their chances of immigrating - to their eventual escape to Brazil, "a nation of color [where] the leaves are always green"; of "saudade", a feeling of melancholia and longing. Having practiced carpentry, entranced by Prague's historical architecture, Alfred's career path was already determined. By the end we get to see Alfred's children and grandchildren, each of whom has been influenced by their father's story; Maria became a designer, her brother an architect.

Willer's film is not without its merits. It deals with the relevant issue of what it means to be a migrant. It's soaked in bitter nostalgia, examining how time corrodes, both metaphorically and literally, as shown in the scenes where the Willers revisit the Czech Republic and the once-flourishing factories, now rusting and disheveled. One factory cloakroom, filled with lifeless, hanging uniforms is particularly striking. Pigott-Smith conveys the intensity of Alfred's writing, especially in the scenes of the bombs dropping on Prague, missing a 15-year-old Alfred by an inch.

Yet "Red Trees" can't escape the tropes of a typical autobiographical doc: swirling piano music, voice-over driving the narrative, B-roll footage of fields, buildings, factories, soap bubbles, telephone wires, ocean waves and grey skies. Dull, self-indulgent passages, such as Alfred bonding with his grandchildren or Maria wondering, "what would the world be like?", are borderline groan-inducing. Sophisticated but unoriginal, "Red Trees" is yet another substandard reminder of both the evil humans are capable of, as well as the perseverance it takes to overcome such evil. Saudade, indeed.

2.5 out of 5 stars

"That Sugar Film" Fails to Incite a Rush

Synopsis: *Damon Gameau embarks on an experiment to document the effects of a high sugar diet on a human body.*

Damon Gameau's study on the effects of sugar on a healthy human body starts with a montage of colorful confectionery products, scored to Depeche Mode's "I Just Can't Get Enough". This is both an effective and obvious way of establishing the somewhat-playful, (very mildly) satirical tone the flawed but well-meaning "That Sugar Film" adopts, to approach the serious issue of sugar-caused obesity in contemporary societies.

Gameau, who wrote, directed, produced and picked himself as the subject of the documentary, takes viewers on a journey, from his home in Australia to the United States and back, wherein he starts at an above-average health and then literally sweetens his way into a near-psychotic frenzy, by eating an average of 40 teaspoons of sugar a day. Supervised by doctors and nutritionists, this rapid switch from a no-sugar regiment to a high-sugar diet results in mood swings, visceral fat around his waist, clearly visible after just 12 days; after 28 days, his liver "turns to fat". His pregnant partner Zoe comments he's very easily distracted - but his preoccupied state of mind could also be - at least partially - justified by the making of this elaborate documentary… while Zoe is pregnant, mind you. (Great timing to purposefully screw up your health, Damon! Tsk-tsk.) At the end, it's not about the actual calories - though he gained weight and had a variety of hazardous effects on his body, Gameau's calorie intake hasn't changed from before he embarked on this "adventure" - it's about the source of those calories.

Celebrities like Hugh Jackman and Stephen Fry show up briefly in fragmentary, historical - and irritatingly pedagogical - interludes. Actor Brenton Thwaites appears for all of 30 seconds, just so the host can go inside his toned body in a badly-animated sequence, riding glucose cells. I felt like I was back in my high school biology class, watching an educational video. The addition of celebrities is a gimmick that adds no value, except potentially drawing in a wider audience.

While in the United States, which we all know is the land of obesity, Gameau marvels at Jamba Juice's sugar content for a good several minutes. He also encounters country bumpkin Larry, who is addicted to Mountain Dew, and proceeds to get dentures, shown in graphic, painful detail - and then resolutely keeps drinking Mountain Dew, the stubborn loon. Our host's incisive US adventure concludes with a half-baked inquiry into the machinations that go on behind the curtains of sugar industries, who (gasp!) fund research studies on sugar's health effects. My mind was blown at the possibility of such corruption in a country known for its straightforwardness.

The highlight of "That Sugar Film" comes when Gameau ventures into the small aborigine town of Amata and witnesses a high consumption of sugar in a culture that's historically been known for barely having any sugar in their diet. Introduction of Coca-Cola changed that forever: obesity prevailed, along with a slew of long-term health effects, which led to the small town rebelling… But even with Coke gone, without a proper regiment, they started to resort to other sugary products, and their health now continues to deteriorate. The oldest living culture on Earth is in danger of disappearing. This is a much more affecting and relatable fact than the personal experiment of a well-off documentarian.

Some other (questionable) facts along the way are mildly interesting: we eat an average of six kilograms of sugar a week; if we were to remove all sugar items from supermarket shelves, only 20% of products would remain; sugar mood fluctuations can lead to panic attacks; in 1955 Dwight Eisenhower had a heart attack, which led to heart disease research blaming sugar as a highly probable cause. Though mildly diverting, those factoids could also be easily looked up online within seconds.

While some of the science in "That Sugar Film" can't be argued with, Gameau's research methods are dubious: he measures his sugar intake very approximately, as displayed in his "intricately mathematical" calculations at breakfast, or when he eats sugar ON his roasted chicken, which is gross and just unnecessary. Gameau is a TV actor who makes for a surprisingly bland protagonist, jumping around in his yellow briefs a bit too much, and also popping up in a "WTF" dance video at the end. (Seriously, I don't know what to make of that video. It's almost worth watching the entire film for… almost.)

Frequent animations, understated special effects and quirky editing enhance the narrative, but also remind that without those embellishments, the documentary would be quite dull, a rehashed "Supersize Me" about facts we should all already know: corporate giants rule us, excessive sugar consumption is bad… I'm not saying the world doesn't need a reminder, but "That Sugar Film" is too self-indulgent, too diluted in its research and conclusion, and too didactic to truly resonate. It made me (guiltily) want an ice-cream Snickers afterwards.

2.5 out of 5

Thomas Vinterberg's "The Commune" Struggles to Connect

Synopsis: *A story about the clash between personal desires, solidarity and tolerance in a Danish commune in the 1970's.*

Referred to as "kommunalkas", communal apartments appeared in Russia in the early 20th Century, each one housing several families to save living costs, post-revolution. Despite economic struggles (and arguably because of them), those families tended to bond, sharing intimate secrets with each other, along with showers and kitchen sinks. Originally from Russia, I've never actually lived in one, but grew up watching Soviet films, "kommunalkas" serving as a common setting and a plot device / emotional catalyst. Even in the late 1980's and early 1990's, folks still roomed with two or three families - generations that struggled to keep up with the rapid political changes, finding a perverse comfort in the necessity to share home space. They drank vodka and played guitars, reminiscing about the days of yore.

Thomas Vinterberg, a controversial director known for his visceral, "take-no-prisoners" filmmaking style, tones down the shtick big-time in his latest feature, "The Commune", which reveals a similar living arrangement, only in the politically-unstable, 1970's Denmark. Here though, the formation of the titular commune is a conscious decision, made by its lead protagonists. An odd jumble of nostalgia (Vinterberg drew from personal experiences when making this film), "The Commune" is crammed with cultish undertones, half-baked political statements, intense-but-incomplete character studies and a mixed message at the end. Occasional welcome directorial trademarks - an abrupt cut here and there, a resonant, gritty realism to some of the proceedings - spice things up, but "The Commune" is essentially let down by its leader.

Erik (Ulrich Thomsen), an architecture professor, is faced with the choice of either selling his deceased father's house for a good chunk of change or residing in it. His newscaster wife Anna (Trine Dyrholm) pressures Erik to bring together a group of people and stay in the house. She does so with such inexplicable fervor ("I need to hear someone else speak. Otherwise I'll go mad."), possibly affected by the tumultuous cultural and political paradigm shifts, as well as her settled-in life, that her husband reluctantly agrees. A variety of characters - including the financially-strapped, leftist renegade (Lars Ranthe), a big ol' cry-baby (Fares Fares) and a child with a heart condition (Sebastian Grønnegaard Milbrat) - move in, and hilarity ensues.

Only it doesn't. We are firmly in Vinterberg territory here, as soft and confused as the man's "mode" may be. Remember, this is the guy who got his start with Lars von Trier, a fellow bleak cinematic auteur and scathing critic of society. Despite the pop-rock/twangy throwback soundtrack (most of it in Danish and cheesy as hell), outbursts of unexpected sentimentality, especially evident in the maudlin resolution, the overtly 1970's embellishments and the patchy comedy, "The Commune" still manages to intermittently venture into some fascinating, dark places.

Just as alienated at home as he is at work, Erik cheats on his wife with the beautiful young Emma (Helene Reingaard Neumann). When he reveals his infidelity, Anna acts nonchalantly, even going as far as proposing that Emma move in - which leads to Erik growing increasingly distant from Anna, who grows proportionally distant from the very "commune of love" she herself created. Other standouts include Emma's awkward "initiation" into the "Big Love"-like abode, Anna's emotional breakdown before a live broadcast, or the highlight: daughter Freja (Martha Sofie Wallstrøm Hansen), walking in on her father cheating, followed by a phone call from her unsuspecting mother. I also like that Erik's two loves look so much alike, the "new" vs the proverbial "old" ("Your eyes are brown," Anna says. "Your eyes are blue," Emma responds.)

Dyrholm and Thomsen, having worked with Vinterberg on his 1998 masterpiece "The Celebration", do all the heavy lifting. Dyrholm fares better, especially in the second half, when her character starts to disassemble, bit by bit. Thomsen plays a man on the edge, resentful of the new generation, humiliating his students for expressing unconventional ideas, exorcising his demons by sleeping with a girl half his age. Prone to outbursts of seizure-causing hysteria, he holds the screen, but his performance is somewhat one-note, his character not really evolving, save from one emotional breakthrough towards the end. As for the rest of the cast, they play second-fiddle to our heroes; we see them gather at dinner, exchange inconsequential remarks and go skinny-dipping (those Danes and their explicit nudity, gotta love it) - and that's about the extent of it. Those characters' blankness becomes grating over the film's almost two-hour running time - and a particular letdown, considering the helmer's usual deftness when it comes to handling actors.

Vinterberg seems confused here. Is his film about acceptance, the importance of sticking together and the corrosive effects of rejection? Or is it a study about idealism vs reality? Perhaps it's a cautionary tale? A statement on political change and its effects on society? Maybe, it's simply a retrospective glance back at the director's own upbringing. Regardless, its messages are muddled, underdeveloped and dipped into sap.

There is a speech that a character makes at one point, about an experiment, wherein well-fed but untouched-by-human-hand babies perished, most likely due to the lack of human interaction. Ultimately that's what I took away from "The Commune" - it's about our instinctive need to flock together, our fear of being alone, of death. Too bad Vinterberg's latest dies under its own lack of humanity, of a propelling momentum, so evident in his previous work, or those Russian "kommunalka" films I watched as a child (seek out Vladimir Bortko's Bulgakov 1988 adaptation "Heart of a Dog"). It is mired by a lack of focus, an overblown conclusion… and certainly doesn't warrant a "Celebration".

2.5 out of 5 stars

"The Death of Stalin", While Not Without Its Merits, Perfunctorily Dissects an Easy Target

Synopsis: *The film follows the Soviet dictator's last days and depicts the chaos of the regime after his death.*

Armando Iannucci has never been the one to shy away from scathing satire. After co-creating the ingenious British sitcom "Alan Partridge", which followed the travails of a sardonic radio talk-show host (Steve Coogan), his focus shifted to taking merciless jabs at British politics in the TV series "The Thick of It", and consequent film spin-off "In the Loop". Then of course, "Veep" happened, raking in Emmy after Emmy - and deservedly so. Julia Louis-Dreyfus' portrayal of the titular character as an obsessive, vehemently narcissistic, uber-intelligent, defiantly independent and ceaselessly arrogant go-getter anchored the show's hilarity in something substantial and real. Iannucci satirizes U.S. politics, yes, but he also mourns them, carefully deconstructing the system to reveal how futile our struggle for true democracy is, how ideologies and people get swallowed up in the swamps of turgid bureaucracy.

Now he turns his attention to Russia in "The Death of Stalin", a film that revolves around a very real event that occurred over half a decade ago and yet still linger in many people's minds. As I have mentioned in my reviews, though I have lived in America and Germany for well over two decades now, I was born in Russia, speak fluent Russian, have family there. Many Americans seem to forget about Russia's crucial part in winning WWII, producing films stateside that focus primarily on this country's defeat of the Nazi's - while it was the Russians that suffered the most losses and sacrifices, ultimately defeating the Germans during the historic Stalingrad battle. More so, Russians have become the Ultimate Villains, demonized in every news image, social media outlet, film and pop culture mention. I will not delve into the political reasons behind the recent flare-ups - that's a topic for a different article - but there's no denying there's a continuous resentment/hatred imbued in everything Slavic-related.

Now, I may seem a bit defensive, but perhaps rightfully so. In these days of political instability, with so much bias and social-media-inspired hatred spreading like disease, I can't help but feel like films, such as the recent Oscar-winning documentary "Icarus", and now "The Death of Stalin", serve to merely add fuel to the fire as opposed to reminding us of the importance of uniting as nations - two of the most powerful nations, to be precise. "Icarus" isn't well-structured, its narrative rambling, until it resolutely settles on demonizing Russian Olympic athletes. Yet it won the Oscar against way-more-deserving competitors, all pumped up on zeitgeist steroids of its own. In "Stalin", Iannucci depicts the infamous Russian leader as a pathetic, albeit powerful and fear-inducing, little man, shriveled up and dead, covered in his own urine. Whether that's its goal or not, it reinforces the image of Russia as a weak, dumb, politically unstable nation, with a history to back it up. If my grandmother, who worships the man and also happens to be a wonderful, ethical woman, saw this, she would have a heart attack.

Does that mean the film should not exist? No, because I am a true proponent of not applying any sort of censorship when it comes to humor. We should be able to laugh at humanity's flaws, no matter how atrocious - yet if we venture into very real territories, subjects that may prove truly offensive, we should tread carefully - otherwise it becomes crass. At this point, it's less about censorship and more about sensitivity.

Iannucci knows American politics. The cast in "Veep" is all-American. He nails it on the head with the jokes in "Veep", his scathing humor rightfully aimed at the politicians who resolutely guide us to annihilation. Yet it is difficult to satirize a complicated historical event of a country you have never lived in, because a) you will never truly have empirical knowledge of the contexts and details of the event, and b) you weren't there to live it. So while the director is witty, wise and experienced enough to pull off some delightful feats with his cast and set-pieces, the film leaves a bitter aftertaste of yet another example of America - or England, for that matter - poking fun at painful history, while at the same time crumbling itself WHILE preaching about equality/prejudice, feminism, etc.

I had the same issue with "Inglourious Basterds", which not only shamelessly rewrote history (still fresh in the minds of many human beings), it also depicted Hitler - an undoubtedly evil but cunning, highly intelligent man - as a mere spastic caricature. Like Iannucci, Tarantino was skillful enough to pull off a film that even fooled me into thinking it was a classic upon my first viewing - until the dust settled and that nasty taste seeped in. As talented as Tarantino is, who is he to mock tragedy? It made me badly wish he just stuck to the sincerity and intensity of that first sequence with Christoph Waltz and the milk.

Iannucci pretends to not even go for authenticity. With a mostly-British cast playing real-life figures - Michael Palin is the sniveling Vyacheslav Molotov, Simon Russell Beale is the vile Lavrenti Beria, Paul Whitehouse is the iniquitous Anastas Mikoyan, Andrea Riseborough is Stalin's pragmatic daughter Svetlana - and some American names thrown in to dilute the image even more: Steve Buscemi as the scheming Nikita Khrushchev and Jeffrey Tambor as the dumb-as-nails Georgy Malenkov, "The Death of Stalin" reduces those real-life figures to one-or-two-adjective caricatures. At the same time, in the background, folks "hilariously" get butchered, strangled and thrown down the stairs under Stalin's orders - but, as Iannucci said in the Q&A I attended, he never intended for the "people" to be the targets of his satire, just the political leaders running the show.

And one could argue the absurdity of the film - the very "Veep"-like hustle and bustle and power-grabbing games that ensue after the Great Leader perishes - serves as a good enough reason not to scrutinize it the way I'm doing. Thankfully, Iannucci happens to be a master of comic dialogue and the stalwart cast lives up to his words. Vasily Stalin (Rupert Friend), a constantly-intoxicated shell of a man, utters at one point, "I know the drill. Smile, shake hands and try not to call them cunts." Georgy Zhukov (Jason Isaacs), at a different point, exclaims, "What's a war hero got to do to get some lubrication around here?" It's this juxtaposition of British slang / humor and Russian reality that both scathes and amuses.

The film is also well-shot and edited, although it does come off as a bit theatrical and Aaron Sorkin-y, its constant freeze-frame introductions of main and supplementary characters grating. The film is worth watching for its individual set-pieces rather than the overall narrative arc, which proves anticlimactic.

Yes, Stalin was inarguably a despot. But to many Russians he was - and still is - the Savior - clearly, as the film was banned in my Motherland, which I believe is too harsh, evoking the aforementioned censorship. However, I wouldn't blame the older Russian generation for avoiding theaters if it had been released. Why would they want to see some middle-aged British guy pissing all over their god? Perhaps Iannucci should keep focusing on taking stabs at the imbeciles running this country, instead of laughing at dug-up pieces of the past that still resonate painfully with millions of people. Just a thought.

2.5 out of 5 stars

"The Finest Hours" Fails to Conjure the Perfect Storm

Synopsis: The Coast Guard makes a daring rescue attempt off the coast of Cape Cod after a pair of oil tankers are destroyed during a blizzard in 1952.

"Disheartening" would be a gross underestimation when it comes to describing Hollywood's tendency to corrupt aspiring, talented filmmakers. While there are a few directors who, despite the gold-plated allure of the system, stay true to their original visions and keep the independent spirit alive (thank you, Tom McCarthy), others simply cannot resist the temptation to, for lack of a better term, "sell out".

And who can blame them, really? If you were, say, Colin Trevorrow, and made a $750,000 charming indie, "Safety Not Guaranteed", would you say "no" to directing two of the biggest sequels of all time (the $150 mil. "Jurassic World" and the upcoming "Star Wars: Episode IX", whose budget is so large, they could build an eighth continent with it)? High-powered execs pluck cheap talent, with reservoirs of potential - Sundance hits, like "Looper" (whose director, Rian Johnson, is now busy working on "Star Wars: Episode VIII") - but instead of maximizing on that potential, they restrict directors, distorting their imaginations with preconceived notions of what the general public wants. The extent to which a director can express his creative vision is inversely proportional to the budget of the film. The filmmakers' hands are therefore cuffed, and they have no choice but to bow at the producers' whim. Movies are chopped and rewritten, to appease everyone, to bombard with forgettable, PG-13 thrills.

Though it's getting progressively more difficult in this day and age of studio-driven cinema, some filmmakers still manage to have creative control over big-budget product (Quentin Tarantino, Steven Spielberg, Christopher Nolan, and, to a lesser degree, Joss Whedon, come to mind), and/or to use the profits from those films to keep making their art. Craig Gillespie's coastguard action drama "The Finest Hours" unfortunately signals the aforementioned corruption of a talented artist. The man who once directed the sensitive and warm-hearted "Lars and the Real Girl" and showed some promise with the bigger-budget remake "Fright Night", now bombards his audience with the most stereotypical genre tropes, wasting an intriguingly unconventional cast in a "been-there-seen-that-a-million-times" sappy Hollywood "thrill ride". A few moments of adrenaline notwithstanding - it's Disney, after all, and we're on a roller-coaster - your finest hours will be spent avoiding this film, and watching one of Gillespie's older "United States of Tara" episodes instead.

Bernie Webber (Chris Pine) is the somewhat-shy-but-determined-and-handsome hero, a Cape Cod coastguard. Early in the film, Bernie falls for Miriam

(Holliday Grainger), a local naive-but-loyal-and-beautiful young woman. When she proposes to him at a spectacularly romantic dance, he looks her straight in the eye and says, "No." Distraught, Miriam runs out into the wintry night, yet it doesn't take long for Bernie to explain to her, Spider Man-style, that his job is too dangerous, and he simply cares too much for her… so, oh well, okay, yes, he'll marry her. Miriam falls into Bernie's arms again, willing to take the risk and dedicate her one-dimensional existence to this young lad with a penchant for danger.

In the meantime, maritime drama occurs off the Cape Cod coast: after a captain's refusal to slow down in a storm, an oil tanker capsizes, snapping into two pieces. One half sinks immediately; the other stays afloat. The remaining crew, led by the blank-faced Ray Sybert (Casey Affleck) - pronounced "sea-bird" - begin arguing about life boats, before Sybert silences them with an axe (yep, it happens), and some grim facts: "We're sinking. (Beat.) If we lose the power, we lose the pumps. (Beat.)" They have about "four or five hours", during which they build a manual tiller, to steer the boat to shallow waters. For those of us who don't understand the concept of "steering", Sybert, taking cues from "Interstellar"'s "wormhole pencil" sequence, uses an egg to helpfully demonstrate the tiller's effects.

When another oil tanker capsizes in the area nearby, the crew worries, "If everyone's getting them, who's gonna come for us?" Well, Chris motherfuckin' Pine, that's who! Ordered by insecure commander Daniel Cluff (Eric Bana) to assemble a team, Bernie picks his friend Richie (Ben Foster) and a few other heroic misfits, and they embark on a perilous journey, on the tiniest boat, through the most vicious of snowstorms this side of Jonas. "They're sending you out to death," the local wise fishermen warn them. And so the rescue begins.

Chris Pine's Bernie gets most of the film's unintentionally funny lines. "Sometimes people go out and don't come back", Bernie says, to which Miriam tearfully (and sensibly) responds, "Are you talking about the storm or the marriage?" When confronted to turn back by Richie halfway through their adventure, Bernie hesitates, then solemnly intones, "Not on my watch." Later, he addresses a potential sinking situation: "We all live, we all die… right?" Um, have you seen "Titanic"? There's no room on that lifeboat, Bernie.

Speaking of which, at least the freezing temperature was more-or-less accurately rendered in Cameron's beloved epic, with DiCaprio's face turning white before icing up and disappearing underwater. No one seems truly cold in "The Finest Hours", all rosy cheeks and maybe - just maybe - the occasional tremble. Aren't those supposed to be below-freezing temperatures?

The film's subplot stinks. I find it offensive how they just had to add a talented actress to play "the wife", in this testosterone-driven story of men in peril. There's even a scene that lousily attempts to address 1950s bigotry, in which Miriam begs Daniel Cuff, at least 800 times, to "please call them back", to no avail. The issue here is that her character - and her storyline - is so underdeveloped, the film, in its thickheaded determination to avoid accusations of sexism for not including a woman at all, instead becomes that much more sexist by reducing its one female part to a peripheral footnote. "The Finest Hours" reiterates the point that Hollywood is going about the whole "casting women" thing in a completely wrong way - but that's a subject for a different essay.

Eric Bana and Ben Foster, both highly talented actors, are wildly underused. Casey Affleck literally sleepwalks through the blizzard - the guy's normally got infinitely more screen presence than his famous brother, but here seems to be cashing it way in. Characters remain at arm's length, displaying no real chemistry, no dynamic or intrigue - they are only slightly less disposable than the fools inhabiting Michael Bay universes.

In typical Hollywood fashion, characterization comes second - or third, or fourth - to the spectacle, and "The Finest Hours" does deliver in some scenes, particularly the ones involving Bernie's boat crashing, rolling and piercing through the giant waves, as well as some sequences involving Sybert's crew. That said, the whole "massive-wave-flips-boat" vs. "men-yelling" thing gets repetitive quite fast. There is also one cool, memorable shot, tracking the crew, as they yell out an order to change the boat's speed and direction, passing it along until its execution, which only serves as a reminder that it's THE one cool, memorable shot in the entire film.

"The Finest Hours" provides no real insight into what it means to be a coastguard, or a crew member of an oil tanker. It reduces its one female role to a redundant subplot. Every beat is predictable, making one wish Gillespie added at least a few colorful lines or unexpected plot twists. Guess the studio took the reign on this one.

2.5 out of 5 stars

Faux Documentary "The Landing" Meticulously Examines a Lunar Mission that Never Happened

Synopsis: *An investigation into the tragic end of Apollo 18, the last US mission to the moon in 1973. In interviews conducted in 1998, on the 25th anniversary of the incident, witnesses and participants peel back the layers of mystery surrounding the events that nearly destroyed an American institution.*

NASA's final scheduled manned journey to the moon, Apollo 18, got scrapped due to budgetary constraints. The US had beat the Russians to our satellite - if not to space - and, content, moved on from cosmos exploration. David and Mark Dodson's faux documentary "The Landing" imagines what it would be like if the mission did take place. The bulk of the film revolves around conspiracies resulting in its consequent, mysterious landing, way off its marked site, back on Earth. While impeccably produced, with the combination of archival footage, reenactments and talking heads making it all seem very real, and somewhat absorbing, the mockumentary ultimately doesn't present a compelling enough reason to sit through 90 minutes of adults playing make-believe.

It certainly got me at first. Fully aware that the Apollo 18 mission never took place, I nevertheless found myself looking up the facts five minutes into the doc. Living out his life isolated in the blizzard mountains, Lt. Cmdr. Bo Cunningham, USN, Ret. (Don Hannah), speaks very earnestly about his early dreams to fly and the disappointment he felt over finding out he was NOT going to fly the lunar module - as in, actually feel his heavily-insulated feet sink into the lunar soil. Destined to pilot the command module over the moon's surface instead, his eyes almost well up. How could I NOT look up if that shit was real? Having reaffirmed my suspicions, I kept watching, a bit frustrated, but with a newly-found appreciation for the mockumentary's authenticity.

Who did the much-coveted role go to? The popular and good-looking Al Borden (Jeff McVey), "America's First Surfer Geologist Hippie Poet Golden Boy Spaceman", as Look magazine accurately described him, a man who "could stare at a rock for hours", such was his fascination with the world. The third member of the Apollo 18 trio was Ed Lovett (Warren Farina), whose political affiliations may have helped him become the Commander of the mission. "We saw ourselves as being flyers," Bo says, "and this was the ultimate ride."

Having made it to the moon and back, the Apollo 18 "landed far off course in the Takla Makan desert of Western China". Disoriented and shaken but convinced that they were being tracked down by the US government, the astronauts set up camp, Al and Ed stinging themselves on a wild poisonous bush in the process. Ed started throwing up, hallucinating, accusing Bo of messing up the landing - or intentionally changing course. "They were clearly affected by something and I wasn't," Bo comments.

The damn bush ended up killing both of Bo's partners… or did it? Upon his return to the US, it didn't take long for the question to arise - which, of course, led to a government-issued investigation. Was there a glitch in the system? Did Bo mess up the landing? The details of their stay in the desert were heavily scrutinized. Bo denies any allegations. So what, he contaminated some moon rocks! The conspiracies got more and more far-fetched, with Bo being accused of working for the Chinese and killing the men. His very sanity was called into question: "Did America Send a Madman into Space?" proclaimed one magazine article.

The film works wonders as a faux documentary, down to an Apollo XVIII pin one of the interviewees wears. It's chockfull of stylistic flourishes - such as 1970's-style magazine clippings, archival recreations, a 1970's score - which help generate that authentic feel. All the actors shine, including "CHIPs" star Robert Pine as Peter S. Pellarin, US House of Representatives. It asks pertinent questions about the nature of truth and shows how Earth can be more alienating than its moon, with its merciless deserts, corrupt politicians and suspicious federal agents.

A fake documentary about alleged facts, it's quite meta indeed. That said, it's difficult to disregard the notion that, as a real doc, it would've been endlessly more fascinating. Once the realization - and then novelty - that you're watching a reenactment of one sinks in - an impeccable reenactment, but a reenactment nonetheless - it becomes a bit of a slog to sit through. The Dodsons ask us to get involved in conspiracies and allegations in a fabricated story, where we know nothing is real. If "The Landing" were presented as a feature-length fiction film, with developed characters we grew to care about, perhaps it would have worked. If they condensed it down to a short, it may have been a nifty little cinematic exercise. As it stands, the film, despite its cleverness, never quite lands.

2.5 out of 5 stars

"The Man Who Knew Infinity" Showcases Slumdog's Beautiful Mind

Synopsis: *Growing up poor in Madras, India, Srinivasa Ramanujan Iyengar earns admittance to Cambridge University during WWI, where he becomes a pioneer in mathematical theories with the guidance of his professor, G.H. Hardy.*

Some films are so old-fashioned in plot and structure, their predictability can either be reassuring (the lack of shocking developments is akin to a warm cup of tea; see: "About a Boy") or frustrating (the lack of originality rendering the entire thing utterly redundant; see: this month's "Mother's Day"), depending on your predisposition to this sort of fare. Matt Brown's "The Man Who Knew Infinity" perfectly exemplifies such a film, with a by-the-numbers biopic plot that lacks forward momentum and ultimately gets bogged down in sentimentality. What could have been a fascinating account of a man whose theories and formulas are still used in deciphering black holes, ends up being a run-of-the-mill, nauseatingly clichéd, "turn-off-your-brain", pseudo-uplifting melodrama (ironic, considering it's a film about math and geniuses) that will "reassure" only those seeking the most basic and, yes, formulaic sources of inspiration. I, for one, was very frustrated.

The film opens in Trinity College, Cambridge, England, 1920: Professor G.H. Hardy (Jeremy Irons) ruminates on his relationship with Ramanujan (Dev Patel), looking out of his window nostalgically: "I suppose it's always a little difficult for an Englishman and an Indian to understand one another properly. I owe more to him than to anyone else in the world. And my association with him," he adds despondently, "is the one romantic incident of my life." (Damn, this dude needs to set aside his calculations and get laid!)

The film then transports us to Madras, India, 1914: Ramanujan is a young math genius; he gets a job with the bigoted Sir Francis Spring (Stephen Fry), who at first bellows, "This man looks like he lives on the street. Get him out of here!" Ramanujan promises him that he's skilled, and what may be glass now will eventually turn into a diamond (I'm slightly paraphrasing, but that's quite literally what he says). With nothing but an abacus at his disposal, Ramanujan pursues his dream of moving to England to make new, earth-shattering mathematical discoveries and prove that Indian culture spawns geniuses just as qualified as the Brits. He receives hesitant support from his wife - and even less support from his mother. "What nonsense are you talking?" the latter says over dinner vehemently. "It is forbidden to cross the seas!"

Ramanujan's breakthrough formulas eventually reach the attention of Hardy, a "man of numbers" who desperately wants to leave a legacy, and his scholarly mate

Littlewood (Tobey Jones). Both are so impressed with the young lad's talents, they hastily recruit him. Upon hearing the news, Ramanujan ceremoniously cuts off his long hair, signifying the upcoming change in his life - thereby horrifying his mother - and, after a tearful goodbye, embarks on the 6,000-mile journey across the ocean.

Hardy and Littlewood greet Ramanujan - somewhat awkwardly. After being thoroughly impressed by all the privileges of Civilized Living, Ramanujan is shocked when, during their first session, Hardy tells him he wants the boy to attend some lectures, instead of, you know, publishing his groundbreaking work on infinite numbers right away. "First, we need proofs of your work," Hardy sternly stays. Even Littlewood exclaims at one point: "This will take a lifetime!" "Maybe two" - Ramanujan responds, with a knowing grin. (Yes, the film is chockfull of references to infinity.)

Together, Hardy and Ramanujan (spoiler alert!) overcome the raging prejudice, bond (Hardy: "What an unlikely team we make!"), share moments of uplift and face more obstacles (tuberculosis, war, suicide), which they overcome against all odds, as they pursue the solution to the central elusive formula. It all ends with a Big Speech scene, and a sprinkle of tragedy - both great Oscar bait. There is also the underdeveloped subplot of Ramanujan's wife, longing for her husband, into which I won't delve too deeply here, due simply to its blandness and worthlessness.

Dev Patel is a bit muted in the central role, his performance not so much understated as simply blank, especially in contrast to the British stalwarts that surround him. "The Man Who Knew Infinity" comes alive whenever screen veteran Jeremy Irons is on screen, his by turns weary, forceful, passionate and insecure professor portraying more with single expressions than the filmmakers seemingly ever intended. Stephen Fry is suitably sleazy, but he's on screen for literally two or three minutes. Tobey Jones is always reliable, and here convincingly plays a man whom Jeremy Northam's character, Hardy's nemesis/mentor Bertrand Russell, refers to as "a figment of Hardy's imagination", getting blamed for all of Hardy's mistakes. His trajectory is perhaps the most poignant aspect of this film. Director Matt Brown wisely - or perhaps unknowingly (happy accident?) - lets the actors handle the rougher patches, or the film would have been a complete disaster.

I am harsh. No one sets out to make a bad film, and this one at least deals with grand issues, such as diversity, faith vs science, prejudice, pursuing your dreams despite all odds… Old, worn-out themes, but commendable nonetheless. The world of grumpy British professors competing for intellectual fame is also well portrayed.

But then there's all the hokey dialogue ("Your accounts better be half as polished as your ego"; "I was told you like numbers more than people"; "You are my everything", "My God puts formulas on my tongue when I speak" - wait, is this a faith-based film?). There are the foreseeable beats (during his first class, the teacher calls Ramanujan out because the kid's not taking any notes, but guess what - Ramanujan aces the crap out of that formula on the blackboard, embarrassing the racist teacher). There are scenes that are way OTT, like the young man's first British lunch experience, where he accidentally eats some animal lard (he's from India! c'mon, he's vegetarian!) and storms off - CULTURE CLASH, spelled out, for those of us who can't read.

Larry Smith's cinematography is intermittently eye-catching: the man who shot "Only God Forgives" paints the British campus in golden, autumn hues, and the Indian parts in kaleidoscopic colors. Matt Brown's direction is smooth but unremarkable - but, like I said, at least it doesn't get in the way of the performances, ultimately letting them carry the film over its muddy waters. The "infinity of math vs the infinity of legacy" concept is hammered into your head constantly - and I wish they added another layer to that notion, say, the futility of striving for infinity due to the brevity of existence, and whether posthumous recognition even matters. The central formula/theory that Hardy and Ramanujan are trying to prove is not compelling enough to sustain interest, and the film contains long, dull patches.

If it's a heart-warming, cheesy, predictable and uplifting story you're looking for, say, while ironing or doing dishes, then "The Man Who Knew Infinity" is right up your alley. Make it a double-billing with "A Brilliant Young Mind" (read my review here) for a night of middling underdog stories - or rather don't, and watch Ben Wheatley's brilliant "High-Rise" (out in theaters this weekend) instead.

2.5 out of 5 stars

Blair Witch Moves to Sweden in David Bruckner's Wooden Horror "The Ritual"

Synopsis: *A group of college friends reunite for a trip to the forest, but encounter a menacing presence in the woods that's stalking them.*

I remember watching "The Signal", a 2007 sci-fi horror-comedy hybrid split into three parts, each written and helmed by a different filmmaker. The pseudo-zombie triptych, while flawed, was memorable for its unexpectedly clever bits, most of them contained within David Bruckner's segment. The fact that it was made for less than $100K made the vividly-rendered, intensely-paced project that much more impressive. Since then, I have eagerly followed the man's career, yet - aside from a few mildly diverting projects, such as a contribution to the lo-fi "V/H/S" gore anthology and the ambitious "Twilight Zone"-ish thriller "Southbound" - it seems to have taken him ten years to come up with a proper follow-up.

At the showing I attended, which took place at the Netflix screening room in Hollywood, Bruckner introduced the film himself, referring to it as "masculinity and Norse weirdness". The former, I got plenty of in a 90-minute visual sausage fest (at least the man's self-aware); as for the latter, while there was, I believe, one reference to Norse mythology, the film certainly could have used more weirdness and gallows humor. As it stands, it's neither here nor there: not quite uncanny and subliminally frightening enough to evoke such works as Jeff VanderMeer's "Southern Reach" trilogy (the first of which, "Annihilation", has been adapted by Alex Garland and is coming out this month - coincidence?), nor is it goofy and satirical in the vein of Christopher Smith's 2006 cheeky "Severance".

A bunch of mates plan a trip somewhere cool, like Amsterdam or Ibiza (pronounced "I-bee-tha"). When Luke (Rafe Spall) goes into a convenience store with one of them, a robbery leads to a tragic murder, and Luke spends the rest of the film haunted by guilt, wondering if he could have done anything to change the outcome of that evening. For whatever reason, six months later he, along with his friends Phil (Arsher Ali), Hutch (Robert James-Collier) and Dom (Sam Troughton), decide to honor their dead mate's memory in cold, rural Sweden, of all places. They camp out in the flatland wilderness, exchanging cheeky, very British quips ("One, two, three… Brexit!" they exclaim for a selfie). Due to a minor injury, they take a shortcut back through the deep Swedish woods, where ancient evil lurks.

The ancient evil comes in form of a well-designed monster, which (spoiler alert) Bruckner cleverly doesn't reveal until the end, first showing us the horror it leaves in its wake - gutted creatures, suspended from tree branches - then slowly providing glimpses of the hooved creature. Odd things happen, such as our hapless heroes ending up in a cabin, where they all awake from intense nightmares in ritualistic poses, one of them praying to a headless wicker man. They proceed deeper and deeper into the woods, until... well, I don't want to spoil the end, though to be honest, there's not much to spoil: you get to see the monster in its fully glory. The hint to the so-called "twist" lies in the title.

The film could have been so much more. It touches upon ideas of guilt manifesting itself in physical horror, something the film half-assedly explores. The sub-plot is just not well-interweaved into the story, halting any semblance of suspense in a desperate attempt at some sort of resonant ethical subtext. Shame - this could have been a much more enticing, not to mention psychologically-affecting, running thread, than just a ritualistic, sacrifice-seeking monster. The characters are not developed enough, despite giving it their best effort. Rate Spall in the lead is the standout (check him out in the Christmas Special episode of "Black Mirror" to see him at the top of his game). "The Ritual" is stuffed with redundant bits of dialogue, characters stating the obvious, in the vein of: "Something's not right here". There's a LOT of walking through the woods, and though Andrew Shulkind does wonders with his camerawork, creating a pastel-like, foggy and saturated palette, it feels like those pretty images of trees are just filler, not really driving the momentum forward.

There are some nifty moments of suspense interspersed throughout the film. The monster itself is worth the wait... almost. Bruckner knows how to position the camera and has a pretty good grasp at building tension. One just can't help but wish "The Ritual" had something more otherworldly about it, a shocking development or two, a memorable character - or at least the tongue-in-cheek humor and inventiveness Bruckner displayed in "The Signal". As it stands, file "The Ritual" - along with "Troll Hunter" and "Dead Snow" - in the "Mediocre Scandinavian Horror" drawer.

2.5 out of 5 stars

"The Take" 'Elbas' Its Way Through a Herd of Cliches

Synopsis: A young con artist and former CIA agent embark on an anti-terrorist mission in France.

Idris Elba is so fervently beloved by his fans, it makes one wonder where the adoration stems from. No disrespect to the charming actor who can certainly hold the screen, but which film was it, exactly, that propelled Elba to that Don Cheadle status? One glance at his resume reveals a slew of duds ("The Reaping", "The Unborn", "Obsessed", "The Losers", "Ghost Rider: Spirit of Vengeance", "The Gunman"), some mid-grade stuff ("Takers", "Thor", "Prometheus", "Mandela: Long Walk to Freedom", "Finding Dory"), and only a few moderate gems in-between ("Zootopia", "The Jungle Book", "Star Trek Beyond"), most of the good ones' high quality having little to do with Elba's actual performance.

The only standout that comes to mind is Elba chewing scenery in the gratuitous-but-effective "Beasts of No Nation", a powerhouse role that verged on - but never slipped into - parody. My personal favorite Elba performance is his memorable appearance in several episodes of TV's "The Office", as the uptight and sexy boss Charles Miner.

The main reason for his recognition has to be the TV show "Luther", which I admit I haven't yet seen, having heard nothing but raves about it - and hence distanced myself from it. (A tendency of mine is to avoid whatever is deemed wildly trendy by the masses: I was late on "Harry Potter", "Star Trek", "Sopranos" and "The Wire"). Similarly to how Benedict Cumberbatch's sling-shot career move was "Sherlock Holmes", "Luther" must have instantly cemented Elba's status as a serious stalwart. (The British crime show has been on my Netflix cue for months now; as my British friend next to me reassures me, "he's the shit in it.") I'll make it a point to watch "Luther" ASAP. For now, I have writer/director James Watkins' "The Take" as the most recent example of a mediocre film that doesn't do its star justice. Why Elba would pick this project, which gives off a distinct, stale, straight-to-video whiff, is beyond anyone's guess.

Formerly titled "Bastille Day" (France's version of Independence Day - and a catchier name, if you ask me), "The Take" (not to be confused with the 2007 John Leguizamo vehicle) doesn't take its time plunging us into the action: Michael Mason ("Game of Thrones'" Richard Madden), a pickpocket, storms through some sort of a Paris gathering that features a nude girl descending a red-carpet staircase. Cut to: CIA agent Sean Briar (Elba) is being grilled by his superiors, Tom Luddy (Anatol Yusef) and Karen Dacre (Kelly Reilly), for his questionable actions in the field. "Reckless, insubordinate and irresponsible towards human assets", Briar is immediately established as a badass who disregards authority and yields results through, ahem, unconventional methods.

In direct contrast to his methods, a conventional plot unravels, wherein rookie terrorist Zoe Naville's (Charlotte Le Bon) explosive suitcase accidentally ends up in Michael's hands and goes off, barely gracing him. He's caught on camera; Briar and his team run down the young man's profile, which includes gambling, bad childhood, lice - same spiel you've seen a million times. Michael is "always running away from something, mostly from himself." After an intense chase that takes them from the Paris rooftops to the street markets (where you can apparently easily shoplift with no consequences), Briar busts Michael, with the highly memorable line, "Yeah mothefucker, now what?" It doesn't take long for Michael to convince Briar it wasn't his bag - and of his outrageously proficient thieving skills. With 36 hours to comply to the terrorists' demands, leading up to - you guessed it - the Bastille Day parade, they team up, utilizing their respective talents to take down the bad guys.

Protests within the city abound, French and U.S. authorities clash, traitors are revealed within the evil French government, political hashtags spread like cancer, and plenty of arbitrary banter ensues between the two leads, some of it mildly amusing, most of it been-there-seen-that stuff, recycled from dozens of better buddy films. "You think I got a chance at the agency?" Michael wonders after pulling off an elaborate little heist. "You got potential," Briar replies. Love is in the air. It all ends in a massive shoot-out, with Briar a one-man army against dozens of armed officers - until hundreds of protesters get involved.

The film comes alive during its action sequences, which are well-choreographed and suspenseful. Unlike Watkins' previous effort, the somnambulant Daniel Radcliffe horror smash "Woman in Black", "The Take" moves at a breakneck pace. It's got a nice international flavor to it, the setting being Paris and all. Elba is stoic and invulnerable, an amalgamation of all tightly-jawed action heroes of yore, with hints of sorrow behind his eyes. Madden fares worse - while never terrible, he comes off as whiny and one-dimensional. The chemistry between them is minimal - but it's there, glimmering dimly.

On the flip side, the film is stuffed with conventional villains, its plot nonsensical, containing holes large enough for Elba to power a Jaeger through them. "The Take" shamelessly channels everything from "The French Connection" to "From Paris With Love", with no hints at depth or meaning. The infusion of "relevant" political themes is laughable in what is essentially a B-movie extravaganza of shoot-outs and cheap explosions. Suspend your disbelief, get stoned, and - for those of you enamored by the lead - bask in the Tao of Elba.

2.5 out of 5 stars

"The Timber" Needs a Good Polish

Synopsis: *In the wild west, two brothers embark on a journey to collect a bounty in a desperate attempt to save their home... but what they find along the way is more than they bargained for.*

The Western genre is a tricky one to tackle these days. Harkening all the way back to Edwin S. Porter's 1903 classic "The Great Train Robbery", the Western has since witnessed a variety of incarnations. Master filmmakers like John Ford, Howard Hawks, John Huston, Sergio Leone and Sam Peckinpah have produced some of the best shoot-'em-ups in cinematic history. It's a hefty task, to compete with those guys.

In 1995, Jim Jarmusch took a radical approach with "Dead Man", a minimalist, black-and-white spiritual odyssey that stripped the genre down to its core elements. In "Ravenous", Antonia Bird took another subversive route and amped up the depravity, violence and sexism inherent to the genre. A darkly-comedic horror, "Ravenous" turned cowboys into flesh-craving cannibals. Kevin Costner brought gravitas to the more recent "Open Range", and his experience, stemming from an extensive history of acting in Westerns ("Silverado", "Dances with Wolves", "Wyatt Earp") was evident. Now we have "The Timber", director Anthony O'Brien's low-budget attempt to wholeheartedly embrace the genre, and the film's earnestness almost outweighs its numerous flaws.

The story begins somewhere in the cold, cold, Wild, Wild West. Wyatt (James Ransone, so memorably hilarious in "Sinister", but very somber here) brings a stash of money to the bank. He is told it's not enough and has one week to vacate his premises... unless he kills Jebediah (William Gaunt), a wanted man, and a mysterious-but-evidently-dangerous-and-borderline-mythical figure, who hides up in the ice-cold Timber, a mysterious-but-evidently-dangerous-and-borderline-mythical place.

So Wyatt relays the news to his brother Samuel (Josh Peck, so memorably subtle in "The Wackness"), who immediately gets all cocky and ready for battle. The brothers will do anything to protect their mother Maggie (Maria Doyle Kennedy), Samuel's wife Lisa (Elisa Lasowski) and Samuel's baby. And so they embark on a journey to find Jebediah (who, by the way - minor point - also happens to be their father), accompanied by a suspicious representative of the bank, Colonel Rupert Thomas (Mark Caven). The Colonel, of course, ends up having secrets (or, in this case, "traumas" would be more accurate) of his own. In the meantime, the local Sheriff (David Bailie) helps the poor ladies fend off against persistent bank reps.

Throughout their journey, the brothers lose their horses, encounter sadistic bandits and almost die of cold and starvation. When they finally get to the Timber, they coincidentally stumble upon a revolt, which saves them at a crucial point, and allows them to confront their evil father.

One of the film's issues is its lack of empathy. The characters remain at arm's length, and that's not the actors' fault: both Josh Peck and James Ransone are admirable leads. It's that the cast is given so little to work with, the script riddled with clunky dialogue, delivered in even clunkier, uneven accents, ranging from Russian to English to Irish to a very Texan drawl.

And when I say "clunky dialogue", I mean borderline-crude and often hilarious. Here are a few tidbits: "He's a murderer, Sammy." Pause. "Well, who ain't." Or how about: "What's Timber like, Colonel?" Long pause. "Eventful." There are outbursts of emotion, here and there: "I don't want to raise my son in this kind of world!" Extensively long pause. "It ain't easy, this world…" Okay, finally, my favorite: "You must be Wyatt, the prodigal son!" Pause. "Prodigal or not, I'm here. And I'm looking for him. Where's my father?"

O'Brien's film is filled with formulaic touches, from the "man who has to go on a mission, leaving his child and wife behind (rather thoughtlessly, if you ask me)" staple of the genre, to the repeated shots of Samuel's wife, holding the baby while longingly staring out the window. The sudden outbursts of action are badly choreographed and highly disorienting. One hilarious scene involves a baddie shooting a random guy for no apparent reason, then tilting his head back and laughing uproariously, like he just witnessed a mime exploding. Also, I'd like to point out how well-groomed Samuel's stubble is, never quite reaching that beard stage, while his silky hair always lands smoothly on the side (I wish I could say the same about poor Samuel).

I'm also not sure about the film's morals. What is it saying, exactly? That violence is the only way to combat violence? That one would - and should - go to extreme lengths to protect his family? Is it a story of family redemption through vengeance? Its overall theme is somewhat muddled - a big "no-no" in all the classic Westerns it tries so hard to emulate.

The director proves much more adept at the silent, lyrical sequences. There is a beautiful, slow-motion sequence of one of the horses hitting a snow wall, and the carriage breaking. The cinematography, courtesy of Phil Parmet ("The Devil's Rejects") is sporadically stunning - the cold is palpable, especially in a shot of the brothers walking through blinding snow. The narrative's languid pauses work in achieving a mythical, contemplative atmosphere. And the ending, that cuts between Samuel's confrontation with his father, and his wife fighting off evil bankers, is suitably suspenseful.

Anthony O'Brien has probably studied the classics: "The Treasure of the Sierra Madre", "Red River", "The Wild Bunch", "The Good, the Bad, and the Ugly", "Unforgiven", "No Country for Old Men", "Django Unchained"... His effort is evident. But I couldn't help thinking of those films, even when marveling at "The Timber"'s uncompromising, gritty vibe. Those films' budgets were sky-high, I get it. But in a genre like the Western, it's all about sparse landscapes and leathery faces and deadly betrayals - and a mystique that's haunted the genre since its origins. One can get away with making a beautiful Western on a low budget. O'Brien should aim for more ingenuity next time around. And get a better team of screenwriters.

2.5 out of 5

Fans of 1980's Horror May Enjoy "The Void", but They've Probably Seen Stranger Things

Synopsis: *In the middle of a routine patrol, officer Daniel Carter happens upon a blood-soaked figure limping down a deserted stretch of road. He rushes the young man to a nearby rural hospital staffed by a skeleton crew, only to discover that patients and personnel are transforming into something inhuman.*

Disclaimer: *I make it a point never to read any reviews prior to writing one, in fear of being influenced by someone else's opinion. Upon finishing this review, I was somewhat surprised to discover a 100% score on Rotten Tomatoes (granted, based on six reviews so far). I would therefore like to take this opportunity to address the filmmakers:*

Dear Steven & Jeremy,

I ask you to please not hold a grudge against my somewhat-negative (albeit well-informed and eloquently written) review for the following reasons:

1. I am taking advantage of the freedom of speech in this country, before speech gets banned and sent into exile. (Poetic waxing aside, it's just an opinion, dudes.)
2. You are still much richer than I am.
3. This review will in no way affect the traction of the film, if it gets one (which I hope it will; I always root for ambitious independent filmmakers to attain success in this cruel, cruel cinematic world). The commies at Rotten Tomatoes don't pay attention to us lowlifes at IFC anyway.

(Disclaimer: Dear RT Staff, we don't think you're commies, nor is anyone in our highly talented staff a "lowlife"; this was meant to reassure Steven & Jeremy - please do include us in your roster of prolific critics.)

Sincerely,

Alex Saveliev

In Hollywood, a talented artist sometimes has to find a niche, before gaining enough experience to exhibit their true potential. Take Jeremy Gillespie and Steven Kowalski. They are steadily achieving prominence in Hollywood, in the (respectively) art direction and make-up FX departments. While the former assisted in ensuring that films like "Pacific Rim" and "Suicide Squad" looked frightening and painterly, the latter painted the frightening creatures and baddies in those films.

Prior to resuming their day jobs (and collaboration) on the upcoming Stephen King adaptation / remake of Tommy Lee Wallace's 1980's "classic" "It", Jeremy and Steven team up to helm the horror flick "The Void", utilizing what they've learned in their years in the industry, with mixed results. While there is no shortage of ambition or mayhem, Gillespie and Kowalski struggle with an all-over-the-place, laughably silly plot and seem lost in countless homages to all-things-1980's.

Things start off swell, prior to getting bogged down in contrivances. Evil-looking men with rifles chase a young man and woman out of a dark house. James (Evan Stern) makes a narrow escape; the girl isn't so lucky, shot and lit on fire. Officer Daniel Carter (Aaron Poole, bearing a striking resemblance to Aaron Paul) stumbles upon the crawling James on the side of the road. He takes him to an Arkham-like hospital, headed by the Vincent Price-like Dr. Richard Powell (Kenneth Welsh). As James convulses on his cot, nurse Allison (Kathleen Munroe) converses with Daniel, revealing a traumatic past that will later play a crucial role in the film. You with me so far?

Better be, because things get progressively more convoluted - though not necessarily complex - from here. Next thing he knows, Daniel stumbles upon nurse Beverly (Stephanie Belding) slooowly puling a knife out of a patient's eye. Having skinned her own face, Beverly turn to a terrified Daniel. "Can you help me?" she asks, reaching out... Therein, the insanity ensues.

Daniel experiences cosmic visions of another dimension, a hazy triangle forming in its viscous black clouds. A no-nonsense state trooper, Mitchell (Art Hindle) arrives on the scene - but not for long. Monk-like figures in white gowns, triangles sketched on their faces, trap everyone inside the hospital. Slimy creatures, consisting mostly of tentacles, emerge out of people's bodies. Static phone calls from the "Perpetrator" assure Daniel that His "intentions are altruistic".

There's also a bored-but-sassy nurse (the under-appreciated, and here underused, Ellen Wong), the pregnant Maggie (Grace Munro) and a slew of other characters too disposable to name. Oh, and have I mentioned the triangle, which pops up everywhere, an occult key to the "mystery". It all leads to a denouement that is both very silly and grotesque, and contains the following line of dialogue: "I lost my daughter to the abyss and tonight I'm calling her back!"

I do have to mention some positive stuff first. The film is predictably well art-directed, the make-up FX gruesome and believable. It does have its share of genuinely unnerving moments, such as Daniel's first encounter with the figures in white. 1980's are back, folks, and after "It Follows", "Neon Demon" and the mega-popular series

"Stranger Things", here's another horror project supplemented by a synth revivalist score. It works (mostly) to its advantage, complementing the film - but the originality of using Giorgio Moroder / John Carpenter-style music is beginning to wane.

Gillespie and Kowalski struggle with an over-abundance of characters and some major pacing issues, revealing their inexperience behind the camera, while showcasing their imagination and wit. "The Void" is wildly uneven. Not a single character is memorable, but there are memorable one-liners. Scenes with more than three people tend to be shrill and poorly edited, but then they are followed by quieter, subtler and more effective sequences. As the directors try to find their footing, so does the audience, lost in the (literal) murk on-screen.

And damn, this film is dark. Yes, the FX are cool, but most of the scenes involving them are either cut with a buzz saw or dimly lit - so that one would notice the flaws, I assume, or the multiple plot holes, for that matter (e.g. how did the hospital staff - and Daniel, who's supposedly a frequent visitor - never notice the, ahem, "happenings" in the basement?).

The dialogue, while not atrocious, isn't exactly Shakespeare either (example of an exchange: "We're gonna die!" "No, we're not gonna die. You're gonna die!") - but nor does it try to be. Themes of resurrection and mourning are tacked on, but nowhere close to fully-fleshed out, further rendered silly by said dialogue ("I defy God! I spent my life resisting death, but now I understand - I must embrace it.") "The Void" also relies too heavily on exposition, with characters explaining plot points as they unravel. This film would be much more effective if 50% of the dialogue were eliminated. John Carpenter, to whom this film is heavily indebted, knew when to shut the fuck up and let his imagery do the talking.

Obviously inspired by the hip new thing, "Stranger Things", the directors pay homage to "The Thing", "Aliens", "Hellraiser", "The Fly", and add a dash of the more recent "Martyrs" and "Event Horizon". As a result, we get an unholy amalgamation, a midnight stoner B-flick nowhere near as assured as the films to which it aspires, be it the prestige or the cult classics. The intriguing imagery, impressive production design and some moments of sheer terror are all there - but that's to be expected from the film's two craftsmen. Perhaps Jeremy and Steven should stick to their day jobs. Their palpable passion and ambition get lost in the void of lackluster execution.

2.5 out of 5 stars

"The Wilde Wedding" Has Nothing to Do with Oscar

Synopsis: A retired film star's wedding to her fourth husband brings chaos when their families (and her ex-husband) shows up for the festivities.

"Patchy" would be one way to describe Damian Harris's cinematic trajectory; "unpredictable" would also apply. Briefly appearing as Miles in Dick Clement's 1969 crime comedy "Otley", Harris didn't truly resurface until two decades later, when he wrote and directed the sex dramedy "The Rachel Papers". Despite a venerable cast - Jonathan Pryce, James Spader, Michael Gambon, Dexter Fletcher and Jared Harris (Damien's brother) - the film failed to live up to its acerbic source novel's wit and barely made a dent in both the box-office and public consciousness.

That didn't stop Harris from somehow snagging the then-hot Goldie Hawn for the lead of schlock-fest "Deceived" in 1991, followed by the even-schlockier Ellen Barkin bomb "Bad Company" four years later. Things seemed dire for Harris, not helped by a short string of forgettable TV credits and the awful 2000 erotic thriller "Mercy" - also starring Barkin - which put an end to his lustrous career for eight years.

Then came child abuse drama "Gardens of the Night" - boasting a restrained John Malkovich and a surprisingly terrific turn from Tom Arnold - whose earnestness and reliance on cheap tactics outweighed its genuine ambition. Now, after another decade of radio silence, Harris attempts a comeback with "The Wilde Wedding", a lukewarm romantic comedy that reunites the writer/director with Malkovich, and adds Glenn Close, Patrick Stewart, Minnie Driver and Noah Emmerich to the head-scratching roster of top-notch actors with whom Harris has worked.

The ingredients of a mature, May-December / December-December rom-com are there. "The Wilde Wedding" contains memorable lines of dialogue, some real chemistry courtesy of its formidable cast, and a sustained melancholy tone, a palpable sense of longing one experiences in their twilight years. Yet it also cannot escape its Lifetime roots, missteps and clichés pulling it back from… if not greatness, then at least adequacy.

From the get-go, if one manages to overlook the whole "family gets together for special occasion" chestnut, the film's framing device - daughter Mackenzie (Grace Van Patten) narrating a wedding video - works against it, infusing the otherwise quite mature film with a juvenile tone. Mackenzie has a crush on her cousin Dylan (Tim Boardman) and asks every member of the family what true love means to them. Saccharine, cheesy and generally distasteful, this plot-line clashes with the much more sophisticated - if, again, "patchy" (ugh, all that family singing, pass me the puke bag) - sequences involving the three leads. Perhaps if it were utilized more consistently, it may have had a stronger effect, but Harris starts and ends his film with Mackenzie's video, while just sort of brushing upon it in-between.

Eve (Close) is a film star, about to marry famous writer Harold (Stewart - with hair!) after stealing the spotlight from her ex-husband and actor Laurence (Malkovich) years ago. By turns sophisticated and saucy, Eve greets both gentlemen at her abode with grace and humor, their rapport knowingly sharp. Laurence in particular is quite the character: an erudite eccentric, a cynic and a wine connoisseur, prone to extended, very Malkovichian monologues. "I, for one, would like to commend Eve on her optimism and her perseverance and, of course, her courage in taking this plunge yet again," he toasts drily during the wedding rehearsal. "The sofa looks like Gorbachev's forehead," he comments at the wine stain he had inflicted. There's real chemistry between him and Eve, especially in the few scenes where they let go and embrace the good old days in bouts of sweet-tinged nostalgia.

Wily and philosophical, Harold is also somewhat of a rabble-rouser and serves as a great - if somewhat underdeveloped - counterpoint to Eve and Laurence. "Our time is nearly done," he muses. "Sometimes I wonder if we should really be saying no to anything before we face the long night." At another point, he exclaims to Eve, "How can you leave me to languish on this moonlit night, alone in my bed?" If Harris made a film about those three, it may have been a fine theatrical piece.

Trouble is, the film has about a dozen plot lines, most inconsequential, like Mackenzie's crush / quest to find the meaning of true love. More and more characters and their little "intrigues" snowball as they arrive for the wedding, until an incident involving a misplaced box of hallucinogenic mushrooms by the rebel, motorcycle-riding playboy son Ethan (Peter Facinelli) changes everything. How inventive, to use drugs as the pivotal means to existential understanding. It's like "Crystal Fairy & the Magical Cactus" had awkward sex with "Mother's Day".

Characters hook up, Malkovich trips out, and Stewart, after his Poo Emoji appearance in the dreadful "The Emoji Movie" this year, shows up in another sequence not quite befitting of an actor of his age and eminence. Minnie Driver has her moments as the chain-smoking, meditating mother Priscilla, a self-proclaimed "rock goddess" who sings covers at every occasion. All this crisscrossing between storylines and tones allows for little room to breathe though. It's as if Harris were testing himself, to see how many characters and plots he can he stuff into one 90-minute film.

Most of the dialogue is neither terrible nor terribly memorable - and that applies to most aspects of this film: music, lighting, its cinematic techniques and ideas about, well, love. The momentum never gets going, the film swirling around those white privileged people and their "problems" until it just ends, never getting too anything remotely revelatory. With "The Wilde Wedding", Damian Harris stays true to his "patchy" and "unpredictable" status - perhaps he could replace those adjectives with "consistent" and "wise"... you know, when he makes another film in five-to-ten years.

2.5 out of 5 stars

"Zoology" Tries to Spin a Mighty Tail but Ends Up Shriveled

Synopsis: *Middle-aged zoo worker Natasha still lives with her mother in a small coastal town. She is stuck and it seems that life has no surprises for her - until one day she grows a tail and turns her life around.*

Ivan I. Tverdovskiy's "Zoology" promises a Lynchian dissection of humanity, a world seen through a Cronenbergian body-horror lens, where matters of flesh and soul are one of the same. After all, it deals with an inexplicable mutation that leads to a major character transformation. Alas, the director keeps it low-key - as was clearly his intention. There are no spilling guts or visceral moments of terror and/or poignancy, no embellishments. "Zoology" tells it like it is, and as a result falls flat on its tail.

Lonely recluse Natasha (Natalya Pavlenkova) lives with her mom in a small apartment somewhere in coastal Russia. She is soft-spoken and shy - and hence the object of ridicule from her coworkers at the zoo, who play pranks on her, like filling up her cabinet drawers with live rats. One day Natasha faints at work. Consequently, she starts feeling weak and experiencing lower back pains. When a fleshy tail finally sprouts out of her butt, Natasha goes through countless inconclusive X-Rays and tests.

At the same time, she falls for a local, dashing young doctor, Peter (Dmitriy Groshev). Along with her tail sprouts a gradually unveiling sexuality, a discovery of self. Natasha dyes and cuts her hair, trims her skirts, goes sledding and clubbing with Peter, and makes out with him in public. Only her tail accidentally pops out at the club, freaking everyone out - except Peter that is, whose main object of affection may very well be the tail and not the person to whom it's attached.

Since the appearance of the extra body part, Natasha also seems to have formed a relationship with animals, touching hands with monkeys and whispering sweet nothings to the wild cats at the zoo. Deemed demonic, she's not allowed in church. Her ultimate violent action, which comes at the end, although drastic, can be foreseen a mile away.

The film, while sometimes charming and innovative, as a whole is as unostentatious as its protagonist, a fleeting experience whose imagery and themes remain blank, as flat as the ocean in its grey frames. I happen to speak Russian fluently and while some of the dialogue is natural, other bits seem needlessly improvised, in need of a good polish (which the U.S. subtitles, weirdly, do quite well). "Zoology"'s production values sometimes reveal themselves in garishly lit scenes or odd framing and lighting. There are also some inexplicable creative choices, of which I'll name one: why is Natasha's boss at the zoo so freakin' cruel? She makes all of the Horrible Bosses seem like Gandhi in comparison.

"Zoology" shows that a blossoming comes from within. It's a story of alienation and our lack of acceptance - folks either treat Natasha as a monster or as a sexual curiosity. It contains a subdued central performance that verges on impassive. It's basically a Slavic "Slice" or "Raw" - except not as compelling as either.

2.5 out of 5 stars

2-STAR REVIEWS

"A Boy Called Po" Says Nothing New and Moves So Slow

Synopsis: *When David Wilson's young wife falls victim to cancer, he is left a single working dad with the sole responsibility of caring for his sixth grade son with autism.*

It's difficult to criticize a film with intentions as earnest as those of John Asher's palpably are in "A Boy Called Po." Like its protagonist, Asher is the father of an autistic boy, and he gets all the details seemingly right - the child sporadically running away from their parent, isolating themselves in imaginary worlds, being highly sensitive and overall challenging - but while those intermittent scenes may ring somewhat true, the rest of the film doesn't. For anyone who has ever seen a "disease-of-the-week" TV drama, it's a predictable bore to endure, altruistic intentions be damned.

Chalk it up to cheap, sappy, manipulative tactics Asher employs to string the audience along. You've seen it all before, and done better. Five months after David's (Christopher Gorham) wife passes away, he and his autistic son Patrick, a.k.a. Po (Julian Feder), are deeply immersed in grief, Po drawing rainbows on the wall with ketchup and mustard. At school, bullies punch Po, stuff him into lockers and call him Spaceman. Consequently, he "isolates himself more and more", drifting into imaginary fantasy worlds. The ethereal Amelia (Caitlin Carmichael) becomes Po's first "real" friend, with whom he escapes into a magical secret garden.

In the meantime, David faces dire financial straits, having spent most of his money on his dying wife's medical bills. The school principal insists on special education. When a rep from the Child Protective Services, Ben (Brian George), advises David to submit Po to a Special Care facility, the torn father faces a difficult choice: listen to Ben or keep fighting for his son, possibly allowing the boy to "drift away" completely. Of course, there's Amy (Kaitlin Doubleday), a beautiful blonde teacher, who comes into their lives to infuse the story with some romantic sparkles.

If it all sounds morbid and somewhat uninvolving, it's because it so deeply is. With no room for levity, scenes unravel at a snail's pace, with their outcomes seen a mile away. Here's an example: David flies planes with Po, Po gets hurt, Child Services dude Ben arrives at the scene promptly and goes off on a prolonged spiel about how good he is at his job - which, much like the rest of this film's dialogue, just sits there admiring itself without moving the story forward.

If "A Boy Called Po" does achieve something quite remarkable, it manages to check almost every cliché in the film book. Derivative funereal opening? Check. Hazy flashbacks to dead wife? Check. Exasperated father yelling at son to shut up, then feeling sorry right after? Check. Kind traffic cop tearing up the ticket after seeing the autistic kid? Check. A "funny" bodily humor sequence? Check (here, it involves burping). Burt Bacharach's twinkling piano music, which sounds like it was composed as a schizoid Lifetime lullaby, grates like the moldiest cheese. As for the "Rainman" "twist" at the end, my jaw literally dropped open - it's so casually thrown it at the last minute, it's almost impressive in its audacity, but remains utterly ridiculous and nonsensical.

"If I was you, I'd keep my retarded kid on a leash," the security guard, who was strangely compassionate up until this point, advises. "That way, he wouldn't get away from you." He receives a well-deserved punch, although whether it's for being offensive or for not using the more proper subjunctive mood when speaking, remains to be seen. Screenwriter Colin Goldman is, after all, famous for scribbling segments of "Mickey's Twice Upon a Christmas", so let's not question his literacy.

One redeeming factor of Asher's film is Julian Feder's titular performance. He really quite excels as the mac-and-cheese loving Po, a compassionate, sincere and lost child. Too bad the imaginary worlds to which he escapes are populated by cheaply rendered pirates, cowboys, knights and astronauts. The kid's intentions, unlike the director's, actually manifested themselves in an effective performance, one that belongs in a better film than Asher's.

2 out of 5 stars

"Aimy in a Cage" Aims for Hallucinatory but Winds Up Rabid

Synopsis: A creative teenage girl is placed into a mind-altering procedure to civilize her, while news of a virus epidemic spreads throughout the world.

Once in a while, a film comes along that is so purely insane, both structurally and visually, it defies description. Some such films succeed, others fail miserably - the endeavor to give conventional film structure the finger and venture into the unknown is a brave one. While one may certainly applaud Hooroo Jackson's ballsy first foray into filmmaking (an adaptation of his own graphic novel "Aimy Micry") for thinking outside the box, "Aimy in a Cage" fails to live up to its grandiose ambitions.

Imagine the rapid-flow, demented editing of Oliver Stone's "Natural Born Killers". Now throw in the ballistic, ultra-close-up, heightened performances of Terry Gilliam's "Fear and Loathing in Las Vegas." Mix in a dash of Wed Anderson camera pans, quirky musical cues, chapter title cards and production design. Set the entire film in one apartment. Boom - you get "Aimy in a Cage". Yes, it sounds almost intriguingly crazy, and I'd say see it for yourself to believe it, but watching Jackson combining those three auteurs' most extreme elements is like subjecting yourself to over an hour of eye-scorching, eardrum-drilling nonsense. Occasional inspired moments only reinforce the theory of how much better the film would have been, had one of the aforementioned directors taken the reigns.

The first segment introduces us to Aimy's demented world, set in an apartment decorated by crackheads and Cirque Du Soleil performers. Aimy (Allisyn Ashley Arm) argues with her Grandma Micry (Academy Award Nominee Terry Moore, in late-Vincent Price (read: "balls-out nuts, made me super uncomfortable") mode) about "touching grandma's possessions" - specifically, a broken wooden doll. Aimy's brother, Steve (Michael William Hunter), can't imbue any sense into Amy either - she can't spend her whole life, holed up in that room, making useless art!

Things get progressively crazier from here. Crispin Glover pops up, wearing a top hat, as Claude Bohringer, a gentleman hell-bent on getting Grandma Micry's fortune. At night, Aimy sees a ship captain (??) arrive and accuse her of having, I'm paraphrasing, "mind problems of astounding proportions". Her father, Gruzzlebird (Theodore Bouloukos), extra-protective of Grandma Micry, decides to give Aimy an operation, to bring her back to the real world.

Despite Aimy's crazed resistance, they proceed with the surgery - and next thing she knows, Aimy is being spoon-fed nasty porridge by Caroline (Paz de la

Huerta, whose exact role I'm still trying to figure out). Aimy's wearing a giant helmet, her brain fried, her ambition eradicated…. but, um, not really, as she keeps ranting about being a snake charmer and dancing and jumping on tables, until the family ties her up on a chair. At this point, the film becomes a progressively darker, torture-porn, psychedelic retread of Yorgos Lanthimos' "Dogtooth", with lots of shrill screaming… and exactly one memorable line: "Even a rodent gets a wheel".

As if that were not enough lunacy, a TV anchorman informs of a zombie-like "Apollo virus" outbreak in the city, making folks "confront social Darwinism at its finest" - and the characters are quarantined inside the apartment. The two storylines - the apocalypse outside, and Aimy's personal doom - never quite gel, even when the former literally infiltrates the latter at the end, Hazmat suits and all.

The main issue with Jackson's film is that there is no distinction between Aimy's world and the real one - we never get that she's talented and crazy, while her family is sensible and boring. They're all equally unhinged. Is the tale told from her eyes? Is this film a throwback to late-1960s - early-1970s psychedelic fare? Does all of this take place inside a music box? (Frequent clues, such as the apartment's boxy structure, cutesy musical cues and Aimy's doll-like dancing, imply that's the case.)

On any account, Hooroo Jackson's film fails to elicit much more than a pounding headache. Add brain-scathing interludes (quick-cuts of random paintings), slapdash editing and an ultra-high-pitched tone, and the film's short running time (barely over an hour) begins to feel like an eternity in bad-movie hell. I'm glad I watched "Aimy in a Cage" on my computer - the experience of seeing it in a theater would have been borderline unbearable.

I haven't read the graphic novel, but I assume what worked on page just doesn't translate to the screen here, at least not in the hands of the person who wrote it. The madness is not inspired like the best of Jodorowsky or Gilliam, and quickly gets tiresome and repetitive. The bad acting, especially from the shrill lead, and poor production values certainly don't help matters.

Unless, of course, I were to take a powerful blend of mind-altering substances. Perhaps then Daphne Quin Wu's intermittently interesting camera movements, and Chloe Barcelou's insanely trippy production design would have complemented the nonsense, and perhaps even some of the nonsense would make sense.

Like, say, I'd see how the whole dreamlike narrative is actually an allegory, a universal story of living up to your artistic aspirations, not letting them be suppressed by familial - or societal - expectations. It could also be a parable about coming out of the closet - be it a closet of suppressed ambition or homosexuality, whatever. Or maybe it's a statement on the collapse of the nuclear family, with Hazmat suits at the end representing the new era, an ever-shifting generational leap.

I'd try it out, but something tells me there are better films out there - say, Roy Andersson's "A Pigeon Sat on a Branch Reflecting on Existence" - that may be much more fulfilling and memorable.

2 out of 5 stars

"Alleycats" (Premium) Rushes to the Finish Line

Synopsis: *When bike courier Chris witnesses what looks like a murder, his first instinct is to cut and run. But when his curiosity draws him back in, he's soon embroiled in a world of corruption, political power, and illegal bike racing.*

In 2012, David Koepp directed the Joseph Gordon-Levitt starrer "Premium Rush", a high-concept film whose premise could be summarized in four words: "bike messenger vs. cop". While entertaining, it rushed out of your mind as swiftly as its hero cyclist dropped off packages. It was simple and effective entertainment, one that was meant to be ephemeral. Director Ian Bonhôte delivers a cheapo British version of "PR", but needlessly overcomplicates the plot, infusing it with a wildly hipster mentality, a political subplot and illegal bike racing. As a result, we get a weird, half-baked concoction that doesn't provide an incisive look into the dark world of rebel cyclists, or work as a thriller, or political commentary for that matter.

The film gets right down to business. While delivering a package, Chris (Josh Whitehouse), a struggling bike courier with a GoPro on his helmet, stumbles upon Yates (John Hannah, hamming it up), a Member of Parliament, leaning over a corpse. The GoPro conveniently serves two purposes: it records the alleged murder and provides us with shaky POV shots, a staple that's been stapled to death. Several days later, a newspaper article reveals that the body belonged to the MP's intern. Chris's sister Danni (Eleanor Tomlinson) comes back into his life - and we're promptly introduced to their gang of Alleycats, a renegade group of illegal bike racers who hang out in clubs that play hard-pounding drum'n'bass, and sprays graffiti and tattoos like there's no tomorrow. They party and bond and race illegally. "The one rule is that there are no rules," one character proclaims. It's all so forcefully badass, all middle fingers, anarchy and punk rock, as seen through the eyes of a misfit angsty teen. So far, so fast, so furious - with the Hollywood franchise's glossy sheen stripped off and shredded, then reassembled by a group of amateurs.

Anyway, Chris gets run over by a car, the hit ordered by - you guessed it - Mr. Yates. Distraught, Danni and her gang give him a ceremonial burial - complete with a bike studded with photos of Chris, and buckets of black eye shadow. Dannie decides to investigate, with the help of the dead intern's father, George (John Lynch), who's all disheveled, stammering, "Yates, that fucking bastard has something to do with it, I know it… I saw some emails…" Well, of course you did. And so, about 48 minutes into this 100-minute feature, the plot kicks into high gear (clever, I know), as Danni and George's trail leads them into a dark world of corruption, and a finale that involves a grisly murder, a sex scandal, unexpected betrayal and a masked (!) bike race. It's all boring as fuck.

Aside from the fact that "Alleycats" marks the curious reunion of John Hannah and John Lynch, who shared the screen 18 years ago in the romcom "Sliding Doors" (and don't actually share it here, come to think of it), and a few mildly diverting scenes here and there, Bonhôte's film is a disaster. It's cheaply and crudely shot. It's horridly scored, as if the world's worst DJ picked the track list - save for one song choice, which happens to supplement the best sequence in the film, involving Danni following someone in the underground station. The gang painfully overacts, trying to "out-cool" and/or "out-hipster" each other. I instantly disliked the characters, all of whom are underdeveloped twits. "It's just a hit and run," Danni speaks bitterly of the police's negligence. "Another stupid courier." This is a real issue, folks! Pay attention please.

Eleanor Tomlinson, whose stunning big eyes and porcelain complexion certainly captivate, lacks any semblance of depth underneath the beauty. A romantic subplot (because this film doesn't have enough going on) between Danni and Jake (Sam Keeley), the one member of the Alleycats who helps her, is uninvolving and utterly lacking in chemistry. Oh, and there's a French character called… French. This is as inventive as the film gets.

"Alleycats" should have taken some cues from its Hollywood big brother and stuck to simplicity. Aimed at a very narrow target demographic who are too busy changing gears, this dud pedals away, but never gains momentum. Go rent a Cannondale instead.

2 out of 5 stars

Disney's Live-Action Remake of "Beauty & The Beast" Doesn't Hold a Lumière to the Original Animated Classic

Synopsis: *An adaptation of the Disney fairy tale about a monstrous-looking prince and a young woman who fall in love.*

Sigh.

Do I really need to go over the plot? If Bill Condon's "Beauty and the Beast" diverted from the well-known fairy tale at least a little bit, it may be worth the time. As it resolutely sticks to the original - only adding a few unnecessary tidbits to make it seem like an "update" - reading the synopsis again should do the trick: "A monstrous-looking prince and a young woman fall in love." Neat, right?

What it does is accentuate the story's multiple nonsensical aspects: Why do all the characters speak in different accents, if the events take place in France? Why would Belle attempt a complex escape from the Beast through a window, when nothing is really preventing her from walking out the door a few moments later? Why is her first escape attempt thwarted by wolves, while when the Beast finally lets her go, she gallops away with no issues? What's up with her father stumbling upon the Beast's castle, then being unable to find it, then Gaston finding it with the use of a mirror as a GPS device; the convenience of the castle's geographical location fluctuates, depending on who's traveling to or from it. Also: who lights the Beast's candles? If you say "magic" is the answer to all those questions, I'll have Cadenza shoot you with a piano key.

The film's main theme is questionable, too. Let's look at the Beast's trajectory. At the start, he is a handsome, pompous, condescending and self-absorbed rich bastard. It takes the worst torture ever to be inflicted upon a human - being turned in a gnarly werewolf - to make him abscond into isolation, delve into literature and discover humanity (it's either that or suicide, I'd assume). And then Belle is rewarded by having him turn back into the handsome jock that he was - and the film trails off with a "happily ever after". My guess is, a few months later, Beast will have a few "Belles" on the side - you know once the shock wears off and all. So much for the whole "beauty is sound within" thing.

The key to Gary Trousdale and Kirk Wise's animated classic was its simplicity and brevity. This is a very straightforward tale of acceptance, of not judging a book by its cover. The Hollywood remake tacks on an extra 40 minutes to the original's 80-minute running length, packing it with fillers, such as redundant characters, a needless detour that deals with Belle's mother's death, and even more needless musical numbers. The Beast himself breaks into a morose song at one point; Dan Stevens may be a talented actor, but his nails-on-a-chalkboard crooning proves he should stick to his day job. It's as if the filmmakers realized they couldn't improve on the original so they just added padding, hoping audiences will see it as "fleshing out" the story.

After her stint as Hermione on the Harry Potter series, Emma Watson steadily rose to fame as the next "it" actress, for no discernible reason - unless one considers her roles in "The Bling Ring", "This Is the End" and "Noah" as revelatory. Finally getting the chance to step into the shoes of an iconic character, little Watson freezes up, emoting little beyond what's on the surface. She never brings Belle to life, not for a moment making one believe she is a strong-willed Disney princess, something Auli'i Carvalho pulled off with aplomb in the recent "Moana" - by just using her voice, mind you! - or, say, Amy Adams did with a healthy dose of self-awareness and wit in "Enchanted".

What's even worse, Belle's relationship with the pile of digital goo that is the Beast doesn't come close to emulating the epic romantic swoop of the 1991 classic. Despite Dan Stevens' best efforts, he gets utterly lost underneath the pixels (watch him in the astonishing FX show "Legion" instead). When it came to THAT ballroom dancing scene, all I could think about was Watson in the embrace of a green-suited Stevens, a large team of computer nerds making sure his digital hair coils around her fingertips just so.

Josh Gad, the voice of Olaf in "Frozen", is better off behind the camera, once again coming off as a low-rate Jack Black. He mugs it up as LeFou, whose homosexuality apparently wasn't obvious enough in the original film and needed to be amped up, Hollywood-style, for 2017. Gad's flamboyant approach to the role sparked controversy in some right-wing states for the wrong reason - if there's anything to be offended by, it's how poorly he represents homosexuals, his character a starry-eyed fool, a back-stabber lacking intelligence, individuality and self-awareness.

The object of LeFou's utterly unjustified affection, Gaston, is played by Luke Evans, who annunciates each evil sentence with so much evil, he is evil incarnate. I love Emma Thompson, but she doesn't quite nail the gargantuan task of honoring Angela Lansbury's Mrs. Potts, whose performance of the titular number was so memorable. The new iteration? Emma's vocal chords just aren't there, I'm afraid. The two actors who come out unscathed are the great Ian McKellen, infusing the curmudgeon Cogsworth with much charm, and Kevin Kline, who manages to somehow work his magic and, in the few scenes he's in, lend Maurice some real gravitas.

The production design is predictably incredible, although again, heavily relying on obvious CGI to move the story along. The colors are vibrant, the film is chockfull of diversity - both racial, sexual, bestial, you name it - and everything is polished to a T, as we've come to expect from films, whose budgets could bankroll a small African country for decades. A "strong feminist role-model", Belle is told by Gaston that "the only children [she] should be concerned with are [her] own", causing a reverberating gasp in the theater. The bigwigs made sure all the boxes were ticked and a "perfect" confection was presented to the viewer, designed to illicit such reactions.

However, it's the imperfections that sometimes accentuate the beauty, and here it/she gets lost in all the superficial gloss. The film doesn't strive to shock, awe or inspire with a never-before-seen sequence, shot or effect - something totally doable in a reportedly $160 million production. The press screening I attended was continuously filled with annoying applause (literally at the end of each grand statement or musical number!), as if the audience were celebrating how well the new one pays tribute to the original, instead of being silently mesmerized by the originality of the approach, like, say, "The Jungle Book" audiences were. While I oppose the idea of remakes in general, at least Favreau put an interesting spin on the proceedings, paying homage to both the book and the Disney classic - oh, and it had BILL MURRAY as BALOO.

"Snow White and the Huntsman", "Maleficent", "Cinderella", "The Jungle Book" (which I actually liked - read my review here - but I repeat, that was John Favreau at the helm), now this, and we have "The Little Mermaid" and "The Lion King" coming up. One could argue that the reasoning behind remaking all those animated classics into mega-budget, live-action fare is to introduce them to a new generation, remind them that those stories are timeless and important. I'd argue: those remakes proved highly successful, and the hacks' wallets started buzzin', *"more! more!"*. I'd argue: there's no real reason behind remaking "Beauty and the Beast", pretty much shot-by-shot, except to cash in on a well-known property's success. I'd argue: let those kids watch the originals, for chrissakes. They are readily available on Blu-ray at the Amazon website near you.

2 out of 5 stars

"Black Panther" isn't Quite as Revolutionary as the Movement after Which It's Named

Synopsis: *T'Challa, after the death of his father, the King of Wakanda, returns home to the isolated, technologically advanced African nation to succeed to the throne and take his rightful place as king.*

What are DC/Marvel films, exactly? Are they reflections of our tumultuous times, the superheroes our modern gods, embodying our hopes and dreams of a united civilization? Are they parables on humanity's continuous war with itself? What genre are they, exactly? While, say, "Iron Man" or (Christopher Nolan's) "Batman" lean towards science fiction and thriller territory, "Deadpool" and "Guardians of the Galaxy" could be considered comedies, and the campy "Thor" or "Wonder Woman" are more like fantasies, taking place in different realms and dimensions. Underneath all those glossy veneers, it all boils down to a simple three-act structure: 1) hero/villain/McGuffin (re)introduction; 2) obstacles faced to get to the Ultimate Showdown; 3) the Ultimate Showdown.

Both studios desperately and unsuccessfully try to create tangible cinematic universes with intertwined storylines, where all the characters connect - DC falling behind recently with their apocalyptic misstep, "Justice League". As the films get more bloated, they attempt to incorporate traces of wit and character development, by way of hiring visionary independent directors and handing them budgets 50 times the size of their previous feature, with the hope that their auteur brilliance will shine through. They admirably try to incorporate zeitgeist themes like those of political unrest ("Captain America; Civil War"), feminism ("Wonder Woman"), 1980's nostalgia ("The Amazing Spider-Man") and now, with "Black Panther", racial equality. (They seem to only manage one or two at a time though.) Marvel hired Ryan Coogler, the young black filmmaker behind indie darling "Fruitvale Station" and the small (by Hollywood standards) Rocky follow-up "Creed", to direct and co-write this multi-billion Marvel enterprise.

Kudos to Coogler for at least including a semblance of an original story, pedestrian as it may be, and not making the film JUST about social injustice, or what it's like being transgender, or the throes of French-Polynesians, etc. T'Challa (an earnest but (or hence) forgettable Chadwick Boseman) succeeds his father as King of Wakanda, an Atlantis-like nation hidden from view in Africa by some sort of a shield thing and run on ultra-special Unobtanium/Adamantium-like metal/energy thing, the name of which I forget and is frankly irrelevant. What's relevant is that Wakanda wants it all to itself, while the magical metal/energy thing could potentially solve all the third-world problems. In comes Erik Killmonger (Coogler mainstay Michael B. Jordan, beefed up, making for a slightly more compelling villain than the standard norm). He claims that he's the true successor to the throne, his arguably commendable goal being to help the prejudiced stand up against their oppressors with the help of the UnobtAmantium.

"Black Panther" has superheroes wearing cool costumes, pulling nifty digital stunts. It's got commendable themes of prejudice and injustice, addressed with a blunt-edged Mjollnir-like hammer. It's got action - but more interspersed, counting on its dramatic scenes to be as breathtaking as those of panther claws bloodlessly slicing flesh. (Bravo, Marvel, you've achieved the drama/action balance - only "bland" would be a more accurate word to define it than "breathtaking"; the pixelated thrill-bits are as dull as the dialogue exchanges.) There wasn't a single moment I wasn't expecting, a single line that made me well up with emotion or want to get up and cheer, a single adrenalin-pumping instant that resonated. To compare, I recently watched S. Craig Zahler's "Brawl in Cell Block 99". Featuring a searing Vince Vaughn performance and made for a millionth of "Black Panther"'s budget, the film is 100 times more entertaining, visceral, socially conscious and memorable.

So what are Marvel films, exactly? They are repetitive cash cows, advertising machines, genre-less reflections of our collective consciousness, simplified to trendy themes, a few bright moments courtesy of their indie directors, increasingly slick (and increasingly appalling) special effects and the same goddamn narrative structure, over and over again. At least "Guardians of the Galaxy, "Deadpool" and the recent "Thor: Ragnarok" acknowledge their own goofiness. The more overly serious and impassioned those films get - again, with the exception of Nolan's trilogy - the more ridiculous they tend to seem.

It's great that DC/Marvel films are now socially-conscious and all-inclusive. I appreciated that about "Black Panther", I really did. Yet I had a hard time sitting through the same trite, "relevant" good vs. evil storyline, the same quips, the same campy visuals and solemn speechifying, the same beats, the same final battle - and the same freakin' Stan Lee cameo. All power to the people, sure - just as long as those people aren't cash-grabbing studio execs, capitalizing on trends.

2 out of 5 stars

"Blackbird" Awkwardly Blends Cheesy Musical Numbers, Repressed Homosexuality… and Jesus

Synopsis: *A young singer struggles with his sexuality and the treatment of others while coming of age in a small Southern Baptist community.*

At first glance, director Patrik-Ian Polk's tale of Randy, a closeted gay black kid living in a religious community, is a commendable, valiant and timely endeavor. Bloodcurdling prejudice still reigns in many parts of America, and light needs to be shed on those injustices. Unfortunately, upon closer scrutiny, the film - an adaptation of Larry Duplechan's 1986 book - reveals itself to be off-putting and overstuffed; perhaps they stuck too close to the rhetoric and many plot points of a novel written 30 years ago, which was well-meaning but now feels somewhat outdated.

The very first sequence throws you off-balance, introducing Randy (newcomer Julian Walker) singing at a church choir. His eyes meet Todd's (Torrey Lamar), chemistry sparks, and they make out, causing choir members to gasp and faint. It's all relatively amusing and promising, but then the tone swiftly shifts to somber, as Randy awakens from his wet dream and prays to the Lord to forgive him for his sins.

This constant shifting of tones remains prevalent throughout the film. And how could it not? The filmmakers, instead of focusing on this kid's intimate plight, tackle an incredible variety of themes and plot points. It's about (get ready for this) a boy who is gay *and* in love with his friend's boyfriend, *and* sings in a choir, *and* stars in a local (hysterically cheesy) film production, *and* works on an all-male adaptation of "Romeo and Juliet", *and* meets a filmmaking hunk; (deep breath) his sister is missing, with an ongoing investigation functioning as a "minor" subplot; Randy has an estranged father (Isaiah Washington), while his mother (Mo'Nique) is a borderline-crazy religious fanatic; Randy's friend is pregnant, which causes a furor in the community; and he has premonitions, some of them involving dead people… Plus, there are nods to Shakespeare, John Cassavetes (which, within the film's context, are borderline sacrilegious - it's like the filmmakers are letting us know they're aware of Cassavetes, but have learned nothing from seeing his films), and there are even semen sequences straight out of a Farrelly brothers film.

Most of the young cast - with a few exceptions, including the lead - give amateurish performances, but the overwritten, obvious script, by Polk and his co-writer Rikki Beadle Blair (both worked on the short-lived Logo show "Noah's Arc"), doesn't make the job any easier for them - *you* try saying the following lines and make them sound plausible: Randy: "I wake up and I'm soaked in… in…" His friend: "Say it!" Randy: "Sin!" Or how about this insightful outburst: "My virginity is nothing but a curse!" The following line summarizes the film's bogus, misguided solemnity, as well as, I believe, its main point: "What's wrong with the occasional dream?"

"Dream? Dream about what?" Randy exclaims early on in the film; before he can answer, Todd rides in on a bicycle, shirtless, and starts pouring water on his head in slow-motion. "Blackbird" is full of such jarring, ridiculous moments. Randy's first sexual experience with a young man just happens to be in front of his own, fanatically-religious and grieving mother's house (you can guess where that leads). Todd keeps climbing through Randy's window to chat with him, in obvious nods to the Shakespeare play they're staging (hey, at least you can't fault the filmmakers for having low aspirations!).

Some scenes almost transcend their ludicrousness, such as the "You Suck… But in The Most Attractive Way" song Randy sings to Todd, as he's cuddling with his girlfriend (the rest of the film's many songs sound like they've been written by Mandy Moore). The final sequence, where Todd gives Randy a speech through the window, is so stretched-out and laughable and out-of-context, one wonders what the "F" the filmmakers were thinking.

This precarious mix of campiness, crassness and earnestness makes for an uneasy but strangely-compelling watch. "Blackbird" tries to satisfy a variety of demographics: Bible-Belt folks, contemporary hip teens, Academy Award voters… As a result, it alienates them all. One character says "Jesus is there, in everything we do." Same applies to this film - Jesus is mentioned at least 300 times - but it contains too many F-bombs to appeal to the stringent faith-based audiences, who would also balk at certain sequences, such as one involving a simulated male rape, and another portraying a male threesome (both played for comedic effect).

It's a shame, as the film had potential. Isaiah Washington and Mo'Nique are top-billed, but rarely appear, though in some of the film's best - and painfully short - scenes. Washington atones for his "Grey's Anatomy" debacle with a sequence where he talks about kissing a boy, "tongues and everything" (he also produced "Blackbird", further establishing his gay-friendly cred); Mo'Nique has to utter some terrible, pseudo-Biblical lines, but also has a somewhat-powerful sequence, where she tries to exorcize the homosexuality out of her son. Julian Walker does a commendable job in the lead. Most importantly, the film's heart is in the right place, its powerful messages of religion, tolerance and sexuality well-intentioned but inadequately relayed, diluted by too many head-scratching moments and half-explored themes.

It seems like "Blackbird"'s filmmakers were unsure of which direction to take it; a firmer stance was needed. The film is as at war with itself as its main character. As a result, the soapy mixture, at least in tone and substance, is much more "A Walk to Remember" than "A Woman Under the Influence".

2 out of 5 stars

"Cars 3" Stalls, Drags... and Disturbs in Equal Measures

Synopsis: *Lightning McQueen sets out to prove to a new generation of racers that he's still the best race car in the world.*

Pixar has always dared to anthropomorphize the unlikeliest of heroes: an ant in "A Bug's Life", a rat in "Ratatouille", a cockroach and a robot in "Wall-E", human emotions in "Inside Out"... Not only did those animated features make us feel for something with which we wouldn't normally identify, they made us believe, within the context of those worlds, that a sentient rat could, indeed, become a chef, or that a robot could love.

"Cars", and its consequent three sequels, fails on both accounts. Its mechanical protagonists are rarely endearing, due to their soulless nature (we don't imbue a vehicle with the same affection as we do a living thing, even if it's a cockroach), nor does it make us believe in its universe.

Where does it take place, exactly? Is it on Earth? Must be, right - there's the Roman Colosseum, and Florida's Florida... Then where are all the humans? Is it set in the future, post-apocalypse, after the machines took over, Skynet-style? Wouldn't everything in a world inhabited solely by cars be intuitive for a car to, you know, utilize? After all, it would be impossible - not to mention impractical - for cars to build cathedrals and shopping malls, film theaters and hotels, not to mention the uselessness of have doors or windows... Are the rearview mirrors ears? What function do they serve, since they cars' windshields are essentially their eyes?

The questions don't end there. In Brian Fee's "Cars 3", there's a training sequence involving an actual animal (though we never see it): Cruz Ramirez (voiced by Cristela Alonzo) doesn't want to run over a crab. However, in a different sequence, cows in the film are represented by herd-like tractors. So what's the deal here? Was that a mechanical crab? Was the crab even there? Where are all the humans and animals? Upon further research, I stumbled on <u>this</u> website, which has a deeply disturbing "Cars" theory of its own.

Putting aside the film's creepy world and creepier protagonists, as difficult as it may be, the story itself if as rusty as Mater's (Larry the Cable Guy) exterior. At least the original "Cars" had the saving grace of Paul Newman's wise ol' voice as Doc Hudson bringing gravitas to the proceedings. I must've seen the sequel twice and still have no idea what it was about. The plot of the third one is starting to evaporate as I write this, so I better get to it quick.

Lightning McQueen's (a bland Owen Wilson) streak of success comes to an abrupt end with the emergence of next-gen, aerodynamic, computer-modulated race cars, led by the Bugatti-looking, snarky Jackson Storm (Armie Hammer). After an accident and consequent rehabilitation, Lightning gets back on the proverbial track, with the help of a bureaucratic sponsor, Sterling (Nathan Fillion) and his main trainer, Cristela. It all comes down to a crucial race in Florida, with perfunctory adventures on the way.

So perfunctory were the adventures, even the calmest of kids grew restless at the press screening I attended. Enraptured intermittently by the gorgeous visuals, their attention drifted during the long, painful sequences of characters "flash-backing", moralizing and baring their souls. The film's almost two hours, for NASCAR's sake! For a film about racing, it sure trots a lot.

We've seen it all before: themes of new generations learning from the old, while the old generations come to terms embracing the new ("It's futile to resist change, man," a character proclaims at one point); stale, pseudo-inspirational speeches ("Don't fear failure - be afraid of not having the chance"; "It's my last chance to give you your first chance"), the new characters fail to bring anything new to the table, while the old ones are cardboard, Mater's hillbilly shtick wearing particularly thin. Pixar even relies on pratfalls and lazy stereotypes - this marks the first time I haven't had a single genuine laugh throughout an Pixar film since the infinitely-better "Brave".

My theory is that John Lasseter, who directed the original "Cars", wanted to expand upon the "Toy Story" concept, delve deeper into that world only children inhabit… The difference is, "Toy Story" had humans. The toys had eyes where they belonged. Their universe made sense. "Cars 3" amounts to a colossal miscalculation on Pixar's part, a world devoid of animals, a world of sentient gears that just expects us to accept it. And perhaps you do. But I defy you to accept its lack of depth, insights, heart and propulsive stories, so prevalent in the best of the company's oeuvre. Instead of going to Disney's Vault, this franchise needs to be left rusting in Pixar's junkyard.

2 out of 5 stars

Sitting Through "Decanted" is Like Watching Wine Ferment

Synopsis: *Look inside one of the most intimate wine growing regions in the world, Napa Valley, as we follow the journey of new beginnings and mastering a craft.*

While no wine connoisseur by any means, I appreciate and respect the biblical liquid, not only for the history it represents but also for its artistic qualities: the colors, ranging from crimson to a translucent honeydew; the fragrance, soul-like in its ephemeral nature, delicate and pure, bringing to mind love, passion, sophistication and a plethora of distant, exotic places. Wine could potentially be very cinematic, especially in the hands of a capable and romantic filmmaker. It served as a backdrop for films like Alexander Payne's bittersweet existential comedy "Sideways" and Ridley Scott's by-the-numbers "oh-la-la, we're so French" Hollywood farce (read: flop/fiasco/fuck-up) "A Good Year".

A naked Thomas Haden Church does not get rescued by a heartbroken Paul Giamatti in Nick Kovacic's vino documentary "Decanted", nor does it have a hammy Russell Crowe woo a bashful Marion Cotillard in seemingly endless vineyards. Kovacic doesn't strive to juxtapose winemaking against life's existential issues or draw parallels between the fleeting awe of a wine sip to that of love-at-fist-sight, or infuse another metaphor about how wine gets better with age. It doesn't even compare the winemakers of Napa Valley to those of, say, the French, Argentinian or Italian vineyards. What the doc does do, efficiently and pragmatically, is showcase the craft, step-by-step, in one of the wine meccas of the world. It took me four bottles of Pinot to sit through it.

Get ready for a plethora of aerial shots of Napa Valley, which resembles "a patchwork quilt", as one of the winemakers refers to it lovingly. The beauty of this California region, the "geologic epicenter for wine growing", cannot be argued, and Kovacic portrays it well, courtesy of cinematographer Caleb Stine. Vibrant, juicy purple grapes, shiny bottles, dark-red wine being poured and gushed out of sterile faucets, green pastures and vineyards, of course - all those things are caught in meticulous detail, as we follow the process, from growing to fermenting to drinking, and delve into "price point vs quality level" and "Sulphur content" conversations. Are you on the edge of your seat yet? Skip "Split" (the demented Shyamalan thriller, out in theaters now) and watch "Decanted" for the REAL thrills!

"How can I deconstruct and then reconstruct the perfect wine?" one fervent fan wonders. "It's a beautiful business, because it becomes a part of your life," another remarks. "The great thing about winemaking," one gentleman states, "is that you get to do something different every day." The film could have used a touch of that variety, as it tends to stick to one flavor. The most fascinating tidbit comes from a woman, whose 6-liter bottle of wine sold for half a million dollars.

As someone who doesn't drink much wine, but appreciates its beauty, I'd rather see it be used as a metaphor than be dissected and scrutinized. For a documentary about the thirst-quenching, mythical liquid, it's dry-as-sand. Werner Herzog this ain't (I can see it clearly: [German accent] "The rich soil I tasted made me think of the soil that birthed Jesus, who incidentally claimed to turn water into this blood-like liquid - and I couldn't help but wonder about those isolated people, and whether their blissful, intoxicated isolation is a sign of utopia.") As it stands, it doesn't delve behind the minds of the winemakers, doesn't examine wine's history or impact on other cultures and/or arts, doesn't look into the effects of global warming on the vineyard, neglects the reasons behind wine's allure… It has no momentum, nothing at stake - it simply displays the process, no more, no less - a pleasant, extended screen-shot. Wine fans looking to geek out may rejoice. For me… well, I'd rather glare at the swooning, crooning Crowe and Cotillard all day.

2 out of 5 stars

"Frank the Bastard" Meanders Through Genre Tropes While Claiming to Defy Them

Synopsis: A young woman returns to a small, murky New England community where she grew up, to uncover the mystery behind her mother's untimely death. Some of the locals intend to stop her, and a conspiracy unravels.

At the screening I attended, "Frank the Bastard" was introduced as a "gothic regional noir", which got me both excited and confused, as I had studied, reviewed and made films for years, and yet never heard of such a genre. The lights dimmed, and the film's title wedged onto the screen in a grisly, menacing font, suggesting a dark and intense journey into the human psyche. As the film progressed, my excitement quickly waned. Calling "Frank the Bastard" a "gothic regional noir" is as misleading as calling "Drive" a "non-stop throwback action thriller"; though both films contain references and brief flashes that could be described as such, those are certainly not their genres.

The reason why I brought up "Drive", a much-disputed film, is because I happen to fall under the category of disappointed folks, who expected it to live up to the hype ("award-winner that redefined modern cinema", bla-bla), but instead were met by an overly-rigid slog through a neon-lit, pseudo-1980s non-plot, which, granted, was beautifully shot, but featured characters so boilerplate you almost wondered if it were all a joke, an elaborate prank Nicolas Winding Refn pulled to test our gullibility. "Frank the Bastard", I'm afraid, will not provoke a comparable debate.

There's nothing technically wrong with its production values - it's decently shot, edited and lit. Brad Coley's sophomore effort's heart is in the right place, but his story of a young woman, Claire, who reluctantly responds to the unexplained urges from her shallow best friend and revisits her childhood commune to uncover hidden truths, follows all the well-worn tropes of hundreds of similar films. Tortured protagonist? Check. A "David vs. Goliath" story of a community uprising against evil corporate forces? Check. Clumsy, expository dialogue? Double-check. Tie in a little murder mystery, and you got all the ingredients of the blandest soup at a drive-through deli. The most fundamental issue is that "Frank" lacks a novel hook, which is sadly ironic, considering the film's pre-screening "pitch".

And lord, does it move slow. The somnambulant pacing gets livened up from time to time by touches of relatively interesting themes, such as reliving your past in order to embrace it, but the film never has anything truly profound to say. Clichés abound: in this town, everyone knows everyone, and everyone is incredibly sinister;

there is a bar fight, with racist hicks spewing out slurs; and it all ultimately comes down to the ownership of Claire's farm, as well as a pipeline coming through and polluting the crap out of everyone. There are so many stories of family trees and town histories, told in a monotone by so many characters, the film is both derivative and needlessly complex. The experience is like sifting through an old small-town newspaper. Oh, and William Sadler's sketchy New England accent doesn't help matters much, either.

As for the title character, Frank? What's his role? His schizophrenic so-called protagonist (he's on-screen for all of ten minutes) seems to function as some sort of metaphor, personifying the Christ-like nature for which we should all strive; he's an uncomfortable, under-developed blend of every similar character in film history, from Michael Fassbender's titular "Frank" (coincidence?) to Juliette Lewis's Carla in "The Other Sister". Regardless, Frank obviously - spoiler alert - saves the day, in a jarring, almost-rape sequence that implausibly takes place in a jail-cell. The ending is downright silly, involving improbable coincidences, hallucinogens (!) and an extended fiery flashback.

Some of the supporting players effortlessly steal scenes from the two leads, particularly Chris Sarandon (Academy Award Nominee for "Dog Day Afternoon"), who has way too little screen time, but makes the most use out of it, and the wonderful theater actress Wendy Vanden Heuvel, who, if there is any justice in this world, will be a prominent screen presence in the near future (her grief-stricken Alice is by far the film's highlight). Next to those two pros, Rachel Miner's spaced-out vapidity, which worked to her advantage in Larry Clark's cult classic "Bully", becomes that much more of a detriment, as does Shamika Cotton's amateurish line readings, especially in the few scenes she shares with Sarandon.

"Frank the Bastard" comes off as a low-rent "Erin Brockovich", with Miner instead of Julia Roberts, and Brad Coley instead of Steven Soderbergh; or call it "Promised Land", without Matt Damon or Gus Van Sant. Both of those films were flawed in their own ways, but the filmmakers brought years of experience and truly committed to their "underdog on a crusade" stories. Brad Coley, despite the earnestness and evident effort he displays in "Frank", still has a long way to go.

2 out of 5 stars

"Front Cover" Airbrushes Serious Issues and Lacks Depth

Synopsis: When a gay fashion stylist works with a renowned foreign actor, they both embark on a journey of self-discovery.

While it's highly commendable that more gay-themed films and TV shows are being produced, so far the subject matters have mostly revolved around the fact that the protagonist(s) is/are gay. Yes, "Transparent" delicately and wisely dealt with the repercussions of a patriarch coming face-to-face with being transgender, but it was solely ABOUT that, with some less-memorable sub-plots thrown in. Same with "The Danish Girl", a beautifully-shot but sterile film that examines what it was like to switch gender for an early-20th-Century artist Lili Elbe. Take a look at Laverne Cox's character in Netflix's imminently watchable "Orange is the New Black": a heart-wrenching couple of episodes deal with Sophia's transformation; with that out of the way, the poor girl is saddled with a (literally) murky, basement-level sub-plot. HBO's otherwise-flawed "Looking", centering around a group of gay friends, came closest to depicting everyday life, gay or straight.

It's spawned by Hollywood's love of hammering themes into our heads. Feminism? Instead of providing us with an original film driven by strong, proactive, independent women, we get "Ghostbusters" - "look, women can hunt ghosts too! Take this little slice of stale cake and choke on it!" I dealt with this issue myself, when one of my own scripts - that had a transgender character (gasp!) have a story NOT related to her sexuality or gender - at first piqued the interest of studio execs due to its high concept, and then scared the shit out of them due to its protagonist. It's "either or" - either you focus on the plight of being transgender, or don't include transgender characters at all.

I'm not trying to diminish the importance of those features - people, especially ignorant ones, do need to be aware of the historical, personal and societal implications of being transgender and/or gay. But I just wish that there were more films where being gay - like being black or Korean or a woman or disabled - wasn't the centerpiece of a film, or where a gay character's sole personality wasn't that one trait. There is light at the end of the tunnel: smaller, indie films - like Craig Johnson's "The Skeleton Twins" - have begun to surface, which include colorful characters with depth who just also HAPPEN to be gay. And hey, at least we're past the days of atrocities like "Boat Trip" and "I Now Pronounce You Chuck and Larry".

Unfortunately, Ray Yeung's "Front Cover" is a love story that ends up being a half-assed study of what it means to be gay and Asian in today's America. Why couldn't it JUST be a subtle, tender love story about two young Asian men? My feelings - and mind you, I'm straight and white - is that it would be significantly more memorable, had it just focused on fleshing out its heroes and making their plights original, heartbreaking, new. "Front Cover" does not. The fact that Yeung attempts to deal with a rarely-dealt subject is actually the only thing going for "Front Cover", the film's flimsy plot, paper-thin characters and lack of novelty ultimately rendering it a failure.

Ryan (Jake Choi) is a fashion stylist for an unnamed corporation. A self-proclaimed "not very social person", he's upset he didn't get the Front Cover ("It's because I'm Asian," he says, fully confident that his impeccable looks or immediately-appealing personality had nothing to do with it). Out of touch with his Chinese roots, he meets Ning (James Chen), a famous star flown in from China to replace him as the model, whom he now has to style. It takes about five seconds for Ning to call Ryan out on his lack of cultural awareness - in a Chinese restaurant, no less, where poor Ryan gets served crab and has no idea how to eat it. He also doesn't know how to speak Chinese, play Mahjong (a great game, by the way) or, most importantly, doesn't have a clue about the Chinese fashion style - but all that doesn't get in the way of Love. Ning may be homophobic to start with, but the closet doors fling open fast, he sheds his strict Communist upbringing and embraces Western civilization (with some coitus thrown in for good measure). In a wildly unpredictable twist of events, their relationship becomes public, cultures clash, yet Love prevails.

Any earnest intentions are scrubbed with hilarious scenes, such as Ryan begging Ning to take his underwear off during a shoot, which ends in Ryan scrubbing Ning's feet. "Hey, have you ever tried weed?" Ryan inquires, before the requisite munchies, dancing and... well, you know what they say about pot being the gateway drug to homosexuality. One of the few highlights comes in the "parents visiting" scene: "Chinese [are] like water," the wise, old father states, "takes long time to boil but once hot, takes lifetime to cool down." Profound. But then the scene drags on. And on and on, with a background flute making things that much more... resonant. This wouldn't be a sexy romantic film without the obligatory club scene, Ryan and Ning dancing to some 1990s Love Parade-style electronica, complemented by a sex montage that brings to mind THAT club/sex scene from "The Matrix". Not a good thing. As for the sappy ending, with its messages spelled out like we were in kindergarten eating chalk... let's just say my gag reflex was getting a workout.

In case you didn't catch my sarcasm earlier in the review, Ryan is a total brat. "I'm almost 30," he complains early in the film, "and what do I have to show for it, besides some designer clothes, magazine spreads..." (He goes on to mention a dozen other accomplishments that a vast majority of population would consider "life goals".) Right after agreeing that he knows next to nothing about Chinese culture, Ryan exclaims, "Who does he think he is, Mao Tse-tung?" - as if he has the slightest clue about the founding father of the People's Republic of China. As the love affair blossoms, Jake Choi attempts to infuse his character with some likability, but I'll be frank, the actor is just not up to the task. He lacks charisma and screen presence. James Chen comes off a bit better as Ning, the pompous-but-highly-acute superstar who wants to "represent the New China". His brashness, juxtaposed against the sweetness, works for the most part; he dominates the scenes with Choi, and part of it is surely due to his character: it's much easier to cast an impression as the cocky superstar than the quiet, fragile stylist. He fares worse in the later sequences, where subtlety comes creeping in. Both leads lack outstanding features, quirks or memorable personalities.

The sentimental piano interludes, awkward editing and pace, and by-the-numbers plot don't help matters. "Front Page"'s politics are questionable, its examination of cultural differences shallow and at times misguided and muddled. Yeung's film scores points for having Asian, gay protagonists not SOLELY as a gimmick to appease a still sadly overlooked demographic. Too bad the craft isn't there. Too bad the plot and the characters kinda suck.

2 out of 5 stars

"Gurukulam" Subjects Itself (and Its Viewers) to a Pseudo-Meditative Stupor

Synopsis: *Follow a group of students and their teacher, as they confront fundamental questions about the nature of reality and self-identity at a remote forest ashram in southern India.*

"Gurukulam", the debut directorial feature of husband-and-wife team Neil Dalal and Jillian Elizabeth, comes close to being the cinematic equivalent of watching grass grow. While its intention - to reiterate the importance of finding peace within yourself - is commendable, the documentary struggles to attain an existential mood, or provide any revelatory testimonies. As it stands, "Gurukulam" is a pretty, almost 2-hour-long screensaver.

The "film" (I hesitate to describe this... um, footage as such, for it lacks any sort of narrative) follows a group of nameless, unmemorable students, who study Advaita Vedanta in South India for three months. In the beginning, the titles solemnly announce that "some will stay for three years" (which, coincidentally, was the amount of time it took me to get through this doc). For the first 12 minutes or so, literally nothing happens. The small, woody commune is shown. A teacher gives students grammar lessons. Coconuts are being chopped up. A woman cooks. Another woman in a shawl attends a class. All of this culminates in a nearly 30-second shot of... a door slowly closing. As we hear the students speak about their reasons for escaping to this paradise - from atheists to the deeply religious - a remnant of traction is gained, but the pace remains somnambulant for the rest of the doc's excessive running time.

A few mildly interesting philosophical tidbits pop up periodically, such as Swami Dayananda (the village's guru) proclaiming, "I am reality... The whole thing is me. The subject and object should be included". Those kinds of statements are potentially powerful, but here come off as disjointed and borderline-silly, taken out of the lesson's context. In fact, a lot of it sounds like finger-wagging mumbo-jumbo from a bad Dr. Phil episode. A student with a British accent trumpets his satisfaction with finding this commune, after years of traveling through India in search of spiritual salvation: "Personally, I wouldn't settle for anything less than the universe." (Good for you, man - I'll settle with "galaxy".) He later talks about understanding "the truth of everything".

The whole "you are the universe"/"infinite power" rhetoric is repeated numerous times throughout the film, which liberally throws around grandiose statements, but never backs them up with anything approaching spiritual enlightenment on-screen. At one point, a woman reveals that she's been reading Buddhist texts for a long time, but it wasn't until she arrived here that she fully understood the meaning of it all; "Because it was just reading. I wasn't able to assimilate and understand." The same issue seems to apply to "Gurukulam": we are just watching blankly, with no assimilation or understanding.

There are a few pretty shots, but then again, the location is so magnificent, a 1998 flip-phone would have a difficult time snapping a bad picture. There's no structure, no real protagonist to follow, no story arc or compelling hook... The all-too-brief highlight comes at about the halfway point, when an elephant wonders into the commune... with no consequences. Perhaps it was just a relief to see something actually happen.

"Gurukulam" was clearly aiming for "meditative and quietly observant", but ended up "pointless and disjointed", like sauntering through a large empty field, where you may spot something of passing interest, but ultimately it's a slog to get to the shade. Any film, no matter how artistic/independent or ostentatious/big-budget it is, needs to primarily entertain, whether with its images, sound, performances, action - whatever. Godfrey Reggio's "Koyaanisqatsi" did so marvelously in 1982, spanning the entire world, achieving a transcendent rhythm, akin to a beating heart, its series of stunning images powered by an unforgettable Philip Glass score. Ron Fricke's "Samsara" is a more recent example of a film that relies on sensory overload of music and imagery, as opposed to a clearly defined narrative structure, to portray the fragility, beauty, ugliness and briskness of life.

What will "Gurukulam"'s already-niche audience take away from this project? That it's important to "be one with everything"? Is the goal to attract Westerners to remote and holy parts of the world? It doesn't even entirely convince of its guru's practices' efficiency, especially after a character voices a concern, late in the film, that his parents don't "get" his journey. If he truly achieved an "inner peace", would his mom's disapproval even matter?

I'm all about escaping societal expectations and embracing life to the fullest, and I love Indian culture and what Buddhist teachings represent, but this doc made me want to embrace reality by watching a verbally-dexterous episode of "Veep"... and then, maybe, doing a little yoga.

2 out of 5 stars

"Ismael's Ghosts" Provides Further Proof That Its Director May Be Too Haunted to Tell a Coherent Story

Synopsis: *The story follows a filmmaker whose life is sent into a tailspin by the return of a former lover just as he is about to embark on the shoot of a new film.*

Arnaud Desplechin and I just don't seem to be on the same wavelength. His 2015 coming-of-age drama "My Golden Days" had so much potential, had it stuck to the leads and developed one or two strands properly, instead of veering off in multiple directions. I couldn't keep up with his rambling rhetoric - evident in my own somewhat rambling review - and, although I liked the film, I wished Desplechin would hone in his predilection for self-indulgence in his next features, and just focus.

Judging by "Ismael's Ghost", not only has that not happened, the filmmaker's ventured deeper into showcasing his personal preoccupations, with little thought to clear character development and a disregard for his audience. Clearly literate and passionate, Desplechin has trouble stuffing all of his existential musings, political diatribes and heartfelt tendencies towards melodrama into a coherent narrative. Despite compelling lead performances - which only make you wish the film cohered better - "Ismael's Ghosts" ends up a turgid mess.

Ismael (Mathieu Amalric) is a middle-aged filmmaker, working on his next artsy spy thriller. It involves a secret agent, Ivan (Louis Garrel), being recruited by the Ministry of Foreign Affairs. In real life, Ivan happens to be Ismael's prodigal (read: mythical) diplomat brother, haunting him.

Ismael, who lives with girlfriend Sylvia (Charlotte Gainsbourg) by the seaside, visits the still-grieving father of his long-missing wife, Carlotta (Marion Cotillard). It's been 20 years since she left into nowhere, but Ismael is - you guess it - haunted by the ghost of Carlotta - sometimes literally, in nightmares that make him fall out of bed, screaming. Then Carlotta nonchalantly appears on the beach, claiming to be homeless and wanting to reclaim her husband.

"Sleep with her and I'll kill you," Sylvia threatens when Ismael rushes over to his wife. As he rages and smashes furniture around Carlotta, demanding an explanation for her disappearance, Carlotta provides a long, dreamy one, summed up in her final statement: "I abandoned all of you. You weighed too heavy. Or I weighed too heavy." Apparently, one day she "became light" in India, and even married a man, who died three weeks ago. Emotions flare up. Everything seems to lead to a kinky *ménage à trois* - but then Sylvia leaves Ismael in his chateau by the sea, with the gorgeous wife reincarnated from his past.

Up until this point the film may be melodramatic, but it's eloquently written and focused, building towards some sort of a cataclysmic climax. Then, in an odd twist, Desplechin decides to instead deviate off the path - the focus not so much blurring as switching off entirely - and the film becomes a rambling mess of half-formed ideas and unfinished threads. Carlotta sort of disappears again, to reappear later and haunt her poor father. Ismael runs off his set, leaving his film incomplete, and goes into hiding, while Sylvia elopes to the mountains.

When a producer tries to lure Ismael back, the borderline-mad, delusional director shoots him with a gun. The film becomes a psycho-study of Ismael, with dashes of his (excruciatingly long) cinematic visions and immaterial sociopolitical context thrown in for good measure.

The dialogue is eloquently written, which is to be expected from Desplechin. Especially in the first half, the filmmaker skillfully involves you, despite the sentimental flourishes, which would have perhaps fared better onstage - all this spastic screaming and heightened emotion, *mon Dieu*! But the trio - Amalric, Cotillard and especially Gainsbourg - are highly watchable, the scenery is beautiful, and we succumb to the "Nicholas-Sparks-by-way-of-Jean-Paul-Sartre" narrative.

But then it all becomes too much. "Ismael's Ghosts" switches perspectives - from the protagonist's visualized fictional script, to his hallucinatory visions, to Sylvia's narration, to all the flashbacks - so many times, it becomes tiresome, repetitive and confusing. Artistic flourishes, like the odd intermittent fades within the same scenes and over-saturated flashbacks, add little to enhance or stabilize the story. There are unexpected, strange deviations, such as the long, long rant that Carlotta's father embarks on while boarding a plane and the consequent, even longer, politically-infused speech at a film festival.

"Ismael's Ghosts" tries hard to avoid sentimentality, but Desplechin can't help it, with characters screaming out things like, "A thousand times I thought you were dead!" As if that weren't enough, the film contains a character breaking the fourth wall and directly addressing the audience - oh, and lest I forget, there's an exploding head.

Reign it in, Arnaud. Watching your films is like reading someone's essay, which starts off focused and involving and then becomes scattered with fervent footnotes and digressions. As it stands, "Ismael's Ghosts", despite the star cast and prestige filmmaking team, is bound to become a specter in the filmmaker's ever-growing filmography.

2 out of 5 stars

"LBJ" Sees WH Going OTT

Synopsis: *The story of U.S. President Lyndon Baines Johnson from his young days in West Texas to the White House.*

What happened to Rob Reiner? The once-great director, responsible for a streak of instant classics - "This Is Spinal Tap", "Stand by Me", "The Princess Bride", "When Harry Met Sally…", "Misery", "A Few Good Men" - suddenly popped some sort of pill that twisted his vision and resulted in 1994's "North", the abysmal musical flop infamous for Bruce Willis sporting a pink bunny suit. As the pill's effect took hold, Reiner mustered one more decent feature - the Aaron Sorkin-scripted ode to democracy, "The American President" - before delving deep into bland romcom murk.

The titles speak for themselves: "The Story of Us", "Alex & Emma", "Rumor Has It…", "The Bucket List", and so it goes… As in, "And So It Goes", Reiner's 2014 stab at Nancy Meyers fare - but even the presence of such stalwarts as Michael Douglas and Diane Keaton couldn't alleviate the sour odor of a once-great mind grown stale. Aside from the intermittent amusing acting turn (see: Max Belfort in "The Wolf of Wall Street"), Reiner's career seems to have dwindled into oblivion.

All these romcoms tried hard to recapture the spontaneity and charm of "When Harry Met Sally…", while 2010's "Flipped" and 2015's "Being Charlie" saw the director struggling to revisit the grit and nostalgia of "Stand by Me."

Now here comes "LBJ", Rob Reiner's spiritual successor to "The American President", and another presidential biopic in a cascade of cinematic depictions of historical political figures ("J. Edgar", "Lincoln", "Hyde Park on Hudson", "Jackie", "Churchill", among others). Reiner seems to have rediscovered the pill container that made him trip out in 1994 - and shared them with his cast, who ham up a storm.

The story begins with Lyndon B. Johnson (Woody Harrelson, in heavy prosthetics), accompanied by his right-hand Walter Jenkins (C. Thomas Howell) and wife Lady Bird (Jennifer Jason Leigh), greeting the Kennedys - John, Bobby and Jackie (Jeffrey Donovan, Michael Stahl-David and Kim Allen, respectively) - during their famous arrival at Dallas Love Field (that pink dress!). Johnson, desperate to winch election but "afraid people won't love him", compares the beautiful Kennedys to show horses, while seeing himself as a Texas work stallion; a man of great ideas vs. a man "who can deliver."

After a slew of proceedings, consisting mostly of men scheming / speechifying in darkly lit rooms, LBJ loses the election to Kennedy. In his role as VP, he becomes the liaison between the "progressive" Kennedys and the South, led by sleazy, racist senator Richard Russell (Richard Jenkins). The passing of the Civil Rights bill becomes the running thread through the dragging narrative.

Things do pick up a little at about the halfway point, with yet another all-too-quick depiction of that horrible day at Dealey Plaza. With a sudden shift in character, Johnson becomes a focused hero, fighting for what's right - until, that is, a lengthy afterword reminds us about, you know, his whole stance on the Vietnam War (he was an avid supporter). Guess there are two sides to every coin.

Problem is, neither side is well examined. The film seems to struggle to make itself relevant in light of the current presidency, spending a significant amount of its running time emphasizing Johnson's Southern arrogance and contrasting him against the righteous Kennedys - yet it backs out at the last minute, making him a hero. Reiner also seems to forget to develop three-dimensional supporting characters and, most importantly, a compelling plot.

The director relies so heavily on schmaltz to mask the lack of actual emotion, the feature becomes increasingly difficult to digest. The same sentimental trappings befell "The American President", but that film was at least saved by Sorkin's script and its restrained performances - particularly Annette Benning's, a strong female character who led us through the chauvinist world of the White House. Here, poor Jennifer Jason Leigh is delegated to the loving/supporting wife role. Way to regress, Reiner!

Harrelson is unleashed here, a disrespectful, conniving egomaniac who defecates with the door open. While he's imminently watchable, despite the atrocious make-up, the actor is at the mercy of his confused leader here, trying his best to make his loathable character turn compelling and likable.

Everyone else struggles to catch up with him, Ralph Yarborough / Bill Pullman's reaction shots during the final rousing speech particularly priceless. Unsurprisingly, Richard Jenkins comes off best in a thankless role - he and Harrelson get one memorable - and highly uncomfortable - exchange featuring a black servant.

Despite all the overacting, the film is as dull as a congressional hearing, ticking off all the biopic clichés in the book: archive footage, glamorized lighting and patriotic lectures. That said, the film is handsomely shot by Barry Markowitz. It's not utterly horrible or offensive. It's just... unnecessary. "Power is where power goes," LBJ says in one scene. Rob Reiner's power as a filmmaker seems to have shut down entirely.

2 out of 5 stars

"Les Cowboys" Gallops Its Way into Pure Nonsense

Synopsis: When his daughter goes missing from their prairie town east of France, Alain and his young son, Kid, head out to find her. The journey takes the men to some far-off and unsettling places in what begins to feel like an endless quest.

French screenwriter Thomas Bidegain has quite the resume. After gaining skills with a few shorts, Bidegain achieved notoriety in 2009 with his first feature-length script, "A Prophet". The film won the Grand Prize of the Jury in Cannes and was nominated for an Academy Award for Best Foreign Language Feature. He went on to write the lyrical-but-flawed "Where Do We Go Now", the heart-wrenching "Rust and Bone" with Marion Cotillard, the vastly underrated drama "Our Children", the fashion mogul biopic "Saint Laurent", and the sorrowful "Dheepan", which won the Palme d'Or in Cannes last year. An enviable career, to say the least… So what the hell was he thinking when he decided to direct "Les Cowboys", a messy, pointless thriller with a muddled political message? Put it this way - while Bidegain may be a terrific writer, he's no Jacques Audiard when it comes to helming duties.

Bidegain's tale opens with a U.S.A.-worshipping cowboy convention, where Alain Balland (François Damiens) sings Patti Page's "The Tennessee Waltz" (badly) on stage to an adoring, cult-like crowd, all sporting wide-brimmed cowboy hats, American flags and denim. His wife Nicole (Agathe Dronne), and siblings Georges, a.k.a. Kid (Maxim Driessen) and Kelly (Iliana Zabeth), are among them, the latter of whom dances with her father, in a sequence that lasts way too long for its own good. We get it - they love country music, as much as each other! It runs through their freakin' veins! Something bad is about to happen to her!

Lo and behold, Kelly disappears without a trace. Alain finds out from her friends that she's been seeing a guy called Ahmed (Mounir Margoum) instead of attending her Tuesday swimming classes (argh, the horrors of teenagedom!). Somewhat presumptuously, Alain reprimands Ahmed's taken-aback parents, then proceeds to pretty much dismantle Kelly's room, piss off the local cops, and racially profile Ahmed's family and work colleagues. We're at minute 15 here, and I already love this guy!

And how about this town? Bidegain's version of a saloon is frequented by a Native American character, referred to derogatorily as "L'Indien" (Jean-Luis Coulloc'h), who serves no apparent purpose but to enigmatically wander in and out of the place. What IS this place, for Christ's sake - Shyamalan's "The Village"?

A Sherlock Holmes-like, weirdly elusive gentleman from the Ministry of the Interior asks enigmatic questions and inspects Kelly's room, then leaves with no answers. When the Ballands gets a letter from Kelly, saying something in the vein of, "I'm fine, don't look for me", Alain goes all Liam Neeson, interrogating folks in impoverished neighborhoods. "I don't give a shit," he tells a guy serving him tea. "All that, your life, I don't give a shit! I'm looking for my daughter." He then nearly assaults a child in a "gypsy" camp outside town, because she's wearing Kelly's bandanna, and consequently gets kicked out by the "gypsies". When he returns to get the "gypsies" (where's Borat when you need him?) with the cops, the place is empty.

Years of worldwide searching (Yemen, Denmark, Turkey) apparently pass. Next thing we know, after a brief fade-out, Alain and the much-older Kid (Finnegan Oldfield) travel by boat to Antwerp, following a trail, which then leads them to Dangerous Syrians. Why Alain would endanger his kid is never fully explained or even hinted upon - wouldn't it be wiser to have him stay with his mother and her new boo? 'Cos if Alain is dragging poor Kid along out of pure envy, that's just selfish, if you ask me.

From this point on the film gains momentum at a directly proportional rate to its preposterousness. A purportedly shocking development halfway through the film, and the consequent shifting of gears, tonally and thematically, will most likely throw you off rather than make you admire the filmmakers' audacity. I'll let you discover whether or not Kelly is found in Chaman, Pakistan, with the help of a mysterious "L'Américain". By this point the film lost me, big time. It's as if "The Vanishing" copulated with "Taken" and gave birth to a French little "Syriana". I will, however, say that a girl named Shazhana (Ellora Torchia) comes into the picture, a portion of the film dedicated to her adjustment to this weird cowboy/French culture.

Despite being a French production, "Les Cowboys" has all-American sensibilities: blatant racism under the guise of "incisive exploration", a Dirty Harry-like Caucasian protagonist who takes the law into his own hands and passes it on to his kid (or, should I say, Kid), unwarranted allusions to 9/11 and terrorism… François Damiens raves and shouts and offends - it's a one-note performance that displays minimal range. Finnegan Oldfield fares better in a quieter, subtler role that manages to convey more - but not enough to save the film, or even buoy it.

If it's supposed to be a satire of the genre, it's certainly too somber to be classified as such. If it's a portrayal of an obsessed man gone berserk, it's way too "been-there-done-that", and the jarring shift in the middle of the plot doesn't help matters. If it makes some sort of a political statement, it's too diffuse and unintentionally (?) xenophobic to get its point across.

The film moves at a brisk pace, I'll give it that. The filmmaking team know how to frame a shot and piece together a movie. John C. Reilly pops up briefly, providing a welcome little glimpse into how wonderful this film could have been, if it were just about his character (doesn't that apply to every film starring John C. Reilly?). Cinematographer Arnaud Potier may depend a bit too much on blurry backgrounds, but does contrast the visual feel of a classical Western (lots of pretty prairie / forest scenery) against the "grayness of today" admirably.

That said, this attempt to transport an old-fashioned Western story into a contemporary setting is both too literal and obtuse, too straightforward and complicated - and just too strange, confused and discombobulated to function. Bidegain should stick to his day job.

2 out of 5 stars

"Ozzy & Jack's World Tour" is Reality TV 101

Synopsis: *The self-proclaimed history nerds hit the road on a father-son journey they've waited years to take.*

I have a confession to make. For all my waxing poetic about how the entertainment industry needs to elevate our collective consciousness instead of pandering to audiences' tastes, for all my extended monologues about how even escapist entertainment should be original and intellectually stimulating, I myself am a sucker for reality TV. I don't necessarily find the characters compelling, nor do I revel in the lifestyles of the rich and famous. I watch those shows for their technical accomplishments, particularly the sly editing (it's like the makers of VH1's "I Love New York" were in on the joke, cutting away at just the perfect time for comedic effect). I watch them for the borderline-theatrical, superficial drama (my favorite bits of CW's "America's Next Top Model" involved catty fights and buckets of tears)... And you can't deny the entertainment factor. Switch off your brain, lie back, and immerse yourself into the utterly brain-numbing world of "Survivor". That said, I do have to use an extensive amount of mouthwash (and read a passage James Joyce's "Ulysses") to rinse out the foul odor of trash heaped upon me in 42-odd minutes.

Unless I'm mistaken (and feel free to lock me in a cubicle of snakes for 10 minutes if I am), the first such show was the Dutch "Big Brother", back in the mid-1990s. One could argue "The Osbournes", which premiered on MTV back in 2002 (about five-or-so years after that channel turned to crap, with a capital shit), set the standard for all the consequent reality TV shows that followed celebrities' daily lives: "The Simple Life", "Keeping Up with the Kardashians", etc. The inherent appeal of watching a well-known public figure - in this case, a nearly-comatose rock legend Ozzy Osbourne - reveal their intimate details, (heavily-edited) warts and all, proved a major success, spawning dozens of imitators. A critic such as myself has to put his prejudices and morals aside when reviewing a show like "Ozzy & Jack's World Tour", A&E's latest attempt to reinvent the formula by sending the even-more-comatose father and his son on a nationwide historical adventure. Like in Sky1's "An Idiot Abroad", but without Gervais's genius (or infectious laugh), we are left to gape and laugh at the two hapless protagonists and guiltily reward ourselves with a Godard film afterwards.

I had the privilege of screening the first two episodes, and what can I say - they blew my mind. I'll never be the same person again. Thank you, A&E, for making me reconsider my place in the universe and ponder existential questions. Sarcasm aside, what you see is pretty much what you get: a somewhat-entertaining slice of "reality", with the self-professed "history nerd", the Prince of Darkness, and his (very hairy) son traveling to random U.S. locales: the museum of military tanks (Ozzy rides a tank!), a gun range (Ozzy fires a powder rifle!), a Williamsburg wig store (Ozzy wears an 18th-Century wig!), the NASA headquarters (Ozzy goes to Space Camp!) and the Alamo (on which Ozzy allegedly peed in the 1980s)... and so on and so forth.

Standouts, if you can call anything a "standout" in what essentially amounts to total dreck, include: Jack and Ozzy in a Chick fil A, listening to one of Ozzy's hits on the radio while munching on those pickle-marinated slices of heaven; Ozzy's obsession with cannibalism; Ozzy perking up at the mention of opium ("I wish I had a time machine, he says, then stating plainly: "I want opium"); and all the stuff involving NASA (but I'm a space buff - a screenshot of a nebula would mesmerize me for hours). I never thought I'd say this, but Sharon and Kelly are sorely missing from this show, which could use some of the former's wisecracks and the latter's eccentricity. It gets pretty tedious, watching father and son touching historical rocks and encountering apathetic experts of their respective fields. There are pieces of historical wisdom, mind you: "The civil war kinda started around here... and ended around here"; "This town has been restored... complete with poop"; "Your bones have feelings"; "I got more piss than spit"; "I've always wondered if they have sex in space" - and my favorite, a prolonged scene of Jack trying to explain to his father what a kilobyte is.

Peter Weir's brilliant "The Truman Show" predicted the reality TV trend right before it gained traction, its stratospheric rise led by "The Osbournes". The film nailed everything that's wrong with the genre. Morally and ethically, one can't do worse than subjecting themselves to crap like "Ozzy and Jack's World Tour." It teaches us nothing about history, it makes us smirk at its protagonist, it underestimates our intelligence, it's a cash-in and just another excuse to gawk at C-list celebrities... do stuff. Who's the target audience here? Metalheads-slash-history-buffs-slash-reality-show-fans? The fact that Ozzy doesn't seem to have a clue what's happening 80% of the time is cringe-worthy and doesn't help matters. Please note on record: I DO NOT recommend this show. Yet, secretly, when no one - except maybe your lovely and understanding spouse - are watching, you may want to curl up in front of the TV - and it becomes a drug. Whether you can handle the withdrawal is up to you.

2 out of 5 stars

"Phantom of the Theatre" is No Webber's Opera

Synopsis: *A haunted theatre, filled with the vengeful spirits of a tragically-trapped performance troupe murdered in a fire 13 years ago, waits for the once-grand palatial playhouse to re-open with a new show - and bring in new victims.*

China is rapidly becoming a major global player in the cinematic world, its significant theatrical sales saving the likes of, say, "Terminator: Genisys" from flopping at the worldwide box-office. The breakneck theater expansion in the country led to a high demand of Hollywood product, as well as local productions that emulate the gloss and style of Western blockbusters (obviously with toned-down violence and sex). As a result, we get Wai Man Yip's "Phantom of the Theatre", China's "Crimson Peak" with a dash of (or with allusions to) Webber's classic musical - a romantic, pseudo-gothic horror, basked in red and golden hues, old, vengeful ghosts and scandalous drama. Unfortunately, just like Guillermo Del Toro's admirable failure, "Phantom of the Theatre" fails to balance out all those elements and achieve the grandeur for which it was aiming. Despite being a discombobulated mess, Yip's berserk film does have its redeeming qualities, the primary one being: for the most part, it's rather beguiling, if for all the wrong reasons.

From the first second, "Phantom" moves at a brisk pace, to say the least. A thief escapes from hesitant cops into an old, abandoned movie theater. Before he can bite into an apple (don't ask), numerous ghosts materialize, accuse him of murdering them, and set the man on fire. All of this happens in less than three minutes - next thing you know, the film cuts to an Oscar-like ceremony, called the "First Film Queen Awards", where the most popular actresses in the country are celebrated. Among them is Meng Si Fan (Ruby Lin, "The Way We Were"), who gets the "Most Photogenic" award, an uncomfortably sexist sequence that made me wonder whether it was intentionally satirical, a statement on Hollywood's system, or just blatantly chauvinistic.

In the meantime, forensics inspect the thief's burnt body and discover embers inside - "the fire was internal". Wei Bang (Tony Yo-ning Yang, "Formula 17") is the forensic scientist's boyfriend, a screenwriter just back from France, whose horror script caused "quite a stir" at the award ceremony. He is looking for a lead actress; "You will get what you want", his girlfriend reassures him. Inspired, Wei Bang goes to a meeting with Mr. Tang, a film investor, who is having a meeting of his own with Meng, promising her support for all her films. Wei Bang catches Mr. Tang slipping a roofie-like substance into Meng's wine and stops her from drinking it at the last minute - but she drinks the tainted wine demonstratively in front of Tang (dangerous move, if you ask me - and another example of questionable sexism in the film) and consequently passes out in Wei Bang's arms. Right then and there, Wei Bang decides he wants her as his lead actress.

Soon Wei Bang wanders into the haunted theater, location scouting, and witnesses a ghostly scene from the past. Despite finding out that there was a fire at the theater 13 years ago that killed an acrobatic troupe, an energized Wei Bang quickly decides to shoot his film at - and even move his office to - the haunted mansion. "Aren't you worried that the rumors are true?" the theater owner asks him. "Only the guilty are afraid of ghosts," Wei Bang calmly responds. He visits his mother's grave, who committed suicide, which prompted him to move to France and abandon his father, Commander Gu Ming Shan (Simon Yam, "Ip Man"). They meet at the cemetery; it becomes apparent that Ming Shan is against the whole filming endeavor, his military upbringing clashing with his son's creative ambitions, and he resents his son for leaving him.

The shooting commences. Meng's lead male co-star apparently only picked the script because "there are intimate scenes between us" (yet another example of the film's confusion with its sexual politics). "In that case," Meng responds, "you better go easy on me." Before he has the chance to do so, the set lights explode during the shooting of the first scene, and the actor is set on fire, after inhaling the scent of a flower that may or may not contains an evil powder. The incident sends the crew into a disarray, but they resolutely (and inexplicably) proceed. "Running away won't solve anything," Meng tells Wei Bang at one point... Um, yes it would - get the fuck outta that theater, girl! Even after Mr. Tang, the producer who tried to roofie her, attempts to once again rape Meng, and after she is chased around the theater by a slew of ghosts - including the twins from "The Shining" - and a masked killer - even then, Meng sticks to her "running away won't solve anything" theory.

As the rest of the film progresses, mysteries and past secrets are unveiled - Meng's sister died in the fire; Ming Shan reenters the picture to marry Meng (scandalous!); the phantom surfaces; an extended flashback towards the end derails the plot while also somehow furthering it; and Wei Bang's film premieres… which leads to an unintentionally hilarious, overblown stand-off.

The film's primary fault is that it's not frightening in the least - a big "no-no" for a horror film. The plot lurches from scene to scene without much coherence or character development, frustratingly confusing at times. The ultra-silly dialogue is blankly delivered by the wooden actors. Tony Yo-ning Yang fares the worst as the lead, particularly in scenes where he has to react to crazy shit - his expression is totally vacant. Ruby Lin fares better, but flings to the other end of the spectrum by overacting in some scenes. Their romance is unbelievable and cheesy: "You have nothing to be afraid of tonight," Wei Bang tells her on a dimly lit street cafe, "just be yourself." Mind you, most of the scene is played out in slow motion, I guess to accentuate the subtleties of their romantic exchange.

Speaking of, there are about 20 slow motion sequences, 30 horror dream sequences, and so many flashbacks that one would get alcohol poisoning if they were to take a shot each time one of the aforementioned things occurred. "Phantom of the Theatre" is clogged with nausea-inducing, soapy sentimentality. And I'll mention it again, just to beat a dead horse: the sexism, whether it's meant to be satirical or not, is wince-inducing throughout ("A woman isn't worth getting blood on my hands," a character proclaims at one point).

That said, there is some effective imagery: Meng lying on a sheer-white, satin-like material, surrounded by dozens of ghostly faces that swallow her up; a man on stage, engulfed in flames, bent back and frozen still; a burning man causing a vehicle to explode; a female performer, soaring over the stage on silk strings… A few mild references to "Phantom of the Opera" kinda work, the carnivalesque atmosphere is well-sustained, the set design is beautiful, the quirky score helps move things along briskly (though sometimes it swelters with "Gone with the Wind"-style grandiosity), and the cinematography is beautiful. Oh, and there is a nifty little message about the dream-like power of film.

Above all, the unabashed commitment and passion of the filmmakers is palpable. Yes, "Phantom of the Theatre" is deeply flawed, but it's jarring of tones and heightened stylistic flourishes render it entertaining, in a B-movie, "so-bad-it's-good" sort of way, like a cult classic with good production values. If you're looking for an evening of pot-fueled goofiness, then look no further than "Phantom". Its end theme song alone is worth the price of admission for lovers of ultra-camp. But if you are looking to see an actually scary Chinese film (well, technically from Hong Kong), Fruit Chan's creepy "Dumplings" will satisfy your craving.

2 out of 5 stars

Saban's "Power Rangers: Dino Supercharge" Evokes Nostalgia for the Giddy Imbecility of the Original Series... but Not Much Else

Synopsis: Join the Power Rangers as they face extreme dangers and impossible odds to protect the ten Energems. They must summon all their Dino Super Charge powers to become stronger than ever and battle the evil alien Heckyl and his alter ego Snide, but a force even greater than Heckyl stands in their way: The Dark Energem!

Let's get this out of the way: the target audience for "Power Rangers: Dino Supercharge" are pre-teens, ADD-addled kids craving colorful action, simple characters and a straightforward premise that could repeat itself, episode after episode. Hence, applying legitimate criticism to this show is akin to reviewing the Teletubbies or Flintstones based on their artistic merit (ironically, all three of these simplest-of-shows have had dimwitted feature-length adaptations). More of a tool for parents to distract annoying offspring than a fully-fleshed out, intricately-plotted series, "The Power Rangers'" predictability has always been reassuring. As a child, watching the original series while getting ready for school, I knew for a fact that the Rangers were ultimately going to save the day from the Big Bad (Most Likely Robotic) Enemy - and that's all I needed to know.

Saban claims the reason for its recent big-screen "Power Rangers" flop was the PG-13 rating, but the franchise was doomed from the start: perhaps certain things are best left in the nostalgic drawer. Kids these days have been raised on "Transformers", and let's face it, if you're looking for robots battling it out, "Power Rangers" resembles "Transformers-Light", with a bunch of teens replacing Mark Wahlberg and Elizabeth Banks standing in for the Decepticons. The cheap-o TV series embraces some of the campy aspects that made the original sorta endearing, but updates everything with a shiny, Lego-like polish. It's morphing time, indeed.

"Power Rangers: Dino Supercharge" is actually the second season of the Dino Charge "saga" - or at least, that's where I started. Within the first minute of the first episode, titled "When Evil Stirs", I was overwhelmed with so much mega-confusing exposition, I had to pause and write this down:

Tyler Navarro (a.k.a. the Red Dino Charge Ranger a.k.a. Adrian Grenier-lookalike Brennan Mejia), bonded with Shelby Watkins (a.k.a. the Pink Dino Charge Ranger a.k.a. Meagan Good-lookalike Camille Hyde) over some glowing magical stones called Energems, consequently becoming the Dino Power Rangers.

They met Keeper (a creepy-looking 6-foot Yoda in a monk outfit) and gave away their remaining Energems to fellow Rangers.

A villain called Sledge "sent monster after monster" to steal the Energems, until he finally managed to do it himself - but the Rangers weren't going down without a fight. They defeated Sledge and went back to their normal lives.

But, as Tyler writes in his diary (aww!), though he knows "it's good that the world is safe" and is "glad to be looking for [his] dad again", he misses having his Energem and being a Power Ranger. Of course, now that Sledge is gone, an even more powerful enemy surfaces.

Did you get all that? Good, 'cos, like I said, that's just the first 60 seconds of a four-and-a-half-hour season. The new villain turns out to be an angsty teenager with a Dr. Jekyll syndrome - he even goes by the name Heckyl (Ryan Carter, turning the "ham" dial to 1,000), morphing into his "rather uncouth" alter ego Snide when ready for battle. And man, he's ready, hunting down the Rangers one by one: the aforementioned Pink and Red leaders, but also the Blue one (Yoshi Sudarso, whose pseudo-Asian (supposedly prehistoric?) accent/speech impediment is terribly distracting), the Green one (Michael Taber), the Black one (James Davies), the Gold one (Davi Santos) and the Purple one (Claire Blackwelder).

Their Dino equipment includes Dino-Steel armor, Power Blades, and they utilize a variety of techniques, such as the Rapid Blast, which involves swiveling around while laser-shooting enemies, and the titular Dino Charge - an... explosion, I guess. Each episode ends with the obligatory giant robotic fusion of all seven Power Rangers going face-to-face with equally gargantuan foes.

The special effects range from godawful to surprisingly-decent for a low-budget kiddie TV production. I can't decide whether I prefer the former (which at least reminds me of the camp of the original series) or the latter - the series is stuck in the "neither-here-nor-there" zone. Some of the robo-costumes are kinda cool, including a Harley Quinn-esque female bot - but the Power Rangers' suits could've used a little more stitchin'. The dialogue is predictably childish ("My heart is empty but my tummy doesn't have to be!" a Ranger exclaims, while a villain freezes a Ranger into an ice-cube and proclaims: "Easy peasy Ranger freezy!")

Look, I have clearly way outgrown this kind of stuff, and Saban's series threw me off-guard. Do I treasure the fond memories of watching "Power Rangers"? Do I hope that the current generation of kids have a similar opportunity to put their brains on hold, while simultaneously giving their folks a much-needed break? Or do I stick to my convictions that entertainment, no matter its target audience or level of silliness, should still stimulate on some cerebral level? Like the show itself, I'm neither here nor there, so I'll give it a rating as ambiguous as its intentions.

2 out of 5 stars

"Radio America" Loses Its Signal Before You Can Tune In

Synopsis: *After being discovered at a music competition, two young farmers find themselves living the rock star life. As their national tour becomes a massive success, they begin to lose track of their true selves until a tragic accident brings everything back into focus.*

Once in a blue moon, a film comes along that is so adherent to its genre's tropes, it's baffling. Christopher Showerman's rock biopic, "Radio America", is a low-budget example of such a film, earnestly attempting to emulate every stereotypical underdog-rise-to-fame story ever made, from "Country Strong" to "Rock Star".

An avalanche of clichés smothers us from the get-go: two young hillbilly boys, sporting overalls, plaid shirt and John Deere hats, play the guitar out in the cornfields. It really doesn't get any more "country" than that. The child acting is so bad, it comes as a relief that within minutes, a savvy pan ages the boys a decade or so; now in their twenties, Dave (Christopher Alice) and Eric (Jacob Motsinger) sneak in to rock concerts, dreaming of making it big.

One day, while they're tending to their livestock, their friend (and Dave's object of affection), Jane (Kristi Engelmann), swings by to let them know about an upcoming Battle of the Bands. The boys agree to audition – but only if Jane agrees to be their manager. They buy new guitars and hire a drummer, Donny (Wayne Bastrup).

Cut to: they are signing a deal with a sleazy record label honcho, Simon Weinreib (played quite terribly by the film's writer/director Christopher Showerman, wearing shirts so silky and shiny, one can almost catch the camera's reflection in them). A live performance on the local Radio America station showers the band with immediate success. Before they know it, The Rockness Monster (yes, seriously), later shortened to just "Monster", are performing in front of crowds consisting of 30,000 fans (15 of which seemed to actually show up on set). A quick rise to national fame, infidelity and heartbreak, arrogance and greed, and an unexpected death - all the prosaic elements of a rock biopic are here, delivered clumsily.

Where do I start? There are too many fundamental missteps to count. The script – the "backbone" of any film – is predictable, sometimes incoherent, and filled with ridiculous lines ("You are a cockless monster" is one of the gut-busting punch lines; "You're in Washington." "D.C.?" "State!" is another example of the film's polished dialogue; or my favorite: "He's gone! I'm all that's left. But I still love you.").

Cinematographer Terrance Stewart fails to evoke a true country/rock vibe, despite all the cornfields, cows and overalls. I see what he was aiming for: a delicate balance of warmth and nihilism – but his imagery fails at displaying either. Jessie S.

Marlon's editing also leaves a lot to be desired: the transitions are wonky, there are countless fade-outs, and the film's flow often stumbles.

Showerman's struggles to elicit decent performances out of the amateur cast – including himself – are painfully evident. The characters never have room to develop, so their relationships, particularly the love triangle, feel fabricated. In fact, the leads look stoned, which probably made it easier for them to get through this shoot, but doesn't do their dialogue exchanges any favors.

Most crucially, the music feels cheap and inauthentic – especially the grating titular track. Some scenes verge on the "so-bad-it's-good" realm, especially the making of the "Radio America" music video, supplemented by a montage of farmland - and horrid, horrid singing (think low-rent Nickelback). It's the most unintentionally funny film since Angie and Brad recent frolic "By the Sea" – a wildly different creature, mind you, but equally earnest and equally ridiculous.

"Risky Business" is another musical highlight (the lyrics are almost worth hearing for their sheer ludicrousness… almost), the umpteenth montage showing the boys livin' that rockstar life, which apparently involves going into the wrong hotel room by mistake, playing air guitar, sleeping with groupies (duh, can't leave that out), and signing autographs outside lonely supermarkets. I loved the bit where Jane busts Dave in the middle of an orgy, and he runs after her, exclaiming, "It's not what you think!"

Also, what's up with all the DVDs, CDs and CD players? Was this film made in 1998 and shelved for 17 years? Simon's abrasively silky shirts and wide, colorful ties certainly support that theory.

Read MacGuirtose, the actor playing English Joe (whose exact role remains unclear to me), is a sight to behold, overacting as if he stumbled in from the set of SNL. If I had to name one highlight, it would have to be the practical joke that the band members play on English Joe about midway through the film. It involves a lot of duct tape and a loudspeaker, and cuts at just the right time. The ending, with its suicide attempt and mending of a broken guitar, also comes close to approaching true poignancy – it's just that the events leading up to it haven't earned our investment, so it's not as resonant as was oh-so-clearly intended.

I can't fault the film's grand ambitions, but this is a case where budget limitations, along with a basic lack of film continuity and character development, really bog down the entire project. You'll be better off re-watching the sanitized-but-infinitely better visual rock ballad "Almost Famous" – an obvious inspiration for

"Radio America". Which leads me to a side-note: was Christopher Alice cast based on his resemblance to Patrick Fugit?

2 out of 5 stars

"*Suburban Cowboy*" Beats a Dead Horse

Synopsis: A drug dealer on Long Island finds himself over his head when one of his soldiers robs a connection to ruthless Serbian gangsters. When the debt falls on his shoulders he is forced to take drastic measures.

Quentin Tarantino influenced a splurge of mid-to-late-1990s films that attempted to emulate his poetic, highly cinematic dialogue and defiance of conventional narrative structure. From utter trash ("The Boondocks Saints", "The Big Hit", "Suicide Kings") to flawed-but-valiant attempts ("Things to Do in Denver When You're Dead", "2 Days in The Valley", "Go"), no one quite got away with it. The eloquent vulgarity, the darkly humorous violence, the racist rhetoric his characters spout, the little references to films of yore - it's all essentially an extension of QT's persona, shaped by countless years of sifting through cinematic treasures; it comes naturally to the geeky tall genius. Attempting to plagiarize THE master plagiarist is futile.

While QT's influence can still be felt today (look no further than the recent, admittedly entertaining "Seven Psychopaths" for a "Tarantino-lite" experience), his impact has lessened, or rather morphed into that of a different, more commendable kind - directors trying to "out-Tarantino" Tarantino and, in an ocean of constant regurgitation, stand out with auterish trademarks of their own (see: Alejandro González Iñarritu, Alfonso Cuarón, Richard Linklater (who just keeps getting better at being Richard Linklater)). I can't say for sure whether that was one of the intentions of the filmmakers behind the deplorable, grimy thriller "Suburban Cowboy", but the film certainly gives off a stale whiff of a director resorting to cheap shock tactics and blatant provocation to make a name for himself, bringing to mind last decade's cheap QT knock-offs. Crammed with filthy characters, filthier language and next to no plot, this "Cowboy" should have stayed in the stable.

Blank-faced Jeremy Sisto doppelgänger Frank Raducz Jr. plays Jay, a werewolf-obsessed Long Island drug dealer with a stripper girlfriend, Victoria (Alandrea Martin), and a traitor henchman, Alex (Matty Finochio), who used Jay's product to pay off his own debts. Alex swears to stop gambling and begs Jay to front him some more product - or "spark plugs", as the drugs are referred to. But "Alex is bad news, always has been", according to Jay's boxing coach. Next thing Jay knows, he's on the run with Victoria from some vicious Serbian gangsters. He has no choice but to confront Vuk (Zoran Radanovich), the boss, trying to justify Alex's mistake. The Serbians want $150 grand and - why not - throw in Victoria too.

So Jay goes around collecting money, spouting pseudo-intellectual talk about werewolves and vampires. "Be the wolf," Jay tells himself at wrestling practice (is there a form of contact sport he is NOT into?). If the parallel isn't obvious enough, he exclaims at another point: "Me? I'm like a werewolf - gnarly in every way. And when I turn..." - and he trails off, letting his "prey" fill in the blanks. To further emphasize Jay's canine nature, a shadow on a wall morphs into a werewolf as he goes berserk on said "prey" - it's hilarious in its spontaneity and pretentiousness, and wrongheadedness of the chosen soundtrack to accompany the sequence. Victoria finally comes up with a plan... Will she and Jay come out of this mess alive? Does anyone give a shit?

It's jaw-dropping how misogynistic and racist "Suburban Cowboy" is. If it was intended to be ironic or knowingly referential, it doesn't back it up with any semblance of character development, wisdom or poignant moments. The very first shot is that of a naked female body; soon after, the same young woman dances in an unnecessary, icky strip scene, covered in Wonder Woman body paint. She is the only female character of any worth in the entire narrative. Oh hell, I'll let the film's dialogue speak for itself: "I cream-pied the bitch"; "She lets me put it in her ass, so I keep her in my back pocket"; "I turned her face into a Van Gogh, it was beautiful."; "I got a roll of duct tape with her name on it"; "You better have your wet snatch, 'cos I'm about to face-fuck you"; "You're coming in like a spick at the end of the month"; "I like to do my drugs the way I fuck - when I pound the pussy, I like to hurt it"... Lovely. No race seems to go unscathed - "The [Jews] are so cheap..."; "I'll go to war with that Greek motherfucker"; "What's up with the Mexican standoff?" "Yo, we're Dominican, alright?" - and no derogatory, sexist statement left unsaid. Bravo.

If I had to point out some redeeming things, under gunpoint, it would have to be the inventive, graphic novel-like title credit sequence, and the cool electronic soundtrack by Dirty South (a.k.a. the film's producer Dragan Roganovic). Otherwise, "Suburban Cowboy" has next-to-no driving momentum, its dialogue lacking Tarantino's wit and grace - it just sits there, as ugly as the characters spouting it. The film doesn't have a lot to say, reemphasizing its point (or lack thereof) over and over again, as we follow the coke-sniffing protagonist round and round in circles, his charcoal-black eyes revealing a deep dearth of feeling. On a technical level, the film is more-or-less proficient, but there's just no reason to ride into the sunset with this cowboy.

2 out of 5 stars

"The Backseat" Never Gets to Ride Shotgun

Synopsis: *A feature length coming of age story about high school love, punk rock, and hemorrhoids.*

Once in a while, along comes an ultra-low budget independent film that manages to transcend its lack of production values with either top-notch acting, an involving plot, bracing humor, real insight into the human condition - or, in best cases, all of the above. I remember watching a screener for such a film, John Wick's "Francis of Brooklyn", which dealt with PTSD, religion, homelessness, and despite its evident micro-budget, brought to mind classics like Terry Gilliam's "The Fisher King".

Unfortunately, "The Backseat" is not one of those films. While it outwardly strives to cite cult favorites, such as "Empire Records", "American Pie" and even, dare I say, "Sid and Nancy", with its flagrant concoction of vulgarity, sweetness and a lumbering, pseudo-nihilistic approach, it falls short of attaining those films' status in the cinematic pantheon of rebellious teen fare. Perhaps it would have worked better as a satire, as its earnestness violently clashes with blatant sexism and offensive throwaway statements.

Ryan O'Learey's feature directorial debut starts promisingly. Our hero, Roy, is a young outcast, brainstorming potential band names with his friend, Larry (Craig McDonald-Kelly). Their list includes standouts like "Schindler's Clit", "Jesus Christ Sex Machine" and "Secret Hitler" (it's like Secret Santa, you see, and "everyone loves Secret Santa"). They finally agree on "Witness My Jehovah", and start posting flyers, looking for a drummer. The script, by O'Leary, so far is sharp, crammed with zingers and snappy one-liners. Roy and Larry finally find the perfect drummer: the sexist, brash Mike Peterson (Costa Nicholas defines "OTT" in his one-note performance).

Things go downhill from here, into the dark depths of stereotype. Roy's mother Debra (Lori Hamilton) is an eternally-cheerful, nuclear-family staple, who nonchalantly cleans up her son's post-masturbatory semen. His dad David (John Thomas Cramer) generally just doesn't give a shit (his response to his son's sudden happiness: "It's probably drugs"). Roy's gym teacher, Mr. Hennrick, is abrasive and overbearing, played quite terribly by Matt Van Orden, who, at one point, loudly announces that Roy has hemorrhoids, making sure Roy's bully classmates can hear him, and yes, consequently make fun of Roy.

Roy encounters the girl of his dreams, Samantha (Allyson Reilly), after an unnecessarily extended and nauseating sequence at the doctor's, because, lo and behold, they both have hemorrhoids! Sharing absolutely zero chemistry, Roy and Samantha embark on a romance. The film becomes a love-story-cum-coming-of-age--cum-underdog-punk-rock-flick-cum-lots-of-cum. It all leads up to a small show at a local tiny club.

Because the plot is so deeply rooted in clichés, the film's budget limitations become that much more obvious. Some transitions are wonky (take a whiskey shot for each fade out, and you will be annihilated by the time credits roll), the camerawork is cheap, Roy's school consists of exactly eight students…

To be fair, at least O'Leary seems to have tried, intermittently. There are a few mildly diverting sequences, my favorite involving Larry's fascination with Terrence Malick's "The Thin Red Line" (Roy's sleepy response: "Literally like watching grass grow"). Chris Bellant makes for an adequately awkward and sardonic protagonist. But there are too many forcefully raunchy and obnoxious jokes - e.g. "what the fuck, you threw up on my penis!", classy - and amateur, one-note performances.

I wonder if O'Leary watched the recent "Wetlands", which dealt with similar issues, also crassly, but its originality and compelling heroine outweighed - and one can even say complemented - it nastiness. Perhaps the director is finding his footing, and if he focuses more on character development and visual innovation in his next feature, maybe, just maybe, he can truly steer a race-car. For now, he's in the backseat of an old Chevy.

2 out of 5 stars

"The Light Between Oceans" Shimmers and Flickers Dimly

Synopsis: *A lighthouse keeper and his wife living off the coast of Western Australia raise a baby they rescue from an adrift rowboat.*

Writer/director Derek Cianfrance made his presence known with the impressive feature length debut "Blue Valentine" - an erotic, challenging and desolate cinematic haiku, which featured one of Michelle Williams's best performances. High on the accolades and attention the film received, Cianfrance went on to make the rambling-but-ambitious "The Place Beyond the Pines". The film had its intense and graceful moments, suggesting (or rather leading one to hope) that this was a misstep, rather than an unraveling of a once-promising artist. Unfortunately, the latter proved to be the case. Little did I expect the dreck that is "The Light Between Oceans" to be the follow-up "Pines" foreshadowed.

Let's start with the trailer, which not only rightfully suggests a perhaps teeny-bit-more-polished Nicholas Sparks adaptation, but also reveals the entire plot of the film in less than two minutes. So why sit through over two hours of it, you ask? Aside from a few redeeming factors on which I will elaborate below, having patiently endured the ordeal, the answer eludes me, as does the answer to another, equally imposing inquiry: what the hell was the director thinking? What made him pick M.L. Steersman's debut historical novel, a well-written but somewhat predictable and half-baked tale that seared its wings by soaring to unreachable heights? Apart from the whole affair clearly being Oscar bait, with its swooping score and camerawork, at what point did Cianfrance decide that this material would correspond perfectly with his anything-but-sappy sensibility? He wrote the damn thing too - either the paycheck was impressive enough to set aside artistic integrity, or Cianfrance has officially morphed into just another Nick Cassavetes.

1918, December. A traumatized Australian WWI soldier Tom Sherbourne (Michael Fassbender) returns home from France after four years of witnessing unimaginable terrors (luckily, the actor does a persuasive job insinuating what those might have been). He agrees to look after a lighthouse on a remote and desolate island, taking over from another keeper, who committed suicide after sending signals to his dead wife and getting "cabin fever". Sounds like the beginning of a horror film - and one could make a case that "The Light Between Oceans" is just that, based on the number of miscarriages, stormy nights and tears featured in the narrative. Only it would make for the most boring horror film ever, its most frightening aspect being the director's indulgence in Hollywood staples.

I digress. Totally enamored by this handsome, broken man, young Isabel (Alicia Vikander) soon finds herself marrying and moving in with Tom, a ray of bright light in his otherwise-dim existence (yes, there are a lot of those subtle metaphors scattered through each freakin' frame of the film). Darkness does eventually seep back into the light: during a brutally stormy night, Isabel has a miscarriage, the lighthouse proving to be futile when it comes to guiding her to safety. After a second miscarriage (Cianfrance should've gone three for three; it's like we're watching "4 Months, 3 Weeks and 2 Days"), poor Isabel is on the verge of a breakdown… when, by some celestial miracle, Tom spots a boat out in the ocean, with a baby girl and a dead man inside. How convenient!

"Can we leave her awhile?" Isabel asks, eyes glazed over with motherly love. "Give her time to catch her breath?" His face all, "I see where this is going", Tom reluctantly agrees. Next thing they know, many months pass by. Just as Tom reads to his child, "there came a sudden cry out of the darkness", he spots Hannah (Rachel Weisz), kneeling and weeping by a tombstone, with a plaque that says something in the vein of "Father and Child, Lost at Sea". Tom puts two and two together, and then, well, I won't spoil it for those who, after reading all this, still want to watch "The Light Between Oceans". I will say that a baby monkey rattle is crucial to the plot, that Tom ends up in jail, and (okay, SPOILER ALERT) there's an extended, gag-inducing prologue featuring a daughter visiting her surrogate father.

Aside from the hard-to-buy premise of the plot, there are the constant run-ins between Tom and Hannah at just the right time. Everything in the film seems to unravel like your average fruit: in the beginning you hope for a maracuya but nope, all you get is a basic orange. The "cabin fever" that the initial keeper of the lighthouse experienced (may his soul rest in peace) is never touched upon - the couple seems perfectly happy, frolicking away from humanity with nothing but each other and the wind to keep them company. The film doesn't tighten its scope, or framing, or pace as it progresses, which would potentially make it more of a claustrophobic experience.

And dammit, the tears. Every main character in the film cries in at least 18 scenes. I don't remember the last time I saw that many close-ups of watery eyes and snotty upper lips. And wouldn't YOU cry, if you had such dialogue to enunciate? "You're still a mother and a father, even when you no longer have a child," Isabel shares wisely, as the two of them sit on a cliff-side, gazing over an endless ocean. "There's a light inside of you," Tom writes, "and it shines as bright as the light in the skies." "You…" she stammers. "You make me feel like… peace." "When it comes to the ocean, anything's possible," Tom observes. My favorite exchange happens early on in the film: "We can't talk about the future, only what we imagine we wish for," Tom says elusively. "So what do you wish for?" Isabel wonders, moving in closer to him. "Life"," he says. The film is generally very wet: aside from the tears, there's all the rain, ocean, mist and sap that drags you down, making it the definition of a slog to sit through.

And dammit, the metaphors. The film starts with a sunrise and ends with a sunset. Numbed by death, Tom runs away from the darkness of war; "Out here," he says, "I am only responsible for the light." The film's soundtrack is overbearing to the max; in fact, I blame Alexandre Desplat's score for the film's triteness as much as I blame the director. "The Light Between Oceans'" best moments are the quiet ones, where only the whistling of the wind and the rustling of the grass can be heard. The same exact film without thunderous music guiding you through its emotion terrain would have arguably made for a much less manipulative and more contemplative experience (key word being "arguably"). Curiously, for a film filled with so much tears and drama, I never felt anything but aggravation and the excruciating passing of time.

Michael Fassbender, one of our great actors, is reduced to a caricature of a man scarred by war. He does what he can with his expressive eyes, but his performance is one-note, revealing little dimension beyond "seeking solace". Alicia Vikander is effective in a couple of scenes but again, her character isn't fleshed out enough, given enough backstory or motivation for us to truly care about Isabel. Weisz casts the most memorable impression in an all-too-brief role as Hannah, but yet again, she did much more with way less in "The Lobster." Cinematographer Adam Arkapaw, who shot last year's "Macbeth" - a much better film starring Fassbender - saves the film from being utterly worthless with his breathtaking scenic shots, evoking painters of that period like Gerhard Bakenhaus and Granville Redmond.

While "Blue Valentine" was succinct, raw and subtle, "The Light Between Oceans" is bloated, glossy and obvious. Whatever noble intent it may have had to hark back to the glory days of filmmaking are overshadowed by its dullness and predictability. The actors and production values barely save it from hitting rock bottom, but this is just as shameless as your run-of-the-mill Sparks adaptation, only with the pretense of being a major award contender, as if Cianfrance watched "Kramer vs. Kramer" and decided to fuse it with "Atonement". In one word: ugh.

2 out of 5 stars

Critique of Critical Critique of Raoul Peck's "The Young Karl Marx"

 Synopsis: *The early years of Karl Marx, Friedrich Engels and Jenny Marx, between Paris, Brussels and London.*

 Raoul Peck is a political filmmaker. His films all have a uniting theme, one of social injustices, which he explores from all angles, from the eyes of Independent Congo's leader Patrice Lumumba in the confusingly-titled "Lumumba" to the recent, Oscar-nominated documentary "I Am Not Your Negro", which again, as the title suggest, deals with the history of race in America. Now Peck depicts the events leading up to the writing of "The Communist Manifesto" and consequently "Das Kapital". Quite the subject to tackle then, but the filmmaker goes about it in the most painstakingly detailed and impassive way as is cinematically possible. Were it not for splendid production design and costumes - those top hats! - one could mistake this for a documentary reenactment, told in a theatrical, pedagogical manner.

 Welcome to the mid-19th Century. Karl Marx (August Diehl), the "son of a converted Jew", proudly refuses to surrender after authorities bash in the front door of his little publishing house. He writes scathing anti-authoritarian articles ("the people see the punishment and not the crime"); shackled for expressing his beliefs, Marx makes the decision to move to Paris.

 Accompanied by "the prettiest aristocrat in Trier", his wife Jenny von Westphalen-Marx (Vicky Krieps), Marx smokes cheap cigars at a Parisian republican convention, publicly calling out the famous anarchist and founder of mutualist theology Pierre-Joseph Proudhon (the Dardenne Brothers mainstay, Olivier Gourmet). Marx claims that the man's speechifying amounts to nothing but mere abstractions. Introduced to him by another revolutionary anarchist, Mikhail Bakunin (Ivan Franek), Jenny proceeds to define Proudhon's statements as "an image chasing its own tail."

 In the meantime, Mary Burns (Hannah Steele), an outspoken, self-described "slave worker" and leader of sorts at a spinning mill in Manchester, causes a stir of her own with the authorities. The son of the evil factory owner happens to be the compassionate Friedrich Engels (Stefan Konarske), who "despises gentlemen", referring to the upper-class leeches feeding off the laborers. After an unsuccessful attempt to "enlist" said laborers in helping him write a book about the conditions of the working class in Manchester - which results in a bloody nose - Friedrich seeks out liberalist Arnold Ruge (Hans-Uwe Bauer), wherein the Great Meeting of the Minds happens: Marx meets Engels.

Both broke, they start writing an essay, fueled by Proudhon's speech and Jenny, their muse. They morph Proudhon's abstract notions into an "appalling reality". Marx speaks fervidly to factory workers of equality, spouting hatred about the bourgeoisie. He soon gets expelled from France and joins Friedrich, along with Mary Burns, in London's League of the Just. Together, along with their growing crew of revolutionaries, they have heated debates over smoky cigars until the Communist League is formed, to much fanfare and swelling music.

Prone to heated outbursts and offending peace resistant leaders, Diehl is a marvelous Marx stuck in a dry film. He and Konarske do their best to ignite the screen yet, given the over-written dialogue and snail-like pacing, there's little they can do. Their characters spout their rhetoric but what truly drives them, scenes of tenderness and humanity, are curiously missing. Vicky Krieps, so mysterious and alluring in P.T. Anderson's recent "Phantom Thread", comes off a bit bland here, her character, apart from a few moments of slight empowerment, delegated to the "supporting wife" role. (I feel like I've written this sentence about women playing the trite "helpful wife" role in my reviews more than once - feels strange to write it in one of a film made by such a socially-conscious director.)

Scenes feel artificial and staged, but worst of all, didactic. The film is so boring, it made me want to bang my forehead with "The Communist Manifesto". Scratch that, it made me want to READ "The Communist Manifesto", so long as it would detract from watching another uneventful, talky scene unfold. The script - by three people! - lacks a forward momentum, an exhilarating highlight, at least a trace or two of wit. It's just one long, monotonous slog through this particular, important tough not quite cinematic moment in history. The few brief moments of spontaneous inspiration - the violent, slow-motion opening, repeated in Marx's dreams; Marx and Engels running away from authorities down narrow paved streets - are dulled by the rest of this film, akin to a few drops of spice making next-to-difference in a watery soup.

I guess Peck's film serves as a decent introduction to Karl Marx and a half-decent juxtaposition of the tumultuous, politically and socially charged climate in which he lived against our own. That said, "The Young Karl Marx" feels like it should be taught in history classes instead of shown in theaters.

2 out of 5 stars

1.5-STAR REVIEWS

The Faith-Based "A Family Man" Puts Its Audience Through Hell

Synopsis: *A headhunter whose life revolves around closing deals in a survival-of-the-fittest boiler room, battles his top rival for control of their job placement company – his dream of owning the company clashing with the needs of his family.*

God sure is mentioned a lot in "A Family Man", a faith-based cancer drama, which, as this critic's 12 faithful readers know, is my favorite cinematic genre. In Mark Williams' hilariously earnest and disastrously misguided tearjerker, God, Faith and Being Good ultimately preside over Evil - though not before buckets of tears are shed, and a plethora of Positive Messages is spelled out. Its target Bible Belt audience may nod their heads in approval, but even they are bound to clutch their crosses in horror at some of the most unintentionally hilarious blowjob dialogue in cinematic history.

The story in a nutshell: the prototypically selfish/arrogant, Chicago headhunter Dane Jensen (Gerard Butler) says things like, "This job is a desk, a phone, a chair... and your ass" and ""I am who I say I am." (Eminem?) A self-proclaimed "American hero", Dane cheats, scams, lies to his clients, manipulates deals – and worst of all, misses Halloween with the kids. "You know what would be nice?" he tells his loving but neglected wife Elise (Gretchen Mol), after she gives him a blowjob for hours. "If I could cum."

Dane mixes Red Bull with his coffee (a line of cocaine would probably be healthier, or at least better-tasting, I, ahem, assume). His greatest competitor is his young, determined coworker Lynn (Alison Brie); his most challenging client - Lou (Alfred Molina), 59 and unemployable. Taunted by his Nazi-like boss (Willem Dafoe), on the verge of a major raise, Dane will stop at nothing to get what he wants… Except, of course, the Big C. The second half of "A Family Man" goes tumbling down into the charcoal abyss of morbid, crass manipulation.

Headhunter-turned-screenwriter Bill Dubuque has a real knack for maudlin exchanges - and none for snappy one-liners. "Every family has its issues," Lou tells Dane at one point, as the music swells, "but you've only got one family." What. A. Revelation. As for Gerard Butler, he just isn't likeable, no matter how many times his lips twitch and his baggy eyes water. The actor seems exhausted, cashing his paycheck in-between cocaine-fueled Hollywood parties. The film expects us to hate him at one point and relate to / root for him the next. The whole affair is as cheap as its protagonist's job tactics, as misguided and lunkheaded as its lead star - sorry - former star. It does an atrocious job portraying true grief, without ever coming close to encompassing the implications of a terminal illness. Worst of all, "A Family Man" fails at even trying to be original or entertaining.

Apart from the lead, the cast comes off relatively unscathed. Gretchen Mol, in a thankless "nagging wife / grieving mother" role, does her darnedest with the crappiest of lines. "Maybe if we spent more time out of the bedroom," she manages to utter with some conviction, "we'd spend more time in it." Stalwarts Alfred Molina and Willem Dafoe both seem to think they are in a different film. While Dafoe, in full-on "Gordon Gekko mode", plays the Devil Incarnate Himself and manages to somehow stick true to his character, Molina - particularly in an honestly emotional, seemingly improvised bathroom scene - is a stark contrast to the ugly, fabricated cinematic reality surrounding him. If this entire film revolved around just following his character silently around the house, it would have made for an infinitely more entertaining experience.

For a film wholly about morals and ethics, it's astoundingly morally/ethically wrong. It puts its child character through unimaginable grief and gives its audience undeserved redemption. It contains sequences such as Dane lying next to his comatose son as he headhunts over the phone - not to mention THAT whole blowjob exchange. I hope its target demographic isn't too offended by all that sex stuff. The rest of us are better off re-watching "Up in the Air", or even "Boiler Room", instead.

1.5 out of 5 stars

"Abe and Phil's Last Poker Game" Has Very Little at Stake

Synopsis: Dr. Abe Mandelbaum has just moved into a new manor with his ailing wife. After forming an unlikely friendship with a womanizing gambler, their relationship is tested when they each try to convince a mysterious nurse that they are her long-lost father.

There's no denying the legendary status of Martin Landau and Paul Sorvino, the leads of Howard Weiner's dramedy "Abe and Phil's Last Poker Game". The former - who passed away earlier this year - has graced the silver screens since the late 1950's, with such unforgettable performances as the Academy Award-nominated turn as Judah in Woody Allen's "Crimes and Misdemeanors" and the role that finally brought him the long-deserved Oscar, his heartbreaking Bela Lugosi in Tim Burton's black-and-white masterpiece, "Ed Wood". The latter has appeared in over 100 film and video titles since the early 1970's, in such roles as Henry Kissinger in Oliver Stone's "Nixon", Fulgencio Capulet in Baz Luhramann's "Romeo + Juliet" and, of course, Paul Cicero in Martin Scorsese's "Goodfellas".

Among the two of them, they've covered everything from Dostoevsky to Shakespeare (with, admittedly, some less, ahem, literary choices in-between). Now the stalwarts come head to head in what I assume is Landau's last screen performance. This Meeting of the Greats is orchestrated by none other than… Howard Weiner, who wrote and directed this feature, and whose only other credit is a low-budget religious documentary titled "What Is Life? The Movie." My expectations skyrocketed upon stumbling upon this little factoid.

After a languid, flatly-shot opening, the "made-for-TV" vibe continues throughout the film, with boring framing devices and a maudlin soundtrack. After a minor stroke, Abe (Landau), a doctor who snaps anytime anyone refers to him as "mister", moves to Cliffside Manor, a home for the elderly, ruled by the "old-man-hating" Grollman (Alexander Cook). He brings his wife Molly (Ann Marie Shea) along, but soon forms a friendship with the disease-ridden Phil (Sorvino), and the two get into shenanigans, most of them involving getting laid. "The things that gave me pleasure in my life," Phil says, "were baseball, poker and fucking, but not in that order." While Phil is humorously/tragically dying, Abe is pursuing the hot 50-something intern who gets him "harder than I've ever been!"

In a house full of clichéd inhabitants - the womanizer, the seductive volunteer with painful "pits" in her face (don't ask) - the chain-smoking Angela (Maria Dizza) is just another stereotype: a lost 30-something, looking for her father. Upon meeting Abe for the second time, Angela bears her soul to him, involving adoption and nightmares and existential angst. Both old men are potential - though unlikely -

fathers. Abe, Phil and Angela converge at a poker table (albeit very briefly, rendering the title misleading), truths surface, words are spewed, folks die, blablabla.

It would be pleasure to watch the two actors emote were - except that they are emoting in a sap-infested melodrama. Landau looks into a mirror, all nostalgic, decades of life passing through his eyes, and one can't help but imagine the actor going out on a less sour note. Similarly, Sorvino is underserved here - he tries his best, his dying character never losing the sparkle in his eye, yet he's put through the motions. Their old people back-and-forth rapport is somewhat charming, but also eye-rolling and sometimes gag-inducing. Speaking of, there are not one or two but THREE lovemaking scenes that are lunkheaded and uncomfortable and misguided.

And the music swells and swells. Filled with stilted dialogue, such as "How am I supposed to know who I am if I don't know where I came from?" and "Follow your heart", Howard Weiner's film fails on most accounts. As a rumination on death and cosmic questions, it's lackluster. As a sobering, wistful comedy, it's next-to-worthless: it's blatant, borderline-vulgar in its lack of subtlety. As a treatise on dying, it says nothing new. I've mentioned Michael Haneke's "Amour" in my reviews before, a devastating masterpiece about Love and Dying. Forget "Abe and Phill…" - which ticks off so many clichés, the book's not thick enough - and watch "Amour" instead. If you would like to see the two stalwarts, Landau and Sorvino, at their peak, be sure to add "Ed Wood" and "Goodfellas" to that eclectic cinematic trifecta.

1.5 out of 5 stars

Don't Let "Doobious Sources" Fool You into Smoking Schwag

Synopsis: *A pair of weed-loving, free lance video journalists find themselves targeted by a mark they slandered in one of their exposes.*

It's rare for a film that revolves around potheads smoking weed to hold any sort of artistic merit. The somewhat-decent among them - the "Harold and Kumar" entries, "Half Baked", "Smiley Face", the Cheech & Chong saga - have a giddiness to them, where plot becomes irrelevant and you follow the protagonists' stoner logic, be it the search of a White Castle or the consumption of laced cupcakes. Director Cliff Lord makes the crucial mistake of infusing too much plot into "Doobious Sources", which could have been a midnight delight, but ends up being, like, a total downer, dude.

Zorn Tappadapo (Jason Weissbrod) and Reginald Block-Hunsleigh (Jeff Lorch) are BFFs, who have an affinity for freelance journalism (hard emphasis on "bullshit" here), the former's job description condensed to "shoot news, rolls dime bag blunts", the latter acting as the "news reporter". The "Instant Karma Investigative News Service" specializes in real estate fraud, exposés and the like, "bringing the scumbags of the Earth to the public's attention for over five years", as they exclaim proudly in unison. Surprisingly, the local news channel picks up their stories, because they are supposedly brilliant. They embark on their biggest assignment yet: to expose a crooked politician and consequently "bring down the whole government". They bring along Ky Kittridge (Creagen Dow), who brings down the whole movie with terrible acting.

From this point on, the plot gets too tangled and messy and pointless to depict in detail. Zorn, Reginald and Ty travel around in a giant bus, smoking pot, stealing safes, infiltrating people's lives - and so on and so forth. The film is like a nerd that tries too hard to be cool, from its characters' wacky names to the handheld approach, which must be discussed. Here it stands as a backbone for the entire film, told solely from the perspective of the friends' two cameras, and while arguably ambitious, the British TV series "Peep Show" did it better, to a much higher comedic effect. Here the approach proves lunkheaded, as editing is crucial to comedy.

"You guys and these cameras, they're like appendages!" one character exclaims. The handheld narrative is also a metaphor: the heroes' lives are "merging with art". Issue is: there's no "art" in what they're doing, quite the opposite in fact (though one may argue art's in the eye of the beholder, I defy anyone to argue me on that point when it comes to "Doobious Sources"). The whole production gives off a whiff of cheapness, and I'm not just speaking about the budget, which by itself would be forgivable.

> Yo, bros, check out some of this dope dialogue from "Doobious":
> "Zorn, man, never forget - a vagina is a cul-de-sac."
> "Journalism delayed is journalism denied."
> "The fact that you're afraid almost makes me cum in my pants."
> "There is a reason for everything, if you just have faith."
> "How about you lick my balls."

On second thought, I change my mind about the film's artistic merits.

The plotting's choppy, and the "Gregslist" side-plot brings the film further down into the miasma of incompetence. It's probably for the best you do smoke a ton of weed before watching this, just so that it evaporates from your mind soon after. It's a shame, because there are glimpses of chemistry between the two leads, along with a few clever exchanges along the way.

The film starts by quoting an imaginary figure, Dubois (get it?) LeToque (which, in reality weirdly belongs to either Hugh Grant or Milos Forman, according to my Google search - am I missing something here?): "A free press is the cornerstone of democracy." I'd like to refer to another, more fitting quote, by the very real advocate for democracy, Mr. Martin Luther King, Jr.: "Nothing in the world is more dangerous than sincere ignorance and conscientious stupidity."

1.5 out of 5 stars

"Freedom" is as Trite and Manipulative as Its Title Suggests

Synopsis: A tale of two men, separated by time and circumstance, but united in their search for freedom and redemption.

Since his Academy Award victory for "Jerry McGuire", Cuba Gooding Jr.'s career as a leading man has been patchy, at best. Laughably-terrible Hollywood flops "Chill Factor", "Boat Trip" and "Dirty" led to a series of straight-to-video fare, like "End Game", "Hero Wanted", "Line Watch", "Hardwired", "Ticking Clock", "Sacrifice"… Those generic titles, resembling mid-1990s Mark Dacascos films ("Sanctuary", anyone?), speak for themselves: the poor guy's career, save for a few minor supporting turns in Hollywood flicks, has been on a steady decline. Unfortunately, his latest starring vehicle, "Freedom" - which he also executive produced - gives little sign of a much-needed comeback for the once-inspired actor.

The feature-length debut of Peter Cousins, known mostly for his role as "Luke Carlyle" on the obscure 1980's soap "Sons and Daughters", "Freedom" was also written by Timothy A. Chey, whose credits sure strike a pattern: "Impact: The Passion of the Christ", "David and Goliath", "Final: The Rapture"… I have absolutely nothing against religious beliefs, nor have I seen any of Chey's films, but this whole project gives off a mild riff of propaganda, the similar kind witnessed in the recent array of "faith-based", creatively bankrupt pictures (see: "God Is Not Dead"), driven by a forceful moral message, aimed at specific groups of religious fanatics, most of whom have no appreciation of true cinema. That's not to say "Freedom" lacks any semblance of creative ambition - it's certainly earnest and pretty to look at - it just constantly steps wrong, displaying an evident absence of filmmaking proficiency, screenwriting prowess and, as a result, originality, laying on its goodwill message way too thick.

The film jumps incoherently between two disparate storylines. The first, taking place in 1856, sees Cuba Gooding Jr. sleepwalking through his role as Samuel who, along with his family, attempts to escape from the Monroe foundation in Virginia, assisted on their way by the Underground Railroad, a secret organization that helped slaves flee to Canada. A potentially-fascinating and harrowing journey is rendered monotonous and cliché-ridden, led by indifferent performances, with the sole exceptions of William Sadler ("The Shawshank Redemption"), who almost saves this storyline with his sneering, impassioned portrayal of Plimpton, a morally-torn slave hunter, and the great character actor David Rasche ("Burn After Reading"), who provides solid, albeit very brief, support as Jefferson Monroe, the owner of the estate from which the Woodward family escaped.

The other storyline, narrated by Samuel's mother over a crackling fire, takes place in 1748, and follows John Newton's journey back from Africa; he's the captain of a slave ship, and observes their miserable fates dejectedly (Bernhard Forcher in the role is as wooden as his ship)… But it's really about how he came up with the song "Amazing Grace", and how the song went on to influence millions to drop arms and have faith in humanity. Hallelujah.

To say that the film is riddled with clichés would be a gross underestimation. Within the very first minute, there are four glaring ones: the "inspired by a true story" chestnut; the unnecessary, exceedingly schmaltzy voice-over narration; the thunderous score; the old scrolls, depicting the characters' journey with "Indiana Jones"-style traceable lines…

Some "memorable" bits of dialogue include the following "gems": "In the smallest of things, I see a glimmer of hope"; "If I don't come back, I want you to be careful"; "We must go quickly, there's not much time!"; "Hope can be found in the darkest of places" (…wait, I thought hope was "in the smallest of things?"); "With forgiveness comes true freedom"; and, my personal favorite, the somehow wildly inappropriate, "My dear, we are slaves to the critics!" The words "freedom", "faith" and "hope" are persistently uttered on so many different occasions, one truly begins to feel like the filmmakers are shoving their doctrine down their throat, as earnest as the director's and screenwriter's efforts may be.

Both storylines are regularly disrupted by musical numbers which, though thankfully toned down and avoid the exuberance normally prevalent in musicals, come off as misguided and unfinished, and do nothing to help drive the story or evoke any emotion (if in doubt, just check out Cuba Gooding Jr.'s own blank reaction to a particularly over-stretched choral piece). A story like this should be powerful enough on its own merits and does not need to be embellished by such flatulent, oddly contemporary touches.

But "Freedom"'s greatest flaw is its resolute lack of complexity; the film provides no real insight into the origins of slavery or the psychology behind it. It lacks "Amistad"'s epic scope, "12 Years A Slave"'s power and intelligence, and "Django Unchained"'s humor and drive. The dark irony lies in the fact that the story "Freedom" tells about the depths of human depravity and prejudice is in itself riddled with stereotypes and sermonizing, rendering it inconsequential, and further tarnishing Cuba Gooding Jr.'s ever-fledging resume.

1.5 out of 5 stars

"Sweethearts of the Gridiron" Induces Groans Instead of Cheers

Synopsis: On September 12, 1940, when they took the field for the first time, the Rangerettes made history, and changed the future of football halftime entertainment across Texas and the United States.

Fair warning: this review may enrage die-hard football fans, especially those residing in Texas.

I am not a fan of the game, nor the clone-like films that are based on it. Perhaps it's my European roots (right, blame it on heritage) or general lack of interest in competitive sport (tennis and, to some degree, basketball being the two graceful exceptions to the rule). No matter how many times I tried to get into it, spurred by the cheers and enraged, drunken frenzy of friends, football never made sense to me. From my perspective, all those rules and regulations amount to a bunch of moderately-to-extremely-ignorant oafs running at each other at full speed. I've personally been through the U.S. college experience, where I witnessed those oafs being fabricated for glory: you get to skip all the classes you want and still get a good GPA, as long as you work out and attend practice and, most importantly, represent this great nation by ramming into your opponent - and, if you're lucky, shattering some his bones.

Now, I'm not arguing that competitive sports bring a sense of camaraderie in hard times: the Super Bowl, the Olympics, Wimbledon - people from all across the world unite and cheer and forget about wars, I get it. On the flip side, it can be argued that competitive sports also lead to fans' massacring each other over a team, as can be witnessed in the hooligan culture in countries like Britain and Russia, or the recent debacle over the Russians' presence in the Rio Olympics - sports and politics fusing in the worst way imaginable. I would rather watch a searing film (preferably not a pseudo-inspirational, trite-as-fuck tale about an underdog sports team) or go to a potentially mind/life-altering concert than sit for over two hours in an overcrowded stadium, crammed with roaring twin-like fans, having beer spilled on me and… Am I an old curmudgeon or what?

If I ever do watch football, it's for the half-time show. Filled with highly extravagant and silly antics, such as a mega-popular star belting it out, cheerleaders stacking themselves on top of each other like cards and the occasional nipple slip, this IS America, folks: elated for no reason, drunk on its own glory, silly - and very entertaining. Chip Hale's run-of-the-mill documentary, "Sweethearts of the Gridiron", takes a look at the "world-famous Kilgore College Rangerettes", a group of cheerleaders who awed a nation with their mind-boggling routines (forget Stephen

Hawking, THIS is some stimulating stuff) back in 1940 and "changed football halftime forever." The synopsis is misleading however, giving the impression that the doc will throw a retrospective glance back at the history of the Rangerettes - instead, it briefly lingers on the past and focuses mostly on the present. Perhaps the cheerleaders' story is not worthy of a full-length doc itself - but neither is this heap of trash.

We follow a group of young, athletic girls in Texas, trying out for the Rangerettes cheerleading team. They go through their daily practice sessions, which the doc sometimes portrays as arduous as army training. Both determined and a bit shallow - think high-school brats with potential - they share their trepidation and wisdom with us throughout. "I wanna be here so badly," is repeated over and over again, emphasizing how badly they wanna be here. "If you want to get there, you have to work hard for it," is one of the defining lines of the doc. (Shit, really? I have to reevaluate my life now.) Two of the girls decorate their room with "streamers, dangly stars and flag banners", an explosion of red-white-and-blue to keep those patriotic spirits soarin'. "It is meant to be pretty," Shelley Wayne, the Rangerette choreographer declares during practice. "Pretty and regal." Re-reading this paragraph, I just came to an epiphany: this would have made a perfect Christopher Guest satire. "Best in Show II: This Is Spinal Bend", anyone?

The only semi-diverting parts come from the original Rangerettes themselves, nostalgically reflecting on the good old days. "We were the first ever, and when we were there, we were the best ever," one says, chuckling. The Mayor of Kilgore, Ronnie Spradlin, comments, "They were unique here and, like anything successful, they were copied over and over… Every high school in the nation has dancing girls." In other words, the gargantuan degree of their influence on this nation is, well, unfathomable. If I dig real deeply for more redeeming characteristics, I'd point out some cool archival footage and a few instances of graceful, almost-balletic moves.

But that's really about it. I wish I could "high-kick" this documentary. "Sweethearts of Gridiron" is a dull experience, akin to watching a third-rate reality series compressed into 90 uneventful minutes. It would have made a much more interesting doc if it examined the somewhat-sexist implications behind cheerleading (one could argue the entire thing amounts to scantily-clad women twerking to cheer up the boys; even historically, as the doc points out, women never got to mingle with the boys, and this was their opportunity to stand out, be the "dancing girls" along with the marching band), its ramifications, relationship to the sport itself (which is barely ever mentioned), the impact of cheerleading, and sports in general in contemporary society. It does not succeed at portraying two potentially-intriguing trajectories: the cheerleader experience and how it evolved between 1940 and today;

and the paths of the current-day girls to becoming Rangerettes. There are no standout personalities or memorable character trajectories, no subdued context, no filmmaking flourishes and no suspense to the proceedings - this is a straightforward account of a bunch of well-meaning, hard-working high school graduates who just want to cheer.

The documentary, like the sport it reveres, remains vacuous, a waste of time and potential on both the filmmakers' part and the hard-working girls, who in my mind at least, could project their skills into something more substantial, like ballet, an art form that has the potential to change lives. On the other hand, if there were no cheerleaders, there would be no half-time show, and that would take away my experience of tuning in, in hopes of another boob slipping out, or Beyoncé tripping over a cheerleader, or Pink hitting the wrong note. It's all scandalous and entertaining, and this nation would be a horrid, horrid place without it.

1.5 out of 5 stars

"The Automatic Hate" Triggers Instant Viewer Animosity

Synopsis: *When Davis Green's alluring young cousin Alexis shows up on his doorstep, he discovers a side of his family that had been kept secret his entire life. As the two get closer, they set out to uncover the shocking secret that tore their families apart.*

Justin Lerner's "The Automatic Hate" scoops in a wide variety of flavors - lofty family drama, incestuous romance, dark comedy, a study of obsession - into one nasty-tasting mix, failing on all accounts. Its shock value - the one thing it had going for it - is diminished by the vacuous, insipid filmmaking, wooden performances and a pacing so languid it would make anyone's eyes wander towards their cousin's cleavage (juuust kiddin').

One lovely evening, as Davis Green's (Joseph Cross) girlfriend Cassie (Deborah Ann Woll, of "True Blood" fame) breaks up with him over a traumatic event, Alexis (Michelle Williams-lookalike Adelaide Clemens, physical resemblance being their sole similarity) shows up, all hysterical, on his porch. She impulsively asks for a hug, then informs Davis that she's his cousin. He doesn't believe her: "We have the last name, but it's pretty common. Please leave." She does - but not before dropping off her card, with her number scribbled on it.

A troubled Davis finds a painting in the basement, depicting his father with another man, which leads him to visiting his dying grandfather who, upon gazing at the painting, chokes out, "We don't talk about Joshua" - and proceeds to have a panic attack. An even more troubled Davis confronts his father Ronald (Richard Schiff), a professor at a local university, about the mysterious Joshua, but when daddy tells him to leave it alone, Davis embarks on a quest, tracking down Alexis in a tiny suburban town, filled with thrift stores, lose girls and nudist gardeners.

Joshua turns out to be Davis's gun-toting uncle, played with manic, psychotic relish by Ricky Jay, who confronts Davis at the breakfast table: "You're fucking my daughter, the least you can do is keep me company while I kill a pig." The man quickly figures Davis out. "Did he send you here to spy on me?" he asks about his brother. You see, something happened between the brothers, and therein lies the central mystery of the film.

Only it's really not that compelling, at least not enough to sustain interest for over 90 minutes, which here feel like 90 hours. Secrets lead to more secrets, family history unveils itself, an icky romance blossoms, Cassie comes back into Davis's life after an expected death - until all gets revealed, if not necessarily resolved. Compelling stuff, I know. Get in line, 'cos the tickets are sold out.

The film's shaky, awkward dialogue rings false every time a character opens their mouth. Here are just some quotable bits: "So you have any brothers or sisters? No? That's too bad"; "That guy in the bar? That's not shitty luck, that's shitty taste"; "I know you have to go now, but please promise me this is not the last time I see you"; "I love you… more than just family"; "Mind your business, you jealous c**t." (Okay, that last one I actually kinda liked.)

The acting is all over the place. Joseph Cross is okay, if a bit blank, in the lead, but the secondary characters are mostly played amateurishly. Richard Schiff and Ricky Jay, who have worked with the Coen brothers and David Mamet, respectively, have seen better days, but both do what they can to hold our interest in their poorly-written scenes. The fluctuations in tone are as borderline-bipolar as Alexis, who cries at whim, slices off chunks of people's beards with a serrated knife, and almost goes Alex Forrest on Davis's ass towards the film's end (for those of you unaware, that's a "Fatal Attraction" reference).

Some particularly off-putting, sleep-inducing and tonally jarring scenes include a bar-fight that seems to have started from nowhere; a clichéd "bonding in the country-side" sequence; an extended viewing of a roll of old film discovered in an attic; an incestuous and dispassionate sex scene; a dinner sequence inexplicably scored to Jacques Brel's French ballad "Quand On N'a Que L'amour" that results in a slapstick fight; and an ending that leaves a particularly sour taste in your mouth.

Oh, "The Automatic Hate,", how much do I loathe thee? Let me count the ways. You keep cutting away frustratingly, never letting scenes reach their culmination. You move at a snail's pace. Your pseudo-ominous undertones just underline how straightforward, pretentious and predictable you are. You provide no fresh insight into family reconciliation, obsession or family ties; you lack subtlety, though you strive for it oh-so-hard.

At times, Lerner's film, with its off-kilter (to say the least) love triangle and piling-on of stereotypes, approaches satire, or farce, but never quite reaches it, its incest vibe a particularly peculiar choice. I automatically hated this film from its first clichéd, poorly-written moment.

1.5 out of 5 stars

"The Bet" Represents Independent Filmmaking at Its Worst

Synopsis: A teenage boy and his grandfather wager a bet: which of them will be the first to 'score' with a woman.

Audiences are used to Hollywood dramas pandering to their baser instincts and bombarding them with easy-digestible sentiments, instead of trying to elevate their collective consciousness with insightful, potentially life-changing existential introspections. Of course, (increasingly rare) exceptions to the rule exist, but there is a clear dearth of such fare, the few truly good dramas being delegated to the low-budget, indie market.

It's especially disheartening when independent features, free of studio interference, attempt to appeal to the lowest common denominator and emulate Hollywood's worst tendencies. Finola Hughes' borderline-offensive feature directorial debut fails to exhibit any sense of vivacity, novelty or basic filmmaking proficiency that, say, small-budget films like Lenny Abrahamson's recent, visceral "Room" display. The film resembles the kind of sappy crap the Dream Factory churns out on a weekly basis - imagine a Katherine Heigl / Nicholas Sparks adaptation, made on a shoestring budget, with neither Heigl nor Sparks, and you'll have an idea of what to expect from "The Bet".

Scott Hagood plays Addison, the film's hapless protagonist, who, in the very first shot, types "I'm 18 and still a virgin" into Yaggle - what, I assume, is the clever result of combining the words "Google" and "Yahoo" (I can almost hear the clap of high-fives at the table-read). Addison plays video games with his socially-awkward friends Tyler (T.J. Alvarado) and Raul (Peter Isaac). His raunchy playboy grandpa, Collier (Tim T. Whitcomb), sports a stud in his ear and eyeball-scalding Hawaiian shirts, and gives Addison valuable life advice, like the following driving tip: "Women love a man who can handle a stick". Addison's widowed mother, Libby (Portia Thomas), worries about being left alone when her son goes off to college. She is dating a man but has been out of the game for a long time, her social rustiness weirdly exemplified in her inability to pick a household accessory (her choices include ugly, ceramic leprechauns, woodpeckers and eagles). Libby misses her husband; "I still don't get how someone can just get leukemia," is one of her piercingly keen observations.

One day, Collier challenges his grandson: if Addison gets laid before him, he gets Collier's old, slick Pontiac; if Addison loses, he has to fix the porch and do landscaping work (the horror!). They get to choose each other's victims - sorry! - love interests: "three choices a piece, three weeks to do it." Grandpa's "selections" for the young man include an unattainable sex bomb, who only sleeps with jocks; a goth dominatrix, who only sleeps with college students; and Jennifer (Mary O'Connor), the cute-as-a-button, blue-eyed girl of Addison's - and, let's face it, folks - everyone's dreams. Grandpa's "picks" are determined at a retirement home: a horny cougar, a grieving widow, and an uptight world traveler.

What ensues is a protracted and predictable journey of self-discovery, chockfull of stereotypical characters, inadvertent sexism, sappy montages and misjudged advice, such as when Grandpa Collier tells Addison to "just grab 'em and kiss 'em" (I'm not so sure most women would agree with that strategy). Some scenes, like the one where Addison flirts with the sultry bombshell for the first time, or visits the "bad girl" at a pseudo-gothic club (the director is obviously completely out of touch with contemporary youth) are borderline unwatchable.

Desperate attempts to elicit laughs - an impromptu face licking, forced lines like "my soul hurts when I breathe" - are so cringe-worthy, they would make David Brent shudder in revulsion. The tonal shifts are jarring, Finola Hughes' background as a soap actress (300 episodes of "General Hospital", no less!) particularly evident in "The Bet"'s dramatic scenes, which are so soapy, I felt like I dropped a bar and was being bent over in a jail shower room.

At the very least, I expected the cinematography to be decent, considering Craig Kohlhoff has worked on the sets of "Mr. & Mrs. Smith" and "Punch-Drunk Love", but it's rudimentary at best, with some shots seemingly blocked to purposefully obscure actors… Which is probably for the best - the performances here are more wooden than Grandpa Collier's Viagra-induced erection.

The concept of competing against a family member to get some action is inherently creepy. "The Bet"'s misogynistic approach is baffling, considering the director is a woman. When you combine creepiness with misogyny (behold the sequence where Grandpa Collier chooses high-school girls for his grandson on campus!), and add a dash of ageism, the resulting effect is similar to that of chugging a cup of rotten prunes - you'll be washing the sour taste from your mouth for days to come.

"The Bet" is a rare example of independent filmmaking where the goal was seemingly to appease every demographic with the most trite, manipulative tactics. The whole project should have been left alone. The film offers no new insight into human relationships, generational disparity or coming of age, in addition to being distasteful - but it's worst offense is its underestimation of contemporary audiences' intelligence.

Perhaps Hughes' will learn from her mistakes, and her next effort will be more honest and shrewd - but if I were you, I wouldn't bet on it.

1.5 out of 5 stars

1-STAR REVIEWS

"A Wrinkle in Time" May Be the Worst Disney Film in Over a Decade

Synopsis: *After the disappearance of her scientist father, three peculiar beings send Meg, her brother, and her friend to space in order to find him.*

An abomination. A travesty. A disaster, a bomb, celluloid excrement. Call it what you will, except don't call Ava DuVernay's latest collection of cobbled-together, eye-scorching images a film.

Because a film has to have a coherent plot. What we get here instead is a hip/nerdy young heroine, Meg (Storm Reid, lost in this vortex of nonsense), hopping through dimensions in search of her scientist father (Chris Pine), with the help of three nutty tramps - sorry - "The Misses" (Oprah Winfrey, Reese Witherspoon and Mindy Kaling), and her uber-annoying young brother Charles Wallace (Deric McCabe, spending way too much time on screen). How does Meg cross worlds? What determines which world she comes upon next (one consists of endless fields straight out of "What Dreams May Come", while others seem to hail from Aronofsky's nightmares)? Where did "The Misses" come from and why do they disappear halfway through? What is the all-encompassing darkness, exactly? How is Meg supposed to find her father, provided with next-to-no clues, in this chaotic psychedelia of incomprehensible nonsense?

Beats me. The plot makes zero sense. Zilch. I have not read Madeleine L'Engle's 1962 award-winning novel, upon which this film is based. I am sure it answers a lot of those questions. Or it doesn't. Books sometimes don't have to. But a film cannot rely on our knowledge of a book to coast along from one half-baked sequence to the next. Worse even, it brought back memories of infinitely more magical films like "The Neverending Story" and "The Chronicles of Narnia", what with its evocation of the Nothing, its young heroine stepping through a portal in search of her parent and encountering god-like deities in the process… Only instead of Falkor, we get a flying piece of lettuce - yes, lettuce. Go see it for yourself, if you don't believe me - or rather go buy a $16 Caesar salad and have a healthy dinner tonight.

Let's talk about the "deities", a.k.a. "The Misses", a.k.a. the tramps. First, Reese Witherspoon's Mrs. Whatsit pops up in Meg's bedroom in a horrific ginger wig and a dress that looks like a madman's origami collage. She hams it up so much, she puts her pig Rosita from "Sing" to shame. Mindy Kaling's Mrs. Who joins, in wigs of varying awfulness, grinning idiotically, batting her three-foot-long eyelashes and enunciating the film's themes by quoting random historical figures. And then - just when the lunkheaded costume design and casting choices seem to have reached their zenith - Oprah friggin' Winfrey's Mrs. Which shows up, wrapped in tinfoil, the size of a three-story building, towering over her... sisters? Lovers? Children? Regardless, Lady O wouldn't have it any other way. All three women - and their hair/eyebrows - have seen better days.

Happy Medium - a character of unknown origin in a weird, pixelated hell-like cave, played by a stoned Zach Galifianakis in what amounts to a glorified cameo - is barely worth mentioning, except for the fact that he tries his best to infuse the semblance of a narrative with some much-needed irreverence and humor. It's too little, much too late. Chris Pine is pretty smarmy to begin with - it takes the actor a lot to push past the smart and exhibit charm - and in "Wrinkle" his character does something so irredeemable towards the end, the fact that it's brushed under the rug minutes later and all is forgotten is astoundingly nonsensical.

The special effects rival the costumes for sheer awfulness. It's clear Ms. DuVernay is out of her league with digital trickery, as the CGI barely serves any purpose except background, with occasional flourishes, such as the aforementioned, badly-rendered flying lettuce leaf.

"A Wrinkle in Time" is, at-best, a C-list production with a $100+ million budget, an incoherent mess, with wooden characters processing cardboard instead of emoting, logic be damned. It's awkwardly paced, poorly acted and directed, it's messages are muddled and worst of all, it's ugly, with no sense of style or substance. I watched the "film" at a press screening with my wife. Both of our jaws remained dropped at the ineptness of it all, the sheer circus of failure on display. It was one of the only screenings where I almost walked out of the theater at about the halfway point - and I would have missed nothing if I did.

I was never a huge fan of Ava DuVernay's chest-thumping "Selma" or the pedantic doc "13th", but they displayed some real filmmaking chops, an acute knowledge of plot advancement and the importance of creating strong characters. It's as if, swallowed by the massive corporation that is Disney, Ava lost track of herself, popped twelve tabs of acid... and pieced together this entire "pastiche" the next day, during the comedown.

1 out of 5 stars

"Dark Moon Rising" Marks Another Disaster in Eric Roberts' Overstuffed Filmography

Synopsis: *A group of shape-shifting werewolves descend upon a small town in search of a girl who is re-born once every 2000 years. She holds the key to their survival and all will die who stand in their way.*

Eric Roberts' films should come with an "Enter at Your Own Risk" warning. At the time of writing this review, the actor boasts - get this - 259 titles on his resume, with 34 currently in production, and 11 more in development, amongst them the bound-to-be-classics "Santa's Boot Camp" and "Sicilian Vampire". It would take over a month of marathoning through Eric Roberts films, if you were to watch them back-to-back; by the time you reached "A Talking Cat!?!", you would most probably have given up on cinema forever and/or committed yourself to a mental institution.

Eric Roberts' was once fantastic in Andrey Konchalovsky's 1985 thriller "Runaway Train". The hard-working man joins the mighty pantheon of once-promising American actors, who, after giving at least one mesmerizing performance, somehow lost their path. There's Michael Madsen, and his razor-blade dance in "Reservoir Dogs" - despite Tarantino keeping him afloat in intermittent, high-profile projects, Madsen seems to say yes to every horrendous script that lands on his agent's desk ("Vigilante Diaries", anyone? No? How about "Lady Psycho Killer"?) Then there's Tom Sizemore: after his unforgettable turn in "True Romance", he went through some, ahem, personal stuff, and now his most recent project in production is… "Halloweed", whose gimmick you can probably guess. I won't even go into tracing he careers of Gary Busey or Tony Todd - you get the idea.

You also may have noticed that I spent the first two paragraphs avoiding writing about "Dark Moon Rising". That's because the career of Eric Roberts (and his revered peers) opens doors to an endlessly more fascinating and complex discussion than anything this lackluster effort can potentially warrant. Roberts is only in a few relatively brief sequences, but his manic scenery-chewing is more vicious than any of the film's werewolves, at least providing those scenes with a "so-bad-it's-hilariously-bad" vibe. It's difficult to figure out whether his character - a werewolf hunter / Vietnam vet - is drunk, or whether Roberts showed up on set annihilated, which makes observing this fiasco moderately fun. The rest of the film is unwatchable.

Where do I start? Do I go into analyzing how the opening scene establishes the prevailing murkiness of the film, which evidently makes the terrible effects - along with the shoddy acting and blurry cinematography - less noticeable? Should I talk about the dialogue, chock-full of lines that were apparently written by an inebriated monkey ("Don't let your mind create sympathy for the beast" is one of my favorites - and most deeply felt - statements)?

I could talk about the opening credits that spell out the actors' names, along with their characters' names (because you will surely not remember them); or the reoccurring "WTF" "mind-surfing" sequences, that plunge the protagonists into a theater-stage-like setting, with a blatantly fake moon and even more blatantly fake floating critters, who vaguely resemble the forest spirits from "Princess Mononoke" or the, um, forest spirits in "Avatar". I was compelled to discuss the soundtrack, a jarringly intrusive fusion of Gothic rock, drum-and-bass and ear-splitting dub-step.

But what's the point? Everything in this film - from the central vacuous hole of a performance by Cameron White, who imbues his goth/hipster character with zero personality, to the abundant horror-film clichés that pile on top of each other in a rapid succession - was clearly made by amateurs with no real understanding of narrative structure, character development, forward momentum, lighting, effects, and so on. The climactic showdown (letdown?) at an abandoned factory with an evil guy sporting a Wolverine hairdo puts the final nail in this coffin.

Faintly resembling a very cheap version of those 1990's Kevin Williamson "teen-slaughter" pics, "Dark Moon Rising" makes "I Still Know What You Did Last Summer" look like "The Night of the Hunter" (or "Twilight" look like "Citizen Kane", or… oh, I could go on forever). If you want to see how to make a good werewolf flick on a tight budget, you'll be better off checking out Neil Marshall's "Dog Soldiers". Rest assured, that one doesn't have Eric Roberts in it.

1 out of 5 stars

"Honeyglue" Sets a New Low for Cancer Dramas

Synopsis: *After learning she only has three months to live, Morgan flips her conservative protected life upside down. That is where she meets Jordan, a rebellious gender-defying artist, who takes her on adventure of a lifetime.*

I have always had a big issue with cancer dramas. For whom are they made, and why? If you have a terminal disease, and the main character lives at the end, it may give you false hope, the last thing you need. If the central protagonist dies, then it just reiterates the point that struggle/hope is futile for us all. If you don't have a terminal disease, whatever the outcome of the film, it reminds you that it can happen to you any day.

There are so many of them, too. "Love Story", "Sweet November", "Stepmom", "My Sister's Keeper" and the recent "The Fault in Our Stars", with its "you-have-to-see-it-to-believe-it Anne Frank sequence", instantly come to mind as the most jarring. While some valiantly try to sidestep sentimentality and deal with the subject sensitively (if you MUST watch a cancer film, see "Terms of Endearment" (which is at least well-written, acted and directed) or "50/50" (which is at least somewhat funny)), the disease, like intellectual disability (see - or rather don't: "The Other Sister", "I Am Sam"), or faith (see - or rather don't: "God's Not Dead", "Miracles from Heaven") is the trickiest of subjects; those films' borderline-offensive, relentless mushiness blatantly manipulating one into sobbing and/or gagging. They pander to their respective demos, capitalizing on the most personal of issues by stomping them to death. It's cruel and incredibly offensive.

One can never depict, in 2 hours or less, what it's truly like to face certain death, to slowly deteriorate, to feel yourself disappear. (Sidenote: Michael Haneke came closest with his heart-shredding "Amour" - but it dealt with Death head-on, artfully, inspiring profound existential rumination, and he is the only filmmaker I can think of that can pull off such a feat). I'm still struggling to find a reason for why one would even attempt such an endeavor. James Bird clearly had good intentions - and the guts - to contribute to the aforementioned line-up of terminal-illness features. His laughably terrible "gender-defying" cancer drama "Honeyglue" further reiterates my point. I have absolutely nothing against gay-themed films, but do YOU want to see a "gender-defying" cancer drama? Case closed.

This one may actually be worth a look, just for how disastrously misguided it is. From the get go, it unabashedly dives into phoniness, with Morgan (Adriana Mather) and Jordan (Zach Villa) making a suicide video, "a farewell video to our family", followed by the oh-so-poignant credits: "A dragonfly's lifespan is three months long.

In that lifetime, our love story takes place." (Can't you just see the filmmaking team, arduously researching the lifespans of different animals, until one stumbles upon the dragonfly, which also –gasp! - happens to be a phrase some transgender people use to refer to themselves – BINGO!) Lo and behold, the damn dragonfly gets another shout-out less than 2 minutes later, in a boisterous techno nightclub, during the following "lyrical meet-cute" that had me in stitches: "What are you?" "What do you mean, what am I?" "Are you a dragonfly?" "I look like an insect?" "Like a dragonfly." This dialogue, which would make Charlie Kaufman implode with envy, goes on, but I'll spare you the juicy details (or let you discover them yourselves – unless you have paint drying or grass growing that requires your immediate attention).

After a night of clubbin' and making out, Morgan and the "rebellious gender-defying artist" Jordan (by the way, note the subtle symbolism in their name similarity – very much in line with the whole "gender-defying" theme) exchange numbers "I'll always remember this night, kissing the very attractive boy-girl," Morgan says sexily. "It's girl-boy," comes the solemn response. "Your 8s looks like 9s," he then says, watching her scribble the number. "My 9s look like 8s," she corrects him. Excuse me while I go wash out all the metaphorical stench out of my mouth. Turns out, Jordan stole Morgan's wallet – on her birthday, no less, which – you guessed it – happens to be on the same day as his - and proceeds to converse with a bee (no joke!) in the shockingly empty nightclub parking lot, before absconding to his tent on a high-rise roof.

Next day, a doctor informs Morgan's distressed parents Dennis (Christopher Heyerdahl) and Janet (Jessica Tuck) of the grave news: Morgan's cancer is spreading – and fast. "I'm afraid it's irreversible," the doctor says oh-so-gently. "The swelling in her brain is only going to get worse… It's difficult to say how long… Three months, maybe…" What a bomb to drop! Bailey (Booboo Stewart), Morgan's brother, doesn't want to "hear this shit" and storms off, while the parents weep at the futility of it all.

Jordan returns Morgan's wallet, and a romance ensues, filled with all the aspects you'd expect in a love story between a transgender artist and a cancer-stricken patient: prejudice (racism, sexism, ageism, metabolism – you name it, it's here), high-pitched melodrama that makes "The Young and the Restless" seem Fincher-esque by comparison – and dragged-out, painful scenes of atrocious acting. Adriana Mather fares worst in the central role, her lips barely moving when she tries to emote, her expressions static as her character disintegrates on screen. The fact that Zach Villa, his character an embodiment of every "gay artist" cliché in the book, pulls off some of his lines and actually casts a semblance of an impression in this dreck just makes me wish he were in a project better suited to his talents. Poor guy. He valiantly tries – and fails – to develop any chemistry with his on-screen partner. The rest of the cast have seen better days too, especially the great Amanda Plummer, stuck here in a thankless role as Alice, Jordan's trailer-trash mother.

There are too many ill-judged sequences to count; in fact, I don't think there was a single moment that worked. There's the scene of Morgan playing Inspector Clouseau with the "dragonfly boy" that is so atrocious you really kinda have to see it to believe it. Same applies to the dinner scene, where Morgan introduces Jordan to her family, the camera wildly spinning around the table as if it were on drugs. "Honeyglue"'s poor production values are especially apparent in the animated interludes, which hammer the film's themes into your head remorselessly.

The sub-plot involving Jordan owing money to his ex-girlfriend Misty (a shrill Fernanda Romero) drags the film further into the pits of hell. The obligatory head-shaving sequence is scored to the worst-possible song they could have picked. There is a wedding ceremony – another musical montage of archival footage designed to melt your heartstrings but instead plucking at them till they're shredded. Morgan and Jordan's wedding night is yet another lovemaking montage (there are 398 montages in this film). At the end they become "outlaw bandits", and the film completely skids off the rails (it involves a kidnapping, and the most idiotic request ever committed to celluloid). And really, shut the fuck up about the damn dragonflies already – it's bringing back memories of that horrid 2003 Kevin Costner film, which doesn't help matters at all! I threw up more times during "Honeyglue" than its protagonist did from the chemotherapy.

As for the dialogue, I'll just let the following Shakespearean verses speak for themselves: "It's not what I got, it's what I want." "And what is that?" "You." (Gag reflex, full throttle!); "He expresses himself, that's what's important. Not everyone is brave enough to do that." (True that!); "It's about self-liberation, freeing yourself from the shackles of conformity." (How poetic!); "Morgan is a gay lesbian." "I'm so confused – does that mean he's a straight homosexual?" (I'm confused too, but for many other reasons); "I have a brain tumor." "A brain tumor? Like what, a tumor in your brain?" (No silly, I'm talking about unicorn confetti); "What happened to your face?" "Someone broke my heart, and it spread to my face." (Hahahaha!); "I just want to put her back inside me so we can start all over again." (Yuck!); "She needs to be outside so she can fly" (No comment on this one) … One line particularly reminded me of a scene from the classic comedy "Airplane": "Jordan, have you ever been arrested?" ("Have you ever seen a grown man naked, Billy?")

No amount of good will can save this repetitive film from being an utter bomb, an insulting, confused mess that displays zero understanding of what it truly feels like to rapidly approach the inevitable. Based on this evidence, director James Bird (who also wrote and produced) should stick to his day job… let's just hope it has nothing to do with oncology.

1 out of 5 stars

Move Aside, Denis Villeneuve: "Ripped" Announces a New Auteur in Town

Synopsis: The story of two free spirited stoners who, after smoking some top secret pot created by the CIA in 1986, find themselves catapulted into 2016. With 30 years of their lives lost, our now balding and overweight friends use their uncomplicated enthusiasm to get their lives back on track and figure out the modern world.

Brad Epstein's career as a producer of romantic comedies ("About a Boy", "Dan in Real Life", "Ghost of Girlfriends Past") may lead one to assume that his directorial debut would delve into similar "girl-meets-boy-or-vice-versa" territory. Yet a closer look at his earlier choices (Q-Tip's "Prison Song", "The Adventures of Rocky & Bullwinkle", "Ed") reveals a filmography as riveting and flawless as his latest film "Ripped", coming out now, in 2017, hot on the heels of 2009's "Ghost of Girlfriends Past". Either some big studio fallout occurred, or it really took Brad eight years of absolute focus (and heavy marijuana consumption) to create this masterpiece.

And a gem this is, a radiant emerald beckoning us in those murky waters of worthless indie filth, like "Norman" (read review <u>here</u>) or "Chuck" or "The Wall", littering our minds with their incisive commentaries, thought-provoking ideas and character studies. Simplicity is key, see. The effort and time Epstein must have dedicated to bringing this concept to fruition were absolutely worth it. "Ripped" is bound to go down - scratch that - it's already been catapulted into the anal canals of cinematic history as perhaps the best film to grace (VOD) screens since… well, since sand scalded Lawrence's feet in Arabia. Yes, it is this terrific.

I'll tightly pack the plot summary for you into the bowl, so you can take it all in one bong hit. Ready? Sparking. Harris (Vandit Bhatt) and Reeves (Kyle Massey) smoke a lot of weed, live out of their van and dream big - until their van gets stuck in a ditch, and they wake up 30 years later in the bodies of Russell Peters and Faizon Love. This must be the cleverest midway twist since Tom Stall killed Carl Fogarty in "The History of Violence", and if we're not on the same page, you may as well stop reading this review.

Still with me? Spark it again. When they see everyone on their cell-phones - obviously strange, new devices to our aged, stoned protagonists - they react in the most poignant and knee-snappingly funny way possible: "Why is everyone on their calculators?" Kudos to Epstein and his co-writer Billiam Coronel for sharpening their dialogue and flair for memorable one-liners. I'll get back to those - the plot is just so involving.

We follow Reeves and Harris on their misadventures, as they encounter modern technology, get prescription marijuana medication, come up with an intricate business plan and - get ready for this whammy - find love. Alex Meneses' performances as Debbie, Harris' love interest, is unforgettable, up there with Hepburn' and Streep's best work. When the two of them are on screen, such as when they delve into their past at a record shop, sparks fly that haven't scathed as harshly since Demi Moore met eyes with Robert Redford in "Indecent Proposal".

It's the way Epstein weaves complexities into the seemingly-simple proceedings that really gives "Ripped" its edge. From the get go, the film starts off with a controversial quote: "Marijuana is not a drug. I used to suck cock for cocaine. You never suck cock for marijuana." It says it's from an "Unknown 80's Television Star", but I think Epstein is being modest - this is clearly a passage from James Joyce's "Odyssey".

A prostate exam halfway through the film made me laugh so hard, I thought I'd lose control over my own bowel movements (damn you, Epstein!). When Harris and Debbie's son discover Skrillex and turntables, it reminded me of the pure, unadulterated joy cinema can evoke in audiences. Hilarious scenes like the young protagonists stripping in front of a drug dealer or being confused by a contemporary urinal emphasize the way society suppresses the drug culture, and how all the money we spend on the war on drugs should be delegated to the War on Garbage Cinema. The final presentation Harris and Reeves give tops the film off on the highest (pun intended) note imaginable.

As for the aforementioned dialogue, I'll let those ores of pure gold speak for themselves: "If you go down on me, I'll take off 10%. If you make me squirt, I'll take off 20." "I could hear my ears listening to things." "I hope that the glutens eat free." "Better to be pissed off than pissed on." "Back in the day, the only people who used to wear helmets and pads were retards and women on their periods."

Though, according to a passage in the film involving a newspaper, the project may have been laying on the shelf for close to a year now, looks like there will be a lucky few who will see and appreciate its glory. I'm glad Brad Epstein left his romantic comedy streak in the past, along with those pesky ghosts of girlfriends.

Clearly, his "stop-and-go" slew of extraordinary projects all led to this impeccable study of humanity, carefully wrapped under the guise of a stupid stoner comedy - and only the uninitiated, those who don't appreciate true art, will mistake it for a stupid stoner comedy. Hopefully, there aren't too many of "those" among us.

That would probably upset Mr. Epstein, and I wouldn't want to distract him - who knows what kind of masterpiece he will drop on us eight years from now.

1 out of 5 stars

"Tales of Poe"'s Tell Tale Heart Lacks a Pulse

Synopsis: *Based on the classic works of Edgar Allan Poe - a unique spin on three of Poe's popular stories.*

Directors Bart Mastronardi and Alan Rowe Kelly clearly adore horror. One look at their credits reveals a slew of Z-list slasher flicks with obvious titles that speak for themselves: "Vindication", "Gallery of Fear", "She Wolf Rising", "Grindsploitation"… Unfortunately, their affection of the genre does not translate to technical prowess. Another horror film aficionado, heavy metal musician Rob Zombie, displayed surprising directorial chops with the "The Devil's Rejects" and his remake of "Halloween" - both flawed-but-ambitious films, dripping with throwback style and a wretched/depraved/sick aura that has since become the director's trademark. "Tales of Poe" strives hard to match that level of assuredness, but Mastronardi and Kelly's attempt to "pull a Zombie" fails drastically. None of the bearded filmmaker's skill is evident, showcasing the two directors as eager fans who perhaps need to take a film class or two to hone their craft behind the camera.

Split into three parts, "Tales of Poe" starts with the best one (and that's saying a lot, considering how sub-par it is), "The Tell-Tale Heart", whose heartbeat plot will be known to anyone at all familiar with Poe. A middle-aged nurse (C-list horror mainstay Debbie Rochon), freshly committed to a mental hospital, encounters a wildly unhinged patient, Evelyn (Lesleh Donaldson), who corners her, rasping: "Tell me what you've done or I'll rip out your cunt, like I did with all my husband's other sluts." (Classy!) So our hero reveals the story of how she used to work for an aging Hollywood star, Miss Lamarr (co-director Alan Rowe Kelly, hamming it up), in a giant Gothic mansion. The nurse quickly becomes obsessed with Miss Lamarr's "empty, lifeless" eye, making it her goal to "rid herself of it forever". And so she does - using her stiletto, no less! Before she has time to seduce and mount an oblivious police officer, the floors begin to shake, and Miss Lamarr's beating heart sends the nurse on a rapid downward spiral.

The second story, "The Cask", begins at a vineyard (we know this, because there is a repeated close-up of a green grape that graces the screen between each scene transition). The wealthy Fortunato Montresor (a flamboyant Randy Jones) is getting married to the deceitful Gogo (Alan Rowe Kelly, again). He takes Gogo, along with some friends and family, down to his wine cellar, where they encounter the mysterious Marco Lechresi (Brewster McCall). Before he knows it, Fortunato awakes paralyzed, and helplessly watches Gogo and Marco entomb him within the building's walls. Mired in atrocious dialogue, FX and acting, "The Cask" has next to no redeeming value.

But it's a masterpiece compared to the final story, if you can even call it that, entitled "Dreams". The protagonist, a young woman (Bette Cassatt) is immersed into a variety of different trippy environments, supplemented by a sometimes-ominous, sometimes-lunatic musical score. Inherently, the concept of visualizing someone's nightmares is a tricky task - it's akin to the utterly tedious chore of listening to someone recounting their dreams - and the third part of this anthology is a near-wordless hallucinatory mess, a jumbled montage of cheap, distorted shots, demons dancing behind white bed sheets, 19th-Century frolicking/picnicking in a garden, grotesque "The Cell"-like torture and crimson-red roses - all seemingly edited by someone deep into week three of a massive cocaine binge.

"Tales of Poe" contains all the hallmarks of a made-for-TV production: cheap title credits, bad acting, shoddy effects, nails-on-a-chalkboard dialogue… The mental hospital is straight out of TV's campy "American Horror Story", filled with belligerent maniacs and crazed, murderous psychos. Even Poe's lovely prose, injected intermittently to add some sophistication to the proceedings, can't save the film, which substitutes their subliminal terror with a blood-and-gore-soaked orgy. Think of an extended, particularly cheap "Tales of the Crypt" episode, and you'll be close to imagining what the experience of sitting through "Tales of Poe" is like. Among the esteemed author's many adaptations ("The Raven", "The Pit and the Pendulum" "Extraordinary Tales", etc.), "Tales of Poe" crumples to pieces like the House of Usher. Here's hoping Mastronardi and Kelly leave H.P. Lovecraft alone.

1 out of 5 stars

"The River Thief" Shamelessly Steals Your Time

Synopsis: *Diz is a reckless teenage drifter living life on the run. When Diz floats into a small town on the Snake River, he is confronted by an unflappable old man named Marty, falls for Marty's guarded granddaughter Selah, and robs a local drug-dealing crazy. With more money than he knows what to do with, and criminals at his heels, Diz puts the people he's learned to care about in danger.*

Sometimes films turn out to be so bad, they defy categorization. What were the filmmakers behind "The River Thief" thinking? The whole affair strongly whiffs of pseudo-inspirational, target-audience-pandering faith-based fare, where things like proper character development, originality, tension, nuance and so forth get swept away by wild efforts to please the Bible crowd with finger-wagging messages. If, however, director N.D. Wilson's intention was to make a sobering drama with thriller elements, he failed miserably on both accounts, filling his ridiculous plot with such a rapid succession of genre staples, one would be hard-pressed to pinpoint each one. In fact, that's probably the only thing this film is good for: playing a drinking game called "Spot the Stereotype!" Warning: rapid intoxication will occur.

It all starts well with a series of beautiful images of a Grand Canyon-like valley. We follow young Diz (Joel Courtney) down the Snake River as he robs people, stealing everything that comes his way - from small things, like shirts, to guns and boats. He gets by and seems content, one with the river, always escaping into its safety. The first five minutes or so, I was perked up, somewhat intrigued by where the film was taking me.

Turns out, into a swampy land of atrocious dialogue and amateur acting. Diz meets Selah (Raleigh Cain), a waitress, and pays her with a candle and a porcelain girl ("She reminds me of you," he says.) When Selah kicks him out, Diz proceeds to spy on her singing gospel tunes with her God-loving grandfather Marty (a wooden Tommy Cash - the late Johnny's younger brother). When Diz stumbles on a drug deal, unknowingly stealing the thugs' car, he barely makes an escape in the all-cleansing river. Now Clyde (Bas Rutten) and Saul (Paul Johansson) are on his tail.

One boring thing leads to an even duller one, until Marty and Selah eventually get kidnapped for ransom - along with Diz later - and two twists, one more ridiculous than the other, occur in rapid succession, in a desperate attempt to tie everything together neatly and tack on a profound message at the end. Long story short, what initially starts as a somewhat-unusual study of a young, confident, rebellious kid with potential, swiftly becomes mired in half-assed filmmaking - the type of which I've seen too many times, having worked in the distribution business.

No one sets out to make a bad film? People who want to make money with their no-name, low-budget endeavors, that's who. Lacking the talent to produce anything that would be artful or worthwhile, they are keen to be in the industry and/or monetize their product by targeting specific demos - in this case, I presume, secluded church-goers, righteous families and ignorant hillbillies. Anyone with an above-average intelligence would dismiss this crap, which has nothing to offer, except for maybe its funky soundtrack and a basic sequencing/editing prowess.

I mentioned horrid acting and dialogue. Perhaps the former would be better if the latter was polished (or entirely rewritten) a few more times. Here are a few shining examples of the wisdom "The River Thief" imparts: "You think stealing gives you control? Well, gratitude gives you freedom." "You are my family. I've been given to you and you've been given to me." "I don't believe in money," Diz declares defiantly at one point. "The only thing dumber than a guy is a girl," a bartender says. "That's just rude," Selah replies, the quick-witted firecracker that she is. "I don't believe in sermon, old man," Diz proclaims (he generally doesn't "believe", you see). Marty's enigmatic response? "Well, that's a matter of opinion." The thugs are especially memorable, with quips like, "That's when I'll catch him. And when I do… then you can skin him" rendering them supremely threatening.

Whether you're a devout churchgoer or not, if you've ever seen a decent film or read a good book - or even if you haven't - avoid this thief at all cost.

1 out of 5 stars

Blackface, Necromancy & Lovesick Caribbean Mummies: Revisiting Manuel Caño's Demented "Voodoo Black Exorcist"

Synopsis: *The mummy of a long dormant but powerful Caribbean voodoo priest Gatanebo gets revived on a luxury South Seas ocean liner and proceeds to terrorize the passengers. He falls for the ravishing Sylvia, who reminds him of his old flame Kenya.*

I can see the advertisements for Manuel Caño's 1974 Spanish "voodoosploitation" flick, "Voodoo Black Exorcist", clearly: "The director of "The Swamp of the Ravens" Unleashes A Horrifying Tale of Savage Murder, Witchcraft and… Love!" Okay, I made that tagline up - there was no way I was going to one-up the real thing: "This Dude Means Business, So Watch Out When Your Nerves Start to Shatter!"

Coming from the same bottomless reserve of Z-list exploitation films as the one Robert Rodriguez and Quentin Tarantino dug into for grainy, crude and cheap "Grindhouse" inspirations, "Voodoo Black Exorcist" lives up to its genre in every conceivable way. It's poorly made, from top to bottom: horrific acting from leads Aldo Sambrell, Fernando Sancho and Eva León; little-to-no sense of camera positioning, lens focusing or, you know, narrative structure; laughable English dubbing; editing so choppy it makes the chopping in the film pale in comparison… And that's of course, disregarding the blatant racism, white actors shamelessly strolling around in full "blackface" make up; the glorified violence; the senseless nudity and frequent objectification of women… So bad it's good? Not really. If "Voodoo"'s got one thing for it, it's this: predictable it's not.

In other words, you'll have little-to-no clue what's going on and/or you won't give a rat's ass. I'll throw some expletives at you, in true grindhouse tradition. Woman's Head Gets Sliced Off in A Sinister Island Voodoo Ritual! Blatantly Caucasian Head Swiftly Turns Dark-Skinned Once Detached From Body! A U.S.S.R. Rocket Departs to Space! An Ancient Mummy Inexplicably Ends Up on A Luxury Ocean Liner! A Woman's Mystical Tribal Belly-Dance Awakens Mummy! Mummy Kills Innocent Kitten! Mummy Sees White Woman, Experiences Flashbacks To Its Blackface Lover! Mummy Chops Off Innocent Man's Papier-Mâché Head! White Woman Wakes Up Next To Disembodied Head ("Godfather" homage, anyone?) Filmmakers Take Ayahuasca!
All Hell Breaks Lose!

Some exploitation classics deserve resurrecting. Examples include: "Night of The Living Dead", "The Texas Chainsaw Massacre", Dario Argento's stuff, all the

Pam Grier blaxploitation stuff, "Dirty Mary, Crazy Larry" and "Vanishing Point", if you're a fan of car flicks… I'll even go so far as to find redeeming value in video "nasties", such as "Cannibal Holocaust" and "Last House on The Left". Those cult classics possessed a sort of rugged, dark charm and basic filmmaking proficiency. "Voodoo Black Exorcist" has all the production/ethical values of a cheap 1970's porn, minus the titillation. It's a truly painful-to-sit-through mess of a film. No wonder it's been brought back to life by The Film Detective, known for resurrecting cult-ish duds (see: "Dementia 13", "A Bucket of Blood", etc). Criterion wouldn't touch this with a ten-foot beeswax candle.

1 out of 5 stars

0-STAR REVIEW

"We Make Movies" Gives the Finger to the Art of Filmmaking

Synopsis: *A heartfelt and hilarious comedy chronicling the ups and downs of a group of college students who spend their summer making a movie for their town's Film Festival.*

Once in a blue moon, a film comes by that is so unabashedly misguided, it defies description - or a coherent review. What in the world was Matt Tory thinking when he put together his lame excuse for a crew and proceeded to shoot the incoherent mess that is "We Make Movies"? In my mind, he got high, binge-watched "The Office", thought, "Hey, I could do that Michael Scott thing, but, like, about making movies and shit". He then called his film-nerd friend, who was, like, "Totally, dude, it'll be like a micro-budget 'For Your Consideration' meets 'Ed Wood'!". They then got high together while working on the script, and decided, screw it, we'll do the Larry David thing and just come up with random outlines, sketches and puns - mostly revolving around character names ("Stevphen"), town names ("Boehring"), riffs on Hollywood franchises ("Dreidel to the Grave") - and so on, so forth. As a result, they produced a film so awkward in pacing, intent, acting - literally very aspect of production - that it falls under that rarefied "zero-star" film category, having absolutely no merit for existing. Only due to my unadulterated love of filmmaking did I cringe through the entire almost two-hour (!) length of this garbage.

One of the main issues is that Tory's just not NEARLY wise/savvy enough to satirize popular films, rendering his jokes futile and tasteless. From the get-go, "We Make Movies" starts with two cinematic tropes in one second: the pointless "Based on a True Story" gimmick, instantly follow by a California desert shot, with the titles proclaiming "Arabia". Do they mean the entire Arabian Peninsula, spanning 3.2 million square miles? I wish that were the joke of the scene - how redundant location credits in films can get - but no, the plot swerves wildly, "panning back" to reveal that it's director extraordinaire Stevphen's (Matt Tory, tackling the mighty task of writing/producing/directing AND starring) crew working on an ultra-ultra-micro-budget film set. A wild vortex forms - an abysmal director, Matt Tory, making a film about abysmal filmmaking that satirizes abysmal Hollywood productions - sucking the entire enterprise, and its audience, into a dark, dark abyss of cinematic depravity. Tory's purportedly incisive stabs at clichés, if that's what they actually are, happen to make one long for the clichés he satirizes.

Stevphen and his right hand, Donny (Jordan Hopewell), argue about executive producer credit and coax their "star" friends Garth (Jonathan Holmes) and method actor Leonard (pronounced "Lee-o-nahrd") into being in their new film (the latter starved himself for six hours once for a role - are your sides splittin' yet?). Stevphen's "film" is titled "A New Don: Part II" ("It's like 'Star Wars'; after they see this one, they're gonna be dying to see what happened in the first one"), and Tory makes us follow the characters through a painfully-unfunny table-read, acting in front of a green curtain, etc. "He's like my Sundance Kid, the Burt to my Ernie… Tonto, to my Walker Texas Ranger" is just an example of a line reading, which probably made Tory's crew's guts bust with uproarious laughter. "Shalom, suckers!" a rabbi yelps, machine-gunning away - trust me, it sounds way more amusing than it is.

I'm all about supportive micro-budget filmmakers whose ambition and skill overshadows a lack of production values - see my review of the minuscule-budget "People" here. Yet when a film, as earnest as its goals may be, is done this poorly, with no sense of pacing or comedic timing, it makes me sad that we live in an era where anyone with a bit of cash can grab a camera and consequently pollute Amazon Prime with their crap. While there are certainly benefits to talented filmmakers having the ability to publicly express themselves, the downside is, turds like "We Make Movies" are churned out on a daily basis, polluting VOD "Recently Added" lists. Time is precious, as is the art of filmmaking - "We Make Movies", which could have been shot by my 12-year-old sister, is a sad waste in regards to both.

There's absolutely no reason for anyone to see "We Make Movies", a flimsy, cheap and poorly acted so-called "satire" on filmmaking, especially when great films, like David Mamet's "State and Main", Tim Burton's "Ed Wood", Robert Altman's "The Player", or even Tom DiCillo's micro-budget mini-masterpiece "Living in Oblivion", deal with the subject in much more artful, confident - and most importantly, bitingly witty and entertaining - ways. Those directors know the cinematic world they inhabit and satirize. Matt Tory either needs to stick to his day job or "make way more movies" - and much better ones than this heap of junk - before he can claim the right to poke fun at the industry. Let's hope he spares us.

0 out of 5 stars

ALEX'S BEST & WORST FILMS OF 2016

Best Films of 2016

1. The Handmaiden
2. The Red Turtle
3. The Lobster
4. Hell or High Water
5. Manchester by the Sea
6. Arrival
7. Neruda
8. Kubo and the Two Strings
9. Aquarius
10. Things to Come

Honorable Mentions:

Miss Sharon Jones!
People
Morris from America
13th
The Music of Strangers
Sky Ladder: The Art of Cai Guo-Qiang
Embrace of the Serpent
Son of Saul
Hunt for the Wilderpeople
Midnight Special
Deadpool
Lemonade

Potential Contenders I Haven't Seen Yet:

Martin Scorsese's "Silence" (Note: did not end up making the list)
Jim Jarmusch's "Paterson" (Note: did not end up making the list)
Morten Tyldum's "Passengers" (Note: DEFINITELY did not end up making the list)
J. A. Bayona's "A Monster Calls" (Note: added to "Honorable Mentions")
Denzel Washington's "Fences" (Note: added to "Honorable Mentions")
Aren Ade's "Toni Erdmann" (Note: added to "Honorable Mentions")
Tom Ford's "Nocturnal Animals" (Note: added as #7 Best Film of 2016, moving the rest of the list down respectively)

Paul Verhoeven's "Elle" (Note: still haven't seen the film at the time of this book's publication.)

Alex's Worst Films of 2016

1. Mother's Day
2. Honeyglue
3. Boo! A Madea Halloween
4. Billy Lynn's Long Halftime Walk
5. Dirty Grandpa
6. Zoolander 2
7. Ride Along 2
8. London Has Fallen
9. Gods of Egypt
10. My Big Fat Greek Wedding 2

Dishonorable Mentions:

Les Cowboys
The River Thief
Collateral Beauty
Adam Sandler's Netflix excrements: The Do-Over / The Ridiculous 8 / True Memoirs of an International Assassin

Missed Opportunities

Miss Peregrine's Home for Peculiar Children
The Witch
Desierto
Max Rose
The Light Between Oceans
Voyage of Time: The IMAX Experience
The Birth of a Nation
Mifune: The Last Samurai
Moonlight
La La Land
Allied
Independence Day: Resurgence
Suicide Squad
Batman v. Superman: Dawn of Justice
Rogue One: A Star Wars Story

ALEX'S BEST & WORST FILMS OF 2017

Best Films of 2016

1. mother!
2. The Florida Project
3. Call Me by Your Name
4. The Shape of Water
5. Three Posters Outside Ebbing, Missouri
6. Coco
7. BPM
8. Personal Shopper
9. Ladybird
10. It Comes Out at Night

10 Honorable Mentions

1. Dunkirk
2. Raw
3. The Meyerowitz Stories
4. Good Time
5. Tragedy Girls
6. Thor: Ragnarok
7. The Bad Batch
8. Thelma
9. The Lost City of Z
10. Jim & Andy: A Look Beyond

10 Likely Contenders I'm Yet to See

1. Faces Places (Note: still haven't seen the film at the time of this book's publication)
2. A Fantastic Woman (Note: did not end up making the list)
3. Phantom Thread (Note: added as #6 Best Film of 2017, moving the rest of the list down respectively)
4. You Were Never Really Here (Note: still haven't seen the film at the time of this book's publication)
5. The Death of Stalin (Note: did not end up making the list)
6. Brawl in Cell Block 99 (Note: added as #8 Best Film of 2017, moving the rest of the list down respectively)

7. I, Tonya (Note: did not end up making the list)

8. God's Own Country (Note: still haven't seen the film at the time of this book's publication)

9. Loveless (Note: still haven't seen the film at the time of this book's publication)

10. Quest (Note: still haven't seen the film at the time of this book's publication)

10 Biggest Disappointments and Near Misses

1. The Killing of a Sacred Deer
2. Blade Runner 2049
3. Battle of the Sexes
4. Star Wars: The Last Jedi
5. Film Stars Don't Die in Liverpool
6. Justice League
7. In the Fade
8. It
9. Valerian and the City of a Thousand Planets
10. Free Fire

10 Worst Films of the Year

1. We Make Movies
2. Emoji Movie
3. Boo 2
4. Ripped
5. A Family Man / Geostorm (Gerard Butler double-bill)
6. Why Him?
7. Beauty and the Beast
8. The Mummy
9. Fifty Shades Darker
10. Life

Alex's Top 38 Horror Films Of All Time

Anyone who's ever compiled a list will tell you it's an arduous (but fun) task. While it's next to impossible to include every horror gem - nor have I had the opportunity to see a great deal of films that should be on this list but, well, aren't (including ones that have been released since I published this book) - I did my best to share my own, personal preferences, as well as some reasoning behind each choice. Feel free to comment, complain - or slay me in the darkest of nights in a Shatner mask.

38. Grindhouse
Granted, this ode to exploitation classics may not be everyone's cup of tea – it's lurid, gratuitous, eccentric, badly shot – but if you like this sort of thing, as I do, you may discover a gem, a knowing homage to grimy cinema of yore, 1970s splatterfests (it even contains missing reels!). The hilarious mock-trailers by Rob Zombie ("House of 1000 Corpses"), Eli Roth ("Hostel") and Edgar Wright ("Shaun of the Dead") are the standouts; Robert Rodriguez's zombie gore-fest "Planet Terror" is fun but all over the place; Quentin Tarantino's foot/car fetishes are in full display in "Death-Proof", a talky female-empowerment tale and direct homage to the infamous car chase sequence in 1971's "Vanishing Point", with a stellar Kurt Russell in his 1980s badass mode. The rest of the cast is nothing to smirk at either: Bruce Willis, Josh Brolin, Freddy Rodriguez, Rose McGowan (okay, you can smirk at this one), Jeff Fahey, Michael Biehn, Rosario Dawson, Michael Parks, Mary Elizabeth Winstead and the indelible Zoë Bell, formerly a stunt woman, who proves that she's got some acting chops up her sleeves. If it's refinement and subtlety you're looking for, look elsewhere – otherwise, leave your good taste at the door and delve into this extremely entertaining trash-fest head-first.

37. Phantasm
Cult director Don Coscarelli made a comeback of sorts with the frankly atrocious "John Dies at the End", but let's not forget this odd classic from 1979, which established him as a cult auteur, and spawned countless direct-to-video sequels. The Tall Man, gnomes, parallel dimensions, flying orbs that drill through people's brains… Perhaps "odd" was an underestimation – the film is downright batshit nuts, but also terrifying and very, very funny. "The ice cream is gonna be flyin' fast and furious." Erm, yes, yes it will, indeed.

36. Jacob's Ladder
Adrien Lyne, best known for directing sexual psycho-dramas in the 1980s ("9 1/2 Weeks", "Fatal Attraction"), took most by surprise with this foray into

psychological horror. What's even more shocking is that "Jacob's Ladder", a brutal examination of post-Vietnam traumas, personified in the brooding, haunted central performance by the never-better Tim Robbins, is so assured and relentlessly terrifying, striking resounding notes of existential anguish. The ending may be a tad on the sentimental side, but you'll never be able to get the images of those lanky, faceless, reverberating demons out of your head.

35. The Texas Chainsaw Massacre (1974)

You may remember Tobe Hooper's classic as one of the goriest horror flicks of the 1970s, but watch it again and marvel at how understated it actually is. Most of the violence is off-screen, but its ferocious pacing, grainy cinematography, cunning editing / sound design and depraved characters - with no discernible reasoning for their atrocious behavior – are the elements that make it seem so savage. Incredibly influential (not in the best way, unfortunately – it spawned countless gratuitous slash-fests, including sequels, remakes, and remakes of sequels that pointlessly delved into the events leading to Leatherface's depravity (he was abused as a child, you see)), TCM remains a chilling masterpiece of gritty, suffocating horror.

34. A Nightmare on Elm Street

Is there a more iconic horror character than Robert Englund's Freddy Krueger? That eye-searing, red-and-green striped sweater, those claws, the cackle – his demonic sadist, infiltrating teenagers' dreams, is the stuff of legends (and nightmares… literally). But what's arguably more demented and powerful is how the director, Wes Craven, nailed the angst and terror of post-puberty years, when the darkest fantasies have the potential to alter into hideous, lethal and utterly pointless attempts to run away from… yourself. TNOES carved the path to countless, inferior sequels, but the original remains the greatest, most subliminally terrifying. Plus, it introduced the world to Johnny Depp.

33. The Orphanage

Guillermo del Toro produced this spooky Spanish ghost story about a young boy's imaginary friend that is a masterful example of "less is more". Without relying on cheap scares, director J.A. Bayona's ("The Impossible") debut is boosted by the pseudo-gothic atmosphere, beautiful cinematography, a transcendent, lyrical performance by its lead (Belén Rueda) and slow-building tension. Winner of seven Goya Awards, this is a gem worth seeking out.

32. Three... Extremes

Three tales by three Asian masters of horror: Fruit Chan's "Dumplings", about an aging actress wishing to reclaim her youth by eating the titular dumplings, whose ingredients contain (SPOILER ALERT!) human flesh; Park Chan-wook's "Cut", a twisted homage to Roald Dahl's "Man From the South", about an extra who kidnaps his director and forces him to play out sadistic scenarios; and Takashi Miike's "Box", a surrealistic study of a woman's reoccurring dreams about being buried alive (arguably an homage to 1988's "The Vanishing"). Check out the worthy sequel as well.

31. Scream

Wes Craven's tongue-in-cheek horror film dissects/satirizes the genre as much as it pays tribute to all the staples that form it. It may have been imitated countless times since its release, but very few hold a candle to this fast-paced, hilarious – and very 1990s – roller-coaster ride. Courtney Cox, Drew Barrymore, Rose McGowan (second time on this list!), David Arquette and Skeet Ulrich (yes, as I said – VERY 1990's) ham it up in all the right ways, and that Ghostface mask is as recognizable as a certain red-and-green striped sweater from the director's earlier classic (see #23 on my list). Skip the sub-par sequels and re-watch the original. "Surprrrrise, Sydney!"

30. The Descent

Neil Marshall's female-driven horror about a bunch of adventure-seeking gals exploring a maze of dank caves, only to stumble upon a nest of evil subterranean creatures, gets more and more claustrophobic as it progresses. The performances are all top-notch, the incessant suffocation palpable – especially during the latter half, when the young ladies, driven to the brink of madness, start to turn on each other. Seek out the version with the original, downbeat ending, which (SPOIER ALERT!) offers a tiny sliver of hope before engulfing you, along with its last remaining survivor, in pitch-black, inescapable gloom.

29. The Cabin in the Woods

A bunch of dumb teens venture into a remote, dark cabin in the woods… Sounds familiar, right? Shelved for several years due to MGM's bankruptcy, Drew Goddard' & Joss Whedon's ultra-meta horror flick was finally released in 2012, and it totally snuck up on audiences; it's so unexpected, sly and ingenious, the less said about it, the better. I will state this: TCITW is as much a love-letter to pretty much every single horror flick ever made, as it is a criticism of the genre's stereotypes. The delightful duo of Richard Jenkins and Bradley Whitford propels the film forward, while the blood-soaked, gleeful insanity that ensues in its last half-hour will drop jaws and twist minds of unaware viewers. Oh, and the unexpected cameo is sure to make genre aficionados cheer in delight – apparently, she's a fan of werewolves…

28. The Dead Zone

David Cronenberg. Christopher Walken. Stephen King. Need I say more? Based on King's novel, the film details the protagonist's torment after he awakens from a coma to discover he's developed psychic powers. Shot in the Greater Toronto Area during a scathing deep-freeze (which, at times, became borderline-intolerable for the cast and crew), the chilly environments certainly complement the narrative's perfectly-sustained, icy-cold tone and mounting dread, leading to a downbeat ending that is somehow both tragic and uplifting. Holding back on the blood and gore, so prevalent in his previous outings, Cronenberg smartly utilizes subtler techniques to accentuate the dismal mood of the proceedings. A cult classic that remains remarkably timeless.

27. From Dusk till Dawn

Directed by Robert Rodriguez, written by Quentin Tarantino, this knowing homage to exploitation classics starts off as a mesmerizing road-trip thriller about a sibling team of bank robbers on the run, who take a family hostage. Once they arrive at a grimy Southern club hilariously called Titty Twister, the plot rapidly descends into utter insanity, which involves vampires, giant mutant rats and a blood-fest of epic proportions. George Clooney, in his big-screen debut (if you disregard – as you should! – "The Return of the Killer Tomatoes!"), exudes charisma galore (he's never been so badass); he, like so many other actors, owes a debt to QT for jump-starting his career. Harvey Keitel is in fine form, Juliette Lewis is at her weirdest, and "FDTD" boasts the one actually decent performance by QT himself. The special effects and make-up are fantastic, the pace is unforgiving… The one slight issue I have with the film is that I can't help feeling its first part – before the vampire orgy unravels – is significantly better directed and paced than the second - which I know is the point, but nevertheless makes me wonder what it would be like if they just stuck to it.
Oh, and be sure to check out the ridiculously entertaining Blu-ray commentary by the two directors, who counter-balance each other so well – Rodriguez, suave, relaxed, macho, and Tarantino, gushing a mile-a-second; their love of movies and film-making is so palpable you can't help but feel inspired.

26. The Thing

John Carpenter's Antarctic horror masterpiece flopped at the box-office and received a mixed critical reception at the time of its release in 1982, but time has been kind to the film: it rapidly developed a cult following on VHS and is now widely considered to be one of the most influential genre pieces ever made. The paranoia that envelops the snowbound crew (led by a gruff, bearded Kurt Russel) after they realize that they've been infiltrated by a parasitic extraterrestrial life form – with the ability to assimilate other organisms – is almost unbearably palpable. After a slow-burner intro, the film kicks into high gear (the "mutated dog" and the "head on legs" sequences are master-class filmmaking, while THAT blood test is one of the most brilliant displays of sustained tension in cinema history), and the ending is uncompromisingly grim. Skip the lackluster remake and watch the badass original again to marvel at the exquisite make-up and creature effects by Rob Bottin and the great, late Stan Winston, which, over 30 years, have lost none of their jaw-dropping power.

25. Dawn of the Dead (both versions)

Many consider George A. Romero's original "Night of the Living Dead" the true masterpiece, but while it certainly remains the first "legit" zombie flick, its black-and-white, somewhat amateurish cinematography, poor acting and clumsy editing haven't aged well, and the scares are few and far between. Having directed several mediocre-at-best horror flicks in the 1970s, he returned to the series with this infinitely better sequel, which satirized the consumer society and introduced a larger-scale zombie apocalypse. The film was later remade by Zack Snyder, who amped up the energy and terror, but dialed down the satirical aspects of the original. Both are equally excellent and worth watching as a double-feature to compare and contrast.

24. Kill List

British director Ben Wheatley announced - or more like blared - his arrival as one of the most promising talents in contemporary horror by fusing together ostensibly disparate elements into a coherent whole. "Kill List", an extraordinary mind-fuck of a film, starts off as a run-of-the-mill, talky British gangster flick, proceeds to escalate into a vicious torture-thriller (be warned: the hammering-of-fingers sequence is not for the faint-hearted), and ends cloaked in satanic blackness. In lesser hands, it would be an incoherent, laughable mish-mash of genres, but Wheatley clearly has a plan, manipulating and leading his audience into the jaws of hell itself. ALSO: see the director's follow-up, the comedy-road-trip-cum-horror, "Sightseers".

23. The Omen

Before "Mama", "Orphan", "Hide and Seek", "Joshua" and, um, "Children of the Corn", there was "The Omen", the "creepy kid from hell" movie to top them all. Richard Donner's ("Lethal Weapon", "Superman") big-screen feature debut showcased the director's knack for sustained suspense. The gist: Gregory Peck plays an American ambassador who learns that his son, Damien (Harvey Stephens) is the Antichrist. The John Moore remake with Live Schreiber and Julia Stiles strips away all the subliminal horror and excellent cinematography of the original.

22. Carrie

Sissy Spacek (in an Oscar-nominated performance) shines as the outcast, extremely vulnerable high-school teenager, abused by classmates and tormented by her Jesus-freak mother (another 1976 Oscar nominee, Piper Laurie). Brian De Palma's flair for staging elaborate set pieces is in full display here, especially in the grandiose, blood-drenched finale, when Carrie finally… snaps. Quentin Tarantino placed "Carrie" at number 8 in a list of his favorite films ever, and for a good reason: in the words of New West Magazine's Stephen Farber, "it's a horror classic, and years from now it will still be written and argued about, and it will still be scaring the daylights out of new generations of moviegoers." Skip Kimberly Pierce's remake (starring Chloë Grace Moretz as Carrie and Julianne Moore as her mom); do yourselves a favor and re-watch De Palma's flawless original.

21. Funny Games (both versions)

In the words of Austrian Michael Haneke, gloomy auteur / director extraordinaire, "Funny Games" (both the original, and the US shot-by-shot remake) "is a film about the representation of violence in the media, not about violence per se. It is a self-reflexive film." When asked whether or not he actually watches films that "Funny Games" is directed against, he replied: "I don't watch that sort of thing because it makes me sick. I'm not a masochist after all!" The insinuation here is that we, the audience, are indeed masochists, if we are able to sit through this 90-minute ordeal, a relentless assault on our preconceptions of silver-screen violence, as well as a brutal statement on how desensitized we've become to people getting hurt in movies. We relish violence when it happens in "Die Hard" or "Hostel". I guarantee you there is no pleasure to be had in watching people being tortured in "Funny Games"; Haneke shows us violence for what it actually is: an abhorrent, irrational behavior that results in ugly consequences.

The plot is so simple, it can be described in a one-sentence pitch: Two young men break into a family home and proceed to inflict psychological and physical pain on the innocent inhabitants. Haneke deconstructs torture porn down to its minimalist basics, and yet his mastery of technique, his unflinching, sterile cinematography, and the frequent meta quirks inserted here and there (such as the sequence where one of the protagonists seems to have a shot at escaping her wrath, just to be literally rewound to the beginning of that scene by one of the smirking evildoers, after which her attempt fails miserably) make us both uncomfortably aware of the overall visceral effect and the fact that we, the audiences, are the ones to blame. Not a lot of people can sit through this film (during the screening I attended with a friend, most of the initially-crowded theater was empty towards the end of the movie), but if you are a fan of horror, and film-making in general, it may just make you reevaluate your own stance on media violence. Or perhaps, like me, you are a masochist. ;)

20. The Babadook

The best, most cerebral - and most overlooked - horror film of 2014 was a tiny Australian picture called "The Babadook". Truly frightening, emotionally resonant - and with a stellar central performance from Essie Davis (who should've received a

Golden Globe nomination instead of freakin' Jennifer Aniston), "The Babadook" teaches us that sometimes, one's deepest traumas cannot be eradicated, but kept at bay… if fed from time to time.

19. The Evil Dead Trilogy

It's hard to believe now, after over 30 years of its release, that "The Evil Dead" was declared a "video nasty" and consequently banned in some countries due to all the gore and violence. In comparison to some of the recent torture porn, the original, and especially its two sequels are remarkably tame and frequently hilarious due to obvious budget limitations – but that doesn't take away from the trilogy's inventive camera trickery, ghoulish make-up effects, and a performance-for-the-ages by the one-and-only Bruce Campbell. Sam Raimi went on to establish himself as the king of horror in Hollywood ("Darkman", "Drag Me to Hell"; he also produces the upcoming remake (scroll down to see the trailer)), but "The Evil Dead" remains his crowning achievement, paving the way to numerous low-budget filmmakers utilizing the ingenious techniques. No wonder Stephen King himself cited it as one of his favorite horror movies of all time. In the words of Ash: "… Groovy."

18. Audition

The best way to watch Takashi Miike's "Audition" is to know nothing about it going in (as is the case with most of the Japanese auteur's filmography – take "Gozu" and its lactating minotaur). Skip the spoiler-filled reviews and dissections of its female-empowerment themes; the less you've heard about "Audition", the better. The film's several major shocks sneak up on you; it starts off as an almost-cheerful rom-com – and then gracefully slides into madness. That bulky sack… I've already said too much. Watch it, then get back to me, and we shall discuss whether it is in fact a statement on our contemporary male-dominated society, or simply Miike fuckin' with your head. One guarantee: you will not soon forget the extended finale.

17. (Tie) Videodrome, Dead Ringers, Scanners

I picked David Cronenberg's "The Fly" (#3) and "Dead Zone" (#20) for my "Top 25 Horror Films" list, but these three features equally represent the director working at his peak: all three are classics of "body horror"; Kafkaesque studies of man's relationship with technology (Cronenberg loves merging humans with machines, sometimes in ghastly, literal ways); insightful social commentaries; brainy explorations of sex, phobias, atheism and obsession; and, above all, just superb entertainment. Recently Mr. Cronenberg has strayed away from all the fluids and gore, focusing on more accessible (read: commercial) fare - but that does not render those classics any less psychologically acute or sophisticated.

16. **The Shining**

The documentary "Room 237" explores the numerous potential meanings behind Stanley Kubrick's adaptation of the Stephen King novel but, while there are certainly many ways a viewer can interpret this masterpiece (I personally think of it as an allegorical examination of obsession and the perils of creative writing), one thing is indisputably a fact: the genius director's meticulous study of a man's descent into madness is unparalleled in its mastery of technique and manipulation of audiences' senses. The introductory helicopter shot, the jarring soundtrack, Jack Nicholson's crazed performance, the blood-filled elevators, the twins, the labyrinthine finale – every aspect of "The Shining" burrows its way into your subconscious (as all Kubrick's films do) and remains there forever. Altogether now: "All work and no play makes Jack a dull boy."

15. **Halloween**

Who can forget the legendary score to John Carpenter's horror classic? That subdued piano chime (composed by the director himself) is only one of the many reasons his film is so effective; putting an expressionless William Shatner (!) mask on the villain and implying rather than showing considerable violence are amongst many others. According to Wikipedia, "critics have suggested the film is a social critique of the immorality of youth and teenagers in 1970s America, with many of Myers's victims being sexually promiscuous substance abusers, while the lone heroine is depicted as innocent and pure, hence her survival"; however, Carpenter dismissed those claims – it is essentially an intrinsic exercise in creating subliminal terror. Many slasher flicks followed, including countless sequels, but few matched the original's flawless pacing and unadulterated dread.

14. **The Host**

A smash hit in South Korea, cult auteur Joon-ho Bong's 2006 feature about a slimy creature than comes out of Seoul's Han River and starts terrorizing folks is a cautionary environmental tale, absurd slapstick comedy and deranged monster feature all rolled into one – and somehow it works. Superbly entertaining and imminently re-watchable, with numerous standout sequences (the crossbow-wielding warrior woman particularly comes to mind.)

13. **"Dikaya Okhota Korolya Stakha" ("Savage Hunt of King Stakh")**

None of you have heard of this 1979 Soviet film, but try to seek it out – it's a testament to the fact that big budgets and a prolific Hollywood cast aren't necessary ingredients for a quality horror feature. Based on the King Stach legend (according to the myth, the said King was murdered by the powerful magnate Raman Janouski back in the 17th Century and swore eternal vengeance against the entire Janouski line, consequently rampaging through the area each night on ghostly horses), the film steadily gathers momentum, resulting in a face-off of epic proportions. I remember watching "Savage Hunt..." as a child and having the shit scared out of me; more than three decades later, the film lost none of its power. I'd personally love to see a remake Valeri Rubinchik's weird and beautiful movie, but would also hesitate to touch it, because it does such a great job of nailing the anxiety of being stuck in a middle-of-nowhere mansion, with the constant dreadful anticipation of the apocalyptic horde of horses. Think Edgar Allan Poe meets Werner Herzog, with a dash of Guillermo del Toro atmospherics, made on a shoestring budget, and you'll get an idea of what you're in for.

12. Rosemary's Baby

Pregnancy can be terrifying. Sure, it's generally regarded as a beautiful thing, an almost-celestial occurrence, so to speak – but one can't deny that the thought of a tiny human offspring developing inside of a womb, the inevitability / unpredictability of it, the physical and psychological pain that is entails – not to mention the actual process of child-birth – may also induce nightmares. Now imagine if you're not quite sure whether the thing evolving inside of you is human. Roman Polanski masterfully explored those gruesome aspects of child-bearing in "Rosemary's Baby", a chillingly subtle study of a woman who becomes increasingly aware of her future offspring's demonic nature, all the while suspecting her husband's involvement in a satanic cult. Mia Farrow wasn't the director's first choice – Polanski initially envisioned Rosemary as a full-figured, girl-next-door type, and wanted his own wife Sharon Tate for the role – but he ultimately made the right one by casting the frail, delicate, little-known actress as the titular character. It's hard to imagine anyone else playing the part; as the film progresses, her mental and physical deterioration is so convincing, her fear so visceral (perhaps made more so by Farrow's real-life trauma, a nasty divorce from husband Frank Sinatra), you can't help feeling absolutely devastated as you watch her crumble. To quote Roger Ebert, "Rosemary makes her dreadful discovery, and we are wrenched because we knew what was going to happen – and couldn't help her." And let's not forget the nightmare sequence, one of the scariest ever made, in which Rosemary is raped by Satan. Talk about celestial.

11. Tie: 28 Days Later & 28 Weeks Later

Danny Boyle can do no wrong: the British director has played with every cinema genre – from science fiction ("Sunshine") to survival drama ("127 Hours"), from dark comedy ("Shallow Grave") to children fantasy ("Millions") to bio-drama ("Jobs") – each time imbuing the project with his trademark ceaseless energy, terrific soundtrack, distinctive visual flair and superior performances (he even staged the 2012 Olympics, and totally crushed it). While it's hard to pinpoint a standout in Boyle's filmography, "28 Days Later", an apocalyptic drama / zombie horror, is certainly one of his most memorable and unexpected achievements. The narrative commences with the prolonged, quietly mournful sequence, in which the protagonist (played by the criminally underrated Cillian Murphy) discovers, upon waking up in an emptied hospital, that the world has been devoured by a killer virus. Filmed on Standard-Def video that was intentionally processed and degraded to look as cruddy as possible, Boyle captures an unforgettable, desolate majesty with his shots of an abandoned London, wind whistling through its hollow streets and vacant windows. The film then promptly shifts into high gear, chronicling his, and several other survivors' (one of which is played by the extraordinary Brendan Gleeson), attempts to fight off the rabid infected. The POV shot of a blood-drop plummeting into a character's eyeball is just one of the many highlights that display Boyle's knack for memorable visuals. Juan Carlos Fresnadillo's follow-up, "28 Weeks Later", happens to be one of the singular cases where the sequel is just as good as the predecessor; the director wisely doesn't stray too far from the original, maintaining the tone and pace of Boyle's film, while dialing down on the poetic lyricism and catalyzing the horror elements. My advice to you is to make it a double-feature; watch the two films back-to-back, ideally with the lights off, and the sound turned way up.

10. Eyes Without a Face

A famous doctor gets into a car crash, whereby his daughter's face is mutilated. Guilt-ridden and maniacal, he begins to stalk innocent victims and transplant their faces onto his daughter's. Though not overly graphic, the oppressive mood sneaks up on you, the gradual and torturous disintegration of the heroine almost unbearable to watch – and that's what ultimately makes the film so indelible. The way it utilizes sound – uncannily cheerful (and hence that much more menacing) carousel music, jarring dog barks – enhances the overall effect. Undeniably influential on such films as Pedro Almodovar's "The Skin I Live In" and John Carpenter's "Halloween", Georges Franju's "Eyes Without a Face" was way ahead of its time, dealing with issues of identity, cruelty, imprisonment and obsession in a controversially artful, restrained manner, which may have been the reason for the initial mixed response it received. The Frankensteinian fable was also quite prophetic: plastic surgery as a subject of debate is more relevant today than ever. With time the film gained cult status, and is now rightfully regarded as a masterpiece.

9. Ring (Ringu)

The highest-grossing – and widely considered the most frightening – horror film in Japan, Hideo Nakata's shocking "Ringu" ("The Ring") is based on a popular book by Kōji Suzuki, which in turn draws on the Japanese folk tale Banchō Sarayashiki. Propelled by its creepy atmosphere, the film is one of the best examples of how horror does not need to rely on gratuitous gore and geysers of blood to petrify an audience. The simple story of an investigative reporter researching an evil tape will leave audiences with expressions similar to those of the film's twisted victims', who have seen the unspeakable contents of the tape, and consequently died of fright. The tension mounts and mounts until it reaches a nearly unbearable apex – I watched this film by myself in a dark Chicago apartment, and as a result couldn't sleep a wink that night. Employing a variety of brilliant techniques, such as shooting actress Rie Inō walking backwards in a jerky, exaggerated motion, then playing the film in reverse, Nakata knew that distorted perceptions of reality can be much more powerful than sadistic violence. As for the final half-hour... let's just say you'll never look at your TV screen the same way again.

8. The Birds

I still hesitate to classify it as "horror" (I like to think of it as an allegorical study of, to quote the humanities scholar Camille Paglia, "the many facets of female sexuality and, by extension, nature itself") but Hitch's adaptation of Daphne du Maurier's story (also see "Don't Look Now", #1 on my list) certainly unsettles with its depiction of a town inexplicably attacked by a herd of demented birds. Arguably one of his better films, unhinged to the max, with great special effects and a tormented Tippi Hedren (watch HBO's "The Girl" to witness the seven gates of hell Hitch put his actress through during filming), "The Birds" is timeless and extremely influential.

7. Jaws

Steven Spielberg's masterpiece isn't technically a "horror film" per say, but there's no denying the lasting impact of its unrelenting tension and dread that oozes from every frame – and how about that ominous John Williams score ("duh-dum...duh-dum...") The (unavoidable) decision to keep the shark hidden underwater for most of the film's duration proved to be superbly effective, Spielberg's subliminal direction has never been better, the acting is top-notch – all those aspects add up to one of the most effective "monster flicks" ever made. It's also the first official "blockbuster" of our era, paving the path to "Star Wars", "Indiana Jones" and many others. "We're going to need a bigger boat", indeed.

6. The Exorcist

I remember watching William Friedkin's ("The French Connection") horror epic "The Exorcist" with a close friend in a crowded Munich theater, when it was re-released in all its digitally-remastered glory. At about the halfway mark, my friend leaned over to me, his face pale, lips quivering, and whispered, "I can't take this anymore. I gotta go." He bolted out of the theater. Mind you, he is a horror movie fan; this just goes to show how powerful Friedkin's masterpiece remains – its relentless atmosphere of anxiety and impending calamity literally made him sick. Throughout the years, "The Exorcist" clearly lost none of its effect. There are several reasons for that. The possessed protagonist, subjected to indescribable agony, happens to be a little girl (who, at one point, stabs herself repeatedly between the legs with a crucifix) – Friedkin boldly gave the finger to the common predisposition that children shouldn't be tortured on-screen, putting his young actress through the wringer, and hence making the audience squirm uncomfortably in their seats. The constant presence of evil – Satan – permeates every frame, even – and perhaps more effectively – those that don't blatantly show the horror (one of the most effective and spine-chilling sequences sees the priest slowly walking up to the haunted room, from which milk-curdling shrieks emanate – we know the demon is in there, and the images it invokes in our minds are much more terrifying than anything we could actually see); it's almost as if the production itself was demonically possessed. Ellen Burstyn gives a stellar, uber-authentic performance as the grieving mother, grounding the film in reality and personifying every mother's fear of her child being subjected to an affliction. The tension builds to the final exorcism sequence, where it reaches an apotheosis and, like a resonant note being stricken over and over, the director sustains it – this is top-notch film-making.

William Friedkin had a series of flops after "The Exorcist", vanishing into obscurity, resurfacing briefly with 1985's "To Live and Die in L.A." After a long absence, he seems to have found his muse – playwright Tracy Letts – and made his comeback with the glorious adaptations: the paranoia thriller "Bug" and "Southern-fried noir" "Killer Joe". Hopefully, Hollywood's notorious "bad boy" (he's known to be a bit of an ass on set) keeps at it; "The Exorcist" remains his magnum opus, and one of the most inspiring films in my life.

5. Psycho

There has been a slew of Hitchcock homages, including two simultaneously-released biographical features: HBO's "The Girl", which focuses on the tumultuous relationship between Hitch (Tobey Jones) and Tippi Hedren (Sienna Miller), and Fox Searchlight Pictures' theatrical release "Hitchcock", which details the production of "Psycho", with Anthony Hopkins wearing layers of prosthetics as the titular character, Hellen Mirren playing his wife Alma Reville, and Scarlett Johansson in the role of Janet Leigh. Unfortunately, neither of those films managed to do justice to the formidable, delirious, fetishistic filmmaker, possibly the most influential one in the history of cinema. The latter picture was particularly disappointing, despite respectable performances by Hopkins and Mirren, as the production crew was denied access to any of the actual footage from the 1960 horror masterpiece (and who could blame them, after the fiasco that was Gus Van Sant's shot-by-shot remake – with Anne freakin' Heche in the epochal Janet Leigh role, and, Vince Vaughn (!!) as Norman Bates).

All right, so the original's ending was somewhat redundant, a forensic psychiatrist Dr. Fred Richmond (Simon Oakland) dissecting Norman Bates' fractured psyche, but forget the ending: the way the director defied cinematic conventions by brutally killing off the main (anti) heroine in the first half-hour of the film – Janet Leigh was a major star at the time, and to see her mutilated in the shower so soon and unexpectedly was a jarring shock to the audiences' systems – was incredibly revolutionary. Hitch also shrewdly manipulates our emotions, at one point making us sympathize with the villain: when Norman methodically cleans off the blood, or when he watches his victim's car sink half-way into the lake and then momentarily halt – we are rooting for him despite our apprehensions. Sadistic? Yes, but also a virtuoso achievement, previously unparalleled, and rarely matched since. From Anthony Perkins' performance (his best, by a long stretch) as the charming and creepy Bates, to the sensational shower sequence (70 shots in 45 seconds), "Psycho", in the words of critic David Thomson, let "the subversive secret out," after which "censorship crumpled like an old lady's parasol."

Made for just $800,000, "Psycho" went on to gross $32 million, marking it as the biggest hit of Hitchcock's career.

Numerous directors have tried to emulate Hitch's style, from Brian De Palma to Atom Egoyan, but few have been successful (Kubrick and Scorsese are among the select few that come to mind.) To this day "Psycho" hasn't aged a bit, terrifying even when watched in broad daylight. Anthony Hopkins recalls his first viewing: "It was packed. I sat down and I didn't know what the hell I was in for. I had heard stories about it. When it got to the shower scene, I don't think I've ever been so scared in my life."

When Hannibal Lecter himself admits to being scared, you know you're in for a treat.

4. Let the Right One In
A beautifully shot, atmospheric masterpiece, "Let the Right One In" cunningly deconstructs the recently all-the-rage "vampire flick" by foregoing the hackneyed staples of the genre in favor of a novel, artistic approach, drenched in desolation and breathtaking poignancy. Set in a small, wintry Swedish town, where the only light seems to come from flickering lamp-posts, the sun obscured by a thick blanket of low-hanging clouds, the story follows a young, bullied boy, Oskar, who leads a life of anonymity, obsessing over murder articles in the newspapers. When a neighbor moves in next door, an ethereal young girl named Eli who walks barefoot through the snow, he becomes increasingly enthralled by her mysterious aura. Casting is key here: Kåre Hedebrant's fragility and Lina Leandersson's wise-beyond-her-years, entrancing eyes and demeanor (at times her features are subtly – but very effectively – transformed with CGI to make her look older) correspond perfectly, in a ying-yang sort of way. I don't want to spoil too much of the plot, but, while several sequences – the bursting-into-flame hospital bed; Eli's visit to Håkan, her lover/servant, after he gets horribly disfigured; the cat-attack; Eli entering Oskar's apartment without being invited; the heartbreaking conclusion – particularly stand out, it's the central love story of a boy

and a girl finding salvation in each other that resonates the most. The film was remade in Hollywood, but while "Let Me In" is adequate, I strongly urge you to watch the original instead. "Twilight" should have taken notes – THIS is how it's done.

3. The Fly

Infinitely better than the original 1958 film, and the epitome of David Cronenberg's exploration of his favorite "body horror" sub-genre, "The Fly" boldly takes Kafka's "Metamorphosis" and twists it on its head, detailing a man's gradual – and torturous – transformation into an insect. Jeff Goldblum is astounding as Seth Brundle, a scientist that invents a teleportation machine. He meets a journalist, Veronika (Geena Davis, equally brilliant); their first sexual encounter prompts Seth to successfully reprogram the computer to cope with living creatures. Stricken by jealousy, he decides to teleport himself, unaware that a fly got caught in the machine with him. What follows is a deft study of obsession, love, identity and self-mutilation; "The Fly" aggressively transgresses against the model of the conventional, shallow Hollywood horror movie.

While I could go on for pages and pages analyzing this brilliant achievement in horror film-making – and arguably Cronenberg's best – I'll let one of its fabulous, chilling quotes (uttered by the protagonist as "Brundlefly", on the verge of self-destruction) speak for itself:

"You're afraid to dive into the plasma pool, aren't you? You're afraid to be destroyed and recreated, aren't you? I'll bet you think that you woke me up about the flesh, don't you? But you only know society's straight line about the flesh. You can't penetrate beyond society's sick, gray, fear of the flesh. Drink deep, or taste not, the plasma spring! Y'see what I'm saying? And I'm not just talking about sex and penetration. I'm talking about penetration beyond the veil of the flesh! A deep penetrating dive into the plasma pool!"

Heavy stuff, but don't hesitate for a second to dive into this plasma pool.

2. Martyrs

Pascal Laugier's existential "Martyrs" is not for everyone. Those who can stomach its unflinching assault of uber-violent imagery will discover an absolutely stunning achievement in film-making, which transcends its torture-porn roots – a genuinely artistic revelation. Similarly to Michael Haneke's "Funny Games", "Martyrs" dares us to stare into the abyss, challenging our preconceptions of violence and its consequences. It starts off with the viciously cold-blooded massacre of a seemingly-normal family, and then gives us the reasons for why it happened – and then… Well, let's just say to spoil all the twists and turns of this remarkable picture would be to do you a huge disservice. With stellar technique, and standout performances by its two lead actresses, Laugier takes us on a wrenching journey that serves as a study of female empowerment, a dissection of our contemporary views on cruelty (both cinematic cruelty, and the cruelty exhibited throughout human history) and a lyrical ode to the limits of pain a human being can endure before she achieves celestial ecstasy. Controversial? Very much so, but also uncompromising, disturbingly beautiful, and very, very emotional, without ever so much as flirting with sentimentality.

I watched this with two close friends – both cried, and half-way through begged me to pause it so that they could collect their breath, but then urged me to keep playing it, for it's a visceral experience you simply cannot disregard. As hard to watch as it is unmissable, "Martyrs" ends with a pseudo-"2001" phantasmagoric light-show journey into the protagonist's eye, which will never – I repeat, NEVER – leave your subconscious.

If you can get that far, that is.

1. Don't Look Now
There are too many reasons for why I chose Nicholas Roeg's 1973 masterpiece "Don't Look Now" (adapted from the short story by Daphne du Maurier) as my #1 all-time favorite horror film to list here, so I'll focus on a select few.
Let's start with the indelible lovemaking sequence (I know that's what you want, you horny bastards) – by far the most erotic, beautiful one of its kind ever made. Rumors have it that the leading couple – Donald Sutherland and Julie Christie – were alone in the bedroom with the cinematographer, Anthony B. Richmond, and Roeg, to create an authentic sense of intimacy; allegedly, what we are witnessing is actual intercourse. The way it's filmed, with constant inter-cutting between the sex and the two reminiscing about it as they get dressed post-coitally, is so impeccably done, so affecting and genuine, it makes every other sex scene look glorified and amateur in comparison. Of course, this is a horror movie, so this scene serves a purpose: it emphasizes the growing detachment the grief-stricken couple later experiences.

The film begins with a devastating sequence of John and Laura Baxter's daughter tragically drowning. The couple flees to Venice, where John gets offered a job to restore an old church. In the meantime, Laura comes across two psychic ladies, who tell her they can see her daughter, she is here, now, with them. This leads to a growing sense of paranoia, especially after John spots what seems to be a little girl, running through the labyrinthine Venice alleys. When his wife leaves Venice, John starts seeing things that may or may not be there – or perhaps they are premonitions of an impending doom.

Roeg was a master who, like Hitchcock, happened to be way ahead of his time at creating tension through gorgeous, impressionist, reoccurring imagery (e.g. the red jacket their daughter wore during the accident keeps reappearing throughout the film; streaks of red almost jarringly stand out in an otherwise muted, pastel-colored Venice; Venice's water canals are like reminders of the tragedy, and at one point John Baxter fishes a doll out of one of them, which is a grim mirroring of the startling opening sequence); Roeg employed flashbacks and flash-forwards, blurred scenes together, using color and patterns to disorient and engage the audience in equal measures. This is more than just an "occult horror" – it's a lyrical, poetic, timeless meditation on grief's ability to manifest itself in irrational fear, an allegorical study of how guilt can alter into paranoia, with career-best performances from both Sutherland and Christie (and that's saying something). As for the ending – it will sear itself into your brain forever.

No wonder "Don't Look Now" inspired some of my favorite contemporary filmmakers: Danny Boyle (who counts it as one of his favorite films), Alfonso Cuarón (who included "Don't Look Now" in his Top 10 Time Out British Films poll), Lars von Trier ("Antichrist" pays homage to "Don't Look Now"), Martin McDonagh (who said that the Venice of "Don't Look Now" was the template for the depiction of Bruges in his film); the film's imagery and stylistic techniques have served as an inspiration to films such as Spielberg's "Schindler's List", "The Brood" by David Cronenberg, "Memento" by Christopher Nolan… The list goes on. It's one of the most inspirational films in my life, and one that I can constantly re-watch, and find new, subtle intricacies with each viewing. It is, in my opinion, the best horror film ever made, and one that will be extremely difficult, if not impossible, to top.

Honorable Mentions:

Lars von Trier's dread-infused, allegorical, Satanic "Antichrist"; Jacques Tourner's classic "Cat People"; Henri-Georges Clouzot's "Diabolique" (which is really more of a thriller with horror elements); "Fright Night" (both the original and the remake); the original torture-porn, Eli Roth's claustrophobic "Hostel", the original "Paranormal Activity"; and the punk-infused splatter-fest "The Green Room", which features Patrick Stewart playing a modern-day Nazi.

About the Author

Alex Saveliev is a produced, multiple award-winning screenwriter and published author of short stories. One of Alex's short stories, "Maid", was featured on Roger Ebert's literary blog. Alex is an established film critic for a Dallas-based entertainment website, with close to 200 published reviews. Having spearheaded international film distribution at several Los Angeles-based companies, Alex has attended every film market and edited hundreds of stories and scripts. He has an entertainment blog with over 6,000 fans.

Having lived in Russia, England, Germany, Thailand and all over the United States, Alex has finally settled - at least for the time being - in Los Angeles with his wife and two cats.

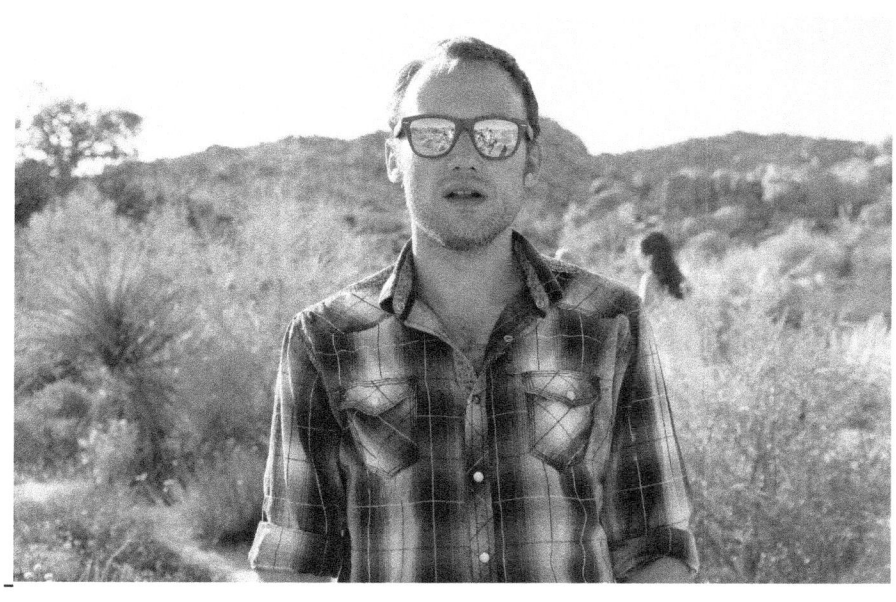

www.ingramcontent.com/pod-product-compliance
Lightning Source LLC
Chambersburg PA
CBHW062059220526

45471CB00010B/3543